IS THIS OKAY? . . . AM I A FREAK? . . . AM I THE ONLY ONE? . . . HOW FAR CAN YOU GO? . . . SHOULD I DO IT?

Dr. Judy answers all these questions and hundreds more in her down-to-earth and open-minded way. A truly honest and straightforward question/answer and quiz book, *Generation Sex* gets to the heart of what's on everybody's mind—sex. Discover the New G-Spots for men *and* women, new Secrets to Attraction, the Hottest Places to meet Mr./Ms. Right, Ten Top Ways to Rev Up Slacker Sex, the Four Key Steps to solving any sexual problem, and the Two New Golden Rules of Sex. Take the Sexual Attraction and Sex Style Tests and learn how—in these complex and risky times—to find cosmic sexual love.

Generation

S e x

AMERICA'S HOTTEST SEX THERAPIST ANSWERS THE HOTTEST QUESTIONS ABOUT SEX

by

"Dr. Judy" Kuriansky

HarperPaperbacks
A Division of HarperCollinsPublishers

HarperPaperbacks   *A Division of* HarperCollins*Publishers*
                    10 East 53rd Street, New York, N.Y. 10022

Copyright © 1995 by Dr. Judy Kuriansky
All rights reserved. No part of this book may be used or reproduced in any manner whatsoever without written permission of the publisher, except in the case of brief quotations embodied in critical articles and reviews. For information address HarperCollins*Publishers*,
10 East 53rd Street, New York, N.Y. 10022.

Cover photograph by AP/Wide World
Author photo © 1994 by Trix Rosen

First printing: June 1995

Printed in the United States of America

HarperPaperbacks and colophon are trademarks of HarperCollins*Publishers*

❖ 10 9 8 7 6 5 4 3 2

To all the blessed men and women who call me on the radio, come hear me speak, read my articles, and go on the TV shows I do, I extend my heart and my love. You are each a gift to me. Your trust and sharing proves over and over that from deep connection comes healing and joy.

■   ■   ■

There's an angel dressed in white satin with sparkling gold wings and a golden halo, holding a gold baton with a star on top, perched on my computer. She smiled at me through writing this book. Her light, love, wisdom, and playfulness inspired me, as did every soul of every person who has reached out to me and whose life I've touched, and who is very alive in the pages of this book.

The angel was a gift from my friend Reverend Ruth Green, offering valued spiritual counsel at the crescendo of this most treasured creation.

Other special angels have graced my professional and personal life. There is my first radio program director, Jay Clark, who believed from the start that if I could play in a rock band I could do talk-radio. And my hero and radio guru now, Steve Kingston, truly the "King" in every way, whose brilliance, energy, and love inspires me to be, as is so idiosyncratically his style, "in the pocket." There's Edward and my mom, to whom I turn for advice, with their precious unconditional love and unfailing good judgment. There's my inimitable *LovePhones* team: Chris Jagger, a dream-come-true on-air partner with his sharp wit raging from the warmest heart; my cherished producer, Sam, advising vibrators and attempting phone sex while keeping us all in the spirit of *The Lion King*'s "Hakuna Matata;" Fuzzball, Frank C., and Mousie, the great boys on the front line; Cathy Donovan backing us up; my driver, Sal, who introduced me to the brilliance of TAFKAP; all the gang at Z100, WMMS, and Rocket 107; and our *LovePhones* intern/researchers, Joann Ricovero, who sifted through everyone's needs, and Audrey Sorgen and Brett Kopelan, *crème de la crème* of the new generation, there for the callers (and me) with dedication and uncanny intelligence at all hours; and my valued assistant, Alissa Pollack, whose cherished loyalty and enthusiasm helped me 24/7 in the home stretch, as always. There's my *Newsday* editor, Barbara Schuler, with her friendship and smarts, and my team at HarperCollins, from Geoff Hannell to Gretchen Young and my stellar editors, Katie Tso, Karen Klein, and Carolyn Pittis, with such support, talent, and care for all the aspects of this project. There are my valued colleagues with their brilliant contributions, Drs. E. Douglas Whitehead, Sandra Leiblum, Michael Perelman, and Gaetano Bello. And there's Tony Leroy, whose spiritual guidance ignited the launch, my friend Mitch, for his inspiration, the inimitable David Sittenfeld, and all my Bey buddies for celebrating all the roles (from Tink the Shrink through Catwoman), Amy Rosenblum and all my good friends at the *Sally* show, cherished treasures Teri Whitcraft, Fred Barron, and Frank Hagan, and trusted "soul sisters" Laurie Sue Brockway, Edie Hand, Jill Marti, Madeline DeVries, Rhea Ross, and Voltage, whose energy, support, and love through this process and all my life shine brightly in my heart and soul. On a purple throne, sits the regal Al Lowman, whose vision sparks any idea to stratospheric heights. I love you all deeply and appreciate your love for me.

CONTENTS

Note: *Generation Sex* covers many real questions from real people, but in the interests of compacting as much information as possible, and protecting individual's confidentiality, many situations and names have been changed or collated. Offering general guidelines for solutions to common problems about love and sex, it is meant to encourage you to talk with your family and friends, partners and physicians, clergy and counselors. An independent study on callers to *LovePhones* proved talking about sex did not make kids do it more; instead those who were not having sex felt more supported, and those who already were, thought more about safe sex. Since everyone is individual, and not every answer can cover every aspect of every issue, make sure you consider all the factors in your situation, and seek the necessary personal help. Also, *always* practice safe sex and take that advice as a given in *every* situation. And please note, this book is intended for a *mature* audience!

The author and the publisher disclaim responsibility for any effects resulting from the information contained herein, which is also not meant to endorse any institution or product. Given the author's background and training as a psychologist, the advice focuses on emotional concerns; but many sexual questions are related to medical conditions, so you are urged to see a medical doctor for general check-ups and specific problems. Don't hesitate—like Victor who couldn't imagine telling a doctor he had a rash on his penis from dipping it into Crisco, or Pam who feared going to the gynecologist to have her missing condom removed because then her mother would find out she was no longer a virgin. Take care of your health!

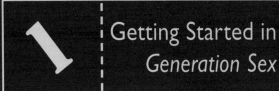

1 Getting Started in *Generation Sex*

"DR. JUDY, I WANT TO DO IT FIVE TIMES A DAY, IS that normal?" "She wants to tie me up, should I do it?" "I can't get to second base, what do I do?" "How can I get my teeth to tingle in orgasm?" "Where's the male G-spot?"

These are questions about sex today that try men's and women's souls, questions I field constantly from my nightly radio call-in advice show, *LovePhones*, as well as my many television appearances, speeches, magazine articles, and newspaper columns.

Some questions—from aphrodisiacs to performance anxiety—have perennially plagued people over the decades I've been in this sex field. Others—from sex with animals and aliens, to sex buddies, betrayal and blackmail—are freshly spawned from today's ever-more troubling times.

Some questions show the lighter side of sex: "How do you do the pogo-stick position?" "Does touching yourself give you zits?" "What's a zebra penis?" But imaginations have gotten kinkier—from "I put a friend's ferret down my pants" to "I want to watch two hermaphrodites doing each other" and "I'm having sex with dead bodies." And then there are the heart-wrenching stories. Michelle got AIDS from a one-night stand. Ashley's father and his friend put a gun up her vagina. Charles was inserting pencils in his rear, not because he was freaky, but because he was so depressed when his girlfriend rejected him, he threw himself off the top of a building.

The tragedies and comedies are here for you in *Generation Sex*, to answer your most common concerns: "Am I normal?" "Am I the only one?" "What can I do to solve this problem?"

Keep this book on your bedstand. Read it before you fall asleep. Quiz your love partners and your friends. Know everything you can about sex that can be riddled with anxiety or laced with love. It's a guide about sex for generation X and *all* generations.

I would have liked to know all this when I was growing up. I had a happy childhood, in a loving but puritanical family, where sex before marriage was taboo, where my father, a dentist, thought anything but dental instruments in your mouth was unhygienic and my mother thought you could get pregnant from kissing. I majored in math and French at first in college, then, fascinated by the mind, switched to psychology. Working in London and at the New York State Psychiatric Institute at Columbia Medical Center with problems like depression and schizophrenia, my unit got involved with the beginning of sex therapy, and my career evolved from there. In the midst of the sexual revolution, I was getting my degree in clinical psychology, acting out a long-time fantasy of playing in a rock band, leading consciousness raising groups, and doing research with the Scientists Committee for Public Information that became news and led to my being hired as a feature reporter on TV.

From that first TV job, I was asked to do a radio call-in show five nights a week three hours a night. Since then, I've heard it all—in so many years as a media psychologist and sex therapist, answering thousands of questions . . . Okay, I have been stumped lately about a few things, like trunkbutt (it's not picking peanuts up with your rear) and fellching. You'll get to know about all of it here. I've spent a lot of years training and working as a psychologist with all types of people using all kinds of techniques. So I promise, you'll learn a lot not only about sex, but love, your self, and life in general.

As a bonus, you'll get some sex advice from the stars—from "bad" boys and girls like Sandra Bernhard on fantasies, Aerosmith's Steven Tyler on threesomes, and Van Halen's Sammy Hagar on hot spots, to the "good" boys and girls like Sheryl Crow on what's sexy, Fabio on romance, and Richard Marx on sexual confidence. Heed Salt-N-Pepa on rough sex: "If he gets too rough, scratch that game." And comic Pauly Shore on masturbation: "Look at five Playboy centerfolds one at a time, and talk to each, 'Come on, honey, it's your turn.'"

Goodness knows, today everything goes. Indeed, Seinfeld extolled the pleasures of masturbation and exposed fake orgasms on national TV. Madonna put a stiletto at her crotch in her *Sex* book and her panties on Letterman's head. Howard Stern did "pussy-sniffing" and lesbian dating contests. A tennis star revealed she's gay and an Olympic champ confessed he competed with HIV. The President was accused of sexual harassment and O. J. Simpson went on trial for sex-obsessed murder. John Bobbitt got emasculated and Mike Tyson got a prison term. Bloodthirst is "in" from movies to S&M fashion chic. There's hardly a sexual stone left unturned.

"They've pierced all the body parts they can pierce," Grateful Dead's Bob Weir said. "They've done just about everything they can do with their hair. They have adopted just about as revolting an attitude as they can adopt. So how much further can you push it?" Hang on Bob, even Guns N' Roses found something they've never seen before (read about it later).

Truth is, the sexual revolution isn't over. Now we need an ongoing sexual *evolution,* and lots of education. That's evident, when I hear Reed thinks a girl can't get pregnant unless she has an orgasm, or Steven thinks you can't have an orgasm until you're eighteen. Or when Laura thinks she has to have sex with some guy or he'll dump her. Or when Jessica does it with half the frat because she feels fat and unwanted.

My cure is the **Three R's** to rule your sex life: **Respect** (for yourself and others), **Responsibility** (you control your thoughts and your acts, they don't control you), and the **Right to Say Yes or No**. You'll find these Rules woven throughout *Generation Sex*.

And more, you'll also find the 4 T's: Trust, Talking, Touch, Taking Time (some have added Tits, Torture, Toys, Tongue, Teasing). Then there's the Five F's: freeing up Feelings, facing Fears, accepting Fantasies, expressing aFFection, and having Fun.

Apply these to common themes throughout *Generation Sex.*

Am I a freak? This is a common question. Scot likes to sniff girls' rear ends to get turned on. Francesca wants to hold her boyfriend's penis all the time and fell asleep with her head down his pants on a plane to California but wonders if there's something wrong with her. Kevin's girlfriend likes him to insert his two webbed toes into her vagina. Heather is worried about her belly-button fetish since seven guys liked it but three didn't. In most cases, you're not abnormal to feel the way you do, to have the fears, desires, fantasies you have.

Is this okay? You'll find lots of permission, encouragement, and support here. Trisha can rub herself over her panties but feels "immoral" putting her finger inside her body. There's nothing wrong or bad about that, she can still consider herself a virgin, and doing it can help her feel comfortable with a boyfriend. Jessie was upset that her boyfriend looked at her funny after oral sex, and she wanted to know if she was doing it right. Any way you do it is fine. Brenda worried about her fantasy about Nine Inch Nails' Trent Reznor. "Go ahead and imagine him on his knees before you. Tell him what you want him to do," I encouraged her. "Okay, I'm tying you up," she finally blurted out. "I'm on top of you, sitting on you, and you're doing it as I'm on your face, riding you . . . " If all your life you've pleased others, now it's your turn to be pleased, using anyone as your sexual muse.

Am I the only one? I hear it so often: "I'm the only one with this problem . . . " and it turns out not so unusual at all: "I'm in love with my soccer coach," "I think about having sex with my boyfriend's boss," "I want to do it in public,"

"I tried to go down on myself." Whatever you come up with, someone else has been there, done that.

In a survey of over three thousand six hundred questions to *LovePhones,* the biggest cluster was about dating: "Why am I such a loser with girls?" "I slept with him but he likes someone else," "Since we broke up I can't turn on with anyone else." The next most common category contained body complaints: "My penis is bent," "My vagina hurts," "One breast is smaller," "I only have one nut." Questions about masturbation, and wondering "Am I normal" and "Am I gay?" also abounded.

How far can you go? Permission aside, there are some unacceptable acts. Read about the "no-no's" that make my blood boil, from sexual blackmail to betrayal to self-abuse (like the ever-prevailing refrain: "He beats me, cheats on me, mistreats me . . . but I love him"). Corinna's boyfriend puts a brown paper bag over her head when they have sex and calls out the name of his ex-girlfriend who was also her ex-best friend, but she doesn't say anything because she loves him. That isn't love, it's abuse and low self-esteem. Remember Respect and the Right to Say Yes or No Rules.

Another "no-no": the "it just happened" excuse. Like Brian, who went to visit his girlfriend and she wasn't home but her sister was, so as he says, "I went in her room and we talked and before I knew it we were doing it on her bed. It just happened . . . " Nothing just happens. Remember Responsibility Rules.

Another "no-no": settling for crumbs. Marissa lost her virginity to an older guy who doesn't call often but tells her, "Don't go with other guys." She has to learn she deserves more. Similarly, Felicia does everything for her man: "I even had sex with his ex-girlfriend and let him tape it. But he won't eat me. He said he can't because he has a daughter to kiss." She has to learn "you got to receive, or leave . . . and believe . . . in yourself."

Should I do it? The all-too-common scenario has a new twist; it's sexual blackmail. "My boyfriend said if I don't do what he wants (have anal sex, do it with another woman or his two friends), he'll tell the whole school I swallow." She doesn't want to do whatever, but says he says he'll find someone else if she doesn't. Or she's stuck on him because he was her first. And surprise: today more men also feel pressured, by women turning them into sex objects, demanding they do it with another guy, or however and whenever they want. You don't have to be a gas station, letting someone "fill 'er up" at your expense. That's being used, not loved.

Remember, Respect Rules. I recall going to a 2 Live Crew concert to see what it was like, since the group had been the subject of so much scandal and arrests for lewd behavior. Women were thrust through the mosh pit onto the stage like Christians thrown to the lions, made to drop to their knees in front of the band who unzipped their pants and shoved the women's heads into their groins. Other simulations accompanied a song with the refrain, "Head down, butt up, that's the way I like to fuck." The only thing more upsetting than the guys' treatment of the women, was that some of the girls volunteered to go on stage, pleased to do anything for their five minutes of touching rap-star celebritydom.

(It reminded me of Howard Stern's gig at a Manhattan club years ago where girls fought to be on stage or their guys pushed them up there, for the "pussy-sniffing contest" where Howard would guess which one had her period.)

You'll find my favorite therapy techniques and my philosophy of life in this book.

- **RETRAIN YOUR BRAIN.** Reprogram your mental computer. Change your mental TV channel. It's the technological age, so treat your mind like a TV or computer: if it's telling you something unhealthy, delete the program and type in a new one, or simply switch the channel of your mind. Replace the image of one guy you think you love but who treats you badly, with the mental picture of someone else who treats you royally. Change "No girl likes me," "I can't hook up," "My breasts are ant hills," to "I'm awesome," "Whoever gets with me will luck out," and "I love my body."
- **REALITY-CHECK.** Always phrase things right. The way

you say things affects how you see things and how they are. Richie was upset, saying, "My girlfriend talked to me for hours and now she won't mind me at all." "How long have you known her?" I asked. "Three days," was the answer. Three days does not a girlfriend make. Just calling her his "girlfriend" made Richie more miserable than if he said, more accurately, that someone he knew for three days fell out. Don't blow it up and your upset will go down.

- **READ YOUR BODY.** One of my favorite questions is: "If your (penis/breasts/any body part) could talk . . . what would it say?" If you can't last long, your penis could be saying, "I can't be in here, it's too dangerous, I could get her pregnant, get trapped, or not perform." It's a proven Gestalt therapy technique: seeing the message from your actions is more than half the battle to changing it.

- **REVERSE ROLES.** Walk a mile in the other person's shoes. Joey has been going out with his girlfriend for three years, but two weeks ago he followed her brother into the basement, had oral sex, and ejaculated on his back. It felt good and now he wants to do it again. "How would you feel if your girlfriend did that with your brother?" I asked. "Not good," he answered, finally considering his behavior.

- **REVEAL YOUR SECRET AGENDA.** Get to the "Aha"—the real truth without fear, shame, self-blame. Half the cure is facing the problem openly. Rick caught an eighteen-year-old family friend watching in the doorway when he and his wife were having sex, but what was he really worried about? He confessed, "I think about her when I'm having sex with my wife." Becky's boyfriend tricked her into admitting she'd had sex with ten guys before him, and called her a "slut" when really he was angry figuring she had sex three hundred times before but only wanted him twice a month.

- **REACH YOUR DEEPER ISSUE.** Put yourself "on the couch." Like Freud said, everything has a deeper meaning. Peel the layers of the onion and find out what you really fear or need (control, love, attention, being part of the crowd).

Raven is a hairdresser who called to say she runs her hands over guys in her chair and gets so turned on she has to go masturbate. "No, you don't *have* to," I told her. "What does your cutting hair mean? It means you're in control . . . so, enjoy feeling in control and you won't need to go masturbate." You'll always ultimately get more satisfaction and freedom fulfilling the deeper need.

Bill said his wife refused to have sex, so he went in another room, masturbated, and came back in the bedroom and ejaculated on her face while she was sleeping. Call that low, but to get to the core, I asked, "What do you do when people tell you 'no'?" Apparently he can't stand frustration and manipulates in order to get his way.

Interpret the symbols of your behavior. Francesca hugs her boyfriend's penis like a pacifier when she needs comfort, Heather binges on belly buttons because she needs to be nurtured, Scot wears diapers because he felt turned on when he was toilet trained, and Kevin's girlfriend focuses on his feet because she's frightened of his penis. Once you understand, you don't feel like a freak.

(Unless, of course, you are a freak—though even then there's a lesson—as when Mike reported getting off on wiping his bowel movements all over himself while his girlfriend watched . . . and we busted him for pranking. You don't have to be Freud to know that his life is probably filled with shit!)

- **REVEAL YOUR GHOSTS FROM THE PAST—THEY CLOUD YOUR PRESENT.** Janine needs rough sex, so we listed all the men from her past at whom she's really angry for not loving her enough. Jeff was bewildered by his desire to act like a baby girl with his wife until we jogged his memory of being eight years old and playing baby with a little girl. Now taking on more responsibility as a man made him dream of being taken care of like in the childhood game. Scot acts like a second "wife" and slave to a married man who doesn't want him to see anyone else. Turned out his father was never around and he was overly close to his mother who had polio and made him do errands, laundry, and dishes in an apron. "Cool," he said, seeing the connection between serving his lover as a way to symbolically stay faithful to his mommy. Seeing the source releases you from the slavery of repeating the past.

- **REPAIR YOUR HURTS.** Finish unfinished business. Tell an old lover off. Ask your father for love you never got.

- **REHEARSE WHAT YOU WANT TO SAY.** John wants to ask a girl he has a crush on for a date. Leila wants her boyfriend to go down on her. Pretend you're in the situation and say what you want. Practice builds your confidence. Here's how the progression goes: Think It, Feel It, Say It, Do It.

- **REVERSE PROBLEMS INTO POSSIBILITIES, BLOCKS INTO BLESSINGS.** Danielle's boyfriend went off to school, but rather than fear flirtations he may face, she's better off considering the distance between them as lending enchantment, or freeing her up for something better.

- **REFLECT ON POSITIVE THINGS.** Whatever the mind can conceive, you can achieve. "Dream it and you can be it." Lisa found a pile of porn videos in her boyfriend's drawer and refused to have sex with him anymore because she didn't think she looked as good in garters as the video porn stars did. Do affirmations: "I am beautiful. My body is beautiful. I deserve to have what I want. I am worthy."

You'll learn, here, too, about my special therapy tricks:

- **THE MIRROR LAW OF ATTRACTION:** Review every relationship as a mirror of yourself. If you think that no one wants a commitment, it's YOU who doesn't. If others treat you badly, you're treating yourself badly. There is no enemy without if there is no enemy within.

- **THE TWO NEW GOLDEN RULES OF SEX:** "Do unto others as you would have others do unto you" (people please others often as they would like to be pleased), and "Do unto others as they would have done unto them" (your preferences are not always the same as your partner's; find out what s/he likes or dislikes).

- **THE FOUR STEPS TO RESPONSIBLE SEX:** Stop and think. Recognize your needs. Assess the potential consequences.

Do something healthier. Before you act on an urge (for a teacher, neighbor's spouse, coworker), think, "What do I need (attention, ego food)? What could happen as a result of doing this? Who could get hurt?" Then accept the consequences of your actions and always learn a lesson. Joey should have thought before he followed his girlfriend's brother into the basement. Now he's ruined both her, and his own, trust. What could he have done instead?

Many times it's important to see the funny side of whatever's torturing you. Laughing about sex eases anxieties and guilt. That's why we joke around on *LovePhones*. One of the funniest times on *LovePhones* was when Paul called to say he once did it with a sheep when he was growing up on a farm in Ireland and now he can't do it with women because he keeps thinking of the sheep. I suggested he needed to confess. Read about what our precious producer, Sam, told him in the chapter on Am I A Freak.

People always want to know whether people lie on *LovePhones* and how I feel about it. I don't care—because it's true for somebody and because every made up story reveals a hint of your real fears or needs. When John says his penis caught on fire at a barbecue, I "hear" that he's afraid to get burned by his newfound sexual feelings. When Alan boasts his girlfriend rubbed his penis under the table during dinner at her parents' house, I say he clearly needs to rub his nose at authority. If Willy worries about putting beetles in his boxer shorts, he's likely really worried about what else is NOT in them.

Most importantly, find the love and spirituality in sex. Connect with others on that deep level. Therein lies the relief from pain and the hope for happiness. Take heart from knowing that rock stars who have done it all—Vince Neil had five women, Steven Tyler really did it in an elevator— say that after all the drug and sex orgies, watching, being watched, threesomes, foursomes, and acting out of all kinds, they have come to the conclusion that the best sex is a four-letter word—LOVE. Save it for someone you love.

Come to it all with self-esteem and self-empowerment—the ultimate sex appeal.

As Steven Tyler said at Woodstock, at end of his set, "The light at the end of the tunnel is you."

JAKE: *"BIG HOOTERS, MAN. IF SHE DOESN'T HAVE big ones, count me out."*

Pat: *"He has to be sensitive. That's number one."*

Jesse, 18: *"I like this guy Pete but his eyes are too close together and it turns me off. I don't want to have sex with him and look into those eyes."*

We all have an idea of what we like in someone. I call it a sexual script: a movie in your head of what your perfect partner should look like, and how the attraction goes. The most unusual or common characteristics can turn a person on or off. Know what your hot and cold buttons are.

Even if you think you can't explain why you are drawn to someone, if you stop and think about it, you can name the top things that attract you to or repel you from someone. What are they? Write them here.

MY LOVE CRITERIA

My Top Three Turn-ons:

1) _____

2) _____

3) _____

My Top Three Turn-offs:

1) _____

2) _____

3) _____

Very individual things can turn you on or off. Enrique, for example, called to say that he had a blind date and thought he liked the girl until they were sitting in the movies, and she blew in his ear. "I wasn't with that," he said, and dumped her.

After asking this question of hundreds of guys and girls, here's how it stacks up: guys always put some physical attribute into the top ten, if not number one. Girls rarely rate it number one; sometimes his looks are third, more often fourth. Usually in the top three for both males and females: sense of humor. Top three things women want: caring, intelligent, good sense of humor. A *New Woman* magazine survey found that after love, what women value most in men is that he respect her (72 percent) and be a true friend (66 percent). (Of course, you could add that he calls when he says he will and relinquishes the remote control sometimes.)

In a survey of hundreds of my students at N.Y.U., what her body was like mattered most to guys—eight out of ten made it number one—even though guys usually despair when the shoe is on the other foot (since they often don't think they measure up physically).

Here are the top attraction criteria for some rock stars and celebrities:

Sheryl Crow: "Intelligence, funny, wants to grow."

Lisa Loeb: "He has to have a good heart and listen."

R.E.M. lead singer Michael Stipe says sex appeal comes from the mouth and the eyes.

Gilbey Clarke, Guns N' Roses: "I like thin girls who are funny and hooters of course. Gotta have 'em."

Robin Wilson, Gin Blossoms' vocalist, said he's "romantically dysfunctional" but looks for: looks, intelligence, ambition (he'd prefer a biology major more than a Penthouse Pet), and a sense of humor.

Vince Neil, formerly of Mötley Crüe, now out on his own, pays attention to the eyes, boobs, and butt, but "legs and the face matter, too, and conversation comes into it somewhere."

Comedian/actor Pauly Shore: "I like naughty girls,

brightly colored clothes, and waist-length hair. My perfect woman would be a combination of Sherilyn Fenn, because she's mystic and glossy, with Sarah Jessica Parker because she's innocent."

Romance king Fabio, in search of a "twin soul," is attracted to feminine women, beautiful eyes, and personality (funny, sincere, and outgoing), and turned off by lying and women attracted to him for money.

Bret Michaels, Poison's lead singer, said he looks for "magnetism, personality, beautiful eyes and shoulders, and nice supple breasts" (does this describe his once-girlfriend, *Baywatch*'s Pamela Anderson?)

Joey Lawrence, from the TV show *Blossom*, is attracted to honesty, loyalty (he's been cheated on but never cheated!), and complete understanding. "Being in love means you would die for the other person."

Singer/songwriter Freedy Johnston wants a "sense of humor, someone shorter than me (at 5'7"), not overweight."

Bon Jovi guitarist Richie Sambora: "Good looks, with a personality shining through, sense of humor, and intelligence (guess wife Heather Locklear fits that bill)." (By the way, Richie told me he's not a party boy, doesn't like crowds, and prefers a quiet life, watching sports—what a difference from Heather's last wild man, Mötley Crüe rocker Tommy Lee.)

David Lee Roth: "Smarts, humor, and fury."

Aerosmith's Steven Tyler: "I really like the sluts. I have a thing for girls who just strut their stuff and have skinny little butts."

Broadway and TV soap actor Ricky Paull Goldin: "I love someone very witty who makes me laugh. And somebody I can sort of look up to in what they have done and what they want to do. It's a chemical thing. I never needed to have a brunette or blond girl in my life. The beauty thing is awesome but that only lasts a week or two." (Note his new fiancée, *Baywatch* babe, Yasmine Bleeth).

Urge Overkill lead singer Nash Kato: "She must have a sense of humor and be willing to talk about different subjects. She shouldn't care about what guys think and must love me for who I am and not for what I do."

Fred Schneider from the B52s: "Nice personality, good looks, car to drive around in."

Whitfield Crane, lead singer of Ugly Kid Joe: "Personality, cheekbones, and a good neck."

Bill Bellamy from MTV also watches the look in the eyes, as well as "how she carries herself. Is she sophisticated? Does she have charisma, good karma, good teeth? How is her body—is it healthy, does she work out? Is she fun?"

First Brother Roger Clinton: "The first is superficial, a visual attraction, 'two smiles' (breasts), then she has to be a good person, since I see a lot of beautiful people in L.A. and I got over that."

Van Halen's lead singer Sammy Hagar: "A beautiful face is wonderful, obviously that's all you see walking down the street. And then a nice body, a really nice butt in clothes. I'm into the crotch area, like in jeans or tight pants. The perfect crotch is what I call 'two fingers,' where, if they are in a normal standing position, I can put two fingers between the thighs and go all the way up and barely skim the two sides. But truly, I'm more attracted to the charisma of a body because there are some gorgeous women I wouldn't be interested in."

Many rock stars seem to value looks, because they pair up with models: Mick Jagger has Jeri Hall, Ric Ocasek has Paulina Porizkova. Billy Joel had Christie Brinkley. Steven Tyler's first wife was a model. David Bowie picked Iman. Rod Stewart married Rachel Hunter (and two similarly tall, blonds every ten years before that).

But many new alternative rockers eschew that trend. As Urge Overkill drummer Blackie said, "There's no reason for rock guys to be into models. You'd want a girl you can talk to. It'd be great if she were a CEO. Probably you just don't meet other types of girls in the course of your work."

Smarts over beauty is in. As Soundgarden's guitarist Kim Thayill says, "You can meet a beautiful woman but if she opens her mouth and a high squeaky voice comes out, it ruins it—the voice is everything for me, to tell if she's confident and smart." R.E.M. guitarist Peter Buck likes older women because they have more life experience to share, ideas to talk about in or out of bed.

Of all the rockers I've interviewed, one of the sweetest is Green Day bassist Mike Dirnt, all lovey-dovey with his sweet girlfriend of two years (now fiancée) when I met up with them in the artist camp at Woodstock II. "Everyone tells me he's the best boyfriend," she told me. "He does get nervous performing sometimes (like at the '94 MTV Awards), but other than that he's wonderful." No wonder, in answer to "What do women want?" Mike said, "Whatever they want, you have to ask them, and then give it to them."

You go, boy.

"What is the one sure sign someone is sexually attracted to you when you meet them for the first time?"

Research shows people get attracted to one another in the first fifteen seconds. Here's a quick test to tell if they like what they see:

SEXUAL ATTRACTION TEST

❑ Eye contact that lingers. Research shows the best seduction glance is 60 to 70 percent of the time in lingering looks, the rest glancing away.

❑ Body language (facing you, moving closer, mimicking your body positions).

❑ Slight touches that invade the safer "personal distance" people usually maintain.

❑ Smiles.

❑ Suggestive movements (licking lips, touching finger to mouth).

❑ Questions (where you live, what you like).

❑ Direct openings for further contact ("Have you seen this movie?" "Do you like concerts?").

STRIKE WHILE THE IRON IS HOT

Cerise: *"What do you think of females making the first move? Has society changed enough so they won't be seen as sleazy? I saw this guy at a concert but didn't go up to him. Should I have?"*

Yes. Go for it. Don't hesitate. Let this be the rule: do it if you think that later you would regret not having done it. Candlebox lead singer Kevin Martin advised Cerise, "You should have talked to him. I stop people on the street to talk to them. So does Madonna."

LOVE AT FIRST SIGHT

"I met this guy at a party and it was that typical story that I saw him across the crowded room and that was 'it.' Is that stupid? We only talked a little bit, and now we have our first date coming up. Is there such a thing as love at first sight?"

There are definitely people who claim as soon as they saw each other, they knew that was "the one." R.E.M. bassist Mike Mills and his girlfriend felt "intense energy" when they spotted each other across the room as she was shooting pool at a South Beach restaurant. They are still together after a few years.

Other famous couples didn't make it far after instant attraction. *Beverly Hills 90210* bad girl Shannen Doherty and hunky Ashley Hamilton wed two weeks after meeting, and separated within weeks. Actress Drew Barrymore proposed to clubowner Jerry Thomas in an alleyway after knowing him five weeks; in three hours they were wed in his bar and six weeks later, were divorced.

For others, instant attraction shows all the signs of lasting. Talk show host/actress Ricki Lake became engaged to businessman Rob Sussman three weeks after meeting, and wed son thereafter, feeling their love was so powerful, it just made sense. It happened to Hammer, who told me at an Aspen club that he went up to his now-wife at a church revival meeting and said, "Hello, you're from out of town," looked in her eyes and felt love at first sight. Bill Cosby proposed the second week of knowing his now long-wed wife.

Julie: *"I met a guy the other night at a party at a friend's house and I fell head over heels for him. We had a perfect time together, spending the whole night watching the stars and talking, and having breakfast in the morning. He was so perfect for me in every way, so cute and fun to talk to. He told me I was the prettiest girl he's ever seen and that he can't wait to see me again. But now I haven't heard from him in three weeks. Maybe he's busy. Should I call him?"*

By all means call him. Rather than waste time fretting, always ask for an explanation. Even in a worst-case scenario that someone you want is not interested, it's better to get the truth than suffer imaginary rejections or intense anxiety. Keep in mind that "love at first sight" can be blind and not love, but lust or infatuation. Falling too hard too fast is often evidence more of desperation than destiny.

For some lucky ones, love at first sight blossoms and lasts, but generally real love needs time to grow from sharing and supporting one another through happy and sad times. Have six dates before deciding s/he's "perfect" for you. Then be cautious for six months, observing how s/he treats parents, friends, other men and women, coworkers, children, and animals. Is s/he caring, truthful, able to cope with stress, there for you in an emergency? Does s/he keep his word? Your guy has already failed miserably on that one. Don't make excuses for him or overestimate his initial enthusiasm; actions speak louder than words.

SEXUAL CHEMISTRY

Tammy: *"What is chemistry between two people? I've been dating this guy and I really like him. We've had sex a few times and it's thrilling to share what we really like and to feel real close and sexy. Last time we were together I told him my fantasy of doing it with another girl and I went down on him for the first time and he loved it. He told me he wanted to run away with me. That rang in my ears for days. When he called me, I got such a pounding in my heart that I had to go lie down for a while. I figure that means I'm crazy about him. I only had that feeling once before. Is this what they call chemistry?"*

Chemistry is that exhilarating feeling of mutual magnetism that's actually a magical combination of psychological and physical factors. Psychologically, you seem to read one another's minds and feel your souls are in sync, but the surges you feel also arise from chemicals that flow in the body when you are in a state of arousal, and set off a complex interaction of the brain and various body organs—from the heart to the sexual organs.

For example, adrenaline makes your heart beat faster and your palms sweat. Triggered by someone's look or voice, another love hormone, oxytocin (the same chemical that's stimulated during breast-feeding), stimulates the smooth muscles and sensitizes your nerves that make you more sensitive to pleasure and emotionally attracted. When you add up these reactions, you then decide you're "in love," which makes you more physically turned on, and the cycle escalates! You get so conditioned to this cycle, that someone's "look" or the sound of their voice can set it off!

"I like two guys but with one of them I feel this real sexual chemistry. When we make love, he seems to know what I think and we talk in shorthand. He just looks at me and knows where to touch me. The other one is sweet, but I have to spell it out to him. Should I drop this one?"

Some people are just on the same sexual, and general, wavelength. There are a hundred different explanations for this, from personality types to horoscopes, brain style preferences, or sound wave frequencies. We are attracted to people who fill our needs. You have to decide how important this sexual compatibility is to you in the overall scheme of things. Make your list of love criteria, prioritize the qualities, and compare the balance sheet.

"I like to smell my boyfriend's body, particularly in his armpits and after we had sex. He said he likes to smell my fluids on his hands after sex. Are we weird? Can this really turn you on?"

Yes, it works in the animal world. Chemicals called pheromones (found in sweat glands, armpits, genitals, around the nipples, face, soles of the feet) are a natural, odorless, scent of attraction. In one study men gravitated more to seats in a movie house doused with pheromones. In another, men rated photographs of women as more attractive when scented with pheromones. Attraction is built on the interplay of all the senses, but the sense of smell can be the most powerful because the impulses from the olfactory bulb go more directly to the part of the brain that controls memory and pleasure.

Having your lover's lingering smell is a wonderful reminder of your good time and how much you care about each other. In Greek dances, like in the famous movie *Zorba the Greek,* the men put handkerchiefs under their arms to get it soaked with their perspiration, and then wave it in front of a woman's nose to attract her. Lovers wear amulets around their necks of their lover's sweat, and take a whiff every now and then. Scent is one of the most powerful, yet ignored, senses in attraction.

WANTING WHAT YOU CAN'T HAVE

Too many women go for the one that's unavailable and unattainable. In the old days they did this for the challenge and because of low self-esteem. The "new woman" consciously picks such a man when she *knows* she doesn't want a commitment!

But, as women get more independent, more men are falling into the same old trap.

Eric, 23: *"I always seem to go for the girls I can't get. They're all tall, blond and real lookers. But they don't notice me. And I don't care for the girls who like me, the real sweet ones who don't look as good. What's up?"*

You're in a vicious "Daisy Chain of Attraction," wanting ones who don't want you, not wanting ones you want you. In the dating game, people have a score in their head of how much they're worth in the dating market, and whom they can attract. The most obvious factors that go into their score (called their "eligibility factor") are looks, power, money, personality, lifestyle. If you can't change your bank account or beauty, the best way to up your worth is by inflating your self-esteem, projecting that you are a terrific person.

Poison's Bret Michaels thinks his hair attracts. "I look better with long hair. Unless I had headlights, I'll keep it as long as I can. God's honest truth, When I was fourteen, an older friend of mine had long hair, looked cool, played in a rock band and was dating a beautiful girl. I figured the long hair had something to do with his dating a beautiful girl."

What are your strong scoring points?

WHY AREN'T THEY ATTRACTED TO ME?

Eugene: *"I was in love with this woman and thought she was the one. Then she went off on a business trip to California and called me and said she met someone else. This is the third time this has happened to me. What's wrong with women? I'm giving up."*

Nothing's wrong with women. Your love antennae need adjusting because you're being attracted to the wrong women. Watch for your patterns and the early signs that they're not committed, so you don't repeat yourself.

Remember my Mirror Law of Attraction: love interests are a mirror of yourself, and reflect your needs or wants. If they run off, you're symbolically running off.

MADONNA-WHORE SYNDROME

David: *"I'm a clean-cut guy with a really sweet girlfriend, so how come I see girls in slutty dresses and I think about doing it with them? I don't want to ruin things with my girlfriend. What's up with me?"*

Steve has a similar problem: *"I used to be a love-'em-and-leave-'em guy, but now I want to settle down. The trouble is every time I meet a nice girl, the kind my mother would love and who would make a good wife and mother, I lose sexual interest in her. What can I do to fix this?"*

Steve and David are among the scores of men with the "Madonna-Whore Syndrome" (the Madonna Virgin Mary, that is, not the rock star), where they separate sex and love, and "split" women into the "good girls" (the good wife and mother) and the "bad girls" (who are wild and sexy). Usually the problem emerges after marriage and childbirth, when the man stops feeling sexual toward his wife, and focuses his sexual fantasies on another woman he can "allow" to be wanton.

Not unsurprisingly, some rock stars make this split. A *LovePhones* caller asked Poison's Bret Michaels, "I've been seeing this guy for three years and then he dumped me for a stripper. What's guys' attraction to strippers?" Michaels admitted he could identify with the attraction. "I've dated a stripper. Some have complete relationships but it would bother me for my girlfriend to strip." Poison drummer Rikki Rocket added, "The guys go to look, but don't touch. It's a male bonding thing. To some strippers, sex is a turn-off. I appreciate the strippers. For me, it's a release." Former Mötley Crüe Vince Neil also feels the draw.

To escape this cycle, be aware that what's turning you on sexually is blinding you to what's important in a long-lasting relationship. Mix sex and love. Let a woman be sweet and also sexy.

Some men are threatened by more refined women, and feel safer going for ones they don't fear would reject them, or wouldn't care about hurting or being hurt by.

But, the woman has to do her part, too.

Rebecca: *"How do you stop guys from getting into that Madonna-whore thing?"*

Be an angel in the kitchen and a devil in the bedroom. Ex-Blondie Deborah Harry merges her two heroines: Doris Day and Marilyn Monroe. And *Playboy* centerfold and TV host Rhonda Schear also plays both ends against the middle. "On my show I play with dolls, so I combine the sexy vamp with the little girl mind. It drives guys wild to have both!"

DADDY–DON JUAN DILEMMA

Surprise: women make the same split! Like Tia: *"I'm dating two guys. One is sweet and funny, always does nice things for me, and my parents love him, but he's not my type and I'm not sexually attracted to him. The other is gorgeous and exciting and my friends are all jealous, but he doesn't call me when he says he will and he's a real flirt with other women. How can I get out of this trap?"*

You are in a trap, but you can get out. You have the equivalent of the "Madonna-Whore Syndrome" in men, called the "Daddy–Don Juan Dilemma" in women, meaning you separate sex and love and "split" men into two types: the nice guy-daddy figure whom you treat as a friend and not a lover, and the Don Juan who wines and dines and then dumps you, but whom you wildly desire. Younger women often go for the Don Juan type, attracted by superficial looks, what car he drives, or who their friends drool over. They become addicted to the challenge of making the unavailable, unattainable man want them, to prove they are worthy or desirable when deep down they're insecure. When you mature, you learn more about the difference between that short-lived adrenaline high and the more lasting intimacy of a stable love with a nice guy.

To repair the split, make the nice guy sexually satisfying by imagining him instead of the Don Juan in your most erotic fantasies. When you treat him as you would the most exciting lover, you give him a chance to be that way. Instead of being drawn to the "bad boy" to get free of being such a "good girl," allow yourself to express sweetness and also naughtiness. Own your own power instead of living through the guy.

FAKE NICE GUY

"I met a guy at a wild party who made a big play for me in front of all his friends. I was so lonely, I slept with him on the second date, even though he said he had a "sometime gal pal." He called a few times, being very friendly, but the next time we bumped into each other, he ignored me and flirted with others. When I asked why, he said he had to pay attention to his friends and didn't like public displays. That didn't stop him the first time, so is he a jerk, or am I, for going for him?"

If he really cared about you, he would be more consistently affectionate no matter what the circumstances. Like many desperate, lonely, or naive women, you fall too quickly for any man who shows interest. Too often these guys turn out to be what I call "fake nice guys," who say what you want to hear ("I'll call you tomorrow," "You're the most exciting woman I ever met") but have no follow-through and leave you frustrated. Rather than be angry at him or at yourself, see this experience as a stepping-stone to developing higher self-esteem and tougher criteria for men. Be more suspicious of early warning signs, like his admission of a sometime-girlfriend and his wild pursuit of you while drunk; that doesn't foreshadow long-term interest.

Watch out for signs of the true nice guy: he has girlfriends he doesn't have sex with, guy friends who are happily married, and lets you listen to his answering machine.

DO NICE GUYS FINISH LAST?

Too many nice guys think rats who treat women poorly, win. Like Greg, 22: *"I'm a nice guy. I lost 75 pounds and look good. But why can't I get a girl when the guys who treat women bad get them in the sack right away?"*

Forget those guys. The girls they attract anyway are ones you wouldn't want because they want to be treated badly. Hold out for the girl who appreciates being treated well—she'll have higher self-esteem, which bodes better for a good relationship in the long run. As long as you're not a doormat, stay as you are.

John Henton from the TV show *Living Single* endorsed Greg staying the Nice Guy who pleases women. "You say you are going to call, you call. No games. No screening your messages. All my relationships have been real." And in sex, "I got no problem telling her what I want so it's like 'what you need?' That way if you are satisfied in bed you don't have to go any place else. I make sure she is fine and dandy."

Take heart from the classic movie *When Harry Met Sally,* where the Meg Ryan character eventually realizes her best friend (played by Billy Crystal) was better for her than all the heart-breakers she cried to him over.

The nice guy can be real sexy. Take Tom Hanks. With several hit movies, he's a sex symbol, even though he never saw himself as a real-life sex magnet and has only slept with seven women. "When the sex thing (the sexual revolution) happened," he said, "I was totally crippled when it came down to confidence . . . There was a long period of time where I swear to God being funny just didn't get you laid, no matter how funny you were." But his Nice Guy personality has paid off. It will for you, too.

ARE YOU A BUTTHEAD MAGNET?

Lisa loves jerks. *"The guys I like are always too cool for words. They think they're so good-looking and they never call me after we go out. It really hurts if we've had sex."*

Nicole, 21, is another jerk magnet. *"The guy I'm crazy about told me I could lose a few pounds and that he wouldn't mind sleeping with my best friend because she's got a hot bod and tight buns. When we go to clubs, he takes other girls' numbers right in front of me, even though he says he won't call them. The guy I was sleeping with before borrowed my credit card to buy a necklace for his grandmother but I found out later he gave it to another girl he was seeing, and he never paid me back nor got me anything."*

Jeannie, 17: *"I only attract losers, dorks who don't take me out nice, and just want sex, or who get with other girls, like real male 'hos. Where can I get a pocket porker protector?"*

Reach inside your head—that's where you get your love antennae that attract the pigs who only want to pork you. What a great idea—imagine a pocket spray that you can spritz in the face of any guy who just wants to get in your pants, and he's gone.

Take the "Jerk Magnet Sex Test" to recognize the bed-hopping buttheads before you fall:

JERK MAGNET TEST

- ❏ Are you always attracted to guys who have slept with many women?
- ❏ Do they tell you in the heat of sex what you want to hear but not follow through?
- ❏ Do they please themselves first in sex?
- ❏ Do they always get you to do what they want in sex?
- ❏ Do they not listen when you talk?
- ❏ Do you catch them in lies?
- ❏ Do they cheat on you?

Score: Just two "yes" answers and you need one of those pocket porker protectors that Jeannie wants.

The ultimate Bad Boys of rock, Mötley Crüe, during their "Girls, Girls, Girls" tour supposedly had a contest for who could do the most women without showering or bathing. Nikki Siss won, going seventeen days and taking thirty women without washing.

Entertainment Tonight host, Leeza Gibbons, is a self-confessed "recovering bad boy addict," who suffered because of low self-esteem. Two similar addicts I met doing her TV talk show did an amusing cheer: "Bad boys, they have lust in their lips, grind in their hips, bump in their rump, passion in their eyes and fire in their thighs . . . making them devastatingly . . . motivationally . . . fine." But, to audience cheers, Leeza revealed she realized real excitement comes from a sense of security in a relationship.

JERKETTE MAGNETS

Here's where the nice guy becomes a doormat. Like Danny: *"I try to be nice and girls treat me mean. They promise to go out and then stand me up. Or they let me buy them presents, make me please them in bed, and then don't take my call. What's wrong with me?"*

What's wrong is your low self-esteem and poor self-image that keeps drawing you to women who treat you poorly. Expect to be appreciated. Avoid the "jerkettes"— who criticize, cheat, expect to be catered to, and care more about what you do for them than who you are.

MANIZERS

Talk shows love to trash guys who are womanizers. But guess what—women are manizers, too. Like Kate: *"I'm a manizer and proud of it. I'm a 36-C with seductive skills to match my cup size. I have no respect for men, so I just get them and do them. I had some rock stars and some professors. I told the last one I needed help in class, and seduced him, married and all, over coffee, dressed in a skirt with a big slit up the side. I give them head and control them. But I'm worried that I don't really like sex. What's wrong?"*

You're frightened to feel anything so you control men instead. Men must have really hurt and controlled you, so you're getting revenge. Resist the temptation to seduce. Just as an experiment, find a nice guy you can pour your heart out to.

Ex-Blondie Deborah Harry, making a recent comeback with "Def, Dumb and Blond," admitted to Kate, "at various times I, too, have been in the Man-hater's Club. Guys wear me out. Their male egos get me."

Solution: as the Pearl Jam song title suggests, get a "Better Man."

FEMALE SPUR POSSE

A few years ago there was a big news story about a group of guys in a California school who joined a secret club called the "Spur Posse" where they'd score how many girls they could have sex with. To get even with such men, Michelle and Barbara (whom I met on a *Richard Bey* TV show) started an equivalent group for women, the "HomeGirls," to collect, conquer, and dog, guys. In notebooks and diaries they rated guys' penises and performance.

"We've been the butt of buttheads too long," Michelle explained. "Men have all cheated on us so it's time we're in charge. We go up to a guy in a bar and snow him, take him back to our place, do it, and get up and leave right away with no explanation, telling him we'll call the next day but never doing it. He misses us bad because the sex was so hot. We are not 'hos—we're just out to set the record straight and have a good time in doing it."

In psychology we say these women were "identifying with the aggressor," taking on the qualities of those they feel victimized by. Revenge may be sweet, but living well is the best revenge.

WHY DOES HE LOVE ME?

"How do I know if someone likes me for my intelligence or just for my body?"

Find out what their love criteria are. Ask, "Why do you like me—tell me the top three reasons." Or watch how they behave. If they want more time in bed and less time sharing other experiences, there's your answer.

BETTER MAN

Chris: *"I'm a nice guy. I met a girl I thought was ugly at first but we talked and went to the movies and had a great time and she got sexier to me. But my friends make fun of me and say she's ugly. Should I stop going out with her?"*

No. You discovered a valuable lesson—people can become sexually attractive when they listen and care, and when you share good times and feelings. Ignore your friends—sex appeal is in the eyes of the beholder. Someday maybe they, too, will see beyond the obvious.

QUIRKY TURN-ONS

"For me, girls have to be tall and leggy and beautiful with full lips like Julia Roberts."

"I'm blond and bubbly but I like moody Hispanic boys. I feel safer with them, like they'll protect me."

"I like bald-headed guys in their forties. They remind me of my father."

"I like women with big nipples and a lot of pubic hair. Otherwise I don't want to have sex with the girl." (Aereolas and hairy holes—what a combo, said my LovePhones producer Sam.)

"I'm a chubby chaser. I get erections thinking of sex with fat chicks. I'm 5'8" and 130 pounds. My first girlfriend was fat. My friends make fun of me. What should I do?"

Specific preferences are conditioned by experience. If a favorite aunt was overweight, you might like similarly full-figured women (or the opposite, if your father was heavy and you had a bad relationship, you might go for skinny men). If your first love had lots of hair, you'll be attracted to hair. Ignore others' teasing; make up your own mind. Examine how your criteria serve you: to earn others' envy, avoid competition and rejection, rebel against parents, prove your independence.

If your criteria limit you, make up three new characteristics that appeal to you and find people who fit them.

HOMEWORK: Write them here:

NEW LOVE CRITERIA

1. _____

2. _____

3. _____

John weighs 150 pounds and is 5'9" tall and likes women who are Rubenesque but wanted to know, *"Where can I find these women?"*

Ex-Blondie Deborah Harry, Honorary Love Doctor on *LovePhones* that night, suggested: "At the fat farm. Be happy that something turns you on. Some people don't get turned on to anything."

NOT COLOR BLIND

April: *"I'm black and only attracted to white men. Black men boss and diss me, telling me 'you're my girl' and then messing with my homegirls. I had a kid with a white boy and now we're having trouble anyway. I'm dark-complexioned and always felt bad about it until recently when people say I have beautiful skin."*

That should prove to you that looks don't ensure a happy relationship. Examine what your preference means (being cool, increasing your status) and see the loopholes in stereotypes. Build your self-esteem instead of banking it on who you're with.

Living Single's John Henton advised, "You gotta give brothers a chance."

TURN-OFFS

Most of us have inclusion criteria essential for us to turn on. Other people operate on exclusion criteria—what turns them off!

Jim: *"I liked this girl I hadn't had sex with yet, until I went to the beach with her. She had all this black hair hanging outside her bathing-suit bottom. It grossed me out. Now I don't want to have sex with her. Should I tell her?"*

If you care about her, this is easily correctable. Pubic hair can be removed (many girls get a "bikini wax" to shape their public hair just as a guy shaves his beard). Hair naturally grows down many a girl's leg—those women in the sex magazines and videos who have such small triangles of hair have it styled that way!

If you want her to coif, break it to her in a gentle, fun way. For example, take a shower together and suggest she shave you, to take the focus off her. Then suggest you trim together.

FOR LOVE OR MONEY?

Heather, 17: *"The guy I've been seeing gives me a lot of love and even once got arrested for me for a silly thing, but I met another guy that I like now. He opens doors for me, took me to an expensive dinner, bought me some CDs, and even put money in my parking meter, while my boyfriend has no car and just takes me out for pizza. Should I leave my boyfriend for him?"*

What are your values? As in the famous movie *Indecent Proposal* with Demi Moore and Robert Redford, would you sleep with someone for a million dollars? Sounds like you're seduced by bucks now. But since you once valued love, if this richer guy doesn't give you that, too, you're headed for feeling empty.

John, 18: *"I go to school in Florida and my father got me a Ferrari. Do girls want to have sex with me just for my car?"*

Pick them up in a jalopy and put your sex appeal to the test.

GETTING OVER A PRETTY FACE

George: *"How do I stop just looking at a girl to get her in the sack by how she looks, and look at what kind of girl she is? I've only gone for 10's."*

Give yourself a challenge: for a month, purposefully date only "6's." Do you think others measure you by how pretty the girl on your arm is? Recognize it if you do, and value who you're with for themselves, not what your friends will think of them.

Use the bag test: put a bag over their head. (So you pay attention to their heart.) Or put a bag over *your* head (accomplishes the same). Or make it a two-bagger.

GAP WALK

Rasheed, 15: *"I'm looking for a girl who will have sex with me, and the guys in school said that if a girl walks with a big gap in her legs, like bowlegged, it means she's had a lot of sex, like she's had to spread her legs a lot and they got more stuck that way. Is that true?"*

If you buy that, you'd probably buy hot coffee in the desert. But, true enough, after a long, hard horseback ride, anybody's thighs feel bowed. And cowboys do walk bowlegged, after years of straddling a horse. You can feel a little sore after a long, acrobatic sex marathon, but no girl would have permanent bowlegs from sex, no matter how much she had, or how tough the lover to ride!

MAMA'S BOYS

Francine: *"I like this guy but he's always saying he has to spend time with his mother. When we have sex he even talks about his mother."*

You got a mama's boy. Some men are so attached to their mothers they can't marry or have sex, because they feel married to their mothers. Or they can only be with a young woman, and once she becomes a mother, they get "incest" fears (like supposedly Elvis Presley had). On the other hand, First Brother Roger Clinton admitted as an Honorary Love

Doctor that he was a mama's boy, and proud of it, but he claimed it made him more, rather than less, able to fall in love with a woman.

VACATION GOGGLES

"I went on a vacation and wasn't looking for anyone but I met a guy I fell in love with. We had some of the most romantic evenings I ever dreamed about. Now that I'm back, I'm not happy with my boyfriend. I've talked to the other guy every night, but he lives a few hours away in another city. Can that last, and should I break up with my boyfriend?"

Obviously if you fell so hard so fast, you were not so committed to your boyfriend to begin with. What's missing that this new romance fulfilled? See if your current relationship can be saved with the attention and romance you experienced on vacation before you pursue this new man further. "Vacation goggles" can cloud your judgment, making you intoxicated with movie-set moonlit beaches and freedom from expectations, rigid roles, and everyday stresses. You'd have to spend as much time, in regular (not romantic) daily life, to see if your relationship with the new guy can withstand reality.

LOSERS—NOT

Alan, 15: *"I'm a loser. I can't get a girl to look at me. What can I do?"*

It's common when you're young or unsure of yourself to feel like a loser, even if you're not! *LovePhones* Honorary Love Doctor, pop star/singer Richard Marx offered some great support: "I know what it feels like to be insecure and in high school. I was the king of girls saying 'Let's just be friends' and you know how painful that can be. I felt like a conversational wreck and undesirable. No matter how many women throw themselves at me now when I play, I never let it go to my head because I remember what it was like when I couldn't get them to notice me in high school. It's not me they want, it's the music and some idea in their head of who I am. The best part about going through that pain is that I'm not caught up in how I look. And being the king of 'Let's just be friends' made me develop female friendships that made me a better husband."

Christina needs to get that. *"I have a friend all guys want to do. But when I rap them, they run. I blow kisses like her and dare them to come and get it, but no bites. What am I doing wrong?"*

Nothing is right or wrong. Some people have natural charisma and ooze sex appeal—that comes from confidence. Don't copy your friend. Be yourself.

WHERE TO GO?

"Where do I go to meet someone?"

It's one of the most common questions I get. It depends on your style. If you're a quiet sort, taking a course, working on a fund-raiser, or going to a bookstore or coffee shop is a great way to meet someone of like interest and mellow speed. But if you're an excitable risk-taker, my favorite suggestions are concerts, sports events, and amusement parks. As a spokesperson for Universal Studios Florida, I developed Theme Park Therapy, observing couples falling prey to seduction after going on action-packed rides, the result of a powerful cocktail of chemicals released in the body—adrenaline (the energizer), phenylethylamine (a natural high), oxytocin (the cuddle chemical), and endorphins (the pleasure chemicals). Just a little bit of fear and a lot of energy, and you find the one next to you thrilling.

INAPPROPRIATE ATTRACTIONS

"My boyfriend of seven months is very sweet but not for me. He's too old, still lives with his parents, has no college education and goes from job to job, while I'm the opposite. Now, I've become attracted to one of his closest friends who's more my type. He likes me, too. How should I break up with my boyfriend and approach his friend?"

Acting too impulsively on an attraction to your boyfriend's friend—however compelling—would be selfish and hurtful.

It's okay to want someone who seems more "right" for you (research supports that, while any match can work if you want it to, having compatible lifestyles is the best predictor for a long-lasting marriage) but I commend your desire not to hurt your current boyfriend. Save his ego by reminding him of his good points and that you cared. Wait a reasonable "grace period"—three months or so—before you start up with his friend, to give him time to heal and everyone to re-adjust.

WEIRDOS

"Wherever I go, guys offer to pay me for sex or expose themselves to me. I hitched and a guy exposed himself to me. I met an old guy and he asked me if I wanted to see his pig, so I went to his house and his wife came home and threw me out, calling me a 'ho. Where are the decent guys?"

Where is your judgment? Hitching is dangerous. Going with strangers is dangerous. You've been lucky so far. Remember my Mirror Law of Attraction: everyone in your life is a mirror reflection of yourself. How are you an exhibitionist? You're drawing these men to you to see something about yourself. What do you want to expose in yourself? How do you see yourself as a sex object that can be bought?

ATTRACTED TO OLD BOYFRIEND

"I'm getting married but I'm attracted to my old boyfriend. He was my first. What can I do about this?"

People often carry a flame for the first person they had sex with. That doesn't mean you have to marry him. You probably also have marriage jitters—anxieties about whether your fiancée is right for you. Endure them. It's best not to see your old boyfriend in order to resist temptation, or if you do see him, resolve your incomplete feelings—unless you really want to marry him, in which case, cancel this wedding fast.

BOSS ATTRACTION

Steve: *"My boss asked me to work late one night and called me into her office. She said she had to find out more about me to see if I could get a promotion and asked me if I was seeing anyone, and if I was stable, which included knowing whether I was sexually satisfied. Before I knew it, she pulled up her skirt and got in my face. When it was all over, she said she was going to give me five hours of overtime instead of an hour. I really liked it but what should I do if she wants to do it again?"*

You may have enjoyed your evening of sex but you're embroiled in a sexual harassment situation, with your boss using her position of power to entice you into sex. Continuing this could make your days on the job hellish. Tell her you prefer "no," and if she persists, look for another job.

TEACHER CRUSH

Amber: *"My friend is infatuated with our math teacher. His wife just had a baby. Her father died when she was ten. How do I help her?"*

Crushes can be healthy but help her understand that a ghost from her past is driving her present. Losing her father at an early age was traumatic; it's most likely the reason she's drawn to men who could be a substitute father for her and why his just having a baby makes him even more attracted.

Dave was able to overcome an inappropriate attraction to his teacher with the brain-retraining technique I taught him. He had been masturbating thinking about her and had to stop making that pleasurable association. "I switched her picture to someone else with different hair and eyes and personality," he explained, "just someone I made up." It's simple learning theory. Associate something with pleasure (through orgasm) and you want to repeat it; if that connection is dangerous, form a different association that works better for you. Change the TV channel in your brain.

MOTHER'S BEST FRIEND

Robert, 20: *"I'm sleeping with my mother's best friend, but I feel guilty about it. She has known me since I was seven and tells me, 'I'd never do anything to hurt you because you're my son.' It started six weeks ago when we were drinking and started to kiss. She tells everyone in front of me, 'He's like my son.' How can I get out of this?"*

Just tell her, "No more." It's been so ingrained that you're like her son, likely you feel sex with her is like incest. Also, you may feel used since she's bragging about you. It's good that you don't like deceit. Be honest and tell her that you're not comfortable with that game and don't want to play anymore.

GAYDAR

Lisa, 22: *"I became best friends with this guy and then found out he is gay. We do everything together and have lots of fun and I can tell him anything. When he tells me about guys he goes with, I get very jealous. But I know we can never be together because I'm a girl. Why do I always seem attracted to gay guys? A friend says I have a radar for them, and calls it 'gaydar.'"*

You're on the right track—that you start falling in love by forming a friendship. Sharing with someone is the best basis for a friendship and a sexual attraction. Obviously he's a nice guy, so use that criterion to find a heterosexual guy who can love you.

Women fall in love with gay men partly because they're fun, they understand and appreciate women, and they aren't threatening. Since the relationship has built-in limits, neither person fears rejection or worries how you act; consequently, you are yourself, which makes you appear sexy and feel appreciated.

Examine whether you are both concentrating on your relationship in order to avoid the fears that come from dating potential mates. Get up your courage to face the dating wars.

NARCISSISTIC GUY

Q. What's the definition of a narcissist?
A. A person who says, "Enough talk about me, now let's talk about what you think about me."

Did you hear the joke about the woman who filed for divorce because her husband was too in love with someone else—himself!

"My boyfriend is a Peter Pan. How do I get him to grow up?"

The Peter Pan guys can't and won't make a commitment. They usually don't change until late in life, or when they can't attract the lovers they want. The ultimate narcissist, Warren Beatty, didn't stop his big-time playing around until in his fifties (when he had a baby with actress Annette Bening).

Lemonheads' Evan Dando sings of a classic commitment-phobe in "Confetti": "He kinda, shoulda sorta woulda loved her if he could've/He'd rather be alone than pretend."

PASSIVE-AGGRESSIVE GUY

"The guy I'm dating makes me crazy. One day he tells me I'm different in sex from any other woman because I make him feel so relaxed and I say what I want, but the next day if I ask him to do anything, like kiss me in certain places, he slams me for being demanding. If I get angry, he goes and sleeps on the couch. If I ask him what's wrong, he says everything's fine. Am I wrong to get upset and why does he act like this?"

He's a classic passive-aggressive man who gives double messages, leaving you on an emotional seesaw between hope and frustration. Passive-aggressive people seethe with anger inside but veil it behind innocence or good intentions, or withdraw into the "silent treatment" when challenged. The passive-aggressive guy will forget your birthday, show up chronically late for dates, or refuse to say "I love you." He treats you that way because you allow him to. Examine whether you pick men who keep you at a safe distance. Don't blame yourself—he has a problem. Don't let him talk you out of getting angry when he makes you mad or twists stories.

BORDERLINE

Jay, 26: *"My girlfriend flies off the handle. One minute we'll be having sex, and she's laughing and smiling, and the next, she seems to fly into a rage. What's wrong with her?"*

Such volatile emotions could mean she's intensely guilty about sex. Or they could be the sign of hormonal imbalances, that happen in PMS (premenstrual syndrome), or the result of a more serious psychiatric disorder like manic depression, or borderline personality. People with a borderline personality "split" into good or bad, or vacillate dramatically between the two. They have never learned that people can be constant in their emotions, so they are never constant themselves. Check with a psychiatrist, who can diagnose both physical and psychological problems.

IN LOVE WITH STRIPPER

"I went to a nudie bar last week and this gorgeous girl on stage made eyes at me. Then she slinked over and leaned down and stuck her breasts in my face. All the other guys were looking at me with envy. It was great because I never had much luck with girls before and here was this girl who was so hot and picked me. Later she came over and did a lap dance and let me kiss her nipples. Then she whispered in my ear, 'Will you be my boyfriend?' She told me to meet her after she got off. I waited 'til three a.m. and met her in the parking lot. We went for a drive in my car and she told me lots of other guys have given her big presents like bracelets and one guy even took her on a trip to the Bahamas, but that she liked me best of all. She said it's against the rules for the girls to see the guys who come into the club, but that if we were going out it would be okay and that she really wanted to have sex with me. Should I do it?"

Can't you tell when you're being taken for a ride? A strip bar is the wrong place to measure your attractiveness. The girls are out for your money. How could she fall for you that fast? Sure, maybe you are sweet but imagine that is not a compliment, but an insult that you are a sucker an experienced girl like her can smell a mile away. Enjoy your quick ego hit and go find yourself a girl in real life who will enjoy your company without milking you for gifts on the first date.

A number of celebrities and rockers like to hang out at strip clubs—after all, the atmosphere is conducive to carousing, flaming libidos, and machismo.

DOES HE LIKE ME?

"I like this guy at the supermarket. We're both baggers. I get excited about how he leans the bag against his leg when he packs. I got an earring for him. He rolls his eyes when he looks at me. Does that mean he likes me?"

You have to do what's called "reality testing": finding out if what you imagine is shared by another person. So say, "I saw you roll your eyes. Was that a signal to me of hello?" Unless you "reality test," you can make up a whole misguided story in your head interpreting someone else's actions.

AGE-APPROPRIATE

John, 19: *"Younger girls and older chicks want me, but girls my age, seventeen to twenty-one, won't go for me. How come?"*

Likely your love antennae are not whirring for girls your age. You're probably scared of them. You don't have to worry about impressing younger girls, and you don't care what happens with older women, so you're not anxious about the outcome and ironically that makes you more attractive. But you care too much, and are frightened, about girls your own age, so they pick up your withdrawal and your anxiety and it doesn't work out. Just relax. Be yourself. Be with girls your age as you would with younger or older women and they'll flock to you.

"I'm sixteen and I like only older women in their thirties. I think about them all the time. How can I get myself to think about younger women, when I don't want to."

What do you think about when you think of older women? Usually young men desire the older woman to be a sexual teacher. They think she knows more, and feels more confident about sex than younger girls—and they're usually right. If you want to also like younger women your age, pick one who has the qualities you would want in the older woman. Anyway, it's okay to be attracted to older women; it can work even better for you in a few years.

TRIANGLES

Mary, 17: *"I liked this guy who was bisexual and then he fell in love with another guy I was dating. What should I do?"*

If the guy you were dating likes him back, then drop both of them and find another playground that isn't so complicated. You remind me of that movie *Threesome* where the girl liked the gay guy who liked the heterosexual guy who loved the girl. Nobody got what they wanted! After graduation, they all went their separate ways.

DEALING WITH GROUPIES

Stephanie: *"I have a friend who is a major groupie. She gets involved with sex with all these guys and gets emotionally involved and hurt when they dump her."*

A lot of alternative rock groups, like guys in Spin Doctors and Candlebox, have told me the groupie approach doesn't work; they want to be appreciated for their music, not stardom. As Candlebox's Kevin Martin explained, "We've grown up and way past the stage of carrying on with groupies. We don't bother talking to them. I am involved with someone in L.A. who I care for a lot. Your friend needs to slow down and to be careful—it could lead to death. She must have low self-esteem. We have some songs that deal with co-dependence in a round-about way."

Bob called *LovePhones* telling Debbie Gibson he fantasized about her since he was seventeen and compares all girls to her. Debbie didn't want to be put on a pedestal. "I'm far from perfect. I'm approachable like a normal human being."

Many rockers I've interviewed told me they originally went into music, though, to meet girls. The scene was tempting. Poison's Bret Michaels had a girlfriend at home for almost four years, but admitted, "There is temptation around you every night. It's human nature to be attracted to others. It messes you up a bit."

So how do you cope? According to Guns N' Roses rhythm guitarist Gilbey Clarke: "Girls come up and go right after you even if your girlfriend is there watching you. What you can do is introduce them to your girlfriend. I say, 'Have you met my wife?' and let them talk to her awhile. The thing is you gotta have some trust with your girlfriend, but then again there's nothing wrong with a little flirting."

So with all the hassles of having the hots, or not, here's the bottom line: always have hope. There can be very unlikely pairs:

UNLIKELY PAIR

"I met a girl in rehab. We were both into drugs and she had tried to kill herself. We had sex a few times. Now I'm out and I can't see her, but I miss her. The funniest part is that she wasn't the type I thought I'd go for."

Look at Elizabeth Taylor and Larry Fortensky. She is the world's most famous actress, he is a much younger carpenter from the other side of the tracks. They met in rehab and married, to the world's surprise. Going through rehab together can forge a strong bond between people as treatment breaks down barriers and defenses most people have. What could be more seductive than someone seeing the "real you" when you are at rock bottom, exposing all your skeletons, and still wanting you? Get to that without rehab.

"MY PENIS IS TOO SMALL. I'M SCARED WHAT GIRLS will say when they see it."

"I have a fresh stomach and a bubble butt. Does that turn guys on?"

"One breast is an 'A' and the other fits a training bra. I won't get undressed in gym."

"My right toe is so big and ugly, I won't let my boyfriend see it, so I keep my socks on during sex. He thinks it's stupid, but I tell him my feet are cold."

"One nut is missing. They call me 'peanut man' around school."

Hey, Peanut Man, Pencil Dick, Noodle Man, and Bullet Boobs . . . you can love yourself, ya know.

Feeling good about your body is key to confidence and enjoying sex. It breaks my heart to hear so much distress about looks. In the survey of over three thousand listeners to *LovePhones,* nearly one in five had a question or complaint about their body, from penises that are too small or bent, to breasts too small or lopsided, to upset over all kinds of sizes and shapes of noses, toes, or anything else you can imagine.

You're not alone. Studies have shown that over eight out of ten people despise something about their bodies. That includes even the sexiest stars. But, some of their stories can show you that what you worry about can now be turned into quite an advantage!

For example, one supermodel drives herself crazy about

being fat in that area right under the butt, but millions of guys still bought her calendar. And as a kid, Kim Basinger was self-conscious about her big lips, but look where they've gotten her; other actresses get collagen injections to make their lips look like hers! Guess who also felt tortured growing up with big lips. None other than Aerosmith's Steven Tyler, but look what happened to him. "I got made fun of a lot in school for having big lips," he told me, "and my mother said just to tell them all the better to kiss the girls with. But then, when I was fifteen or sixteen years old, I went to this beach upstate and somebody in the crowd said, 'It's Mick Jagger's brother,' and I decided to 'become' him and pretended for the rest of the afternoon so I got a dose of what it would be like. Big lips are the ticket."

Whichever part of your body bugs you, in this chapter, I'll give you a new view of it—so you can feel better about yourself.

BODY WORKS

Have you ever looked under the casing of your VCR? Or under the hood of your car? Or inside your computer? Maybe you don't need to, to get the best out of that machine. But when it comes to your body, you can't get away with not knowing how it works. Otherwise, guys worry whether masturbating will use up their sperm, and girls panic if too much wet seems to pour out when they get excited. Research has proven that the more you know and the better you feel about your body, the better off you are in sex and love.

What's the part of their body guys are most obsessed about? Right, their penis. This obsession happened way before the fervor over John Wayne Bobbitt's dismembering at the hands of his punishing, knife-wielding, wife Lorena. But the media attention to that made everybody more open to talking about the perils of the penis.

BONER PRIMER

"Why do they say a guy gets a boner? I don't feel any bone there. So what makes an erection?"

There is no bone in the penis, despite this slang term. There are also no muscles. The inside of the penile shaft is made up of three cylinders of spongy tissue and tiny chambers—like a river with lots of tributaries—that fill with blood to create the erection. One tube, called the corpus spongiosum, runs along the bottom of the penis and the other two, called the corpus cavernosa, run side by side along the upper part. The tubes are encased by a sheath. It's the capacity of these tissues, limited by the sheath, to fill with blood that makes for the penis size. When you touch the penis, nerve receptors send messages to the brain, which then reports back to the blood vessels, telling them to open up, to allow blood to fill those cavities.

IS BIGGER BETTER?

Penis size has been said to cause wars and control Wall Street. As a psychologist once said during the nuclear-buildup war era, "If missiles were shaped like cups (vaginas), would men be as likely to use them?" Large, powerful phalluses have been hailed since antiquity, as a sign of fertility. On one of my trips to Japan, I went to a penis parade (actually an annual fertility festival) outside Tokyo, where large pink papier-mâché penises and others made of wood and steel, are paraded through the streets as marchers chant, "Isn't it big, isn't it beautiful?"

Men are obsessed with their penis size—it's one of the most common questions I've gotten over the years of doing call-in advice talk on the radio. Guys are devastated if they think they don't measure up.

COMING UP SHORT

"I'm freaked. My tool is too small. I don't want any girl to see."

"My penis is only four inches when I'm erect. Girls laugh

*when they see it. The last one said, 'I don't want that little
thing in me,' and put her clothes on and left. I'm miserable.
I saw that John Holmes guy in a porn video with a fourteen-
incher. Do all women really care how big you are? What's
the average amount?"*

I don't want you to get obsessed with numbers, but doctors report the average size when soft is about four inches
long, one-and-an-eighth inches wide, and three-and-three-
eighths inches around. When hard, the average penis is
about five-and-a-half to five-and-three-quarters inches long
(with the majority of guys between five and seven inches),
about one-and-five-eighths inches wide, and about four-
and-a-half inches around. But please, learn to love your
penis any size that it is.

I'm so sad you've been hurt by women telling you you're
not enough. It's mean of them to make you feel bad about your
body. I'll never forget a guy who once called me on the radio
saying this was the third time a woman said she "couldn't feel
him inside her." He was so distraught, he was planning to take
pills and liquor and drive to a secluded spot and kill himself.
Please don't measure your value by your penis size. As my
friend, Beverly Hills urologist Dudley Danoff says in his terrific book, *Superpotency,* penis power comes not from your
size or performance, but from self-confidence, feeling good
about yourself, and giving freely to your partner.

Remember these funny reminders:

"It's not the size of the wave but the motion of the
ocean."

"It's not how much you have but how well you use it."

"It's not the size of the tool but how well it screws."

"It's not the size of his penis but how well he uses
his tongue."

"It's not the size of the ship that matters, but how
long it takes the 'seamen' to disembark." (This is
my favorite.)

Sex can still be great with any size penis. Find a good
position. Have the girl tighten her vaginal muscles for more

grip. Enjoy other things besides intercourse (many women come faster with oral sex, anyway).

Of course, some women care how big he is. There's a dance tune that goes, "Don't want no short dick man." And as one woman put it, "There are a lot of fish in the sea. You throw the small ones back and the big ones you mount." You can also throw her back in, if she doesn't accept you.

In short, your ego has to get bigger, not your penis. Really tiny ones (micropenises) are rare, but some guys do have a structural problem, for example, in one condition, called chordee, the urethra—the tube from the bladder through the penis and out the head—is short and pulls the penis back to the body, making it appear shorter. In those cases, a doctor might recommend surgery on the urethra that will result in a longer penis.

DICKEY MOUSE

"Guys tease me in the locker room and call me 'Little Dick' and 'Dickey Mouse.' It's about three inches long. But does it mean they're always bigger than me?"

Don't get so upset. The size of the penis when it's flaccid doesn't always predict the size erect; so one three-incher can grow to six inches, while another three-incher may only grow an inch. Guys always rank on each other, especially as teenagers, so instead of being bullied, don't give them the rise they want, ignore them or say something cocky back (like "When it swings into action it knows what size to be") and then get on with what you're doing.

LONGER OR THICKER?

"Which is better—longer or thicker—to please a woman?"

Thicker, generally, because the muscles that grip the penis are at the outer two thirds of the woman's vagina. Moving these are what tugs on the clitoris and all other structures and *bingo*, triggers her pleasure.

MEASURING UP

"Where do you measure the guy's size from?"

Sex researchers Masters and Johnson measured from the top, but actually if you measure from underneath, where the penis meets the testicles, the penis can be up to an inch longer. Some women claim that when they are on top, they can feel a longer size.

HATES SHAPE

Jimmy: *"My penis is really long and thin. They call me 'pencil dick.' What can I do?"*

Joe: *"I don't have a 'German helmet' on my penis. I wish it had a Darth Vader hat. Is there any way to fix my headless penis? The guys in gym call me Mr. Probosis."*

A video called *Dick* shows about a thousand varieties of guys' genitals, long and thin, short and squat, big or small heads, pulled left, pointed up, balls hanging low, wrinkly scrotum.

Accept your genitals as they are. Imagine them as a child: would you dump on it and make it feel bad about itself? If your genitals could talk, what would they say? Have them say, "Stop criticizing me, man." What do you say back? You better say, "You're okay."

Change your body hate to body love with brain retrain homework: change the computer program, or TV channel, in your brain from "I'm not enough" to "I'm fine the way I am." More homework: do the "Mirror Exercise." Look in the mirror and review your body parts, noticing good things (a defined muscle, smooth skin), and ignoring what you always criticize.

UNDER THE KNIFE

"Can I get that surgery I heard about to make my schlong bigger?"

Women have been spending billions bolstering their breasts (before the implant scandals), so now it's the guys' turn. Lots of doctors now offer what's called "enhancement phalloplasty" or penis enlargement surgery. One doctor got three hundred calls in a week in response to his new advertisement. Some critics charge it's just another way for doctors to make money—five thousand dollars on average for a longer and fatter one—but some guys who have it done are happy with the results.

Still, it's not for everybody, and don't get your fantasies out of hand. You can't double in size—the average you can add is about an inch in width and length (an inch and a half longer is possible but hard to predict).

The procedures make more length (called "penile elongation," "corporal advancement phalloplasty," or CAP) by removing fat deposits around the pubic bone, grafting skin flaps above the pubic bone, and cutting the suspensory ligament of the penis that holds it to the pubic bone. Interestingly, this makes your penis LOOK longer since it exposes more of the one-third to one-half of the penis that is normally inside the body under the pubic bone.

Making it fatter ("circumferential autologous penile engorgement," or CAPE), comes from grafting skin with fat from the groin or buttocks into the penile shaft, or removing fat through liposuction from one area of the body (such as "love handles") and injecting it underneath the penile skin.

There are risks: irregular shapes and angles, lost gains, nerve damage, or ironically, shortening due to scarring. But satisfied post-ops say things like, "It made me the happiest man, I feel I can conquer the world."

A friend of mine, urologist E. Douglas Whitehead, director of the Association for Male Sexual Dysfunction in New York, backs me up that you must have counseling beforehand to sort out problems in how you see your body, sexual identity, and love life. If you're already average in size, you need an attitude enlargement, not a penis enlargement.

Anyway, short of surgery, try making your penis look bigger by trimming your pubic hair, losing weight, and getting in shape.

A big Hollywood celeb also supposedly got a "testicle tuck" to make his scrotum hang higher so his penis looked longer in proportion. Without dangling balls, his whole package looked perkier, too.

Janine: *"I want my boyfriend to go under the knife, to make his thing bigger. How do I convince him?"*

Just like guys who want their girls to get breast enlargement surgery, examine your own need for his sexual characteristic to be more prominent (to fire up your own flagging interest, inflate your own ego)? You'd be doing him a huge favor if you let him know you desire him as he is. People are always motivated to make changes in a better frame of mind when they know they're loved as they are.

Extreme lead singer Gary Cherone advised against it: "You're just looking for sexual pleasure. Sounds like you don't love the guy. When you fall in love, all that doesn't matter."

PREDICTING SIZE

"I heard your shoe size divided by two equal your penis size? Is that true?"

"If your penis grows proportionately with your body, do midgets have small penises?"

"Are guys of different races smaller or bigger?"

Usually your body is proportionate. For example, some urologists estimate that Caucasian men are about an inch more than Asian men, just like their overall size is bigger. One study showed the average Black man is the same as others, but when they're big, they're bigger. But some short, slender guys have large ones and some tall big guys are real small (which really freaks them out), so body size is not a sure indicator of penis size.

PUMP IT UP

"I have a small schmingee. It's about four inches when big. I saw ads in those magazines for pumps you can buy. Do they work?"

Remember an erection is caused by blood flowing into hollow caverns in the penis, making it grow in size and become stiffer until the caverns are filled to capacity. With a vacuum pump, you insert the penis in a clear acrylic cylinder and press a pump to create suction that draws blood into the penis, and then slip a band around the base (like a cock ring, or tourniquet—one guys uses his leather watchband) to trap the blood inside. The erection goes down when the blood drains, but some guys insist the results last—(could be they got more confident, so their blood flows better!). Most doctors warn of dangers of hurting your penis if you're just trying to inflate it to pump up your ego.

The pumps cost about $14 to $50. You can also get prostheses advertised in sex magazines that are penis-shaped molds made of latex that you fit over your penis (like you would a condom), making it appear longer.

Injections that also inflate your penis have been medically tested, but those are supposed to be for erection problems, not to make you macho man (see chapter on What's Up With Him). As my *LovePhones* jock, Chris Jagger, advises, "Make him bigger by wrapping your big lips around it!"

THIS JUST IN: Just in case you had any doubt that men will go to any lengths to be longer, the latest in penis enlargement is **weights**, yes, weights, to stretch the penis and make it look longer. The weights attach to the head of the penis in a nooselike rubber tube that goes over the tip, and stretch the suspensory ligament (that holds the penis to the body). Originally the weights were used after the enlargement surgeries, to ensure the results, but now they're used on their own. Though you should be supervised by a doctor, you can buy these on your own. (They're sold as "novelty items" for a little over $100). The routine: you start with a 4 oz. weight 2–5 minutes with twenty minute breaks and work up to 2 lbs. for 6–8 hours, for up to two years—but with no guarantees!

GROWING PAINS

Steve: *"I heard you only get an orgasm when you're eighteen or older. Is that true?"*

No. You can have an orgasm from the time you're an infant. But you can only ejaculate semen when you reach puberty, because that's when the testicles produce testosterone, which triggers the growth of the prostate gland which contributes to the manufacture of the ejaculate.

David: "I'm 5'7" and look like a little gorilla, I'm so hairy. I'm on the wrestling team. What I want to know is if masturbating will increase my testosterone and my penis size? When will it grow until?"

Your body produces testosterone on its own (whether or not you masturbate). Obviously you have it, because testosterone governs hair growth, and you have a lot.

Masturbation does not make the penis grow or stop growing. Your genitals grow in five stages. They start slowly from the time you're born and change slowly in childhood. In stage 2, at about age 11, the beginning of puberty, the testicles get larger and the male hormone starts to be produced, causing some pubic hair and larger nipples. The scrotum starts to hang lower and gets baggier or more wrinkly. In stage 3, about age 13, the penis gets noticeably longer and wider. In stage 4, about age 14, the head of the penis is more developed and the testicles reach about one and a half inches long, and the skin color deepens. The pubic hair is usually obvious, and gets progressively curlier and coarser. In stage 5, at about age 16 to 18, all these changes continue. They can also get tweaked in your early twenties.

Melissa: "Will a guy's penis get bigger if he uses it more? We've been having sex for about a year, and in the last few months I thought my boyfriend's penis got about an inch longer."

Figure it out. The penis's insides are like a sponge that gets bigger when it fills with blood, but only to a certain capacity. However, if your boyfriend relaxes more, and gets more excited, more blood will rush in there, and it will *seem* bigger than before, when he may have been more anxious.

"I heard women want a guy with a banker's dick . . . that makes big deposits and small withdrawals and guarantees no loss of interest."

WHAT DO WOMEN WANT?

"How important is penis size to most women?"

Surveys in women's magazines show that up to half of women think penis size matters. Always ask them, "What does a big penis mean to you—more power, prowess, pleasure?" Size doesn't *have* to matter. Remember the Sex Rule: **Sex is 90 percent between your ears and only 10 percent between your legs.**

To get pleasure with a small penis, you can change your position in sex, change your attitude, focus on pleasure other than intercourse, or the woman can exercise her love muscles to make a tighter grip (see chapter on What's Up With Her)!

But there's a club in Los Angeles, called the "Hung Jury," started by a guy who argues with me and insists size matters. An eight-incher, he wanted to get laid more often. Members are eight inches or more (the average being nine inches long and six inches around). Of several thousand members, half are men advertising themselves, 30 percent are couples looking for extra partners, and 20 percent are women looking for big men.

> *If you're not built like a horse,*
> *you better have a tongue like a rattlesnake.*
> —Chris Robinson
> Lead singer, Black Crowes

CAN A GUY BE TOO BIG?

Curiosity abounds in Hollywood about who's manhood is big. Ex-*China Beach* actress Dana Delaney told *Details* if you put actors Willem Dafoe, Liam Neeson, and Jimmy Woods in a room together, there wouldn't be room for anyone else.

But is bigger always better? Some guys who have it don't think so.

Like Curtis: *"For all the guys who complain about being too small, I gotta tell you having too much can be an albatross, too. You'd think it'd be great to be eleven inches, but I'm nearly nine, and it hasn't gotten me anywhere. Guys make fun of me, calling me Hangman, Elephant Man, and Robodick. And women hate it. I got with this girl, and when she saw me naked she screamed, 'I don't want that thing in me, it'll hurt.' I don't blame her because it hurt women before."*

Even the adorable, hunky, 1995 *Playgirl* Man of the Year, John Holliday, told me he was always afraid his nine inches would be too much for a girl.

Women complain too: *"My boyfriend's penis is too large and he gets so greedy, my insides can't handle it. We tried it a few times and he couldn't gain entry. What can we do?"*

Too much can hurt. The vagina starts out about three to five inches in length unaroused, but being elastic and expanding like a balloon when it gets excited, it can get to about five to seven inches. Even so, it has limits. When a long penis bumps up against the cervix (at the end of the vaginal barrel), it can be painful. Also, a really wide penis can strain her muscles at the opening. A small-penis guy once insisted, "Dr. Judy, there's no way you can tell me having a Cadillac isn't better than having a Volkswagen," and I replied, "But there are places you can park a bug that you can't park a mack truck."

A really big guy should never force his penis all the way in. How revolting would that be! He and his partner should accept that he doesn't have to fully penetrate to make sex good, prove he's a man, ejaculate, or make her have orgasm.

HOMEWORK: Use the "baseball grip"—choke up on his bat, holding the part of his penis at the base that's still exposed, with your hands—so he feels contained. Wet your hands so he feels the warmth and wetness, like he would inside you.

Agree on a word that means, "stop" (it's too deep).

PEARL NECKLACE

Find other means of pleasure, like Jennifer: *"I had sex for the first time with my boyfriend and his penis was too big. It was thirteen inches long and two inches wide. So we oiled my breasts and rubbed it between them. Was that a good idea? What else can he do?"*

Good idea. Rubbing the penis between your breasts (frottage) can feel like he's "inside" you. Or do "shadow stroking"—rubbing the penis up and down against the vaginal lips at the opening, down between the thighs. This gives you confidence he won't penetrate too deep or too hard without your being prepared. Use a position where the woman is in control of the depth of penetration: woman-on-top rather than man-on-top or him immobilizing her hips during doggie style.

Also, since the clitoris is a woman's hot spot, let him hold his penis and rub it in circles or strokes on your clitoris, to drive you wild.

> It ain't easy being a dick . . . I've got a head I can't think with and an eye I can't see out with . . . I have to hang around two nuts all day, my best friend is a pussy, and my closest neighbor is an asshole. Worst of all, my owner beats me all the time. And now because of AIDS, I have to wear this rubber suit and throw up all over myself. It ain't easy being a dick.

SHE'S SCARED

Crystal, 18: *"I'm scared to look at this guy's penis. I got a peek once and it had like a mushroom head. How can he put that ugly thing in me?"*

Guys' penises are different shapes, just like their faces. Some noses and heads are bigger. They all still work, and it doesn't have to hurt, or displease, you.

Maybe you're afraid of sex, or not ready, or were once forced or abused. HOMEWORK: Brain retrain by changing your mental computer program from "this is ugly" to "penises are beautiful," as you would want him to think *your* body is beautiful. Instead of how it looks, think about how good it feels, and how he treats you with it.

AM I A FREAK?

Examining your body for any changes or unusual things

is good—everybody should do it. Don't freak out unnecessarily if you notice something awry, but always check it out.

<u>ONE BALL</u>: *"They call me 'una cahuna'—I have one testicle. Other guys tease me, calling me Cyclops, and saying, 'You're only half the man you used to be.' I'm afraid that if a girl feels me, she'll know."*

You're not the only guy with one testicle. Be reassured you only need one testicle to go through puberty and function quite normally sexually, manufacturing sperm and fathering babies. You could have an undescended testicle inside your body (that happens in about 3 percent of full term baby boys), or it could have retracted back into the body (that happens for some young boys until puberty). If so, a doctor should bring it down because it's too hot up there in your body (that could cause later problems with your sperm, and cancer risk). You can get different size implants, too—but don't be so self-conscious. Live with it. Don't feel like a freak.

<u>THREE BALLS</u>: *"I have a third nut. How weird is that?"*

Stop worrying and see a urologist. You could have a condition a famous actor had, where a third testicle grew after a painful childhood accident. He impaled himself on a fence when he was ten years old and scar tissue built up around the wound to look like another testicle. It was removed surgically.

<u>UNEVEN</u>: *"One of my testicles is smaller. I'm ashamed."*

You're also not a freak. One that grows faster is often larger. And the bigger one (often the left) usually hangs lower, to keep them from crushing one another when you walk. Be careful, though, because a change in size or a lump could mean cancer of the testicles, so watch it and check it out.

<u>NOODLE MAN</u>: Salvatore: *"Guys call me Noodle Man because my balls are all bubbly like a bag of noodles. What is it?"*

You could have varicose veins in your testicles, called a varicocele. Some guys also call this a "bag of marbles." See a urologist.

BIG BAG: *"I went to this nude beach and saw an old guy with a bag as big as a grapefruit. Me and my friends couldn't stop staring. Yuk, will we get that way when we're old?"* It happened to Tim at seventeen: *"I have a huge testicle. It looks so ugly. The girl I had sex with calls me E.T.— for extra-testicular. What is it?"*

Very cute—her calling you E.T. It's always nice to take an anxiety-provoking problem about sex and turn it into something humorous. A big scrotum could mean any number of conditions, from a hernia to infections to a tumor, to conditions like a varicocele (enlargement of the veins in the scrotum), a hematocele (accumulation of blood from injury), a spermatocele (accumulation of sperm), or a hydrocele (extra fluid in the testicles). A doctor can correct them. With age the scrotum çan droop but not grow gigundo, so don't freak. Some guys wear a big sac like a badge of honor, as if bigger is better.

BUMPS: *"I have bumps on my penis. Did I ruin it by jerking it?"*

Your bumps could be oil or sweat glands, tiny pubic hairs trying to push through, or a very common and harmless condition of fibrous tissue that looks like pen-points, called pearly penile papules. But bumps can come from a sexually transmitted disease, so to be sure, get a medical check-up. If you attach the problem to masturbating, then consider whether you feel so guilty about doing that, that you think you're being punished. (If so, give yourself permission.)

TWO-HOLES: *"I have two holes in my penis. One is on the tip but nothing comes out of it. The other is underneath the head, where the urine and ejaculate comes out. It's even twisted. Will a girl think I'm a freak?"*

I hope you will have understanding partners. In oral or manual sexual activity, the girl may notice, but not in intercourse. Called hypospadias, the urethra (the tube that carries the urine and ejaculate through the penis) didn't fuse properly in the womb, so the opening appears somewhere along the penile shaft. Because it's shortened, it can pull the penis shorter to the body, or twist. Surgery can help in most cases. Feel reassured—you can still have normal sex and make babies.

<u>DOUBLE DONG</u>: *"I saw a guy in a public toilet who had two penises. Is he a circus freak or something? My friend called it a double dong. Can having a twin turbo give you double the pleasure and double the fun? Like, can you go up both holes of a girl at the same time?"*

You were probably seeing things. Fewer than eighty cases of this, called diphallasparatus, have been reported in nearly four hundred years. Somewhat of a medical mystery, it's likely some abnormal lack of fusion of the genital structures in the womb.

<u>HOOKED</u>: *"They call me Captain Hook because my penis hooks up. Is that better than a straight one?"* *"When I get erect, it points sideways like a hockey stick. I've been masturbating for years and pulling it to the right. Could that do it?"* Pete also has a curve: *"The angle of the dangle is about eighty-two degrees. Is that normal?"*

Don't get bent out of shape if your penis leans like the tower of Pisa. Varieties of directions and elevations are normal. It can go up, down, and sideways. Florida urologist Harold M. Reed says that 80 percent of erections turn one way or the other. They grow that way and you can't pull it out of shape by how you tug, pull, or masturbate. You can still have normal intercourse, though some positions may feel better than others. Tell your penis it's okay, and prepare your partner that it's curved but normal.

There is a serious condition, though, called Peyronie's disease, where severe curves are caused by fibrous tissue and calcium deposits in the cylinders in the penis. It can cause pain and may interfere with erection and intercourse. Surgery may be necessary.

<u>ZEBRA MAN</u>: *"They call me Zebra Man because I have blue lines down my penis. What's wrong?"*

Blue, red, or black lines can be perfectly normal, the result of blood vessels that react with skin color (as on any other body part). They could get more pronounced when you get excited and more blood flows to the area.

<u>CUT OR UNCUT</u>: Jennifer, 18: *"My boyfriend is uncut and I don't like how it looks like deformed mushrooms. A friend of mine said they call it an elephant trunk or a turtle head. What can I do?"*

People have preferences for how genitals look, just like they do for how a person looks in general. Do you prefer brown or blue eyes, long or short hair? Do you prefer lots or little pubic hair, circumcised or uncircumcised penises? Learn to love how he looks, just as you would want him to like your breasts as they are. Focus on something you do like.

OUT IN THE COLD

"Does a guy's penis and balls shrink in the cold?"

Yes, think about how you shiver in the cold (outdoors or in cold water) and huddle into your body, to keep warm. Your genitals do the same, especially since the testicles need a certain temperature—about five degrees below your body temperature (98.6°F)—to produce healthy sperm. If they get too hot, the cremasteric muscle that suspends them relaxes and they drop to cool off. If it's too cold, the muscle snuggles them closer to home (to the body)—this also happens when you get turned on.

SEEP OR SPURT

Michael: *"Sometimes when I ejaculate it seeps, and sometimes it spurts. Is this normal?"*

Yes. Men can vary in the amount and projectile of their ejaculate, depending on their excitement level, stress, physical state, and condition. However, if you have pain, trouble urinating, or ongoing reduction in force, have a urologist check it out.

UNLOADING

"I'm afraid if I don't shoot my load, it'll back up. Where do the sperm go?"

The sperm mature and get stored in a coiled tube on the back surface of the testicles, called the epididymis, where they can remain for weeks. If they're not ejaculated, they get absorbed into the surrounding tissue. You won't burst.

SEMEN SOURCE

"Where does my semen come from?"

The fluid comes mainly from the seminal vesicles but also from the prostate and Cowper's gland. The sperm is only one percent of the mixture.

TITTY BOY

"Girls are supposed to have big boobs, not guys. But I got 'em. I'm fat, too. The guys in school call me 'titty boy.' Why do I have them?"

When guys get big breasts it's called gynecomastia. But don't freak, up to half of guys when they're growing up (going through puberty) can have spurts of their breasts looking bigger, because of hormone changes, where the balance of estrogen (the female hormone) and testosterone (the male hormone) tips. This can sort out over time. You're also overweight, so that adds to the problem. Maybe both the weight and breasts are a hormone problem—see your doctor. Guys over seventeen can also get big breasts, caused by many things—too much alcohol, use of some types of drugs, or tumors, that should always be checked out with a doctor. When you were a baby, did you have big breasts? That comes from having a lot of estrogen (female hormone) from the mother.

CASE OF THE MISSING CONDOM

T.J.: *"The other day, after sex with my girlfriend, I went to remove the condom we were using and it wasn't there. We searched all over the bed and couldn't find it. She said it wasn't inside her. I even poked around myself. Have you ever heard of this? Where did it go?"*

Don't worry, the condom didn't get sucked into her body (the small opening to the uterus at the back wall isn't big or open enough, except during childbirth, for the condom to go through). Make sure it didn't slip off when you withdrew, and you just can't find it. But it could be inside, and you just can't reach it because you're too nervous, guilty about having sex, or don't know her body, or you can't feel it because the thin material could be balled up or flattened against the side of her vaginal barrel (that feels similar to the condom material). Calm down and explore again. Have her squat (to help shorten the vaginal barrel) and stick your finger way in and fish around the sides and back. If no luck, go to the gynecologist to remove it, since leaving it in causes odor, discharge, and ultimately infection that can spell serious problems.

ORGANIC FIT FOR SEX

"I just got my period and started using tampons. They seem to go inside only a little way. I heard the vagina is only three inches long, so if man averages six inches, how can they possibly fit?"

The average tampon is about two inches long, held in place in your vaginal canal by the outer third muscles. As I mentioned before, your vagina is normally a tube but can expand like a balloon when you're excited and grows from about three to five inches long, to being wider and about two inches longer. Certain Eastern sex ideologies believe there are three sizes and fits of male and female sex organs, with matched ones making the best sex: Small, medium, and large male (lingam) sizes are called the hare man, bull man, and horse man, equivalent to the three female (yoni) sizes (determined by the depth of the vagina) called the deer, mare, and elephant.

EXAMINING HER BODY

Tito: *"Is it normal to want to see how far you can stretch your partner's pussy, to see what is inside? I expect to find some strange thing inside."*

It is normal to be curious about what's inside the vagina. Many men and women have fears and misconceptions about that great cavern or tunnel. Some guys have trouble staying erect for fear they'll be swallowed up, sucked in, or bitten off (by mythical teeth called "vagina dentata"). You should both look. Get a plastic speculum (the instrument the gynecologist uses to examine a woman's insides) and have her sit up in bed with her legs spread. Insert it and open the tongs to create a tunnel. Shine a light inside to see the walls, their ridges and pinkish color, and the cervical opening at the very end. Prop a mirror between her legs so she can see, too.

SHAME ABOUT SHAPE

Don't fall victim to the "beauty myth" (for men or women), thinking you have to look as thin as Kate Moss or as stacked as Demi Moore, as sexy as Brad Pitt, or as hung as the rockers Cynthia Plaster Caster made casts of. Turn body loathing into body love—by loving every part of you—for a good sex life.

SMALL BREASTS: Marie: *"I'm a 34C, but my boyfriend is obsessed with magazines like* Busty, *but I'm small. What if I don't please him?"*

Guns N' Roses guitarist Gilbey Clarke, as *LovePhones* Honorary Love Doctor, admitted such magazines are part of the band's contract to be planted on the tour bus and part of the reading material while they're waiting to go on, but offered reassurance that "guys do change their fetishes after a while."

The guys from the British band Blur were more adamant in response to another girl complaining about her breasts. Lucy: *"I hate my breasts. They're so small. They're size 34B but I want them bigger, so they have that great cleavage when you look at them at the opening of a shirt. I'm thinking about getting breast implants."*

All four band members went ballistic, telling Lucy not to do it: "That is a lot of rubbish. Thirty-four-B is my favorite, love." "Small tits are more juicy. I'd rather see no breasts than false breasts. Gnat bites are fine." "I think the pressure everyone is under to sort of look exactly right is too much. Be happy with what you got because it is lovely. Would you expect your man to get a penis extension?"

No matter what your breast size, get attention for your personality instead of your cleavage even though lots of stars have drawn attention to bigger breasts, from Demi Moore, Alana Hamilton (when she was married to Rod Stewart), and Melanie Griffith, to Heather Locklear and Hole's Courtney Love. You can consider plastic surgery, but review the scandals about implants; TV talk show host, Jenny Jones, had a nightmare from hers. Make sure you see a qualified doctor; and don't expect them to bring you happiness or the perfect mate. Tell your breasts you love them, before you do anything!

IS BIGGER BETTER: *"Why do men like big hooters?"*

Movies, TV, and advertisements tell them big breasts are sexy, and from historical times, big breasts symbolized fertility. Guys learn to joke about getting a girl with big ones as a conquest when they're adolescents, like showing off to other guys, "Look what I got," which you can translate into "look how (powerful, studly) I am, compared to you."

But too big can be a pain for the girl who's got 'em, like Gina. *"I was very happy to hear Kathie Lee Gifford, when she returned to her TV show after having her baby, joke about what's between her breasts now—her belly button! My breasts are big and they've always been saggy like that, too. I look like something out of* National Geographic *magazine! When I was ten, the other girls in school used to make fun of me. Now I'm shapely, but overall I'm 'full figured.' I'm so ashamed, I haven't ever gotten fully nude in front of my husband. Is there something wrong with me?"*

Women's low self-esteem over their body costs over $50 billion a year in the weight-loss, fitness, cosmetics, and plastic-surgery industries. Not surprisingly, surveys show more women hate their big hips and thighs (called the "Venus syndrome"), than their rear end and breasts. For your poor beleaguered breasts, do upper-body exercises to tighten the suspensory muscles. Of course, if they're too damaging to your back, shoulders, and ego, you may want to consider plastic surgery (make sure you see a qualified plastic or cosmetic surgeon). Apparently, TV's Roseanne was happy with her breast reduction.

But brain retraining exercises are what you need to change your attitude. HOMEWORK: Look at your nude self in a full-length mirror. Neutralize your criticisms ("My stomach is flabby" becomes "My stomach skin is soft"). Focus on positive parts ("I love being curvy"). Feel special. I'm glad Kathie Lee's confession gives you reassurance you're not alone, but don't compare yourself. Get that inner self in shape and then reveal both it—and your outer self—to your husband!

Learn from Melissa, who was upset about her 38DD until she read that her heartthrob, Extreme's bassist, Pat Badger, liked full-figured women. Thinking her hero would like her breasts made her like them more. Be your own hero.

BULLET BOOBS: Karen, 15: *"My breasts are pointy, like cones, and boys make fun of me. They're a 'B' now, but I'm afraid they won't grow and be rounder like other girls'."*

Cones are fashionable, remember Madonna's cone-shaped tops from haute designer Jean Paul Gautier. Love your breasts as they are. I know all kids compare, but you have to avoid getting sucked into others' ranking on you.

LOPSIDED: Samantha is miserable about the size of her breasts. *"It's a secret all my life. One breast is bigger than the other and droops. I don't think any man will ever want me. One guy laughed."*

Mercy! You are more than your breasts. If you don't love you, for sure a man won't be able to. Don't hinge your self-esteem on your breasts. It's normal for one to be at least a little smaller or bigger than the other. If we give the guy who laughed the benefit of the doubt, we'd realize he's just being immature and maybe he doesn't realize he's hurting you. Instead of feeling badly, you should respond with confidence, and educate him for his and every other girl's sake, by telling him, "I feel sensitive when you do that, please don't laugh about my breasts. I know they're a little different, but there's nothing wrong with them." Remember my favorite phrase about how to deal with being teased or bullied, "There is no enemy without if there is no enemy within." Meditate on what that means.

BREAST GROWTH

Rochelle, 16: *"I think my breasts are getting smaller. Will they grow back?"*

Priscilla, 17: *"At what age do your breasts stop growing. Mine are only a 'B' and I want them to be bigger. What can I do?"*

Your breasts will reach their optimal size after your body stops growing in general. You can make them look bigger and change the contour and shape with exercise that make the muscles under them firmer; practice good posture so they stand out; or get one of those new push-up bras that enhance what you have.

Breasts can change size slightly throughout life. If you get fat, they enlarge; if you lose weight, they shrink. When you get pregnant, they engorge with milk. If your breasts seem to shrink, your period is irregular, and you are dieting or exercising excessively, you could have a hormonal imbalance, and you need to go to a gynecologist for tests.

CUNT POSITIVE

"I hate the way my vagina looks. It's ugly. It reminds me of that Andrew Dice Clay routine about how a middle-aged woman's cunt looks like an old veal cutlet. I have big skin that hangs down and it's brown. The lips don't match. I saw once in a dirty magazine that my boyfriend hid under his bed that other girls are pink little things with little tight lips. I'm sick. I'm too ashamed for any guy to ever look at me. What's wrong with me?"

Nothing, honey. Genitals are like faces; they're all different. The inner lips (the labia minora) may stick down out of the outer lips (labia majora) and can be any of a number of colors, from pink to brownish (no matter what the color of your skin). Some are fairly taut skin, others are very fleshy and folded. Look at Georgia O'Keefe's beautiful paintings of flowers that look like genitalia, and get the book *Femalia* (Down There Press), a photo album of vaginal close-ups that shows that female genitalia are as varied as our faces. Check out Doug Johns's beautiful sculptures that celebrate the variety of genital shapes (he's shown in Aspen and New York's Erotic Gallery). Get Betty Dodsen's Self-Loving video from her Bodysex workshops. Betty is a long-time feminist, author, and masturbation teacher who wants women to be "cunt positive." When she first discovered her own genitals, she was horrified, thinking, "They were like those funny-looking things that dangle from a chicken's neck," until a lover convinced her they were beautiful. Love your genitals as you must learn to love yourself in general. Examine them, notice nice parts, talk to them as you would to a cherished friend.

CLITORIS SIZE

Tina, 19: *"Is there an average size for a clitoris? Mine is big and I love it, but guys don't. They've said, 'It's too big' and 'What's wrong with that, I never saw a girl that big, is it swollen, did something happen when you were born?'"*

I'm proud of you that you love it, and how it gives you pleasure. Don't pay any mind to such rude guys. Imagine if you cringed at their penises. All genitalia are unique. You may have a larger clitoris because of having a lot of testosterone when you were born, but tell them you're still a woman, and beautiful to enjoy yourself!

BABY GOT BACK

"I hate my big butt. I wish I had a flat one that looks real good in pants. Thank goodness some guys like women with big butts. How come?"

Some guys say, "the bigger the cushion, the better the pushin'."

Body preferences vary, like tastes for certain foods. Some like little tight buns, like on most of those centerfolds in *Penthouse* and *Playboy*. Others like big butts. It depends on many factors, including cultural preferences, what the media say is attractive, and personal experience (if your first experience with something was good, you tend to want to repeat it).

HAIRY MARY

Yvonne: *"I have hair on parts of my body where it shouldn't be, like around the nipples on my breasts, and growing down my thighs. There's even fuzz on my bottom. I've been called Hairy Mary. It disgusts me so much that I won't let my new boyfriend see me without my T-shirt and shorts on, and I keep making excuses about why I can't go to the shore with him. We argue about it all the time and he's getting fed up with me. He's already joked about my having a mustache, so I'm scared to show him the rest, but I also don't want to lose him. What should I do?"*

In a perfect world, you wouldn't be ashamed about extra hair on your body and would enjoy your relationship and summer fun. Hirsutism, or excessive hair growth—particularly on the upper lip, chin, nipples, extremities and crotch area—can be inherited family or racial traits (certain Latin, Mediterranean, and Semitic women are hairier than Anglo-Saxons, Nordics, Asians, and American Indians). Some men are even turned on by a woman's body hair. Given our cultural norms of beauty, I understand your concern, so consider bleaching to conceal it, or removing it by trimming, shaving, or electrolysis. Waxing is great because it lasts longer and the hair grows back softer.

Since excessive hair growth can signal that you have a large amount of the male hormone testosterone, some hairy girls worry they are "masculine" or not "womanly," but you should still feel perfectly "feminine." It may be within normal limits; however, if you also have menstrual irregularities, you should have a medical check-up.

Q: What do you call an adolescent rabbit?
A: A pubic hare.

CUTTING PUBES

"If I cut my pubic hair, will it grow like hair on my head?"

Yes. Pubic hair is coarser and sometimes darker than other body hair, but it does grow back if cut. Some people like to keep it trimmed, for personal taste. Or they cut it for fun and sexual play. Some guys like trimming their pubic hair to make their penis look bigger, because more is exposed. You can enjoy grooming your genitalia just like shaving or primping. Don't be embarrassed.

LOST

Teresa, 17: *"I tried to have sex with my boyfriend but he couldn't find the hole. He was putting it far back and I kept saying, no, not there. He was letting it slip into my rear end. He said it was because my hole is not open enough and the two holes are too close to one another. Is that true? How does he find the hole?"*

I'm glad you asked. There's not a homing device in the vagina. You both have to know where it goes and you may have to guide him with your hands if he's confused. Also move your body into position so his penis goes in the right place. Some guys think the penis going into the right hole should come easy, but if they don't know what the female anatomy looks like, they may be confused. And if the woman is nervous, even if his penis goes near the vaginal opening, the opening may be tight, so the penis won't slide in easily, and he and his poor penis may get disoriented, not knowing where to go.

Don't be embarrassed. Take a look at some textbooks to see where a woman's vaginal opening is, and where her anal opening is. Then examine your own. Say, 'Let's look at each other' as if you were playing doctor like kids do. You can even make it a little clinical, by having the text nearby and pointing out the different parts.

Beware, though: some guys try to trick the girl into anal sex by pretending 'it just slipped into the back door.' Or blame her for something wrong with her anatomy! Hogwash! Your guy sounds that way, since he's trying to put the blame on you and make you think something's wrong with your body. If he's that kind of sneaky bum, call him on it.

POST-BABY BODY

Christina, 20: *"Since I had my baby, I got stretch marks and flabby, and now I don't like my boyfriend to see me nude and I don't feel as good in sex."*

Get over it. You had a child, so your body will naturally go through some changes that you have to accept. Be inspired: fitness guru Voltage has whipped major models back into runway shape shortly after childbirth, by exercise and eating right! Congratulate yourself for bringing a gift of life into this world!

A WEIGHTY PROBLEM

"When my husband and I got married, we both got fat. I'm up to 195 pounds and he hits 250, and now the 'missionary' position is uncomfortable because of our big bellies. I can't get him to let me be on top. What can I do?"

By all means, change position (because of weight, pregnancy, soreness, injuries, tiredness) for more comfort and pleasure. Experiment with what feels best for both of you—try leaning on a chair or bed, straddling, or lying on your sides. If he's unhappy about a certain position, what does it mean to him? Does your being on top make him think you're the one in control, and that he's not a man? If so, he has to change that belief.

Marital bliss does not have to lead to weight gain. Just because you are secure with one another does not mean you should become complacent or take each other for granted; strive always to look your best and stay fit. Fill each other with love instead of with food.

Julie: *"My boyfriend was thin when I met him but now he's fat and I'm turned off. I said I'd go down on him if he lost weight. Shouldn't he want to be attractive for me?"*

Yes—for you, and himself! He needs to examine the frustrations that make him overeat (fear of performing in sex or other parts of his life, holding back his feelings. But don't bribe with sex. That's not fair. Let him know you love him for who he is. HOMEWORK: When you have sex, picture him in your mind as thin as you'd like him to be. Threatening deals or criticizing him will only frustrate and make him withdraw more into food. He has to want to get thin himself.

FEAR BARING IT ALL

Brad: *"My girlfriend is taking me to a nude beach. I'm getting cold feet. She says I'm a wuss. How do I get over this?"*

HOMEWORK: Practice imagining people watching you take your clothes off. Then take them off. Walk around the room now casually, thinking of people there. Likely you're afraid your penis won't measure up or maybe will get hard and you'll be embarrassed. Now strut your stuff! Stick your chest out and enjoy displaying your body. Tell your penis it looks great the way it is. Imagine people casually looking at it, then imagine them admiring it. What else are you afraid of? Maybe looking at the other people's bodies and genitals, or maybe getting turned on. Go ahead, look. Some may enjoy being looked at, or they wouldn't be there. You're not a pervert.

Closing Note: For Body Love (that applies to guys and girls), remember this limerick from a *LovePhones* listener:

My penis is slightly unsightly,
when erect it protrudes impolitely,
It curves and it dips, when out on its trips,
But it serves me quite well, despitely.

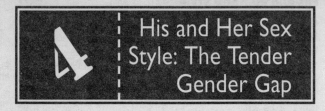

His and Her Sex Style: The Tender Gender Gap

JOCELYN: *"WHY ARE MEN SUCH PIGS? THEY WANT to screw and scram."*

Alex: *"Why don't girls seem to like sex as much as guys? We call the ones who just lay there "refrigerator girls" because they're frigid, or "cemetery girls" because they act like they're dead when you do them."*

That's nasty, but it hits the point home about the complaints between the sexes.

Earthworms may be lucky because they have both sets of sex organs and don't have to deal with the differences between males and females. We do.

The wall between the sexes is coming down. Stereotypes are dissolving, as more men are getting in touch with their "female" (sensitive) side and more women are getting in touch with their "male" (assertive) side.

But there are some differences. Treat them with the three A's: Acknowledge, Accept, Appreciate.

The biggest difference is in timing. Lots of people ask me: *"Why does it take longer for a girl to get to it than a guy?"*

Several reasons:

1) It takes a woman fifteen minutes to get to the same level of excitement it takes a man three minutes to achieve. It's just the way the sexual-response cycles work. So, he has to slow down, or she needs a head start.

2) The guy's most sensitive part—his penis—is usually stimulated more easily and readily, while the woman's hot buttons are less obvious or often ignored. Also, the way the organs are stimulated in intercourse—the man's penis and

the woman's vagina—normally gives the man more physiological pleasure. Imagine what it would be like if sex meant rubbing the man's scrotum against the woman's clitoris. She'd get more turned on than he!

3) Women usually require more mental stimulation to get turned on (feeling loved by their partner), and that emotional state takes longer to reach.

4) Women generally have more hang-ups to get over about letting loose.

HOMEWORK: Match your timing. The guy has to learn more control over the timing of his sexual responses, slowing down to allow her more time. And she can give herself a "jump start" getting in the mood, like taking a bath, reading a sexy novel, or practice some "quickies" on her own (it's easiest using a vibrator, which can bring you higher faster).

Men are like a microwave oven, women are like a crock pot.

"Why are women less willing to try new things than guys? My girlfriend is so scared to do new things in sex, but my guy friends are all hot to experiment."

Surprise, some women these days are even more experimental about sex than guys—and scare the guys off! But traditionally, girls are supposed to be "good" or "proper," not wanting sex as much or not being as wild. Find out what your girl's fears and resistances are. What did she learn about how she—and women in general—are supposed to behave? Some girls do whatever guys want, to please them so they won't leave them, and others are afraid that if they give in, he'll think she's a slut or will leave her after he gets what he wants.

"What do women really want in sex?"

Remember my Sex Rule #2: Do unto others as they would have done unto them. Find out what she likes, and give her what she wants how she wants it for however long she wants it.

Most want cuddling and loving, love, intimacy, trust, respect, caring, sharing. Men need to know that penetration is not the be all and end all of sex; it's all in the buildup. But many women also want good sex. They want to be pleasured and to come and feel satisfied. Here's the deal: "If I let you into my body, let me into your mind."

A woman on a TV show I did in Minneapolis put it well:

A man needs to know that a woman is like a frying pan— you have to heat it up before you put the meat in.

"What really turns a woman on?"
- Being told or made to feel she's wanted, adored, special.
- Being given attention. Surprises.
- Saying things to her like, "I'm crazy about you," "You're the only one for me," "I never felt like this toward anyone," "You're beautiful," "I can love you forever," "I don't have eyes for anyone but you."
- Before, after, and during sex, tell her or make her feel, "You can have all the time you need," "I'm here for you forever," "I love you."

Said British band Bush lead singer Gavin Rossdale, as Honorary Love Doctor, "I tell my girlfriend that I miss her, that there's nowhere I'd rather be than with her."

To please her physically, spend time in foreplay and afterplay. In sex, pay attention to her needs. Don't you go, 'til you're one down. Ask or find out what she particularly likes, since many women are different. If she likes oral sex, go down on her for as long as she likes. Send her love notes. Play her favorite music, light scented candles, pour champagne, bathe her in rose petals, towel her dry lovingly. Start out by embracing her, sharing feelings, kissing her all over, stroking her body for hours, commenting on its appeal. Spend lots of time massaging—her mind and her body.

I asked Offspring lead singer Dexter Holland at their after-concert party what men should do for women. He deferred to his girlfriend, whereupon, she gave him a look, and said, "You know, monogamy!" ("But what would *you* say," I insisted. He relented, and offered, "A penis enlarger.")

"Why is it that women need a reason to have sex while men just need a place? Why don't women want sex as much as men?"

Only because they've been taught that they're not supposed to want sex so much, and because they are usually more careful about knowing that they like the person before they have sex. Testosterone, the male hormone, does make men very active, and often this includes sexual activity as well as energy in other things, like sports. But women's sexual drives can be as strong as men's. These days, in fact, there are men who complain she wants sex more than he does, when it used to be the other way around.

LOVE VS. SEX

"Do men have a real need to be romantic like women, or do they only need wham-bam-thank-you-ma'am?"

Anthropologically speaking, males' primary task was just to get their sperm in the female, but females had to get the male committed enough so he'd protect and feed the young. So there's some basis for men just wanting sex and women wanting more relationship. But today, men are more interested and see the value of romance.

Adam Ant was adamant. On *LovePhones* he explained he thinks men are downright "carnal," but have to learn how great it is to emote and really want a woman and feel all those softy feelings. It expands your soul.

My friend Lou says too many men think, "A load is just a load" but they really should be more discriminating about where they put it.

SEX BRAIN STYLE

Bobby: *"She's always bugging me to talk about what we do and how I feel. Why can't she just mess around and let it go at that?"*

Natasha: *"He's making me nuts. He doesn't ever tell me nice things. Why is he making me so miserable?"*

He's not DOING it to you! You both have different what we call brain style preferences. Men are traditionally more dominant in the left-brain (left for logical) and women in the right-brain (right for romantic). Figure out which one you both are, and then appreciate one another's style. Take this quick test of your brain style in sex. Do it for you and your partner.

SEX BRAIN STYLE		
Would you prefer:	<u>Me</u>	<u>Him/ Her</u>
1. (a) going to new places and meeting new people, or (b) having a quiet dinner at home with close friends		
2. (a) talking about feelings, or (b) keeping feelings to myself		
3. (a) falling madly in love, or (b) being careful it's "right"		
4. (a) a partner who feels like a soul mate, or (b) who wants the same things in life		
5. (a) rushing into something, or (b) taking my time		
6. (a) being reckless and romantic, or (b) reasonable and reliable		
7. (a) saying "I love you," or (b) admitting "I think about you when we're apart"		
8. (a) experimenting with new things in sex, or (b) sticking with what worked before		
9. (a) fantasizing about being seduced, or (b) giving or taking orders		
10. (a) after sex, cuddling or (b) chilling out		

Scoring: If you scored more (a)'s, you're right-brained—romantic, spontaneous, emotional, fun-loving, free-spirited—and you like feelings, communicating, and exploring. More (b)'s mean you're left-brained—logical, reliable, reasonable, practical—and like thinking before you act, doing the right thing, and playing it safe. Neither is better; they're just different.

Apply the **Three A's: Acknowledge** your differences (without making one another right or wrong), **Accept** one another, and **Appreciate** one another's good qualities.

HOMEWORK #1: Walk a mile in the other guy's shoes. Make love pretending you're each other. For example, you mimic his fast movements and he copies your slow ones. Switching roles makes you more open to find the middle ground.

HOMEWORK #2: To seduce the other type, (a)'s should be more patient, ask advice, don't demand feelings. To return the favors, (b)'s should tolerate talking, plan surprises, share more feelings.

A *LovePhones* listener faxed in these New Rules for Males and Females:

> The female always makes the rules.
> The rules are subject to change at any time.
> If the female is wrong, it is due to a misunderstanding which was a direct result of something the male did or said wrong.
> The female has every right to be angry or upset at any time.
> The male is expected to mind read at all times.
> The female is ready when she is ready. The male must be ready at all times.

"What really turns a guy on?

It's the same rule as for women. Dr. Judy's Sex Rule #2: Do unto others as they would have done unto them. Give him what he wants how he wants for however long he wants.

Guys love to be respected and looked up to. If you want surefire fireworks, give him oral sex. Guys lose their head when you give them head. Very few don't crave and love it. If you swallow, you're a goddess. Most love the fantasy of being with two women, so you can whisper to them about it without doing it, so he'll think you're open. Otherwise, find out what he really likes.

"Whose orgasm is more intense—a man's or a woman's?"

Either can be intense. Women more often allow themselves more emotional investment in the experience, so they get a more "total" experience of pleasure out of it. Men tend to be more focused on just their penis or ejaculation, although if they let themselves feel more emotional, and concentrate on feeling pleasure in other body parts, they can experience more pleasure in the whole experience. Both can get higher by focusing on sensations, fantasizing, asking for what pleases them, thinking glowing thoughts, and exercising their love muscles.

"How are men's and women's contractions different?"

There are many similarities. Each has about six to ten quick contractions that last only a few seconds, but can be made to last longer or feel more intense by exercising those "love muscles"—women's are around her vaginal opening; men's are near the prostate gland.

"Are men more visual—like looking at women's naked bodies in magazines—than women?"

Not necessarily. Guys have been conditioned to look at magazines with pictures of nude women from the time they were young, while girls did not do that growing up. Guys are also more comfortable with being nude alone and in front of others, while girls are brought up shy and modest, not looking at themselves or others or walking nude around each other. People have different styles—either visual, auditory, or kinesthetic (focused on looking, hearing, or touching) regardless of their sex. And while people think men get more sexually turned on visually and women by talking or touching, research has proved that women also get turned on by looking. So put on a show for her.

FOOTBALL SEX: Roger, 20: *"I want to go all the way in my girlfriend, but she backs up. What's wrong with her?"*

What's wrong with you? I love football, but guys are wrong when they think all girls want football sex (Go deep . . . !). It can hurt, if he's big or pushing against your insides. And some women get the most pleasure from the outside, rubbing around the opening and the clitoris where the most nerve endings are, or from shallow thrusting, since the outer third of their vagina has the most muscles. If she backs up, she's giving you a message to back off; respect it.

HOMEWORK: To work up to it comfortably, try the Oriental "Thrusting of Nines" technique in intercourse, where you first thrust shallow nine times, then eight shallow and one deeper, then seven shallow and two deeper, and so on.

Sex is like a gun, you aim, you shoot, you run.
—Steven Tyler

"My boyfriend says I'm too hung up on foreplay, and should get to it. Is he right?"

No. You both should enjoy all the activities that build to intercourse. But my hunch is that he is too hung up on getting down to penetration, possibly because he doesn't know what to do or is uncomfortable being intimate and seductive.

I don't like the word "foreplay"—it implies something before the "real" thing, intercourse, in this case. Tell your boyfriend that all of what happens in the lovemaking is legitimate: kissing, caressing, oral, manual, and other play, can be as pleasurable as "the main event." Start by suggesting you give each other massages and offer his turn first, telling him he doesn't have to respond, or be sexual at all. It'll inevitably grow into being more genital anyway, but give him a chance to enjoy touching and slower lovemaking.

Torrie: *"After we do it, I want my boyfriend to talk to me and he just wants to roll over and go to sleep. Why? My friend tells me her boyfriend lays his head on her chest after sex and they talk about how great it was and how much they love each other. I want that."*

Mark: *"Why is it that a girl always wants that cuddling stuff after sex, when the guy wants to just chill or play Sega?"*

Oh, come on, he should do some cooing, kissing, holding, saying how great it was, just for her sometimes. There's no rule that says men have to roll over and fall asleep, pull away and chill, get up and play video games or watch TV after sex. They can enjoy the soft stuff, too. In the resolution phase of the sexual-response cycle, after excitement and orgasm, a guy can go either way: he can withdraw and feel tired, or he can feel more intimate and active. The reasons are both physical and psychological. Sex can work like a sedative. The physical buildup and release of tension (like a good workout) and the mental distraction from daily stresses can relax your muscles and mind enough to lull you into a sleepy state. But sex can also be a stimulant as pumping adrenaline and blood from exercising your muscles as well as the mental feeling of being loved can fire you up so you have more energy, confidence, and desire to keep going.

Look back at your Sex Style scores. Remember those different styles. Neither cuddling or chilling is right or wrong, better or worse; you just have to resolve your differences. The proper amount of play (before, during, and after) depends on what you both feel comfortable with. Give each person a turn to get what s/he wants. Don't start sex too late or when you're too tired. Also, examine your relationship. Does his pulling away just trigger your more general feeling of being neglected or deprived? If so, ask for more time and attention together at times other than sex.

"What can I do to make my girlfriend feel better—and leave me alone—after sex when I'm tired and want to go to bed. I love her and don't like to hurt her feelings."

Bless you for *wanting* to be a great guy lover. Most girls want you to hang in there so they don't feel abandoned (which they're prone to feel). Use the three-pronged coulda, woulda, shoulda approach:

- "I coulda done anything for you ("If I felt better," "we started earlier") reassures her you are capable of giving her what she wants.
- "I woulda made love more if I had the energy but I love you dearly and I enjoyed our sex tremendously." Knowing you wanted to do it makes her feel wanted, so she can let you fall asleep.
- "I shoulda spent more time together" makes her hopeful it'll happen next time. Follow this up with specifying when you'll do it.

CONTROL BATTLES

Jane, 24: *"My boyfriend says I'm too aggressive. He said he wanted to have sex in a public place, so I dragged him into the ladies' room. Then he complained. What's up with him?"*

You're an assertive woman, who also likes fun, picking up on a suggestion and running with it. He obviously got threatened. If this behavior shows up at other times and in other circumstances, he may not be the man for you. He needs to be in control and you need someone who lets you fully express your own inner power.

"Is it possible for a girl to be a feminist and to enjoy a passive role? Can it destroy her being equal to the guy outside sex?"

Of course she can. Being comfortable with yourself means being able to be active and passive in sex. Being active or passive has nothing to do with being masculine or feminine. It's not politically incorrect for a woman who believes in women's rights and equality with men to like being passive *and* let him be in charge. It's healthy to be passive *and* active, to give in to others' needs in sex *and* to initiate to get your own needs met.

JEALOUS OF MEN

Sonja, 24: *"I envy men and have since I'm thirteen years old. They can pee standing up. They have something to go in, and we have to receive. We're the sex objects."*

It's all a matter of your perspective. There are men who feel they are sex objects now! Instead of envying men—or anyone—become the person you want to be!

Also, in the highest state of sex, there is no separate receiver and penetrator—you experience being both simultaneously.

MEN FEEL USED

The roles have definitely reversed. A new trend in the nineties: men who feel women are using them! Usually it's the woman who complains that the guy wants sex all the time and demands it and makes her feel bad if she doesn't do it. And I'm always telling these women that they're not a filling station where the guy can pull up and say "fill me up" and drive off, leaving her pump emptier.

Now guys call up, like Phil: *"This girl I know always makes booty calls to me and I get with her, and then when I see her she don't pay me no mind. I'm not up with that. She don't care nothing about me. I feel like she just uses me for sex, you know."*

You don't have to be a filling station either. If you sense you're being used and don't like it, don't do it. Wait for a better, more equal deal.

GIVERS AND TAKERS

"Why am I always the one who does everything for him? Are men always such takers in sex? I'm sick of it."

Traditionally, women give more than they take in sex, and men do the opposite. From my clinical experience, most men admit they are 60 to 75 percent takers and only 25 to 40 percent givers in sex. But the good news is, there are more men who are more interested in giving. They're gems! It's great to hear a guy say, "I want to see the woman get off first. I get off on giving her pleasure." Ferret out those men: interrogate any guy and ask if they like to please a woman and who they think should come first.

But women need to cooperate; that means letting him pleasure you. Some women can't take it! HOMEWORK: Do the "give-and-take" exercise, where you take turns pleasuring each other (using a timer so you don't worry, "When is my time up?" "Am I taking too long?" "Is he tired or bored doing this?") Expect to receive as well as give.

My last word on bridging the Sex Style gap: The best sex is where sex differences blur, where you achieve the Zen state of giver and receiver, penetrated and penetrator, romantic and logical. You and me become we and one.

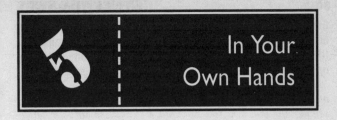

STEVEN TYLER, ACCEPTING THE AWARD FOR BEST
Video from Madonna at the 1994 MTV Music Video Awards,
held up his two fingers. "Madonna, baby, I saw your book,
Sex. Why do you use these two fingers to masturbate?" he
asked, and then answered himself, "because they're mine."

Madonna hesitated a moment and then countered, "If I
were to use your two fingers, it would not be masturbation . . .
it would be child abuse."

Clever, Madonna. But isn't it nice that both Tyler and
Madonna endorse the "M" word—masturbation—that poor
former Surgeon General Jocelyn Elders got fired for using.

Self-pleasuring—masturbation—is healthy. Tyler, as
well as a lot of other rockers, admit that while they were
once into lots of orgies and women, now they're being more
careful and spend more time in their own hands.

Terence Trent D'Arby admits he does it. Punk's first sex
symbol, Blondie's Deborah Harry, is also a fan. Ugly Kid
Joe's Whitfield Crane endorsed it highly when he was an
Honorary Love Doctor on *LovePhones*. He said he started
doing it when he was "prepubescent," until Mom found his
*Playboy*s! Now, he does a lot of it on the road. "Play with
that forever," he advised a caller, "it's totally safe and it
feels good." To keep themselves amused on the road, to
prevent giving in to sex with groupies, and to stay true to
their girlfriends, he and his band mates make up masturbation games. One is the "brain-stretch combo" (wrapping the
penis around the scrotum), another is the "inverted penis"
(making the head go in instead of out), and another which

he proceeded to demonstrate in the studio, is the "belt buckle." Crane turned away from the microphone during a break, and when he faced me again, he had pulled his scrotum out to hang over his pants, looking like a belt buckle! Look out Calvin Klein!

"Safe sex," Crane said, laughing.

"I'm a jackaholic. I like to masturbate five times a day, is that too much?"
"I choke my chicken twice a day, is that okay?"
"How often is it normal to masturbate? Is twice a night too much?"
"I spend more time with Pamela and her five sisters than any other girl. What's up with me?" (Pamela and her five sisters is your hand.)

So many guys who do it a lot worry about whether they do it too much. Fewer women than guys do it, but some female master masturbators worry about doing it too much, too. Usually in the course of discussing another problem about sex, like not having orgasm, I discover that a woman not only isn't masturbating, but thinks it's "nasty." And some guys don't do it either—hard as that may be to believe—thinking it's nasty, too.

How much is too much? Generally, it's okay even if you do it a lot. Some times in life you may want to touch yourself more than at other times, either because you're tense, or really want a sexual experience. It can be okay to do this sometimes three times a day, to make yourself feel better or to learn about your sexuality. How often you like to do it is as individual as how often you like sex with a partner.

But there is a limit: several times a day over long periods of time would indicate that you have a problem. The cutoffs include: Do you do it to avoid a relationship with another person? Do you do it to escape other responsibilities in life (work, school)? Do you do it to avoid facing other problems (like loneliness, depression, family problems)? Do others in your life complain about your doing it?

Why you do it, how it can be helpful or harmful, and what to do about it, is what you'll learn in this chapter.

The son says to the father, "I know you told me if I masturbate I could go blind. How 'bout if I do it just 'til I have to wear glasses."

"Can you ruin your body by masturbating?"

No. Masturbation used to be called "abusing yourself," but if you do it like making love to yourself, there's no danger. Of course guys shouldn't whack themselves around, pulling or yanking. There is no bone in the penis, so you can't break a bone, but you can rupture by pulling too hard. (see the chapter, Check It Out). Both males and females can make the skin sensitive or raw, or get abrasions (which can lead to infections) by too vigorous yanking or stroking. Ease up on that thing, and use cream to avoid this.

"Every time I jerk off I stain the ceiling. Is there a special cleaner for cum stains?"

Congratulations for being able to shoot so far. I'm sure you want me (and everyone) to be in awe of you. Some guys think how far they can shoot their load, or how much it is, is a sign of their potency, power, superiority over other guys (like having a bigger penis), and attractiveness. How can you put your projectile talent to use? Why not project your mind as far as your ejaculate?

"Do women masturbate as often as men, or just not talk about it?"
"What percentage of women eighteen to twenty-five masturbate?"

Lots of girls tell me they've never touched themselves because it's "nasty." Guys have an easier time masturbating because they're more used to touching themselves (since they have to, when they urinate), and society is less negative about all aspects of men being sexual. Girls have not been encouraged to explore their bodies, but they should.

Kinsey's data from the 1950s showed that 94 percent of males and 40 percent of females reported having masturbated to orgasm. More recent studies report about the same percentage of men, but up to about 70 percent of women. So more women are getting the hang of it.

DOING THE NASTY

Tricia: *"My girlfriends were talking about masturbation, but I don't do it. I think it's nasty. Is there something wrong with me?"*

You don't *have* to masturbate, but there also doesn't have to be anything wrong, bad, or nasty about it, and you don't have to feel guilty about doing it (as long as it does not conflict with your religious beliefs). It's important to feel good about your genitals, to have high self-esteem. Where did you learn that touching yourself is wrong? Maybe your mother was uncomfortable about it, and yelled at you, or punished you for it. If so, maybe she was uncomfortable about sex herself or was told by her parents not to do it and just repeated that message to you. It's not disrespectful to make a different decision that it's okay for you. Kellogg, the guy who started the cereal empire, lectured extensively about how masturbation spread foul humors through your body and mind, and made elaborate devices, like harnesses, to prevent people from touching themselves (the movie about him also showed his perverse delight in subjecting people to enemas).

Research has proven that learning how to pleasure yourself is one of the key first steps for women to overcome problems enjoying sex or having orgasms. Believe that your body is beautiful, all parts of it.

Have you ever picked your nose or dug wax out of your ears? Then why not put your fingers in other orifices to explore? Your vagina is just another opening like your nose, and your lubrication is even more interesting than your snot. They're all your body products. You just decided that one place is nastier than the other. You can decide differently.

Masturbation helps you to learn what turns you on, and trains your body to respond. HOMEWORK:
  • Masturbation Relaxation #1: Touch yourself in sexual ways to relax your body and mind. Put your hand on

your sexual parts (breasts or genitals). Stroke or pat gently as you take a deep breath in, to the slow count of three, and breathe out, to a count of four. Inhale and exhale slowly ten times.

- Masturbation Relaxation #2: Do the above, then continue to pleasure yourself to orgasm. The increase and final release of tension results in a calm state.
- Masturbation as Pleasure Exploration: Pleasure yourself to find out what you like, what thoughts and touches turn you on or off.
- Masturbation as Sexual Response Training: As with working out, weight training, or aerobics, masturbation builds up your sexual responses. Practice certain touches and thoughts, and allow your body to respond. As in anything, practice makes perfect.
- Masturbation Training as a "Dress Rehearsal" for Sex with a Partner: Once you are comfortable with how you respond alone, you can be more comfortable with a partner, and also be able to guide him/her in what you like. In basketball, wouldn't you want to practice shooting hoops from all parts of the court before you play horse or get in a game?

Don't procrastinate, masturbate.

"Why should I do it?" Tricia wanted to know.

Remember the **3 M's of Masturbation**:

- **Masturbation as Motivation:** Besides calming you down, masturbation can also rev you up. How? Chemicals flow in your body from the sexual high that you can harness to get activated to do what you want (write a paper, run a mile, clean the garage).
- **Masturbation as Meditation:** Pleasuring yourself is a great meditation tool to enhance self-esteem. HOMEWORK: As you pleasure yourself, repeat over and over, "I am wonderful," "I am loved," "You love me," "I am terrific," and other affirmations. Associating the physical pleasure of self-touching reinforces the thought in your brain, to make you really feel that way.

Similarly, it's a great behavior training tool. HOMEWORK: Think of something pleasurable you want to accomplish—doing well on an exam, making a great presentation, playing in a band, etc. Think that thought while you masturbate.

- **Masturbation as Massage:** HOMEWORK: Caress your body to feel the sensation of touching and also being touched. Experiment with different strokes: long flowing ones versus quicker, shorter repetitions; light and soft, barely touching, and deeper, more intense rubs. Try out different massage techniques—what is your favorite if you were going to a professional masseuse? There are many kinds. For example, Swedish massages firmly trace muscles to relax or stimulate them. Shiatsu stimulates pressure points to move energy in your body. Make up your own variety.

A bush in the hand is worth two birds.

"Is it okay to hone your bone when you're eighteen?"

If you consider masturbating as touching yourself for pleasure, kids start as infants as their hands flail about, land on a body part, and explore. It feels good and they do it again. They touch their genitals just like they do their toes, nose, and ears. They don't think it's nasty or bad.

You learn as a kid that genitals feel good when they get stimulated, like when you're rocked on your tummy in your crib, when you straddle a bike seat, vibrate on a motorcycle, ride a horse bopping up and down and thrusting into the saddle, or even ride in a car with not-so-great-suspension over bumpy roads. Only later, when you're growing up, do you learn it's wrong or bad. By the time you're eighteen (or even younger) you're certainly old enough to know about your body.

"If I don't think about getting turned on, why would I even begin to masturbate? How can I make myself get in the mood?"

Sometimes the cart comes before the horse and sometimes vice versa. That means you can have sexy thoughts and feel tingling in your body and decide to masturbate. Or, you can decide you want to masturbate and then think sexy thoughts and proceed to touch yourself—just like the picture isn't on the tube until you decide to turn the TV on!

Think of masturbation as taking yourself out on a date with your favorite lover—only that lover is you.

Be Prepared. What would you do to prepare for that date? **Prepare your environment.** Make your room cozy, comfortable and sexy—clean up, display your favorite pictures or whatever you want to be noticed about yourself. Buy flowers. Set up mood lighting: move lights around, dim them, put in colored bulbs. Light candles. **Prepare yourself.** Get lingerie (a teddy or silk boxers), and something sexy to wear over it (a lounging outfit or cool overshirt). **Prepare your props.** Go shopping for fun, stimulating things. Have a sex toy chest near your bed for easy access to your paraphernalia, like feathers, fur, vibrators, creams, powders, books, videos, handcuffs, whatever.

"I wouldn't know how to get started to do that thing to myself. What do I do?"

For starters, let's call it body pleasuring, or Body Love, because after all, it means making love to your body.

Phase I is not about your sexual organs, but your whole body, because every part of your body is potentially a sensual zone, and because you have to love it all to feel comfortable being exposed or moving about in sex with a partner.

To start, Look and Appreciate. Stand in front of the mirror, slowly take your clothes off, and appreciate every part of your body without criticizing. Linger on parts you find attractive. Make sexy poses (raise your leg up, turn to the side and caress your upper thigh, turn around and look over your shoulder). Mimic scenes you've seen in films, have read about, or that spontaneously come to you.

The next step: take a bath and instead of soaping up quickly, linger and feel the sensations. Towel off as if you were drying a partner lovingly. Remember you are your best love partner tonight. Next, lie down in bed and smooth a rich body cream all over your body, lingering to feel different sensations on your arms, legs, stomach, chest, neck, face. Feel where the skin is thinner or fleshier. Pretend you're the one being touched, and then pretend you're just the one doing the touching. Massage the cream everywhere, avoiding the genital area, then add touching your genitals. Step three: self-examination, looking at your private parts on the outside and inside. It happens in the movies. In the 1976 movie *The Sailor Who Fell from Grace with the Sea,* actress Sarah Miles does it, and in the 1991 film *Fried Green Tomatoes* the feisty females are instructed to drop their panties and straddle their mirrors.

Longtime feminist and masturbation educator Betty Dodsen spells out how to do it in her book *Sex for One* and shows women the exact steps in her Self-Loving video.

"How do most guys choke their chicken?"

Some guys like stroking their penis with their thumb opposing their index finger alone or together with the middle finger, (I call this the "Scuba OK" technique, since that's the familiar OK shape you make with your fingers, and the sign you use in scuba diving to signal all's well.) Others use their whole hand, or two hands (one to stroke their penis and the other to fondle their scrotum or other body parts, like stomach, chest, or anal area).

Confucius say man with hole in pocket
feel cocky all day.

Richard is a rap deejay. He uses his hands a lot. He also likes to masturbate, so he calls himself a "peejay." His suggestion:

To get in it, exercise your digit, to learn to fidget,
and whack your widget, get into the motion,
    with or without lotion,
polish your helmet and present your p.

EXPANDING MASTURBATION TECHNIQUES

Amanda, 17: *"I only masturbate with my legs closed. I imagine this is a problem because when I have sex, I'll have to keep my legs open. What can I do?"*

Tom, 18: *"I've been knuckling my knob since I'm eleven. I*

lay on my stomach. It's not the greatest way because I can't keep my penis erect against the mattress, and I can't see how I can do it with someone this way. What can I do?"
Claudia, 19: *"I just started having sex, but so far I can't make love right. I've been masturbating on the corner of the sink. How do I move up?"*

We often get "stuck" masturbating in one way that works, and stay with it. But the key is to expand the number of ways you get pleasure, both on your own and with a partner. Some masturbation techniques, like lying on your stomach or under the bathtub faucet, don't lend themselves easily to being with a partner, so it would be best to learn other ways. You have to experiment.

Use some conditioning and relaxation techniques. That means, relax . . . start the way you normally like it (on your stomach, or with your legs locked, etc.) . . . feel yourself getting excited . . . relax . . . keep the same touch and thoughts going as you change position a little at a time (open your legs slightly, or roll on your side a little . . . continue to relax . . . now roll back on your stomach where you're comfortable . . . now get up on your knees). Work up to the way it would be with a partner.

Don't think it's not possible. You have to *just do it*.

Let your mind focus on the new way and add some extra fantasy to up the excitement.

What does your technique of masturbating mean? For example, if you can only do it lying down, but want to do it standing up, does standing up make you feel more aggressive or more powerful? Picture someone on their knees in front of you kissing you there. Take a deep breath and stick out your chest. Affirm to yourself, "I feel good, I can allow myself this pleasure."

NIAGARA FALLS

Daria: *"I like to masturbate in the bathtub. I run the faucet and stick my legs up in the air. Is this okay to do and can I ruin my vagina by the water being too hot?"*

Letting water from the bathtub faucet run over their genitals is one of the most popular ways for women to masturbate and reach orgasm. Why do you like this method? If it makes you feel "clean," do you think masturbation is dirty? If it feels less deliberate in the tub than purposefully touching yourself, then do you feel guilty about it? Confront those feelings. Enjoy yourself. But be a little careful; water shouldn't harm you, but the inner vaginal lips are very sensitive, so don't make the water temperature too hot or they could get irritated. Also, don't let water pour into your vaginal opening; like a douche, as it can disturb what's called the natural pH balance (on acidity) in the vaginal canal, leading to infections.

Another common way for women to masturbate and reach orgasm is to rub the bedsheets or a pillow between their legs. It's okay to do these, but it's best to expand from these "hands-off" ways to "hands-on" touching that is a more deliberate way of saying, "It's okay for me to be sexual," and that is closer to the way you would have sex with a partner. After all, you can make wonderful love in the bathtub with someone, but you can't bring the faucet into the bed; so touch yourself on your bed to reach the same high you get under the water. Usually women like you have an easier time using a vibrator, because they're used to constant intense stimulation that the machine can provide on dry land!

To make changing positions easier, use a vibrator, because the orgasm comes more quickly and reliably, so you don't get discouraged, and the new position is rewarded more easily.

TOOL SENSE

People put all kinds of things on and in their body. Chad grabs a bathbrush. Sheila uses the shower nozzle. Paul cut a hole in a cantaloupe. Rick put a long-necked beer bottle up his girlfriend. Big no-no!

Katherine is most creative. "I pour jelly on the corner of my bed and rub against it. Sometimes I use whipped cream between my legs and then take it off with my fingers and eat it. Sometimes I insert the feet of my doll inside me. Once I put a condom on a banana."

Creativity is fine—but watch out which toys you use—

never use anything dangerous like glass (like long-neck beer bottles), or wood (things on your desk like pencils, bathroom items like a plunger or backbrush, or kitchen utensils like a spatula handle or broomstick). It's no excuse to put a condom on it! Some items around different rooms in the house—like a loofa sponge (for women) or toilet-paper roll (for men) in the bathroom—might be okay as long as they don't scratch or cut you. Bananas have the right shape, but in their skin they can be scratchy (especially the tip) or sting; peeled, they can be too mushy. Frozen hot dogs can be smooth and stay firm enough to work.

Charlie wanted to insert a "D" battery in himself. Come on, man. That might flick your lights, but what if the battery fluid leaked out? Lighten up.

Jimmy: *"When I mash my monster I smack my balls with a spoon. Is this bad?"*

I can see where that stimulation can be exciting, since slapping your face lightly brings blood to your face, so blood would also rush to your genital area if you tap it. An aluminum or silver spoon can feel cold, giving an extra sting of pleasure. But if you do it hard, are you trying to hurt or punish yourself? If you like that cool sensation, stick your fingers in ice and use your hands.

I was more worried about Jimmy's inability to eat out, because he couldn't resist the spoons. What's behind this? Turns out when he was bad as a little boy, mommy would hit his behind with a spoon, and he got a sexual rush from it. Seeing this connection helped him stop beating himself that way.

C.J. called *LovePhones* upset. *"My boyfriend is using my toothbrush up his butt when he jerks off. What can I do about it?"*

Oooh, most distressing, unsanitary, and hostile! My producer, Sam, cut the tension by suggesting that he "consider it a visit from the tooth fairy."

Seriously speaking, turns out C.J. and his boyfriend were always arguing, so this was the guy's way to get back at

C.J. My advice was to have it out with him, or give him the real brush-off.

Dave: *"I got a latex tube from a magazine ad and milked my banana in it and got a rash. What can I do?"*

Likely you got a temporary irritation, or rash, or allergic reaction to the material of the product you bought. Ask the pharmacist for a remedy or see a dermatologist.

Penelope: *"When I was thirteen I found my father's dirty magazines under the bed. Now I sneak looking at them when I masturbate. Is there anything wrong with this?"*

No. You can get some new ideas and build your confidence. HOMEWORK: Pose as the magazine models to really enjoy yourself. Imagine how the sexy models feel inside, and feel the same way. Picture a partner looking at you with the same admiration as they would look at those girls. To be sure not to get hooked on the magazines, make up some new pictures in your mind, with you as the main character.

Bud masturbates onto the poster of TV's *Married with Children* Christina Applegate. That's okay, as long as he's doing it in a loving, not aggressive way. But Pat, 18, is taking it too far. *"I like to whack off in dressing rooms in malls and ejaculate onto the mirror. I can't do it any other way."*

What are you feeling when you do this? Is it your need to show off (because you are intimidated that you are not enough), defy authority (because you were punished for masturbating), or insult others (by defiling them unsuspectingly)? You're being an exhibitionist, who wants to shock people and get a reaction because you feel insignificant and impotent inside.

Remember my four-step program: Stop and think. Identify your need. Assess the consequences. Satisfy the need in a constructive way. HOMEWORK: Go home and do it in front of your own mirror, if you have to, and imagine people being there. Say to the mirror whatever you need to say to yourself ("I'm so big, strong, powerful") and feel like the narcissistic king in one of my favorite poems: "My name is Ozymandias, King of Kings, Look up my works ye mighty, and despair." If you get your inner need satisfied, then you won't be a victim of your compulsive behavior.

NOT MY JOB

James: *"I'm a guy and I wouldn't buff my own helmet. That's for a girl to do me."*

Don't do it if you don't want to, but about 4 percent of guys are like you. You're missing out on a lot of opportunity for pleasure, and learning about yourself as well as what to teach a girl to do to please you. Most guys can't believe there's a guy alive who doesn't choke his chicken; about 96 percent of guys do. Someone can do it for you, but you can also do it yourself.

Girls feel this way, too. Jennifer, 22: *"You're not supposed to do it because your boyfriend does it for you."*

Your boyfriend doesn't have first rights to it: you do. You need to know what pleases you, to help him know what to do. If women think just men can give them pleasure, and not themselves, they become desperate and dependent—you don't want that, do you?

John: *"Isn't it disgusting for a guy to taste his own semen?"*

Absolutely not. Aren't you curious? Why don't you try it and see what your partner would be tasting so you can come to your own conclusions about how it tastes. Get to like it, so when you're with a partner you want to go down on you or swallow, you can think to yourself, "I taste good."

It's just your own body fluid. You swallow your own saliva, don't you? Maybe even you ate a booger or your earwax once. It's all in your mind whether it's disgusting. Decide it's nice.

"If you do it too much, can you get sick of it?"

Sometimes masturbating a lot makes you more turned on and you want to do it more. But you can reach a point of no return—of physical and mental satiation—so you get less turned on. This can last hours or days. There's nothing wrong. Give it a rest. It'll come back.

"I have been milking my own banana since I'm twelve years old. Now I want to marry a girl and I'm worried. If you masturbate a lot, can you use up your sperm? I heard old man's sperm turns to sawdust."

When I was in India speaking at the Third Asian Conference on Sexology, I learned that Indian men freak if they masturbate too often or have morning emissions, thinking, like you, that you'll use it up. It's called the DHAT syndrome. Certain Eastern Taoist sex ideologists do teach that a man has only five thousand ejaculations in his lifetime. (That's all part of the theory that you should recycle your sexual energy in your body without expelling it). Some teachings in the Jewish religion say you should not spill your seed. But as long as you stay healthy, your semen (and sperm in it) will continue to replenish, so don't worry about drying up.

"I lift weights; if you pull your pud too often, will you lose your strength?"
"I play sports, if I toss the javelin before a match, will I lose?"

Yes is the answer to your question if you go along with those Eastern sexologists who believe that ejecting sperm expends vital male energy that should be recycled through the body. Indeed, masturbating can make you less able to lift heavy weights or less motivated to beat the other guy because you get more relaxed. But I think timing matters. If you masturbate over three to four hours before you have to perform well at something, you could do even better because you've had needed stress release and a surge of pleasure chemicals through your body, and enough time to build up your energy or aggression necessary for the competition.

There has been debate over whether sportsmen should have sex before a match or game. In the recent World Cup soccer matches some coaches insisted players' not have sex before the match, claiming it sapped their drive. Curtis Sliwa, founder of the Guardian Angels, refuses to let his street patrollers listen to *LovePhones* before they go out on the streets because he thinks it makes them less aggressive. Other sportsmen want sex before a match, because they want to relax or feel powerful. Many coaches and sex stars

I've talked to say it's individual, depending on what motivates the individual player—frustration or fulfillment.

"I'd like to masturbate, but it's against my religion."

Therapists who specialize in helping people with strict religious beliefs help them interpret the doctrines. For example, New York sex therapists Norman and Ester Fertel helped a man with erection problems get over his no-no about touching himself (necessary homework for his cure) by considering that he needed to massage his penis to improve his circulation. The idea of massage for a medical purpose was acceptable, while masturbation for pleasure was not.

Some religious leaders pose the question, Why would God make us the only animal that feels sexual at any time unless we were intended to feel pleasure? Why did God make the female with a clitoris, whose only function is to have pleasure, unless he meant such a gift to be used?

Patty, 24: "I masturbate a lot—two or three times a week. Will this interfere with having an orgasm with a guy? I was twenty-one when a guy gave me my first orgasm and I haven't had one since."

First off, a guy does not give you an orgasm—he helps, but you take responsibility—by your ability to respond—yourself. So change your attitude, or you won't be able to come because you'll depend on his technique, and you might purposefully not come so you don't owe anything to him.

Second, self-pleasure is as good a practice for having an orgasm with a partner as running a few miles a day is for preparing for a marathon.

Lots of myths about masturbating still prevail. Justin wanted to know, *"Can you get zits from jerking off?"* and Paul wanted to know why, *"After I ejaculate a couple of times, the following day my face breaks out."*

At times when you masturbate you may be going through body changes that seem causal but are really coincidental. In puberty, your oil glands are secreting, so you can get pimples. The more active you are, as in masturbating, the more your sweat and oil glands are activated, as they would be in any activity, so pimples can erupt. Pimple eruptions can be caused by what's called SWAT syndrome: stress, worry, anxiety, and tension. Just one of these can trigger a chain reaction, whereby the pituitary gland signals the adrenal gland to produce more androgens (hormones) and the excess of androgen can cause an acne outbreak.

Dave was actually worried, *"Can you lose your hair from masturbating?"*

Doubtful. Pattern hair loss is mostly hereditary, unrelated to any activity. But, it's possible that hormone levels connect both events, since testosterone levels affect your hair growth and also your sex drive.

Leroy: *"I touch myself wherever I am: in classrooms, the living room, the kitchen, so I can't do nothing else. Is this normal?"*
Sandy: *"I know a girl who is always holding her breast, even in class, and especially when people talk to her. It looks weird. What's wrong with her?"*

Excessively touching or holding yourself, whether in public or private, is like a baby using a pacifier—to make yourself feel better, to comfort or calm yourself. Use the four step program: Stop and think. Identify your needs and feelings, like "I need to be held" or "I'm scared and need someone to help me now." Assess the outcome of different actions. Satisfy that feeling in a better way (get attention from others).

If you get turned on, or an erection, in inconvenient places, you don't have to touch yourself. Every urge does not need to be satisfied. Just notice it, say, "Oops, there it is," and get on with your business.

"My penis is bent to the left. I masturbate a lot by pulling it that way. Did I make it bend that way?"

No. Penises bent in different directions are normal variations. You couldn't yank it and fix it in a position. Likely it was just more comfortable for you to masturbate in the direction it was already leaning (see chapter on What's Up With My Body).

JERK-OFF NOT A JERK

"We've had great sex for a year, but the other night I walked in on my guy in the bathroom masturbating. Why does he do this? Aren't I enough for him?"

"My wife and I have sex about fifteen times a week. Am I cheating on her when I do it on my own, also ten or fifteen times?"

Don't take it so personally. It's unrealistic to think that one person's sexuality is wrapped up totally in another person. Even if you're satisfied with your relationship, you're entitled and healthy to pleasure yourself—to explore private fantasies, release tension, tone up like any "working out," or learn what you like so you can share it. Sometimes a guy masturbates when he wants sex more often than the partner and doesn't want to be too demanding; if that's the case, be happy he's doing it with himself instead of having an affair! If you want to be sure he's not doing it because you don't satisfy him, ask what he would *really* love in sex—and promise to do it. By the way, women in love masturbate, too!

Caveat: there is a chance he retreats into himself because he is not fully expressing himself and therefore not being totally satisfied with you. Usually, there is a private fantasy the person who does it is afraid to share (like wanting to make love to two people, imagining being the opposite sex, being whipped, etc.). Tell him you want to share anything and everything—at least talking about it.

In Dan's case, masturbating when he had a partner indicates a problem. *"My girlfriend is mad because I masturbate too much and I can't get hard with her. Why?"*

Your girlfriend's reasoning is reversed. She thinks your masturbating makes you not get hard with her when it's likely the opposite—you masturbate because you can't get hard with her. Tell her that you're not doing it to hurt her, or because she's not attractive to you. Tell her you'd like to have sex with her without getting hard. Just taking the pressure off will help you. See the chapter on What's Up With Him for lots of suggestions about getting your erection firm. What are you doing to yourself that she's not doing? My friend, sex therapist Michael Perelman, warns that some guys who masturbate too often can get "stuck" coming too quickly, ruining sex with a partner, so should hold off 48 hours before a sex date in order to build desire for release, and do a "hand switch" (if rightie, do it leftie), to be aware of his technique in order to teach his partner.

"One time I was masturbating and my mother came in my room. I was too far along, so I had to finish. What should I have done? We haven't talked since then."

Your mother should have knocked. You deserve privacy. But it was audacious to finish in front of her. You should have stopped and said, "Mom, you interrupted me when I was doing something private. Obviously we're both embarrassed. Let's just forget it. It's a normal thing for me to do." Next time, lock your door. Now, talk about it with her. Practice what you'd say, to get over your embarrassment. Say, "Mom, I'm embarrassed, and so are you, at what you saw. But it was normal and I was in my room, not bothering anybody. I'm sorry if I shocked or offended you. What are you feeling about it?"

SHOW-OFF

Steve, 19: *"I masturbate on the bus, in the train and while I'm driving my '88 Chevy station wagon. I come all over myself. Is this okay?"*

I'm sure you think it's fun, but it's not smart. When you have orgasm, your brain state changes, and your driving judgment and alertness can be impaired, leaving you open to an accident. HOMEWORK: Examine why you need such a thrill and the potential of being seen. Get attention in more socially acceptable ways. Make a list of ten things you think people can like you for. When you get the urge to do it in public, like on the bus, stop and think. An exhibitionist needs to shock people or to get attention. Ask yourself, "What do I really need now?" If the answer is, "I want someone to notice me, to hold me," do something ingratiating, like get up and offer your seat to an elderly person and talk about how they feel that day, to feel like a good person. Think of the consequences and choose a wise action.

Watch out, you could get arrested. It happened to

Joe: *"I was arrested for indecent exposure. I really like driving by and pulling myself while women look in the car. I was stopped at a stoplight doing it and these two women saw; they must have reported me because the police came. It was really embarrassing. It was enough to make me think I don't want to do this anymore, even though I get a real rush out of it."*

One technique would be to scale it down, and do it in your garage, and then just imagine it while you're in bed. Another treatment technique (like for other unwanted behaviors in the Am I A Freak? and Not Down With That chapters) is called extinction, where you would masturbate to the thought of women seeing you doing it in the car until your penis hurts, thereby associating pain and unpleasantness with the previously stimulating thought. (It's a step beyond getting too much of a good thing where you get sick of it.) Then you replace that thought with a positive one—like you and an appropriate partner in front of a fire, professing your love.

SOLO SEX SHY

Simon is the opposite: he's shy about sex in front of others. *"I can't masturbate in front of my girlfriend. I'm too shy about it. But she wants me to. How do I get to do this?"*

If I put you on the Freudian couch to interpret your behavior, I'd ask: What does masturbating in front of someone else mean to you? Does it mean that you are full of yourself, that you don't need her, that you look silly, that you shouldn't be doing this?

BRAIN RETRAIN: Turn every negative into the exact opposite (positive) and play it up. "I look silly" becomes "I look exciting, cool." "I shouldn't be doing this, she should be doing this to me" becomes "This is perfect to do. She loves it and I love pleasing her and myself."

HOMEWORK: Practice by masturbating alone and imagining that she's there. Also, do it in front of a mirror and watch yourself, to see how you look and to get over the self-consciousness of being looked at.

Girls fear such self displays, too. *"My boyfriend wants me to masturbate in front of him. I don't want to do it. Is there something wrong with me? Why do men get turned on by watching women masturbate?"*

Of course, don't do what you don't want to. But lots of guys get really turned on to a woman touching herself in front of him. There's a thrill to watching her overcome a taboo, like watching a "good girl" do something naughty because he knows that girls haven't traditionally been as comfortable "doing themselves" as men are. Also, if she masturbates, it means she's more comfortable with her body, so he doesn't have to worry that she's uptight about sex—and he can feel he has more permission to be sexually free. Watching her probably restimulates those first adolescent stirrings when he wasn't supposed to touch a girl, but got so turned on thinking about and anticipating it. Also, seeing what she does to herself gives the guy a rare insight into what a woman really likes. There's nothing wrong with doing it in front of your partner, so why not give both of you that pleasure. Get over your embarrassment about your body or displaying it.

BRAIN RETRAIN: Believe your body and your genitals are beautiful and that self-display is good.

HOMEWORK: Let him watch you masturbate. Do "the masturbation seduction." Dress in a provocative outfit and lie him down on the bed. Strip for him and stand in front of him, rubbing yourself. Improvise. Put your finger in you, and open your mouth slightly and trace your lips with your finger. Put it inside you again, and lean over to rub it on his lips.

Teach your partner how you touch yourself.
Darryl: *"I masturbate a lot, three or four times a day. I'm going out with this girl, and when she tries to masturbate me or give me oral sex, I can't get off."*

Don't expect your partner to know how you like it. HOMEWORK: Play "Show and Tell." Work it while she's there, showing her and talking her through what you're doing, like a demonstration. Let her get up close and watch. Put your partner's hand over yours while you do it so the other person gets the hang of what you're doing. Then put your hand on top, so they're in contact with your skin. Talk them through it. It's called "guided feedback."

Extreme's Gary Cherone, as a *LovePhones* Honorary Love Doctor, disagreed with me about recommending masturbation to help Darryl's problem. "I would suggest you quit masturbating for a while so when you're with her, you might be a little more excited." But he went for the idea of showing off: "Have you ever done it watching her? You could do wonderful things with her in front of you. Try it, man," he advised.

If masturbation is called choking your chicken, then when you get to intercourse is it stuffing the turkey?

Sal: *"Why is it that sometimes during masturbation my girlfriend tells me to stop and give her the real thing and other times she just wants to have an orgasm from me masturbating her?"*

There's nothing wrong with that. It doesn't mean she loves you or your penis any less. Sometimes she just may be in a groove from the feeling, and want to stay with it. Maybe she's afraid she won't reach orgasm in intercourse that time (it doesn't always happen for most women). Each time of sex is a unique experience. Allow different things to happen, especially if you trust that you care for one another.

BLOW YOUR OWN HORN

Anthony: *"Can a guy go down on himself? Why would he want to do that?"*

The answer is like asking, "Why does a dog lick his balls?" Because he can.

Some guys might find it disgusting, others wish they could do it. There's even a video, *Come Blow Your Horn*, of guys doing it in various positions. It takes being flexible. You can brace yourself against a wall from sitting on the floor or on the bed, or under something like a sink. Some guys can just bend and do it. If you can't bend over and touch your knees with your head, then likely you can't reach. You can practice stretching exercises, but some people just aren't flexible enough. Sorry.

Final Word: Feel confident you're in your own good hands.

"I'M TIED TO THE BEDPOST WITH HANDCUFFS and scarves while he does whatever he wants to me."
"We're walking on the beach holding hands and stop to kiss as the warm ocean waves lap our feet."
"We're in a hot tub doing it."
"Two girls do each other while I watch."
"A big-breasted girl comes up to me in a club and opens my zipper without saying a word."
"The bare-chested gardener with sweat beads glistening on his muscled chest eats me out for hours in the freshly cut grass."

Do you make up exciting sexual stories in your mind? Fine. Are these thoughts perverted or sick? Not (usually). Your mind is your personal playground where you can be and do anything, as long as it doesn't hurt anyone. Sexual fantasies can purge your fears and fuel your desire. Let your mind wander. What scenes do you come up with?

WHAT'S A SEXUAL FANTASY AND DOES EVERYBODY DO IT?

Steven: *"My girlfriend always makes up these stories and gets angry when I don't. Is there something wrong with me or her?"*

A sexual fantasy includes everything from a fleeting thought to a long involved story, like scenes in a movie or book. As soon as you say, "I'd like to do it on the beach," you have an image in your head that qualifies as a fantasy. Sexual fantasies can be real (something you already experienced) or totally made up. They can be consciously conjured-up daydreams or unconscious nighttime dreams. They can be exciting or embarrassing, titillating or troubling. They can be romantic or erotic, rated from PG to XXX.

Since most everyone has some fleeting thought, it's probably fair to say that everyone fantasizes. And, about a third of people do it often. People who have a more mental sexual style (who like using their imagination) conjure up stories more than those who prefer seeing, hearing, or touching things to turn them on. New Order bassist Peter Hook, looking at the tall, slim, thirteen-years-his-junior girl he met at his Manchester club Hacienda, reassured Steven: "I'm not into stories either, man. I'm strictly visual. Just *seeing* my girlfriend does it for me."

Neither style is better, though whichever you are, fantasies can help your sex life. Studies show women have as rich fantasies as guys.

ARE MY THOUGHTS OKAY?

People always ask me whether their fantasies are okay. They'll say, "I think about another guy I know while I'm making love to my boyfriend," or "I want my girlfriend to do something she says is nasty," and then they ask, "Am I normal? Is this okay?" Since sex is still considered sinful by some factions in our society, people have a lot of guilt and shame about their sexual thoughts. I want you to feel free of that shame or guilt.

Go ahead—pretend you are two strangers on a train, a rock star grinding your groin to thousands of adoring fans, or a dominatrix ordering her slave to lick her boots. But there are some caveats:

- Thinking is not the same as doing. You're on safer ground letting your mind roam free if you can control your actions. If you feel driven to act out something that could lead to trouble, don't keep rehearsing the fantasy in mind, since that makes it more likely it'll come true.

- Hurting anyone (yourself, children, others) is off-limits, including having sex with inappropriate partners (like teachers, best friends' lovers, family members).
- Beware of unrealistic expectations, like fantasizing that you can seduce anyone and being disappointed it doesn't happen in real life.
- Use fantasy to enhance rather than escape being with a real person.

HOW FAR WILL IT GO?

John: *"Am I coming into my sexuality by fantasizing about masturbating and being sexual in public places? Or will it go too far—like having sex in the mall?"*

Advice from Lemonheads' lead singer Evan Dando, as Honorary Love Doctor: "There are so many worse things going on right now that you don't have to worry that much. You are exploring new things. Good for you. I think you aren't in serious danger at the moment. (Just) don't get arrested. I wouldn't hit the fountains, though. Stay in the dark."

The queen of sexual fantasy is, of course, Madonna. In an interview with a gay magazine after the release of her film *Truth or Dare,* she said, "I am aroused by two men kissing. Is that kinky? I am aroused by the idea of a woman making love to me while either a man or another woman watches. Is that kinky?" No, and she's acted out those fantasies with gusto!

Read the following fantasies and check your reactions. Which do you find stimulating, strange, or sick?

FANTASY #1: "I'm at a party and walk into a backroom. Two models are there touching each other. They look at me and smile. I watch for a while and then they motion for me to come over and join them."

FANTASY #2: "My boyfriend and I are camping along the coast. We stop at a secluded cove and take out a picnic. The sun is shining and clear blue water is lapping at our feet. He starts spreading the food on my body."

FANTASY #3: "I'm wearing new lacy underwear and all of a sudden I get this idea that I'd like to put the underpants on my boyfriend."

FANTASY #4: "My girlfriend isn't in her dorm one afternoon when I go to see her, but her roommate is there in a towel, and winks at me to come in. I always thought she was hot."

FANTASY #5: "A woman dressed in black leather makes me crawl around and bark like a dog. Then, she drips hot wax on me."

FANTASY #6: "I want to make this guy freak over me. I think about tweaking his twizzler until he screams. I ride him like a mechanical pony in front of a grocery store, bouncing up and down until his balls are so tight he could play tennis with them. Then he bursts into me."

Let your mind trip. Your thoughts can revel in being irresistible, in control or out of control, from watching to being watched; doing forbidden things or fetishes; having sex with strangers or a host of other characters. The possibilities are as endless as your imagination.

MOST COMMON FANTASIES
Percent of Men/Women

• Sex with a loved partner (an ex or imaginary)	75/50
• Oral sex	60/50
• Being irresistible	50/50
• Someone giving in after resisting	33/25
• Sex with two or more partners	33/20
• Forcing someone to have sex	25/16
• Being forced to have sex	20/33
• Things you wouldn't do in real life	20/30
• Being watched having sex	15/20
• Observing others having sex	18/13

SCHOOLGIRL FANTASY

Debbie: *"My boyfriend has a fantasy about me being a Catholic schoolgirl, with knee-high socks and the skirt and the whole thing. He wants me to wear my hair in pigtails and get the clothes. Should I do it?"*

The schoolgirl fantasy is newly popular these days in America, though if you go to Japan, you'll see outdoor vending machines that sell schoolgirl outfits and underpants, and all-aged guys reading comic books with the schoolgirl "Lolita" theme on their long commuter train rides to and from work. Ask your boyfriend what turns him on about this fantasy. Is it the idea of corrupting an innocent virgin, or is it to overcome guilt? How could it be fun or freeing for him—and you?

TOO MUCH FANTASY?

"I fantasize a lot, is that okay?"

As long as you're not escaping your real life, or avoiding real sex with realistic partners, studies show people who fantasize more are more interested in sex and more easily turned on than those who don't have a lot of sexual fantasies.

BREAKING OUT

Fantasies can help you break out of inhibitions. Like for Samantha, who was brought up to be such a "good little girl" who always thought of pleasing a man first:

"I have this thought that this really hot-looking guy comes into my room and leans over me and says I'm here to do whatever you like, and he spends hours licking and sucking me 'til I have orgasms like I never had before."

People worry that if they make up stories, it must mean something's missing in real life. Instead, fantasies can expand your pleasure and creativity.

STAR-TREK SEX

Fantasy can literally and figuratively transport you into new galaxies.

Like for Jake: *"When I have sex, I daydream about flying through the stars and space, walking into the sun, being a samurai or a cowboy fighting five guys and saving three girls."*

Or Lisette: *"When I have sex with the guy I love, I time travel. I see us in a barn, covered in hay, laughing. Or I'm in a rocket ship. One time, I was an Egyptian lady-in-waiting caressing the princess while giving her a bath. Another time, I was in a Roman arena and the winning warrior's prize was to do me in my box. Is there something wrong with me?"*

How about the exact opposite: right on! What imagination. Write all your stories down and maybe you'll use them in a creative writing project some day. Explore how each of these lives (the samurai, cowboy, sun-walker, star-trekker) expresses a part of you and your sexuality: being powerful, exciting, desired. Be that way in your real sex life. Next step: so you're not always lost alone in your mind space, include a love partner in your mind trips.

SAME OLD, SAME OLD

Fantasies can spice up your love life when you've been together a long time. Doug, twenty-six, has a most common question: *"I'm beginning to feel the old sex life with my girlfriend dragging. Does this mean it's over?"*

Don't give up yet. Use fantasy to perk you up. Re-enact the way you first were excited by each other. Singer Richard Marx offers this suggestion: "Pretend you're strangers who never did it before."

GETTING YOU OR YOUR PARTNER INTO IT

What if you want to fantasize more? Or want your partner to fantasize more, like Frankie? At least, he's on the right track.

"I'm the kind of guy that likes to talk about all kinds of wild things, like my T-shirt says, 'Whip me, beat me, bite my ear, call me a slut, tear me to shreds, just do me' and then on the back, 'Who says romance is dead?' The problem is my girlfriend says she has absolutely no fantasies. So, tonight I was trying to break her down and was like, 'Come on, there has got to be a time you think about sex like when I am not around.' And she said, 'Okay, sometimes at night, when I'm

*going to bed, I think about you,' so I asked, 'What happens?'
and she said, 'Well, I get warm all over and picture you next
to me.' And I said, 'Oh yeah, then what do you do?' And she
said, 'I go to sleep, what do you expect me do?' I would like
her to go more and open up and talk to me about it."*

STEPS TO INCREASE (YOUR OWN OR A PARTNER'S) FANTASIZING:

- Positive encouragement. Anytime a storyline is expressed, jump on it enthusiastically.
- Practice right-brained activities (as opposed to left-brained or logical, rational thinking). For example, look at unusual patterns or symbols (in materials, videos, snowflakes, clouds), put an outfit together with unusually matched colors, listen to mind-expanding music (Pink Floyd, Grateful Dead, Queen, Artist Formerly Known as Prince).
- Read sexy novels or watch sexy videos. For my money, one of the sexiest movie scenes is the back-of-the-limo sex between Sean Young and Kevin Costner in *No Way Out.* Sean told me when she saw the dailies she even said, "This is too intense for me. I can't watch this . . . " and they ended up taming it down a lot for the movie.
- Relax in a warm bath, lie on a couch, play relaxing or stimulating music, review a sexy scene in your mind, and expand on it. For example, suppose you met a stranger at a party but nothing happened; picture the guy taking you into the bedroom and tearing off your clothes in urgent passion.
- Mind conditioning: imagine a sexy scene before you go to bed and picture it over and over in your mind, programming your subconscious so it will more likely happen during sleep and get "set" in your mind.
- Keep a fantasy or dream journal. Write them down and read them over.

One warning: you might have a high sex drive and purposefully pick an inhibited lover (to put a leash on you, prove you're right that others are losers, or justify complaining). Or, the inhibited one may purposefully pick a higher-sexed partner for similar reasons.

ROCKIN' SEX FANTASIES

It's as true as the answer to "Does a bear sh— in the woods?" that rock stars get to live out their fantasies. Here are some rockers' favorites:

Steven Tyler. Surprise, he's done it all, so now he fancies the idea of being on a desert island with just one woman, with no clothes, and feeding off the land.

Aerosmith's bassist tom Hamilton: "Being in a treehouse in a jungle, really hot, Tarzan-like."

Urge Overkill drummer Blackie: "A great movie, home-cooked meal for two, cocktail music (Burt Bacharach), some nice champagne and afterwards a cup of expresso or maybe out for a drink and a quiet dance, then back home for some real fireworks."

UO bassist "Eddie" King Roesser: "Golden showers and Disneyland."

Guns N' Roses guitarist Gilbey Clarke: "I'm one of those standard guys where guys like seeing girls with girls and things like that. Being in a rock band I've pretty much seen it all. It's like I really gotta start thinking of some new things. I thought the pregnant wife might be something. But there is one new thing. I was in Lars's limo and saw a porno that was pretty wild. There was two guys with one girl and I've never seen them do it in the same place like that before. I tried to buy it but it was the limo driver's and he wouldn't let it go. That's how he gets people to go in his car."

Ugly Kid Joe's lead singer Whitfield Crane had to suspend his favorite double mint two-girl thing now that he was in love with girlfriend MTV-jay Duff. The new fantasy: "Wanting to go down a slide into a pool of jello while friends would be behind a glass watching."

Simon Le Bon of Duran Duran had the two girls and the

jello thing, too! He liked the idea of two girls in a Santa suit. And at our Z100 10th birthday bash in Madison Square Garden, I asked him on stage in front of 16,000 people what his fantasy was. He wanted to be in a hot tub filled with jello with all important male and female politicians around. He'd be wearing just a tie and suspenders and would jump out to serve them tea. Simon seems to have a real clothes thing: backstage, he said he loves the idea of wearing stockings. (*Cute*, but can that beat the Red Hot Chili Peppers on-stage with just socks on their penises?).

Singer Terence Trent D'Arby upped the numbers. Feeding his fantasy by being on *LovePhones* with *four* Penthouse Pets (so much so that he wrote on our bathroom wall, "For a good time, call Terence Trent D'Arby . . ." with his L.A. phone number), Terence said he's has done it all, but the one thing left he'd like is having *three* girls, "one at my head, one at my foot and one sitting on me."

Comic actor Pauly Shore wants "to pose naked for *Playgirl* because I am more comfortable naked. I'd be looking over the back of my shoulder, head arched, down at my naked butt (like I showed my butt in *Son In Law* even though it was a Disney movie), hayseed in my mouth, on a farm, with my dong between my legs (because I don't want anyone to see it, or see it shriveled, and it should be private)."

My buddy, singer Sophie B. Hawkins fancies the idea of teaming up (note, she's a basketball player) with another woman to have a guy do what they request . . .

First Brother Roger Clinton, whose first CD is called "Nothing Good Comes Easy," would welcome the challenge of doing it in the Rose Garden (easier, he figured, than the Lincoln Room or any other room in the White House because the phone rings too often).

MEN VS. WOMEN

Are men's and women's fantasies different?

They used to be more different than they are now. Surveys years ago showed that while women relished lingering romantic encounters with admirers or faceless strangers, or submission after a struggle, men traditionally fantasized about fast and uninhibited sex (probably because they learned as kids to do it fast in the bathroom), sex in public places, being seduced by older women, and women performing oral sex on them. And there is no question that sex with two women topped the list (watching two women do each other or both doing him).

> A genie tells a guy he can have any wish fulfilled and he says he wants three women. *Poof,* his wish is granted. But it turns out the three women are Lorena Bobbitt, Tonya Harding, and Hillary Clinton. So he gets his penis cut off, his knees smashed, and to top it all off, he has no health coverage.

But the themes of both men's and women's fantasies are expanding, spilling over into each other's traditional domains. While two women and oral sex still top men's list, good news for women: research is proving that his top romantic fantasies match hers—candlelit dinners, moonlit beach strolls.

Like Matt: *"The other night I was lying in bed thinking about my girlfriend and I got this idea that she was at her window and I was on the lawn reciting poetry and then I climbed up the scaffolding—because there was construction on the house—and we made love on the ledge. It was really strange because she was wearing a big flouncy dress like in the old days. If I told my friends about this, they'd laugh at me and think I'm a wuss."*

Cheers to you for thinking of such a romantic scene—sounds like the balcony scene from Shakespeare's *Romeo and Juliet.* (Did you just read it in class, since our real experiences sneak into our fantasies all the time?). How does this love on the ledge relate to wishes—or fears—in your real life? Do you want or fear danger, the risk of discovery or disapproval, or proving the extent of your passion? Build on the romantic themes in your fantasy. I'm sure your girlfriend would welcome that.

All those "New Man" role models in the media and weekend Iron John retreats and bad press about casual sex are helping men get more in touch with that sensitive, caring, committed side, after all.

It's rubbed off on rock stars. Even the "bad boys" espouse romantic sex with their spouse! After having nearly every fantasy fulfilled, guys like Steven Tyler, Vince Neil, and Sammy Hagar love love best. They've all done it with many girls (try five) at a time (for Neil and Hagar the women knew each other). Now, they advise you can explore as many dimensions with just one. Says Tyler, "I can go as many places with my wife." And Hagar, "My girlfriend sets off just the right buttons in my head." And Neil, "I'd like one girl to do it all."

Women's fantasies have also changed—to cross over into men's favorite themes. Top of women's list used to be what was called the "rape fantasy"—really not rape, but "submission"—where the guy wanted her so much that he "made" her give in to sex. This theme was popular years ago when women did not want to take responsibility for sex, when they had to be "good girls," so they liked imagining that the man insisted she "had" to submit. But since women have become more economically and emotionally independent and connected with their more (albeit stereotypic) "masculine" as well as "feminine" selves, they feel freer about having more fantasies where they are in control. So now women's sexual thoughts are more voyeuristic (looking at bodies or other people having sex) and unconventional (like having two-on-one themselves).

There are three new popular themes for women's fantasies, based on a quarter century of research by author Nancy Friday: the woman on top; women with multiple partners; and women fantasizing about other women.

Kelly is typical of the new woman who likes the idea of being in control: *"I picture myself ordering a guy around and telling him what to do. But I worry, is this okay?"*

Yes, it's certainly okay. You're the modern woman, who through her sexual fantasies can now allow herself to be on top—literally and figuratively.

Megan, 21, wants many-on-one (her!): *"I have a recurring dream about being in an orgy, with tongues and lips all over me."*

Great! Let yourself enjoy being loved by a cast of thousands!

And Dawn is typical of the new woman who thinks about another woman while with her boyfriend: *"I think about this other girl when my boyfriend is making love to me. In regular life, I don't want another woman, because I'm not gay and I don't want him to be with anyone. But at the point when he penetrates me, I think of her. She's tall and blond and pretty and I'm kissing her. She holds my breasts in her hand and rubs them gently. I want her to go down on me but don't know how to ask her. I say, 'I love you,' and she says she loves me back. She looks at me and sees it in my eyes, so she puts her head there. Then she tells me I'm real pretty, like my boyfriend never did, and tells me that she loves it and will do anything I want. She does and I rub my hands through her hair as I moan. Is this wrong?"*

What a lovely fantasy. You created this woman in your fantasy to give you certain messages about how you would like lovemaking to go. She is a better example of the lover you would like, because your boyfriend doesn't "read" you the way she does and you are not as comfortable asking him to do what you want. HOMEWORK: Whatever she does to you, ask your boyfriend to do. Tell him to tell you (as she does) "You're beautiful, I love pleasing you like this, I'll do anything you want."

The people we make up in our fantasies are either like how we are or how we would like to be. HOMEWORK: Feel as sexy as you imagine she does. Her appreciating your genitals is a lesson to you that you would like to appreciate your own, and your boyfriend's, genitals. Try treating him as she treated you in the fantasy.

VICTOR/VICTORIA

Karen, 19: *"In my fantasy I was a man having intercourse. I had a penis. In another one I'm with a woman who has a dildo on. Is this wrong?"*

You're not abnormal or wrong. Fantasy is a place to be anybody and have anything you want! Think: what does your fantasy mean about how it's different being a guy or a girl?

Karen: *"It's better being a guy. Guys get more satisfaction in life and in sex. They get immediate gratification. Women take longer, and don't get what they want. In real life I don't come but guys always ejaculate."*

Aha, you need to take your satisfaction more! You created a woman with a dildo in your fantasy to show you that in real life you need to be more like the "man" who has the power and control you want.

LIGHTS, CAMERA, ACTION: IT'S YOUR FANTASY PLAY. WHAT DOES IT MEAN?

You made up your fantasy, therefore you are the producer, director, writer, and all the "actors" and "objects" in your fantasy. They are all parts of you, so if you were each player or object, what would that reveal?

Heather fantasizes about biker women: *"We do it on this shiny motorcycle. She's all in leather and holds me real tight."*

How would you feel if you were the biker babe and the bike? Likely, "I'm wild, I'm tough. I'm cool." Be those things in your real life or in sex with your partner.

Andy: *"I dream I have large breasts. They feel good. I show them off. Does that make me want to be a girl?"*

Not necessarily. Be the breasts. If your breasts could talk, what would they say? Possibly, "feed me," or "love me." You are the breasts, so you need to feed (nurture, give to others) or to be fed (loved, given to). Get in touch with a more nurturing side of yourself, or get more nurturing from others in your life.

MORE CLUES TO WHAT THE
FANTASY MEANS

To find out what a fantasy or dream means, focus on five different elements: where it takes place; who's in it (people or animals); what's in it (objects); what happens (the action); and how you feel about it (happy, relieved, sad, etc.).

Another technique: free associate—say the first thing that comes to your mind when you think of the fantasy or dream. This helps you relate the main elements of the dream to your real experiences and particularly to your past.

This is how it worked with Paul: *"I'm always thinking about having sex with very large women. I wouldn't like this in real life but in my fantasy they're very fat. What does this mean?"*

What's the first thing you think of when you think of large women? Who reminds you of that?

Paul: *"Big breasts, holding on to them, drowning in them, not having to do anything because she's all over me. That reminds me of the lady who used to come help my mother around the house. She caught me masturbating in the bathroom, and I always thought she was looking at me funny after that. She washed her bra and left it hanging in the bathroom and I used to jerk off into it."*

See how free association helped Paul get to the root of his fantasy. Large women make him feel comforted (as in childhood) and safe (like he doesn't have to perform in sex). Sexual fantasies often have sources in childhood experience, like Paul having his first sexual feelings in conjunction with a large-bodied woman (it could be a mother, sister, nanny, or teacher) that makes him attracted to this type now.

How do themes of your fantasy trigger past real experiences?

How does your fantasy protect you? I am a great believer that fantasies protect you, as Tiffany's story proves.

Tiffany, 18: *"I fantasize about having sex with bums. I think about saying to them, 'If you suck my pussy I'll buy you a bottle.' It's like that Jethro Tull song, 'Sitting on a Park Bench.' Is there something wrong with this?"*

Somebody might cringe at your thought, but think about

what it means. You have no problem letting bums please you, because you don't care about pleasing them back and you can exert your power over them without fear. But gorgeous men would scare you—they may not want you!

Since you are every character in your fantasy, as the bum, you have low self-esteem, and rely on others too much. HOMEWORK: When you think about the bum, stop, and change the program in your brain to a really studly wealthy guy going down on you. To work up to it, first look at a magazine picture of a stud, while you masturbate (using a vibrator will help so you don't let your mind wander). Switch from the picture to looking down at yourself and imagining a real guy there.

If you want to change these thinking patterns, you'll need to force your mind to think of the real object of your desire, and masturbate while you do so, training yourself to be comfortable. Tell yourself, "I can have who and what I want."

FOURSOME AWESOME

Figure out the need you have that is symbolized by the action in the fantasy.

Gina: *"I have a fantasy about having sex with three men. One puts his penis in my mouth, one in my vagina, and one in my rear. Is this bad?"*

What need does the fantasy reveal? You want to be filled up! How can you feel filled up—adored, wanted, loved in other ways, besides having penises in every hole?

STAR-STRUCK

Fantasizing about stars can be healthy. As long as it doesn't become an obsession, it shows you value yourself enough to be desired by someone you value.

Louis is obsessed with Janet Jackson. *"She's so sexy and beautiful. I dream about her grinding her groin against mine. She says I'm sexy and 'I love you, I want you' to me. My mother is sick that I have posters of her all over my room. Am I sick?"*

No. You're using Janet Jackson to raise your self-esteem. Imagining the woman of your dreams treating you well teaches you that you deserve to be adored. Approach real girls with that same confidence. Also, feel how confident it would feel to *be* Janet herself.

Timothy has fantasies about Madonna. *"We're in a dark hallway, she tells me I can do anything I want to her. She lets me put on the leather clothes and I tie her to a chair and stand in front of her."*

Good on you. On her Girlie tour, Madonna acted out those similar dominance and submission scenes. By identifying with her power, you are getting in touch with your own power.

Stars think of other stars, too. Actress Sean Young's fantasy lovers would be Patrick Swayze and Clark Gable. "Clark Gable reminds me of my husband with that big barrel chest, dark hair and lots of teeth, and you know he's handsome and quirky. I'd like to be in a movie with Clark Gable where I could be grabbed by him and kissed by him and have some sort of torrid scene with him. (So Sean, treat your husband like Clark Gable!). Or I'd like to be in a dancing movie with Patrick Swayze because I love to dance and it would be really fun to get some sort of swirling, dervish energy going with him, you know."

Comic/actor Pauly Shore likes the two woman thing; "the perfect duo would be Sherilyn Finn because she's very sexy, because she has mystique and glossiness about her and Sarah Jessica Parker because she's an intense little girl, boom, very smart, a lot of energy, a young woman in charge." But Pauly worries, "they would probably get very jealous of each other." (Yup, Pauly, you can't always tell how people acting out your threesome in real life will act.)

POWER TRIPS

Many fantasies are power plays. Julie and Kaye get turned on thinking of servicing powerful men.

Julie: *"I've not been interested in sex, but watching People's Court turned me back on. I guess I get aroused by the power and the tension in the courtroom. It got me into a fantasy, that I got sued for not dry-cleaning a guy's clothes, and for the punishment I go into the judge's room and I hand him the evidence and he gets aroused, and I have to perform fellatio. Is this sick?"*

Kaye: *"I'm married a year and a half and I have a problem getting excited unless I'm using a forced sex fantasy. I like thinking I'm driving in my car. A cop pulls me over for no reason and forces me to have sex with him to get off being arrested. So I service him and he lets me go. What can I do to get past this? My husband is a good guy and I want to please him and show him he is desirable."*

Courtroom and cop dramas are about power, so have fun. You've been the defendant, fearing punishment, having to please the judges in your life too long. Since you created the fantasy, you choose to play one role, but are capable of being the others. Imagine being the cop or the judge, the one pleased, and in power, yourself.

Many women still grow up learning to exclusively please men to get what they need (love, protection), at the expense of being pleased themselves. It reflects low self-esteem. And it's also a way to stay in control by being needed and never feeling indebted.

HOMEWORK: Change the story to bring out something new you want in real life: for example, the cop pulls you over, but as you get excited, another car pulls up and it's your husband and he fights the cop to win you, and throws you on the hood of the car and makes passionate love to you.

GET OVER SHAME

Mike, 15: *"When I masturbate fantasizing about people, I get angry when I see them in real life. Why?"*

Don't feel guilty and ashamed; you're allowed to fantasize about real people and they can't read your mind. Have fun with them in your imagination as long as you know the thoughts won't hurt you or them. If it's someone you're uncomfortable thinking about, switch the image in your head, like changing the TV channel.

WHY ARE FANTASIES GOOD?

- They're fun.
- They're a key to what you want to happen in real life. Rehearsing something in your mind makes it more likely to really happen. Fantasizing flirting helps you be more confident. Imagining someone going down on you helps you get over embarrassment to ask for it in real life.
- They boost your self-image, letting you be as powerful and desirable as you want. If you picture five men undressing your admiringly, it's a sign you want to be adored, so allow yourself to be adored by even one man in real life.
- They help you break out of social stereotypes, letting you be male or female.
- They jump-start your excitement if you're tired or slower than your partner. Imagined sex can turn you on like real touch. Research shows a woman's vaginal tissues can swell as quickly as twenty seconds after having a sexual thought.
- They help you get over sexual problems by distracting you from anxiety-provoking thoughts. For example, instead of worrying about how hard or wet you are, or whether you're having orgasm, think about a sexual fantasy that makes you excited.

IS FANTASIZING WHEN YOU'RE WITH A PARTNER OKAY?

Jessica: *"When my boyfriend and I have sex, I have elaborate stories in my head. I imagine I'm a rich girl and he's my gorgeous tennis instructor who takes me on the court. Sometimes I think he's Johnny Depp. If I love my boyfriend, shouldn't I just be thinking of him?"*

Romance king Fabio's advice: "Fantasy is the key to romance. No fantasy is taboo between two lovers, whether you think it or do it."

It's a common worry that fantasy is a sign something's missing in real life. But any woman or man can have a good relationship and still occasionally imagine a different face—or place—without it meaning that you love that person less. See it as a sign of your creativity or as an aphrodisiac. One caveat: be truthful if something's really missing with that person.

SHOULD YOU SHARE YOUR FANTASIES WITH YOUR PARTNER?

Caroline: *"I have this fantasy that three men are all fighting over me. Won't my boyfriend think he's not enough for me if I tell him?"*

Hopefully not. The fantasy means you want to be more desired, so ask your boyfriend to desire you more. What are the three men telling you or doing to you? Share that with your boyfriend and have him say or do those things.

Some people like to keep their fantasies private, fearing they would be ruined or criticized, but sharing can help you find out new things about what you each want to have happen and help you keep pace together if one person gets excited faster or slower than the other.

However, if you share, make sure you don't do it in spite, or to incite jealousy. Be prepared for the reaction. Insecure partners will freak, hearing about someone else. When Lauren told Tom that she had a fantasy about a carpenter who did some work for her, he pouted and refused to have sex with her for weeks, tortured about whether she'd really do it and angry that he didn't measure up. It took much reassurance on her part for him to believe that she would not act out the fantasy and that he was the man of her dreams.

"If I tell, won't he think I'm perverted or disgusting?"

Of course your partner may judge your fantasy, but you should both follow this rule: no fantasy (except those that hurt someone or abuse children) is perverted, wrong or bad. You could be surprised. Lance fantasized about his girlfriend Laura being with another girl he knew and when he got up the gumption to tell her, he was shocked to discover that Laura wasn't shocked at all. Expecting your partner to object can also reflect your own fear of letting go. Janet fantasized being an exotic dancer but always thought if she told her boyfriend he'd secretly think she didn't have the body for it when really it was *she* who thought her butt was too big and her thighs too fat.

"If I talk about my fantasy, it'll ruin it."

You can keep your fantasy private. But even if you think it to yourself, it will influence the way you make love. For example, if you're imagining being "taken," you will move in submissive ways that make your partner be assertive, so you are "telling" anyway. Sharing it may indeed change it, to be better and more exciting . . . and your partner may add something new and fresh to your idea.

GETTING ON THE SAME WAVELENGTH

Jay: *"I like to think about tying my girlfriend up but she's such a bore she just wants to do it the straight way. She always talks about that silly beach stuff. Is this not going to work out?"*

You need to get into the same, as I call it, sex script. HOMEWORK: Do one of my favorite techniques, called "shared storytelling," where you weave a sexual fantasy together by taking turns adding parts to the story. Co-writing the story helps you find scenes you both enjoy. Start with the best lovemaking time you ever had, thought up, saw, or read about. Relate it in detail in the present, as if it's happening at that moment. Stop after two sentences, to let the other person pick up the story, adding details, taking turns.

Jade started, "We're picnicking in a beautiful meadow. The sun is beaming as you lean over and draw me down on the blanket." Then it's Jay's turn: "I bury my head in your breasts, moving your bathing suit top aside." For her turn, Jade "slows" the story down again, giving Jay clues that she likes a lingering seduction. "You brush my lips ever so lightly as I caress your face lovingly." After doing this several times, Jay and Jade could "enter" each other's fantasies easier; he recounting romantic scenes and she more erotic ones.

Other tips to get her/him into what you want:

- Introduce the fantasy slowly to your partner, bringing up only part of the story line without the detail you think might be too upsetting, insulting, threatening, or jealousy-provoking.
- Appreciate each other's tastes, even if you are not turned on by the idea. You'd be surprised how you might grow if you get into it.
- Make a deal. This is one of my favorite techniques. You negotiate what you'll do, just like business. Lay out the problem, and get to the stakes for each person. Bill wanted Tracy to be a cheerleader and he the fantasy football player. Tracy wouldn't think of it. Why? Because she hated her body, thinking she was fat. "You'd be better off if you got into liking your body like Bill does," I told her. In the bargain, each gives and makes a sacrifice so both win. Bill could have part of the fantasy fulfilled (Tracy would wear part of the cheerleader outfit but not the skirt that made her feel fat), and she wouldn't have to do it on a real football field.

SHOULD YOU ACT YOUR FANTASIES OUT?

It's a common question people ask me. The answer: it depends on how comfortable and trusting you are with your desires and your partner, and what the potential outcome is. Acting out a fantasy can free you.

George: *"I want Sarah to wear those black garter things and go around with a whip, not to use it on me but to look really tough. She won't do it."*

"It's not me," Sarah protested. But under much duress, she finally agreed to try. Though she felt awkward the first time, the second time she got real into strutting her stuff, and a new vamp was born, to both George's—and her—delight!

Desiree, 20: *"My husband wants me to have sex with other guys while he watches, hidden in the closet. I caught him once having an affair, but he broke it off. Should I or shouldn't I do it for him?"*

Find out what's behind his fantasy first. Does he want to justify his past—or future—affairs? Is this a way to keep distance from you or pretend he's not married to avoid feeling trapped by responsibilities? What does hiding in the closet mean to him—does he get off being a voyeur who gets excited watching others have sex, and imagining that you're being naughty doing what you're not supposed to. If so, he gets a double turn-on of you being caught and him being caught!

You know guys' #1 sex fantasy is the two girl thing. Well, when it comes to acting it out, they all want it; but lots of rock stars who have done it, like Steven Tyler and Sammy Hagar, as I mentioned to you already, say now that it's lost its appeal (granted, once you've done something, it's easier to give it up).

And when it comes to any combo of people, be careful—while you can write the lines for every character in your mind trip, in real life you cannot orchestrate how everyone will feel or behave. For example, Vince Neil told me how he invited a Penthouse Pet to visit him in Hawaii, and she asked if she could bring a friend. Yeh, he thought. So he flew them both out First Class, but when they got there they ended up into each other the whole time and he was left out in the cold.

Besides, when it comes to acting out some fantasies, some rockers now put more consideration into their commitment. Guns N' Roses rhythm guitarist Gilbey Clarke explained how the band often sat around in the dressing room waiting for Axl to arrive, with walkie-talkies directing the camera to show girls taking off their shirts, saying 'zoom in, get that one there,' but now when the girls come backstage, Clarke thinks, "Uh, um. But I'm married."

Can acting out a fantasy mess you up? It did for Ricardo: *"Call me pokey. I screwed up with a girl I like. My brother and I had been talking about what it would be like to order an escort service, so we did. We saw them so often on TV. The girl came and did us both. It was okay but not great. My girlfriend found out. It was a great time when we did it but now I'm sorry."*

Well, you found out the hard way that sometimes acting out the fantasy is not worth it.

Kayla also found it can lead to trouble—big time:

"I always wanted to just meet a guy and have him take me to a hotel and have wild sex. It seemed so exciting to go with someone I didn't know and just be carried away with passion. So I went on a trip with my friend to a car race and met this guy and he took me into the back of his van that he and his friends had driven to the race. We had sex and now I'm petrified. Maybe he has AIDS or I'd get pregnant and I don't know where to reach him. It didn't turn out at all like I wanted."

You see, you have to be careful. Take a pregnancy and AIDS test. Now that you've seen where impulsivity can lead, you'll certainly Stop-and-Think next time. Sometimes it takes being real scared before you change your behavior.

GOOD SEX GLUE

Jerry, 18: *"I had sex with this girl and she was engaged. Then she wrote me a letter that she still wants to see me. She's not the right girl for me but I'm tempted to see her because she's played into all my fantasies that are so far out. She played nurse and gave me an enema. She brought her cousin in on the action. And she worked in a supermarket so I played the stock boy and she was the check-out girl, doing me in the back room on the crates of fruits, when her boss walked in. Should I see her?"*

No. She isn't good for you, remember. It's a myth that only one person can fit even your wildest fantasy. There are others who can!

SETTING LIMITS

Susan, 20: *"I can't talk my boyfriend into having sex in a cemetery. He says people might see us. But we do other things he likes, like when I slip my hand under the table-cloth at a restaurant and do him. Why can't we do mine?"*

Likely he's concerned that you're going too far, and he's insecure when you're the one taking the lead. Does he always need to be the one in control? If so, he'll have to learn to let you take the lead sometimes. Agree on the limits you will go to, as he may also be afraid of how far this will go, that is, what you'll want after the cemetery. The more scared partner always has to be reassured and made comfortable, or give it up and just live it out in your mind or by talking about it.

Some fantasies can lead to trouble if you repeat them in your mind.

Jeremy, 19: *"I went over my friend Mike's house and his mother is really hot. When I went to the bathroom, I jerked off and thought of taking her husband's place. Now I think about it all the time. Is that bad?"*

Not bad, but it's dangerous to keep repeating it, as you're fixing it in your brain and you're likely to start seeing her that way in real life. HOMEWORK: Use her as inspiration, but replace her face with someone else's.

Victor: *"I'm engaged and live with my best friend, who's also engaged, and we're all close because we're going to have a double wedding. We're both bodybuilders, and lately when I have anal sex with my fiancée, I think of him. Is this dangerous?"*

I'd say so, if you really want to go through with the marriage. Does this imply you just have marriage jitters or that you really want to change your orientation? Or, since he is so like you, and working out together stimulates such eroticism, is this a narcissistic, ego-boosting fantasy? Not all attractions have to be acted upon. If you keep thinking about this one, since you two have so much contact and in such a sensual way by working out, you are prone to take it one step further.

Brian, 20, also has to consider limits: *"I drive an ambulance and lately I've been getting off on the wrecks. Someone came in with their head sliced so blood was oozing out and I got hard. I wanted to do things to the person. Is this weird?"*

Yes. Not a fantasy to encourage having. If you're so obsessed with morbid thoughts, are you frightened of real, mature relationships? When faced with death, people do get sexy, to affirm life. Change your mental channel: as soon as you think of the injured person and notice your erection, switch your attention to think of a live body.

Both males and females may really need to zip it up. Pat said, *"I'm nineteen but I like to think about having sex with twelve-year-old girls. I like their innocence but I'm scared I'll do it. I don't want to be accused of rape. What's wrong and how can I stop?"* Pris's dilemma was similar: *"I like to fantasize that I'm a little girl having my first orgasm. When I was four or five years old, I masturbated with a boy for the first time and saw his penis. Then I did something with a boy when I was twelve and he was only ten and not even in puberty yet. Now I'm afraid I'll really do it. How can I stop?"*

A fantasy is not always a coming attraction, but I'm glad you're thinking about this one before you let it go further, since it can get you into trouble. Always analyze what a fantasy does for you so you can get control over the impulse in real life. Probably you like younger kids' innocence because you can have control over them, and fear being rejected by peers. You might feel like you're also young, or resent more adult responsibilities and loss of your own innocence. Adjust your real life to satisfy some of the fantasy without hurting you. That can mean finding girls or guys your own age who are innocent, or asking a girl or guy your age to act innocent for you. Fantasize about the freedom and joy that children express without having to be with a child. (P.S. See chapter on Guys Who Like Guys Who Like Girls . . .)

Be careful fantasizing about aggression toward others or yourself. Find out what you feel and need, and turn the stories around so you don't get consumed or hurt.

Damian, 22: *"I'm falling in love with my girlfriend, but I have terrible dreams about running her over and stabbing her repeatedly in the breasts and head. They scare me."*

Of course such violence in your dreams would terrify you, especially when directed at someone you think you love. The dream is a safe place to purge real terror and danger you feel—in this case, the fear of falling in love. Why is falling in love so dangerous that you have to kill? When was falling in love dangerous before? When were you hurt or abused by someone you got close to? Get your anger out toward those ghosts in your past, by imagining them in your room and letting them have it!

You can change the dream by purposefully replacing your girlfriend's face with someone else's. Think through a new conscious "dream" where the action transforms from hitting her to handing her flowers, caressing her, falling into her arms, kissing her passionately, and professing your love.

"I used to have fantasies of torturing women," John Lennon is quoted as saying in the book *The Last Days of John Lennon*. Though learning to control them, he admitted that when he really let his mind go wild, he would think about crucifying women, actually nailing them to a cross. Lennon supposedly kept young girls in the wings during Beatle concerts to have a "knee trembler" (quick sex) with them before, after, or even during concerts (running backstage between songs for a quickie).

Mike has horrific sexual fantasies because of his past: *"I have sex fantasies of torture and blood and am obsessed with an actress. My brother's friend who was homosexual masturbated me when I was eight. Then my mother beat me with a nightstick and burned my penis with a cigarette lighter whenever she caught me masturbating and said if I ejaculate, she'll shoot me or drown me. Now I think about those things and get turned on. I was in a mental hospital because I tried to kill myself when I was fifteen. Then I stalked my high school teacher and the police arrested me. Are these fantasies okay?"*

Purposefully having sexual fantasies about horrific memories can be a way to repair old hurts, giving you a sense of control over previously uncontrollable abuses. In your case, however, it is not good to rehearse them. Talk to a therapist or counselor to purge your fears and anger, so you can be free to trust people again. I'm sorry your past was so painful, but you are entitled to new happier thoughts about yourself and sex.

WHAT'S NEXT?

"My wife and I have done every fantasy, I think—on the L train, in school yards, in a dressing room. Where else can we do it?"

How about instead of looking outward, look inward, toward some spiritual place you can go?

SEXUAL DREAMS

Sexual dreams are similar to fantasies except they happen in the more unconscious mind and therefore have more symbolism and complex plot twists. Because they occur in different brain states, they can also reveal more intense pleasure, or more unpleasant, guilt-ridden, or unacceptable thoughts (from being unfaithful to killing ex-lovers for being with someone else). But you can interpret and use them in similar ways to the more conscious fantasies. Dreams are always connected to things we feel or fear in real life, and it's exciting to find that magical connection to unlock your real feelings.

Yvonne: *"I have this recurring dream that bothers me: I dream about jerking off a guy and his dick falls off and I bury it and feel jubilant. What does the dream mean?"*

Why are you so angry at men?

Yvonne: *"I have big breasts and they only love me for that and what I do for them."*

Look what men have done to hurt you. You think they only like you for your big breasts and for pleasing them, without you getting anything in return. So you get back at them, seducing them and punishing them. I picture you wringing your hands and saying, "So there, you jerk, there's your just deserts for using me." Bury your resentment—instead of his penis—and only go for men who treat you well and whom you respect.

MAKING SENSE OF NONSENSE

Ron, 18: *"I dreamed I went bowling and there was only one pin standing. I put a beeper in-between my girlfriend's legs and woke her up. She wrapped a bathrobe around her ankles and tied it to my testicles. What does all this mean?"*

There are many ways to interpret dreams. In a Freudian interpretation, I would say that you are worried about your potency and being controlled by women (since you couldn't make a strike and got tied up by your girlfriend), and that probably as a child, you felt tied to mother's apron strings. Since one pin is left standing, maybe you feel unsatisfied in sex, left with an erection. Since you want to get your girlfriend's attention by waking her up with your beeper, you probably feel she isn't giving you enough (in sex or anything else). Yet you feel trapped by her because she has you literally by the balls! Probably that means you're afraid that marriage would be a trap, and wonder what sex would be like if you got married. Free-associate—what comes to mind when I say the key words: bowling, pin, beeper between her legs, bathrobe, tied to your testicles? Use my friend Gerri Leigh's dream analysis technique, and string those new words together in a story to get a new meaning.

Kathy: *"I have a recurring dream that a dog is biting my hand. There's no blood when I pull away my hand. Does this mean I want to have sex with a dog?"*

How do you feel about the dog? What's the dog's name? And what do you think the dog wants from you?

Kathy: *"I like the dog but she's tugging at me and won't leave me alone. Her name is Sasha. She wants to play."*

Since the dog in your dream is a part of you, the dream means you want to play more in your life. There's a part of you that needs to come out that is fun and cuddly and affectionate. You don't trust people as much as you do animals. You have to look for people you can be open with and get affection from, and to whom you can express your own affection, as openly and cuddly as you would to a pet.

Sean: *"I dreamt my girlfriend has a penis and I went down on it. Is there something wrong with this? Does that make me gay?"*

Not necessarily. Empathy is a great quality in a relationship. In your dream, you get to experience giving what you get, feeling what your girlfriend feels. HOMEWORK: Imagine you have a vagina and what that feels like. The best sex, anyway, is when you merge both bodies so penis and vagina are indistinguishable.

Playgirl magazine's Man of the Decade, Darren Fox, starring in a male revue (called "Man Alive") told me he thinks lots of men fantasize about women having penises, that it's a way to safely experiment while knowing you're still with a woman (he's married and has a child).

DREAM REPAIR

Dreams can repair hurts or condition us for good things. Karen's boyfriend left her:

"I've been having dreams about my ex-boyfriend and they're tearing me apart. In every one, he's having sex with another girl and I wake up soaked in sweat. I love him so much and I'm afraid to find out he found someone new and doesn't want me back. What can I do?"

Dreams are a safe stage on which the mind can play out what we wish or fear will happen. I know you're hurt about losing your boyfriend, but since he says your relationship is definitely over, welcome your dream as a help rather than as a nightmare.

HOMEWORK: Instead of denying it's over, or twisting yourself into a pretzel trying to get him back (as many do, in futility) review the unpleasant scenario of your ex with someone else in your mind so you get accustomed to the painful reality that it's over while you feel strong inside. Secondly, do what's called "dream-retraining": before you go to sleep, think through the painful event, but put a new ending on it that makes you feel good. Researchers at the University of Chicago trained jilted women to rewrite their dreams of being rejected by imagining meeting their ex while they're with a new lover who adores them. One last step: you must then live out your new ending, by letting him go and moving on to better things in real life.

Remember sex is 90 percent between your ears and only 10 percent between your legs, so use that 90 percent richly.

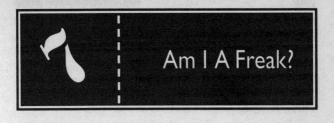

Q: What is the difference between sensual and kinky?
A: Sensual is taking a feather and doing someone's
body. Kinky is using the whole chicken.

"I LIKE TO SUCK GIRLS' TOES. AM I A FREAK?"
"I get excited when I look at my sister's guitar. Is that perverted?"
"I get off when guys call me slut. Is that normal?"

Everybody wants to know if they're normal. Sometimes the answer is no. Sometimes it's yes. It depends on whether or not the thought or behavior has to happen for you to get turned on; whether you can control it; whether it's an escape from an intimate loving relationship; and whether it gets you in trouble physically, psychologically, or legally.

Many behaviors are okay that may seem unusual but that are done with love and that follow the 3 R's: Respect, Responsibility, and the Right to say yes or no.

In this chapter we'll go over things that do and do not cross the line. Some people think they're going to shock me when they tell me something weird they're doing. There have been new ones, like "Ferret Man" (a guy who puts his friend's furry ferret down his pants) and the new twist on "Mortuary Raiderman" (the guy who has sex with not just dead bodies but *ugly* dead bodies—to do them a favor), but generally I've heard nearly everything. I don't say that just to make you think I'm smart or so experienced, but to let you know that most people think they're the only one with a particular inclination, when in fact, there's always someone else who has been there, done that.

To stop doing something, change the TV channel or computer program in your mind, and simply stop doing the behavior and replace it with something else.

"What is tea-bagging?"

When the partner lies on her/his back and the guy straddles her face and dips his scrotum into his partner's mouth, like dunking a tea bag.

"What is shrimping?"

A favorite of a drag-queen friend, who claims it is a "gourmet sex delight"—sucking toes!

"What's one of the most disgusting things in sex you've heard about?"

I get asked this question a lot. It's gotta be people like Mortuary Raiderman wanting to have sex with dead bodies. When people call about this, it may sound like they're making it up, but people really *do* these things. For example, a Washington state guy was found guilty of breaking into funeral homes and doing it with four female corpses. Something else that offended and grossed me out: the kid who called to say he put a toilet paper roll up his rear and then shoved a gerbil in it and took the roll out so the animal could try and scratch it's way out, until it suffocated to death (what animal abuse). Fisting—putting a fist up one's rear even all the way to the elbow—makes me groan. And some bathroom acts turn me off.

Other things turn some people on, and others off! What do you think about all the following?

FELLCHING (AKA GREEK BLOW JOB)

Frankie: *"The other night in sex my girlfriend told me she wanted to have anal sex, and have me ejaculate in her and then kiss it and suck it out and then kiss her mouth and spit it into her mouth. It sounds pretty gross to me, but she's insisting. Is she a freak?"*

A drag queen I know thinks fellching is the best! He loves it and says, "It tastes like Fresca, it gets all foamy when it's inside there and then you suck it out." Fellching is not a safe sex behavior, so you should be careful, but heterosexual and homosexual people have been known to do it and enjoy it. Some people think it is an ultimate sign of sharing your body products, like ABC (already been chewed) gum. The important thing with partner's requests for atypical behaviors is not to make them wrong for their fantasy, but to find out what it means to them, and then see whether, or which part of it, you can share. Remember the Right to say yes or no Rules.

Here's something that is incredibly rude to others:

SEMEN TRICKS

"I've been dating this guy who likes oral sex too much. He's always making me do it. Then I found out he was ejaculating in his ice-cube tray and serving the ice to people in drinks. Is he weird?"

I'd say he's hostile, to trick people into drinking his sperm when they're unaware. Unconsciously, he obviously has a need to be accepted for his sexuality, and probably for his inner self. His practical joke betrays insecurities and real hidden personal problems.

But the next problem is even sweet.

EAR LOVE

Bob: *"My girlfriend has an ear fetish. She likes to lick and suck on my ear, and has a hard time going anywhere else. What's wrong with her?"*

She learned the ear is a safe place to act out her sexual fantasies and energy. The ear is an erotic zone. The Asians know that, because in some sex clubs having your ears cleaned is part of the "treatment." Enjoy doing her ears! Remember Dr. Judy's Sex Rule #1: Do unto others as they do unto you, and Sex Rule #2: Do unto others as they would have done unto them. Do *her* ears. And to desensitize and recondition her, when she is relaxed, have her gently lick your mouth and nipple while imagining they are your ear, and work her way to other body parts.

PIMPLE POPPER

Raoul: *"I'm sexually aroused popping pimples. I have acne on my ass but it turns my girlfriend off. How can I get her to like it like I do?"*

You probably can't. Enjoy your fetish yourself. Why do like to pop your pimples? Does it give you a sense of power, getting that ooze out? Does it make you feel you are taking care of yourself? See if you can get these same feelings in another way.

Any number of body parts or activities can do it for some people.

"I have to lick my partner's eyeball to get turned on."

"I have to look at my sister's guitar to get turned on."

" I like to be spanked."

"I like to rub against strangers in the bus."

"I can't get turned on unless my girlfriend says dirty words to me."

"I like to put bees on my penis to get that sting before I come."

"Whenever I have sex, I think about a large crowd of people watching."

"I can only enjoy sex when I wear a bathing cap on my head."

They're called fetishes (body parts or objects often symbolic of body parts that take on sexual gratification), or paraphilias (acts you have to do to get turned on), where *para* is a Greek word for "beyond" or "outside the usual" and *philia* means "love." So you're outside the usual love norm. Sometimes the quirk is perfectly harmless and even exciting (like wanting her to wear garters) or it's mildly odd (like wanting him to make horse noises). Or it can progress to be kinky and objectionable. In some cases, it can be hostile, dangerous, or outright illegal (like rape or sex murders). You can have these quirks regardless of your age, background (stable childhood or not), whether you're homosexual or heterosexual. More often men have them, although women do, too. Why we get these ideas is not totally known, but thirty years of research on unusual behaviors by famous sexologist John Money at Johns Hopkins Hospital in Baltimore shows these "lovemaps" can be present at birth (from hormonal or developmental factors that affect brain chemistry) or result from diseases or injuries later in life. More often than not they develop in childhood, when sexual feelings happen to occur in the presence of a particular unusual object or event. The two get connected, and the child seeks to repeat the experience. Then the adolescent masturbates with the particular object, or thinking about the particular event, forging an association between the two, and the dye is cast. Often, escaping fears of rejection and intimacy, the person retreats into the fetish at the expense of a real relationship.

VCR ERECTION

"Every time I masturbate, I watch a videotape. Now when I just look at a tape or VCR, I get an erection. Is this normal?"

Ex-4 Non Blondes Linda Perry suggests you don't feel guilty. "It's great if you feel good with it. Maybe you can move on to other appliances, like microwaves or Stairmasters."

Knock yourself out, but get attached to something you can share with a partner, to make a step toward relating to real people.

TICKLING

Mike, 26: *"I like to tie girls up so I can tickle them all over. I like to see them laugh. Am I sick?"*

Your fetish starts out sounding harmless enough. Tickling can be used to stimulate, or to make someone giggle in fun. Called titillagna, it is often used with bondage in S&M games, where the person cannot recoil from what becomes uncomfortable tickling. Your tickling is an act of control, not play or giving pleasure. Get help. When you have the urge to tickle, lie close and feel vulnerable and needy instead, to get in touch with your deeper feelings. Love and sex is not about control, but sharing pleasure.

SMELLORAMA

"I don't like to shower after sex. I like to walk around with the smell on me . . . is this sick?

No. You obviously like the lingering aroma and you like to advertise! Do you want to shock the world or do you want them to know you're loved, or that you're a stud! I bet you enjoy seeing whether anyone sniffs or looks at you funny.

BEST FOOT FORWARD

"My husband likes to rub my feet. He says it turns him on. I put up with it for a while, but finally I told him it's disgusting. Now he won't have sex with me at all. How can I get him to kick this habit?"

I'm afraid you put your foot in your mouth! If you so rudely put down his turn-on, of course he got hurt. Apologize. Everyone is entitled to their personal erotic preferences as long as it doesn't hurt another person. Understand why he finds feet so attractive. If feet are a safer erogenous zone, so he can avoid other contact, there's a legitimate intimacy problem. But it could be harmless. Talk to him more about it.

Why are you so unpleasantly disposed to your feet? Are you embarrassed? One girl called *LovePhones* saying her big toes were so ugly she refused to take her socks off during sex. Spend time alone washing, pampering, preening, and creaming your feet so you feel better about them. Of course, if it's only your feet that get him sexually excited, and he can't get pleasure from kissing your mouth, or intercourse, then he does have a problem.

SHOE FETISH

Vance: *"I have a weird problem. I read the news that Marla Trump's ex-publicist was found guilty of stealing her shoes. I have the same attraction. I ask girls for their shoes and I don't ever see the girls again, but I use their things when I'm alone. I'm ashamed and now scared of this and want some help."*

Legally, you're safer that you ask the girls' permission to keep their things. When someone gets sexual gratification from certain articles of clothing or body part, they are usually a substitute for a relationship with a real person, showing that you have to become less frightened of intimacy. Trace back when you first found shoes sexy—probably when you masturbated with your mother's heels, or wore them when she wasn't home. Resist taking them and ask for a hug from a real person instead.

"Why do men have more weird sex behaviors, like being obsessed with women's shoes or legs or breasts, and women don't get as crazed?"

Freud, the father of psychoanalysis, had an interesting explanation: men develop fetishistic attachments to protect against fears of losing mother (the object symbolizes her) or their penis (the object replaces the penis he sees girls lack). Since little girls stay closer to mother, and don't have a penis to protect, they don't need the object. In one study 15 percent of men compared with 2 percent of women said they would find it thrilling to possess an undergarment or other object belonging to their partner.

SHOPLIFTING SEX

Sharon: *"I got caught shoplifting a necklace from a store a year ago, and my parents bailed me out. It's the biggest thing they ever did for me, they're always so busy because they both run a big business together. But now I still steal necklaces, from my friend's houses. It gives me a sexual thrill between my legs. Sometimes I wear the necklaces and look at my nude body in the mirror. I usually hate the way my body looks, but with them on, I feel pretty. I remember when I used to wear my mother's necklace when I was a little girl."*

Girls shoplift (even when they can afford the items) because they need attention and love. Obviously you feel neglected by your parents, and inferior to your friends. Ask for the love you need instead of making necklaces the symbol of getting mother's love. Imagine the love of a person instead of thinking about the object. Do affirmations: "My body is beautiful." "I am loved."

SEX TOKENS

Zack: *"I like to save girls' panties. After I sleep with them, I hide their panties and they can't find them, so they leave without them. Then I collect them in my drawer. Is there something wrong with me?"*

Olivia: *"I like to ask guys to ejaculate in a jar and then I save it on my shelf—I put their names on it. Is there something wrong with this?"*

Both of you are collectors, needing to hold on to some symbol of a relationship, as a sign of not losing it, protecting yourself from rejection, maintaining power over others. The clothes are a safer substitute for a relationship. What is the symbolism of the type of trophy you pick? These sound like signs of your sexual conquests, needed as proof of your desirability, necessary for your self-esteem. It is common for people to collect pictures of past lovers, matchbooks from places they've been, friendship rings, or other mementos, to remind them of the experience and the person. If the keepsake is more personal, like panties or semen, then obviously sex was an important part of the relationship and probably also your definition of yourself.

"My boyfriend wanted me to shave my pubic hair. I did it for him but now it feels itchy when it's growing back. Was it stupid to do?"

If it was fun for both of you, fine. Use powder and wear cotton panties while it's growing back. If you ever do it again, get it waxed, so the hair grows back softer.

Find out why he wants to do it (kicks, the sensation of skin-on-skin) and what his fantasy is (controlling you, imagining you as a young girl).

Be careful about blood-drawing behaviors that are unsafe sex.

Morris takes it further: *"I shave girls' pubic hair when they're asleep and when they wake up I'm gone. I saw it in a porno movie. I save it in a plastic bag and label it. Is there something wrong with this?"*

Shaving the pubic hair without the girls' knowledge is hostile; you are stealing a very personal part of them. I would guess that you've been hurt by women and have stored up anger toward them. Cutting off their hair, like in the biblical Samson story, is likely a way to take their power from them, because you feel powerless, and to make them into the little child you feel inside. Be aware of these deep inner needs, and resist doing this. (You'll need serious therapy.)

COME ON

"When I have sex with my girlfriend, I like to come on her. Is this weird?"

No. If she likes it, it can be fun, trying all sorts of places. She can also rub it in! Enjoy the delights. It's only a problem if you have to do it to humiliate her. How about using a more charming phrase, "arrive all over you," like the British say, and also the title of Danielle Brisboise's album (she played the little girl neighbor in the famous TV series *Archie Bunker's Place*).

Danny: *"My girlfriend wants me to come on my own face. Then she likes to lick it off. Is this normal?"*

Sure. It's a cute twist on what couples can do. Just check that she isn't opting for it because she doesn't want you to come on or in her instead, in which case she might have some inhibitions about those activities. Why don't you also try it in reverse—spread some of her lubrication on her own face and you lick it off.

Here's a time when it was a problem.

"I wanted to have sex with my wife, but she refused. So I went down to the den and watched a video till I got real hard and then I came upstairs, and while she was sleeping I came all over her face and hair. Was that bad?"

You were angry and got back at her. Do you always have to get your way? Are you always so sneaky? How do you handle frustration tolerance in other situations? Do you always get back at people who tell you no? If so, you better learn to accept no for an answer. Instead of your sneak attack on your wife, talk it through with her and explain how you feel. Come to a mutually respectable resolution.

PUBLIC PLACES

"I like to have sex in public places, like in the bathroom of a train, in a galleria, a park, or a club. The best time was driving in my boyfriend's Jeep. I had my head between his legs under the wheel and was going down on him while he was driving. The Jeep is kind of high, so a lot of cars couldn't quite see in the window, so we really liked it when a truck would go by and the guy would look over and see us. The truck drivers always made a great cheer and honked the horn. I'd look up and smile at them. It's lots of fun. We keep wanting to get more daring. Next time we want to be in the super-market, or the elevator. Is there anything wrong with this?"

Some people would never dream of having sex in anything but a private place, but wanting to have sex in public places is a common fantasy. Many people attach a sexual thrill to the possibility of being discovered, probably awakening feelings from childhood when you weren't supposed to be discovered being sexual and you had to hide for fear of being punished.

There is nothing wrong with having this fantasy—being a risk-taker can be a good quality. But acting it out is a different matter; in moderation and within limits is okay. That means don't impose on other people's morals or privacy. A lot of observers might say anyway, "Why don't you go home or get a room?" Be careful about how a fantasy of sex in public escalates—you could get in trouble with other people or the law. A couple inspired to have sex at a Nine Inch Nails concert in L.A. while Trent Reznor sang "Closer" with the infamous line, "I want to fuck you like an animal," got arrested.

Aerosmith's "Love In An Elevator" is a real popular song, and Tyler really did it. As he told me, he and two girls were on the floor of an elevator, one girl was doing him while he was doing another, and when the door opened at the ground floor, they didn't even notice the people looking in.

James, 25: *I'm in love with my fiancée and we're planning to get married next year, but I only get an erection when we have sex with her parents in the next room. If we're in a place that's private, I can't get erect."*

You've learned to associate sex with danger and getting away with it—from early experiences masturbating, no doubt. Fear and anxiety have physiological effects that cause erection, dilating blood vessels, and making the blood rush faster as the heart beats faster. Stop having sex in her parents' house with them in the next room. Go to a private place and imagine that people are next door, as a "bridge" technique to enjoying it when no one's around.

EXHIBITIONISM AND VOYEURISM: SEEING AND BEING SEEN

Jack: *"I like to go to clubs and get up on the bar and dance wildly and take my pants down. Is there something wrong with this?"*

Getting drunk and dancing wildly and exposing body parts is sometimes tolerated and even encouraged in certain bars, so I can't fault you entirely for doing this when your inner urges are supported by the social situation. But there is something to be interpreted about your need to exhibit yourself nude. Likely you desperately need attention, and have to flaunt your body to get it.

Suzanne: *"I like to leave my window open; it faces another condo across the way. I like the thought that someone could be watching me touching myself. It reminds me of the movie* Body Double *where the guy is mesmerized watching Melanie Griffith through his telescope. Is this sick?"*

Recognize the dangers of doing this; you could attract a weirdo. And if you get lost in doing this, you'd be an exhibitionist that desperately needs attention but can't allow anyone to really be close. Otherwise, indulge the needs behind your fantasy. Do a slow seductive strip. Let yourself tease and tempt. Say out loud to an imaginary admirer, "Look at me. I am beautiful. You want me, don't you, but you can't have me." Revel in being admired.

Eddie: *"I just moved in this apartment and the girl across the way is so hot. She purposefully bends over the stove to show me her butt. Another time, I invited a girl over and had sex with her in front of my window and I saw the girl across the way watching. Should I go across the hall and really do it?"*

You'd probably be disappointed and ruin your little voyeur and exhibitionism fantasy. I'm concerned that sex is just an act with you, and devoid of real intimacy. You ought to get to know who this girl is before you have sex.

Pat: *"My boyfriend likes to stay in the closet while I have sex with other guys. I've only done it once and the guy didn't know. But my boyfriend wants me to do it again. Should I do it again? He was great in bed after that."*

Sounds mean to take advantage of an unsuspecting third party. That's a sign of an abusive voyeurism, using sex to manipulate and control other people. Examine why you would do this: rebelliousness, a need to get away with something, the thrill of being naughty, the fear of losing this guy you're seeing. Is any of that worth it? Resist this "scene" until sex is "great" without it.

Thomas: *"I masturbate in my car while driving. I want some girl to see me do it and come over and get in. I do it all the time in the summer, when I can wear shorts and girls wear skimpy clothes, but not in the winter. After I do it I feel terrible. I'm really a nice guy, even though I do this. Ten years ago a woman got me arrested for indecent exposure, but I still keep doing it. When I was younger I wanted to be a Hell's Angel, to ride around on those big bikes and get the girls. I've been alone so long, my wife left me years ago. But now I want to stop this behavior and can't."*

You have a sex addiction (albeit a seasonal one) because you are out of control, you end up more miserable and guilty after you've done it, and it gets you in trouble. Follow my four steps: instead of instant gratification, stop and think, recognize the deeper need underneath your impulse, assess the consequences, and choose a healthier outlet. If you're lonely, make friends. Since you're insecure about being able to attract a nice woman, say, "I can be loved for me." Get out all your anger toward women. You don't have to be overly "nice," nor the "bad boy" Hell's Angel, but in-between. You need therapy and treatment from a specialty sex therapy clinic.

Harold: *"I like to scare women in the elevator. I flash them and then laugh when they squirm and can't wait to get out of the elevator."*

Watch out. You're going to get caught someday. Obviously you can't form a loving relationship with a woman, and instead of looking for warmth, you go for shock. This is more about getting a reaction from women than about being sexual, but you're headed for danger. To stop this behavior you need specialized treatment that is usually only available in medical center clinics especially for such sexual dysfunction.

Julia, 19: *"I have a neighbor who calls and says he wants to jerk off over the phone with me. I don't want to. How do I get rid of him?"*

Firmly say no, without getting upset or angry or having a

conversation with him. Next time, just hang up. If he persists, calmly say you'll have to report him to the phone company.

One technique to treat people who do such things is aversive conditioning, where you look at pictures of people doing the unwanted act and pair it with an unpleasant experience (like a shock) and follow that with pictures of a more socially appropriate behavior, like two adults looking at each other lovingly.

In another technique, the person is made to masturbate to a tape recording of the unacceptable behavior until they are so "exhausted," the experience becomes unpleasant.

In serious cases, a hormone drug (medroxy-progesterone acetate) has been given to reduce the sex drive and fantasy and need to act out the behavior.

DYEING DOWN THERE

"My boyfriend dyed his pubic hair red and I think it's disgusting. Shouldn't he dye it back?"

He was just having fun by drawing attention to his pubic hair. Why do you think it's disgusting? It doesn't have to be. You're just more conservative about sex than he is. If that extends into other areas of your sex life, then you might not be compatible.

BATHROOM ACTS

Some people are fascinated with what's called "water sports." Like Pam:

"The guy I'm dating asked me if he can watch me urinate. I finally said okay, but then he wanted to masturbate as he watched me. Wasn't that weird?"

A guy can develop an association between urinating and sex from childhood, when as a boy he held or fondled his penis when he urinated or wiped himself and first felt some sexual stimulation in his genitals. The association between pleasure and elimination may also have originated from mother's wiping, diaper changing, or toilet training.

Aiisha: *"My boyfriend suggested the other day that I uri-nate on him. I tried it once and then he wanted to do it to me."*

Using urine for sex is called "golden showers." Doing it once for sexual curiosity doesn't have to be a problem. But like other fetishes, it is a problem if you have to do it to get turned on, or if it's meant to humiliate or dominate your partner. Some people who like to do it claim they enjoy the warm sensations and trust that it makes them feel. They tend to do it on the bed, or in the shower. What does it mean? Since urine is waste, does it imply he wants to domi-nate or degrade you?

"I met a guy who said he went to a support group for peo-ple who like to drink their own urine. There was a couple there who drank each other's urine and bathed in it together and said it was very sexual. That it turned them on, but it was not kinky because it was very healthy. Are these people crazy?"

Drinking urine is accepted in Eastern Ayurvedic prac-tices; the former Indian Prime Minister, Morarji Desai, claims it has kept him young and healthy into his nineties. Some urine extracts are used in modern medicine for such things as heart trouble. People in urine-drinking support groups eat cheese and crackers and drink urine to cure everything from AIDS to toothaches. One guy said he improved his eyesight from 20 over 400 to 20 over 75. Another treats his asthma by pouring urine down his nose. Apparently the "first catch of the day" is the best. Personally, I can't see how it can be free of bacteria, as it is a by-product of body waste, and I don't recommend it.

Frank has a fascination with feces. He wonders, *"Which feels more pleasurable—having sex or a dump. I like it when it hangs half in and half out."*

I bet you turn people off, but I can see some metaphor in what you're saying. Think of the symbolism—in life you're probably half there and half not, pulling people in and push-ing them away! You're still locked in the battle over the potty that two-year-olds go through when mommy wants them to go. Decide to let it go.

Doing number two can become eroticized because when you eliminate (and squeeze), you're exercising muscles that do cause sexual excitement, and because the anus has nerve endings, like the mouth, nipple, and genitals, that when stimulated, release opiates or pleasure chemicals in the brain.

Adam is also fascinated with elimination. *"After I masturbate, I have this urge to go to the bathroom. I get fascinated with how it comes out."* Adam sent these definitions:

Drinker duty: the kind after a night of drinking that leaves skid marks on the bowl.

Lincoln Log poopie: so huge you can't flush until you break it in little pieces with the toilet brush.

Wet cheeks poopie: it's so liquid, it splashes in the bowl and hits your ass.

Dangling duty: it won't drop loose and hangs there, so you try to shake it out.

Cuckoo crap: you strain so hard, when you stop straining, it goes back in.

Your fascination with feces suggests you are stuck at the anal phase of psychosexual development, which means issues of control concern you. That's clear, because you are exploring how your body works, and what powers it has. When someone is sexually aroused by feces, it's called cophrophilia. The variations are people masturbating while defecating (called chezolagnia) or getting aroused watching someone defecate (a coproscopist). One type reenacts feeling like a child who has been taught that playing with feces is dirty or filthy and is now getting off defying mommy (or authority).

Some people have a fascination with their butts, like Alex: *"I like to show off my butt. I drop my pants to my ankles at parties. And I trip on purpose to put my butt in the air."* But Darrell takes it even further: *"I got this idea that I'd like to take a dump on my girlfriend after we have sex. She thought it was disgusting and refused to do it. What's so wrong?"*

Mike takes it one step further: *"My girlfriend put Saran*

*Wrap on her face and asked me to take a dump on her face.
We did it four times. I was embarrassed at first but now it
turns me on. She's a pig, she likes anal sex and says it feels
better. Should I keep doing it?"*

You can do any gross thing you want. I guess it would
serve you right if the Saran Wrap ripped one time and it
landed on her face. I suspect your girlfriend has a fascination with defecation. Like others with anally focused sexual
preferences, she must be fixated at the anal stage of development (which usually takes place at around age two) and is
therefore "stuck" in issues about control.

Of course you're two consenting adults, so you can do
anything you want. Just realize the deeper implications of
your actions. In taking a dump over her face, what do you
feel? Do you enjoy having her watch your intimate act to
feel appreciated, or do you like the idea of "dirtying"
(insulting, humiliating) her, disciplining her, or putting her
down? What is *her* hidden agenda (to be insulted, humiliated, punished, outrageous)?

Brad: *"I have bad gas in intercourse. I farted in my girl's
face and now she won't have sex with me anymore. I like her
a lot. It never happened before. Why now? What can I do?"*

What did you eat before sex? Foods like broccoli give
you gas because of how they affect the enzymes in your
stomach. Or you may have passed gas because you like this
girl and your stomach got nervous, in which case you
should tell her that, and relax for next time, reassuring yourself that she likes you.

EATING SELF-CONSCIOUSNESS

*"My boyfriend won't eat in front of me, even after sex. I
gorge on a Domino's pizza, but he won't have any. What's
wrong with him?"*

Likely he had some childhood trauma around eating. I
picture him sitting at the dinner table and his father criticizing him about the way he eats, so now he's afraid to eat in
front of people. But eating together can be very sensuous.

Remember the movie *9 1/2 Weeks*, where Mickey Rourke suggestively poured all kinds of foods down Kim Basinger's throat? Raw eggs topped with jalapeño peppers! And there's a classic meat-devouring scene in the movie *Tom Jones*, with the couple tearing at bones as if they were tearing at each other's flesh.

KINKY INSERTION

Maurice: *"When I eat my girlfriend she likes me to vomit rice into her vagina. I like the Uncle Ben's with curry goat on it. She likes the grains in there. Is there something wrong because when I put my penis in with the rice, it comes out chafed?"*

You could be pulling my leg with the curried rice bit, but I understand your thinking that something inside her, along with your penis, could add some extra titillation, rubbing against her vaginal walls. Better for her to concentrate on the real stimulation of your penis. When you're not inside her she can trade Uncle Ben for another Ben—Ben Wa balls, the Chinese vibrating balls that are specifically designed to be inserted for sexual pleasure.

DANGEROUS SEX TOYS

Sex toys are great to spice up your sex life. I'm all in favor of them. Vibrators are the best! But some things don't belong in your body.

Hernando: *"I read about some pumps in those men's magazines, but since I couldn't afford one, I took out the vacuum cleaner and put it on my penis and turned it on. I'm glad my mother asked me to vacuum the other day because it gave me the idea. The air sucked it in. If I do it more, will my penis get bigger? Was that a good idea?"*

My *LovePhones* producer Sam's response: "Beavis and Butt-head may say, "that sucks," but what you did was so stupid, you must have a small brain, and a small penis to match, so you must have used a small vacuum. I bet it was a Dick Dirt Devil."

I have to add, a vacuum cleaner blows dust and all you

need is for that to get inside the opening in your penis and travel up your urethra and give you an infection!

Another guy was driving in his car and felt sex urges. *"I got the idea to put my penis in the exhaust pipe. It seemed like a warm place."*

Puleeze!!! You're exhausting me with the absurdity of this. Have a little more respect for your penis's safety.

WILD RELEASE

Dan, 19: *"My girlfriend likes to punch and kick and scream every time she has an orgasm. I like passionate sex, but not this crazy. What can I do?"*

It's likely she's like a lot of women who have grown up being "good" girls and are so guilty about sex, that they are thrashing it out with themselves by having wild episodes. They're like Don Quixote, dueling with the ghosts of their conscience telling them they shouldn't be having sex. Or perhaps subconsciously they are working through some pain about sex, like having been abused. It would be ideal if you could be "there" with her as she experiences these flights into her deeper emotional wells, holding her and being a stable foundation. But if you don't like it, please don't criticize her; that would only lead to her feeling embarrassed and inhibited. If you love her, tell her, "Tell me what feelings you are having when you thrash about," "What angry memories do you have about sex?" Tell her you'd like to experiment with trying it one time being real quiet and soft, just for fun.

HOT ROCKS

Nicole: *"I'm seeing this guy who wants to put ice cubes in my vagina and then burn me with hot wax. He wants to be behind me and surprise me because he says it's better that way. Should I?"*

The ice cubes—sex on the rocks—are one thing, but the hot wax sounds like he's more aggressive than you may suspect. In fact, he sounds like a guy who blows hot and cold, so to speak. I'd be suspicious that he's using you for games, and you'll end up not feeling very loved in the end. If you want to know if hot wax hurts, though, drip some on your finger to try it out.

World-renowned expert in outer-limits sex behavior, Gene Abel, at the Behavioral Medicine Institute of Atlanta, warns that such things can be fun and erotic at first, but ten years down the line—when the kink replaces a live person, relationships and love come to a dead end.

ROUGH RIDER

John, 26: *"My girlfriend claims I'm too gentle in sex. She wants me to do something rough. She told me to pretend I was raping her so I twisted her arm and she loved it. I grabbed her hair and said, 'This is what you like' while I penetrated her real hard. I threw her legs over her neck and bit her breast and it scared me. She yelled for me to stop and I said, 'This is what you like' and kept going, and she threw me off. But she asked for it."*

Yes, she did, but you have to know where your limits are and honor them when you play with fire like this. Agree on words that signal when she's really had enough, like "time out." I'm sure she was surprised to have unleashed a monster in you. Try playing a milder "love slaves" game instead of "rape."

THE 3 B'S OF KINKY SEX: BONDAGE, BURNING, AND BLOODSHED

Kinsey found one in four men and women got turned on to being bitten in foreplay, and a British survey showed nearly one in three people use some sort of power play in sex. Another survey found 10 percent of single women and 6 percent of single men got some pleasure from pain. One third of women enjoyed the fantasy of being forced to submit to sex. Although men outnumber women twenty to one in the more serious bondage sex, women are getting more into it as they become more independent and assertive and in touch with their sexual power.

LEAVES ME BRUISED

Sean: *"I have great sex with my girlfriend but she bites so hard sometimes it leaves bruises. She says, he wants me to have them so I won't go for other girls. I don't think it's her fault, maybe it's because I arouse her so much. She said her ex-boyfriend would never do stuff like that. I want to please her."*

Obviously she bites because she's scared of losing you. Reassure her you won't leave her. Biting is also a sign of aggression: What is the mouth saying? "You hurt me." Who are the other men in her life who hurt or left her (many times a father died or was abusive)? What does she want from you (to be more loving, giving, assertive)?

Try having just "straight" or "vanilla" sex with her—just loving sex in simple positions, and see what happens. You need to feel she loves you for you, not because you do kinky things.

Rough sex has become chic these days. It's part of S&M (meaning sado-masochism) or getting off on pain and power in sex. S&M behavior and paraphernalia is coming out of the closet and going mainstream. Outfits by Madonna's favorite designers Jean Paul Gautier and Versace popularized leather straps, cupped breasts, and bound bodices. S&M toys for beginners include padded fur and Velcro handcuffs in Day-Glo colors, silk blindfolds and soft suede whips in fuchsia and teal. Cher has a new mail-order shopping guide of Gothic items (chain mail helmets, candle stands, crosses).

The National Coalition on Television Violence found almost half of music videos they rated had violence or S&M, with U-2 scoring the least, and heavy metal groups like Mötley Crüe and Twisted Sister, the most. Nine Inch Nails' industrial rocker Trent Reznor sings, "You let me violate you, you let me desecrate you, you let me penetrate you . . . I want to fuck you like an animal." MTV rejected his video "Happiness in Slavery," depicting a man eviscerated by a clawed machine.

Some of it is image. Danzig sings of violence and sadomasochism and is touted in his press as into Satanism, but he told me he's not, and that the tattoo on his back is not an evil symbol as some thought, but an Eastern message.

But the flavor of the times is that bondage is cool. That can be tricky for people who don't know how to set limits, like Natalie, Chris, and others who follow. I worry about them. Here are their stories:

Natalie: *"I love rough sex with my boyfriend. I like to choke and bite him, and run a nail file across his penis until it bleeds. I have fun seeing his face turn colors. I know I'm in command. I like the feeling of raping him so he can see how it feels."*

You've probably been abused yourself and want to stick it back to guys. You feel so powerless and helpless inside that you have to be the boss, and a sadistic one at that. You have to uncover and confront the ghosts of your past, and learn to handle your anger differently; affirm: "I deserve to be loved," and pick people who treat you well. I'm frightened about the well of anger stored inside you; you need serious therapy to work it out.

"BOBBICIZED"

Chris: *"I get aroused thinking of what Lorena Bobbitt did to John Bobbitt. I ask girls to rub their nails in my back harder till I bleed. I've thought about them hacking it off. Is this sick?"*

Mild scratches are stimulating to the skin, but you're in over your head, being turned on by a castration. Obviously, you have extreme anger toward some people in your past, turned toward yourself and your penis. Who hurt you? How were you punished for being sexual? What's so hateful about being a man?

AGGRESSION AFTER

Josie: *"When I have sex with a guy, I want to crack his head open. My current boyfriend is nice and shy and I've broken a lot of dishes. Is there something wrong with this?"*

Actress Sean Young, as *LovePhones* Honorary Love Doctor, advised: "Well, I'd say that you are interested in is being in the control position. Have you ever been in a sexual situation where you decided not to be in control? It takes a lot of trust and intimacy to relinquish that control."

Tony feels equally out of control: *"After sex, I want to beat the crap out of the girl I'm seeing. I want to suffocate her, but I feel like a heel because she has such an innocent look on her face and she idealizes me. I hide it from her and I don't do it because of the repercussions, but I want to. Having sex with her is like working out. I don't feel anything but she seems to love it. What's wrong with me? Would it help me to act out some of these feelings by really getting into it?"*

Evan Dando, Lemonheads' lead singer, as *LovePhones* Honorary Love Doctor, advised: "You can use help to tone down your fantasies. You must want to be violently quelled by a woman. You must have been bossed by women too much—beyond the point where you can't take it anymore. My one piece of advice to you is to go to a brick wall, take a whole case of empty beer bottles and throw them one by one against the wall and then sweep them up. You don't hurt anyone."

I'll add: first, you see a part of yourself in your girlfriend's innocence and helplessness, and you are lashing out against it. Likely some time in your past you were naive and hurt, and are furious at yourself for letting that happen. I bet you also had an aggressive or abusive or alcoholic father who dominated a very sweet and helpless mother, and you were furious watching her be abused. So you are re-creating the same dynamic in your relationship now, being infuriated at your girlfriend for being so devoted when you know inside yourself that you are taking advantage of her and don't care about her in the same way as she cares about you. To stop the cycle, recognize these ghosts from your past. Resist deceiving your girlfriend into thinking you care more than you do. Don't have sex with her just as an act, without feeling anything.

People who need aggression need exaggerated stimulation because inside they feel dead. Talking about his fascination with S&M, NIN's Reznor explained: "Maybe my obsessive desire to find extremes has to do with growing up where nothing happens."

DRAWS BLOOD

Rob: *"When my girlfriend goes down on me she gets rough, biting, and lately it has been bleeding. She's obsessed with supernatural things. Could this be scary?"*

Damon, from the British group Blur: "It sounded good until I heard the blood. Are you doing anything to her at the same time? I think you should do the same thing to her. Does she kind of like cast spells? Can you feel the spells on you? What sort of music does she listen to? It doesn't have to be bizarre. Back to the biting of the penis. You are pretty exhilarated by it, are you, in a sort of scary way? It sounds like you quite like it. Have you asked her why she is doing that? You should wear garlic. I once had a girlfriend who would bite my tongue when we kissed, I mean really bite it but it only lasted about six months and then she stopped. So maybe it is just a fad."

DRESSING THE PART

How does what you wear affect the way you act? It does. I know this from playing so many themes on the "Can This Relationship Be Saved" series on the Richard Bey show. As the ever-so-creative producers under David Sittenfeld's helm come up with the brilliant fairy tale and movie themes, I've been getting couples to compromise on everything from sex to anger, while dressed as everything from Dorothy in *The Wizard of Oz* to Catwoman in *Batman*. You can imagine, pigtails and a basket on my arm definitely inspires a different "feel" from a black catsuit so believable the pitbull dog on the show went growling after me.

Who can deny how Gaultier and Madonna set a "look,"

with black straps and studs that said anything goes, be tough, be androgynous. What you find sexy reflects your individual sexuality. Some guys get off on women wearing lacy lingerie, while others prefer a sporty sweatsuit, and still others a conservative three-piece Wall Street suit over lacy underthings. What do your clothes say about you?

Ken: *"I really like girls who look like 'lipstick lesbians,' with short-cropped hair and baggy pants. But inside I imagine that they are tough but sweet. My friend teases me. Is there anything wrong with me?"*

No. There's something exciting to men about a woman trying to look or act like a man but revealing a sensuous femininity inside. This dichotomy was epitomized in the extremely popular *Vanity Fair* magazine cover photo of Cindy Crawford in a man's tuxedo, standing over a barber's chair, cutting the hair of lesbian pop singer k.d. lang.

More Princesses of Power are dressing the part. Like Priscilla: *"I went to a Body Worship store and bought a black latex suit with spiked high boots and straps for my neck and wrists. My boyfriend was shocked, but he got into it when I told him to kneel in front of me and go down on me and ordered him around."*

You go, girl. You were enjoying being powerful. Many women need to take on the external trappings of the dominatrix (a dominating woman) in order to ask for men to please them, especially orally, because they're uncomfortable about asking for their own pleasure. If it took the outfit to allow you to do that, fine. But do be careful with whom, when, and how, you let these feelings out of the closet; make sure you're in a safe relationship and a safe environment.

Vienna is into the dominatrix trip big-time: *"I'm in the sex industry, as a dominatrix. I make good money, $100-$180 an hour, so I like it. Also, there's no nudity, so I don't compromise myself. I get a lot of bankers and CEOs and upscale businessmen who spend their whole day in control so they come to me to escape control and want me to control them. Some like to dress up like a woman. Others I verbally degrade, calling them slime, dirt, garbage, making* *them bark, crawl, and beg, pouring hot wax on them, and tying up their cock, and they love it. It's a way for them to work out their guilt about pushing other people around. One banker likes me to anally penetrate him with a fish. Another guy likes to sniff my feet and have me call him 'porch monkey' and spit on him.*

"I call myself an expert in power dynamics. But I'm developing problems in my real relationship now. I have "vanilla sex" with dates—that means no kinks or S&M— but the feelings from my work seep in and I get the urge to whip the guy. And I find that gay men are attracted to me, so I can't get a heterosexual guy. I also get mad because I think I'm the one with the power but really they have it. How do I get out of this rut?"

You have to get out of the job, to give yourself time for the confusion to clear. You are definitely playing with power and it's inevitable that the games you play are going to influence your life off the job. Recall ghosts from your past when you were dominated. Purge your anger to men. Remember Respect Rules; pick men you can respect and who respect you. Replace the urge to order a man around, with requesting he hold, hug, and love you while you take that feeling into your heart.

The gay men attracted to you may find your power and going to the edge a real draw. You're not ready for a true intimate relationship. Gay men are less threatening because you can't mix sex and love with them. And perhaps because your job is to humiliate heterosexual men, it's difficult for you to respect them.

The masochist says to the sadist, "Beat me, beat me" and the sadist says, "No."

That means for every sadist, there is a masochist. One doesn't exist without the other. You chose one role, but also experience the opposite. To get out of a trap, if you're dominant, play-act being submissive, and vice versa. Then change the game from control to vulnerability in true feelings and being loved.

SERIOUS MASOCHIST

Marianne Faithfull, ex-lover in the 1970s of the Stones' Mick Jagger and Keith Richards, wrote a book about her descent into sex, drugs, and rock n' roll as sado-masochistic addictions. Her great uncle, Leopold von Sacher-Masoch coined the term masochist.

Twenty-three-year-old Richard talks in the high-pitched, singsong voice of a little girl; he is the epitome of a masochist: *"My lover bought me a big dildo for my birthday. He penetrates me real deep with it, and made me bleed. I yelped but he did it deeper and laughed. What else can I do to please him so he'll enjoy himself but won't go too deep? I already wear little short dresses for him, where he makes me tuck my penis into little pink panties. Then I bring him his food on a tray. So what else would he like?"*

Dump him. That'll get a real rise out of him. The fact that he's abusing you, yet you want to know how else you can please him, shows me that you are a real honest-to-goodness serious masochist. That means you've confused love and pleasure with pain. You have to connect with the distortions in your early childhood when you first learned to be a doormat. You can learn that you can be loved by being treated equally, and well.

SEWED UP

Lajoia: *"My boyfriend wants me to close my gaper hole until he gets back from the pen so I won't be with no other man. I love him, we've been going out for two and a half years and have good sex. Should I let him do it?"*

Sometimes people could be making up stories that sound far out, but even if they make it up, the details have some meaning in their real life. Thinking about stitching yourself up obviously shows you have your own deeper guilt about sex (female circumcisions were meant to curb women's desires), fears about infidelity, and ideas that men dominate and control women. Prove your fidelity in words.

PRISON GROUPIES

"I'm in love with this guy who was put in jail for murdering two people. He told me he didn't do it and I believe him. I want to help him with his case and get him out. I'm falling in love with him. Doesn't he deserve love? I didn't think Ted Bundy should have been treated the way he was either, and gone to the chair. Everybody said he was a nice guy."

You're the one who is looking for, and needs to feel she deserves, love, beyond any act that you do. I imagine you remember feeling you were a bad girl as a child for some little transgressions that you never got forgiveness for, and always tortured yourself with, and this is a way you are working that through.

Some women are masochistically attracted to sadistic disturbed men. These are groupies who write love letters to convicted serial murderers, like Ted Bundy before his execution, protesting his innocence, pledging their devotion. The women are projecting their own unacceptable impulses into these bad boys, and vicariously accepting and excusing them. Also, they have such low self-esteem and pathetically boring lives that they are attracted to the notoriety of the criminal, distorting crimes into bravery and excitement. Forgive yourself for anything you did as a child that deserved such punishment. Instead of "saving" the guy, do something to jazz up your own life.

DEVIL WORSHIP

There seems to be quite a trend for young people today to be into witchcraft and vampirism. There certainly have been several movies about it, like the Brad Pitt–Tom Cruise extravaganza, *Interview with the Vampire.*

Bradley: *"I have a problem. I just found out from my girl-friend's best friend, who is also one of my best friends, that she has been into devil worship for a while. I never knew anything about it. She has always hated black cats. They kill them and then they worship them. I want to save her. I know she hates her parents because she was abused by her father. What can I do for her?"*

You can talk to her about what she is into, and why. Say honestly that you noticed her acting a little strangely. I'm glad she trusted you enough to share that she had been abused. I think it is very connected to her being into devil worship, if that's what it is. She had, after all, a devil in her life that she still has to gain control over. Some people who have been abused become abusive to other people or things. When she starts to tell you about why she is doing the devil worship, you can suggest that maybe she has to purge some evil from her own experience.

WITCHCRAFT

"I'm into a brand of witchcraft that says nature is beautiful. We paint our nails black and wear long skirts. My friend's mother got me into it. It's made me feel better about myself. I'm more secure, no matter what others think. My friends are in a coven and they do rituals to purify things."

At least you're not doing evil. Some people need to belong to a cult to increase their self-esteem. Or they need to get involved in rituals to feel powerful or part of a crowd. It would be best if you could feel confident, powerful, capable of doing good without having to formalize it into witchcraft or any other cult. But as long as you're not sucked into it to the point where you lose your independence and identity, and you're doing good, it can't hurt you at this point.

VAMPIRISM

"Since my boyfriend got back from California, he's been into vampirism. He wants to drink my blood. I used to love him. We dressed alike and did everything together. Now I'm afraid to have sex with him. One time he was kissing my leg and breasts and neck and then he bit me real hard. I shrieked. So I told him we could just have oral sex and to stop kissing me. Now he ejaculates in my mouth. My old friends say I should stay away from him, that he's spaced

*and weird. But he's been my best friend. I live near a ceme-
tery and he always wants to go and do it there. What should
I do?"*

Your friends are right. He may have been your best
friend before, but people change. He's into occult things
now, and they scare you. So tell him you need to take a
break. Let him go through this phase—if it is a passing
one—without you so you don't get dragged into something
that's over your head.

ANIMALS

*"While blowing my stuffed monkey, the dog gets jealous.
What should I do?"*

*"I was eating a peanut butter sandwich nude the other day
and some fell in my lap and my dog licked it up and it felt
real good. For breakfast, do you think he'll go for the maple
syrup on my waffles?"*

*"I was cleaning my ears the other night and the cat jumped
up on my lap and I was petting him and then I put a Q-Tip
in the cat."*

Paul took his anger out on his cat: *"I got divorced and
am still angry at my ex-wife. I came home one night and I
got drunk and crazed and saw my wife's face in the cat, so I
raped the cat. The cat used to run to the door when I came
home and now he just hides under the couch. I'm sorry and
I miss his love and attention."*

Now you might think Paul was really pranking. But,
there is a real message in his tale. He hurt the only one who
cared for him (his wife/his cat), isolating himself, and then
feeling sorry for himself. He has to tell a tale of a weird
incident, showing that he can't really be open about his
feelings, hurts and needs—which was probably the problem that led to his divorce in the first place. So, in his
bizarre story, Paul has revealed the turmoil he's about deep
down!

Some people pull my leg when they talk about sex with
animals, but up to 4 percent of males and females have
these fantasies.

When Deborah Harry came to *LovePhones*, she brought Chickie, whom she calls "the love lap dog" or "little licky." Deborah's advice: "Animals can be better friends than people."

Some people find the thought of sex with animals disgusting; others are fascinated and want to do it. An obsession with thoughts about animals, or compulsion to be sexual with animals is a fetish called zoophilia or bestiality. Whatever you're into, figure out what it says about your needs, and what your conflicts or problems are with the real relationships in your life—unrequited loves, unsuccessful dating, or chronic disappointments with people. And remember that animals can scratch or bite, or pass infections.

BEAUTY AND THE BEAST

Marta: *"I've been thinking about having sex with my dog. Georgie Boy is the sweetest terrier who is so good to me. He waits for me at the door every afternoon when I come home and curls up next to me in bed every night, making the cutest growling gurgling noises. He listens to everything I say, and when I cry in my bed, he growls. He's so much nicer than any guy I know. All the guys I've ever liked go out with me once and then never call again. I don't know why. I'm nice to them. I even thought of having sex with a girl I know who's the only girl in school who has been nice to me. When I see my dog lick his pink thing, I think about doing it, too, or having him put it next to me, you know where. The other day I put a pink bow on him and he barked so cute."*

I don't think you're perverted—you're just desperate to be loved, and you see that it hasn't worked out with any person yet. You want to be loved sexually as well, and are using your dog as a substitute boyfriend who adores you unconditionally, and lets you say or do anything to him. The real problem is that guys have been mean to you and rejected you, so you're turning to anything that has made you feel good.

The human–animal companion bond can go too far. In one study, eight out of ten pet owners said they were closer to their animal than to friends or family. Actress Linda Gray (from the TV show *Dallas*) once joked she uses her horse as her shrink, since it's "always available, doesn't talk back, and doesn't charge." The danger is in using the animal as an escape or excuse from the disappointments or anxieties of real life and relationships. You have to face your desires, needs, and fears about affection and sex, build your confidence, and take risks with real people instead of withdrawing to your pet. Or move into the doghouse yourself!

DOG EAT DOG WORLD

Bob, 19: *"My girlfriend doesn't know this but I saw her one night putting dog food on her crotch and having her dog, a St. Bernard named Beethoven, licking it off. I'm upset because she told me I was the King of Cunnilingus."*

Obviously the Keeper of the Crown will get it wherever she can. Curious your girlfriend doesn't have a lap dog. Why is the dog better than a man? Some reasons: it doesn't get tired, you don't have to return the favor.

> If the dog wants to hump your leg,
> make him take you to dinner first.

DOG INTRUDES ON SEX

"I have been seeing a guy I like for about six months. We just started having sex and his dog is always sneaking into the room and watching us while we do it. Now the dog barks at me when I come in the door and whimpers when we go in the bedroom."

I suspect your boyfriend gave his dog lots of undivided attention before you came on the scene. Now, the dog is suffering from a kind of rivalry and sees you as competition for your boyfriend's attention. The dog has to be disciplined to stay out of the bedroom when you are having sex. Then, your boyfriend should spend some quality time walking and playing with the dog so it doesn't feel neglected. You should also spend some play time with the dog, alone, so it gets used to you as a friend rather than thief of your boyfriend's time and love.

FELINE FAVOR

"My boyfriend has a cat and one evening I was laying on his bed nude, watching TV and playing with myself, and his two cats jumped on the bed. I was petting them and one draped itself over my breasts. The fur felt so soft and good. The other one was nuzzling into my stomach. I got up to get a glass of milk and some cheese and crackers, and the cats jumped back on me. When I went to change the channel, I leaned over and some of my milk spilled on my breast. The cat licked it off and I got a little surge through my body that went down into my genitals. So, I poured another drop of milk on my breast and the cat licked it more. Its scratchy little tongue felt so good on my nipple, it made my nipple get erect. Then I decided to spill a little milk on my snatch, and the other cat went to lick it off there. It was such a thrill, having one cat's little scratchy tongue on my breast and the other at my clit. They were purring, but after a while they jumped off and I was very disappointed. I wanted it more. It was so exciting. Do you think I did anything bad to my boyfriend's cats? I'm scared to tell him about it. But I also want to try it again. I'm thinking of not giving the cat the milk he puts out for them one morning and then making them want it so bad they will lick me for a longer time. Would that be a bad thing to do?"

Teach your boyfriend to do it and you won't need the cats. Or masturbate on your own, thinking about your boyfriend doing it. It can get complicated, or abusive, to use animals for your sexual pleasure. One woman in your predicament bought a very low-grade sandpaper and rubbed it very lightly on her nipples to get that scratchy stimulation— but be careful! (P.S. Stroking a cat on the head awakens its sexual feelings.)

FERRET FANCY

"I was over my friend's house and he has a ferret and I put it in my lap and it got into my pants. I liked it going around, it felt all furry around my penis. I got excited. Do you think it's wrong for me to do it again. Will my friend get upset?"

Your friend might think you are taking advantage of his pet. If you like something furry on your genitals, why don't you buy or make a fur mitt and get your girlfriend to touch you with it. Fur does feel pleasurable and exciting.

GUILTY OVER PAST

While city slickers think it's a put-on, it's not uncommon for people to grow up on farms and experiment with animals. Paul called *LovePhones* explaining that he came from a small farm in Ireland, where they say, "the men are men and the sheep are nervous," and confessed, *"I had an experience with a sheep when I was a teen and now I can't have sex with a woman."*

You did what many other guys growing up around animals do. Forgive yourself. Condition yourself to think of being with a person. Use masturbation training, using images that start from nonthreatening ones (like you talking to a woman, having dinner together, making out in the car) to progressively more sexual ones (thinking of a real woman lying next to you, touching you, lying on top of you, you penetrating her). My producer, Sam, offered Paul confession, comforting him: "Don't worry, many of our flock have strayed . . . "

Myron claimed he could only do it with cows—how udderly ridiculous.

FOLLOW THE LEADER

Mark, 27: *"I used to be shy but my wife was into kinky things. I thought she was perverted at first, when she wanted me to tie her up and shoot off in her face, and she'd play cards with her girlfriends and watch pornos while I went to sleep. But she brought me out and made me wild.*

Lately I've been the aggressor, wanting to do other things, like have another girl in bed with us. First she said yes and I called a 976 number and ordered a girl, and my wife went in the bedroom and locked the door and wouldn't let me in, so I called to cancel it. It was her idea, so what's wrong with her?"

She feels out of control. She probably liked being the one who set the pace, but now you've not only caught up but outdone her. You'd better set some limits as to what's okay and not okay between you. And talk about whether she prefers being the one out front and is scared that you are now. You may have to take turns playing the leader and the follower.

THREE-WAYS

Brandon: *"My girlfriend was the one who suggested that we have sex with some of her friends who come over. We do it about one or two times a week. Now when I have sex with her, I have to think about another woman being there, I can't just enjoy it with her."*

You're a perfect example of how what you think expands your sex life—introducing another person—actually restricts it. You got into a sexual habit. To get out of the habit, when you're with your girlfriend alone, and the thought of another woman comes into your mind, change your thought processes. Imagine your mind as a TV. Take the remote control and switch from watching the picture of the three of you to seeing just the two of you. Or delete that computer program in your mind and type in a new one of love between the two of you.

You are using the presence and thought of another person to distance you from your girlfriend. Examine why you are afraid of intimacy with her alone now. Are you angry that she was the one who suggested you bring another person in, and so subconsciously you fear that she doesn't care as much about you, so you're defensively keeping distance from her? Or are you afraid that you can no longer please her?

John: *"I have a problem. I have been going out with this girl and all of a sudden she tells me that she wants to have sex with two guys. I asked her if she'd do it with two girls and she said no."*

TV soap and Broadway actor Ricky Paull Goldin doesn't approve of threesomes: "Hell, no, that's my vote. That could really mess your head up. That would ruin a relationship. This is the type of situation that you really have to stop and think about what is about to happen or what could possibly happen. Ask her how she'd feel about seeing another girl's hands all over you. That's a real good way to get down to the two sets of feelings and if this is something that you guys could ever deal with."

"I want my boyfriend to have sex with another guy. I want the two guys to go down on each other and then one be in my mouth and the other in my vagina, and we all get off that way. I have a bisexual friend Mike who is willing to do it with us and my boyfriend said he'd think about it. Do you think it'll work?"
"I want to have sex with my boyfriend and another girl, but I want him just to watch. I don't want him to do things with her. Can I tell him that he is not allowed to touch her but can touch me only?"

You can request anything you want, but you can't ensure that the real people in the real situation are going to do exactly what you want. The only way to make a threesome work, especially when you're new at it, is for all the participants to be real clear about exactly what everyone's sex scripts, or expectations, are. When you have the sex play written out already in your head, you better be sure they all are willing to go along with their roles as you've written them. You're the author and director of this play but only one of the actors. Even in the confines of a role they agree to play, they are likely going to express themselves and bring up some unexpected feelings in you. That's why the fantasy is often far better than the reality.

You might be interested to know that a lot of "bad boy" rock stars (like Steven Tyler, Sammy Hagar, Vince Neil) who have indulged every fantasy and done the threesomes (and foursomes and more) feel it has lost its luster and are working on loving one person.

Ex-4 Non Blondes' Linda Perry: "I've been involved in a menage, first with another woman and then with another man. It was okay. It was a friend thing—a team effort. But instead of doing it, go get Betty the Blow Up doll and put a little fur on her area. It's safer."

Lisa, 24: *"I'm a manicurist and I do this porn star. As I do her nails, she hits on me, telling me she'd like to run those nails down my chest, and asking how would I like one in my navel and down my stomach. I fantasize her with my husband, all three of us together, but when I told him, he said I could do it with her alone. Should I do it with her first alone, or insist he join us?"*

His suggestion sure threw a crimp in your wheel. Why would he encourage you to be with her alone? He may be afraid of the dynamics of the three of you together, him not being able to perform, him liking her more, you being jealous, whatever . . . find out what it is. Be prepared for complicated aftereffects when you introduce someone else into a relationship. It's rarely ever simple.

The hardest combo to get going is being a girl and wanting your boyfriend to do it with another guy, because it triggers homosexual panic. But sometimes guys have the fantasy for this themselves. They consider it a bonding experience and a power trip. Like Burt, 20: *"Me and my frat bro want to double team this girl. How do we get her to go for it? I heard about liquid panty remover—getting her drunk—on the* Ricki Lake *show."*

Ask her. Don't be jerks and get her drunk so she doesn't know what she's getting into. If she's smart and sober, she'll see she's being used, and refuse.

TRICKED INTO THREESOME TEST

Christina: *"My boyfriend is seventeen and suggested I do his friend, but after I did in order to please him, he said he was trying to test me to see if I'd be unfaithful and I was, so now he said he lost respect for me. He didn't enjoy it and I did it just for him, so now I feel cheap and sleazy."*

You made the mistake of not finding out the truth of how he felt, and he was unfair to try to trick and test you. If that's the way he communicates—showing his dishonesty and insecurity—you're better off without him. I'm infuriated that you'd do anything just to keep your boyfriend. Have more self-respect. Learn from every situation that you should evaluate the possible good and bad outcomes before you act.

THREESOME THREAT

In some cases, wanting to include another person sends a hostile message to the partner.

Kevin: *"My problem is that I have been with my wife a little over a year and lately I have not been satisfying her. One day she said, 'Get yourself ready. I am going to bring a person here so that as you are standing and watching me, you could learn how to make love.' When I make love to her I come in five minutes or something. I pull out and I just work her, and I just try to eat her and by the time I go again I try to stay calm but by the second time I come fast again."*

British singer Alison Moyet advised: "I don't think she has your best interest at heart there. And, I certainly wouldn't be pushed into a situation where you have to watch your wife having sex with somebody else. That is far too damaging and I don't think the relationship can really flourish under that kind of situation. If she was being really intelligent, then she would try and teach you how to make love to her, not by having you watch somebody else."

SWAPPING

"My girlfriends like to talk about sex with their girlfriends, and offer them to have sex with their boyfriends. The guys then do it. Is that sick?"

With women becoming more liberated about sex, they're enjoying doing the things that guys used to do—like talk about how they got laid, how "good" she was in bed, and "male bonding" by doing the same girl. Now some girls find it cool to pass around the guys they've had, as a way of "female bonding" and protecting themselves from being hurt by treating guys like sex objects. Of course, doing that treats people like meat, and if you really loved someone you wouldn't want to share them or pass them around.

SWINGERS

"My ex-boyfriend was involved in the swinging lifestyle. I never really understood why he or someone needs to be part of such an unhealthy scene, especially in this day and age of AIDS. Why would he do this?"

Some people find it arousing to see, hear, smell, or touch others having sex. It can also relieve the pressure of intimacy with just one person. Swingers describe their activities as fun, diverse, and insist that it bonds, rather than distances, them as a couple. They enjoy having sex with others just as they would going to a movie, or playing doubles tennis. But it's dangerous—when I went undercover with the TV show, *A Current Affair,* to do a story about swingers, I saw a lot of people in swing clubs having sex without protection!

The clubs have various rooms. There's an entrance with some food laid out and a locker room for your clothes. You can have sex in a large room with mattresses on the floor, where people lie in twos, or reach over to the person or couple next to them, or you can go into little rooms with various furnishings, like chains to hang from or chairs to straddle for various sex positions and practices. It's dark and hard to see, so groping is in order, but it's light enough to tell what's going on if you focus. People talk in soft tones. Some have an indoor pool. People hang out in the rooms or in the hallways, leaning against walls, sitting on benches, or standing and talking.

Jennifer and Alan are typical of couples I have talked to at swing clubs. She said: *"My husband likes watching me have sex with other people. We go to the sex clubs and he watches me give head to other guys and have sex with them and then we go home and have the best sex. We love each other and have two kids, so we look like regular people, but this wasn't how I was brought up, even though we do this. Are we regular?"*

Obviously you are afraid that you are not regular or normal because of your sexual explorations. You are not alone in this thought, but the idea of what's normal or regular is up to you to redefine. Since you and your husband both agree about this behavior and it seems to work for the both of you, without harming your family, nothing will likely change your view. But do consider: exactly *what* about this really gets you off, and can the thought be enough?

Many couples I interviewed at swing clubs claimed they were very much in love and that watching or joining with others spiced up their sex life without ruining their commitment. The guy often loved the thought that instead of fearing his woman straying, he was choosing for her to be with other guys while she was still his. Basically, he felt in control. And the women loved being the object of great desire.

GROUP SEX

In one survey, 25 percent of single men said they've been involved in group sex, while less than one in ten women had. Also, most people seem to try it only once.

Kevin: *"How do I get into an orgy? I really want to do that thing I heard about that they call 'daisy chaining,' like '69' in a circle, where one girl sucks the guy while he licks another girl while she is going down on another guy who is going down on the first girl. It sounds real cool."*

Some people just hang out with friends, since sharing a fun time (like bowling, concerts, dinner) makes them feel bonded and sexually aroused. Or, they go straight for the jugular (like watching porn videos together as a stimulus). Others seek out partners who are more experienced in the life, by looking in the newspapers and magazines that cater to a swinging crowd. There is an organization called

Lifestyles based in California that holds an actual convention for all types of sexual persuasions and combinations to meet one another and network.

John, 18: *"My buddy and I want to try out each other's girls. We tried making out next to each other and one of us reaching over to touch the other girl, but she moved away and seemed annoyed. I said my girl is better and I want to prove it. How do we get them to do it?"*

You're treating girls like trophies and using them as a game between you and your buddy. Why don't you just be satisfied comparing your penis size and leave the girls alone.

SUCKLE TURN ON

Tony, 22: *"Ever since my wife had a baby, I like suckling on her breasts. After the baby feeds, I get on them. I love it more than beer. Now when I see pregnant women in the street, I look at their breasts and think about suckling at them, and I feel tingles in my groin. I'm afraid I'm going to get with one of these women."*

Having a child has catapulted you back to a baby state yourself. On the simplest, healthiest level, you're a typical guy who is jealous of the attention mother gives to baby. It reminds you of how wonderful it was not to be a man with responsibilities but an adolescent who is free to run around, or a baby who's totally and completely adored and fed—so you want to regress to that. Recognize these feelings, and as soon as the thought about suckling these other women's breasts comes into your head, snap your fingers to interrupt it and punch another thought into your computer mind—make it a mature thought, for example, being on an exotic beach with your wife with no cares in the world, or playing with your baby.

Paul has another twist on new fatherhood: *"I want to have intercourse with my wife as she is nursing our new baby."*

What does this desire mean? On a deep psychological

level, you may be merging the two sides of the female figure (the lover and the mother parts), which is a healthy sign.
But you may also be competing with the child: as it nurses,
you want your wife's attention.

PLAYING BABY

*"I've been married two years and we just had our first
baby. I'm a good father and husband and I just started my
own business, but I am ashamed and scared that I am
consumed with thinking about talking baby talk, wearing
diapers, and drinking from bottles, and can't seem to
enjoy sex the regular way anymore. Why do I feel this
way?"*

Some amount of regressing to babyhood can be within the
range of normal love play between two trusting partners who
allow each other to express hidden and/or forbidden wishes
and primal needs to be pampered or protected. This can
include using baby talk and play-acting being baby or
mommy. Such pretending in the safety of a permissive love
relationship can help you re-experience early pleasurable
experiences or replay painful ones to repair them, but
becomes a problem—a paraphilia called infantilism—when
you have to use baby clothing or experiences (bottle-feeding,
burping, diapering, powdering, sleeping in a crib) to get
turned on. Undoubtedly for you as for Tony and Paul, having
a baby and becoming a father, and starting a new business,
has triggered an intense desire to be nurtured and protected,
and escape all the mounting responsibilities you have at
home and in business. Admit those needs and fears, limit
your pressures, practice relaxation, and openly request the
nurturance you need.

Your behavior sounds mild. When men are compelled to
act like babies, it usually means early sexual feelings (like
erections) happened in childhood, when wearing diapers or
rubber pants. In one study only a third wanted to stop the
behavior. If you do, learn more mature behavior by masturbating while touching or wearing adult items. (Infantilists
have appeared on TV talk shows, and have support groups

like the Diaper Pail Fraternity and newsletters like Crib Sheet. In Japan there are clubs for men who like to wear diapers.)

"My wife likes me to play the daddy role and she likes to be the little girl. She likes me to say things like, 'What will Daddy do to his little girl if she's bad?' and she says, 'Oh Daddy, I'm so sorry I was bad, but don't you love me, Daddy?' and then I say things like, 'Daddy's going to give it to you harder.' Is something wrong with this?"

As long as you know you are not really stuck in playing the roles of child and parent and can also have sex as adults, it can be a safe way to allow yourself to role-play. Such pretending can help you both work out unresolved feelings from childhood, and your needs to be adored. Play variations—mommy and her little boy, daddy and his girl, being "bad" or "good." But getting lost in the roles can distort your relationship. The best way to use these games is to spend nonsexual time reflecting on what you wanted or missed in your childhood. Treat the game as a key to your psyche.

PORN MAG ADDICT

Dawn, 24: *"My boyfriend won't give up his dirty magazines. He says I'm insecure and maybe that's true, but I feel like it's taking away from our sex life. We have sex once a week and it's normal and plain. I ask him whether I can dress up for him and what fantasy he has and he says he doesn't have any. So why does he go to the magazines?"*

You're right. If you are willing to participate in a fantasy and he refuses, obviously he doesn't want to open up to you and feels safer with imaginary women in the magazines. He's entitled to his private fantasies, but not when he totally shuts you out. He could have that infamous Madonna-Whore Syndrome men get about keeping their wives "pure" and seeking wild sex elsewhere. Don't blame yourself but tell him you want to make your sex life more exciting. Dress up without his permission. Read the magazine with him and suggest a fantasy you can both get into.

PORN MOVIE ADDICT

There's nothing wrong with some good erotic entertainment in the VCR to spice up your love life—after all, there's plenty of it on the silver screen these days—but there is such a thing as addiction to porn.

Kelly, 22: *"My boyfriend has to watch a porn when we have sex. If I get in the way of the picture, he pushes me away. I'm no beauty queen, but is this too much?"*

Yes, he can't stand the intimacy with you. That's his problem. And if he pushes you away, he's being abusive. Don't stand for it. If he can't get into you, get away from him! And stop putting yourself down comparing yourself with the video vixens, by saying you're not pretty enough.

PORNO ANTICS

Since porno films are so popular, a lot of guys want to mimic what they see in their own life.

Mike: *"I saw a porno of a girl doing a 'humpty dance' I want my girlfriend to do. She was gyrating around and then she threw out white stuff from her. She spurted what looked like Jergens lotion out of her vagina. Can women do that?"*

If they exercise their vaginal muscles, yes, they can expel—or take in—something. It's like the trick of "snaking," being able to undulate the vaginal muscles, to make a guy feel like he's being "milked." The actress probably spurted some sort of lotion, to look like ejaculate.

900 LINES

Katie, 23: *"I'm married but I call the 900 numbers. I get off on the phone. I can't stop 'cuz I'm real bored at home, cleaning the house. Where is this leading?"*

You're out of control. HOMEWORK: As soon as you get bored, do something else with your time. Make a list of ten things you can enjoy and feel good about yourself over. Do one of those instead. Sex phone lines, escort services, nudie bars, go-go bars, table dancing, lap dancing, and all such diversions have proliferated in the past few years because they're safe sex. And because in this age of more repression, people seek expression of their desires.

PHONE BONE

Tracy, 24: *"I like to call guys and give them a 'phone bone.' I act like a woman on the 900 lines. I tell them all kinds of fantasies, like being with another woman and they love it. I don't know if I can be with a guy in person."*

You're using the phone as a less anxiety-provoking way to share your fantasies. It's okay to practice like this, but you have to transfer that safety into face-to-face contact or you'll forever be lonely.

Billy Baldwin (brother of Alec) told *Cosmo* magazine, "all of this is not kinky . . . it's just a different form of expressing yourself sexually without putting yourself at risk."

GO-GO BARS

The Sex in America study of almost 3,500 adults showed that 22 percent of men visited a club with nude or seminude dancers. Four percent of women also admitted to it. Women have gone to clubs where men dance (from Chippendales to Adonis and Man Alive), to various male strip revue clubs and, less common, they have gone along with men to clubs where women strip (Cleveland's Tiffany's Cabaret encourages couples as customers).

Some women, like Pam, enjoy it: *"I love going to those strip joints with my boyfriend. He gets really hot and screws my brains out when we get home. And, I love looking at the women's bodies, too, and learning how they flaunt themselves since I don't have the nerve to stick my pussy or my rear end in his face and I sure would love to do that. Is there anything wrong with that?"*

No, they sound like two valid reasons. If he's going to go, why not go along with him, so you are associated with his excitement; it's simple learning theory. And if in the process you learn to enjoy displaying your body and asking for pleasure, that's a valuable lesson.

Danielle feels exactly the opposite: *"I hate that my boyfriend goes to go-go bars with his friends. Can I insist he stop?"*

Many men who go to higher class "gentleman's clubs" are not perverts, but businessmen, college guys, regular Joes. Celebrities and rock stars also hang out at strip clubs. As Vince Neil, a real devotee, says, "It's a party atmosphere and I love to party. I also love women's bodies." The reasons vary from expressing fantasies to frustrations. After playing around there, they can go home to their girlfriends and wives and think they didn't cheat, even though they got turned on.

The visit can be innocent, but if he seems addicted, and you feel abandoned, frustrated, and unfulfilled, something is wrong with your relationship that you have to confront directly instead of arguing about the club. Find out what fantasy he's into there, that you can share.

IS GO-GO FAR GONE?

Starlight: *"I lost my job as a bank clerk and I couldn't find another job, so a friend suggested I go be a dancer at a club. I did and I love it. A lot of the girls there had been abused as kids, I know, but not me. I love being seen as a piece of meat. I parade in front of guys and they drool for me. I feel great about my body, as I knew I had a tight butt and firm breasts, but it's a thrill when I can go out there and bend over and spread my butt cheeks and I know they're staring longingly at my holes. They're probably not getting it at home. And it's real safe sex. I love teasing them and they loved being teased or they wouldn't come. I also love being judged for my body and not where I went to school and what job I have."*

It sounds like you want to convince me, and have me give you approval. I still maintain that such a power play shows the contempt the sexes have for each other and perpetuates lack of intimacy and true relationships. How can I argue with you—that there are other more respectable ways to earn money—when girls like you always insist that the payoff stuffed into your G-string is incomparable. You have to consider how this experience is really affecting you, and see that you do have other alternatives.

You think you have power over men (a reason abused girls go into it) since you tempt and tease them, but ultimately they have power (to pay, abandon, use) over you.

Amber, seventeen, wants to stop: *"I was working as a waitress in a strip bar but then I started stripping because I can make so much more money to pay for school— $3,000 a week. But it's going too far. The owners of the club asked me if I wanted a line of coke. And I'm getting into girls because the girls touch each other and try to kiss me. I like to show off my body and it's hard to give up but the atmosphere is getting crazy. I never felt very good about myself, and this really boosts my ego, so how can I give it up?"*

Remember that you're not comfortable with it, you're going to get into trouble, and there are better ways to raise your self-esteem. I feel scared for you. You're so desperate for attention and being admired, you could go over the edge. I'm glad you're stopping and thinking. It shows you're smart. Girls who have worked this scene and gotten out, say the money isn't worth the danger (drugs, rape, emotional confusion) and they feel such higher self-esteem when they get a job they can be proud of. Learn from my assistant, Alissa, who gave up her top-paying barmaid job because she realized the attention she got was not for *her* but for her body. Being penniless, back in school working on her career, felt better than men ogling her tits and treating her like a piece of meat. Do affirmations: "I am worthy, I am a good person, I can make a living doing something else that gives me respect."

ESCORT SERVICES

Greg: *"I pay a hundred dollars to these girls in an escort service to get tickled on my feet. I had a friend take me to a club one night and he went up to a girl and asked if she would go out with his friend, me, and she looked over and laughed. I usually keep my socks on. Is it safe to take my socks off?"*

Yes. But you need to let someone get close to you. Then you won't have to resort to paying for sex. Everyone gets rejected. Keep on 'til you find a real person who will like you.

MALE PROSTITUTE

Stopping prostitution is equally tough.

Gibby, 21: *"I've been a male prostitute but I want to get out of the game. I started when I was fourteen when a friend set me up and then I had a pimp. I got lots of money—five dollars for a pig in the blanket and twenty dollars for a vacuum job—and presents out of it. I'm very pretty looking, so the men wanted to go down on me. Then some would ask me to do disgusting things to them. I'm tired of being a sex toy. I wouldn't recommend it to anyone. Now I wonder if I can ever get my self-respect back."*

Yes. It'll be a long road, because you have to overcome the past temptations, and the memories. You'll have to see yourself in a new way, and begin to trust others as liking you for yourself not for how you can service them. I'm proud of you for choosing self-respect and unconditional love over selling your body and soul.

BODY PIERCING

Vince: *"I want to get a Prince Albert—an earring through the hole in my penis and out through the head. What do you think about it?"*

Justine: *"I want to get a ring through my belly button and one through my vaginal lip, but my boyfriend won't let me. He says it's disgusting, and he's afraid it'll rip his penis when we have sex. What should I do? I do worry that maybe it'll affect breast-feeding if I ever have a kid."*

Once a badge of rebellion against authority, body piercing is now becoming a fashion among more mainstream young people, who sport rings through their eyelids, nose, lips, nipples, and even other sexual parts. But before you do it, examine your motives and what the piercing means to you (a sign of your independence, rebelliousness, coolness)? You won't become a sex god from it. Professional piercers will say there are no dangers, but doctors say you can get infections from urine, semen, smegma, or any bacteria caught under the ring. Extra-sensitive nipples during breast-feeding might breed irritation or infection, and babies might not like the interference, although there is enough area for them to suck. Talk it through—discuss your opinions, consider each other's feelings, and make compromises.

Ultimately, if it turns your partner off so much, then give it up; he should matter more. Attach a removable earring or paint on a design. In a *Sassy* magazine poll, 75 percent of boys and girls were repulsed by eyebrow, lip, and tongue rings. Guys said "ouch" and "nasty" to the thought of kissing a girl with a tongue ring.

STUMPED

Stacy: *"My friend's father had an accident at his plant where a big machine fell on his foot. He had to have his leg amputated above the knee, and now he's in a wheelchair. I went over to visit him one day and he rolled up his pants and showed me his leg. I asked him if I could touch it and he said yes. Since then, I was dreaming about it. The next time I went over, I asked him to see it again, and I rubbed it. I felt a tingling in my body and now I keep thinking about how I'd like to have sex with him. I'd like to sit on his chair and hold his leg while we do it. Is there something weird about me?"*

Obviously his injury has touched some part of your soul where you are sympathetic, and are now connecting that sympathy to lovingness and sexuality. I would say that he is a father figure for you and his now being handicapped may also allow you to express nurturing feelings which frighten you otherwise. Some people have fetishes about sex with handicaps and have clubs and magazines to network about it. However, if you are obsessed with erotic attachment to an injury or amputation, this can imply a problem. It may be a safer expression of lust, hiding your guilt about sex. Or it may signify low self-esteem, whereby you can hide your own poor performance, protect yourself from rejection by a more demanding partner, or only feel turned on when a partner is helpless, reflecting your own helplessness. You might have repressed desire to injure, or fears of being injured. Jane Fonda and Jon Voight celebrated able-bodied and physically challenged love in the movie, *Coming Home*. Magazines and clubs exist for people who are interested in amputees.

WHEELCHAIR WHIZ

Jay, 17: *"I had a diving accident two years ago and now I'm in a wheelchair, a quadriplegic. But I have this great girlfriend and we have great sex. I do everything with her. She handcuffs me to the bed and I even put a tampon in my mouth and inserted it in her. She calls me the 'wheeling wizard.' So anybody else can do stuff, don't you think?"*

Good for you! You're an inspiration! You prove that you can make good loving work under any circumstances and with any part of your body, with a little inventiveness! Whiz on!

EYE ON

Tricia, 26: *"I met a guy in a bar and went home with him. I told him I had a glass eye and he asked me to take it out for him. I did and he put his finger in my eye socket and told me he was getting hard, and put my hand on his pants. I told him it was going to far and to get out. Now he called and wants to see me. Should I see him?"*

No. He sounds like a "paraphiliac"—a person who relates to disabilities because he can't be with a real person. He may not be dangerous, but he damaged your self-esteem.

You so desperately need affection, that you need to be careful whom you let into your heart—or your eye! Use your inner eye to be more discriminating.

When Tricia hung up, Butch faxed *LovePhones:* "I want to poke out your eye and make love to your skull." And someone else faxed saying the guy was just trying to see her eye to eye, since the penis is also a one-eyed monster.

SEDUCTION DURING SLEEP

"I like the idea of being half-asleep when my boyfriend has sex with me. It seems to be the only time I can enjoy it."

You have "Sleeping Beauty Syndrome," meaning that you enjoy the fantasy of feeling "awakened" into sexual pleasure by your dashing Prince. Wanting to be half-asleep can mean you don't want to take responsibility for being sexual, so you can either let it be done to you, so you don't have to respond, or you can pretend it's not totally happening. Playing this game can be fun and it's a lot healthier than getting drunk to achieve the same feeling of letting go. But if you have to be semiconscious to have sex, then you must be scared of some feelings. Some "Sleeping Beauties" have been abused as kids, and are used to going outside their body during a sex act, and letting the other person do all the activity and perform sex acts on them.

"My ex-boyfriend told me he had sex with me when I was sleeping and came inside me. I feel like I've been raped because I already have a child and I didn't want to get pregnant, but he wanted to have another child. One time I woke up and he was kissing my vagina. I hate it because I was molested by my father when I was five years old and my boyfriend knew it, so how could he do this to me. I broke up with him but he wants to get back with me. Should I?"

Find out what his motives were for having sex with you while you were sleeping. He is imposing his will without your consent. So, it's understandable you experience it as a violation, even though in kissing your body he may have thought he was being loving. Taking you in sleep is using your body, rather than a consensual act. I would guess that your boyfriend has trouble confronting you as an equal adult. He must have some intimacy and aggression problems. Better know what these are before you can decide if the relationship is a healthy one for you.

ONLY IN THE DARK

"I have to have sex in the dark. I can't do it if the lights are on. Is something wrong with me?"

Some people have sensitive eyes; Elvis Presley didn't like people taking his picture because the flash hurt his eyes. Also, having sex in the dark can be a fun game, encouraging you to be more sensitive to touch. But you could have a problem. Are you that self-conscious about your body? What don't you want to see? It's likely you feel guilty, self-conscious, or insecure about sex, seeing nude bodies, or displaying yourself. Face those feelings and get over them. Love your own body. Accept that you can be sexual. Turn a little night light on, and work up to more light.

A variation of this is when someone needs the other person to keep his/her eyes closed in sex, or to wear a blindfold—which can also be either fun *or* a problem. If it's extreme, then it's a paraphilia called amaurophilia. Progressive steps in severity: needing the person to be asleep, feigning being dead, or really dead.

PLAYING DEAD

> **Q:** What do you call an erection when looking
> at a dead body?
> **A:** A stiffy.

"My boyfriend wants me to play dead when we have sex. He wants me to lay there like a dead body. Is this queer?"

I remember walking in Harvard Yard with a bunch of my Smith classmates and meeting a guy who invited us back to his dorm at Harvard. There, he showed us a big black wood coffin in the middle of the common room. "We like to have sex in it," he announced proudly.

Asking your partner to pretend being dead is a sign of a need for complete control, for objectifying the partner so they're not human and you don't have to consider their needs, feelings, or conflicts. It could just be a temporary kinky kick. But if the fears of intimacy run deep, and the behavior escalates and persists, he's got a serious emotional problem and a sexual paraphilia called necrophilia.

A fascination with death can start in childhood. Tom Petty even danced around with a "dead" Kim Basinger in his "Mary Jane's Last Dance" video. But sex with dead people is sick.

Bill called *LovePhones* to say, *"I work in my father's mortuary since I'm nine years old and I get turned on by having sex with the dead bodies. It started when my girlfriend went away to college. I feel so sorry for them, being so pretty and dead, that I give them half an hour of pleasure."* So what's the problem, I baited him. *"Well, now I seem to be doing it with the ugly ones, too,"* he said.

Bill, you're a real lady-killer, or *wish* you were—the problem is you can't make it with real women!

I asked Bill a lot of questions about how the bodies are laid out. He got some details wrong about the biers. So, Bill was stiffing us, after all, but even though he made it up, people really do this (how abusive!). And since Bill made it up, it shows he really does have problems relating to real people—a real lady-killer!

LATEX LOVE

"My girlfriend is a plastic doll. I got one of those battery operated models, so her hole actually moves. She's made of latex, so it feels real. And she has a wig. I want to make a tape recording where she says how great I am. Is that a problem?"

Quite a Chatty Cathy you want there. Obviously you have a hard time relating to a skin and bones real female. It's a lot less anxiety-provoking or scary to put your penis in a piece of plastic than to face a real person with needs and feelings. Get yourself some of the real thing. Risk it. Research on monkeys showed the babies who grew up on wire mothers were less socially capable than those who had real mothers. Trade your Latex Love for Real Love.

PUSHES LIMITS

Gina: *"I've been with this guy two years and he loves to pleasure me in oral sex. He's very talented and he can make me come up to five times, and keeps pushing it. The last time I was at the point where I said please stop, but he said next time he wants to make me go so far I pass out. Is that possible or is he on an ego trip?"*

He's certainly on an ego trip, to stimulate you beyond where you like it! He must stop if you say stop. Wanting to make you pass out is dangerous, and sounds like he's using you to prove he can control you, not please you. He sounds scary, one step from that dangerous game of sexual asphyxia where you choke the person so they have a powerful orgasm. "He's shooting for the 'Super Bowl of Sex,'" exclaimed USA Network's *Up All Night* host, *Playboy* magazine centerfold, and comedienne Rhonda Schear, playing Honorary Love Doctor that night. "Maybe you could fake passing out just to get it over with and start all over again with one or two smaller orgasms . . . it's not great advice but it's what I'd do because I'm an actress."

VAGINAL LOCK

"I had sex with this girl and about five minutes into intercourse I couldn't pull out. My penis got bigger, and she got tight and it got locked in her. I couldn't pull it out for half an hour. What was that and how can we prevent it next time?"

You could be pulling my leg (because you've seen dogs do this), but it is possible—the vagina "locks," as in the case of vaginismus, when the woman gets nervous and the muscles tighten. But it wouldn't lock for half an hour; so I think this story shows you're scared of sex and being inside a woman.

SOLO SLEEP

Gabrielle: *"I have a problem sleeping in the same room with someone else. I can't go to sleep-away camp for that reason. What's wrong with me? Do I think someone's going to come in my bed?"*

Maybe you had an unwelcome visitor in your bed sometime in your past. Condition yourself to get more comfortable with company. Precondition your mind by going to bed thinking over and over, "I am safe." Start with a teddy bear in your bed, talk to it as if it were a person. Leave the TV on, as a sign of other "people" in the room. To build your tolerance, ask a friend, or sister, if you can stay with her in her room, but have another room to retreat to so you feel in control.

CYBER SEX

"I log onto bulletin-board services as a woman. My handle is 'Lilly White.' It's fun to see what guys say. Why are they so stupid?"

Computer sex services or phone lines allow you to take on a new identity. What you choose is always a projection of a part of you, so examine what that is. Obviously, you need to get in touch with your feminine self, and you use the anonymity of the bulletin-board service to do that. What are those qualities you can express only when you pretend to be a woman? Is it being sensitive, wanted, taken care of, seductive? Allow yourself to express these in your real life.

Unfortunately some perverts are using such computer services to hook up with kids, by pretending different identities. Fortunately, "cybercops" are patrolling the internets to catch these perverts. Please be honest.

SPIRIT SEX

Herb had sex with a spirit.

"I love my wife, but when she went away on a business trip for the first time, I had a weird experience of a ghost coming onto me and having sex with me. My son usually sleeps between us, and that night he urinated on the bed. I turned over the mattress and he did it again, so I took him up to his room, and was sleeping alone for the first time, and this pressure was over me. It was a woman and she had sex with me! Was it a ghost?"

You could have had an erotic dream. Your wife was gone, and you were alone in the bed for the first time, so you were missing her, and created her spirit there. Try this Freudian interpretation: you regressed to being a child with typical ghost dreams. Also, there are kinesthetic dreams, where you actually have physiological reactions that feel real, making you sense a real woman present. Folklore would say you were visited by a succubus who seduces men in their sleep (an incubus gets on top of women) to make you come and take your spirit, and you die. Satanism would suggest a witch put a spell on you, masturbating at bedtime about the man she wants to attract, whereupon he has a wet dream, and when he sees her, he falls in love. In another theory, a witch Lillith was thrown out of heaven and gets revenge visiting men in their sleep.

As a final word: Here's one definitely out of this world that I can heartily endorse.

ALIEN SEX

"I think my boyfriend is into alien sex. He went to a store and bought some books about it. He wanted me to go back to the store with him. Should I?"

Yes, explore what he means by it before you freak out. In the movie *Cocoon,* the alien sex in the pool was a real high—Tahnee Welch sent Steven Guttenberg electrical love charges across the water without even touching.

See if you can project that state now—send orgasmic vibes across the room, across town, through the phone—the Force is with you.

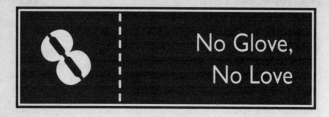

I'VE TOLD YOU HOW OFTEN I HEAR THE "IT JUST happened" story. It makes me nuts. "We were just hanging out . . . I never expected to have sex . . . I was on my way home . . . we were drunk . . . it just happened . . . " URGGHH.

But here's the worst part, "And now I think I'm pregnant!"

It's inexcusable in this day and age to have any mistakes! Inexcusable to get pregnant because you were careless, drunk, or didn't know better. *Stop and Think* before you have sex. Could what you're doing lead to getting pregnant? Are you ready for a baby in your life? Who is this guy, or girl, to you anyway? Many times you hardly know the person. What in the world would getting pregnant do to the relationship, much less to your whole life? It only takes one time. It's easier than you think.

Maybe you'll be more careful when you hear heartbreaking stories from those who weren't careful.

Like Camille: *"I went out with this guy a few times and I liked him, but he hasn't called me. He doesn't even say hello to me in the hallway. It's like I don't exist. Here's the worst part, I think I'm pregnant."*

And Lisa, 16: *"I already had one abortion when my best friend's stepfather raped me, and now I got pregnant again from this guy I went out with. I have nightmares and feel ugly. I feel like killing myself. My parents don't know anything about it."*

Nina, 18: *"I was going out with this guy who's a different race from me and I'm pregnant. He split because when he found out, he said it was against his religion and he couldn't take it. He told me to do whatever I want. My mother and I don't talk and my father is dead. I never finished high school. What should I do?"*

Kevin, 16: *"I just dated this girl a few times and we had sex at a party and now she called me up and told me she's pregnant. This is awful. I don't even like her."*

Camille, Lisa, Marie, Kevin, and so many others like them, need counseling and support to face their situation. But, you have a chance not to end up in that same mess. If you just remember, Responsibility Rules.

Some statistics:

- There are about a million teenage pregnancies every year; it's hard enough growing up, much less being a parent before you're ready.
- About half of all pregnancies to women between the ages of fifteen and forty-four in the U.S. are unintended.

It's important to know how you get pregnant, because believe it or not, so many males and females have myths about it!

WHAT YOU KNOW ABOUT PREGNANCY QUIZ
(Answer P for "possibly" or N for "no" for each)

Can you get pregnant if:

(1) the guy pulls out before he ejaculates	P N
(2) you have sex at any time of the month	P N
(3) his penis is out but you're wearing underwear	P N
(4) you kiss with your mouth open	P N
(5) the guy comes between your legs but not inside you	P N
(6) you have anal intercourse	P N
(7) he comes in your mouth	P N
(8) he touches you after he ejaculates in his hand	P N
(9) you have sex but the girl doesn't have an orgasm	P N
(10) you stand up afterward	P N
(11) the guy jerks off in the water and you're near him	P N
(12) you have sex in the swimming pool	P N
(13) you douche	P N
(14) you wash out with Coke	P N
(15) you use Saran Wrap instead of a condom	P N

Check your answers. Just ONE wrong answer and I'm concerned—because you HAVE to know how you get pregnant and what the risks are!

Answers:

(1) **Possibly**. Melanie: *"I'm scared to death. I had sex with my boyfriend for the first time the other night and we didn't have any protection. But he pulled out right before he spurted. Now I'm late a few days and I'm panicked, but how can I get pregnant if he didn't come inside me?"*

> **Q:** What do you call people who use the rhythm method to prevent pregnancy?
> **A:** Parents

It is not safe to have sex when the guy pulls out when he thinks he's coming. This is one of the biggest myths about pregnancy: thinking the dip and dash, or withdrawal method, works. It doesn't. As the saying goes, "Every basketball player dribbles before he shoots." That means guys have a little ejaculate (called pre-cum) seep out of their penis before they actually ejaculate. When they're excited, it just comes out—they have no control over it—and it has many active sperm in it, though not as many as in ejaculate, but they're just as capable of getting you pregnant. Besides the pre-cum coming out, some guys aren't quick or experienced enough to pull out before they come, and may do it as they're ejaculating already, so you think he pulled out but some sperm already shot inside. By the way, the pre-cum looks clearer and whiter and feels more liquidy than ejaculate. It is manufactured in the Cowper's gland, unlike the ejaculate which comes from other organs. If his penis is outside, you can see the pre-cum at the tip.

(2) **Possibly**. Any day can be a fertile day. *"I'm nineteen and just started having sex with my boyfriend. He says you can't get pregnant three or so days before your period. I disagreed. Who is right?"*

You win. It sounds like your boyfriend is trying to convince you that he doesn't need to wear a condom at certain times during the month since many guys object to condoms and will look for any excuse not to wear them. Don't let him talk you out of it. It's possible that a stray egg is released and travels into the fallopian tube—where it can meet sperm—at any time in your cycle. Clocking the woman's cycle for "safe" days to have sex without contraception, called the rhythm or calendar method, is widely practiced by some religious groups (it's sometimes called playing Vatican roulette) but it is not foolproof. Granted, a woman is most fertile around her midcycle when she is ovulating (when the egg, released by an ovary, travels down the fallopian tube where it can unite with the sperm), which for a woman with a regular twenty-eight–day cycle means about three or four pregnancy-prone days before and after the midpoint (longer for women with irregular cycles). You have up to a one-in-five chance of getting pregnant from unprotected sex during this time. The woman is least fertile during menstruation, when the uterus lining to which a fertilized egg would have attached, sheds. Teens are especially vulnerable because their menstrual cycles are often irregular, making it more difficult to time ovulation.

HOW POTENT ARE SPERM?

There are typically 80 million to 320 million sperm in each average ejaculation. Many surround one egg to try to penetrate its walls; but it only takes *one* to make a baby.

> **Q:** What do a lawyer and sperm have in common?
> **A:** Both have a one in a million chance of
> becoming a person.

Maybe so, but it only takes one sperm in millions to make a baby.

(3) **No**. Your underwear stops sperm from going in your body.

(4) **No**. How would sperm get in your body this way (from kissing)?

(5) **Possibly**. Only if the sperm are deposited right on the labia (vaginal lips), in which case they can swim into the vagina.

(6) **No**. Figure it out. Ejaculating in the anal canal just shoots the sperm up into the anal canal, connected to the digestive system, an entirely different route from the vaginal canal and reproductive system.

(7) **No**. Figure it out. If you swallow semen, it will travel the same route as food—which goes down your throat into your stomach, where it gets digested, and the by-products then go through the small and large intestines, and waste exits in the urine or feces. There is no connection to the reproductive organs.

(8) **Possibly**. Alexis: *"I decided not to have sex yet, but when my boyfriend and I were fooling around the other night, he touched himself until he finished, and then he touched me. Even though we didn't have intercourse, can I get pregnant?"*

In optimum conditions for pregnancy, the sperm are deposited inside the vagina and then swim through the cervical opening to meet the egg in the fallopian tube. Since ejaculate dries quickly outside the body, sperm normally die unless they are in the moist, warm environment of the vagina or reproductive tract. But conceivably fresh sperm can be introduced into the vagina manually, allowing them to then continue their journey, and pregnancy to occur. To be safe, wash thoroughly before continuing any sex play.

(9) **Possibly.** Reed has a unique myth: *"I heard you can't get pregnant unless the girl has an orgasm."* Wrong. The contractions of an orgasm can help the sperm travel up, but as long as they're deposited in the vaginal barrel, those feisty fellas will race up, orgasm or not.

(10) **Possibly.** Some people think you can stand up and it'll all pour out, like Jose wanted to know: *"How does the ejaculate stay in the girl's body? Why doesn't it fall out?"*

Some semen oozes out, but many get right on their way. As soon as the ejaculate enters, the sperm start swimming up through the cervix into the fallopian tube to meet a possibly awaiting egg, aided in their swim by the liquid from the woman's lubrication. A sperm measures a microscopic 1/5,000 of an inch and travels at a speed of 1/8 of a minute and can take 5 minutes to reach its goal. The ejaculate seems to become a little thicker in consistency after release, acting like a plug to keep it from dripping out. Standing up won't get all the sperm to drip out, but lying down can help them stay in, and lifting your pelvis up can aid them in their upward journey.

Sometimes a girl gets long clear gel-like whitish stringy stuff that comes out of her vagina. It's called spinbarkeit, an overabundance of mucus that comes through the cervix, which acts like a rope along which the sperm can attach and travel up the vaginal barrel, through the cervix and into the uterus. It's like Rapunzel's long hair that she let down from the tower where she was trapped, on which the prince climbed up to get to her.

(11) **No**. Splish splash, it can't happen so easily in the bath, unless he is depositing the sperm right at your vaginal opening. But I can see where you might think you could get pregnant if the sperm are in the water and swim over to you and swim in. It doesn't work that way, but actually I grew up with that myth, too.

I was fifteen and my family was vacationing in Florida. My period was due soon. I had a date with the heartthrob lifeguard and he kissed me in the water. Our bathing suits were on, but he pressed against me. A week went by and I still didn't get my period. I panicked, wondering if I had gotten pregnant from that full body press in the ocean. One night, standing at the bathroom sink, trembling, I asked my mother, "Can you get pregnant from being in the water with a guy?" "Yes," she said. "Even if you have your bathing suit on and he is just against you?" I asked, incredulous. "Yes," she answered, "the sperm can go out the side of his bathing suit down his leg, across the water, up your leg, and squeeze inside your suit." "How can that be?" I asked, stunned. "Sperm are very powerful," she answered. I was terrified! Fortunately, I got my period a few days after this. Years later I found out why my mother had that erroneous myth—an aunt had gotten pregnant but insisted she hadn't had intercourse and had just been lying together making out with a man. So, you see, my mother—like parents in general—was just passing along (mis)information that she had learned growing up.

(12) **Possibly.** Having sex around water (in pools, showers, tubs) is certainly erotic, and good advice for couples to spice up their love life, but care should be taken about getting pregnant. While no studies have been done about pregnancy risks from this practice, water in the vagina from immersed sexual activity can act as a douche, flushing sperm out, but also do the opposite, propelling semen upward in the body. If a man ejaculates in a bath, however, it is highly unlikely that the sperm will swim through the water and enter the woman's vagina! The semen will get diluted and the sperm will soon die.

As far as having sex in the pool, information from various condom manufacturers, pharmacies, and chemical companies suggests that the antibacterial purifying agents added to pool water (like chlorine) may kill sperm; if, however, ejaculation occurs inside the vaginal canal, certainly some semen can continue its journey through the cervix unharmed. Condom use under any circumstances is definitely advisable, and while being underwater does not penetrate or weaken latex condoms, it can reduce the condom's effectiveness. Water can seep into the sides of the vagina, loosening the condom's grip, making it more likely to slip off; or it may get inside the condom, further loosening it or diluting the spermicide. The inside-outside pressure from sex under such conditions can also cause seepage of the ejaculation over the top of the condom into the vaginal canal.

(13) **Possibly.** Robin: *"I was going to douche after we had sex, to wash out the sperm. My friend did it and she didn't get pregnant. Is this good to do?"*

No! The water can actually help the sperm move on their journey, through the cervix. Also, the sperm are fast on their way, before you could even try to get them out.

(14) **Possibly.** Putting Alka Seltzer or Pepsi-Cola or Coca-Cola in your vagina as a spermicide—to kill the sperm—does not work!

(15) **Possibly.** Using Saran Wrap as a replacement for a condom's no good. It'll tear and it's too thin so those nasty viruses will go right through.

SPERM SHELF LIFE
"How long do sperm live in the body?"

Sperm can live in the woman's body about forty-eight hours after ejaculation, but they have been known to stay alive for up to eight days. If they're not in a warm, moist, alkaline place, they die quickly. So they die very quickly outside the body.

WHO'S RESPONSIBLE?
"When I told my boyfriend I wanted him to wear a condom, he said he wouldn't. He told me I should do something about not getting pregnant, like wearing a diaphragm. Should I?"

Traditionally it was up to the man to take precautions, but now women have to be equally responsible. Both partners should share the responsibility about pregnancy and prevention. That means both have to accept that they are being sexual and both have to be prepared. She can't assume he has condoms; he can't assume she's on the Pill. Talk about being careful before you have sex. But, I think if he resists wearing the condom, you have to find out what his objections are, and answer them, because all possibilities should be up for grabs.

Don't be a sex dope:

If you don't have a parachute, don't jump
Cover your stump before you hump
Don't be silly, protect your willy
If you're not going to sack it, go home and whack it
If you think she's spunky, cover your monkey
If you slip between her thighs, condomize
If you go into heat, package your meat
If you undress venus, dress your penis
Never deck her with an unwrapped pecker
Don't be a fool, wrap your tool
Take care of business before you get down to
　　pleasure

(SOME COURTESY OF ADAM, *LOVEPHONES* LISTENER)

HIS OBJECTIONS

"My boyfriend doesn't want to wear a condom. He said we either go bareback or there's no ride at all. What should I do?"

Remember, the Right to say yes or no Rules. He's not the boss. This is a mutual deal. Answer his protests with a clever retort: "No glove, no love," or "If you're not ready to wear a condom, you're not ready for sex." People who don't use contraception have negative attitudes or conflicts about being sexual, or they're passive and irresponsible about their own or their partner's health. Use my four-step method. Stop and think. What are your feelings? If you're guilty about sex, don't do it, or get over your guilt. Think about the consequences. Then make a smart decision. Don't you care about your health?

If a guy protests wearing a condom, here's how you can answer him back:

- He insists: "It doesn't feel as good as wearing nothing." (You answer: "Relax, that's what feels good. Use your mind to bump up the excitement." Or tell him, "it'll feel worse to be dead.")

- He insists: "I won't feel as close to you." (You answer: "The fact that we know we're looking out for one another makes up for any physical separation.")
- He insists: "I'm clean—I don't have anything." (You answer: "Fine, then we're extra sure. It's not an insult to you, it's just smart.")
- He insists: "It kills the spontaneity." (You answer: "No, it's another way to play—let's put it on together and make it sexy.")
- He insists: "They cost too much." (You answer: "I'll buy it" or "I'll loan you the money.")
- He insists: "I'll lose my erection, it's not going to work." (You answer: "Stop thinking it'll fail. Expecting it to make you lose your erection makes it so; just relax and enjoy the experience.")

Lance wanted to know, *"Should I put it on soft, or wait 'til I get hard? The problem is, it makes me go soft."*

Poison's Bret Michaels (one of *Baywatch* babe Pam Anderson's ex's) empathized that he doesn't particularly like condoms either, but advised waiting 'til you're hard. "It's a pain to stop in the middle of heavy petting to try and open the condom. It usually falls to the floor. The fear is that you will lose your hard-on. One can only get it on with a proper erection."

But guys are not all to blame. They're not always the one who won't wear a condom. Madonna admitted she doesn't always use one. Bobby put a condom on and the girl he was with got insulted. Steven came across a girl who wouldn't let him be responsible: *"I met this girl on my friend's boat and we were doing it in the hull, and I went to put a condom on and she said no sex if I put it on and that I was the first guy who asked for it. Are there lots of girls like this?"*

No. But there are some. They may want to play Russian roulette, but should you? Don't feel like a wuss if you insist if the girl doesn't want to. She may have motives—either she secretly wants to get pregnant (to feel loved, to trap you, to get back at men), or she wants to prove something (that she likes you, or that she's hot, or she likes living dangerously). Whatever, don't fall into the trap.

Girls don't want guys to wear a condom for all the same reasons as for the guys, because:

- They think it's what the guy wants.
- They're afraid to speak up.
- They don't want to insult the guy.
- They want to prove they really trust him (that he's "clean").
- They don't want to ruin the spontaneous moment.
- They want to feel close to him, with no barriers between them.
- They secretly want to get pregnant—to just have the baby, or to trap the guy into marrying them.

Marie, 16: *"I wanted to have sex, and I slept with this guy and we were drunk and the second time we didn't use a condom. Could I get in trouble?"*

Yes. Look at all the serious errors you made. Getting drunk. Having unprotected sex. Having sex with someone you didn't even care about, just to do it. Separating sex and love and risking your self-esteem. I hope for your sake you don't get burned by this triple whammy. It only takes one mistake to ruin your life with an unplanned pregnancy, or a deadly disease.

Another problem with condom misuse is social resistance against contraception or condom use. Some schools have suspended students who distributed condoms at class events. One distribution company once refused to handle an issue of *Spin* magazine that contained a condom and explicit instructions on its use. But there have been some advances: public-service announcements about condom use (as long as they also talk about abstinence) have been allowed on TV, TV shows have included condom use in plots, and some school districts are re-evaluating sex education programs in conjunction with parent groups.

"Do you honestly think that people are being that stupid these days, with all the stuff that's out there in the media about condoms and getting pregnant and getting diseases?"

Despite all the info out there, people are still not getting it. Surveys show about three in four college seniors and half of freshmen have had sex, yet 40 percent (more men than women) say they did it without birth control in the past year. Similarly, another study showed 40 percent of teens had sex before ninth grade but only 45 percent used a condom the last time. In a poll of twelve to seventeen year olds, almost a third reported having sex, but more than half did not use birth control their first time. Despite the CDC's widely praised 1994 TV ad campaign to encourage condom use, the same number of condoms—137.6 million—were sold as in an equivalent period the year before. Guys seem to be more responsible for the problem by resisting wearing them. Seventy percent of condom purchasers are still men, and a study of four thousand women found that women who relied on the guy to wear condoms had higher rates of sexually transmitted diseases than those who used a contraceptive themselves (like a diaphragm or sponge).

OUTERCOURSE
"What's the most effective birth control other than abstinence?"

Besides not having sex, you can have sexual contact without intercourse. It's been called "outercourse," that includes kissing, touching, petting, and mutual masturbation. You also can't get pregnant from oral or anal sex, though you can transfer diseases just as you would in intercourse.

When it comes to contraceptives, they all have a margin of error that can lead to mistakes. Even ones you think might be foolproof, like having your tubes tied or his getting a vasectomy, have led to surprise pregnancies. Condoms with spermicide have only about a 4 percent chance of a typical user having an accidental pregnancy over a year (like IUDs or birth control pills) though without spermicide, the chances can triple. With the rhythm or withdrawal methods, as well as a diaphragm with spermicide, you have about a 15 to 18 percent risk, which grows with using just foam or suppositories, a sponge, jelly, cream, or film. Unprotected intercourse gives you up to nine out of ten odds of being unsafe . . . a bad deal.

Because most methods are not foolproof, sometimes it's a good idea to use double protection (like a condom and a diaphragm).

Other methods are being tested for contraception. For men: reversible vasectomy; the male pill (hormones that reduce sperm production but may also reduce sex drive); a hormone inhibitor, or sperm immunization (a vaccine, using salmonella bacteria, that prompts the man's body to develop antibodies against his own sperm cells); and gossypol, a compound from seeds, stems, or roots of cotton plants that reduces sperm production (but also risks side effects).

For women: long-lasting hormonal injections in the bloodstream or hormones absorbed through a diaphragm-like ring in the vagina; vaccination to develop immunity to sperm; a hormone inhibitor; sterilization (injecting liquid silicone into the fallopian tubes to block the sperm and egg); and RU-486, a hormonal substance that prevents the sperm and egg from implanting in the uterine wall and induces menstruation within ten days after a missed period.

"What's the best male condom?"

Many condoms are named for ancient warriors, Egyptian leaders, and tribal heads, from Trojan to Ramses to Sheik. The name may draw you, but comfort and safety should be the top criteria. Always use latex; it protects against smaller viruses and is more resistant to tears than the thinner lambskin types. Pleasure Plus, available from Condomania, gets good reviews. You may think ribbed ones give you added sensation, but not all men or women say they make a difference. Colors and tastes and gimmicks—like the John Wayne Bobbitt condom introduced by Condomania because "no man is safe" and called "a cut above the rest"— might seem like fun for diversity, but make sure they don't sacrifice safety.

"Is the female condom better than the guy using a condom?"

The female condom (called Reality) consists of two plastic rings attached to an oversized balloon-shaped loose-fitting sheath, which, when inserted (pushing it up with your index finger as far as it can go), fits against the vaginal walls, providing a tunnel for the penis during intercourse. One ring holds it in place, blocking the entry to the cervix; the other hangs outside the vagina, covering the outer lips and the base of the penis during intercourse. Like a diaphragm, you can put it on before starting to make love, or wear it under your clothes during your date, so you're prepared, and don't have to interrupt the action or wait for him to have an erection, as you would using a male condom.

Women who like it say they feel confident because it's made of a stronger material than male condoms, and they like having another choice about contraception— so they're not at the mercy of the guy who may not want to wear a condom or be as conscientious about protection. But critics don't like that it prevents skin-to-skin contact and say it looks funny with the outer ring hanging outside the vagina. Performer Sandra Bernhard said sex with a female condom sounds like a crinkling garbage bag.

"Me and my girlfriend were having sex in rooms next to each other. Her boyfriend had a condom and we didn't, so after they used it, we washed it out. She said that was okay. I said it wasn't. Who's right?"
"My boyfriend and I were having sex and the condom broke. We didn't have another one, so he tied a knot in it and we tried again, but it broke again. Now I'm worried I could have gotten pregnant."

What's broken is your reasoning! *Never* re-use a condom. Don't tie it up, and don't wash it out and re-use it. Use a new one every time. If you don't have another one, don't have sex. If you can't afford to buy a condom or any other contraception, think about this: You certainly can't afford to get pregnant and have a baby.

"How do you properly use a condom?"
Open the package carefully. Don't use scissors or your teeth. Check the expiration date. If it's brittle, don't use it. Pinch the air from the tip with your thumb and forefinger (an air bubble trapped at the tip increases the possibility of breakage). Place and hold the rolled up condom against the

tip of the penis. Unroll it down to the base of the penis. Never use oil-based lubricants like hand cream, Vaseline, massage oil, or butter, which weaken the latex and are incompatible with what's called the pH factor in the vagina (so could cause an infection). Use only K-Y jelly or spermicidal lubricants. After ejaculating inside, hold the rim of the condom tightly at the base of the penis so no sperm leaks out, and it doesn't come off when you pull out.

"My boyfriend is very large, and condoms don't fit. What can we do?"

Get the magnums. Ask your pharmacist for them.

"I'm on the Pill. My boyfriend wants me to use that most of the month and a condom in the middle of the month. Is that a good idea?"

Absolutely not! Find out why he wants to switch off. Does he feel more confident with the condom when you're supposedly most fertile? He needs the facts: when you're on the Pill, it interrupts your hormonal balances so you are not ovulating—allowing eggs to mature and drop into the fallopian tube to meet with sperm. You have to take the full course of Pills in the dispenser for the month or it's ineffective.

"Where can I go to get protection?"

Ask a pharmacist for a recommendation about condoms, contraceptive jellies, foams, sponges. You need to go to a gynecologist to get fitted for a diaphragm, for an IUD or Norplant, or to get a prescription for contraceptive pills. Planned Parenthood can help you with an examination, advice, and samples. Retail stores like Condomania have a huge selection, with lots of fun carrying cases.

"Is there anything you can do immediately after intercourse to guarantee you won't get pregnant?"

There are two methods. "Morning-after" pills include high doses of hormones (estrogens or progestins), which are supposed to ruin the lining of the uterus so the embryo cannot stay attached to feed off it. Or insert an IUD within five to seven days after having intercourse during your midcycle to prevent any fertilized ovum from implanting. Don't use these as birth control!!!

CONDOM ALLERGIC REACTION

"I agreed to have sex with the man I'm seeing because he finally agreed to wear a condom. I bought him the latex ones lubricated with Nonoxynol-9. Now he's complaining it burns when he urinates after intercourse and he blames the condom. Could he be telling the truth or is he just trying to get out of using one?"

You are a responsible woman of the '90s, not only for insisting on using condoms as long as you decided not to be abstinent, but also for buying them yourself. Wisely, too, you chose latex condoms, as they provide the most secure protection against smaller viruses, such as HIV and hepatitis B, which cause sexually transmitted diseases. Though many men unfairly blame condoms for their losing feeling or their erection, your boyfriend's physical complaints and explanation could be legit. A small percent of people get allergic reactions to the spermicide Nonoxynol-9, which could cause symptoms like he describes. Test this by trying condoms with an alternate spermicide (like its close chemical relative Octoxynol-9) or plain lubricant, following recommendations by your local pharmacist. If he experiences no symptoms—and medical examination rules out other potential causes such as sexually transmitted diseases or other allergies to latex or packaging ingredients—the problem was likely with the spermicide and he can use the new condoms without worry. If the symptoms persist, check it out with a doctor.

An important clarification: condoms are not lubricated with Nonoxynol-9, but with various materials compatible with latex (like surgical lubricant) to which the spermicide is added. Therefore, condoms that are not lubricated do not have spermicide added, and thus do not provide added protection beyond being a barrier.

PREGNANT ON PURPOSE

Tamara, 26: *"I want a baby and my boyfriend doesn't. I want to trick him by going off the Pill. He doesn't listen to what I want anyway. He says he's scared to be a father. And he's been messin' with other girls when I been wasting a few years being his girl and I'm tired of it."*

Getting pregnant would be an irresponsible, immature, and selfish act, and an ultimate disservice to him, you, and the baby. Why should he ever trust you if you trick him into having a baby! He says he's not ready. And his actions also show he isn't ready to settle down and commit to you. Don't think it will be any easier once you have the child.

I worry about this motive for pregnancy. It sounds like you need to be mothered, and you're not getting that mothering, so instead you're turning it around and wanting to mother. Such vicarious nurturing is not ultimately going to be satisfying to you. You will end up frustrated and empty, as you realize how demanding a baby is. Find others who can take care of you—family, friends, maybe a new boyfriend. If you want a kid so badly, wait 'til you're really ready to be a mother and find a partner who wants it, too.

It was too late for Dawn, who got pregnant on purpose to trap her boyfriend into getting married, but it didn't work. Paul said: *"It was the one-night stand from hell, and I don't want to be with her and now she's saddled me with this kid that I have to worry about for the rest of my life. I really hate her for it. Does she think I would want to marry her if she tricked me? She wanted to trap me because she thought I was good-looking and could take care of her because she had problems with her mother at home. But once the baby came, I told her I'd live up to giving her some money, but I didn't want her hanging around me. I already met someone I really liked. She was fussing and screaming at the girl who almost left me over it. How do I get her out of my hair?"*

You can't—you both have a big responsibility now, and have to deal together because of the baby. She's going to need some serious therapy; the problems she had before have only escalated now with the tension of having a child and the abandonment she experiences from you. It's the only way to get her to see that she has to let go of you since you are so adamant about not being with her. Agree to go to counseling with her ostensibly to discuss a plan to take care of the child, but then to talk openly about her obsession with you.

"I had a baby and I gained weight and my boyfriend calls me 'chunky.' I'm terrified to get pregnant again, but I want another baby. What can I do?"

Don't be persecuted by his taunts. Think of yourself as beautiful. Your boyfriend has a problem being sadistic. Likely he's also immature and insecure. Tell him repeatedly, "I get hurt when you say things like that. I cannot accept your saying these hurtful things and ask you to stop once and for all. If you do it purposefully, you have a serious problem and better get help. If you don't, then please be more aware of how what you say affects me." Like I said to Tamara, I am concerned that you want to get pregnant because you really want to be nurtured and loved yourself and so will vicariously give it to a child. You need more love and attention yourself.

INFERTILITY

Many pregnancies are mistakes, but there are also many couples—one in seven, in fact—who cannot conceive.
Kelly: *"I'm trying to get pregnant but my husband is shooting blanks. He's angry. We've spent a lot of money and nothing's working. Now we're arguing. What can we do, this is supposed to make us love each other more."*

Infertility causes great strain on a couple. They blame each other, feel frustrated and insecure about not being a "real" man or woman, get stressed about spending so much money on medical procedures, lose excitement over sex that has to be "performed" (like his ejaculating in jars or having sex on particular days according to her temperature). Boost your husband's ego by telling him, "I want you, you're special." Be patient. Remind each other that these stresses happen to all couples trying to conceive.

Oliviera: *"I got married at fifteen in another country where I'm from and I was supposed to have a baby, but couldn't. I went to an old lady who helped people. She said my uterus was too tilted and put her finger in and fixed it. Then she told me to put soap on my stomach to tighten it. And to burn some special grass in a fire and sit in it to get hot. Then I had to go to a church and collect seven fruits on a stick and make a tea out of it and drink it seven days. It worked and then I got pregnant. Why did it work?"*

True enough, the concoction you made could have had herbs capable of healing. But it may have worked also because you believed it would. Studies show people who take sugar pills improve as much as people who take real medications because they think they're getting something to help. Also, stress can cause infertility, so warmth and hope may have helped you relax. There are many cases where as soon as couples reduced their stress, by accepting the infertility or adopting a baby, they got pregnant.

There are many medical means now to help couples who have trouble conceiving. One that has gotten a lot of public attention is "surrogate mothering," where a woman agrees to be inseminated by another woman's husband and carry the baby. This can be very expensive. One trio in Raleigh, North Carolina, cut costs with a unique method. The husband ejaculated his sperm into a turkey baster and the wife's sister stood on her head against a wall and inserted the turkey baster inside her—and after the second try, it worked. Don't *you* try it or you'd be a turkey.

Keith: *"My fiancée found out that we can't have children because she had a lot of surgeries, and now she's not returning my phone calls. She thinks I want to leave because her last husband cheated on her, though I assure her I want to be with her. I was dating her before she got married, and when I went away she married that other guy.*

I told her it's okay to adopt and I want her to know I'm there for her. What can I do?"

Just keep on telling her. She's devastated and thinking you don't mean it, remembering how disappointed she was with her ex-husband. Also, she likely feels guilty that she hurt you and irrationally thinks she's being punished now, for that and maybe many other things. Some people who mourn a terrible blow, like she is, pull away from others, feeling shame and fear. Don't stop your reassurances. She needs time to get over her upset over not being fertile (and thinking perhaps this means she's not a woman), purge her fears of being deprived of a family (of course you can adopt, but she has to go through this stage first), and dissipate the ghosts of past men who have let her down.

BABY ON OWN

Leon, 23: *"Two chicks I know want to have my baby. One said she just wants me to give it to her and then I don't have to do anything. She has no boyfriend and wants my genes because I'm blond and strong and cute. But wouldn't I want to see my kid after? Should I do it?"*

Better think long and hard before you do this. Can you make a baby and walk away from it? You might be flattered and intrigued by the idea now, but once the real child arrives, you may feel differently—as you suspect. Do you just want to prove you're a man, having your progeny walking around? Are you really ready for fatherhood? And is she really ready for motherhood anyway? What are the motives for having a child—is she frustrated no man loves her, so she'll be "one" with a child instead? I did a study for *New Woman* magazine once about single women, and found of 1,600 women surveyed, 40 percent said they would consider having a child on their own. It's a sign women are getting more emotionally, financially, and sexually independent, but you have to be realistic. If you did consider it, you better get expert legal advice about how it is going to be arranged after the birth, what rights you have or want to give up.

My final word on this subject, thanks to our *LovePhones* fan and buddy, Len the pharmacist, who faxed these in:

NEW YEAR'S RESOLUTIONS

I will always use a condom during sex.

I will use a new condom for every act of intercourse.

I will thoroughly wash before any kind of sex.

I will always be sure there's sufficient lubrication.

If it hurts my partner, I will stop.

If something bothers me, I will check it out.

I will take time to do something pleasurable every day.

If my partner and I are not ready to raise a child, we will not get pregnant.

Every woman should be worshipped as a Love Goddess.
—Comedienne Judy Tenuta,
Squidmistress of Studsicles

You're number one.
—Salt-N-Pepa, in concert

WOMEN HAVE FOR TOO LONG FELT LESS THAN MEN
in sex—less experienced, less in control, less able to have an
orgasm, less able to walk away from sex without longing. There
is no reason to feel less. Value your own experience, concentrate on your own pleasure, assert being in control.

If a woman feels positively about her sexuality, she is
more apt to have fulfilling love relationships. According to
a study of college freshmen at Ohio State University,
women who describe themselves as passionate and comfortable with intimate experiences in relationships are more
likely to have been in love.

So in this chapter we go over some common questions
about women and sex.

One of the biggest questions women *still* have is about
orgasm: how to have it.

The girl who does not have orgasm is not *frigid*. We say she
has anorgasmia, meaning she is *before* orgasm. That means
she can have one, she just hasn't learned, or let it happen yet.
"In all my life, I never had an orgasm. What's wrong with me?"

Nothing is wrong with you that cannot be fixed. Almost
ten million women of all ages have never had orgasm. Even

up to half of happily married women have trouble having orgasm, and 15 percent never have it. So, you're hardly alone! It's rarely a medical problem, and is usually caused by your fears, embarrassment, inexperience, or deeper problems in your life or relationships. But there's hope! You can learn: lots of treatment programs have proven that up to nine out of ten women can learn to have orgasm in just several weeks with a more positive attitude, permission to be sexual, and exploring their responses to stimulation.

HOMEWORK: Here are ten easy steps.

---

10 EASY STEPS TO ORGASM

(1) Review your personal sex history to learn who, what, where, and when you get aroused.

(2) Learn about your body parts and how they work. Examine yourself in a full-length mirror and focus on what you like instead of what you don't like. Examine your genitals, using a mirror between your legs, to see more clearly. (P.S. If you're really adventurous you can get a plastic speculum, like the instrument the gynecologist uses to look *inside*.)

(3) Treat yourself. Once a week give yourself a big treat that makes you feel good.

(4) Do sexual self-pleasure. Two nights a week for an hour spend time alone with your sexual thoughts, feelings, and touches. Start with a relaxing bath and putting lotion all over.

(5) Face your fears about sex. Will he leave you? Will you be doing something wrong?

(6) Do the "yes-no" exercise, saying yes to three things you would say no to and no to three things you would say yes to, to build your assertiveness.

(7) Explore your sexual fantasies. What exciting thoughts turn you on? What turns you off?

(8) Role-play what an orgasm would feel like.

(9) Use a vibrator to pleasure yourself.

(10) Read books and watch videos, both educational and erotic ones, to get ideas and get going.

BACKS OFF GETTING OFF

"Every time I feel I get close to having an orgasm, I pull

back. It's like a fear of going over the edge. Is there a reason for this?"

Feel confident that when you have that feeling of being about to go over the edge, you are real close to the orgasm. Sometimes this hesitation is fear—fear of letting go. It's psychological. Identifying the fear is half the battle. What will happen if you come? Possible answers: He will leave me, I'll feel empty, it won't really be good, the feeling will be over. All of these, of course, are irrational even though you think them. Correct the thinking. Feel the fear and do it anyway.

It's okay to pull back a little, but go forward again. Going too fast can be like becoming anaerobic when exercising. Like driving a car, step on the gas, then let up on the accelerator, then give it gas again; that leads to a stronger orgasm.

Jessica is jealous of her boyfriend. *"He knows what he's doing in sex. He gets hard and goes for it."*

Don't envy him, take a lesson from him. Take your pleasure, too. Like he does, go for it!

Like ex–4 Non Blondes' Linda Perry says, "I'm a woman and I get hard!"

IS IT THE REAL THING?

"How does a woman know she's having orgasm? How does it feel?"

It's not a good idea to score your orgasms. Instead, think that every reaction is legitimate. The general idea is that it's a buildup of tension and then a release; and sometimes you feel contractions. Some women have orgasms without knowing it, because they're so focused on thinking an orgasm is something other than what they're feeling. Some think, for example, it should be an explosion, as for a guy. For some it is, but more often it's different from a man's.

Let yourself go. Studies that measured women's physical responses (the temperature and pressure pulse in the vagina) found that they were responding more than they said they were. In one study, women were asked to describe what they experienced at the height of pleasure, and they said things that sex therapists rated were probably orgasm. This proves that women may have orgasm but not recognize, or admit, it as the real thing. Some of the things the women said they felt: "a warm feeling," "tingling all over," "contractions down there," "feeling so good it hurts," all the way to "I blanked out!"

Guys also want to know how to tell.

Joe: *"How do you know when a girl is having an orgasm? Is it when she shakes a lot and gives me a look like a stare?"*

There are lots of different signs and they vary from woman to woman. And any one woman can react differently on different occasions. Some women like to lie still and feel localized feelings, including contractions, in the vaginal area. They could get stiff and shivery. Others like to move about and their body may go from little quivers or shakes, like your girl's, to extreme thrashing about (like you see at rock concerts in the mosh pit). She could give you signs, by sounds or a look, so you'll know how excited she is.

Some women are self-conscious about how their face looks, because it can get contorted from the muscle tension. They want to keep some perfect smile like they see women have in the movies or in magazines. But it's really important to just let yourself go and feel whatever comes naturally. That's how the best reaction happens. *Decide* that you look great because inside you *feel* great.

SHAKE, RATTLE, AND ROLL: REACTIONS IN SEX

Chad: *"Every time I make love to my girl, she shivers and her teeth chatter. First I thought she was cold. Then I got scared. She told me her knees went jelly. Why does she do this? She won't tell me. Should I get her more blankets? Should I leave her alone?"*

She could be cold, so try the blanket bit, but more likely she's nervous about being excited (and having a mini panic attack). Haven't you ever gotten so excited and nervous at the same time about something that your knees got weak! It's a reaction of the nervous system. She probably doesn't tell you because she's embarrassed or doesn't understand it herself, or is afraid you'll be turned off or upset. Tell her that her reactions are an acceptable part of the buildup of tension. She needs to stop, let the shivers subside, and then build up the tension again. Retrain her brain to "Relax, I can enjoy this."

COMING ALERT

Linda, 23: *"This guy wants me to tell him when I'm coming. Why would I do that?"*

Good guys get pleasure from knowing that they're giving you pleasure. So the more he knows about what you like, the better he can please you. Tell him if you like. But sometimes it can give you too much pressure, called "performance anxiety," to keep him posted on exactly where you're at, especially when you're not sure yourself yet. HOMEWORK: Take one time and *tell* each other exactly how you're feeling, and another time, just *feel* it. That'll give you a good balance. The more you trust him, the more you'll be able to react freely; that's why it's so important to choose wisely and know the guy well before you sleep with him.

LITTLE MAN IN THE CANOE

"Where is that thing they say is the woman's button?"

If you spread open the vaginal lips, making a triangle frame with your fingers, the clitoris, as it's called, is right at the top of the triangle, where the inner lips (the labia minora) meet (that's why it's called the "little man in the canoe"). Since it has a head, hood, and shaft, it's like a penis. The head is the most sensitive part (as it is for most guys) and lies under a fold of skin (like a guy's foreskin) called the clitoral hood. Some peek out and some are hidden when unstimulated. The shaft is usually hidden within the hood, but you can stroke it under the skin, for pleasure, and trace it, like the roots of a tree. As with a man's erection, when the woman gets excited, or when the clitoris is stimulated, it fills up with blood and swells to several times its size. Because it has many nerve endings, it's very sensitive.

FAKING IT

"Ever since I've been with my fiancé I've been faking having orgasms. Lately it bothers me that I'm lying to him, but I'm scared to tell him the truth. Should I tell him, and can men tell whether it's the real thing anyway?"

Many men cannot tell whether a woman is experiencing her peak because they do not know exactly what a woman's orgasm is or because they are too caught up in their own arousal, as was humorously proven by Meg Ryan's simulation of an on-cue orgasm in the movie *When Harry Met Sally*. Most men rely on moans or heavy breathing as signs of a woman's excitement, but her deliberate pelvic thrusting and voluntary vaginal contractions can confuse even the most experienced partner. Since a woman's orgasmic reactions can be less obvious and more varied (from mild flutters to wild frenzies) compared with a man's ejaculations, it is even more difficult for him to tell.

Some women fake for years. A California man sued his wife for faking (on grounds of fraud, that he wouldn't have married her if he knew). She admitted she kept quiet to save his ego, but he won $242,000 (the decision was later reversed)!

Although occasional faking can be okay to save face, protect a partner's feelings, or boost self-esteem, doing it a lot is a problem. Examine why you do it. If you didn't want to be sexual to begin with, be more assertive about saying no. If you want to get it over with because you're tired, accept that orgasm is not necessary in every encounter. If you're dissatisfied, learn what pleases you.

If you fake it because you're embarrassed about how you react, you shouldn't be having sex with him to begin with (because it shows you don't trust him). If you fake to make him feel good, you're actually cheating him, because he's not pleasing you after all, so he's getting the wrong idea of what you like. Guys who find out feel foolish and fooled. Worst of all, faking cheats *you* of pleasure.

If you have faked, don't fess up—start from now, and say what you want.

Having said all that, guess what—faking is good in two situations: to jump start your own or his pleasure, and to practice how to have orgasm. HOMEWORK: Fake it—with extreme body movements, heavy breathing, screams, just to get comfortable with reacting that way.

WANTS IT WITH HIM INSIDE

"I want to have orgasm with just him inside me. What's wrong that I can't?"

You can, you just haven't yet. First know there's nothing wrong with you for not coming in intercourse with his penis alone. Only about a third of women can do that. That means seven out of ten women need other stimulation, usually to the clitoris, which after all is a real sensitive spot. The problem is that intercourse doesn't always stimulate the clitoris enough. Imagine if intercourse involved rubbing the testicles against the clitoris—then women would have more orgasms compared to men, instead of the other way around when it's the penis in the vagina!

Here are the steps:

---

10 STEPS TO ORGASM WITH A PARTNER

(1) Give yourself permission to be sexual with him.

(2) Instead of being embarrassed about your body or about saying what you want, think, "I look great" and, "However I react is fine."

(3) Identify and get over your fears (of getting close, pregnant, rejected). You won't be stuck on him if he "makes" you come, you'll be freer and stronger on your own.

(4) Switch your mind from worrying to concentrate on any spot that feels good.

(5) In self-pleasuring, picture him touching you and practice how you'll feel and behave.

(6) Concentrate on what *you* want instead of just what pleases him.

(7) Get rid of ghosts from the past: delete from your mental program stored up angers of other guys who did you wrong.

(8) Tell him what you want and like.

(9) Do affirmations: "I feel good," "I am loved."

(10) Instead of monitoring how you're performing, throw yourself into the experience.

BRIDGE TECHNIQUE

"I can't have an orgasm unless my boyfriend touches me with his fingers at the same time. I'm missing out on all the fun. What can I do?"

You are not missing out on the fun. Remember most women need clitoral stimulation in order to orgasm, which can happen either by means of his finger, yours, a vibrator, or the kind of penile penetration that pulls on the muscles that stimulate the clitoris anyway.

Use the bridge technique. Practice during masturbation. Stimulate your clitoris with one hand, and penetrate yourself with your other hand or with a dildo. Have an orgasm several times while stimulating on both sites, then over successive times, gradually take away your other finger touching your clitoris. It's called the bridge technique, a gradual conditioning, like using training wheels on a bike! As you withdraw some of the clitoral sensation, continue to imagine the sensation on your clitoris. Then gradually switch your attention to the stimulation of your vagina.

"Is it okay for my boyfriend to rub my breasts or my clitoris when he's inside me?"

Absolutely. That's the point. Pleasure anywhere, and as many places at the same time as you like or as you have hands or mouths or organs for. Some women like to be touched with the palm of the hand, with rotating motions. Others prefer more finger touches. Some like the whole breast rubbed; others like just the nipples held. You may be more or less sensitive on your nipples, preferring light or harder touches. Same variations go for your clitoris. Some women like the side of the shaft touched, others prefer the head. Some like long strokes, others like circular motions. You can mix it all up.

LOTTO SEX

Ginger: *"I have what I call 'Lotto Sex' with my boyfriend, because I have a one in a million chance I'll get turned on, and he never picks the right number! He does his thing and it's over and he doesn't know where anything on me is that moves."*

How sad. You have to write him out a more winning ticket (give him instructions), or decide he's not the right ticket for you! Yup, the guy matters, he doesn't *make* you win, but if you trust him, and he cares, he'll help spin your wheels right, and you'll more likely hit the jackpot.

Tony is a better bet.

HE WANTS TO GIVE HER THE BIG O

Tony: *"I like sex with my girlfriend but she doesn't come with just me inside. She has orgasms by herself and when I do her with my mouth, but not just with my penis. What am I doing wrong? How can I give it to her?"*

Comic Judy Tenuta: "All men should massage women at all times, and be willing to be our furniture."

I'll add, I'm happy you care that your girlfriend has pleasure, and it sounds like you're doing a great job already! Your girlfriend is normal! Many women find it so much easier to reach orgasm by hand or mouth than by intercourse, and that's perfectly fine.

You help, of course, by how much you create an atmosphere of trust and comfort, and by following my Sex Rule #2: Do unto others as they would have done unto them. That means please her as she likes to be pleased. You will help her by doing whatever she says she likes, telling her you care, and boosting her confidence, security, and trust in you and the relationship, which sets the stage for her letting go.

Tell her all the reassuring things women like to hear, "You're beautiful," "You really matter to me," "I want to please you," "I care about you." The safer she feels with you, the more she can let go.

Like lots of good guys, Max wants to do the right thing: *"Sometimes I'm fingering my girl and she gets close to orgasm and then I move and she says it's too much pressure and she loses it and gets discouraged. I feel really hurt. How do I help her get it back?"*

Let her cool down and build up again. Don't get discouraged and stop altogether. Follow her lead and trust she can lose it and get back on track, just like a guy losing and regaining his erection. Start from scratch again, using my "Driving Technique": gas it to 60 mph, then let up on the accelerator to 45, then gas it again, to 55, and so on.

"Do women like it fast and hard or slow?"

There was a popular line in a song that went, "I want a man with a slow hand . . . a lover with an easy touch . . ." A lot of women like a slow buildup, as it takes them longer in the early stages of the sexual-response cycle, and later when they get more turned on, they might like faster, deeper strokes. You have to know your woman and follow her mood at the moment.

CONSTRUCTION SEX

Gloria, 26: *"My boyfriend thinks he has to be like a construction worker in sex—drilling my cavities like a jackhammer. How do I get him to stop slamming me?"*

Get him to talk about what he thinks a man should do—a lot of uneducated guys think that the hard driving is what women like, or that it proves what a man they are! Tell him my Golden Rule #2 about sex: Do unto others as they would have done unto them. Tell him in a nice way—when you're lovey-dovey, that you love it when he does it real soft and slow, and that one time you'd like to try it *real* soft and slow, for fun.

Carly: *"I've had orgasm with different guys but not with this one I'm seeing. Why—is it his fault or mine?"*

It's both. You have to know what you like, feel confident about your body and your reactions, and let yourself go. He has to tune into you, do what you like, and make you feel accepted, appreciated, and loved. If you have an orgasm with other guys but not this one, it could mean either that you don't like him as much, or the exact opposite, that you like him so much, you're scared.

Sonic was one of the most adorable calls to *LovePhones*. He called proud that he followed my advice and "gave" his girl her first orgasm and it was terrific. *"I really gassed her, telling her I love her and she was the only one for me. She loved that. I was 'in like swimwear.' In her mind and her insides."* But, he teased, there was only one problem. You see, *"I had her on the desk, up against the drawer, going upward in her."* So what's the problem? Sounds wonderful. *"Well,"* he replied, *"now my girl wants to do it on the beach."* So, that's great. You got it down. You got it going on. Just let it rip again in a new setting. *"Well, no,"* he answered, *"it worked so well on the desk, I'm trying to figure out, how do I get the desk out to the beach?"*

Sonic's dilemma is a cute example of just how sensitive guys can be to "giving" a woman an orgasm, making it work and wanting it to work again next time.

HIS EGO

"Why do men feel there is something wrong with a woman if she doesn't have an orgasm?"

Men often score their own sexual prowess by whether the woman responds. It's a blow to their ego if he can't "do it to her." So some guys try to make you feel wrong or inadequate, to protect themselves from thinking they're not doing something right. Don't fall into that trap.

"What's the average amount of time most women require in foreplay before they are ready for copulation or orgasm?"

First off, I don't like the word "foreplay" because foreplay and afterplay imply that the activity leading up to and after orgasm is not real play, but it is. Consider all of it as legitimate as orgasm.

Next, remember every woman and each time is different. But remember, too, that it takes her about fifteen minutes to get to the same place it takes you three minutes to get to. Remember, *It's like a man is like a microwave and a woman is like a crock pot.* How quickly her excitement escalates depends on how she feels about you, her physical state, mood, where you are (to name a few). The seduction is critical.

THE LOVE MUSCLES: KEGEL EXERCISES

"When my boyfriend is trying to enter me he groans, 'Oh, Kerry, you're so wet and so tight.' I guess that means that he loves it. I heard him brag to his friend the other day over the phone that I have a 'cherry vagina.' Do men really like it tight? Will it stretch the more I do it? How can I keep it good for him?"

Men do like a vagina that grips their penis—obviously it creates friction and a tight fit that stimulates the penis when it's inside you. Enjoy the compliment. The term "cherry vagina" refers to a virgin's vagina, which, because it has not had sex or babies, is likely to be tight. As you have more sexual experience, it's better to think that your muscles *relax*, rather than stretch. And the vaginal barrel doesn't lose some elasticity until much later in life. Of course, the muscles get looser after childbirth.

HOMEWORK: You can strengthen your love muscles, making yourself tighter, with the Kegel exercises. The exercises were originally developed by a man named Arnold Kegel in 1952 to help women regain control of urination after childbirth. They work out the pelvic-floor muscles that extend from your pubic bone to your tailbone—the pubo-coccygeus (pyoo-bo-cock-see-gee-es) muscles or the love muscles—that contract at orgasm. The steps are:

STEPS TO BUILD LOVE MUSCLES

- Locate the muscles around the vagina by simulating (or actually) forcing yourself to urinate and then stopping the flow of urine to feel which muscles are contracting.
- Insert a finger into your vaginal opening and contract those muscles you located. Feel them squeeze your finger.
- Exercise 1: Like doing reps in lifting weights, squeeze these muscles for three seconds and release. Rest thirty seconds. Then repeat four times quickly again. Rest thirty seconds. Now repeat five times. Continue up to ten quick squeezes.
- Exercise 2: Imagine trying to suck something inside your vagina. Hold for three seconds. Relax. Now imagine trying to expel something from your vagina, hold for three seconds. Relax. Repeat three times.

You can make up your own variations on these exercises, like making your own weight-lifting routine. The best part is, you can do these exercises without anyone noticing—in the car at a stoplight, waiting on line at the movies, watching TV. You can also do the Kegels while he is in you.

"How can I get my boyfriend to satisfy me every time?"

Know what your own needs and sensations are and tell him exactly what to do. Don't expect to be satisfied every time and don't think about orgasm or any other goal, just enjoy each other's company and pleasuring.

FINGERING IS FINE: DIGITAL SEX

Maria, 17: *"I prefer when my boyfriend fingers me. I had a penis once and it hurt. Is this okay?"*

Digital sex is fine. Fingers can reach places and do some actions that a penis can't—just by nature of their flexibility, ability to turn, move into grooves, swivel, vibrate, and do all sorts of motions. But if you avoid a penis, that's a problem. If you had pain during intercourse, you may be nervous and tightening up.

Of course, always have clean hands and well-manicured fingernails with no jagged edges so you don't irritate or tear the lining of the vagina or the outer genitalia.

"Can a woman have thirty-one orgasms in a four-hour period, combining oral, fingering, intercourse?"

Go for it—as many as you want. Women can keep on coming. The orgasms may vary from more concentrated ones with contractions to more "full-body" or "total" ones.

"How do you get multiorgasmic?"

Give yourself a break, allowing little peaks and valleys, which are normal, but don't give up and end the sexual experience. Rest at various points, letting the tension subside a bit and then build it up again. Trust that anything that happens is awesome. Trust that your partner adores you. When they're masturbating, a lot of women find it easier to have several orgasms in a row if they use a vibrator, to keep the stimulation intense.

"Why are some women multiorgasmic and others are not?"

Some people just are more sexual, their sexual drive is higher, they are more comfortable with their body and sex, feel better in the relationship, or have more sexual experience or confidence.

"If you have your period, can you have an orgasm?"

Absolutely. Some women find their sex drive high around that time, although others find it's highest around the time of ovulation (in the middle of your period) because physiologically that's the time that nature seems to want women to desire sex more because that's the time they are most likely to get pregnant. Having orgasm can even ease some of the pelvic congestion, by the releasing of tension. But there is also some suggestion that it may extend your bleeding a bit. Ultimately, when you *feel* better about having sex, it *is* better.

"I've heard about clitoral and vaginal orgasms. Are these the types?"

Experts don't like to distinguish the types of orgasm. But, if you have to know, here's how they've been defined.

Clitoral orgasm. In the past it was believed that this type of orgasm was inferior to vaginal orgasms from intercourse. But that's not true. Orgasms called clitoral usually mean they come from more direct stimulation of the clitoris, orally or manually or with a penis or other object. They usually feel more focused, and therefore the woman can feel contractions easier.

Vaginal orgasm. This term usually refers to an orgasm that comes from stimulation of the vaginal canal, most often from penetration or intercourse. Once considered superior to the orgasm by stimulation from the clitoris, it is now known not to be better, but just another way.

Blended orgasm. This experience feels like a "body" orgasm, with stimulation and reactions seeming to come

from the entire vaginal area, spreading throughout the body.
HOMEWORK: Get one by switching your *focus* and touch.

G-SPOT
"Where is the G-spot?"

The G-spot, named for the German gynecologist Ernest
Grafenberg, who first described it, is a small mass of tissue
on the front wall of the vagina, one third of the way up. You
need to crook a finger toward the front to feel the slightly
rougher tissue there. *The G Spot* book that came out over
ten years ago made it popular as some magical spot, but
please don't think you need to find it or like it, because
many women don't.

Now the latest: when I was in India at the Third Asian
Conference on Sexology, I met researchers from Malaysia
on what they call the AFE (anterior fornex erogenous) zone,
from the top of the G spot to the cervix at the back end of
the vaginal barrel, claiming IT as the hot spot. You're supposed to slide your finger up and down that area and then
hit the G spot and repeat. In the advanced technique, you
stroke the AFE zone and then sweep the sides of the walls
in clockwise and then counterclockwise motions (starting
from the top at twelve o'clock, to six o'clock and back to
twelve). Nine out of ten women in the study got very wet
within ten minutes and a third had multiple orgasms. Other
experts think the excitement also comes from getting so
much attention and ANY spot will do!

"X" MARKS THE SPOT
*"My friend said her boyfriend tugs on something inside her
vagina. He wraps his fingers around it. What is it?"*

Here we go with more hot spots. Sounds like your
boyfriend is tugging on the cervix, the lumplike opening to
the uterus at the end of the vaginal barrel. It protrudes (like
the uvula in your throat) at certain times of the month, so he
can reach it by inserting two or three fingers palm upward.
A Chicago writer I met wrote about it as the "X" spot and

describes these wonderful tricks: the "love slide" where you gently move it back and forth, the "X massage" where you gently tap or probe the rim and opening with incremental pressure, the "love tug" where you pull on the sides, and the "love triangle" where you encircle and rotate it. All these cause stimulation of the surrounding nerves and gentle movement of the uterus—leading to what you could call a "cervical climax." Other fingers are free to stimulate the clitoris or other body parts for "blended orgasms." To trigger "Xtasy," the "horizontal slide" is recommended, where he slides on top of her, while she is lying face down, pillow beneath her hips.

"What's the best position for achieving an orgasm?"

The key to orgasm is like the three rules for real estate: location, location, location. Whichever position pleases you—mentally and physically. Usually it's best for the woman to be on top so she can guide the amount and type of stimulation. Some women like the man on top and their legs in the air or over their shoulders, or doggie-style, for deep penetration; others find these painful (partly because they press on the bladder). Some like the scissors position, with legs intertwined, so both people can move. Whatever position, it is also best to allow some access to her genitalia and clitoris so it can be stimulated along with the penetration, either by his or her hand, by the penis rubbing up against it, or tugging the muscles that pull it.

ON TOP

"My boyfriend wants me to be on top in sex. He got crazed about it when he saw Sharon Stone on top of Michael Douglas in the movie, Basic Instinct. *I'm scared to do it."*

Guys like the woman on top. One good reason is that he can relax more, and she can do more of the "work." It's the most recommended position when a guy has a problem with erection or ejaculating too quickly. Sounds like you have female performance anxiety. We talk easily about male performance anxiety—meaning men who think they have to live up to certain standards in sex, so they get anxious and can't perform at all. But women have it, too. What do you think is expected of you up there? Just relax and do what you like. Get over embarrassment about your body, and fear of being in control. Mount him like you would if you were horseback riding, and unbridle your passion.

ORGASM END

Cheryl: *"How can you tell when an orgasm is over? I don't know when to stop."*

It's generally over when you feel a wave of relaxation after a buildup of tension. But there's no rule about stopping. Keep going as long as you want.

COSMORGASM: THE COSMIC ORGASM

"How can I get that total body orgasm that feels so good? I want to be thrashing about, like my friends describe, where they feel the earth move."

Those are your endorphins—those pleasure chemicals in your brain—flowing. They remind me of my favorite line from *Miami Vice* about being "so high you need clearance to land."

It comes from a high state of excitement on the physical and mental planes. That means a lot of physical stimulation, usually after a long session of lovemaking. Your mind has to be totally relaxed and into the moment. Like listening and swaying to your favorite music, close your eyes and sway to the feel of your body sensations. Set the stage by sharing an experience that you both enjoy so you feel in tune. That could be anything from shooting pool, to a walk in the park, to watching your favorite video. If you like to talk, tell your partner your dreams—that'll get you high. Talk about what you most want in life. Or your biggest success. Let your mind say, "I love this," "I am in ecstasy," "There is nowhere else I would rather be than right here, right now," "This is heaven." Say you love each other.

Make sounds to go with your body motions. Start with

low groans. Feel the sound coming from the center of your gut. Feel you trust each other totally and do or say anything that most excites you. Let your body move as if it is directed by the energy. Give in to it rather than directing it. Then feel the electrical charges going through your body and popping off in your brain. That's the biggest natural "drug" high.

You can also "fake" (really, rehearse) what that ultimate high would feel like so you get comfortable with the way your body moves, and so you condition your mind and body to respond that way.

According to Eastern sexology, a woman's excitement goes in nine stages (compared to a man's sharp peak). After the vaginal orgasm (stage four where most Westerners stop), you stay with the feeling, trying to touch the man with every part of your body, 'til you're united and feel a "little death."

SENSITIVE BREASTS

Carla: *"My girlfriend says she feels electrical charges from being touched on her breasts in lovemaking that lead to orgasm . It sounds so great, but my nipples are flat and I don't feel much there. Is she telling the truth, and if so, what can I do to feel what she does?"*

A small percent of women can achieve orgasm through breast stimulation alone. These women, like your girlfriend, feel nerve connections between their erogenous zones. But rather than comparing yourself with her reactions, enjoy and develop your own. Every woman's sensuality is unique. Keep in mind that breasts and nipples vary in sensitivity (as in size and shape) from woman to woman, and even from your own left and right. Sensitivity is not related to shape or size, nor does it reflect how sensuous you can be. In the excitement phase of the sexual-response cycle, the breasts naturally grow in size, and the nipple, richly supplied with nerve endings, becomes erect when small muscles at its base contract in response to touch, sexual arousal, or cold. HOMEWORK: To develop more responsiveness there or in any area of your body, give yourself permission to enjoy it, focus your attention there, and experiment with different kinds of touch or stimulation while you think sensuous thoughts. Imagine the stimulation traveling throughout your body.

LOVE LIQUIDS

"I'm secreting a white fluid from my vagina when I have sex. It didn't come out with my past boyfriend. What is it?"

This could be cause to celebrate. It could mean you're really turned on. Good for you. Your lubrication is like his erection. Likely you got more comfortable with sex in general, and with this guy in particular, so you're letting yourself go and your body is showing it. Secure guys like when a woman is wet (anxious ones worry, slip out, or get threatened). You can always pump up his excitement and yours by saying, "You make me so wet!" like he would say, "You make me so hard."

Of course, it could also be some discharge from a sexually transmitted disease, or urine that could come from a physical problem, pressure of the penis against the urethra, or just inexperience about which muscles to let go. If you practice having orgasm with a vibrator, you will locate the muscles more clearly. (P.S. If you spread your lips open, you will see that you urinate from a different hole than your vaginal opening—some women, and guys, don't know this.)

Peter: *"I was making love to my girlfriend and all of a sudden liquid spit out of her like a waterfall and the bed was soaked. She got real embarrassed and ran to the bathroom, thinking she had peed; but it didn't smell or taste like urine. What is it?"*

Don't rush for the Depends: she could have ejaculated. Yes, when the G-spot reseachers put little cameras inside women's vaginal canals, they observed such spurts in some women and called it "female ejaculation," with liquid coming from the Skene's glands (different from regular lubrication), that does not smell like urine but can result from stimulating the tissue around the urethra just below the neck of the bladder. But don't strive for this, or any other type of reaction. Love every way you react. (P.S. It *could* be pee, if she isn't controlling her muscles right.)

Lorelie, 20: *"Is it normal to get real wet when you're not with someone? I wake up wet."*

Good for you. Guys get erections, women get wet. It means your body is responding, and when you're with a partner you'll both be real happy about this. A woman lubricates through the night just like guys have nocturnal erections. Some women naturally produce more lubrication than others. Enjoy yours.

Tiffany, 17: *"I get turned on by little things, all kinds of things, guys' eyes, hair, and I sit in class and I get tingly like orgasms and very wet. I have to bring extra panties to school and go to the bathroom and change. How can I stop it?"*

It wouldn't be healthy to try to turn off sex entirely, because then you'll have trouble turning on when you want. But you can learn to retrain your brain. Don't pay attention to the boys' hair and eyes that turn you on; turn your attention to something else. Realize you don't have to have sex whenever you have a sexual thought. You can stop it at any point by controlling your mental sex computer.

TOO WET

John: *"I just started with this girl and I love her and we were both virgins, but every time we make love I slip out and I can't feel myself because she's just so moist. It's a little like swimming in a pool. I didn't know this or maybe I wouldn't get involved."*

That's her lubrication. It's a lot like you having a stiff erection, so don't begrudge her! Some girls would give their eyeteeth for that. Experiment with different positions so you can feel more. Have her exercise her vaginal muscles so she can grip you more. Enjoy other ways of lovemaking. Appreciate her wetness. Say to her, "You are so wet, I love it," even if you don't believe it yet. It will make her feel good, and cycle toward making you feel good, too. Maybe you're worried about not having a big enough erection! Stop thinking about all that and you'll both react in a better way.

The opposite can happen—being too dry—like for Laura.

Laura: *"I'm real worried. I'm bone dry. Intercourse hurts. I can't do it. The more he pushes, the more it hurts."*

Of course. Dyspareunia, pain on intercourse, can come from lots of things. It can signal a physical problem—any one of a number of sexually transmitted diseases or infections (see chapter on Playing It Safe) in which case you should check it out with a doctor. Or it can be in your mind. You could be tightening up because you really don't want to have sex for any number of reasons (fear of pregnancy, not trusting your partner, insecurity). If your vagina could talk, what would it be saying? Likely, "Gimme a break." What does it need most? Maybe being loved, not just penetrated. Remember, love is the best lubricant.

UNRESPONSIVE

> A husband says to his wife, "I married you for life, now show some!"

John is upset: *"I go down on my girlfriend but she just lays there like a dead mackerel. Why?"*

She's either inexperienced, scared to respond, or really not allowing herself to let go. Encourage her and reassure her by telling her she's beautiful and that you love smelling and tasting her, and that you love when she responds!

ORGASM AFTER-EFFECTS:

CRYING: *"I've been having sex with a great guy I'm crazy about. But every time I have sex I cry uncontrollably. I think it's a good experience, because I feel relieved after, but he gets worried, asking me what's wrong and whether he hasn't pleased me and is making me unhappy. I feel it's just the opposite—that he makes me happy. What is going on?"*

I'm happy for you that you are in love and are having fulfilling sex with someone you love. Your crying doesn't have to be bad. Welcome it. Crying is purging; of course you feel relief. Women may cry before, during, or after orgasm or "good sex." Fewer men ever do this, simply because they don't allow themselves to release their emotions as women do. The crying is related to the buildup and release of tension. Women may cry before orgasm as an expression of the body letting go, instead of having a genital response. Crying during and after orgasm can be a continuation—and heightening—of orgasm. Consider it as another sign of your orgasmic expression, like screaming or laughing.

But underneath your joy could be some deeper pain that can be unearthed and purged. You could be crying for your loss of innocence, or guilt, over no longer being the "good little girl" you were brought up to be. Reassure your boyfriend that your crying is a wonderful expression of your love, and his touching your soul. Ask him to hold you, or lie next to you, rather than to pull away. Ask him to allow you to go deeper into the crying, rather than stifling it. Breathe through the tears, feel the security of his presence, and connect with the depths of your soul, heaving and howling. Remember any past losses or pains you've had. What a wonderful experience that deep purging is! How lucky you are to be getting close to it, and having a partner who triggers it and supports you through it.

LAUGHING: *"When I make love to my fiancé whom I love very much, I have the urge to laugh hysterically, but I am afraid to hurt his feelings. Sometimes I let myself giggle and I think he gets annoyed. His face does look funny in sex; he makes all these faces and grimaces. Why do I do this?"*

Because you are having fun! How wonderful! Go ahead and giggle to your heart's content. Like crying, giggling or laughing purges pent-up emotions. Also, people can make funny faces in sex because the muscle tension causes you to grimace in different ways, that you might not otherwise make. As with crying, laughing during and after orgasm is a buildup and release of tension, and thus can be part of your sexual response cycle, and even help you get more excited. Ask your fiancé to enjoy it and not be insulted. You are not laughing *at* him, so can he laugh *with* you?

"After I have an orgasm I get depressed and hate the man who gave me one. I feel 'dirty.' I have intense orgasms, hysterical crying. I wish the guy would be out of here and that I never see him again. What's wrong with me?"

What you really want is for the guy to stay—not to leave you forever. You're terrified of being abandoned—that's why you cry so hysterically—and so you consciously want him to leave so you don't get really hurt by his *really* leaving you. People who are terrified of rejection reject others before the dreaded rejection happens. You may have been abused as a child and harbor some resentment and fear of enjoying sex because of that. Allow yourself to be sexual. It's not dirty. That's an old message from your past.

Make sure you only have sex with someone you care about. Force yourself to let the guy stay. Continue to cry. Or purposefully laugh. Tell him how terrified you are of separating after such an intense experience together.

"After coming from oral sex, I curl into a ball in a fetal position. Is this normal?"

Think about what you're feeling and what that position means to you. It can show that you really got connected to some really deep primal feelings in a good way, maybe even that you felt loved or content as a baby. But it also can signal a withdrawal and a need for protection. Sex can trigger this feeling in some women who have been abused. Ask your partner to hold and cuddle you as you go through those deep emotions.

ALL GIVE AND NO TAKE

"I'm twenty-five and have been married for three years. I had sex with two men before my husband, but in all cases I was always the one giving, and never receiving. Something clicked, though, and for the first time a few months ago I got angry that my husband is so selfish and told him I want more. The real problem is, though, that even when he goes to please me, I stop him. What's wrong with me?"

Do you believe it is more blessed to give than to receive?

But women who are persistently selfless in sex may suffer from low self-esteem, intimacy fears, or co-dependency. HOMEWORK: Retrain your brain from "I don't deserve pleasure" and "If I don't give, he'll get angry and maybe leave me" or "If he does something for me, I owe him" to more constructive thoughts like, "I do deserve pleasure, I won't be afraid to ask for it," and "true love has no strings attached." Holding back denies the other person the satisfaction of contributing to your fulfillment. Why don't you "take"? Are you afraid to owe him or to be needy? Are you ashamed of your body? Practice receiving, imagining him approving and appreciating you. Then, ask for what you want. If he loves you, he'll gladly oblige, and if not, you might as well know the extent of his selfishness.

SHE COMES QUICK

Jim, 25: *"I took this girl out and took her back to my crib and expected to bone her. My cock was harder than Chinese algebra, but soon as I get in, she busts her nuts on me and I didn't get mine. What's up?"*

Some women, like men, have a short sexual-response cycle and get turned on easily, then feel satisfied or so sensitive they don't want further stimulation. Or like men with premature ejaculation, they have what could be called premature orgasm, where they reach orgasm before they really want to—in other words, it's out of their control. The reasons and cure is the same for premature ejaculation in men. It can come from nervousness about performance or distrust or anger in the relationship. If she's cutting out quickly, Jim, then maybe there's a good reason. Could you be pushing for sex too hard, so she senses she's going to be used, and she outsmarted you, and cut out faster?

As Graham Coxon, from the British band Blur wisely advised: "Why can't she come again while you're getting going?"

I usually tell you to connect sex with love, but sometimes, to cure a problem like this, you have to do an interim step and allow yourself to have sex without being overloaded with all the complicated feelings. This works well in cases where you're afraid to feel too much because you might lose the person, or you feel you have to perform in order to please them and you sabotage the experience. Other steps involve spending time in masturbation to learn what turns you on and off, with different touches and thoughts, so you can control your sexual thermostat. If one person finishes before the other, you can finish on your own or ask the partner to do some minimal activity to help you reach your peak. Don't leave the other person high and dry.

As far as not getting the feeling back right away, recognize that a "refractory period" is part of the sexual-response cycle, which means it can take a little time to restart the engine, or to reboot the computer. The amount of time differs for different people. She can keep going, or she can stay in the sexual experience with you until you're satisfed. If she cuts out quicker, likely she's avoiding you or intimacy.

TO SLEEP, PERCHANCE TO ORGASM

"If men have wet dreams, can a woman have an orgasm in her sleep? The other night I woke up in the middle of the night, feeling like my body was twitching, and then I got real relaxed. I never had an orgasm before, but could this be it? How can I make them happen more in my dreams and in real life?"

Yes, good for you, you could have had an orgasm in your sleep. Up to half of women (compared with nine out of ten men) are estimated to have at least one spontaneous orgasm during sleep at some point in their life. While this can happen at any age, some experts claim that women have them more often in their forties (compared with men in their teens and twenties)—probably when they become more confident and experienced. Sometimes women who don't have orgasms in waking life can let go in the safer realm of the unconscious dream state. But there is some suggestion that women who are more turned on in general carry that over to sleep, too! One study of college graduate and undergraduate women found that those most likely to have sleep orgasms were sexually active and had positive attitudes toward sex.

Like wet dreams (nocturnal emissions) in men, spontaneous orgasms in women are reflexes that can be a continuation of incomplete sexual feelings from the day, or part of an erotic dream.

MACHINE SEX

Bridget: *"What's the value of a vibrator and can you get addicted to a vibrator? A friend got me one for my birthday and called it 'Bridget's Widget.'"*

Your friend did you a nice favor—introducing you to a special fun toy. You can get addicted to it if you're scared of relationships and you escape into sex with your machine instead of with a person since the stimulation is so steady, reliable, and quick. But otherwise, the machine is a great way to train you to get excited and induce orgasm; the stimulation is constant because it doesn't hold back like your hand (directed by your brain) can. It's also a great aid if you want a quickie, to shorten the time for you to have orgasm, since for most women it takes longer by other methods, either alone or with a partner. Because using the vibrator helps you have an orgasm, and come quickly, it can build sexual self-confidence. It can also just simply be a sex toy, for you or him, to use on any part of your body, both to relax and to excite.

My friend Reverend Ruth Green is waiting for the talking vibrator that says, "I love you," "You're beautiful," and "Can I see you tomorrow?"

Craig: *"My girlfriend lets me use a vibrator on her, but she won't let me put my penis in her. What's wrong?"*

She obviously has a fear of being penetrated. Lovingly get her to express her fear. Is she afraid it will hurt or get her pregnant? Or that it won't work out well, that you'll lose your erection, that she won't enjoy it, or that she won't have orgasm with your penis and she'll be ashamed? Just voicing fears can make them dissipate. She may also have been sexually abused when younger, and fearful of those memories. Ask her if that's the case.

George: *"My girlfriend uses a vibrator and I want to know whether she likes it better than me."*

You're suffering from the typical threat men have that the machine can supplant them. See it as a helper, not a replacement of you.

USA network's *Up All Night* Rhonda Schear shared that she uses vibrator and her boyfriend has had a similar reaction. "Sometimes he actually mentioned that he gets a little jealous because he feels that it'll take away from our love-making . . . but he'll have to beat that!"

CAN'T FEEL ANYTHING

Michelle, 19: *"I feel dead inside in sex, and can't feel anything. I have so much love to give, but I can't let it out. I can't allow myself to be touched. My father was killed when I was seven. People said he called for me. I have so much anger inside—why did he leave me? I'm afraid to lose someone I care for."*

Any traumatic loss can make you cut off your feelings, both emotionally withdrawing from intimacy and physically desensitizing from touch. It is good you make a connection between this early loss and your pain now, and realize that you have pent-up anger that needs to be released. Have imaginary conversations with your father in which you tell him that you miss and care for him and are furious that he left you. Relieve yourself of the ghosts from the past. For moments live in the present and allow yourself to practice touching yourself and feeling the sensation. HOMEWORK: Allow yourself to feel one thing a day. Say to yourself, "I am risking feeling something. I will not die from doing this."

It's best to have sex with you being on top, to feel the sensations, so you control the amount and type of activity and can focus on what you feel. Practice having your partner's penis inside you, without moving, so you can sense how it feels. While you're on top, move around. Change position. Try the "Yoga Sun Worship" position, where you're on top and arch your back up like a cat stretching, thrusting your pubic bone against his, so you have more contact.

IT HURTS

Sarah: *"My boyfriend goes at it for an hour and I get sore and it hurts. What can I do?"*

Sex Rule: Anytime you have pain, stop, or you can get tears and infections in your vagina. And then you'll turn off to sex, expecting it to hurt next time! Don't be afraid that if you stop he won't like you or that something is wrong with you. Take a break, and do something like hug, kiss, or talk, 'til you're ready again.

Pain on intercourse, called dyspareunia, can come from a physical problem (so see a doctor) or a psychological problem (so see a therapist). Like with dryness, if your vagina hurts, what is it saying? If it's angry at your boyfriend, tell him why (maybe he's pushing you into sex).

CLOSES UP SHOP

Robert, 25: *"I've been married for two years. My wife won't let me play with her vagina. If I put my hand on her buttocks for more than a few minutes, she pulls them away. She closes her legs. I try a lot. What can I do?"*

Get her to explain what she's uncomfortable about—the way she looks, smells, tastes; how her body feels. Maybe she's grown up learning that sex was bad—an attitude hard to change at the snap of your fingers just because you got married. Maybe she fears she won't respond and will disappoint you and her. Reassure her. If she's angry with you, get that out in the open. Don't push her into sex; when guys like you do that, the woman feels used and closes up more. Chill and give her a chance to approach you.

She has to trust you so don't push too hard. She may be scared of sex, so only tenderness from you will help. Tell her you love her. Help her get comfortable by telling her lovemaking is play. Gradually introduce something inside her, by starting with small insertions (a pinky finger), and building to larger ones like your penis.

LOCKED LEGS

Terrance: *"My girlfriend's insides are too tight, I can't 'crack dem legs.' A friend of mine told me to use Adolph's meat tenderizer. He calls it the 'pouting pouch.' How can I soften her up and make the hole bigger so I can get in?"*

Jenna: *"I'm in my early twenties and a virgin. Up until now, I haven't dated very much. Four months ago I met a wonderful man and fell in love. The problem is we've been unable to have sex. We tried vaginal intercourse many times, but he has been unable to penetrate me because I tense up. I'm scared but want to have sex very much. My boyfriend has been patient, but what can I do?"*

Candlebox's lead singer Kevin Martin had advice: "Is he using tons of foreplay? And a condom? Women in the early stages of dealing with sexual experiences should get sex toys like dildos and vibrators to learn about their own bodies. The more you learn about your body, the more you can give your body to someone."

When you keep a-knockin' but you can't get in, the woman likely has vaginismus, a condition like a genital muscle cramp, where the muscles at the vaginal opening tighten involuntarily, not letting anything in (whether it's a penis or a tampon or an examination instrument). Estimated in 2 to 9 percent of women, such spasms usually come from associating penetration with psychological or real physical pain. Women who have been raped or incested often find their bodies tighten in sex. Build your trust with this man, and share your feelings. If you are embarrassed about your inexperience, tell him so; he may enjoy teaching you. If you fear being vulnerable and getting hurt, seek reassurance by clarifying his commitment to you. HOMEWORK: Relax by thinking positive thoughts about sex and closeness. Alternate these relaxing thoughts with mental images of him getting close and entering you. Picture yourself receptive. Once you are comfortable with the idea of penetration and feel adequately aroused, try slim and then progressively bigger insertions with or without his help. Take your time and control the rhythm and depth of penetration by directing his actions and using the woman-on-top or side-to-side positions. All the while, put yourself in an open mood by thinking about how you love each other.

Sometimes it's the opposite problem.

TOO LOOSE

Carl: *"My girlfriend is loosey goosey. How can she tighten up? My friend said to stick a cold cucumber in her. Would that work?"*

As I mentioned, vaginal muscles can stretch and loosen like any set of muscles. It happens after childbirth, when they had to let a baby out! I can see the point of inserting something cold; if you ever had a sports injury, you know applying cold reduces swelling and tightens the muscle, but I don't think this is the lasting cure you're looking for. Doing the Kegel exercises helps, as does changing positions, to get more "gripping" of the vagina around the penis.

VARTS

"I was making love to my boyfriend and got terribly embarrassed when all of a sudden I let out a fart. It kept happening. They were little farts, from his going in and out of me. It sounded like a fart, but it didn't smell like one. He didn't say anything, but after a few of them, he stopped making love and went to sleep. I've been too embarrassed to have sex with him again for fear it would happen."

Likely you didn't fart but had a Vart. The "V" stands for vagina. It's the sound of air expelling from the vagina, which sounds like a fart but comes from the vagina, not the anal canal. So it doesn't smell. It's perfectly normal, so you shouldn't feel embarrassed and you should explain it to your boyfriend so he's not hesitant to have sex with you either. Air sometimes gets trapped in the vaginal canal—especially during certain sexual positions—from persistent thrusting and a "tight" fit of his penis in your vagina. When the vagina loosens, or when the penis comes outside more, the air escapes, creating the sound. To release the air, have him pull out, and gently press on your lower abdomen. Then you can resume sex. Another word for this is "quiffing."

FIRST GYN VISIT

"I'm seventeen and still a virgin, and so is my friend, but she told me her mother took her to a doctor for female things the other day, even though nothing was wrong with her. She said the doctor told her every girl should go. But if I'm not having sex, why should I?"

Most doctors agree that by sixteen to eighteen years of age, girls should start having an annual examination by a gynecologist (a doctor specializing in women's health) even if they are not sexually active, because being a virgin does not protect you from infections, disorders, or diseases of the reproductive system or sexual organs.

Be prepared for what will happen. Have the doctor tell you every step she or he is doing. First you'll fill out health forms, and go into the bathroom and leave a urine sample in a cup. Then you'll go into the examining room and get undressed and put on a hospital gown. You'll sit on a special examining chair, and the doctor will first chat with you, check your heart and pulse, and do a breast exam. Then you'll lie on the table and put your legs over two stirrups so the doctor can look between your legs. S/he'll ask you to relax, and will insert an instrument into your vagina that's shaped like a duck bill (it's called a speculum), which spreads open, so s/he can see inside your vaginal walls. Ask to look inside yourself, and the doctor can give you a mirror to hold up so you, too, can see what's inside: your walls, and even up the end to the cervix. With a swab, s/he'll take a sample of cells to test. Then you'll get dressed and return to the office and talk.

Technically, you are under the care of a pediatrician (a specialist in children's health) until age eighteen, but younger teens can be referred to, or seek, a specialist, especially if they are having menstrual problems. However, young women should see a gynecologist as soon as they become sexually active, advises Dr. Gaetano Bello, Assistant Professor of Gynecology at Manhattan's Mt. Sinai

Medical Center, since the younger you are when you start having sex, and the more sex you have, the greater the risk of sexually transmitted diseases and other problems.

Since your friend says she didn't have any specific medical complaints, it may be that her mother took her to the gynecologist to get her into talking about sex, safe sex, and pregnancy prevention, because she was not comfortable doing it herself. Many teens are afraid that parents will try to find out through a doctor whether they are having sex, even if they deny it. Use your friend's experience to inspire you to reestablish trust with your own mother and to talk openly with her about sex.

Ask your friend what happened in her exam, to prepare you for your own visit. To feel more comfortable, tell the doctor it is your first time and request an explanation of every procedure before it is performed. You may want your mother present in the office discussion after your exam, since it is often difficult to absorb everything you hear, because of anxiety or unfamiliarity with medical terms.

FEMALE CIRCUMCISION

"Why don't women get circumcised like men do?"

Ouch. Female circumcision—also called clitoridectomy—is a horrible thing, removing the clitoris, and possibly parts of the vaginal lips. It's done by certain ethnic groups, mostly in the Middle East and Africa, on girls usually before age ten, in order to make sex less desirable for them. Sometimes, to ensure chastity until a bride is paid for, the opening is stitched over to keep her closed 'til she marries and the husband cuts it open with a knife or his penis.

DOUCHING

"I always worry about being clean for my boyfriend so he'll think I'm fresh. Should I douche to be clean?"

No. The vagina cleans itself. And douching too often can upset the pH balance (the balance of acidity or alkaline) in the vagina, making infections more likely.

WHAT'S SEXY?
"What's the real sexiness in women?"

Confidence. Feeling good about yourself. Feeling secure, so you don't desperately need a man, but just appreciate him when he's there.

Q: Who are the seven most important men in a woman's life?

A: The doctor because he says, "Take your clothes off."
The dentist because he says, "Open wide."
The milkman because he says, "Do you want it in the front or in the back?"
The hairdresser because he says, "Do you want it teased or blown?"
The interior decorator because he says, "Once it's in, you'll love it."
The banker because he says, "If you take it out too soon, you'll lose interest."

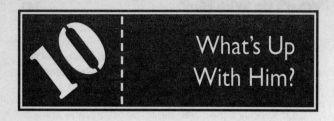

"I TELL GIRLS, 'LET ME SHOW YOU MY HARD DRIVE,' but all I got is a floppy disc."
"I shoot off in two seconds, what's wrong with me?"

Getting it up and keeping it up—men are just too obsessed with that. Get smart: the secret to male performance is not to focus on performance, but to enjoy the experience. And the secret for curing any male problem lies in a paradox: having a problem means you are out of control, but great sex requires being out of control. But the cure involves gaining control, so you can lose it again.

My basic advice is, you gotta go head to head. That means, whenever your penis is not behaving like you want it to, ask one of my favorite questions: "If your penis could talk, what would it say?"

This will help you get over those problems with impotence (not getting or keeping an erection) or premature ejaculation (coming too soon), or the other problems that trouble guys. That means figure out what one head is telling the other. If your penis could talk, what would it be saying to your brain? And what can your brain tell your penis to help it get back on track?

Fear is the first time you can't get it up: the second time is panic.

Scotty, 17: *"The first time I got with my girl, I couldn't get it at attention. It was awful. Now I don't want to do it again."*

You're suffering from the common problem guys have: one failure and they're devastated. The first time you don't have an erection you worry, the second time it happens you panic, so the next time you already are set in your mind that it won't work and it doesn't. You have to break that pattern of expecting failure. Stop thinking about it.

Like shooting hoops, concentrate on what you're doing— on your form, and the feel of the ball, and your body, and your eye on the hoop and the ball, instead of thinking, "I have to make that basket." Don't think about the goal or the outcome, just feel doing it in the best way you know.

Learn to be in the moment without worrying if you'll last. Have confidence it will return. Another day, another erection.

"My boyfriend doesn't have erections. Could it be physical rather than that he isn't into me?"

In young men, erection problems are more often psychological (fears of not performing, getting her pregnant, exposing what he's really like, making a commitment, getting close, guilt over sex, inexperience). But there can be a physical problem at any stage of the complex system involving the brain, nervous system, body chemistry, muscles, and blood flow. You can be tested for blood pressure and flow, and chemical imbalances. One key way to tell if the problem is physical is whether you have erections during the night, because normally you get them every ninety minutes! Urologists can put you in a sleep lab to measure your responses while you sleep; the latest, they give you a portable device (called a RigiScan) you can wear at home. A sloppier do-it-yourself test (called the "stamp test"): loosely wrap a strip of stamps connected with perforations around your penis during the night. If it's broken in the morning, you had an erection and the problem's likely in your head; if not, it could be physical.

Mike: *"I planned a romantic evening, and then when it came time, I lost it. I'm scared to death now. What if it doesn't return?"*

Don't worry about it. Anxiety kills erections. Confidence builds them. BRAIN RETRAIN: Force the thought, "It won't happen" out of your head, delete that mental computer program. Replace it with affirmations: "I am enjoying myself," "I have wonderful erections." HOMEWORK: Do one of my favorite techniques, "paradoxical intention," meaning do the opposite of what you really want: purposefully tell yourself NOT to have an erection. That takes the pressure off your performing, and poof, you'll get one!

There are many emotional reasons why a guy wouldn't have an erection. If your penis could talk, what would it say? "I'm afraid of pregnancy, I'm afraid of getting a sexually transmitted disease. I'm afraid of intimacy. I'm afraid I won't please her or me." You may come up with lots of excuses, not being into it, being self-conscious about people being around, or anything to save your ego.

Build your penis strength and endurance with penis aerobics: that means become aware of how it moves and works. In the shower, touch yourself to get erect and hang a (small) towel on your penis and make it go up and down by tensing the muscles in your groin area. These are similar exercises to the Kegel or pc love muscle exercises for women.

Alex, 21: *"In foreplay I'm hard as a rock, but when it comes to going in, I lose it. It happened with a girl I didn't trust where she'd been because she seemed like too much of a city girl, but it also happened with a girl I loved once. What's wrong?"*

What do those two girls have in common? Do you feel that there's danger of some kind here, that you have to be careful? With the city girl, were you were scared of what you might catch from her, or that she was too fast for you? But maybe you were also scared with the girl you loved, because you could lose her. So, to keep your erection, reassure yourself, and your penis, "I am safe."

HOMEWORK: Try the same "paradoxical intention" technique I suggested for Mike.

As the Dow Jones goes, so go men's erections.

This means guys get hard or not depending on how powerful they feel. There are many reasons a guy can't get, or loses, an erection. If it's not physical, it's fear—of performance, rejection, intimacy—or inexperience, guilt, anger, stress.

When Casey called *LovePhones* with his erection problem, Salt-N-Pepa were Honorary Love Doctors, offering advice.

Casey: *"I had a girlfriend for a year and I cheated on her once with a girl I met at a party and now I can't get an erection with my girlfriend."*

Salt-N-Pepa: "What did she do that your girlfriend didn't do?"

Casey: *"She licked my behind."*

Salt-N-Pepa: "Maybe if you and your girlfriend talked about your relationship and the things you like and the things she likes, maybe you can once again get that erection. A lot of girls have tigers inside and they need somebody to bring it out of them. Just sit down and tell each other what you really love. She may have a few tricks that she wants you to do. So, you tell her one of your boys were telling you about this and you slip out, 'Could you ever do somethin' like that?' and see what her reaction is, 'cause if she looks like she's open to it, then you're in."

Excellent advice. Ultimately, everyone in the studio agreed Casey should do it to her. If you do with your partner what your real fantasy is, then you don't have to find someone else to do it with.

Comedienne Judy Tenuta calls men "dickasauruses" for their Neanderthal obsession with their penises. "Stop thinking about it so much!" she screams.

Mike: *"I kinda go limp during intercourse and stuff, what's up with me?"*

Van Halen's Sammy Hagar advised, "When you're having sex and if you think about anything but good sex and getting horny and if you're not thinking like that, hey, it'll go down. Just like if the phone rings or somebody knocks or says 'the cops are here,' it'll go down. So I'd say, get your mind together and think of dirty pictures or think of the wildest fantasy, what you want so bad that you can't stand to close your eyes and think about nothing but that, and forget that thing going down."

More excellent advice. (Of course, Sammy admits to the opposite problem, always having it up, so that he HAS to get his girlfriend to say, "Hey, Sammy, the cops are here.")

Pressure of any kind can plummet your penis. Figure out, "What does she want from me?" Can you give it without freaking out? Or just say no and calm down.

John: *"My girlfriend wants a baby and, in the middle of sex, keeps saying, 'Hurry up and dump it' and I lose it. What's wrong with me?"*

Nothing, you lose your erection because you're being asked to come, which makes you self-conscious. Also, you probably don't want a child, so you better resolve that decision between you or your sex life is doomed to be the acting-out grounds for your disagreements.

Joanne: *"I dated a guy a while ago and used to feel his big bulge between my legs when we kissed. We split a while back and now we're seeing each other again and this time I don't feel anything. When we kiss, he moves away. I rubbed him there and came up empty. What could be going on?"*

He's obviously afraid and ashamed that you'd discover his problem getting an erection. Likely he had some traumatic experiences while you were broken up, which defeated him. Sometimes a penis can be very soft or small when flaccid, even though it could have been big when erect, so you might not feel it. Don't take it personally; hopefully with increased confidence and security in your relationship, it'll come back.

So many guys lose their erection when they go to put a condom on and then blame the condom.

Aaron: *"Every time I go to have sex, when I put the condom on, it goes down. I lose it. I tried it so many times already and it's like clockwork. I go to slip it on, and I go down. What can I do?"*

Keep it real close to the bed so you don't have big interruptions, like Jagger says, so it's not "like the referee comes in striped shirt, big whistle, and its like 'Time out! Let's get this thing wrapped.' The whole focus is ruined and you roll over and say forget about it!" Make it part of the lovemaking so it's a passionate moment. Have her caressing you constantly, so you don't break the stimulation. Stop thinking, "I know I'm going to lose it," or you will! Instead, refocus on how beautiful her face looks or your breathing, anything but your erection. Try different condoms to find one you like.

Joseph: *"I just got out of a relationship, two years, and the problem is I really can't get hard for anybody else except for the girl. Even when I think about her, I get hard. I've had sex with other girls, but I just really can't get hard. I want to get hard for other people. I want to get so hard you can bounce a nickel off my penis. What can I do about that?"*

First Brother Roger Clinton, as Honorary Love Doctor, advised: "I don't think it matters as long as you're hard enough. The key word here is 'adjust.' You got to distinguish between a hard-on and a hard time."

MR. SOFTEE

Some girls don't care how hard you are. Like Jeanette: *"I actually like it when my boyfriend doesn't have an erection. I like to hold it in my hand and rub his penis head against my clitoris and play with the head at the entrance to my vagina. He gets a little uptight that he isn't hard. Is there anything wrong with me that I like this? I like intercourse, too, but this is fun."*

Good for you and great for him. When it's genuine that you don't mind his not having an erection, and have as much pleasure, then you set the most relaxed stage for him getting an erection after all—by really having the pressure off having to perform—or feeling self-esteem that he's pleased you anyway. In fact, a technique recommended in sex therapy when the guy has an erection problem is called "stuffing"— that means you insert the flaccid, nonerect penis in the vagina anyway. Both of you should be a bit still so you and he can feel the pleasure of "containment"—the penis in the vagina without any motion, just feeling the pleasure sensations of the genitals together. Some guys get hard after this.

Of course, it's possible that women who prefer it soft and don't like when the guy is erect may have fears about intercourse or power struggles with men. But enjoying a softee as an option shows openness. Besides, it gives a woman the added time she usually needs. And she gets to be more in charge of what kind of stimulation she gets by guiding his penis.

For other girls, Mr. Softee matters:

A good man is hard to find,
but a hard man is good to find.

Laura, 25: *"This guy I'm seeing I'm in love with, but he does everything but penetrate me. He says he wants a deeper meaning to our relationship, which I love, but I also want him in me. I walk around in garters and he still doesn't go inside me."*

He may say he wants a deeper relationship between you, but his fear of penetration could suggest that he is actually afraid of deeper intimacy. He may have performance problems and is terrified to reveal them to you, for fear you would reject him. Get him to say what his fear is. Then have him put his fingers inside first, to quell fears of danger (like testing the waters by putting your toe in first). Go slowly in progressive sexual encounters, putting his penis closer and closer to your vagina, and slowly inside. Let him guide his penis with his hand, and yours over it. Once he is inside, experience what's called containment—you lying still and him feeling being inside you, and getting that it's safe, before you move around a lot.

Some guys fear something bad will happen inside that big dark hole. They actually fear "vagina dentata," that the vagina has teeth and will bite them off. (The penis parade outside Tokyo is built on the myth that whenever suitors had sex with a princess, their penises were bitten off until she was "cured" by a common smithy, who carved a steel phallus that removed steel teeth from inside her—and won her as his bride.)

Steve, 28: *"I can't have intercourse with my wife. It turns me off, and I haven't been with her for a year. I think of her more like a sister. But I can get hard with my girlfriend."*

You have the Madonna-Whore Syndrome (see chapter on Got the Hots For . . .). If you can get hard with one partner—your girlfriend—we know you don't have a *physical* problem turning on to your wife. It's in your head. You said the key: you turned your spouse into a sibling. Women do this to their husbands, too, so you become unable to have sex because it seems like incest and you look for an affair where you can have sex without fear of incest.

HOMEWORK: Change the channel in your brain when you see or treat your spouse like a sibling. Deliberately block it out of your mind and replace that picture with that person as a sex object.

HER REACTION

Rich: *"I can't hold an erection for more than thirty seconds and I'm afraid I'm going to lose my girlfriend. She said, 'If this doesn't get better, it's over.' What can I do?"*

Get a new girlfriend. What kind of pressure is that for her to put on you? How would she like it if you told her if she doesn't have an orgasm she's history? The best way for her to react when you don't last long is to tell you she loves sex with you however long it lasts (to build your security) and to make love using the stop-start method, where you tell her to ease up on the excitement a few seconds before you feel you're going to come (the point of ejaculatory inevitability) so you can build up again. Most of all, she should make sure she's satisfied so she's happy, and not attach her ego or measure her attractiveness or your love by your staying hard long. Change the idea that intercourse is the be all and end all, to enjoy all other kinds of contact—like let her play with your penis even when it's flaccid—it can be great stimulation for her to rub it against her clitoris. If she really needs something stiff in her vagina longer, use a dildo. If she supports you and you do your part, then you'll both get what you want.

BLAMES HER

Maria: *"My boyfriend's penis goes dead inside me. He can't stay hard after five minutes. Is it my fault, maybe I'm not good enough for him? He blames me and curses at me saying he never had this problem with other girls."*

He's just trying to save his ass by blaming you. Just like it's the woman's responsibility to have orgasm, it's the man's responsibility to have his erection. You're not the cause. It's mean of him to blame you. He's trying to cover up for his own problem. I don't like that he says that to you; it's a bad sign for the way he is. Blaming others must be a characteristic of his in other ways, too. Not good for your future.

Educate him. Correct him calmly saying it is not your fault. Believe inside yourself that you are attractive. Figure out what he's afraid of, like being close, making you pregnant, not performing well enough. He's going to have to correct his own thinking and distract himself from negative thoughts in his own head to thinking positive, loving, sexy things that will keep him hard.

INJECTION FOR ERECTION

"For the last three years of our marriage I haven't been able to keep a good erection. My doctor said there's nothing wrong with me, and I enjoy sex with my wife, so I'm at my wit's end. Some guys in the office were joking the other day about a shot you can take. Is it for real?"

Yes, shots are actually becoming a rage for erection

problems—and they work! The most effective one used these days is called Prostaglandin E1, which works by dilating the blood vessels to increase blood flow necessary for erection. The shot (called penile injection therapy or PIT) is given directly into the tissue of the penis using a syringe and a small needle—it doesn't hurt. Originally they were only given by doctors, but now guys (or their partners) can do it at home. Also originally it was only for medical problems, but now you can get them (if you qualify) if you can't get it up for emotional reasons, to give you a jump-start. The shot has worked for thousands of men, giving them a stiffy for up to an hour and a half (and more with larger doses!). P.S. If it stays too long—four hours—which can happen, it's called a priapism and it's a red-alert medical emergency!

If a guy has real physical reasons for why he can't get an erection, implants that are surgically put inside the body are a possibility. Stiff rods were once used; now, there are inflatable ones, where the guy can press a spot on the penis or in the scrotum and liquid flows into tubes inside the penis; then he presses another spot and they deflate.

Experts are testing lots of other methods to help erections, including antidepressant medications (think how it makes sense: if you're less depressed, you'll feel sexier), topical creams, gels and suppositories put into the urethra (more expensive than the shots), and things called oral alpha-2 blocking agents that act on the central nervous system.

With any of these, you really should work an any emotional problems you have getting it up, by increasing your confidence, giving yourself permission to be sexual, and getting over any angers or fears. And of course, it's always wise to see a urologist and a sex therapist.

WOOD FOR A WOODY

"I heard about a tree that can help you get an erection. What is it?"

It's a tree extract called yohimbe, from the yohimbine tree, that's supposed to act like a vasodilator, allowing more blood to flow into the penis. It sounds exotic, but it hasn't worked so well so far.

And minoxidil has also been tried, but seems to be better for the hair on your head than swelling your other head!

> *An egg takes three minutes, why does he?*
> —A woman on a Minneapolis TV show I did

Joe: "*I come in two minutes. They call me 'Joe's Garage, screw 'n scram.'*"

MINUTE MAN: PREMATURE EJACULATION

"I was with this girl and I was just kissing and feeling her up on her breasts and I came all over my pants before I even got into her and then she went and told everybody. Now they put a sign over my dorm door that says 'Minute Man.' Hey, that's not fair. How long is a guy supposed to go?"

Minute Man's story is a common one. It happens to men of all ages and in many situations. It's really an "uncontrolled" ejaculation. The key is controlling your timing. It's not about having to last a defined amount of time. Only that it should be when you want to, and long enough to satisfy you and your partner.

So many guys are worried about—and experience— coming too quickly. They want to have the "Energizer" penis that keeps going and going . . . Romance king Fabio warns men, "You should last all night." But most guys have experienced premature ejaculation at least once, if not more. When rocker David Coverdale was an Honorary Love Doctor on *LovePhones*, he admitted the worst sexual experience he ever had was premature ejaculation. It should make you feel better to know all types of guys of all ages and with all types of jobs have had it happen!

Extreme's Gary Cherone knew the "squeeze" technique. When caller Darryl complained that "I can't stop when I'm about to come," Gary suggested he use this special technique. "You have to pinch the head of your penis, like putting a kink in a hose. You hold the head of the penis and pinch it. You'll get it after you practice awhile. Then you

change it around and you have your girlfriend work at it."
New Order bassist Peter Hook recommends doing oral sex
beforehand, to help him, and her.

Besides the squeeze, there's the stop-start, where you
stop stimulating yourself when you feel you are getting too
excited, close to that point of "ejaculatory inevitability"
when you will not be able to control the semen coming out
(you practice in masturbation knowing that point). That
feeling is caused by semen pooling at the ejaculatory duct,
like stallions at the starting gate. Then you start up again.
It's like using the control-alt-delete function on your computer to reboot it gently.

Remember the principle of curing this problem: it's a
matter of control (controlling the level of your excitement),
where you gain control so you can lose control again. That
means you have to pay close attention to what you feel, and
after you know what you're doing, you can give up that
attention and throw yourself into the moment again.

A *LovePhones* caller, Bill, had the hang of the Rolls-
Royce technique: the "Million-Dollar Point" or Jen-Mo
acupuncture point. When you feel that urge coming on, you
push two fingers on the perineum (between the scrotum and
anus) until the throbbing stops. The fluid stays in the
prostate and the semen gets reabsorbed in the blood. In a
look-ma-no-hands variation, you bear down and pull up
your internal muscles. Locate them now by bearing down as
if to force yourself to pee, and now pull up as if to stop the
stream (see details on doing the Kegel exercise reps in the
chapter on What's Up With Her).

Or you do the "Testicle Tug," pulling them gently away
from the body. HOMEWORK: The Dance of the Testes. Take a
bath and relax. When you're done, put on soft lights in your
room, stand feet apart, shoulders rounded, testicles dangling
freely. Inhale freely and visualize the breath going down into
the testes and raising them, exhale and think about lowering
them. Repeat nine times for three repetitions.

Joanne: *"I'm with this guy who is very small and he only
lasts two minutes and I don't have an orgasm. That's a lot*

all put together. But I like him. I think he's feeling badly about it. How do I help him feel better?"

Singer/songwriter Tori Amos: "I think you should seduce him. You know how we as women have this fantasy that the hero is going to come in and just lush us up, know every move with every part of his body, and all we have to do is lay there and moan. I think that we should see the men in that role sometimes and really show *him*. I would give him the most wonderful head he has ever had in his life. And I would say, 'Baby, here. This feels really good.' And just show him constant reinforcement with what feels good. And I wouldn't criticize, I would just keep saying what feels good and show him. And if you are finding resistance, Joanne, then maybe he is not the right sexual partner for you and you might have to look at that down the line. But I would really try and give this a chance."

It's not good to measure yourself against others, but people love to do it anyway. According to the 1994 Sex in America study, 65 percent of men age 18 to 24 said their last sexual event (the whole sexual episode, not just intercourse) lasted fifteen minutes to an hour, 31 percent said it was an hour or more, and only 5 percent said it was less than fifteen minutes. By age 25 to 29, 7 percent said it was less than fifteen minutes, and 26 percent said they went an hour. By age 50, only 5 percent of men went the hour. At all ages, the majority reported fifteen minutes to an hour. Interestingly, the women all reported slightly less time, but still mostly fifteen minutes to an hour.

Bob: *"I come in about thirty seconds and my girlfriend doesn't say anything, but I see the expression in her face and she looks kinda pissed off. Is that normal?"*

It's understandable that she'd be disappointed, but important that she not get upset, because that would escalate the pressure on you. MTV host and comic Bill Bellamy, as Honorary Love Doctor, was supportive: "It's positive that you noticed something in her face. I don't think you should be 'Oh God, I'm bad.' You and your girlfriend can work it out together. Say to her, 'I noticed you looked a little disappointed there, per say, we'd like to hold a meeting here about two-thirty. We need to talk about this because I don't like that face.' Then teach her to touch that spot in your perineum to last longer."

Other good things to do: spend time pleasuring yourself on your own to learn what turns you on and off, with different touches and thoughts, so you can control your sexual thermostat.

HOMEWORK: Use the technique I love, "paradoxical intention." Make yourself come real fast. Say to yourself in masturbation, or to a trusted partner in sex, "We're going to do it real quick. Let me see if I can break my record and come in two seconds. Or before I get in." What this does is take the pressure off, and also help the guy focus on what it feels like to be in control of his timing—so he can work well on the other—squeeze and stop-start and muscle training—techniques.

Coming too soon can be "situational," which means it happens under certain circumstances or with certain partners. Usually it's when you care too much or don't care at all.

Donna: *"My boyfriend has premature ejaculation and said it doesn't happen with other women. But then he also tells me that he loves me more than anyone, so this doesn't jive. Could he be lying that he doesn't love me?"*

A guy may come too fast in many different situations. It depends on what he's thinking. It is entirely possible that he loves you more than anyone and that's why he can't last long inside you. He's terrified that he won't perform or please you or that he'll lose you, which makes him lose control.

Those guys are often able only to last long when they don't care about the woman, because that takes all the pressure off them. He doesn't care what happens, so he can allow himself to behave naturally and nonstressfully. If his penis could talk it would say, "It's safe in here, fella, no worries, who cares what happens." Sounds like this is your boyfriend's case. Reassure him that you know he cares and that he can relax and that sex can be quick or long, it doesn't matter to you.

Then there's the opposite; guys who can function with someone they care about because they feel safe, but ejaculate quickly in a scarier, less secure situation, like in an affair. Their penis says, "Watch out, could be trouble, better get out quick."

"Should I think about the Knicks scores? Or get those creams like Stay Hard, to rub on?"

No. Switch to *less* exciting thoughts, not distracting ones; focus on how your elbow feels, not the ball scores, so you stay in the sexual experience. Desensitizing creams only deaden your senses, and get into your partner to numb him/her, too; you want to *feel* pleasure, not kill it.

"I come too fast. Could it be because I'm uncircumcised? Some people say if you're uncircumcised, the penis is more sensitive in sex. If I got circumcised, would my penis be tougher and I could last longer?"

No. There is no conclusive evidence to prove that the penis is any less sensitive if the foreskin is removed. Some studies have found no difference in men's sexual responsiveness, though self-reports vary greatly, depending on factors like experience, reactions of partners, and preference for appearance.

Corinne: *"I want to help my boyfriend keep his erection and last longer, what do I do?"*

Carry on with lovemaking, no matter what, to place importance on other things. Don't insist on his lasting longer. Tell him he can come quickly the first time, and go again. Do the "stop-start" and "squeeze" with him, with you on top that further takes pressure off him. Over a quiet dinner, get him to talk about his fears (of rejection, pregnancy, commitment). Reassure him you love being with him no matter what.

HOMEWORK: More techniques for getting it up and staying there:

Focus on your sensations in different parts of your body. Do you know the intense concentration of shooting hoops? Do the same in sex. Relax, feel the flow through your shot.

And how's this for a real irony: Do sex without emotion. Yes, just pretending of course. But detach all the emotional baggage ("Will she like it?" "Will I have to make a commitment?" "Will I get rejected?"). Then, do sex flooded with emotion, called "implosion," like flushing all the fears out of you.

Here's something from the Orient most westerners think is silly: the Deer Exercise. Sit on a chair or stand and rub your hands together, grasping your testicles with your right hand, and rubbing your left hand on your stomach an inch below the navel 81 times. Then reverse hands and rub in the opposite directions and finish by pulling in the anal sphincter.

HE RESISTS RELEASE: RETARDED EJACULATION

Many guys are "Minute Men" while some have the opposite problem; they're "Johnnies Come Lately."

"I've been seeing this guy for a few months, but he has come only three times when we have sex. He says that he enjoys everything about our lovemaking and loves women, yet it bothers me to no end that he doesn't come with me when he has admitted that he does on his own, sometimes even three times a day. I can do him orally for a half and hour and finally I said, 'Forget it, I can't do this anymore.' I like him a lot, though he could go for weeks being affectionate without getting close. Is he using himself up on his own or is there another problem?"

So what if it was taking him a long time? He could be suffering from performance anxiety, stress, fears. By being mean, you only made the problem worse. You wouldn't want him to say "forget it" to you if you didn't have an orgasm, would you? Tell him instead that he can have all the time he needs, and that you won't get tired—just like what women need when they don't orgasm with a guy! Switch to another love-making position (to rest your mouth) and then go back to it.

Doing it on his own does not necessarily drain his desire for you; obviously he finds it easier to hide, making me suspect he's frightened of letting you really know him, protecting himself from needing you or from not performing well. Such "retarded ejaculation" is estimated in about 4 to 9 percent of men.

HOMEWORK: As with men who have erection problems, take the pressure off by telling him he doesn't have to perform (permission leads to pleasant surprises!). Don't blame yourself. Stay near him when he does himself (to build your comfort together) and for him to instruct you on how to pleasure him. On some quiet evening, discuss any fears of intimacy he has. Expressing fears can make them evaporate.

"I can't come when I have sex, only when I do it myself. It takes me hours. What can I do?"

Follow my favorite "Penis Talk" technique: if your penis could talk, what would it say? Likely it would say, "Whoa, buddy, be careful. It's dangerous to be in her hands, who knows what you'd owe her if she made you come? Don't get too close. You could get hurt or rejected. You could get her pregnant. You could get a disease. You could get trapped. Don't give her your goods." Then talk back to your penis, saying, "You don't have to withhold your pleasure. Seize the moment" (as women do to learn orgasm). Give yourself permission to be sexual. Fantasize when you are masturbating that you are with someone and letting go. Ask for what you want from a partner. Let out your emotions. Scream what you feel and eventually your ejaculate will spurt out, too! Do the Perelman "hand switch" technique (if you're a rightie, use your left hand), to learn how you do it, so you can get the same stimulation with your partner.

HOLD ON, I'M COMING

"When I masturbate, I get stuff coming out even if I'm not cranked up all the way. How can this be?"

What you got is seepage, not sewage—meaning it's legit stuff! It could be your pre-ejaculate, which is a reflexive emission, but you could also be excited enough that your ejaculation reflex triggered, even without all the blood filling your penile tissues, causing a full erection. Appreciate it and you won't create that anxiety that plunges men into erection problems. But be sure you give yourself enough time between erections.

And it's not a great idea to purposefullly continue to make yourself ejaculate without a full erection, since you'll make your body used to responding this way and then you might have problems when you want to have sex with a partner, and you want to have a stiff erection before you come.

Of course, you should always check out if there's a medical reason why blood doesn't fully fill your penis. Perhaps, too, you are not stimulating yourself enough. If you're using two fingers, try your whole hand, with one hand on the shaft and another on the head. Coordinate orgasm and ejaculation by paying attention to your level of excitement and holding back at the moment you feel you are going to let go, letting it subside, and then building back up again. Gain control, and then lose control again.

COME AGAIN

"How soon after orgasm is a man ready to get an erection again?"

The time between the end of one sexual-response cycle to the beginning of another—the refractory period—is usually about twenty minutes, when the body rebuilds its semen supply. Three different body parts have to get busy! But it varies—some can get it up again right away—usually if they have not totally ejaculated—and others take longer, with the time increasing with age.

WOODY WON'T GO DOWN

"I get hard all the time in class. I'm not thinking about sex.

But then I think I should put my hand down there and do it.
Should I?"

Erections happen sometimes as a reflex, especially when
you're young and have those raging hormones. Just say,
"Oops, there it is," and go about your business. It'll go down
by itself. You don't have to finish it off, nor think it down
(because then you'll have problems when you want it up).

MAN'S MULTIPLE

"You know how women have always been accused of hav-
ing 'penis envy'? Well, my guy admitted to me the other
night that he's jealous of women, because we can have
many orgasms while he can only have one. Please make me
a hero with him by telling me how he, like the Energizer
Bunny, can keep going and going and going."

Any man can have multiple orgasms, though few do.
There are actually two types: discrete, where the heart rate
returns to a resting state, and continuous, where the heart
rate remains high. Here are the two secrets to achieve them.
First, a guy doesn't have to ejaculate to have orgasm.
Redefine orgasm as sustained pleasure, staying in action
during the "downtime." Research showed men rated their
response as only one or two on a scale of ten when they did
not ejaculate, while machine measures of their respiration,
blood flow, and pelvic activity indicated an eight or nine,
proving that without ejaculation, men missed out on their
high.

The second secret is controlling the timing of his release to
delay ejaculation or emit smaller doses using the "stop-start,"
"squeeze," or Kegel exercise techniques. Think of it like
bouncing on a diving board before jumping off. But before you
and he try out for the Orgasm Olympics, do not belittle what
you have; one good go-round can be as fulfilling as a multiple.

CUM AMOUNT

"My boyfriend is obsessed over how much ejaculate he has.
If I use my diaphragm, after we have sex he asks me if I

want a napkin. If we use a condom, he checks the condom to see how much cum he has, and holds it up to me. He wants me to ooh and aah about it. What's wrong with him?"

He's measuring his manhood, ability to please you, power, and whatever by the amount of his ejaculate. He wants you to appreciate him. Your "ooh" about it obviously has great implications for boosting his self-esteem. Do it. He gave you the key to making him feel good.

The average amount of ejaculate a guy emits is about one teaspoonful. But the amount can be genetically determined, and affected by many things, including, age (older men spurt less), how long you're excited before you come, the amount of time since your last ejaculation (if you already came within the last hour, you'll have less this time), and your physical state. Let him repeat, "I am potent" (no matter how big my load is).

NIGHTTIME ACTIVITY

"I often wake up with a stiffy. Usually it's a piss hard-on where I have to urinate right away. But if I got erect, doesn't that mean I was excited in my sleep?"

Not necessarily. All healthy males—from infancy on—get erections during their sleep, every night, in fact, every ninety minutes—usually in conjunction with what's called REM (rapid eye movement) sleep or the dreaming stage of sleep. That means the average penis of a healthy man is "up" almost two hours a night. They happen no matter what you're dreaming, and are frequent for teens, though continue for older men, too. They're often called piss hard-ons just because in the morning you also wake up with the need to urinate.

"I wake up with wet dreams a lot. Once I remembered that I was thinking about four girls all going down on me, and just as I was shooting off, I woke up and I was really coming. Other times it happens I can't remember thinking anything. I just wake up in the wet spot. How come?"

A wet dream doesn't always mean you're horny and want sex. Called nocturnal emissions, wet dreams are reflexive ejaculations that can happen in the middle of sleep or waking up, that are probably triggered by the limbic system in the brain, that you don't have control over. You can have three types of sleep sex reactions—the wet dream (an ejaculation), or an orgasm without an ejaculation (a so-to-speak dry wet dream), or just erections. No one knows why they happen, but it could be due to a build-up of sperm, or a repressed sexual fantasy or behavior (like your fantasy of four women making love to you, a common male fantasy).

Researchers estimate about nine out of ten men (compared with only up to half of women) have had at least one wet dream in their lives, more commonly in teens and twenty year olds (and women in their forties). In one study, some college men worried that wet dreams were sinful or wasted their semen; but they're healthy and pleasurable.

Richard was upset he never had it. *"I never had a wet dream. Is there something wrong with me?"*

No, my *LovePhones* co-host Chris Jagger doesn't have them either, and he's very sensual and sexual. If you have normal night erections, there's nothing physically wrong. You can't necessarily bring them on, but you can make it somewhat more likely by falling asleep thinking sexy thoughts, preconditioning your brain.

"Sometimes my boyfriend gets up in the middle of the night and wakes me up to have sex. I used to give in but now I started to say no, because I get too tired in the day. So just because he had one, does that mean we have to have sex? How can I get him to stop having these erections or to stop waking me up?"

Reassure him that every erection does not have to be satisfied with ejaculation, or intercourse. He won't lose his touch if he lets it go unattended. If he stays sleepy without doing anything to touch himself, the erection will go down. If he needs the release, he can masturbate, letting you sleep.

I'm sure you wouldn't mind being awoken for a nice interlude once in a while—so reassure him that it's not a rejection of him and he can surprise you occasionally, but to please be considerate of your schedule.

PLEASE PLEASE ME

"What makes for a guy's terrific orgasm feeling?"

Pleasure comes from the contractions of the muscles around the urethra and the expansion of the tube from the volume of the semen pulsing through it. Psychologically, it comes from his thinking and feeling that he is having the best time. Hopefully, he adds the spiritual element of feeling intimacy with you.

MALE HOT SPOTS

"Do men have a G-spot like women do?"

Yes, it's their old friend the prostate gland. Funny that it should be associated with pleasure, since it's a site of problems, too (prostatitis, prostate enlargement, or even prostate cancer). Since the prostate is located inside the body at the base of the bladder, you can transport him to heaven by rubbing the "in-between spot"—formally called the perineum, the area between the base of the scrotum and the anus—or by slight insertion into the rectum. It's also called the " 'taint" spot: it " 'taint the penis and 'taint the asshole." This is why some guys may like butt plugs or manual anal stimulation.

Another booster for his bliss: the frenulum—that thin strip of skin on the underside of the penis right where the rim of the head connects to the shaft. Use a well-lubricated tongue or finger, and watch him writhe!

Doing the Kegel exercises can help turn him into a He-Man sex machine. I mentioned them for help with quick shots (premature ejaculation), but they are also good when you have no problem. Exercising the muscles in your groin area makes you more aware of your body, and helps you gain control over how and when you get excited!

DELAYED REACTION

Kyle: *I had a weird experience where I had a great orgasm and five hours later I had another one, when I wasn't having sex. It was really deep. I didn't have an erection but felt this really intense throbbing around the base of my penis. What was it?"*

Great cheers for you! You had a delayed—but cosmic—orgasm. It can happen when the pleasure was interrupted, or when you keep at it so your body is in a continued high state of arousal. The body stores experiences, like sense memories, so just the thought of your extremely pleasurable sexual experience can trigger your physical responses into orgasm at a later time (it's also called "thinking off").

TESTOSTERONE SHOTS

"I'm only twenty-eight and still attracted to my girlfriend I've been with for five years, but where I used to fancy myself a stud, I now feel more like a dud. Can I get some testosterone shots to get back the 'raging hormones' I had when I was younger?"

Testosterone is the so-called male hormone produced in the testes that is responsible for male secondary sex characteristics like body hair, body fat, muscles, and genitalia. It plays a role in sex drive, but should only be prescribed if you don't have enough. Normally, you're producing enough from around age thirteen through the rest of your life (though less as you get into your sixties). Deficiencies in young men are rare, but can be due to various conditions (like undescended testes), illnesses (like mumps, cancer), chronic alcohol or drug use, or accidents. You'd notice low energy, muscle weakness, and disinterest. If you took it and didn't need it, you'd cause a problem—because your glands would STOP producing it, and you could get shrunken testes (called "raisin nuts"), irritability (called "'roid rages"), increased breast size, decreased sperm, hair loss—ugh! Consider other ways to peak your desire—relieving stress, fantasizing, doing fun things.

STILL GOING

Tammy, 25: *"I married a guy who's sixty, originally for his money, but now I fell in love with him. Now he's having problems with his erection and I don't want to cheat on him because I love him. He can only get it up with oral sex. What should I do?"*

Help him get hard with oral sex, and then when his erection is firm, subtly slide over him and insert him inside you. If he loses it, resume oral sex again, alternating the two experiences. Men go through some changes as they get older (erections that are not as quick or hard), but like women, men never have to retire from sex. He may be going through some fears that he is "losing it," so you have to reassure him a lot that he is sexy, that he can still perform, and that he won't lose you. Find out whether any medications he may be taking interfere with his erections. There is always the possibility of using penile injections (or medications to cause erection) as a way to help him restore his confidence.

A hard man may be good to find, but
a good man is hard to find.

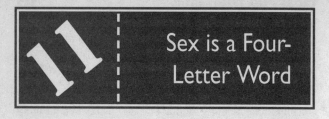

WHAT ARE TWO FOUR-LETTER WORDS FOR SEX? The first ends in K? It's TALK. You have to communicate well to have good sex. The second is LOVE. In this chapter, learn how to do both of those.

When it comes to sex talk, here are Dr. Judy's **Two Rules about Sexual Communication:**

(l) Do unto others as you would have others do unto you. That means treat others the way you would like to be treated. Offer the three R's you would like extended to you: Respect, Responsibility, and the Right to say yes or no. This rule also means you should show your partner what you would like by doing it to them. For example, if you want to be kissed softly, kiss him softly. Another example: don't push anyone into sex, because you wouldn't want to be pushed yourself.

(2) Do unto others as they would have done unto them. In other words, be sensitive to what the other person wants, instead of just doing what you want, or assuming they also like what you like.

(These may sound contradictory, but they're not; follow both.)

In every situation you face, remember also the Dr. Judy Law of Communication About Upsets: what you express can evaporate; what you resist, persists. This means that getting a bad or upset feeling off your chest helps relieve it. But if you try to hide or repress it, it will keep popping up in different forms or disguises.

"How do I get my boyfriend to be responsive to my needs in bed?"

"He doesn't touch me right. How do I tell him to stop?"

"I don't want to do that sex thing with her anymore. What do I say?"

So many people call or write me with things they want to tell a partner but don't. Notice I said they *don't*, because of course they *can*. They just choose not to. They're afraid, embarrassed, worried about the other person's response, or not used to saying what they feel, think, or want. Don't expect your partner to be a mind reader. You have to say what you feel. What are you afraid of? How do you think the other person will respond?

Here are the steps: (1) Recognize what you want from someone. (2) Rehearse saying it. HOMEWORK: Pretend the person is in the room and tell him or her what you want or ask for what you want. (Say it aloud to yourself in the shower so no one hears, or practice with someone you trust.) (3) Feel any fears, but go ahead and say it anyway. BRAIN RETRAIN: Instead of thinking, "I'll be shot down," think, "This'll be awesome."

SPEAK UP

What do women want? Candlebox lead singer Kevin Martin says, "During sex, I ask her what she wants. I'll try anything." Green Day bassist Mike Dirnt agrees, "Ask her what she wants." More likely it's communication.

Cherise: *"My last boyfriend used to go down on me in a particular way with my hips up in the air and sucking on me and this boyfriend doesn't do it. I really miss it. What can I do?"*

It's easy! When you're making love, move yourself in that position, and tell him lovingly you'd love it if he kissed you there and tell or show him what you want. Don't say you did it with someone else, or he'll get threatened. Establish "sexual signals"—messages by sound, looks, touch, words, or movements—that say clearly what you feel, like, and want. Ask for what you want using "I-talk"—

stating what you want by starting the conversation with "I." Repeat after me: "I would like it if you . . . "

Why can't you tell your boyfriend or girlfriend what you want or that you're scared or angry? Why can't you tell your friend how you feel? Why can't you tell your mother or father what you did? So often we need permission, support and encouragement that what we want to say is okay. Have the guts to say it.

Arlette: *"I'm afraid to tell my boyfriend he's fingering me too fast because he has a giant ego that's easily bruised."*

Don't get stuck in the old myth that men don't want to hear a woman say what she likes. More men today welcome a woman being more assertive about sex. Though lovers are sometimes magically in sync, it's a myth that love means never having to ask. But it is also true that guys have fragile egos and can get real sensitive being told what to do—"a few inches to the right, no, not there, move to the left"— because they immediately think that means they're not a good lover. So you have to reassure him first, "You're a great lover," then add directions cloaked as approval, "When you do it that way, it feels best."

Always say what you like, so the person can feel confident they're doing it right, instead of saying what you don't like, because that negative will only get fixed in their head. If you say, "Don't finger me fast like that," what does he think of? Doing it fast. It's like saying "Don't think of a pink elephant," and right away what do you think of?

Take his hand and put it over your hand, showing him what to do. Or put your hand over his and guide the action you like.

"My best friend told me she and her boyfriend made love in the park and I can't stop thinking about it, but I'm afraid to tell my boyfriend in case he won't do it. What should I do?"

Tell him. Otherwise you're depriving him of the chance to know what pleases you and depriving yourself of being pleased. You could be pleasantly surprised that he loves the idea. But, if he nixes it, you'll have to live with it. In that case, here's a win-win compromise: *pretend* you're doing it (so you get excitement), but be in bed instead of in the real park (so he feels safe).

Emma, 20: *"I don't have orgasm but I just let my boyfriend do what he wants. I don't want to destroy his ego because he doesn't satisfy me. I don't need to be satisfied."*

Yes, you do! Girl, you better raise your self-esteem. You deserve pleasure. Besides, you're not doing him a favor by letting him do what he wants if it doesn't please you. Women who don't speak up might be hostile to men, self-sabotaging, or afraid of rejection or commitment. Keeping him at a distance is safe, like saying, "I'm never vulnerable to him because he doesn't please me." Stop selling you both short. (Read the chapter on What's Up With Her to find out about how to have orgasm with a partner.)

Q: Why don't men ask where the clitoris is?
A: Because they hate asking for directions.

"My boyfriend is so sweet. He keeps asking me what he can do to excite me. I don't know what to tell him. What do I say?"

You can tell him to just let himself go, and you'll enjoy whatever he does. Better yet, *you* can learn what you like, and then tell him. Chances are he's also fishing for compliments that he's doing it right, or telling you that he wants you to get more demonstrative. Next time, show him how turned on you are.

Peter proves the importance of getting directions. *"I can't stand that my girlfriend lays there not making a noise. I don't know if she likes what I'm doing, so I don't feel like doing it."*

Invite her to tell. Say, "I want to be the best lover for you. Tell me what would give you the most pleasure." Ask for specific directions with open-ended questions ("How would you like me to touch you now?") or multiple choices ("Should I go fast or slow?"). Also ask for feedback ("Do you like this?"). Tell her men want a woman to show she's aroused by what he says and does.

"How do I help this guy improve his technique of foreplay. I'd rather skip it because it doesn't serve its purpose and usually turns me off."

Unfortunately, some people are just more sensual or sexual than others. And while you can teach someone to be more sexual or to please you, there is such a thing as "chemistry"—you are either tuned in to one another, or more sensual or not. You may also have different sexual styles, just like people have different personality styles (see chapter on His and Her Sex Styles). If you have different styles, you have to know which you are and let the other person know what to do to please you. If he likes to touch, spend time putting your hand over his as you run it over your body in the way you like, to train him. If he is visual, tell him to watch what you do, or dress up for him to admire you. If he is aural (focused on sounds and hearing), whisper into his ear and tell him things you want him to say to you.

"My girlfriend squeals like a rat in sex, and it ruins the mood. How can I get her to stop?"

Sing "Old McDonald had a farm . . ." with her, "with a hee-haw here and a cluck cluck there . . ." No kidding, that turns making noises into a game and gets her to do different ones. Telling her to stop making noise is hurtful and will make her self-conscious. Remember my Sex Rule #1: Do unto others as you would have them do unto you. Model sounds you want her to make. Moan low, growl, purr . . . with her.

"This guy I'm seeing pinches my nipples too hard and sticks his tongue way down my throat. I want to choke. I hate it and want to scream. How do I make him stop?"

Some people don't know how to be sensuous and have to be taught. Make him feel "safe" first by starting the conversation with "I love you a lot and I love making love with you." Then say clearly in a loving tone, "I love those softer kisses on my breasts," or when he's kissing you, say, "I love it when your lips linger on mine more than going inside my mouth right away." This way you let him know in a non-threatening way how you like to be kissed and touched, and he can focus on what pleases you. Kiss *him* the way *you* like—following my Sex Rule #1: Do unto others as you would have others do unto you.

Hopefully, he is just inexperienced and will learn after you do that homework; if he's really insensitive, he may not be right for you.

"My boyfriend asked me for a 'quickie' the other night and I really didn't want to do it, but I gave in anyway. I was tired and thought it would be over quickly. But it turned out to be more involved. I wanted him to just get it over with but was too afraid to hurt his feelings. So I ended up feeling angry and put upon. Should I have told him?"

There's nothing wrong with giving in once in a while to protect the other person's feelings. You can have sex by just being there without being so active. But if this pattern happens a lot, either he's too demanding or you're turned off and you have to find out why. HOMEWORK: Take turns where each of you gets a week where you get your way entirely and the other one goes along with it.

"When my boyfriend doesn't have an erection, I ignore it, but the problem is going on forever. Should I speak up?"

It was good for you to minimize the problem at first, to take pressure off your partner. But when a problem goes on too long (six months or longer) and starts eroding other parts of your lives or relationship, you have to confront it, saying, "We know we really love each other, so let's talk about what we can do about this."

WHEN TO SHUT UP

"My girlfriend is always putting herself down when we have sex. In the middle she'll say, 'Don't touch my stomach, I'm so fat' or 'You hate when I do that, don't you?' How can I get her to stop?"

You're right, she shouldn't put herself down, eroding her self-esteem and eventually your view of her. Tell her she has to give up those thoughts like a bad habit and to stop criticizing herself for both your sakes. Give her re-phrasing homework: Have her replace every criticism with its reverse positive affirmation: "You hate when I do that" becomes "I know you love this," and "Don't touch me there, I'm so fat" becomes "Touch me here, that feels so good." Even if this feels forced at first, with practice the positive statements become real.

Robin, 18: *"My boyfriend told me he had six women before. Now I can't keep it out of my mind when I have sex with him. I'm always wondering what he did with those other girls. Once when we were doing it, I thought he wasn't really into me, so I said, 'You're thinking about those other girls, aren't you?' He wouldn't say so, but I knew he was. I know my breasts aren't as big as his last girlfriend, whom I know. How can I get his mind off them?"*

You need to get your mind off them. Pressing him about his past (especially in bed when defenses are down and emotions raw) is self-defeating; it only highlights your own insecurity to the point where you may even make *him* question your attractiveness—making your worst fears come true! As soon as the thought of her with him comes to your mind, switch it like a TV channel or computer program to say something to him about you and him ("We had such a good time . . . ").

Theresa, 22: *"My boyfriend tells me about other girls, to compare what they do. He asks me how come I never let him do things they do, like one who let him perform oral sex while I never did. It makes me feel bad. Can I tell him not to say these things?"*

Yes! What a hurtful, insensitive way to try to get you to do something. He should never compare you to his past lovers. It'd naturally make you defensive and hurt, and hardly motivated to be better. Even if someone wants to know about the past, hearing it can stick in their craw. You can have a past act you liked in your mind and suggest it, leaving out the part about someone else doing it. If you have to, say you heard about it from a friend, or saw it on TV.

"I've been going out with my boyfriend a year. We have sex twice a day. I'm on top most of the time. He tells me to do it this way or that. Once he told me I was moving too much. I like that he tells me, but if I tell him what to do, he says, 'If I'm not good enough . . .' How can I get him to listen?"

He's being a typical macho lug—able to dish out criticism, but he can't take a suggestion himself. Tell him asking for what you like is a gift, *not* a criticism of him. Since he's so overly sensitive, start with all kinds of compliments about how great he is in bed, then tell him something you love that he does, and then let him know what you'd like him to do. If he can't get off it, get over him.

Shawnee, 21: *"My boyfriend says I'm too wet. The gynecologist said there wasn't anything wrong with me. What do I do?"*

Ask him how he would feel if you told him his erection was too big or hard. Your lubrication is the equivalent of excitement to his erection. He may be intimidated that you're so sexy, or maybe he's afraid his penis will slip out. Find out what he fears. Tell him I said you should feel great about yourself.

TOO MUCH OR TOO LITTLE SEX TALK

José: *"Why does my girl have to do all this yip-yap, he-said, she-said stuff. It's endless the way she wants to go over and over things after, during, before sex, and every time. How do I get her to shut up?"*

Though male and female sexual communication styles are becoming more alike, in general women like to talk about feelings and go over every detail of what happens. Obviously your styles don't match. You'd score big if you talked a little more—you can even just repeat back what she said, so she feels *heard*. Tell her she's beautiful—women *love* that. Acknowledgment is a big aphrodisiac. Or, you can ask her sweetly to please save it and talk to you later, or to write it down and you'll read it later. But it sounds like she's a die-hard talker and you're not even a listener, so that's trouble, and you may not be right for each other.

Bianca: *"My boyfriend doesn't talk in bed. He's very cold. My father was cold, too. I say I want to hear him say something and he says I should know."*

He is copping out by saying "you should know." Sometimes talkers like you purposefully pick the silent types when they're insecure. Because you say your father was cold to you, it's clear that you are repeating a family script. Say to yourself, "My father may not have been a warm, communicative person, but I can have a lover who is."

Guys don't talk in bed partly they're not used to it. They're afraid to admit insecurity or inexperience. They have to be encouraged to talk. You talk first. Ask what they like. Make it a game, telling each other what you like, to take the pressure off doing it spontaneously. Resisting pillow talk comes from inhibitions, religious and social taboos, and fears of rejection, of sounding silly, being criticized, hurting the other person. They can get over these hurdles and learn to talk more if they want to.

Bianca's boyfriend was really cool. He said he'd like to talk more, but asked, "How do I do it?"

You can start by talking about wanting to talk but having trouble, ("I'm not used to being open."). Since she's more talkative, begin with questions to her ("What feels good?"). Read poems or passages from sexy novels aloud. Ask her help ("How do you think I feel?"). HOMEWORK: Make a notebook of "Love Talk." On one page write all the things you would like to say ("I love you; you're the best, I dream of you"). Practice saying these aloud to desensitize yourself to the fear of doing it to her face. Tune in to her head. Study her body signals. Or ask her ("What gives you the most pleasure when we make love?"). Recount for each other and relive in detail the most exciting time you had together in the past. Title a sheet of paper, "Love and Sex Scenes of _____ and _____ ," and write down explicit accounts about what you really would like to have happen as if they were scenes in your favorite movie and read each other's script in bed.

HOMEWORK for you both: Switch roles. You be the talker and let her be the quiet one, so you get a sense of what the other person feels like.

SOME RULES ABOUT SEX TALK

DO:
"walk a mile in the other person's shoes."
learn what you like and don't like.
rehearse in your mind what you would say or do.
ask for specific instructions.
reward what you want repeated.
take the initiative.

DON'T:
ever betray a confidence.
compare your partner to an ex.
criticize.
blame.

MIXED SIGNALS

"This guy tells me I'm the best he ever had in sex one time and that he wants only me real bad and then the next time he seems off on another planet telling me he's always been a player. How do you respond if the guy gives you mixed signals—hot and cold—in a new relationship?"

Believe the second half even though you want to hear only the first half. He wants you and he doesn't. Don't make yourself sick trying to figure out which it is. His ambivalence could be a fear of intimacy, not being ready to settle down, or really not liking you enough. If he's shy, be encouraging, without pressing too hard, to give him a chance to get comfortable. If he's really emotionally unavailable, realize that nothing you can do will change him, and stay with him only if you get enough out of it.

ARGUING KILLS SEX

James: *"I've been going with this girl for four years. We had a baby together, but we both cheated on each other. I got so angry I said I would never have another child with her. She left me for a while, and then came back but she's still angry and we're not having sex. I want to have sex with her, but we're always fighting. What can we do?"*

Bury the hatchet. Write down all your disappointment and resentment toward each other and burn that poison. Start afresh, putting the past behind you. Treat each other tenderly, as if you are seducing each other for the first time. Force yourself to act as you would to a new lover, on your best behavior. When you boil up inside and feel like arguing, stop (bite your tongue!) and think. Recognize your feelings (disappointment, hurt). Think of the consequences (of getting mad, pulling away). Do something else (hug, say how you care). If this is impossible, cut the cord so you don't drive each other crazy and so you can each get on with your lives.

Ed McMahon, *Star Search* host and Johnny Carson's once-sidekick, told me he keeps his marriage great with his (young) wife by making sure they never go to bed arguing! She agreed, they always resolve their disagreements.

THE SILENT TREATMENT

Lori: *"When we have an argument about sex, instead of talking it through like I like to do, my boyfriend gives me the 'silent treatment.' I get so frustrated because he walks away and ignores me. I start screaming more, and he calls me a nag. Then I don't want to have sex with him anyway. Is there any way to get out of this vicious cycle?"*

Yes, vicious cycle it is! You get out of it by behaving differently. Stop seeing his withdrawal as a deprivation of you but rather as a way he copes with frustration and hurt. Say, "I love you and I get hurt when you withdraw. Can we talk this out?" instead of attacking him, "You never talk, you're so frustrating," which only makes him defensive and more likely to clam up. A "cool down" period is not a bad idea on some occasions so you don't say things you regret later.

ASKING FOR IT

"My guy is really gross when he wants sex. He treats me like a piece of meat, saying "Let's fuck," and grabbing his crotch. What's with him?"

Signals to each other about making love have to be

equally appealing. Crude things, "Let's f——" or silly things, "Are you interested in darning socks?" will all be taken in the right spirit if you feel respected—which *you* don't. You'll have to let him know words you like, and that you want him to respect you more. On a Richard Bey "Can This Relationship Be Saved" show we did, the women on the panel all complained about how the guys asked for sex. Nicole said Ben makes it gross and impersonal, saying "Let's do it baby." Heidi said Doug turns her off when he says, "I washed myself, do you want to smell." Another said her husband just drops his pants and says, "Come here and see what I got." They all wanted to be seduced, cajoled, romanced.

IS HONESTY THE BEST POLICY?

Vicki, 19: *"One night we were having sex and my boyfriend asked me to tell him the most exciting thing I had ever done. I didn't want to, but he kept insisting. So I finally told him about the time I was taking an overnight flight to L.A. and I had been talking to the guy next to me. He was really nice and the lights all went out in the plane, as they do on those night flights. I put a blanket over me to go to sleep, and he pulled it over him and put his hand in-between my legs and under my dress. He made me all wet there and fingerfucked me. Then I leaned down and put my head in his lap, and went down on him, with my head under the blanket. The stewardess only walked by once and I stopped and he gasped with excitement until I started again. Then, to my surprise, my boyfriend stopped touching me, and turned over and said he was tired and wanted to go to sleep. I kept asking him what happened and whether he was upset about the story and he said no, he was just tired. What happened?"*

Your boyfriend bit off more than he could chew. And you got hoodwinked. He asked for the story, you told it, and he got upset, jealous, insulted, and hurt. Some couples may enjoy talking about their past experiences in bed as a turn-on, but be careful. Recounting your past with other lovers while in bed with your partner can backfire, making him or her feel threatened.

Certainly singles today should know potential partners' pasts to assess the risk of disease, and to know their "track record" since history tends to repeat itself. And for married as well as singles, in a moment of intimacy while locked in a loved one's arms, sharing a sexual secret—from a most pleasurable experience even to the horror of a past abuse—can be bonding and exhilarating. But be smart about sharing. Some pillow talk is best reserved for a later time, or done over dinner or on a walk in the park (keeping the bed a sanctuary for positive experiences together), or never told.

Lisa, 19: *"I made the mistake of telling my boyfriend about my past relationships. I only slept with a few guys, but now he's calling me a bitch and a slut. What is wrong with him? Why is he doing this to me?"*

Your boyfriend may be projecting his guilt for his own infidelities onto you. He sounds passive-aggressive—men who cajole you sweetly into doing or saying something and then spring a deadly trap. Or maybe he's getting out his stored up anger toward all women. He could be angry because he feels inexperienced—and therefore insecure—compared to you. But tell him you don't have to be a punching bag for his sadism. Say firmly that you refuse to hear those false accusations anymore.

Only about half of readers in a *Glamour* magazine survey said they thought it was good for their relationship to discuss their sexual past with their lovers. Even if they ask, some guys get jealous hearing the answer: "He wanted to know everything but really nothing. He was hoping I was a virgin before I met him." Others say it only to hint about what they want: "She wouldn't wear garters but maybe you will."

The best lovemaking is where you are fully open, emotionally, physically, and spiritually. But when either men or women find out their current love has had many loves before them—or more than they have had—it sets the stage for competition, rejection, and hurt. So think about what impact sharing would have on your partner's feelings.

Cathy, 16: *"I was having sex with my boyfriend and we always said we'd be honest, so when he asked me what I was thinking, I said, 'I'm thinking of Charlie now, get off me' and pushed him off me. He got pissed off and won't talk to me now."*

That was a hurtful and pretty stupid thing to do. You took the honesty rule too far. Of course he was upset. Apologize. Next time, if Charlie comes in your head, keep it to yourself, or change his face to your boyfriend's.

"I lied to my girlfriend and told her that I didn't cheat when I did two years ago. The other relationship is over. Do I have to tell her? I want to get over the guilt."

Usually I advocate honesty, but remember my rule of thumb about telling: know what you expect from confession. Assess your motives and think of the consequences. In some cases (as yours), if you want to be excused and absolved, do it for yourself or in church instead of expecting it from a partner since you might do more damage than good to a solid relationship by raking up the distant past. Live in the now.

"What do you do if your partner is not so hot and asks, 'how was it?' What do you say?"

Consider why he asks the question. Does he feel guilty that he didn't please you enough? Does he need reassurance that he's a good lover? Does he need permission to go to sleep? Say whatever you can that is positive and reassuring while still honest. Use the opportunity to say what you'd like more of in the future, like, "I enjoyed your . . . and I'd love to do more of that . . ."

"I hate sex with fat women. My girlfriend gained weight. How do I tell her it turns me off and I want her to lose weight?"

Better not to tell her what turns you off; that always makes a person defensive and depressed. Close your eyes and imagine her thin. She has to want to change, and people always feel better about changing when they know they're loved the way they are.

TELLING ABOUT RAPE

"Should I tell my boyfriend I was raped? I'm afraid how he'll react."

Since so many women have been sexually abused, and it affects their later sexual interactions with someone they love, sharing the experience during intimate moments can be healing. Reassure him your sexual withdrawal is not his fault. You can say, "If you've noticed I've been withholding from you lately, it's because I'm just remembering I was raped as a child and I'm having a hard time dealing with it. I'm glad I can talk to you about it now."

Be prepared for his reactions to be similar to your experiences of hurt and frustration and helplessness. Or he may not know how to handle it. Be sure you have a great deal of trust and open communication before you share this.

THE SECOND FOUR LETTER WORD FOR SEX: LOVE

Love is the best lubricant. And the essential ingredient to love is intimacy.

As my friend, spiritual adviser Reverend Ruth Green says, intimacy is IN-TO-ME-SEE—meaning look into me and see what's inside.

Many people desperately seek, yet fear, real intimacy in their relationships. It's as if they believe the joke, *What are the three rings of a relationship? The engagement ring, the marriage ring, then the suffering.*

AFRAID

"My girlfriend always complains I can't be intimate in sex. I hear that guys have problems with intimacy. It's true when people get close I back off. My mother wasn't very nice to me. Just what is intimacy anyway so I can tell if I can do it or not."

Intimacy is when two people drop their masks that protect them from getting hurt, and go full throttle into sharing hopes and hurts, dreams and disappointments. You get that feeling "It's just you and me against the world." You feel your insides touch. It's healthy—research shows that people who have long-lasting relationships based on trust have a stronger immune system and live longer—and it's a real high. It's the route to cosmorgasm (see chapter on Slacker Sex to New Rave Sex). Without intimacy, you feel empty, alone, and unfulfilled, vulnerable to depression and escape into drugs.

It sounds like you're scared of, and starved for, affection. Your fear of getting close *is* likely related to growing up without any affection, and feeling rejected by that primary female figure, your mom. I'm so sorry that happened to you. Loving moms help men develop love. As Honorary Love Doctors, Roger Clinton and Ricky Paull Goldin both shared how their fathers left home, but growing up close to their mother had payoffs, helping them become sensitive and understand women.

HOMEWORK: Hug three people a day (getting closer each time). Sleep with a stuffed animal, to develop contact comfort (a stuffed animal is a classic "transitional object" to closeness with a real person). Write down three "secrets" a day you can share with your girlfriend. Trust your girlfriend; she's not your distant mom.

Think of getting close to someone like running rapids. If you're thrown out of the boat and sucked down and you struggle frantically to get to the surface, you will likely drown. But if you go deeper, the water spits you out downstream on the surface.

"How can I tell what type of guy is most capable of intimacy, so I don't get hurt all the time?"

Good bets: men who say they like being involved, they've loved someone before, and they're not scared. Ask directly, "Do you like being real intimate?" If they're enthusiastic, go for it. Bad bets: men who have a history of relationships that didn't last long, are proud of being a player, and say outright they don't want to get involved. These include loners, "control freaks," abusers, self-absorbed narcissists, and romantic idealists endlessly seeking the perfect romance.

"How do I get my boyfriend to be more intimate?"

Reassure him you care. Share deep feelings. Give specific encouragement rather than vague criticism: don't say, "You're not intimate enough with me," but point out when he *is* close and spell out what you *do* want ("I'd like to spend two nights together alone. I'd like us to talk about our dreams. I'd like us to tell each other our deepest fears."). Always reward what you want repeated. As soon as he says something intimate you like ("I had a good time," "You're fun"), play it up. Tell him how you love when he says those things.

Arnette: *"I can be close to a guy, but once I have sex, I feel real deeply involved. Sometimes I try not to be sexual with some men, but I know that I'll care more about them if we have sex. What is that thing that happens? I met a married guy and we were friends and then we had sex and now I think about him more than I do other guys I'm dating but not had sex with yet. Why does this happen?"*

Great sex with intimate love sticks more than Krazy Glue. You can love friends or family, but when there are no limits and you share your body, mind, and spirit, it's a real high! If you're the kind of person who puts sex on that high level, better choose carefully who you sleep with. Obviously you felt safe enough with this married man to let go; next, choose someone who can be there for you even more.

WHAT IS LOVE?

Elizabeth, 17: *"I've been dating a guy for two years. We think we really love each other. How do you know if you really love someone?"*

Comic Bobcat Goldthwait, fresh from being accused of torching the *Tonight Show* chair, and smarting from his good friend Kurt Cobain's suicide, opined: "If you don't check his horoscope every morning, it's not love."

I add, what a sweet feeling. How much from 0 to 100 percent do you feel he loves you?

Elizabeth: *"I'm 99 percent sure."*

That's great. Then really let yourself legitimize it. Feel

the joy of saying, "I'm in love." Feel your chest expand, your heart sing, your step lighten! What are the signs to you of being in love?

Elizabeth: *"He's 'there for me,' he stops if I say so, he always uses protection, he says if he hurts me he'll never forgive himself, he makes me laugh."*

Some commonly mentioned qualities of being in love: being there through good and bad, good communication, being best friends, always having that person on your mind, caring about that person's welfare as much as you do about your own, wanting to be with them forever. To make someone feel loved, spell out exactly what they do that you appreciate, being very specific. Tell them, "I love you because you're (kind, generous, sensitive, loyal)."

THE LOVE TEST

Jennifer: *"I made a wish on our anniversary that I would have a great date with my boyfriend Garrett. It was unbelievable sex. He lay me on my back with my legs up and traced the rim of my vagina. I felt loved and really close to him. Then he made me dinner and sang to me. It was so romantic. Could this be love?"*

You feel a certain kind of love, based on infatuation and lust, but for it to be lasting love, you need time and situations to answer "yes" to these five questions:

LOVE TEST

❑ Do you feel you can share what's in your heart and he will really care about it (openness)?

❑ Can you rely on him to live up to his/her word so you can be open without fear of being betrayed (trust)?

❑ Do you feel like his life and needs matter as much as yours (devotion)?

❑ Can you feel what's inside his skin, and he yours (empathy)?

❑ Do you feel accepted for who you are regardless of what you earn, do, say, look like (unconditional love)?

Carlos, 18: *"I'm in love with my girlfriend and she with me. When I suck on her breasts she says she really feels 'love' with me. Why is that?"*

This is really interesting. People don't often know this, but her "love" could come from a chemical that secretes in women's bodies when they get excited—oxytocin, called the cuddle chemical, because it is responsible for contractions that aid in delivering a baby and also in stimulating breast feeding. Therefore, it is associated with nurturing, caretaking feelings. So this could partly explain why women want to cuddle in sex—when men want to go to sleep. Also, of course, nursing at the breast is symbolically a loving act, so her enjoying that is like saying, 'drink of my nectar, I will feed you.' You both sound in love, so congratulations!

CLAMMED UP

Anthony, 28: *"I do a lot of girls. I think naked chicks are cool. But I get bored after and pick out their faults, like they have flat rears, or I don't like her speech. One girl had my baby and don't let me see her no more. I never feel anything for them. My father was an alcoholic and he always yelled at my mother's faults. Is there any perfect woman?"*

No, but you're sure ensuring that you don't find any woman near perfect. I don't blame you—you have a lot of reasons to be upset. I'm sad you don't see your child— experts now recognize severe father depression when men are separated from their children. Please try to reconcile with the mother of your baby—she's obviously angry with you. As the adult child of an alcoholic (ACOA) and abusive father, you didn't have a good role model. Decide your love with women can be different—more respectful—than your father's. ACOAs think they have to be perfect; no one is. Accept imperfections. HOMEWORK: Make a list of the really important things to you, like caring and sensitivity, and push the other unpleasant qualities out of your mind. Press the delete button on your mental computer when those imperfections come into your head.

THOSE THREE LITTLE WORDS

"When is it right to say 'I love you'?"

When you feel it. Don't worry about the other person's reaction. True love is unconditional, and doesn't expect return. If you get it back, great. If not, deal with it. Trust your own timing.

LOVE CHANGES

Kate: *"I can't understand why I feel so great, so in love, and so great in bed, in the beginning of a relationship and then it dies."*

Van Halen's Sammy Hagar as Honorary Love Doctor advised: "Love changes. Like in '2 Sides of Love,' at first it's real hot and infatuated, y'know. You're so in love and can't stand to be away, not with this person. You have to be with them. And as it fades out, then you find out if you're in love or not, but sex is different. That's when you say, 'I'm going to work on it,' but if it's over it's over . . . things change, go on, find someone else and don't take it personally and don't let it ruin your life. But you have to 'Give to Live.' Everybody goes, 'Well, they never say this to me.' 'Well, you never say it to me either.' Well, someone's got to go, 'I love you,' and then they go, 'Oh God, I love you, too.'"

Somebody's got to make the first move, that's what it's about.

ENDLESS LOVE

"Love is beautiful. How can you make it last forever with one person?"

Constantly support each other to fulfill your individual potentials. Keep sharing—how you feel, your dreams, fears, feelings, experiences. Recognize that love goes through phases—in the beginning you work hard to impress each other. If you both want love to last, it will. It really is a decision first. Everything flows from that decision.

I asked former *Dallas* star Larry Hagman what the secret

to love was. His answer: "Separate bathrooms." Duran Duran's Simon LeBon said he keeps his love alive with wife-model Yasmin, "We don't give each other presents; we just have great sex. That's the most important thing, isn't it?" For the girls in Arrested Development, "love is abstract and misused . . . you really have to respect yourself first, then respect others, and then all will be all right." You go, girls. Respect Rules.

CONFESSING LOVE

The best last word on this subject is about how the four-letter word—talk—mixed with another four-letter word—love—is the best combination.

Brian, 20: *"I have trouble opening up to my girlfriend. She says I treat her like a friend more than a lover. I never say 'I love you.' I feel dumb saying it."*

If you really don't feel it, don't lie; but if you're just scared or afraid, take a deep breath and say it anyway without being comfortable. It'll come more easily with practice. Obviously you have some conflict over those words. Are you afraid it sounds weak or silly or that you could get hurt? You probably never heard such talk when you were growing up. You have to build up your love-talk muscles, like any other exercise. Obviously your girlfriend needs reassurance, so let that motivate you. Start by saying you *feel* as if you really love her.

Adam Ant told me that he once loved and lost a wonderful girlfriend because he always kept pushing her away and never told her that he loved her. She went off and married someone else, and when she called to tell him that she was having a baby, he congratulated her heartily, but when he hung up, a pain shot through him as he realized he had wanted to have that baby with her—but had blown it. So, he wrote the song "Wonderful" to express finally how he felt. It was too late for him with her, but it completed the experience for him, and opened him up for the next time. So what's the morale of the story for you?

"Did I tell you that you're wonderful?"

Front and
Back Door Sex

*Isn't that the way all relationships start—
with a long tongue?*
—Sandra Bernhard

"WHAT'S THE BIG DEAL ABOUT GOING DOWN?"
"Do you have to give a guy head to keep him?" "Why
won't he do me?" These are some of the common questions
I get asked when I make speeches about sex. There are
always more questions about oral sex than any other topic.
Probably because it still is considered a bit of a taboo (in
some states it's still against the law), and because it still
causes anxiety—yet also creates so much pleasure!

"What is oral sex?" Jamie wanted to know. *"I thought it
was when you talk about sex."*
Oral sex is talking of sorts—using your mouth and tongue
to express love for your partner, to show how much you want
to please. Oral sex means using your tongue and mouth to
stimulate your partner anywhere on his or her body. The ear,
armpit, chest, belly button, inner thigh—all can be oral hot
spots. But the *pièce de résistance* of oral sex is the genital
kiss.
Oral sex on a man is clinically called "fellatio," also
known as "doing him," "sucking him off," "skull snapping," and "polishing the helmet." A girl who did it was,
years ago, pejoratively called a "cocksucker."
Oral sex on a woman is clinically called "cunnilingus."
Guys also use phrases like "muffdiving," "going fishing,"

"going downtown." One guy calls it the "Hoover Maneuver," another "scuba diving between her legs."

Doing it to each other simultaneously is called "sixty-nine" because your bodies form that design.

> **Q:** Why can't Miss Piggy count to seventy?
> **A:** Because when she gets to sixty-nine she
> gets a frog in her throat.

"My boyfriend is really into this oral thing. He always wants me to do him, and he thinks I should let him do me back. I think it's nasty, putting your mouth there. Am I weird?"

A lot of people think oral sex is dirty. I disagree, but I can understand how you might have been brought up thinking it wasn't right to do. My own father didn't approve; he was a dentist and he didn't think you should put anything in your mouth other than sterilized dental instruments. Too bad. The day after my mother had her first oral-sex experience with my stepfather (after my father died), she told me, "The girls in the office said my face was glowing and they wanted to know why."

Pris: *"A lot of my friends talk about going down. I've never done it. Does everybody do it or am I the only one? What's the big deal?"*

The big deal is that it's a great pleasure and a high expression of love. In one survey, 90 percent of married couples under twenty-five reported having tried oral sex. Sometimes it's more intimate than intercourse because someone is literally and figuratively "in your face." Pleasing someone orally can make him or her feel real appreciated and loved, and thus can be great glue for a relationship.

Women are too often self-conscious about receiving oral sex. Usually they're embarrassed about their genitals—the way they look, taste, and feel. Be proud of your body. Likely you grew up covering yourself up, learning shame. Or you heard negative things said about your genitals. One patient of mine was told by her stepfather, "Women's vaginas are ugly. They're like frogs' legs you dissect in high-school biology." He's hostile and wrong. Love your genitals. Spread your legs and look at them with a mirror. Pleasure yourself while watching your genitals in a mirror, imagining your partner orally pleasing you. Approach it with an open mind and an open mouth.

> *If you like yourself, lick yourself!*
> —Linda Perry, Ex–4 Non Blondes

Secret Sex Weapon for Men: Many women find it easier to reach orgasm in oral sex than in intercourse. Don't think of it as inferior to regular intercourse. Instead, know it's your secret weapon. Licking and sucking her will be a more surefire way to make her reach orgasm. If you give a woman orgasm through oral stimulation before seeking your own pleasure, you have her in the palm of your hand. She will feel loved and trust you because you cared about her pleasure and then she'll probably *crave* having you in her and can have another orgasm that way!

Secret Sex Weapon for Women: Oral sex is at the top of men's list of what they like done to them. Be aware that some guys will dump a girl if she doesn't do it, and it's one of the top reasons they have affairs—when their woman won't do it to them.

EATIN' 'N' CHEATIN'
"I heard eatin' isn't cheatin'. Is that right?"
Not in my book. Oral sex is just as legitimate, and as intimate a physical and psychological connection, as intercourse. So you can't just get or give a blow job to someone and think you haven't been unfaithful.

STILL A VIRGIN?
"If I give a guy oral sex, can I still be a virgin?"
Technically speaking, virginity is defined by the presence of the hymen, but in my book, a broader definition of

virginity includes any intimate sexual experience (like oral sex). Intercourse isn't the only legitimate sex.

HE'S GOTTA LOVE IT

"Why do guys love oral sex on them?"

Because it feels great to both their heads.

DOWN IN THE MOUTH

Jeff: *"My girlfriend likes oral stuff on her but I get to the point after ten minutes or so where my tongue gets tired and my mouth gets tired and I have to stop before I get her to that point of orgasm."*

Michelle: *"My boyfriend likes me to go down on him for so long my mouth gets tired. What can I do?"*

Take breaks. Of course your mouth muscles could get tired.

Girls doing it on guys don't have to deep-throat or keep a tight grip on his penis the whole time. Take your mouth off, and just keep it at the tip and put your hands around his shaft as if your mouth is there, making sure your hands are real wet (with your saliva) as your mouth would be. He won't lose the enjoyment, and likely he'll be so into the sensation, he won't notice or care about the change for a while. After the break, go back to doing it.

Sandy: *"My boyfriend likes oral sex. He claims I don't do it long enough, but my jaws kill me and feel dislocated. I got this clicking now."*

There are muscles in the jaw that can get strained—see a chiropractor—or you could have a condition called TMJ—see a dentist!

SUCKER FOR BEING SUCKED OFF

"I'm dating this guy and I noticed that in the beginning he wasn't calling me as much as I wanted him to. Then, after about five times of our making love, I sucked him off and let him come in my mouth. The other times I'd gone down on

*him but not for so long and not till he came, but until he
was hard and then we had intercourse. After that, he called
me five times in two days and told me into my machine how
much he loved being with me and couldn't wait till the next
time. Was it because I sucked him off? Are guys such suckers for being sucked?"*

Yes, it would be wonderful if he was getting to like you
for you. But it sounds like sucking him off (and swallowing) added to his enthusiasm and upped your stock. Men
really love it. Now decide if he's really worth it.

GREEDY GUY

Elena: *"My boyfriend has an obsession with me blowing
him. He asks for it when we're alone, or when we're in
clubs, we'll be in a dark spot and he just looks at me with a
certain look and I know what he wants or he'll say, 'Blow
me,' and I get down on my knees or bend down and he
unzips his pants. He's getting to want it all the time, though,
and it's getting too much. Can I tell him that or will he get
upset? I don't want to upset him, because I do like to please
him. He does me about half the time I do him."*

You're not a blow-up doll! Stop acting like a gas station
where he can just demand "fill 'er up" and you do. You're
obviously getting the picture that you're being used, even if
he also loves you. And you're starting to feel humiliated. So
stop it. Tell him he better back off asking you or you'll stop
wanting to do it. Normally I suggest being sweet and positive
when you say what you do and don't want, but you'll have to
be firm to get through to him after he's been so spoiled, and
to overcome your tendency to be so namby-pamby. He
should do himself if he feels he needs it so often. Your fellatio-
cunnilingus ratio is lopsided! Get more equal time.

THE HEADHUNTER

*"I really like going down on guys. I just love sucking a
penis and the way guys love it. My friends call me the
'Headhunter.' Does that make me cheap if I want to do it on*

*the first date? I'm a little overweight, so sometimes I worry
there won't be another date."*

It's fine to enjoy fellatio. Guys will love you for it. But
don't do it so easily—in fact, don't have sex at all so
quickly. Know who you're dealing with. You certainly don't
want to get a reputation for being too easy, or to have guys
bragging about how you sucked them off. You have to be
careful about guys who use you for sex and then spread it
around school to boost their own egos. I worry that you'd
give them head just because you're insecure about your own
body and attractiveness, so you're using this as a way to buy
their attention. I'm afraid it'll only backfire. Resist the urge
to do them and first concentrate on turning your thoughts to
loving your own body even though you're overweight. Or
work on losing weight so you'll feel more confident.

Zelda: *"I have kind of an odd problem. One of my favorite sexual activities is to give head. I happen to be very good at it. The
only problem I have is that once I give them a taste, they get
very spoiled and they don't want to have sexual intercourse."*

You're a guy's dream, loving doing that. What type of
men in the world are you attracting? And you are ending up
feeling empty, used, and deprived? I think deep down you
feel that you are not getting as much as you are giving, and
you need me to tell you to stop doing what you say you enjoy
doing until you are pleasured first. It is wonderful that you
enjoy performing fellatio and that you are so giving, but I
think you are picking guys who are selfish. I don't want you
to have any oral sex or perform fellatio until they have either
done it to you or you have been satisfied in intercourse first.

Actor Ricky Paull Goldin: "And don't show them that magic
talent right off the bat either. Hold back. Make them really
deserve it until you can't control yourself anymore and then you
will probably be further in your relationship with this person and
they will want to make you as happy as you make them."

Q: What's the difference between your bonus
and a penis?
A: You can always count on your wife blowing your bonus.

"Why don't some girls want to go down on a guy? This girl once said to me no way in hell will she stick that in her mouth."

Either they don't know how to do it and are afraid to look silly, or they are afraid to swallow and choke, or they think it's nasty, disgusting, or feel it's degrading. Find out what her fears, resistance, objections, and past experiences are. Once they verbalize a reason, it may instantly dissipate.

Also, once you know the reasons, you can answer them.

SOME REASONS AND ANSWERS

Objection: "I never did it before. I don't know how to do it." (**Answer:** "I'll teach you.")

Objection: "I had a bad past experience. A guy once forced me to do it." (**Answer:** "I'm sorry that happened. We can talk about that. But I'm not the same person, and this is out of love between us.")

Objection: "I'm afraid to choke." (**Answer:** "Do it slow, be in control of how deep you go.")

Objection: "I feel put in a subservient position, with you having power over me." (**Answer:** "Sex is not a power game. It's sharing pleasure.")

Contrary to a report that she never sucks a guy, Madonna told us at the Z100 Madonna Pajama Party introducing her "Bedtime Stories" that she *loves* oral sex—giving and receiving.

Shakeira thinks of oral sex as a power game: *"My boyfriend likes getting his penis sucked. I will not degrade myself doing it. I'm not his 'spit bucket.' How can I get his mind off it?"*

If your partner is not intending to humiliate you, then that thought is in your own head. See it as a sign of love, not degradation. Do it in a way you want to, rather than feeling used. Likely you've done it in the past simply to keep a guy, or you've "done" him and he's dumped you, so you have that unpleasant association. Choose nicer guys and they won't make you do it or humiliate you.

Take a lesson from Heather. After I reassured her it was a good idea to please her husband orally, she decided to give him a surprise. One morning, she woke him up by being down there, gently sniffing and licking him. Still in a sleepy state, he put his hands toward his crotch and buried his fingers in her silken hair. As he stroked her hair and caressed her face, she watched a smile creep over his lips. Waking up to her pleasuring him, he told her, was the most exciting and best present she could have given him.

THE FELLATIO-CUNNILINGUS RATIO: TIT FOR TAT

"My boyfriend wants me to give him head all the time, but he won't go down on me. He says, 'You pee out of that all day and bleed once a month, I'm not going down there.' If I do it to him, then shouldn't he return the favor?"

Steve Stevens, from Vince Neil's band suggested on *LovePhones*: "Why don't you tell him that you won't provide that service if he won't provide that service."

Generally I agree. Fellatio deserves cunnilingus and vice versa. Ideally there would be an equal "fellatio-cunnilingus ratio." Your boyfriend needs an attitude correction, and more factual information. You do not pee out of there. The urinary opening is in front of the vaginal opening. Spread open the lips and take a look and see the tinier hole between the vaginal opening and the clitoris. It's an insult for him to be critical of your most personal parts.

Of course individual feelings have to be respected, but really all guys should learn to love it, just like they expect women to love going down on them. In fact, they pee out of the same hole as they ejaculate—that they expect you to suck!

José is one guy who consciously keeps the score equal. *"Is it too much to expect she do me if I do her? I always suck before I fuck, lick before I stick."*

Of course sex shouldn't be a scoreboard, but often it's only fair if you want it done to you, do it back to your partner. Some people are hogs, they only want to receive. Others are too-much people pleasers, and don't take enough pleasure for themselves. If you're always stuck getting sixty-eight—that's sixty-nine where I owe you one—then reassess whether you feel you deserve pleasure and attention.

> *Eat her 'til her head collapses or her temples touch.*
> —My friend Lou Commesso

> *Show me a man who doesn't eat pussy good and I'll steal his wife.*
> —Dom Commesso, as told to him by a Southern Dude.

Ann: *"I had sex with this guy and he drove me wild going down on me. Is it wrong to want him again just because of that?"*

It makes sense! His being good at it is a good sign: he appreciates women, he wants to please you, he's unselfish, he's not obsessed with power plays.

My buddy Rhonda Schear (USA *Up All Night* host and *Playboy* centerfold) says, "I have girlfriends who won't go out with a guy if he isn't interested in oral sex on a woman. They interview him on the first date!

Find out what his objections are. Once you know the reasons, you can answer them.

Why won't he go down on you?

SOME REASONS AND ANSWERS:

Objection: "I never did it before. I don't know how to do it." (**Answer:** "I'll teach you.")

Objection: "It smells bad." (**Answer:** "I'll wash first, and douse with your favorite scent, but it's my natural scent and I hope you learn to love it.")

Objection: "I feel I am being put in a subservient position, with you having power over me." (**Answer:** "Sex is not a power game. It's sharing pleasure.")

Objection: "It tastes bad." (**Answer:** "Associate it with your favorite taste. Instead of thinking cottage cheese or lumpy oatmeal, think ice cream. Use a tasty food, from honey to whipped cream.")

Objection: "My face gets messy." (**Answer:** "Keep a towel nearby.")

"Do men really enjoy oral sex on a woman or do they per-form it just because the woman wants them to?"

Some men love it. Those men are prizes. It's a sign they appreciate women and are willing to please as well as be pleased. They can like various parts of the experience: bury-ing their head between her legs, doing anything to please her, or sucking out her juices as if drinking nectar of the Gods.

Urge Overkill drummer Blackie, as Honorary Love Doctor, answered: "Oral sex on a girl is the best sex, it's better than rock."

Bandmate, Urge Overkill lead singer Nash Kato, agreed. Natalie called to say, *"My boyfriend has to watch gay porno films to go down on me. Should I let him?"*

UO's Nash told her, "Cunnilingus is the best part of sex. It's one of the most fantastic things in the world. To please you, your boyfriend shouldn't need to see something else. His watching those videos is obviously a bigger deal than you think." That bigger deal *could* mean that he does have feelings toward men.

"A friend told me to use Anbesol and baby oil to numb my gums to give head. Is that a good idea?"

Why would you want to numb your gums, unless you expect it to be unpleasant? Feel it and go at a comfortable pace.

"Sometimes my girlfriend lets me go down on her and then she makes me stop just when I think she's really enjoying it or ready to come. Why?"

Sometimes a woman can get too sensitive from constant or direct stimulation. The clitoris can become too sensitive at different times, as the nerve endings are very rich there. It's fine to let up awhile. You can go back to it after a break or go on to some other stimulation. A lot of women enjoy cunnilingus until they are really hot and about to come, at which point they want to have intercourse. The oral stimula-tion has gotten them excited, so they are more ready to have orgasm on penetration, while it might not have happened as easily with penetration alone.

GIVES IT BUT CAN'T TAKE IT

"When I give my boyfriend oral sex, I can't get him to come even though he says it feels great. I'm getting discouraged. What should I do?"

Don't be discouraged. Just enjoy the activity without expecting he has to come in order to prove you're good or that he's enjoying it. That puts pressure on him to perform. Maybe he's afraid to come in your mouth; reassure him you want it. Then tell him it doesn't matter if he does or not so he won't be pressured. Ask him to identify any other fears he has, or negative thoughts. Maybe he's afraid of intimacy, as if "giving you his sperm" is symbolically giving all of himself to you. Some guys even have a primitive fear that they'll be bitten off, so they withhold really letting themselves go. Or they're afraid of suppressed aggression, that they will use their penis as a weapon and injure the woman. Identifying the fear does a lot to relieve it.

Sometimes guys do girls to hide what they imagine is their inadequate performance. Bobo: *"I could slap on the beard for hours."* You go, Bobo. His girl loves that he loves to do her. But Bobo has a problem: *"She can't do me,"* he says. *"I go limp down there."*

It's great Bobo pleases his partner, but he also has to please himself. He has to get to the bottom of his erection problem. Some women perform oral sex on guys incessantly when they can't have orgasm themselves, so they please him to hide that they can't let themselves be pleased. They have to realize both people deserve their pleasure.

BLACK & DECKER PECKER WRECKER: BRACES

"My girlfriend and I both have braces. Hers hurt me when she goes down on me and mine get her pubic hair caught in them when I do her. What should we do?"

Put your lips over your braces so they don't cut.

STRAY HAIRS

Angie, 18: *"When I deep-throat my boyfriend, I come up with hairs down my throat that make me choke. I get embarrassed for him to know about it, or to cough them up. What can I do?"*

Don't be embarrassed to do what you need to do for your health! If you feel pubic hairs tickling your throat while you're going down on him, stop and say, "I got some of your hairs in my mouth." Cough or pick them out. To prevent them getting in your mouth to begin with, hold the hair aside and take a shower before sex, so, like on your head, loose hairs will get washed away.

OTHER PUBIC COMPLAINT

Andy: *"This girl I'm seeing has pubic hair that's coarse and thick, so it scratches me."*

Tell her to put hair conditioner on it. It can be treated like hair on your head, though it's naturally curlier and coarser.

B.J. AWARD-WINNING TECHNIQUES

"How do you give the best blow job?"
Lisa: *"I want to do it, but I'm afraid I'll do it wrong."*

Madonna in her *Sex* book advised, "have a couple of beers first." I don't agree. Do it sober and experience it.

Sheryl Crow's answer on *LovePhones*: ask him what he likes and he'll tell you, and show you. If you're close to him, you shouldn't be embarrassed. Everybody has to learn. He might love that you're inexperienced. Guys love being with a virgin."

Blur's Damon doesn't think you should tell someone how to do it, "you should just wing it." But Rhonda Schear disagrees. "Start and ask him if this is good, a little hand action, a little tongue action, a little kissing, and then you find the area that works and you just ask him if it works. I tell my boyfriend what I want, so he can do the same. I say, 'this would be really nice if you would do this' and it works."

The term "blow job" is a misnomer. You can blow kisses on his penis, but that is not going to do it for him. It's really more a suck job. Basic mental approach: get into his soul. Sense what he wants. Read his body movements to tell what he likes, whether he likes it slower or deeper. Feel confident that you are doing it fine; or you come off tentative. Really *want* to do it. If you are having a good time, you will do it well and he will enjoy himself, without pressure to perform.

Fantasize. Ask him to touch you while you are doing it, so you are turned on, too.

Brain retrain from "I don't know what to do" or "I'm not doing this well" to "Anything I do is fine." Feel confident. Ask him to give you kudos, or directions. Looking at him in the eyes while you're kissing his genitals can be a great way to get feedback about his pleasure, and to connect with him as you're pleasing him.

Get him excited by rubbing and kissing him through his clothes first. As you undress him, kiss and lick all around his genitals first, teasing him, around the sensitive inner thighs and scrotum. Make sure your mouth is wet, with saliva. Or apply eatable cream or oil (from a specialty sex shop) with your hand. Men like it slippery.

Start licking at the tip, lightly. Circle your tongue around the head, and then slide the head slightly into your mouth. Create suction inside and roll your tongue around the head, lingering on the frenulum (the most sensitive spot on the penis, the underside at the tip where the ridge meets the shaft). Slip your mouth over the tip, licking the frenulum, and run your moistened mouth up and down the sides along the shaft of the penis, first on one side then on the other, remembering that this does not have as many nerve endings, so you should continue caressing the head with your hand, and return to slipping the head inside your mouth again since the head has more sensitivity (not bobbing, but what I call the "quick dip" and "slide"). Some guys like to be held in what I call the "Scuba OK" grip (circled with thumb and forefinger) and some like the whole hand. You can keep your mouth on the tip and hold your hands around the base or move your head up and down, each time taking more into your mouth.

ADVANCED ORAL TECHNIQUES

- Stimulate other parts of his body with one hand, particularly the perineum or "in-between" spot between the back of the scrotum and the anal opening or dart your tongue in and out of the anal opening.

- What I call "Running the Full Mile" technique: run your tongue along the full roadway of his sexual parts, by bending his penis gently up against his abdomen and run your wet tongue from his anal opening, circling it, along the skin (called the perineum) to the underside of his scrotum, then circling the scrotum, and up along the length of the penis, to engulf the head once again. As you lick his penis, fondle the testicles gently (if he likes this), or pull them lightly upward (they will get closer to the body as he gets more excited anyway). Take his testicles in your mouth as you fondle his penis with your hands. Enjoy the sensation of the soft silkiness of the skin combined with the hard stiffness of the erection.

- Either comment on how hard he is, how beautiful his cock is, or how you love sucking him (whatever is honest—always say what's true). If he's soft, reassure him that you love it when he's soft, too. After all, you can take more of him in your mouth. Be reassured that it feels good for him too that way.

- When he ejaculates, place your fingers at his anal opening, or on the perineum, or around the shaft of his penis and suck deeply. He will feel like the life is sucked out of him, but he will be ecstatic. You can heighten his sensation to excruciating points by doing an oral version of a "squeeze" technique (see the chapter on What's Up With Him). Just as he is about to come, continue to suck as you press your thumb on the tube that protrudes along the underside of the penis, so that his reflexes begin to ejaculate semen but you have held up its emission, thereby making the feeling of orgasm last a tad longer. Read the book or get the video *The Ultimate Kiss*.

A *LovePhones* caller, Mike, suggested a "hum job"—putting his penis or testicles in your mouth and humming on them, to create a pleasurable vibration.

DEEP THROAT

Cindy: *"Whenever I try to deep-throat my boyfriend, going down on him all the way, I gag. What can I do about this? He jokes I should go to the circus and take lessons from the sword-swallower."*

Craig: *"When my girlfriend and I engage in oral sex and I come in her mouth, she throws up."*

Singer Linda Perry advised: "Your girlfriend may not be into giving you head. You need to communicate with her. She's not comfortable with it. Sometimes we need to do that for people we love. If she isn't into it, don't be upset. It's pretty common. Some girls just don't like it, it doesn't mean they don't love you."

But maybe she can get into it. You don't have to gag. The steps:

EIGHT STEPS TO DEEP THROAT

(1) Really WANT to do it.
(2) Breathe. Instead of suctioning your mouth around his penis all the time, let some air in the sides. Open your throat like swallowing a pill.
(3) Take gradual steps. Take in as much as you can, stay where you are and take a deep breath. Inch down a little more and repeat the procedure. As you practice this, your throat will relax so you will not gag. You will also build your confidence.
(4) Instead of going down all the way, taking him all in, only go down as far as you feel comfortable.
(5) Use what I call the "baseball grip": grab the shaft of his penis that's left outside your mouth with your hand or hands and mimic the up and down or kneading motion that you are doing with your mouth. He'll likely be so carried away with the feeling, he really won't be able to tell what you're stimulating with what.
(6) Go slowly, altering and quickening your pace as you feel comfortable.
(7) Do what you enjoy!
(8) Since the average penis is five to six inches, and the distance to the back of your throat is about four inches, you have to angle your head to create a straighter line down your throat.

The difference between like and love is spit or swallow.

SPIT OR SWALLOW

Tiffany says her boyfriend is so obsessed with his ejaculate, he puts it in ice cube trays and serves it to unsuspecting people (a "penis colada" he calls it). Okay, that's crude, but guys love it when you honor their ejaculate—by swallowing. Yet many partners still struggle with the spit or swallow dilemma.

"My boyfriend busts on me when we have sex. Should I spit it out or swallow it?"

Keep in mind safe sex: swallowing semen is the transfer of body fluids that could be carrying the AIDS virus. After that consideration, do what you're comfortable with. If you don't want it in or down your mouth, don't. But deep down your man may take it as a sign you really love him and accept his passion and love—by accepting and loving his semen. Reject it and you reject him and he may reject you. Running to the bathroom to spit it out can certainly ruin the mood and his ego.

If you don't want to swallow, you can ask him to let you know before he ejaculates so you can take his penis out of your mouth. Or, if you can let him come inside your mouth but you don't want to swallow, let it seep out the sides of your mouth (if your mouth is very wet, he won't notice the difference). Or, if you can't swallow it all at once, hold it in your mouth and swallow small amounts at a time. Or wipe your mouth into a towel kept right on the bed.

Jackie calls herself the "Queen of Swallows," but it's not a positive thing, because she has a sex addiction: *"I go out with lots of guys to do them. I did it six times a day once. Will I get sick?"*

You likely could get an STD or AIDS, with all that unsafe sex. And you have a sex addiction. I bet you think by swallowing a guy's ejaculate you are getting love, or merging with him, when really you feel empty inside. No amount of semen is going to fill you up—you have to learn to love yourself.

"I don't like swallowing. I feel like the guy has power over me."

That's in your head. If you swallow his sperm, it doesn't mean he has power over you. Maybe that's how guys in the past have treated you, but you have the power because you're the one choosing to do it. Of course, it doesn't have to be a power game at all, just an act of pleasure or, better yet, love. You can do it with the spirit that swallowing his sperm may show that you really love him and everything about him.

"Is it bad for a woman to swallow sperm?"
"I heard if a woman swallows come, the stomach doesn't digest it and it keeps building up. Is that true?"

Semen (with sperm in it) is not dangerous, sickening, or fattening. It doesn't give you a stomachache, acne, or tooth decay. Semen is made out of natural ingredients that get absorbed in the body.

"How many calories are there in come?"

Only about five calories in a teaspoon, an average portion. The calories come mostly from the fructose (a sugar-like substance) secreted from the seminal vesicles, that becomes part of the semen.

Q: What did Jeffrey Dahmer say to Lorena Bobbit?
A: Are you going to eat that?

"DO ME"

"I took this girl out to an expensive dinner and spent a lot of money. Then I took her back to my friend's house and we got busy. She was sucking on me but wouldn't take me all the way in. I'm a big dude, so I wanted her to go all the way down on it. I pushed her head down and she started screaming she's going to call the police. What's wrong with the bitch?"

How dare you force her to go down on you so far. A big penis hurts and she really can choke. You were date-raping her. You have no right to demand sex for spending money, or to force her into anything. I hope she does report you.

For other guys, it is understandable that at the peak of pleasure, they want to thrust deeper and to hold on, but be sensitive to your partner. Unfortunately, the privilege of having it done on him can be abused if he just wants to be "done" and doesn't want to get close to the woman, or please her. The typical horror story: the guy who says, "Give me head," or "Do me," comes in your mouth, then falls asleep, leaves, or worse yet, throws you out. Frankly, it's demeaning. Dump these dudes. If all women didn't let them get away with it, they'd have to change their ways and treat women with more respect.

Betty: *"My boyfriend makes me go far down but I get nauseous."*

Candlebox's Kevin Martin told Betty she doesn't have to do it, and can teach him a lesson. "Next time you take his ejaculate in your mouth, put it back in his mouth or catch it in your hand and rub it on his tummy."

Dee is angry at being forced. *"My boyfriend is always sticking it in my face. I told him next time I'm going to bite it off. Women are such suckers. My mother always caved in on everything my father wanted and that annoys me. Since when do I have to do it?"*

You don't. Remember the Right to say yes or no Rules. But it sounds like your fury is fueled by a build-up of past angers at men for forcing and at women for giving in. Remember my Mirror Rule of Relationships: getting with this guy keeps proving your past, that women are suckers. Move on; find a guy who treats you nice.

"If I want my girlfriend to go down on me and she doesn't do it, how should I ask her?"

Never push her head there. Tell her at a time before you're being sexual (like over dinner) what you like. If she did it once, say, "I loved it when you used your mouth on me." Compliments make a person want to repeat what they did right. If you're in the act already, the best thing would be to do it to her first. If she likes that, after you do it to her, she'll be willing—and anxious—to please you to the hilt. Tell her softly and kindly, "I would really like it if you kissed me there"—point, touch—"whenever you feel like it." The last part gives her the control to do it when she feels the mood come over her—that'll be better for both of you.

> A man is making love to a woman and kissing her breasts, as he repeats over and over, "I love you." Exasperated, and wanting oral sex, she finally whispers to him, "lower, lower," at which point he repeats his refrain "I love you" but in a lower voice. (Poor guy, he just didn't get it.)

THE GUY'S ROLE

Brian: *"I'd like to do my girl but it's rough. The second time I ate her out I got "twatchilism" (a stomachache).*

Ricky wants to please, too, but needs some guidance: *"I'd like to give my girlfriend a birthday present to go down on her, but I never did it before. What should I do?"*

Guys have different feelings about oral sex on a girl. Some love it. Girls who love it love boys who love to do it. So guys, get with it.

Look at her genitals. Remark how beautiful they are. Then keep looking up at her face and into her eyes, and get back down to business. Practice on her mouth, kissing her lips and opening them and inserting your tongue, imagining that her vaginal lips are no different than her mouth lips and your tongue is your penis. Build the anticipation and excitement. Kiss her neck and whisper in her ear, "I want to go down on you and kiss you there forever." Make exotic promises. "I'm going to eat you out so good you'll scream for more." Reduce her anxiety and reassure her by saying, "I love to eat you." Once you're down there, look up and tell her, "You taste so good. You smell so good. I love doing this to you." Most people worry they take too long, so reassure her, "I can do this all day, burying my head between your legs." Work your lips down from her mouth to circling her nipples, to her stomach and belly button. Linger between her thighs and wait 'til she arches herself or moves herself closer to your mouth. Spread the lips apart gently with your fingers, and pull the pubic hairs aside, to expose the clitoris and inner lips, making a triangle like a frame for her jewels.

Remember, some T's:

- **Tease.** Don't just dive in and stay there. Be a dip-and-dive oral lover.
- **Touch** with your fingers, and lightly with the tip of your tongue.
- **Trace** the outline of the lips.
- **Tongue** lapping. Lap as you would an ice-cream cone with longer strokes with a flatter tongue, then alternate with licking with more tip of your tongue. Keep your tongue moist.
- **Tantalize.** Create a steady rhythmic motion. Then gently lift off her and remain poised a few tantalizing inches away, until she feels the excruciating desire for you to touch her again. Then return to licking her, and as you feel her reaching a peak again, lift off again. Repeat this several times, and likely the next light touch will make her orgasm.

Here are some advanced techniques:

- **The Rolls Royce Method:** "Lick, Dip, Slide, Suck." Lick lightly with your tongue around her clitoris, then down to her vaginal opening. Make long lengthwise licks up and down the vaginal opening. Then dip your tongue inside a few times. Then slide your tongue up and down again, and slide to the clitoris. Circle the clitoris, and then catch it in your lips and suck it (as you would imagine she would suck a penis). Do this awhile, then slide down to her vaginal opening again, and start the process over. Each time you slide from the vaginal opening to the clitoris, bring her vaginal juices up to her clitoris and circle it again.

- **The Alphabet Method:** This technique—where the partner traces the letters of the alphabet with his tongue on her genitals—has a reputation, but it doesn't appeal to all women. It gives a guy a pattern if he is not inventive, and focus if he's distractible. But circles or figure eights can be simpler and more effective.

- **Adding a Zinger:** As you lick lengthwise along her vagina, lift your mouth up a little, and make light smacking sounds with your lips. You can even add saying something appreciative, like, "You (smell, taste, are) so good." As the excitement builds, dip your tongue (rolled, if possible) inside deeper, imitating intercourse. Think of your tongue as your penis. As your tongue darts in and out, or plays inside, use your finger to rub her inner thighs, or her breasts, or her clitoris. Or as your tongue plays with her clitoris, insert your finger (or a vibrator) in her vagina. Combine length-long lapping of the vaginal opening with a flattened tongue, with a soft rhythmic tapping on the clitoris with a tipped tongue. Find her particular turn-on. Jasmine likes her clitoris sucked like a baby might suck a nipple, combined with gentle motions (like side to side) of his head. Dara likes his mouth around the top part of her clitoris, near the pubic bone, while he makes munching sounds and motions. Kate likes him to pull the hood back and lick the shaft of her clitoris, then flicking the tip, then taking it all in, just as she would suck his penis. When he pulls outward and downward on her lips, tugging the clitoris, she goes wild.

- **The Double Play:** As you stimulate her clitoris, put a finger around her meatus (urethral opening) or anal opening.

- **The Triple Play:** As you stimulate your clitoris orally, insert one finger in the vaginal opening and another at the anal opening. (Of course, be sure she likes this.)

- **The Full Court Press:** Besides using your lips and tongue, you can bury your whole face in her, or use your chin and nose. You can also use a vibrator to stimulate other parts of her body as you kiss her genitals. With a combination of all these, you'll find out what particularly pleases her; she will greatly appreciate you as a lover, and will be yours. Follow her lead, watch or listen for any subtle changes, or ask her for feedback.

BAD JOB?

Danielle, 16: *"I was obsessed with giving a guy a blow job and I got drunk and did it. But he never came. I'm devastated now that I did a bad job and I feel stupid when I see him. I also heard he told some kids in school I had sex with him, but I didn't."*

He's trying to save face by beating you to the punch and saying he had sex with you to head off you passing rumors that he couldn't come, which would embarrass him. That's wrong of him, so you tell him you heard the rumor and would appreciate that he stop spreading stories and reassure him that you are not telling people he couldn't come.

Don't blame yourself for his not coming. If he was drunk, that would affect him, or if he was uptight or embarrassed. It matters to some extent how good you are to help him ejaculate, but he's the main one in charge of whether or not he lets go. Most important, this should be a lesson to you not to go around having sex just to do it. Wait 'til you really care about someone.

SMELLS AND TASTES

"My girlfriend wants me to eat her out and I don't like the way it tastes. What can I do?"

"I want to swallow my boyfriend's sperm, but it tastes funny. How can I get to like it?"

As my co-host on *LovePhones*, Chris Jagger, says, "It's an acquired taste."

Change your thoughts, tell yourself that she tastes good, not bad. Say, "I like eating her" instead of "I hate this." Associate the taste with something you love. What's your favorite taste? Ice cream (it's been likened to vanilla and pecan flavors), fresh-roasted marshmallows? Spread it on her.

Rhonda Schear advises: "Coax the guy by saying it could be lots of fun even if I had to add things like whipped cream, tasty treats. I would try even if I had to push his head into it and say 'try this.'"

Linda Perry says: "Concoct a 'furburger' like a hamburger, adding ingredients to the meat so it's more tasty."

Vince Neil suggests: "Try edible panties so he has something to munch on first."

Bobby: *"Why does pussy taste like chicken but smells like fish? She cracks her legs and it's like a trip to Sea World."*

Alan: *"I'm in love with this girl. She goes down on me and makes me feel great. But unfortunately, I cannot return the favor. Truth is, she smells really strong. I can smell it even without having my head between her legs. It's like tuna, and I like tuna, but this is more pungent. I get a little nauseous, in fact. I love her and she's so good to me, and I really want to do it to make her feel good because she's been pouting and pestering me about it. What should I do to make it smell better?"*

Diet, medication, and general health (STDs) affect your body scent and taste. Women have different scents. Some have a faint scent or smell like a garden or flowers. Others are really pungent and do smell fishier. This is a natural odor and no amount of douching or washing can eliminate it. A woman's scent can change with her hormones, as during pregnancy. Also, it could be a sign she has an infection, in which case she needs to see a doctor.

To minimize it, she should cleanse the area and dry it carefully, and wear cotton-crotch underpants and panty hose.

BRAIN RETRAIN: Repeat, "I like it." Granted there are scents most people agree are pleasant (rose, jasmine, pine, barbecue, tangerine) and others they dislike. And there are such a thing as pheromones, the natural scent of attraction.

But you can decide you like any scent. Some people like the smell of skunk (I do) or don't cringe at rotten eggs. Mothers don't mind their infant's smelly poop because they love them. What's your favorite smell? Cover her body or douse her genital area with your favorite scent. Use incense or flowers in the room, or put them on her body near your nose, surrounding her in rose petals.

Gin Blossom's vocalist Robin Wilson advises: "Even if you don't like it, do it because you want to pleasure her."

Four Non Blondes' Linda Perry is even more adamant: "Tell him to change the flavor. Practice with a cucumber. My personal thing is that so many girls try to please their boyfriends. Where are the boyfriends trying to please their girlfriends? I don't do that shit. I have taken responsibility to say no. But communication with your lover is the most important thing. I want my lover to respect that I am not into this. Girls don't always have to please their men. Meditate and learn yoga."

LOVING LOVE JUICES

Advice for guys and girls to love love juice: desensitize. Build up to it. Start with some of her lubrication or his semen on your finger and taste it. Tell yourself it tastes good. Put more and more in your mouth, until you can swallow more in this more controlled situation (by hand rather than in the middle of heated sex play, working up to that). Add a piece of candy in your mouth or put a food you love on the genitals so it mixes with the love juices. Associate the most pleasant taste with it, alternating imagining the two tastes in your mouth. What's your favorite food (pick something similar to the consistency of lubrication or semen)? Now think of vanilla ice cream in your mouth, smack your lips, yum, yum, now think of the love juice in your mouth, smack your lips, yum, yum, now think of blue-cheese salad dressing in your mouth, yum, yum, now think of love juices in your mouth, yum, yum, now think of frozen yogurt in your mouth, yummy, yummy, now think of your partner's love juice in your mouth, yummy yummy. Pretty soon the pleasant tastes will spill over onto your thinking of the love juice, and you'll anticipate that pleasantly, too.

"Does guys' semen taste different depending on what they eat? Some taste salty, others are like Clorox and bleach."

Diet can affect the way you taste, but there isn't a direct relationship in the sense that if you eat a chocolate cake, you're going to taste it that night. There are some women who say that celery makes a guy's semen taste good. Think of the ingredients in semen that do have distinctive taste, fructose (sugar) and sodium and chloride (table salt), and small amounts of ammonia and acids. If these are manufactured in greater proportion, it can affect your semen.

Smoking and alcohol can make it bitter. A sharper taste can be due to eating red meats, asparagus, broccoli, spinach, and some vitamins. Vegetarians seem to have milder-tasting ejaculate. A sweet taste can be a sign of a problem like diabetes. Your ejaculate may also seem milder tasting if you've ejaculated a few times. Taste can be affected by smell—which can come from perfumes, making a positive impression, or other things (sweat, smegma, STDs), causing unpleasantness.

RED WINGS

"A few of my friends have joked that they got their 'Red Wings.' Do women like to be eaten out while they have their periods?"

Brenda surely does: *"I had sex with this guy who went down on me when I had my period. It was the best sex I ever had. It made me feel real beautiful and sexy. I told him I had my period and he just smiled and threw me down on the bed and pulled my panties aside and stuck his tongue in me. Then he pulled the tampon out with his teeth. He lapped me up like he was really hungry. I can't stop thinking about it. I would've loved it if he took the tampon out with his hands, much less his teeth. He pulled it out real slow and it felt so exciting as it came out, and my mind exploded thinking that it meant, 'I dig you so much, I'm willing to do even this most wild sign that I love women and love everything about your body.' Where am I going to find more men who do this? Why don't guys get it?"*

Be aware it's blood, and therefore you should be careful about disease transmission, and practice safe sex. Some women—and guys—don't like sex much when a woman has her period. For some, like orthodox Jews, it's against their religious beliefs. Others don't like it because they're embarrassed or ashamed. There's nothing to be embarrassed or ashamed about. If you think you'd like it, do it, or ask him to.

Some think it's disgusting. Like Miguel: *"I was seeing this girl for five months. Recently we got intimate for the first time. I went down on her and she had her period. I had to back off because there were clumps coming out like Ragu chunky-style spaghetti sauce. I got really grossed out. I almost puked. I had to get out fast. I don't think she'll see me again. I haven't called her either."*

Too bad. She's probably really embarrassed and hurt. Call her and tell her you're sorry you were so abrupt, you just weren't prepared for that. Admit you're not that experienced. Reassure her that her period is not gross. Even if you still think it is, I want you to say the opposite: her period is beautiful, the red clumps are tasty. Saying something so extreme will help make your attitude rest somewhere in the middle, and at least you won't have negative feelings about a woman's body floating around in your head. It could get in the way next time with her or anyone else. You'd want her to like your ejaculate, so have the same respect for her period—even if it is blood. It's the blood of life—the shedding of the lining that feeds a baby! Imagine it *is* extra-chunky style Ragu spaghetti sauce, or Manhattan (red sauce) clam chowder.

A friend of my assistant Alissa says, "If Paul Revere could ride through the mud, I can ride through the blood."

69 PREFERENCES

"I prefer not doing sixty-nine, because I get distracted and can't come when he's also doing me. Is there something wrong with me?"

No. Of course when something is being done to you and you're also doing something, you're splitting your attention (sixty-nine, of course refers to both partners orally stimulating each other's genitals at the same time). Suggest to your boyfriend that you take turns so you both can fully enjoy the sensations. Doing it one at a time is probably best when you're just learning, and even in more advanced stages, when your skill can cause such extreme pleasure. While you may hold off mutual genital kisses in favor of taking turns, there's nothing wrong with adding to your own pleasuring, rubbing the clitoris or other body part. In more advanced stages of oral lovemaking, when you do sixty-nine, the experience becomes such a cycle of pleasure—where you become one with each other—that it doesn't matter who and what is doing whom or what.

Heather: *"When I perform fellatio, my eyes water and nose sweats. How come?"*

It could be because having a penis in your mouth makes your throat think it's being irritated, so it sends a message to the brain to lubricate more, and the resulting response is to lubricate the lining of your nasal cavity and your eyes. Being excited also dilates the blood vessels in your skin, and if your linings are sensitive, they are going to lubricate more. It's like what happens to some people when they eat spicy food.

ORAL SURPRISES

"We tried oral sex and my boyfriend said he likes it and that I'm really hot down there and it gets him excited. Then once he gave me a surprise. We were having sex and he suggested we have some Cokes with ice cubes. He showed me some ice cubes in his mouth and then he went down on me and slipped some ice cubes in my vagina. Suddenly I felt a rush, like I came, but I couldn't tell if it was the melted ice cubes. Could I have come?"

Sure, if you enjoyed it. Some women—and men—like the rush of cold on their body or genitals when they're just about to orgasm. It gives them an extra thrill, by the "shock" to their sensitive skin. Likely if he put ice cubes in your vagina, then the sensation was numbed, so physically you couldn't discern whether you were having an orgasm. But if you felt it mentally, great.

I've heard suggestions like Hot Rocks, Alka Seltzer, and Sweet Tarts. A guy at my lecture at F.I.T. suggested ice blue mentholated cough drops for a zinger in your mouth.

"Why does my girlfriend's lubrication taste and look different at different times?"

The consistency and taste of lubrication can vary over the time of the month with a woman's hormone balances.

Guys—and the women, too—have to be knowledgeable about anatomy to enjoy sex of any kind. When you are performing oral sex on a woman, for example, you're particularly aware of the vaginal secretions, so it's best to be prepared for what types they are and what they're like.

William was a little shocked. *"I was going down on my girlfriend and this real stringy stuff that was like a runny nose but viscous, came out. It was like a gooey string. What in the world was that? Was I supposed to swallow that?"*

It's not harmful. It's called spinbarkeit, the mucus that looks long and slimy, and can stretch out from the cervical opening, where it comes from, all the way out the vaginal opening, to the point where the woman may find it dangling down when she urinates, or the man may find it in his mouth going down on her. It is a sign that the estrogen activity from the ovaries is working well, stimulating the production of this ovulatory mucus. Its purpose is to help draw the sperm into the cervix and lead it into the tubes and uterus. It is also a sign of fertility. If her mucus is not clear and watery and the spinbarkeit isn't there, she may not have ovulated (producing an egg that could be fertilized with the sperm).

The more liquid, clearer, thinner ("wetter") the mucus and lubrication, the more likely the woman is ovulating (and can get pregnant). After ovulation the mucus gets thicker, making it harder for the sperm to swim to their destination. (The rhythm method of birth control is based on this.)

"What is the milky-looking stuff?"

It could be normal lubrication (milkier at different times of the month), or the result of vaginal self-cleansing, or it could be yeast, which is not terribly serious and can be easily treated with over-the-counter applications. Yeast is pretty prevalent—in nine out of ten women—at the end of the summer, due to sweating of the vaginal walls, causing the change in the normal pH balance in the vagina.

Enrique: *"I went down on my girlfriend and she had a little piece of shit hanging on to the hair at her asshole. I thought I'd throw up. How can I ever do it again? It was so revolting."*

Yes, that's why I say be very clean. Always scrub in the bath or shower before any kind of sex. People get really sloppy and impatient sometimes when they go to the bathroom. Or they aren't really aware of their body. You should take a mirror and examine all your parts between your legs, not only your genitals, and see where they are and how they have to be cleaned. Believe it or not, some people are totally unaware of where their anal opening is in conjunction with other things, and they don't reach back far enough, so they don't get really clean.

"If you smoke grass and want to do oral sex on your girl, is that munchies?"

Very funny. Smoking grass can make you less inhibited, and so you're inclined to do sexual things you would be uptight about.

"What should you do while a man is orally stimulating you?"

You can gently touch his head, caress his hair. Moan or give other verbal feedback of your pleasure. Talk him through what you're thinking or give him instructions. You can also touch other parts of your own body, like your breasts, or parts of his body. Whatever you do, show him you like it, and enjoy it.

"I don't like to let my boyfriend see me when he's going down on me. Is this bad?"

Better to get over it. Have him turn his head up and look in your eyes every once in a while, and you look down at him. Not looking means you're embarrassed to really enjoy it. Practice while masturbating, imagining his head there and him looking in your eyes. One girl made this work with a training, or "bridge" technique, by putting a picture of a guy from *Playgirl* between her legs, imagining the guy in the photo and then her real guy looking at her. To work up to it: when he's really doing it, alternate closing your eyes with opening them and taking glances at his head between your legs. Then ask him to look at you for fleeting glances.

"Isn't it true that men know best how to give a guy the best blow job as women would know best how to orally please a woman, just because they're the same sex?"

Ideally it shouldn't matter what genitals you have. Anybody can give great head if they're really into the other person and what they want and need. Also, if you're really connected to both the masculine and feminine inside yourself, you could be a great oral-sex partner. Maybe the woman might not know intrinsically, but if the guy showed her and she was a good learner, she could do it as good as any man. And vice versa for the man going down on the woman.

"What's the best position for oral sex?"

The most common positions are where the receiving partner is on his/her back, flat on the bed, leaning against a headboard, or lying at the edge with their legs dangling over the end of the bed, with the giver leaning over, or kneeling between their legs.

To pleasure her, there's what I call the "Suspension Bridge" position: the woman is on her back with her hips arched upward, thrusting her pelvis to the ceiling, with her partner facing down, with upper body arched upward to meet her pelvis in the air, elbows resting on the bed, allowing hands to support her pelvis. In this position the partners can gaze into each other's eyes. "Sit on my face" is another, advanced technique. Some women get uptight about this because they are self-conscious about being so bold. Go ahead, feel like a sexpot. Know he desires you. Actually, in this position you can really control the action more than when he's over you. Rest on your knees and push up and down at will. You can approach from above, or behind.

The best position for fellatio is being between his legs, on top of him. This gives you the most control, especially when he thrusts deeper as he gets more excited and eager. Being underneath him causes more fear of suffocation or gagging. Lying at an angle can also lead to obstruction of the teeth and upper palate.

For analingus, you can be in doggie-style, also stimulating the clitoris or penis with your hand. Or have your partner lie on his/her back, with legs up in the air or over the shoulders, to be able to spread out the buttocks.

DOUBLE PUNCH

Brenda: *"After my boyfriend went down on me for a long time, he wanted to kiss me, but I didn't want to taste myself. I made him go wash his mouth out. Is that silly of me?"*

I think so. Enjoy your own taste. Granted some women may feel it's disgusting, but how horrible to think some part of you is disgusting. Tasting and appreciating your own lubrication is a way to develop sexual confidence and an ultimate sign of high self-esteem. After a bath, lie down and pleasure yourself and put your finger inside and sample it. Imagine how good it tastes. Now imagine your boyfriend doing that to you and telling you how good it and you taste.

Guys can be uptight about it, too.
"My girlfriend did something real disgusting the other day. After we had sex and I came inside her, she said she wasn't finished and wanted me to go down on her. After I had already come inside her, how disgusting would that be, to be sucking on my own come. I'm not gay."

If your girlfriend can eat your come, why can't you? Besides, doing that doesn't mean you're gay at all. I'm proud of your girlfriend that she is willing to ask you for her completion of pleasure after you had yours, if she's not finished. Oblige her.

Think of your come in your mouth as delicious, as a gift from her, and the most intimate transmission of your love for one another. See the previous techniques for a woman enjoying swallowing come, and do that for your own.

CARE

"My boyfriend plays sports and then he wants to get it on with me and me go down on him. But why would I do that if he just came from being all smelly and sweaty between his legs. Even if he were just sitting down in classes all day, it would be sweaty there, but after playing around, it's gotta be gross."

Some people like to go at sex *au naturel*. But I think you should follow the rule "cleanliness is next to godliness" in sex. Follow these conditions before oral sex:

- Always be clean and wash beforehand. Make it part of the love play. It's important for your health, but also for your confidence for you both to feel free to do anything.
- Never do it when one of you has a sexually transmitted disease.
- Practice safe oral sex, because the truth is that there is a chance that the HIV virus can be transmitted if there are any cuts allowing the transfer of body fluids.

"My boyfriend goes down on me when he has stubble on his beard and gives me rug burn. How can I stop this?"

Tell him to shave first. Those sensitive, blood-engorged tissues can really sting and get irritated. If he's real careful and gentle, you might like the slight sting. Talk about this before it's too late.

Q: What do David Koresh, the Phantom of the Opera and Loose Lips Hoolihan have in common?"
A: They've all had major burns on their faces.

THE BACK DOOR: ANAL SEX

I haven't been stumped in years, but at a Hofstra University freshman orientation, someone asked me, "What is trunk-butt?"

I didn't know. I asked the question on *LovePhones* and here are some of the answers people came up with:

Trunkbutt is having sex with an elephant.

Trunkbutt is when someone's penis is so big, and you have anal sex, it feels like an elephant's trunk up your rear.

Trunkbutt is when your butt is so fat you look like an elephant.

The guy who asked the question, John, came up to me after my talk and said he saw it written on a bathroom wall, and found out it's when you have too much anal sex so the anal canal loosens from the connective tissue and starts to collapse, wrinkling like an elephant's trunk, hanging down, even dangling outside the opening. John was worried because he was gay and heard it happens to some gay guys, especially those who engage in fisting (sticking fists up the anal canal).

At my lectures, a lot of questions come up about sex in the "third input" or on the "Hershey Highway," especially these two: *"Is anything wrong with having anal sex?"* No. Except if you're forced into it or can't enjoy sex any other way. The other common question is: *"If I want it, or like it, does it mean I'm gay?"* Not necessarily.

But always remember that anal sex is high-risk behavior for the transmission of HIV, which causes AIDS. This means that you must practice safe sex and know your partner well.

Be careful about a "double whammy"—having anal sex and then putting your penis, finger, or tongue in the vagina or mouth, as you can transmit bacteria and cause a serious infection.

Lots of women aren't keen about anal sex. Guys want to know why, like Charlie: *"Why don't chicks want to take it in the rear door?"*

It can be downright painful, unless they're real relaxed.

Even then it can be too tight. Also, everybody attaches personal meaning to sex acts. Find out her associations. Does being in that position make her feel humiliated or controlled?

But some guys like to do it, and girls like Beth want to know, *"Why are guys so persistent about making a girl turn over?"*

Again, it's a matter of what it means to him. Does he think it's the epitome of what's cool, or proof he's dominating or in control? He could be acting out a homosexual fantasy.

Charise: *"I want to do it for my boyfriend, but how can I get over the pain?"*

Relax. Say to yourself, "Yes, I want to do this," instead of thinking, "Oh no," or worrying whether it's going to hurt. Anticipating pain makes you tense up, so muscles tighten and pain results. Relaxing eases the muscles and makes entry easier. Establish trust. Agree that you will stop if there's pain or you don't want to continue. You can also get used to the feeling by inserting smaller, thinner things first—a finger or anal dildo (never dangerous objects like wood or glass). Use lubrication; vaseline is better than creams that gum or dry up. ALWAYS use condoms.

If you are being penetrated, give instructions about when and how far to enter. Be in a position (on top, kneeling, doggie-style) where you can control the depth, angle, and rhythm of penetration, to feel comfort and confidence.

Train for No Pain. As Sandra asked: *"When my boyfriend puts his finger in my anus it's okay, but when he tries his penis, it hurts. The last time he tried, I got constipated. Why is that?"*

The penis is bigger than his finger, right? So of course it hurts. Your vagina is used to receiving something larger, but your anal canal isn't. The cure is like treating vaginismus (when the vaginal opening closes like a cramp)—where you start with a small insertion like the pinky finger, and build to gradually larger sizes, like two fingers and then the penis. You got constipated because the muscles have tightened since you found it unpleasant; your mind has to say, "relax."

Devon wants to know: *"Why don't girls like their asses eaten?"*

For the same reasons they may not like anal penetration there or oral sex. Figure out the mental association. They may fear smelling or tasting bad, or doing something embarrassing, like letting out gas.

To get over this embarrassment, they have to be fully clean, to reassure themselves of being attractive there. Build self-confidence by thinking positive thoughts ("My rear looks and smells good," "He loves me there"), admiring your rear in a mirror, fantasizing about the act, and asking him to tell you he enjoys it.

Susie and Jerry called *LovePhones* with their disagreement, that he wants to do it, but she is adamant, *"I'm just not into it."*

Remember, the Right to say yes or no Rules. No one should ever force a partner into a sexual behavior they don't want to do, and if they do, they don't love and respect you.

That night, the guys from the band Candlebox were Honorary Love Doctors. Guitarist Peter Klett told Susie: "Don't do it. Is it something he needs for his male ego?" And lead singer Kevin Martin asked Jerry: "Have you ever attempted to feel what it would be like? While in the shower, slip one finger in. Some women love it, some will never be a part of it. We are not all the same. We all don't like the same thing. You'd have to work your way into it slowly."

Get all your arguments out in the open. Jerry thinks it would be fun, the dirtier the better; Susie thinks it's disgusting. Jerry wants her to feel what he feels. That's not necessary; couples can differ about what they like. One person can enjoy doing it and the other person not be into it. Let him assume the position, but insert inside your vagina instead, and think he's elsewhere.

Frank is empathic. *"That place just wasn't made for sex."*

James's girl feels the opposite, as he complains, *"My girl prefers anal sex to intercourse. She calls it a 'noolie coolie.' Since we did this, she doesn't want me in her vagina anymore. At first I liked it, but now I don't. Is something wrong?"*

Possibly. Find out what anal sex means to her, why she prefers it exclusively. Does it mean she's not having "real" sex, so she feels less guilty, or that she enjoys submitting, or that she associates the position with being humiliated? Tell her how you feel about her preference. Maybe you think her wanting that means she doesn't love you as much as if she wanted intercourse. Or maybe you don't like her calling all the shots. Tell her intercourse matters to you, as a sign of love.

Joyce's guy is also into it: *"When we were having sex the other night, my boyfriend turned me over on my knees and jerked my butt in the air and started licking me there. Is this normal or dangerous?"*

Rimming (using the tongue to pleasure the anal opening), anolinctus (licking), or anolingus (inserting the tongue), can transmit diseases, like AIDS, hepatitis, or other STDs, because there is a lot of bacteria in the area. So you should always be thoroughly clean, and use protection. You can even take an enema before sex to feel clean and empty. Some people think it's disgusting, but actually it can be very pleasurable, since there are sensitive nerve endings at the anal opening. Licking or tugging there also stimulates other muscles in the genital area.

John's girl is pulling sexual blackmail on him. *"She says she won't let me in the front door unless I lick her back door. She says, 'If you loved me, you'd do it.' This turns me off, but she does stuff to me like swallow, so shouldn't I do this to her?"*

I can understand that you want to please her, but you don't have to do anything she requests if you really can't get into it. Sexual blackmail is unacceptable. If you want to get over your resistance, examine your fears and what the act means to you and you may change your mind. Or compromise, just licking around the general area. Have her express why she thinks that is the ultimate test of your love. Loving sex respects the other person's limits, without demanding a particular act for selfish pleasure.

The Whacky Whacker, Anal Love Juicer, Anal Passageway Navigator, Funky Butt-Lover, Rectum Raider, and Labia Lover wanted to know: *"Can a guy reach an orgasm with anal stimulation alone, like with an anal vibrator and no penis action?"*

Sure, in fact it stimulates his prostate gland and the male hot spot, so he can have an orgasm. This may or may not be accompanied by an ejaculation, which is a separate experience.

"My boyfriend likes to put my finger up his anus when I give him oral sex. Is this normal? Is he gay?"

He is not necessarily gay. Nor is it abnormal. Some men go wild getting oral pleasure while you also stimulate their anal opening, as the latter stimulates his prostate gland. The combination of the physical sensation and his mental association can drive him to ecstasy. Always be careful to clean your fingers afterwards if you are going to continue sex play, especially touching yourself, and don't do it unless he has cleaned himself all the way up.

SNIFFER SEX

Scot: *"I like to sniff girls' anuses. It turns me on. They call me 'Scot Toilet Tissue.' Does this make me abnormal?"*

Not unless that's all that turns you on. Putting you on the Freudian couch, I'd say you got stuck at the anal phase of development, where you were fascinated with your toilet training, and your ability to produce feces. You may also have enjoyed your own odor in the toilet, and found that stimulating, so now you have transferred that to girls.

REARING UP

Danny, 17: *"When I masturbate, I play with my ass. My girlfriend saw this and it grossed her out. Is this stupid to do?"*

No. You must have learned to enjoy the soothing feeling of rubbing your rear, and started to do it when masturbating. It's like thumb-sucking. Your girlfriend need not be so sensitive about rear ends. We develop masturbation habits though, so if it bothers you or her too much, you can purposefully stop doing it.

DOESN'T GET HINT

Jake, 21: *"I can't get a girl to give me back door action. I go down on them first and do it around their butt, but they don't get the hint. My roommate gets it real easy. He lies to them and tells them anything. What's with me?"*

Don't copy your roommate, who sounds like a jerk. Find someone you can care for and vice versa, without putting conditions on oral sex with paybacks.

BE PREPARED

Jeff: *"When I come I wanted my girlfriend to stick her hand up my butt. But she did it and took her hand out and there were feces on it. She was grossed out. I really dug it, but now I'm afraid she won't do it again. Won't this happen every time?"*

Clean yourself, man. Use the Fleet enema squeegee bottles (the water one, rather than the oil one). Do it a half hour before you have sex, so you're cleaned out but any leftover stuff won't drip out either.

ANAL PORNO VIDEOS

Theresa, 25: *"I walked in and saw my husband on the couch doggie-style with a porno on the TV, and he had a vibrator inserted in his anus. How do I tell him about this?"*

Just be direct. What is your worst fear—that he's gay? It's not necessarily so. Maybe you can get involved in his fantasies and expand the pleasures that you can have together instead of him hiding what he likes.

SEE NO SPERM

"If I ejaculate in her rear and then she has a bowel movement, can I see the sperm in the bowl?"

No. Sperm are microscopic. You can't see them with the naked eye. But the semen can act like a mild enema, by adding some liquidity to the feces.

Final Word: Whichever door you knock on, make sure you're welcome!

JAGGER LIKES TO SAY HE'S "TRY-SEXUAL"—HE'LL try anything.

Candlebox lead singer Kevin Martin echoes, "I'll try anything. I'm tri-sexual."

Whatever you try, remember Dr. Judy's Sex Rule: "Love is the best lubricant."

There are four F's to good sex: Express your Feelings. Get the Facts. Allow your Fantasies. And have Fun. Explore new boundaries in what turns you on, alone and with someone. Heighten all your senses: sight, smell, hearing, touch, taste.

SEX TOYS AND GAMES

"Are sex toys okay to use?"

I am in favor of certain sex toys and games. But fill your heart before the toy chest. Rule: use toys as long as they don't get out of hand (hah, hah). That means, as long as they aren't a replacement for a partner, and as long as both people agree to use them.

MACHINE SEX

"What's the difference between a dildo and a vibrator?"

Dildos are shaped like penises and you put them inside your body openings for pleasure. They can be made of plastic, or latex-like materials that feel very natural and even have veins like real penises. They come in all sizes and colors, and some are battery operated, or electrical, so they vibrate. The Japanese are particularly inventive: "The Beaver" or the "Bull and the Bear" has a phallus-shape you insert that twists, with a ring of ball bearings that vibrate at the vaginal opening, and vibrating rabbit ears or beaver tail that stimulates the clitoral area.

A vibrator usually refers to a larger machine that is used externally and marketed as "a body massager." Popular ones include Homedics' "Body Mate" (with an added bump for clitoral stimulation), Hitachi's "Magic Wand," Windmere's products, and Panasonic's "Panabrator." Nass Toys' "Lady Bug" straps on to vibrate against the clitoris.

"I really want to get one of those vibrators. But is it a good idea and will it help me have an orgasm?"

A vibrator can really help a woman have her first orgasm, or have them more regularly, because the constant stimulation doesn't let her stop short of her peak like she might if she were using her hand. And it's particularly useful in the "bridge" technique, to train her to have orgasm with a partner, by holding it on her genitals while he's inside her, and gradually withdrawing it as she gets closer to her peak.

You can use only one—or try a double whammy: a battery-operated dildo to insert (so you get vibrations in your vagina) and a body massager held over your clitoris (to trigger orgasm) or on another body part (to add excitement).

A guy can get pleasure using a dildo or vibrator anywhere on her, or on himself—guys really like the vibrations on the perineum, behind their scrotum.

Four out of the five members of the all-girl band Fem2Fem admit to loving the electric way! Julie, a self-proclaimed bisexual, has a small hand-held version with various attachments. Christina, a lesbian, got a mini-vibrator that comes from Japan from her new girlfriend; it has knobs on the tip for acupressure. Lynn, also lesbian, uses the biggest machine: "It's an 8000 Harley and I ride it in second gear!"

"I'm afraid to get a vibrator because I may get addicted to it. Can that happen?"

It's easy to see why you could get attached to a vibrator because, in contrast to a relationship, it's always there when you want it, always works, never gets tired, and never wants anything in return. You'll only get addicted if you escape into it and avoid a relationship. Otherwise, consider it a healthy addition to your pleasure alone and together.

Some people think if you use a vibrator too often you can decrease your sensitivity to respond to fingers or a penis. Just the opposite: the stimulation is different, but the vibrator heightens your potential to respond in other ways.

Q: What did the banana say to the vibrator?
A: Why are you shaking, she's going to eat me first.

"I love my vibrator, but when my boyfriend came over and saw it under my bed, he freaked, saying, 'I guess I'm not enough for you. I can't compete with a machine.' How can I convince him he's wrong?"

Advice from Guns N' Roses rhythm guitarist Gilbey Clarke: "Guys love it when women go wild so he shouldn't object. But get one close to his size—that's what might bother him! Maybe it'll give him a hint, 'Baby, I need a little more than you're giving me.' Tell him, let me have this fantasy and I'll let you have one."

Too bad that men get competitive with vibrators. Reassure him that he's a great lover and that the machine doesn't replace him. Most guys get to like it once you put it on *their* body and they feel good. Then, show him how to play with it on your clitoris or other body parts. Then do it while he's penetrating you.

A special treat for some men: use a mini vibrator in his anal region, four inches long and half inch diameter, either at the opening, or inserted to reach the prostate gland.

Ron: "I'm the one who got my girlfriend into the vibrator. I bought her the first one for fun, but now she bought a few

*different types and she's overdoing it. All of a sudden, she's
having an orgy by herself and I'm out. I met her at work
one day for lunch and opened up her purse and the vibrator
was there. What can I do?"*

Like any new toy you get and love, you can want to play
with it all the time, but you eventually get tired of it. You're
not replaced; in fact, you'll also benefit from her current
growth. Don't over-dramatize—the machine can't compete
with you as a responsive, warm body, as long as that's what
you are!

ICE MAN

As hockey fans say, "On the ice is twice as nice."

*Danny: "My girlfriend likes ice cubes inside her vagina at
the peak of her passion. I keep a glass by the bed and as she
gets close to coming, I put some in my mouth and then I
thrust them into her vagina. Is this a good idea?"*

Some girls may like the cold rush on the genitalia,
swollen and heated-up with blood from excitement, but
frankly, I don't think it's a good idea because if you ever
had an injury you know ice reduces the swelling and desen-
sitizes—why would you want that? (Some guys like a cold
rush on the tip of their penis, too).

What about the opposite—heat it up!

*Dave: When I do that oral thing, I put some Hall's in my
mouth, those ice blue mentholated cough drops, and boy
do they tingle. Then, I put them inside her with my
tongue."*

The vaginal barrel is like the inside of the mouth, so similar sensations would happen in those two places. Suckers
can make the tissues tingle; beware they don't irritate.

*"My girl sticks all kinds of things in her—like toothbrush
handles and pens."*

No! Stick to toys made of natural materials, and stay
away from anything (glass bottle necks, wood bathbrush
handles) that could tear your delicate linings.

BENWA BALLS

"What are those little balls you can insert in the woman to turn her on?"

Benwa balls are small balls the size of walnuts, made of steel, plated with chrome or gold, that vibrate inside the vagina, and move around inside as the woman moves. Also, by tensing her muscles around the balls, the woman can exercise her genital (pc or love) muscles, developing stronger "gripping" of the vaginal muscles to make more contact with the penis on penetration, and more intense orgasms.

ANAL BEADS

"Is it safe to use those beads that you put up your ass?"

Anything you put in your body has a potential to irritate, tear the walls, and therefore cause infection. If you're careful, though, you can use anal beads safely and with pleasure. They can be a rope, tied in knots, or with plastic beads at various intervals. People insert them in the anal canal, and pull them out during orgasm to create stimulation.

MAKING NOISE

For ex-Van Halen lead singer David Lee Roth, the secret to really pleasing a woman is "her ears—the best sex is in the ears—talk dirty to her."

British rock group New Order bassist Peter Hook, has the opposite preference: "I prefer nice quiet sex" (ironic, for a guy who owns one of the hottest clubs in England).

Couples can also be divided on the noisy sex factor and dirty talk. Like Melanie and Dan.

Melanie: *"I've been seeing this guy for three years and we just got engaged. I never knew he was dissatisfied with me in bed, but the other night during sex he turned the sound on the stereo way up and when I complained, he said my silence was deafening him! We got into an argument and I nearly broke the engagement. I've only been with a few men before, but they never complained. Am I abnormal to be quiet in sex and am I right being so upset?"*

Certainly Dan was clumsy complaining about your sexual silence; you should never criticize someone in bed, and always say what you like instead. He should whisper in your ear one night when you were feeling especially confident, "Honey, I love when you make noises. It lets me know you are enjoying yourself and that I'm pleasing you." It's fine that he likes feedback. If making noise is not your style, show him he pleases you other ways, like by movements or facial expressions. Many people, like your fiancé, find heavy breathing and orgasmic cries arousing. To please him, can you learn to do it?

Practice. Start with nonsexual sighs while sinking into a hot bath or putting body lotion on. Rehearse different sounds: low purrs, deep sighs. Feel your body vibrate with the sounds. Once you're more comfortable, surprise him.

TALKING DIRTY

"Once in the middle of sex, I shocked a guy out of his wits when he was going down on me and then I pulled him up over me and said in a real gruff voice, 'Fuck me now.' He was so excited, he kept saying 'Oh baby,' over and over after that. Do you think all guys like that?"

"My girlfriend likes me to talk dirty to her, screaming that she's a bitch and a whore, while we're having sex. I'm hesitant to do it. Should I?"

Tess, 26: *I'd like my boyfriend to talk dirty in sex, to use nasty words. I play CDs by the Former Prince to get him in the mood. I want him to say things like 'Tess, you're my bitch' . . . How do I do it?'*

You go, girl! Barry White and The Artist Formerly Known as Prince are brilliant examples of sexy talk on tape. Check out the latter's album "Coming" with the last cut "Orgasm" as he talks a woman through a two-minute orgasm.

Tell your honey outright, 'I'd love you to say, Tess you're my bitch . . . do this or that . . .' Or, you set an example. If he resists, find out what he fears (disrespecting you, going against his upbringing). Tell him it's a game that makes you feel uninhibited because you know you care about each other. What deeper needs do you have to do this: to get over being a "good girl," to heal past times when such words were used to hurt?

Talking dirty (called "coprolalia") was once considered deviant, rude, disrespectful, and unladylike, but the sexual revolution and proliferation of 900-lines has made them more mainstream. One survey showed that over fifty percent of women and men felt talking dirty was normal (with career women liking it the best!), while only one quarter of the women and one fifth of the men thought it was kinky. But beware that it doesn't lead to unsafe sex or misleading messages (for example, saying "beat me" without meaning it, or "Do it now" before precautions are taken).

Sometimes a partner is shocked or disgusted at crude terms, but gets more accepting after realizing the difference between a put-down and raunchy talk meant to be playful, overcome sexual inhibitions, and increase sexual arousal.

If words are said in the love and passion of the moment, anything goes (except another's name!). It is a great release and can be really hot to surprise a lover as a sign of your abandonment. If your mind says, "That's bad or nasty," to anything, imagine WHO would disapprove (mother, priest) and in an imaginary conversation with that person, say, "You may disapprove for you, but I don't consider myself bad for this."

Prince Charles and his lover Camilla Parker-Bowles apparently had no hesitation talking dirty, as revealed in their taped sexy phone conversation, the scandalous "Camillagate" tapes. Said Charles: "I want to feel my way along you, all over you and up and down you and in and out . . ." "I fill up your tank." "Your great achievement is to love me." "Oh God, I'll just live inside your trousers." Camilla: "Oh, you're going to come back as a pair of knickers (panties)." Charles: "Or, God forbid, a Tampax."

LOVE TALK

Stroke the mind before the behind.
—Dr. Rosie Milligan, *Satisfying A Black Woman Sexually*

"My girlfriend wants me to talk more in sex, but what should I say?"

Silence is not golden when it comes to sex. Much research over the years has also proven that couples who talk together have happier marriages and that happily married couples talk more together—particularly saying positive things about each other! Not everyone can be eloquent as Cyrano de Bergerac, but what and how much you say in bed is not as important as just expressing yourself. Sweet nothings ring in your ears, and build self-esteem and desire!

What you say can be an aphrodisiac. If it's exactly what a person wants to hear (their sex script), you hit the jackpot. Remember to whisper in the left ear because it's connected to the right (romantic) side of the brain. Suggestions:

SIX STEAMY SEX TALKS

- "Thank you": Appreciation and acknowledgment, after or during sex, for their time, attention, touching, builds self-esteem.
- "Hmmm": Repetitive sounds facilitate relaxed, meditative states.
- "You're beautiful": Praise and compliments boost confidence. An old Black jazz pianist in San Francisco, renowned for his success with women, had a secret: crying on a woman because of her beauty.
- "I'm glad you're here," "This feels good," "I still love you after all this time," and especially, "I love you. This is only for you. I'm yours," at the moment of orgasm. Reassurance builds confidence and bonding.
- "I can't wait to be with you again," or "I have to get up a few minutes after we're finished, but that doesn't mean I'm leaving you. Feel me still on top of you," "I'm going to lick you all over next time": Promises for the future prevent rejection.
- My favorite technique: "Sexual Play By Play," giving an ongoing description of your sex encounter as it's happening, heightens the experience.

LOVE SLAVE

Janey: *"I have been having sex with a rich guy who rents a hotel room for me to come over for sex. Once I was wearing a really sexy outfit and he got down on his knees in front of me and looked up at me asking what he could do to please me. Normally we have straight sex, and I really feel like equals, and usually he has a really strong voice, but this one time, in a little boy tone, he pleaded, 'Please Janey, I want you so badly, let me suck you down there, please.' At first, I was a little scared but finally I told him, 'Bury your head there,' and he did it, moaning and groaning. It was really exciting. I want to do it again, but I'm a little scared to become like those dominating mistresses. Also, I wonder, considering he's such a powerful guy, does he really like being at my mercy like that?"*

Aerosmith's Steven Tyler: "I like that dominant stuff a little bit, yeah. I like them to rear their beautiful faces and I like them to take control of the situation every now and then. You know—not have to do it all myself . . . See, it's all in the face. As long as I have a face, you have a place to sit."

Playing love slave—with handcuffs, friendly spankings, blindfolds, orders—for one another can be extremely pleasurable, and healthy, to give each person a chance to experience healthy control. Many men today also like women to be more assertive and women are getting more comfortable taking control.

To answer your question, powerful guys can be even more attracted to being ordered around in sex, because they're so busy controlling people in business, that they like to take the opposite role in sex. One study of prostitutes in Washington, D.C. showed that many male clients who held high political posts asked to be ordered around. Congratulations to you for getting in touch with what you like, feeling your power, asking for it, and finding a man who can "play" at it while still treating you as an equal. What a dynamo combination.

S&M GAMES

Dave: *"I have a younger girlfriend who likes being submissive. I blindfold her and spank her. But I want her do it to me, to know what it feels like. But she says she's not good at it and won't. What can I do?"*

Help her understand why she won't do it. She's probably a shy, "good girl" who's scared to take control. Reassure her that it's only a game and that you won't permanently make her take over. You will still take care of her. Have her slowly get into it by telling you minor things to do, like directing you to move your arm to the left or to get her a glass of water.

Lorraine, 18: *"I like my boyfriend to bite me on my nipples and on my vagina when we have sex. He doesn't like to do it. Is there something wrong?"*

Mild biting, scratching, and pinching can be exciting, as it stimulates the nerve endings. Examine why you want this. If you can't feel anything without strong bites, concentrate on tiny sensations. If you feel guilty about sex, give yourself permission. If you're afraid to get close, purposefully resist the bites and feel loved instead.

Sex symbol Brad Pitt supposedly loves leaving "love tattoos" all over lover's bodies, and then connects the hickeys with a marker, making body art (and making it playful).

X-RATED FARE

"My husband enjoys X-rated movies to the max. I don't. He wants me to watch these movies with him and then try the particular sex acts. How do I finesse my way out of this without hurting his feelings? His usual line to me is, 'How do you know you don't like it if you won't try it?'"

His line can also be the truth. Reconsider watching the movies and trying out the acts; could sharing these bring new excitement? Pick a more erotic than explicit one. There's some good "female friendly" fare available, including Femme Productions' videos and even Playboy's series (shot very tastefully). Be appreciative that he wants to share them with you, rather than watching alone secretly, or trying out the acts with someone else!

SHE LOVES CELLULOID SEX

"I know most women complain about men watching "dirty movies" on the VCR, but I'm one man who caught his woman watching. I couldn't help getting upset. Is there something wrong with her or me that she has to do this?"

Your woman is not alone. Polls show that as many as one in four women have sampled X-rated video fare and studies prove that women like looking just as much as men do.

Watching videos can be an escape from intimacy or permission to do some new things yourself once you see couples on screen doing them comfortably.

Research shows that women object to men viewing nude pictures of other women because they feel jealous of the other women's more attractive bodies. Now men face a similar threat! The solution: rather than feel intimidated that you don't measure up to the video hunks or that your woman's viewing means you are inadequate, talk with her about what she finds appealing: What scenes would she like to do with you that you both might otherwise be ashamed or afraid of? Make your real life compelling so any made-up story is merely an addition and not a substitute to your turn-on—alone or together.

LINGERING LOVE

"We've been married for five years and every time we make love it's over so fast. I read about all-day love sessions in romance novels so how can we make it last longer?"

Real life is not like romance novels, but the contrast between the two can seem greater these days when work and family life demands cut in on sex. Prolonged, romantic lovemaking is a great way, though, to boost your ego, bond you together, and relax your body and mind.

Get over any mental blocks (being bored, worrying about repeating it). Make time together a priority and set chunks of it aside. In "It's About Time," Lemonheads' Evan Dando sang about how a couple simply can't get their schedules to jibe.

Plan a seductive evening or an entire weekend day at home together free of interruptions. Pack the kids off to friends. Draw out seduction with touching and flirting.

Focus on tenderness and affection, like in Michael Bolton's song, "Time, Love and Tenderness." Do pleasure touching that isn't intended to be sexual, and it will grow into that.

"How do I make my boyfriend less mechanical and more romantic?"

Tell him how wonderful he already is, to set the foundation of confidence. In reading passages from books or watching movies, point out scenes you like, and mention how you like when he's like that (remember, reward what you want repeated). Always point out when he does it right.

THE ULTIMATE ROMANTIC EVENING

Marion: *"What's the ultimate romantic evening for me to plan for a guy I really like? How do I really seduce him?"*
Laura: *"I've been with this guy for 12 years and I have three kids by him, and now we've split up but he comes over every other day to have sex. I want to do something very different for our anniversary. What could be really hot so he'll keep me burning in his mind?"*

Celebrities suggestions:

Rhonda Schear, USA Network's *Up All Night* hostess, *Playboy* magazine centerfold, actress, and comedienne: "Making out and kissing a lot, in the backseat of a car or someplace naughty. I like all that. Romance is everything. Holding hands in a restaurant or rubbing feet between each other's legs is really good."

Comic/actor Pauly Shore: "Light candles, watch a porno flick, she would talk dirty like girls in film, come on I'm gonna spank you if you're bad . . ."

Richard Marx: "A candlelit dinner or a bubble bath, and

a fantasy pretending you're strangers who never did it before."

Romance novel cover boy Fabio: "A moonlight swim, picnic on a mountain top, a candlelight bath for two."

Van Halen lead singer Sammy Hagar: "A man who can put a great meal on the table on that first date will blow her mind. Guaranteed you will get it that night. You whip up an unbelievable dinner and get a bottle of wine from the year of her birthday (my girlfriend's is 1967). That will open the bedroom door and pull the sheets back."

John Henton, TV's *Living Single*: "Do something different. Get out of wherever you are used to hanging out and making love. Get a hotel room. Do the dinner thing. Walk around. Go to a club if you like dancing or go to a show if you are into that. Have a few drinks and go back to the room and just kick it and do fun things."

"My boyfriend is coming home from jail, how can I make it as romantic as possible for him?"

My *LovePhones* co-host, Chris Jagger, warned: make sure you don't suggest anal sex.

BE FREE AND EXPRESSIVE

"How do I get her in the mood?"
"We get bored in sex. What can we do?"

This is the most common question, in all the years people have sought my advice—through letters, radio or TV shows, newspaper columns, or private consultation. Boredom in bed can happen as soon as two years into the relationship, down from the "seven year itch" of Marilyn Monroe's days, or the four years anthropologists estimate animals keep faithful until the offspring are old enough. In this age of fear of AIDS, and increased male interest in intimacy, more men and women want to make commitments last.

Continued excitement IS possible—if you work at it—breaking old habits, taking risks, overcoming resistance to change (laziness, inexperience, fear, negative attitudes).

SEX TO-DO'S

- Set aside two nights a week with one hour of uninterrupted time to be together.
- Make a list of surprises and do one a week for each other.
- Leave love notes in jacket pockets, daily planner, car seats.
- Verbal foreplay. Call during the day and promise what you'll do.
- Make up a private language of love for positions and fantasies that make you special to each other.
- Focus total attention. Take turns lying back and enjoying it.
- Spend a whole day or night in bed—eating and playing. A couple I met in Tampa won a supermarket contest for the most romantic couple because they spend eight hours in bed every other week, playing.
- Read a sex manual together and try out what they suggest.
- Make love in front of mirrors and watch yourselves.
- Get a sex game from a sex store and play it. Some board games have to-do cards, like, "Tell your partner the time you felt most loved," or, "Kiss a place you never kissed before."
- Make up your own sex games. Play role reversal (be each other for the night). A *LovePhones* caller, Max, suggests "Lotto Sex": "If I win my girlfriend has to warm my erection with saliva and eat me dry. If she wins, I eat her out till my tummy is full."
- Come up with a new sex fantasy. There is always something new in your imagination. Get a costume for each of you that fits the fantasy and play it out.
- Read erotic books aloud.
- Write poems to each other and recite them or recite from romantic poetry.
- Look at erotic pictures in magazines together.

☞

SEX TO-DO'S (CONTINUED)

- Watch romantic movies or erotic videos.
- Try different positions—make them up or follow the Kama Sutra—and giggle! Try "dry humping" and "shadow stroking" (sliding the head of the penis up and down in the groove of the female's genitals).
- Re-create your best times together, from the first wonderful date you had. It takes a little acting, but you can get into it. It'll bring back that thrill you had and long for.
- Make love in a different place or way, or at a different time.
- "The Explorer Exercise" to find new hot spots. Romance heartthrob Fabio's hot spot is his neck. Van Halen's Sammy Hagar suggests the base of the penis or about the first two or three inches down from the top. What he likes on women is "anyplace between the waist and the knees, including the thighs, crotch, butt, and belly button." (But don't put your finger in Sammy's belly button, he hates that).
- Use Sex Aids: creams, oils, Kamasutra dust, feathers, fur, vibrators.
- Play different roles, either as movie characters, or make ones up. For example: playing savior, offering emotional and physical comfort, causes eroticism.

101 USES FOR A PENIS

"My girlfriend likes to use my penis to slap against her face in sex. Is something wrong with her?"

Not necessarily. It can be a sign of great freedom of self-expression in sex to use your penis for any number of sensual acts—against her face, in any orifice, rubbed against her eyes, between breasts, inside bent knees . . . wherever your creativity takes you. Like eating off someone's plate, using your penis shows she's that comfortable, and intimate, with you. When you're turned on, blood rushes to the skin surface and it's sensitive. Slapping something against it gives off tingles that can be pleasurable.

SPERM BATH

"I like my boyfriend to 'whitewash me'—ejaculate on my face—and he loves it. Is this sick?"

No. Unless you do it to humiliate yourself, it can be quite a sign of freedom in sex, and appreciating him. Some women like it on their breasts, or stomach. You can rub it all over your body! Have fun. Just be careful of your eyes. Caution: don't think you can avoid getting pregnant by pulling out just before he comes; remember pre-cum has potent sperm in it.

WHERE

"What are some different places we can try to have sex?"

The sky's the limit. Use your imagination. Start with different rooms in the house: kitchen, den, bathroom. A bath, shower, steam bath, or any body of water, is erotic because you're nude and clean, and water is sexy (its negative ions create positive moods). Outdoors, in a garden, woods, secluded park, in fresh air is exciting. Roger Clinton said on *LovePhones* that he'd like to do it in the Rose Garden.

In "public"—the thrill of possibly being seen or getting caught can add spice. Ex–*China Beach* actress Dana Delaney said she did it in a public pool and joined the "mile high club" by doing it with the pilot of a six-seater plane over the Grand Canyon. People have tried the "mile below" (scuba diving) club, too.

Favorite places for Honorary Love Doctors: Steven Tyler likes a deserted beach, so does Fabio—a "blue lagoon" is where he'd like to be with his "twin soul" woman. Bret Michaels of Poison hated the sand and the cold didn't help him "sizewise" and prefers his room. David Coverdale's favorite place was Bangkok. For Guns N' Roses' Gilbey Clarke, "it was once on my motorcycle, not driving it though, that is a little dangerous." Former Mötley Crüe lead Vince Neil likes sex in weird places. "This girl in Vancouver got me into it, we'd go out and do it in people's boats. I had sex one time on my balcony on Sunset Boulevard on a Friday night. There were hundreds of people walking by. And I had sex in a booth at a club and everyone was walking around and watching us have sex, but it was thrilling. It's like the weirder the place, the better."

WHAT'S THE WILDEST

Lots of callers to *LovePhones* want to hear the Honorary Love Doctors' wildest sex experiences. Here's some:

Candlebox's lead singer Kevin Martin: "Years ago I was quick to get sex over with. Mentally it's easier not to be concerned with a partner's pleasure. One needs to have longer foreplay. The most incredible experience is to come together. The wildest sex was on a bus in Seattle on the way home from work. I came quickly. The girl I was dating was sitting on my lap and I had the Velcro fly going. It was unsafe sex. Sometimes, you do stupid things."

Guns N' Roses' Gilbey Clarke has seen it all and been in a lot of group things, but still got shocked by seeing one girl with two guys in the same place: "two pegs in the same hole." A caller reported his wildest: a video of two hermaphrodites having intercourse and oral sex with their mini-penis/enlarged clitorises.

Poison's lead singer Bret Michaels (once *Baywatch* babe Pam Anderson's beau): "It had something to do with a banana and yogurt. It was very enjoyable and in this day and age very safe. I like gin and tonic, to loosen those inhibitions, and then for the first time, fast, hard, and intense sex. For the second time, slower sex. The third time, that night . . . if everything is still working . . . I don't like public places. I like it in a bedroom, dark, some place I'm familiar with. I like the mattress on the floor."

Poison's drummer Rikki Rockett: "It was with a girl who had her belly button pierced. She couldn't care about anything else I did if I played with that."

The guys from the Brit group Blur: Graham: Try biting his dick. Dress up as Batman and Catgirl. Damon: both wear wigs on your heads or anywhere. Chris says mess with his butt. "There is nothing wrong with sticking your finger up someone's butt. If you don't want to put your fingers up there use a vegetable. You can make it taste a little sweeter. Put a condom on your tongue. Stick a carrot up there and then eat it. Isn't there a place in, up there somewhere that kind of makes blokes come? Isn't that a prostate gland or something?"

Aerosmith's Steven Tyler really DID Love in An Elevator. "It started in a hot tub on the twenty-second floor. We wound up in an elevator and it was with two girls. I was being manipulated by one girl and doing the other and I didn't know what I was doing and I'm not sure why but I went into one of those trance states forgetting that we were in the elevator. I was laying on my back on the floor and, uh, the doors opened up and we were in the lobby. And a bunch of people were standing there and they looked in and they looked down. (A caller finished the story, by suggesting the onlookers noted that's the biggest luggage they've ever seen!). The best sex, Tyler claims now, is with his wife, because "it can happen as many times as it wants to and it doesn't uh, you know when you, after a while, you get to know those little places that get you off all the time. And as long as you keep communication open, that's the secret right there."

"We've tried everything. What are some wilder suggestions about what to do?"
Try these New Rave Sex tips:

TEN NEW RAVE SEX TIPS

1. Home grown porn. It's a trend that couples are filming their own sex—in their backyards, bathrooms, bedrooms—and even selling them! Celebrity skin tapes include: Tonya Harding and her then husband Jeff Gillooly, and the infamous Rob Lowe tape of 1988.

2. His/Her Cross-dressing. Tranvestism is becoming more open both in the U.S. and abroad. (It's also increasingly popular in Japan). Wearing his shorts can give her a sense of power, putting on her panties gives him a new appreciation for her! One of my favorite designers, Norma Kamali, suggests girls raid their brother's closet, and vice versa. Duran Duran's Simon LeBon likes the idea of stockings.

☞

<u>TEN NEW RAVE SEX TIPS</u> (CONTINUED)

3. Erotic stripping. Deliberately struggle with buttons, straps, and buckles that suggest obstacles to overcome. Robert Downey, Jr. would allegedly borrow costumes from his film set (of the 17th century) and do a tantalizing striptease before sex.

4. Dirty dancing together. Rub and hump to rhythmic dance music.

5. Masturbation displays. It's a favorite male fantasy to watch a woman pleasure herself!

6. Resist orgasm. As in Eastern practices, stay at the plateau.

7. Make taboo fantasies okay. Be the opposite sex, pretend to be other people.

8. Sitophilia: using food for sex. Eating is erotic and food is a substitute for love. Feed each other (as Mickey Rourke fed Kim Basinger in *9 1/2 Weeks*). Or eat a meal off each other's bodies. One woman greeted her husband at the door in a lacy tablecloth. When he asked, "What's for dinner?" she answered, "Me," and led him into the bedroom where she draped herself on the bed and lay the meal she had prepared for him on her body.

9. Play "War and Peace": alternate active lovemaking (thrashing about) with passive, slow-motion sex. This alternates the sympathetic nervous system, associated with the racing heart and panting breaths of the "fight or flight" response, with the relaxation associated with the parasympathetic nervous system.

10. "Thinking off." Transmit orgasmic excitement without touching, by just thinking about it! One *LovePhones* caller described making love to a woman standing fully clothed on a moonlit street, pressing bodies against one another and feeling the polar energy of their bodies lifting them to orgasm. Remember the scene in *Cocoon* where Tahnee Welch went electrical spark across the pool to Steve Guttenberg. Honorary Love Doctor actress Sean Young described a similar "Android Sex" when she played a distraught android in Ridley Scott's futuristic *Blade Runner*. "We could just rise above and feel somebody's connection. We did not really need to bother with all that messy, juicy, slippery stuff. All we need to do is get zapped with the basic vibration of a human being."

"What can we do that's different in the actual sex act? We need some new ideas."

Try these:

MORE NEW RAVE SEX TIPS

- **Containment.** Instead of rushing to thrusting, feel what it feels like to have something (a finger, tongue, penis, dildo) inside you. Francine, who works in TV, calls it "still store" (when you put a picture in computer memory to appear on the screen behind the reporter's head).
- **Lovers "bowling."** Insert fingers in both openings, as you would a bowling ball.
- **Love Muscle Maneuvers.** Japanese prostitutes during WWII had this Tantric sex technique down—where they perch on top of the man and "milk" his penis by contractions of their abdominal and vaginal muscles, without moving their body (also known as "snaking," "Kabazzah," "snapping pussy," and by Native American Indians as the "Apache grip," or "Kikaboo twist").
- **"Co-breathing."** Where one breathes in as the other breathes out, exchanging energy.

Practice the Five C's: Concentrate on being calm, content, compassionate, centered, and then cosmic.

PHONE SEX

Jane: *"My boyfriend just moved away for his job. We started to have phone sex but I'm not very good at it. How do I do it?"*

Play-by-play sex! Think of yourself as being a sports announcer on the radio—observing and reporting the action as it is happening. Use your imagination by picturing him right there in the room with you. Talk through what you are doing as if it is in the present, giving a blow-by-blow description of what you are each doing. For example, you say, "Hi, I'm so glad to see you. I'm touching my hand to your cheek and smiling at you, thinking you're so handsome tonight and saying with my eyes that I want you so badly." He says, "Good," so you pick it up more. You say, "I'm unbuttoning your shirt and you put your hands on my hips, running them down my butt, and grabbing the cheeks, whispering in my ear, 'I love grabbing your tight buns, they make me so hard.'"

You can always ask him questions, like, "What are you thinking you would like me to do now?" He may say a suggestion or may say you're doing just fine, so go on. "I unzip your pants and feel your pulsing member in my hand," you continue, "and you pick me up and carry me over to the bed, where you lay me down gently and start unbuttoning my blouse and rubbing your hands over my firm breasts, leaning down to kiss them, as my nipples get hard" . . . and you're on your way . . .

With Gavin Rossdale and the British band Bush as Honorary Love Doctors, we identified the following key questions: "Where are you now (on the couch, in my bed)?" "What are you wearing?" "What would you like to do to me (or me to do to you)?"

British band Bush drummer, Robin Goodridge's great suggestion: "Get a dictaphone" (great pun! but also smart suggestion, to practice in a tape recorder).

DRESS-UP

"I've always wanted to buy one of those wild sex outfits they have in those sex catalogues, either the crotchless panties or the push-ups. But I'm afraid that my boyfriend will think it's silly. Should I get one?"

Absolutely. Dress up in anything. Have fun. Try different outfits. Dressing the part can help you ACT the part; wear a sexy outfit and you'll *feel* more sexy. Try a tight sheath, a frilly nightgown, schoolgirl outfit. Surprise him, too (with a sequin jockstrap, caveman wrap, football jersey).

If he's uncomfortable, reassure and encourage him to enjoy it for you. Even sweet Debbie Gibson is into underwear variety: "Sometimes I'm into silk, sometimes cotton, and sometimes Bugs Bunny boxers."

POSITIONS

"What position is the best?" "Can you suggest some new positions?" "My boyfriend always looks to do it in different positions. How else can I make love to him, so he's not bored in sex?"

Try any way your bodies can move and drape, freestanding or up against anything (walls, beds, chairs). The position you like best—especially to come to orgasm—depends on your physical comfort, excitement, and friction of your body parts.

Since women's orgasm is triggered by the clitoris, the best positions rub the clitoris or pubic bone and leave room for a vibrator: side-to-side with legs intertwined, woman-on-top, or man behind. The woman-on-top takes pressure off the guy to perform, and allows her control over the amount and type of stimulation.

Jazz up the missionary position, with the guy thrusting forward as well as downward. Reposition her legs, open, knees up. Or lift onto your arms, put her legs inside yours, and move downward onto her, sliding down her body and lifting up again, in an elliptical motion, with your penis tightly gripped between her legs. Lots of callers rushed to try the original "3-Eyed Turtle," combining voyeurism and frontage (name thanks to WMMS' Brian and Joe): Rub the penis head (Eye 1) against the clitoris (Eye 2) and enjoy watching with your eyes or in a mirror!

In the "Yoga Sun Worship" position, the person on top arches his/her back up like a cat stretching, thrusting the pubic bone against the partner for more contact.

One of my favorites, the "Inverted Forklift": start out on your backs, rotate to face each other, intertwine your legs, and lift your pelvises into the air. Tense muscles for more grip.

The Kama Sutra, the ancient Eastern guide to lovemaking, depicts innumerable positions with exotic names. For example, in "Bunny Licking Its Fur" the man lies on his back and the woman sits on top. In "Fish Linking Scales" she straddles her thighs against him and slowly inserts him, thrusting forward. In "Stepping Tigers," they advance and retreat in mutual attacks like a pair of tigers, with eight thrusts in five repetitions and a brief resting between each set.

"Twin Phoenixes Dancing" is for a threesome, where one woman lies on top of another woman, face-to-face in the "Gobbling Fish" position (rubbing their jade gates against one another) as the man kneels beside them and inserts himself between them, connecting both above and below.

Dave's girlfriend learned this from cheerleading: the "Pogo Stick," where "she does a handstand and wraps her legs around my hips and I put it in her and she bounces up and down." (They also call his penis "the microphone, since she does interviews talking into it, and then sucks the battery juices out!")

Favorite positions for some Honorary Love Doctors:

Richard Marx: woman on top

MTV's Bill Bellamy: doggie style, face-to-face, and woman on top.

Ugly Kid Joe's Whitfield Crane: "spooning" or "basketing" (cradling stomach to back).

Ed Kowalczyk from the band Live: the wheelbarrow, where one person is behind with the other's legs around his hips, and hands on the ground.

HOT SPOT POSITIONS FOR HIM AND HER

"What's the best position for the best orgasm for him and her?"

Of course, it's always individual. But, for many women, use any position where you can access her clitoris, or rub his pubic bone against hers. For the man, it's any position to allow oral pleasure of the penis and finger massage of the perineum or anal opening, stimulating his hot spot. This includes the woman on top facing toward his feet, kneeling between his legs, or rear entry with the woman bending between his legs. A big bonus in intercourse: as he thrusts in toward orgasm, she squeezes her pc (love) muscles to expand the head of his penis.

Ann: *"This guy I had sex with insisted on doggie style, but I don't like it. Is there anything wrong with me?"*

Honorary Love Doctor Bill Bellamy was sympathetic. "Doggie style is in a man's repertoire and the whole idea of making love to a woman in that position is erotic. But a lot of women don't like it because it's like 'not facing me, I can't see the love in his eyes.'"

Rear entry done lovingly is fine, unless it's meant to dominate, humiliate, or distance the woman. Also some women like the deep penetration of rear entry or lying on their back with their legs above their head, while others (especially those with a tipped uterus) find it painful.

"My girlfriend prefers when I use my fingers. Do you think that's because my penis only does the 'ole in and out? What else can it do?"

The Chinese "Nine Manners" ways of moving the penis (jade stalk) include: striking left and right like a fierce warrior; climbing up and jumping down like a wild horse; emerging and submerging like a flock of gulls over waves; stirring lightly like birds pecking grain; penetrating deep and skimming shallow, like a big rock thrown in the sea; stirring and pushing slowly like a snake through grass; loosening rapidly and piercing suddenly like a frightened mouse dashing into a hole; lifting the head and crooking the feet like a falcon teasing a hare; rearing its top and dipping its base like a sail bucking gusts.

There are six styles of penetration: pressing firmly, cutting the oyster open for its pearl; shoving into the golden gulch; ramming against the jewel; thrusting and withdrawing; grinding and plowing to and fro; grinding against each other. According to the Tao of Nines, the guy performs a pattern of thrusts progressively (nine shallow and one deep, eight shallow and two deep, etc.).

"What's the 'Venus butterfly' that was once mentioned on that TV show L.A.Law?"

It's an oral technique of pleasuring the woman's genitals by using your tongue to trace infinity shapes (like sideways eights) that are like the fluttering motions of a butterfly's wings.

MUTUAL ORGASMS

Brian, 22: *"How do I time my orgasm with my girlfriend's? I don't know if she's coming to it."*

Don't strive for simultaneous orgasms because it can put performance pressure on both of you and end up ruining your enjoyment and response. But here are the secrets to it. As a foundation, you gotta have trust—knowing you really care for one another. That lets you really let loose and feel secure about your responses. HOMEWORK: Each spend time learning about your own responses, so you know when and how you get excited. What are the signs? Then, tell each other your signs, and set up a code to let each other know your excitement level. Then do practice sessions where you each take turns stimulating one another to orgasm, to watch how you respond, giving clues, "I'm getting close," or "slow down a little here." Then you stimulate each other at the same time, still giving feedback, to synchronize your excitement levels.

Another secret to achieving mutual orgasm is the participant-observer technique: That's where you learn to be lost in the sensation of the sexual moment, but at the same time you are also able to observe what is happening.

FOOT FIRST

"I'm obsessed with women's feet. Can I find women who will like this as a real spark to sex?"

Feet add great spice to sex, as long as you're not self-conscious about them (as many people are). One girl who called *LovePhones* was so embarrassed about her big toe, she wouldn't take her socks off in sex. One guy was disgusted by his girlfriend's missing toe, yet another was exquisitely turned on by his girlfriend's webbed foot. We snickered at Fergie's lover sucking her toes—but podoerotica has a long history. As outlined in the book *The Sex Life of the Foot and*

Shoe, the Chinese considered the penis inserted through a folded foot as the most royal sex. And famous reflexologist Laura Norman outlines in her book, *Feet First,* how massaging seven thousand nerves in each foot produces deep relaxation and pressure around the ankles frees blood flow to the sex organs.

MASSAGE

"What are some good tips about how to touch my girlfriend to give her pleasure?"

Touch strengthens the immune system. Research proves babies grow happier and more sociable the more they are held, and older people's heart rates stabilize when they stroke babies or pets.

Massage, or pleasure touching, is basic for good sex. Masters and Johnson called it "sensate focus," or focusing on sensations, also called "non-demand pleasuring." Each takes a turn giving and receiving touching for a set period of time. First exclude, then include, genitals.

Advanced massage techniques include strokes like kneading, percussion (like playing drums), compression, pressing with your forearm, snapping the sides of your hands.

Acupressure points related to sex: four points waist level in the lower back, two and four fingers from the spine, and three and four fingers below the navel.

SET THE STAGE

"My room is a mess. I don't like to have any guys over because there are papers and books all over the place and it's not very sexy. My friend says I'd have better sex if I made up my room."

I agree. Make your room into the sexiest place you can imagine, for seduction. You'll feel great and enjoy having company! Look in magazines for ideas and use your own imagination. It doesn't have to cost a lot. Dressing your room for sex is like dressing yourself.

WEATHER

"Does the temperature of a room enhance sexual pleasure? What's the best?"

Cold can make you cuddle, but warm is generally more conducive to sex, since blood flows more freely, making you feel fit and freer to move.

PET NAMES

In an informal survey we did on *LovePhones,* nine out of ten callers said the best thing they can hear in sex is their own name!

"Do pet names for each other and for your genitals really add to sex? What do they really mean?"

Pet names make you feel special to each other. They also are fun. Remember Gennifer Flowers reported that President Bill Clinton called her breasts "the Girls," and she called his genitals "the Boys." Britain's Princess Diana's male confidante James Gilbey called her "Squidgy." Suggested names for a guy or his penis: Mr. Happy, Mr. Wonderful, Mr. HoHo, Mr. Winkie, Thor, Big Boy, and The King. For her: "Magic Box," "Honey Pot," and "Home Base."

Note, you never see the word "penis" in romance novels; instead it's his pulsating hardness, inflamed velvet steel, mighty crown, stiff member, manroot, engorged manhood, rigid desire, love shaft with the velvet head. The infamous racy comic George Carlin called it the heat-seeking moisture missile, one eyed wonder worm, purple helmeted love warrior, bearded blood sausage. Other names for testicles: love apples, squirrel food. Female genitals: furburger, beaver.

POPPERS

"What are poppers and do they work?"

Poppers are capsules of amyl nitrate, used medically as a resuscitator, that jump start your breathing, so they give you a rush (not surprisingly sold in sex shops under names like

Rush and Locker Room)—watch out, they can be dangerous (from causing headaches to death).

A GOOD SEX DIET

"What should I eat to be good in bed?"

Most American doctors, like radio health expert Dr.
Robert Giller, insist a healthy diet in general is best for sex.
That means fresh fruits and vegetables, low-fat dairy prod-
ucts, veal, chicken, and fish more than fatty red meat.

SEX VITAMINS, MINERALS, AND HERBS

*"What vitamins can I take for my sex drive? I heard
Vitamin E works."*

Vitamins are important to good sex because they help
produce hormones and neurotransmitters crucial for sexual
functioning. Vitamin E got its reputation as the sex vitamin
because it improves circulation and lowers blood pressure,
causing relaxation. One study showed it increased the size
of a rat's scrotum. Also helpful: lecithin (found in semen
and available from grains and fish) and Vitamin A (to
increase sperm count).

Some supposedly helpful herbs: sepia (to increase desire
after childbirth), fuchsia (to release inhibitions), pink mon-
keyflower (to undo body shame), basil and mariposa lily (to
treat the Madonna-Whore Syndrome), and hibiscus (to stimulate orgasm).

APHRODISIACS

"Do oysters really work? What other food turns you on?"

The FDA will not endorse any food as a turn-on. People
have tried everything from crushed rhinoceros horns to
dried hare's womb, to oysters, caviar, and chocolate, and
while none may have magic ingredients, as long as they
stimulate your senses and make you think they turn you on,
they will.

Foods can suggest sex by their shape and consistency

(celery and cucumbers imply the phallus, oysters recall the scrotum or vagina), their reputation (a woman has been called a "hot tomato"), or association (some people say red meat makes them more "animal"). Eggs symbolize sex, and their protein and amino acids can increase ejaculate, as can honey.

Oysters got known as an aphrodisiac because horny sailors returning from sea would eat them, yet oysters, and other seafood, also have mucopolysaccharides (complex sugars and proteins) and zinc (without which a man goes zonk).

CHOCOLATE TURN-ON

Would you prefer chocolate to sex? An eye-popping three out of four women in one survey said yes.

"I'm a chocoholic—I love chocolate. I heard that it has something in it that makes you fall in love. But I'm unlucky in love, so how can this be?"

Chocolate has a long reputation as a gift of love, used to pay homage to Indian love goddesses. Its energy boosting sugar and caffeine is stimulating, and it also contains phenylalanine that can stimulate a "natural high," but not enough of it to make a real difference. Moreover, its cost, consistency ("melting in your mouth"), and covering (strawberries, ice cream), give it associations to love.

SUPERMARKET SEX: SITIPHILIA

"I came home one evening and found my girlfriend in bed with a vegetable inside her. Is that sick? Does that mean I'm not good enough and I should leave her? Or should I try fruits and vegetables on her in sex? Which ones?"

Sex and eating are related; after all, sex is a form of feeding—your sense and your ego. Different foods serve different sex purposes. Firm, phallic foods can be penis substitutes with a partner or in solo sex: squash, cucumbers, corn cobs, even sausages and hot dogs. Be sure to wash them! Some are best unpeeled. Some, like bananas, may have the right shape, but not be as effective: unpeeled they can scratch or sting, peeled they can be too mushy. Some strippers put vegetable between men's thighs and fellate them or bite off the tip. Other foods can be stuffed inside the vagina or other openings, like grapes, cherry tomatoes, or peeled and cooled hard boiled eggs. Practice "safe food sex," to keep the organs free from infection.

Food is used in games. In "Shoot the Plum," guys stand in a circle and masturbate; the last one to ejaculate on the plum has to eat it. In "Spaghetti, Meatballs, and Me," you put a paper plate over his penis and serve spaghetti and meatballs, then sucking up each strand. Dress the penis or vagina like a sundae, with ice cream, or any toppings you like, from hot fudge and cherries to whipped cream. Try supermarket sex before you check out—of the relationship.

SUGARY LOVE

Steve: *"I love whipped cream and chocolate sauce for sex, but can this be dangerous if I get too much of it inside my girl?"*

Yes, the sugar can upset the acid-alkaline balance in the vagina. So put the toppings on top!

SCENTS

Animals attract by scent, and the sense of smell goes more directly to the brain than any other sense. The newly popular aromatherapy uses scented oils from plants inhaled or applied on the body to affect your mood. British aromatherapist Betty Dean gave Urge Overkill's Nash Kato a treatment on *LovePhones* for good sex: ylang-ylang, peppermint, and geranium. He said it was "better than sex."

MUSIC

Music can stimulate or relax for sex, depending on your pleasure. For some, heavy metal Nine Inch Nails, with its techno-industrial thrashing inspires the primal id; artists like Barry White and The Artist Formerly Known as Prince provide sexy "talk-through"; and New Agers like Steven Halpern use rhythms and tonal patterns to change your brain state from the busy beta to the relaxed alpha. Richard Marx's favorite music to make love by is Sade's "No Ordinary Mood."

SUBLIMINALS

"I wanted to get one of those subliminal tapes to make me more sexy. They say you can listen to the music and the words seep in without knowing it."

No one has proved that the subliminal messages on those tapes really work. Certainly the music can be relaxing, and that predisposes you to better sex, by easing physical and psychological tensions and anxieties that get in the way of good sex. Also, expectations create results. If you THINK you are going to improve, you will.

MAGNETS

"Some guy told me you could have a better sex life by sleeping on magnets. Is that true?"

There is such a thing as "vibrational" or "energy" practices that apply the principles of electrical and magnetic forces to healing. We know that the earth emits electromagnetic waves, that these waves in the universe influence our body rhythms, and when a cell's electromagnetic field is disturbed it can result in disease. These theorists maintain that if your body is in balance, you will have a better sex life.

EASTERN SEX

"I have a friend who came back from India and said they do weird sex things there. What can I learn from them?"

The Eastern goal is "magnetic" exchange of energy, becoming one with each other and the universe, instead of the Western fast "electrical" discharge ending in orgasm. To accomplish this, you do not focus on genitals in sex, but on connections between body parts, especially the heart. Bathing, massage, and scents set the stage and intercourse happens after a long time (at least a half hour), or not at all; instead partners do exercises like the Love Tap, facing one another with hands over hearts, feeling energy between you, releasing inspiring emotions or even tears. Western men strive for ejaculation, while the East demands semen retention (called "sealing the penis" or "Sexual Kung Fu") and allows release only once every three days in spring, twice a month in summer and autumn, and not at all in winter. The man serves the woman, considering her satisfaction first. An Eastern slow stimulation sex sequence is kiss, lick, blow, caress, nibble.

SPOILED BY SPICE

"I've been with a guy who opened my eyes to kinky things, like sex toys and wearing my panties and garters to work. He does two to three hours of foreplay. Now that my eyes have been opened, I'm scared that he's spoiled me and I won't be satisfied by any regular guy."

Now that you've tasted filet mignon, you're scared you won't be satisfied with hamburger. Likely true. Rest assured there are some other men out there for you who can be equally as open. Now that you know what you like, your "love antennae" will draw them to you.

THE 12 FANTASY GIFTS OF CHRISTMAS
faxed in to *LovePhones*

12–*LovePhones* stories
11–Porno flicks
10–A surrogate partner or inflatable date
9–Cans of whipped cream
8–Battery-operated double headed vibrators
7–Pairs of hand cuffs
6–Leather whips
5–Benwa balls
4–Nipple rings
3–French ticklers
2–Flavored condoms
And a blow job in the back seat

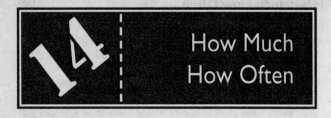

I'M AT THE HOT NEW YORK CLUB, TUNNEL, AND sitting next to me is none other than John Wayne Bobbitt, bragging to me about how he's oversexed. Bobbitt was hosting a party to raise money for his defense and selling "penis protectors"—plastic sheaths to protect your penis from castration. He told me, "I'm really into sex. I think about it all the time. Is there anything wrong with that? I'm so sensitive, that you can just breathe on me and I come."

On *LovePhones* we call it "thinking off"—being able to reach an orgasm without any physical stimulation, just by thinking about sex. I love the concept, and recommend it highly. But somehow the magic of it is lost thinking that John Wayne Bobbitt is a grand practitioner.

"How often is often enough to have sex?"
"What's the normal amount of times you should have sex?"
"I want to do it three times a day. Will that dull my mind?"
"I think about sex all the time. Am I a nymphomaniac?"
"Is there a point when enough is enough or should we get it as much as we can?"

Many people worry about how often it's normal to engage in different sexual behaviors. The answer is generally that whatever feels right to you and works for your partner is okay—from none at all to four times a day.

Some people might argue you can never want sex too much or too little. I disagree; you could be shutting down ("inhibited sexual desire") or you could be too fired up (self-described "nymphomaniacs who really have 'hyper-sexuality' or 'compulsive sexual behavior'"). Or you could be mismatched: one wants it more than the other.

"How many times is it possible physically and mentally to have sex?"

As many as you can stand or want. Some people can go for eight-hour marathons before they get tired and emotionally satisfied, but bounce back the next day. The number of times you want, or have, sex is based on a lot of factors, from your desire, to mental and physical health, time, and availability of partners.

I don't like to give statistics for people to measure themselves against, because that can set up arbitrary goals or expectations that are contrary to healthy sex. Set your own standard. Aerosmith's Steven Tyler says he thinks about sex all the time but only has it about twice a week. What number is right for you? A number of surveys suggest that the average number of times couples have sex is 2.2 times a week; less often for singles. If you're really that curious about how you stack up compared with others, here are the average number of times U.S. adults say they have sex per year, by age group, according to the 1993 National Opinion Research Center:

AVERAGE FREQUENCY OF SEX

18–29 years old: 81x a year—7x a month
30–39 years old: 80x a year—6 1/2x a month
40–49 years old: 65x a year—5 1/2x a month
50–59 years old: 46x a year—4x a month
60–69 years old: 27x a year—2x a month
70+ years old: 9x a year

The Janus Report on Sexual Behavior surveyed eight thousand people over nine years and found that young people are having more sex now than three years ago. More sex was reported by 62 percent of men and 66 percent of women ages eighteen to twenty-six, heralding what the report called a "second sexual revolution"—a resurgence of sexual behavior after a period of fear about AIDS and other sexually transmitted diseases. Ten percent of men and four percent of women had sex with over a hundred partners.

Q: Why do men name their penises?
A: Because they don't want a stranger
making so many of their decisions.

Men do seem—too often—to be guided by the head between their legs rather than the one on their shoulders.

Eighteen-year-old Joe's complaint was: *"I see so many girls I'd like to do. I can't seem to control my 'Timmy,' as I call him. He sees something and he has to have some skin."*

Have a conversation between your two heads—the one between your legs and the one on your shoulders. If Timmy could talk, what would he say?

Joe (as his penis): *"I want that."*

And what would your brain say back?

Joe: *"Watch out, buddy. Keep it under wraps. This will get you in trouble."*

And what does your penis say back?

Joe: *"Shut up, you're bumming me out."*

Let the brain win.

MEN vs. WOMEN

"Why is it that women need a reason, but all men need is a place?"

Women attach more meaning to the sexual act than men, traditionally. Men seem to be more able to separate sex from love, and to act on their sexual impulses without as much consideration, hesitation, fear, emotional investment, or afterthoughts.

Diana: *"I like sex and I'm upset about being put down about it. Is there anything wrong with a woman wanting it a lot? Why is she called a 'slut'?"*

Salt-N-Pepa certainly celebrate the view that women are

allowed to want it as much as they want it. In their single "Shoop," the rap queens let you know that "just because I want a phone number does not make me a 'ho." But they also do odes to pure lust, "Push It," "Shake Your Thing," and "Whatta Man," where women are equal sex partners to men.

"Do men really reach their peak at eighteen?
"Do women really reach their peak sex drive when they're thirty-five?"

As Roseanne joked at the '94 MTV Awards, "I'm forty-one and at my sexual peak, and let me tell you, it's lonely at the top." It's an old wives' tale, but it's certainly a good explanation for the new trend for younger men–older women relationships.

There is some validity to the theory that men are sexual when they're eighteen. They have the time—later they're more tired and stressed with developing their careers, with families, and other responsibilities. They're socialized, given permission, and encouraged to get a lot of it at that age. And, true enough, their hormones do rage.

Compared with women at eighteen, they are more comfortable being wild sexually. Females have been brought up to care more about relationships and to be "good" girls. But, even girls buy into the dichotomy: guys who have a lot of sex are studs and girls are sluts.

The reason that women tend to reach their peak at thirty-five is because by that age they have developed more emotional and financial security and independence, so they feel freer to be themselves in all realms, including the sexual.

HORMONES

"Why do they say guys have raging hormones? Do women have raging hormones?"

Hormones—from the Greek word meaning to excite— play a vital role in sex. There are three types: androgens or testosterone (male) and estrogen and progestins (female). Testosterone in both sexes greatly affects the level of sex drive, though men have probably thirty times more than women. Testosterone peaks in women around the time they ovulate—nature's way of making women want sex more at the time they can be most fertile. And it peaks for men in teenagehood, accounting for their "raging."

Estrogen (also present in men in small amounts) is responsible for women's vaginal wetness and tissue elasticity, as well as mood. Some researchers have given estrogen to male sex offenders to lower their sex drive. Progesterone, tested as a male contraceptive, also lowered sex drive.

OTHER CHEMICALS

"I'm a runner and get those wonderful endorphins in my brain when I hit the wall. That makes me feel so good. Somebody told me that you also get them in orgasm, that it feeds your sex drive. Is that true?"

Yes. Endorphins (endogenous morphines) are the "pleasure chemical" released in the brain from exercise or from orgasm; they are pain blockers and produce a "natural high." Other chemicals that contribute to sex include vasoactive intestinal peptides that dilate the blood vessels and cause erection, and acetylcholine that keeps the arteries relaxed so the erection stays. Neurotransmitters in the brain also affect sex drive. Dopamine, which affects memory, also causes arousal.

Serotonin is a calmative. Too little makes you depressed, but too much (as happens for some people on antidepressants) can inhibit orgasm. And since vitamins support the production of hormones and neurotransmitters, they can also be considered important to sex drive.

LOW URGE

It's been called the biggest sexual problem: no urge, or losing it, clinically called "inhibited sexual desire":

"I don't care about sex. What's wrong with me?"

"My boyfriend used to like it all the time. For the past two weeks he hasn't been on me at all. What's up?"

"I don't seem real interested in sex. Is there something wrong with me? Guys probably won't like me if I'm not into it."

Some people don't put a high priority on sex. Just because our society is obsessed with sex, doesn't mean *you* have to be. On a scale of 0 to 100 (with 0 not at all and 100 a lot), how interested are you? You'll surely find somebody at the same level. Ask them to rate themselves so you don't get into a relationship where you're incompatible.

Reasons for a low sex drive, or drops in drive, run the gamut. Maybe you haven't met the right man to get you turned on. Or maybe you learned sex was bad when you were growing up. Or you could have been abused and repressed your desires. Sexual desire is affected also by your hormones, drug or alcohol use, medications, and physical illnesses. The problem could be in you (stress, anger, depression, fear of intimacy, lack of confidence, lack of knowledge); with your partner (lack of trust, anger, different styles); or due to situations (you don't have a partner, you've been abused). Figure out which, if any, is true of you.

In any case, feel okay about your level of sex drive. You can't change anything until you really accept where you are.

Being too tired is one of the biggest causes of not having sex.

POOPED

"I want good sex with my husband, but by the time we get to bed at night, I'm just too tired. What can I do about it?"

Make time for sex before bedtime. Do it before dinner and dishes and cleaning up and other exhausting home chores. Reorder your priorities so you leave something else for later. Don't expect sex to be a whole exhausting experience. Learn to think of it as energizing, not requiring or draining your energy, so you approach it more willingly. Expectations condition experience.

Life changes—from moving to job stresses to illnesses—can affect how often you have sex. Expect and accept them.

But perhaps two of the biggest transitions that affect sex drive are getting married and having kids.

SHE DOESN'T WANT IT AFTER MARRIAGE

Derrick: *"We hit the skins a lot but since we got hitched, she don't give it up anymore. What's up?"*

Unfortunately, some women use sex to trap their man, and then once they've got him, they feel they don't have to work at it anymore. These women weren't that interested in sex in the first place. If that's the case, it'll be hard to get her going. You'll probably have to accept that you're just not going to have it as often as before. She may come around a little, if you impress upon her how important sex is to you.

Others stop being sexual for psychological reasons that can be changed if you discuss what her blocks, and your needs, are. It may be because she thinks it's inappropriate for a wife to be a lover, or she's copying what her parents did, or the responsibilities of life are draining or distracting her energy. Maybe she's mad at you, or feels turned off because you come on too much. If you're too demanding and she feels used, back off and give her a breather.

"I'm pregnant with twins and sex is uncomfortable. But my husband won't leave me alone. If he doesn't get it, he gets mad. What can I do?"

He has to understand that the hormones of pregnancy can cause changes in your sexual drive and your body is changing. Some positions are more uncomfortable now, so adjust positions. The vagina may be drier, so use a lubricant. Doctors say you can continue to have sex until the last two weeks of your pregnancy, but your husband should respect your feelings. Try having sex without having to go all the way, or without intercourse (fellatio or mutual masturbation) to satisfy him, so he does not feel deprived.

"I'm pregnant and my husband does not want to have sex. I feel devastated. What's wrong?"

Some men get terrified when the woman gets pregnant.

They have fears about injuring the baby, or ejaculating in the baby's eye (this can't happen, the fetus is in a sac floating in amniotic fluid). Psychologically, the guy can get insecure about how to behave as a father-to-be, resentful about impending responsibilities, and fearful about both of you assuming new roles in life. Have him express these fears. Tell him how you feel neglected and unattractive, and that you need his reassurance, especially at this crucial time of impending parenthood when you should be more together.

TURNED OFF AFTER DELIVERY

Mark: My girlfriend had a baby and I wanted to witness the birth, so I coached her through it. I watched the child come out of there and now the thought of sex with her makes me sick. I can't get an erection. She's gone from regular tampons to the super-absorbency kind, too, so it's really big down there. I can't believe a child came out of there, given his big head. It used to be all mine. What can I do?"

Others guys feel like you do. Think of the beauty of the delivery, not the blood and gook of the dripping amniotic sac. Image your girlfriend's vagina, "see" the baby coming out in your mind's eye, and "see" flowers and "hear" wonderful music playing! The truth is that the vagina closes after the birth—it doesn't stay as large as the baby's head that came out of it. It's like an elastic band. Now it is more stretched than before and she does have to heal, but it's not as wide as you're thinking! Are you afraid that your penis won't fill her anymore? It will. Are you afraid you will hurt or rip her? Check first that her episiotomy (stitches for the cut usually made to enlarge the vaginal opening) is healed. Accept her changes. That's what happens after childbirth— best to think it's a small price to pay for your baby. Try different positions. Have her exercise her vaginal muscles to get them back in shape so they can grip your penis better.

All too often when kids come into the house, sex goes out the window. You can't let that happen.

CAN SEX THRIVE AFTER KIDS ARRIVE?

Claudine: *"I'm thrilled to have our first baby, but since I gave birth, my husband and I have had a real hard time with sex. He doesn't come on to me as much, and I'm hardly interested at all. What's wrong and how can we get back to the way it was?"*

Don't fret. It's common to lose your sexual desire when you have your first child (and sometimes with each successive child). You're exhausted, and coping with all the emotions—from excitement to resentment—of your new roles as parents. Solve the practical problems of lack of time alone and exhaustion. Insist on at least one hour two evenings a week or a few hours on the weekend, just for the two of you. Divide chores. Line up baby-sitters so you can have time alone. Plan "dates" where you treat each other as lovers.

Continue to see your body as sexual. Face and dispel any insecurities about being out of shape. Change any negative thoughts about parents not being sexual. Even if your own parents weren't affectionate, you can be. Don't call each other "mommy" and "daddy" which would douse sexual fires.

Q: Why do guys rub their crotches all the time?
A: Because they're lost in thought.

"We have two kids and no sex because they're always on top of us. I'm only twenty, so I don't think I should be giving up sex already in my life—that's for old people. What can we do?"

Brainstorm ways to be alone. A baby-sitter is worth her weight in gold. If you don't have the money, make exchange deals with other parents. If the kids have to be in the house, keep them occupied so they leave you alone. I love this suggestion: tell them to play a Treasure Hunt game. They have an hour to find twenty things in the house that you hid. But here's the hitch: hide only nineteen things, so they take the whole hour to look! Hang a clock on your door that shows when you can be interrupted.

RECOVERING
"I was an alcoholic, but now that I stopped drinking, I'm finding sex not as enjoyable. How can I make it as before?"

Alcohol likely made you more sexual because it lowered your inhibitions, allowing you to act more freely and think about sex more. Now that you are sober, your defenses and fears may have reared their ugly heads again. You can be as sexual as before—and even enjoy it more—by allowing your mind to create the same state as the alcohol did. Where the alcohol once masked certain feelings, you now have an opportunity to truly feel, and relish, them.

Many celebrities who are recovering drug or alcohol addicts acknowledge how sex at first seems less exciting, but ultimately takes on the intense feelings of an aware, alert mind. Aerosmith's Steven Tyler describes how now that he's off hard drugs, sex is better. His feelings are real, not hyped; he can perceive small pleasures and feel more truly connected.

TV WIDOW
"How do you compete with the remote control? He's plastered in front of the TV and doesn't pay no mind to me."

Agree on time the TV will be on, and time for togetherness. One woman dressed in sexy clothes, and sat down next to her guy while he was watching TV, not nagging him to turn it off, but watching with him and enticing him. He soon switched to her channel!

ALL WORK AND NO PLAY
"I used to have a high sex drive but since I'm going to school and trying to start my own business, sex hardly crosses my mind. A cute guy asked me out the other day and I didn't even care. The dry spell worries me. Am I sick and can I get my sex drive back?"

Congratulations on all your new efforts to get ahead—give yourself a break from sex and everything else. There's nothing wrong with pouring your mental and sexual energy into other things now. I'm among those who believe that working excessively hard for some period of time doesn't have to equal a problem but can be a very positive channel for your energy. Doing well at your new endeavor can be just as fulfilling as sex—as long as it doesn't go on end-lessly and as long as you're not using work to escape from sex, dating, relationships, or feelings in general.

Of course, it is a problem if there is a reason why you have turned off. Danielle: *"My boyfriend used to want it every day. Then it dwindled to once a week, then once a month. And now to once in six months. He told me when he was thirteen he was molested by a female cousin who was eighteen and she forced him to touch her. Could this have something to do with it?"*

Absolutely. He has all sorts of stored up feelings about that abuse, including guilt, anger, and shame. Once he works through these feelings, he can get his fire and lust for you back. He should join a therapy group for men who have been abused. When you're making love with him, remind him, "I am with you and love you, it is not her." Build up his confidence that he can be in control, by letting him call the shots. Or if he liked that she ordered him around, tell him that is nothing to be ashamed of, and you would gladly do it, but this time with his permission.

ANHEDONIA

"I can't feel any pleasure. What's wrong with me?"

There are some people who have a condition called anhedonia, where they don't feel any pleasure. While this may be physiological, based on a damaged nervous system, it is more often psychological. Try to identify your fears by attending to all the feelings you have. Keep a journal. Write down whatever small feelings you have. Do activities that heighten your senses—eat strong-smelling foods, touch yourself often with different materials (fur, cotton, metal, glass). Fantasize. Allow your imagination to run free. Have fun.

HE WANTS TURN-OFF

"I am religious and I don't want to have sex before I am married. But I go out with girls and I feel those urges. How can I kill these stirrings in my body and mind? Is there a pill I can take?"

I would not recommend that you try to totally eliminate these urges, since that will make it difficult to revive them when you want (like after you marry). Certain medications dull sexual desire, but they are indicated when you have a medical problem, not to purposefully dampen sexuality. Consider deciding that having such urges is normal and do not make you a "bad" person. Take control: you can experience sexual stirrings without acting on them. When the impulse gets strong, redirect the energy into an activity together or focus your concentration on a different but equally absorbing topic. Enlist your date's help, by talking with her about your religious beliefs and your desire to feel close without having sex. Hopefully she will respect and help you in your efforts.

BUDDIES NOT LOVERS

Bill, 24: *"I've been married three years and we haven't had sex since we got married. I've become a couch potato, and we're like roommates and best friends rather than lovers. It's like puppy love calling each other 'sweet thing' and 'honey bunch' and 'buddy boy' but no sex! I buy her flowers, but it doesn't go anywhere. Why?"*

It happens to more couples than you think—they get married and turn into buddies, best friends, and brother and sister instead of lovers. It comes from repeating your parents' past, laziness, fears of sex ruining your friendship, or unconscious needs for a family more than a lover. (For example, say you had a brother or sister who didn't live up to your expectations, so you turn your spouse into a more perfect sibling.) I know it sounds absurd, but it's true. Bring this out in the open so there's no secret agenda between you, and force yourselves to act like lovers. HOMEWORK: Plan two sex nights a week together, to get into the groove.

LIVING UP TO LOVE FEST

Some people just have a high sex drive or bursts of drive where they can go for a long time. But they may still worry if this is "normal."

George, 15: *"I had a love fest with my girlfriend where we went for seven hours on end and I got off four rounds. Is this normal?"*

Sure. I'm sure you did some talking and playing during that time—that's great. I bet you're worried you won't be able to live up to this again. Don't put that performance anxiety on yourself. Enjoy that it happened, and know that you were great then, so you build your confidence. Then, it WILL happen again without your forcing it (which won't work) or your shying away from it.

SEX FIEND

Gerard: *"I think I'm a sex fiend. I had sex with three or four girls who know each other. Do you think I should talk about it to a new girl I like? She doesn't know my reputation. I don't want to hurt her feelings."*

Sure, warn her how you make the rounds. If she's smart, she'll run like hell.

HIGH SEX DRIVE

"Is there anything wrong with always being horny and enjoying and wanting sex very much?"

No. Some people are very sexual. Enjoy it. As Freud said, there are two drives, Eros—or the life or sex drive—and thanatos—the death or aggression drive. The desire for sex is primal.

"Is it true that the more you have sex, the more you want it? And conversely that the less you have it, the less you want it?"

Certainly if you are sexual and you are deprived of sex for a while, you can build up your passion and be very "hot" for a long-awaited encounter. But it's also true that if you have sex more, you want it more. Psychologically, frequent activity builds up your sexual confidence, so you want it more. It can become a habit like any other activity. And like doing any regular exercise, you come to feel more physically fit as your body becomes acclimated to the activity.

Conversely, like stopping any exercise, if you fall out of the routine, you lose your muscle tone and your psychological drive to do the activity. And psychologically, interruptions can damage your confidence, so you become less willing to try it again.

> *If sex were like fast food,*
> *you'd have an arch over your head.*
> —from the TV show, *Designing Women*

NYMPHOS

People with too much sexual desire call themselves nymphomaniacs. They've been called promiscuous. They could have a sex addiction, also called "compulsive sexual behavior" or "hypersexuality."

Mike, 29, has it: *"My wife is very hot. She's from Brazil, but treats me mean. We do a lot of dangerous sex, in buses, in her parent's front lawn, her giving me head while I'm driving, in a go-go bar. My wife showed pictures of us nude to my stepdaughter and now I'm fantasizing about her. That scares me. I've been a sex addict, but I thought it was over."*

No, buddy. It's not. You still got a sex addiction and better do something about it quick, including stopping fantasizing about your stepdaughter because your lack of control is dangerous.

"I flirt with every man I see," twenty-two-year-old Kim blurted out, *"and usually end up in bed with him. Then I*

wake up in the morning disgusted, wondering, 'What have I done?' Most times I don't even know his name."

Mike, 19: *"I slept with my cousin's girlfriend. She grabbed me, so she wanted it. I have to have sex with every girl who turns me on and shows she wants it."*

No, you don't!

Kim and Mike describe a problem for an increasing number of young men and women today: sex addiction. Like an addiction to alcohol, drugs, or food, being out of control of sexual thoughts and behavior interferes with your life. It means using sex as a drug: an anesthetic to numb pain, a tranquilizer to relax, a mood elevator to feel less depressed, or a mind-altering substance to escape reality— but always as an intoxicant, to get "high." The problem can range from being unable to get sex off your mind to getting in trouble with the law over it. It is estimated that about one in twelve Americans has a sex addiction, including some celebrities.

In her compelling personal account of sex addiction, *Lovesick,* Susan Israelson says Marilyn Monroe had it. Guns N' Roses Slash said before he married his wife Renee (whom he called "a religious fanatic about fidelity"), "I went from being a drug addict to a sex addict," sleeping with any woman he felt like and lying to her. TV child star Danny Bonaduce told me he was a sex addict, on top of drug addiction, too. "I was getting into sex all the time on the set of the *Partridge Family*," he said, "And then when I worked at a radio station I would say on the air that I was having sex in the studio and they wouldn't believe me but a girl would be going down on me while I was talking on the mike. And I'd wake up on the couch after some nights of sex, sometimes many girls in one night."

Eight out of ten sex addicts have other addictions, like alcohol abuse, workaholism, compulsive spending, or eating disorders. Eight out of ten also were sexually abused as children, seven out of ten physically abused, and nearly all emotionally abused. Sixty-five percent of sexaholics are estimated to be professionals with college degrees.

Female sex addicts tend to suffer more than men from

society's attitudes, as men's sexual escapades are seen as a badge of macho virility, while women are labeled "loose" or "sluts." But it's a problem that is becoming more dangerous for both sexes in this age of AIDS, when sleeping with strangers can mean contracting a deadly disease.

Experts disagree: some maintain that sex addiction is a valid disease and others insist there is no such thing as sex addiction since sex can't be considered a disease when it is about life and joy.

Some experts also criticize the self-help programs based on the Alcoholics Anonymous model, where people go to meetings to share stories of their problems and follow "twelve steps" that include submitting to a Higher Power to overcome their addiction—claiming these groups make people dependent and perceive sex as "bad." When I was doing a report for *A Current Affair* about sex addiction, I interviewed a researcher who attended these groups and contended that rather than control sexual activity, people got turned on listening to each other's stories about sexual fantasies and behavior, and used the groups to indulge their obsession with sex and as a pick-up place to meet new sexual partners!

I think the support and reassurance that these groups can offer are helpful. But professional therapy is also essential. In sessions with twenty-two-year-old Kim, I helped her to see sex in a new light: not as a means to get love, but as an outgrowth of a loving relationship that grows over time and is built on trust. I encouraged her to have a more spiritual view of sex, as described by Charlotte Kasl in her wonderful book, *Women, Sex and Addiction,* by moving away from whatever she instinctively felt as "dark" feelings and toward more "light energy" (called Reiki in Japanese), and by coming to each relationship saluting the goddess within her and the holy center within each being (practicing *namaskara,* a Hindustani word meaning "I salute the divinity in you"), to achieve mutual respect and true love.

To get over a sex addiction, you have to realize that having sex is not going to fill the "black hole" you feel inside. Think before you jump into bed; do something else to make you less lonely or more involved (work out, start a project, do a consuming chore). Express deep feelings (shame, fear, rage, hunger for love) with a therapist or friend.

A loving partner can help. Slash credits his wife, a "religious fanatic about fidelity," for bringing him to his senses, by dumping him when she found out about his affairs. He panicked, never knowing his heart could ache so bad, crawled back, and they got married. Bonaduce told me his wife Gretchen helped him stay sober, with her constant devotion and support, and sharing his struggle as she herself is recovering from a compulsive behavior (anorexia).

Sex addiction shows up as emotional desperation and compulsive acting out. It can be related to many other problems, from hormone imbalances to obsessive-compulsive disorder, psychopathy, family dysfunction, panic disorders, and, interestingly, attention deficit disorder. Laura's boyfriend has it: *"My boyfriend is totally hyper. He's always doing three things at one time. When we have sex, he doesn't stay focused, he yaps about all kinds of stuff, or gets up to turn on the TV. He doesn't listen to me when I'm talking, like he's thinking his own thoughts. His mind runs a mile a minute and he can't stick with being lovey dovey at all. What can I do?"*

He's either selfish, stressed-out, or more likely, he has a real disorder, hyperactivity or attention deficit disorder (ADD). Since ADD is a medical disorder that's likely inherited, it's not totally under his control. Some medications (anti-depressants or a stimulant, Ritalin) can help, but you and he have to manage his behavior. Because he's distractible and impulsive, spell things out real carefully and repeat them. Write down what you want so he can read it and study it to prevent forgetting. Plan a schedule of time together and write it on a calendar. Reward him constantly when he sticks to your schedule or pays attention to you. Be more positive: instead of thinking of him as "hyper" think of him as "energetic," instead of "impulsive," say he's "quick on the draw." Make him laugh lovingly about how he jumps from one thing to another.

ADD affects about fifteen million men and women, and often goes undiagnosed more in women because being overemotional is more accepted as a normal "female" trait, and because women don't as often show the unruly, disruptive behaviors guys do.

SEXERCISING

"I was never interested in sex in the past but since I've been working out in the gym after work three times a week, I find that I'm thinking about sex a lot. Does this make sense?"

Exercise can indeed be an aphrodisiac. In one study of over eight thousand exercisers, 89 percent said working out boosted their sexual confidence, and a third said they were making love more often. In another survey of five hundred women, thirty percent felt turned on during or after exercise and seven percent had spontaneous orgasm in class! There were also take-home benefits, since one in four said their work-outs gave them more frequent orgasms in bed, too.

There are many reasons for the erotic effects of exercise. Psychologically, "getting into" your body makes you focus on physical sensations, a precondition for enjoying sex. Working on your figure enhances your confidence in your body, nudity, and overall self, also essential for good sex.

But beware, too much can backfire. In a German study, brutes beefing up their biceps caused a drop in male hormones and sex drive. In a California study of wives who took up running, husbands were threatened by their newfound attractiveness and independence; the happiest couples were those who worked out together.

MISMATCHED

One of the biggest problems of sex drive is whether the two of you match. It's called sexual compatibility.

Apparently the honeymoon is over fast. Nearly half of 345 newlywed couples in one survey said they wished they had sex more often. The book *The First Year of Marriage: What to Expect, What to Accept and What You Can Change* reported that newlywed sex is hardly as romantic and sexually exciting as one would like to believe.

Married or not, couples often disagree about the number of times to have sex and the type of sex they like. It's called sexual incompatibility. I get a lot of complaints from men and women about it.

"My husband can go for two hours, but when he's off he's done, and I can go for twenty-four hours."

"I can wear out any girl. How can I get them to go four or five rounds when they start drying up after two or three?"

Don't push it. Loving sex takes into consideration both people's paces. Give your partner a break, or you'll sabotage yourself. For example, if the guy keeps pushing when the woman is dry or unwilling, she'll only shut down more, physically and emotionally, feeling pressured and worried that she's not responding.

If you want more activity when your partner doesn't, let him or her lie there while you stimulate yourself more actively as long as you want. If you still have to drain off a lot of energy, bounce up and down on the bed and run around the room.

No one is a filling station where you just pull up and say "fill me up" 'til your tank is full. Twenty-two year old Marlin has to learn that lesson. He asked, *"I'm married but my brothers get it more than me. I want it seven times a day but my woman's dry. What's up with her?"*

What's up with you? You're using, not loving her. A marriage license is not a promise you'll be serviced in sex. With that attitude, no wonder she might feel used and turn off. Back off and give her a chance to feel respected and to want it—and you.

Both of you are bound to have fluctuations in your sexual mood and functioning; therefore, there will be times when you feel more or less in sync. Do not despair, rather accept the normal ebb and flow of your sexual response cycle and the stages of love, that can change in major life transitions, like before or after making a commitment, marriage, the birth of a child, job changes. Therapy is indicated if the problems persist longer than a few months or interfere greatly with your life.

Attitudes also affect sex drive. If you think you're supposed to act "proper," you'll inhibit your drive; or if you think a guy's always supposed to be ready, you'll try to act that way.

BRAIN RETRAIN: Switch anxious thoughts to pleasurable ones. Confront real problems like stress or anger that are dampening your desire. Give yourself time to get in the mood. Make "transition time" in bed, where instead of immediately being sexual, you share feelings or events of the day. Hold and cuddle to experience intimacy. Allow the person who feels less sexual to participate only partially in the sexual encounter. Build each other's confidence with statements like, "I enjoy being with you whatever happens."

What if you think your partner is a "nympho" and you don't want it as often?

Crystal: *"My man is bugging me. He wants it 24, 7. How do I get him to chill?"*

Joe, 23: *"I'm with this woman who's a nympho. We used to go at it all the time, but not now. When I don't want it I just say 'no' but she gets pissed. What can I do?"*

You're entitled to say no, but do it the right way and she won't get upset. A flat no is upsetting, rejecting, and hurtful. Instead, reassure her by saying, 'I love you and love making love with you,' promise another time when you will be sexual, or let her be active and you be passive. Also, ask her to describe what she wants from sex and suggest other ways to get that (working out together, or just telling her how wonderful she is!). Make sure you're real clear, instead of just expecting your partner to know when you want it and when you don't.

Gary, 24: *"I'm married three years and we haven't had sex in six months. Now my wife's best friend is coming on to me. I dropped some ice cream on my chest and she came and licked it off. What should I do?"*

You're sexually frustrated. Find out why you and your wife haven't done it and what drove you to consider the affair (maybe you're angry at your wife). Stop seeing the friend so you won't be tempted.

Patsy, 21: *"Me and my boyfriend have sex two to three times a day. If I don't get it, I get grumpy and yell at him. Is this wrong?"*

Yes, because that shows you're just using him to reduce your stress and anxiety. I wouldn't blame him if he started resenting it. Sometimes sex can be for stress reduction, but you shouldn't use a partner for this all the time. Channel some of your sexual energy into sex sessions by yourself.

Sandy: *"My fiancé doesn't like phone sex, hot body oils, cognac in front of the fireplace, pornos, or talking dirty to me. Should I marry him?"*

Presumably you were attracted for other reasons. Decide how important each sexual affinity is to you and him, on a scale of 0 to 100. Then check off which ones you could give up. What are your other top priorities in life? If sex is major to you and you can't give up those activities, then you're in for a sadly deprived marriage.

MORNING OR NIGHT

"I want it in the morning and she seems to want it at night. What can we do?"

Some people are indeed night-owls and others morning glories. It can be physical, due to their different body clocks, called circadian rhythms, making them more alert either in the a.m. or the p.m. Partners who differ have to find a middle ground—like in the early evening or on week-ends. Or you have to switch off, doing it sometimes at her peak time and sometimes at yours.

Some guys think they are interested in sex in the morning because they have early morning erections. But those are a physical response, part of the sleep cycle, that do not necessarily mean he "woke up sexy," so he is not ruining his body or ignoring sex signals by not having sex then.

INITIATING SEX

"I have to wait until my guy wants to make love. If it takes

him five days, that's how long I have to wait. I try to play with him when I have the urge, but he just turns over and says he wants to sleep. I love him but I'm frustrated. What can I do?"

Ideally, both partners in a couple should have a say in when they have sex, even though either one has a right to decline at any time. Agree on taking turns initiating sex—give each person a week to say what they want to happen and the other person goes along with it. This empowers each person with a chance to be assertive without fearing rejection, or to give in if they're too controlling. Like many men, yours may have grown up mistakenly thinking the man is entitled and required to initiate sex, yet he may find it both a pleasure and relief when the woman takes over. If he does not give in to any of your requests, he has a serious power problem that requires counseling. Or he may simply be spoiled by your letting him have his way. Educate him that women have desires, too. Instead of keeping silent or pouting, as many women in your situation do, tell him about your fear and hurt over his rejections. Let him know that you find him desirable at times when he may not be feeling the same way, and that it is important to you that he respond. Reassure him that if he is tired when you want to play with him, he does not have to engage in extended love play, but can take a more passive role.

LONG DISTANCE, PLEASE

"My boyfriend and I had great sex until he got sent to another state for his job. Now he has to commute home, but not often because we don't have the money. What can we do?"

"I've been married three years and work two jobs and never have time for sex anymore. I used to want sex every night. What am I going to do?"

Instead of complaining, celebrate. What is the possibility here? Have phone sex. Or write sexy letters detailing your fantasies. Make a sexy video. Distance lends enchantment. Plan out what you will do for each other. Watch separations build up your excitement to be together. You may find new eroticism for each other.

CAN'T HAVE IT

Even if you want sex, what happens when you can't have it?

Lily, 19: *I broke up with my boyfriend. After two years of lots of sex I'm horny now. What can I do with myself?"*

Jocelyn: *"I used to have lots of sex but I don't want to now because I'm afraid of getting AIDS. But I'm frustrated, so what do I do with my sex drive?"*

If you've been delightfully spoiled, with good sex as well as love, you miss the contact comfort and holding as much as the sex! Whether it's the loss of or separation from a partner, stress, or the fear of catching a disease, many more people today are having spurts when they don't have sex, even after times of fulfilling indulgence. Don't get afraid you'll lose the knack; you'll get back in the saddle fine, like riding a bike, it's a skill you never lose. Now, you just need other outlets for that energy and other ways of satisfying the needs that were met in the loving sexual interchange.

Denying sexual feelings or trying to get rid of them can only lead to problems, like taking drugs, drinking, overeating, even being hostile to people you think have great sex. Instead, redefine sex. Tap into the traditions of Eastern sex, where the highest form of sensual pleasure comes from higher communication between two people where you share souls instead of touching tits. If you always need sex to prove you're lovable, learn you don't need someone to make love to you to feel loved. Talk to friends about writing your dream novel, and get off on them listening attentively and encouragingly. Exercise results in a "high" and relaxation similar to sex. Keep a journal of your feelings—writing down needs and frustrations makes them less pressing. If you feel tense, take a bath, listen to calm music. Touch is healing, so hold hands, hug a friend, stroke an animal. Making love provides contact comfort, so get a massage. Nurture old friendships and family connections neglected while you had a lover and develop new relationships. In short, enjoy life. The more alert you are, the better you will feel without a partner and the better prepared you'll be when someone new comes along.

HOW LONG DOES IT LAST?

"I'm twenty-one and live next door to a woman who's a widow in her early seventies. The other day she was telling me she missed the great sex she had with her husband and asked me if I masturbate and if it was okay if she did it. I was really shocked, because she was already old. What should I have told her?"

Tell her to go for it. Be extremely enthusiastic. She's never too old to enjoy her body. Tell her it would be healthy for her. Older women who stay sexual have less vaginal atrophy (shriveling up of the vaginal canals) and fewer genital problems compared with women who do not engage in such behavior. While people don't often talk openly about it, solitary sex throughout life is more common than you think. Kinsey found about 50 percent of widowed, separated, or divorced women (and more men) in their fifties pleasured themselves about once every three weeks. Those findings have been corroborated by more recent surveys, which report up to a third of eighty-year-olds still enjoy some sex. Experts suspect these statistics would be even higher if we got rid of negative social stereotypes or upbringing, attitudes, guilt, fears, and proscriptions that are likely carryovers from youth.

As I say, you never have to retire from sex!

As a final word: however much, however often you have sex, wouldn't it be nice for it to be spellbinding? Think quality, not quantity.

SPELLBINDING SEX

April: *"My girlfriend is seeing a guy who's married and has five kids. She won't leave him because of the great sex.*

I think he has a voodoo spell on her. Do you think that's possible?"

Great sex can feel like a spell. You can get attached to a person who satisfies your needs in sex because psychologically you're appreciated, and physiologically, the chemicals that flood your body and brain make you feel good. It's no mistake that songs are written about how being in love is like being under a spell: "that old black magic called love."

Once a King alway a King but
Once a Knight is Enough

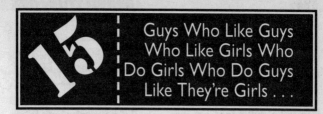

*Girls who are boys who like boys to be girls who do boys
like they're girls who do girls like they're boys . . .*
—Blur, "Girls and Boys"

SO MANY PEOPLE WORRY, "I DID (THIS OR THAT),
does it mean I'm gay?"

Homosexual, bisexual, heterosexual, whatever you call
yourself, I love what my *LovePhones* co-host Chris Jagger
calls himself: "I'm trysexual. That means I'll try anything."

And my buddy, singer Sophie B. Hawkins, calls herself
"omnisexual" (*Omni,* the Latin prefix meaning "all"), which
she says means that "whether I love a man or a woman, I
am inspired to become more of my unique self."

I'm a fag trapped in a woman's body.
—Madonna, on stage on her Girlie tour

Madonna is the epitome of what I'd call "pan-sexuality"
(also Greek for "all")—crossing all sex barriers, refusing to
be labeled, enjoying male and female dress, partners, and
attitudes, from a Marilyn Monroe diva to a leathered dominatrix to a tuxedoed tough guy. Whether or not you think
she goes too far, you can't beat her basic message in all her
work, music, image, clothes, relationships: "It's not about
being male or female, but being a person."

QUIZ: AM I GAY?   0 •-•-•-•-•-•-• 6

1. How often do you have sex fantasies about the same
   sex?   0 •-•-•-•-•-•-• 6
2. How intense are the love feelings you feel for people
   of the same sex?   0 •-•-•-•-•-•-• 6
3. How many times have you kissed someone of the same
   sex and wanted to go further?   0 •-•-•-•-•-•-• 6
4. How many times have you had sexual experiences
   with someone of the same sex? 0 •-•-•-•-•-•-• 6
5. How pleasant or unpleasant is the thought of sex with
   a same sex person?   0 •-•-•-•-•-•-• 6

Rate yourself from 0 (not at all) to 6 (a lot or often).
Connect your dots to see a pattern, and read on for explanation of what it can mean.

A common fear both guys and girls have is about
whether or not they are gay, especially if they've had sexual
thoughts or experiences with someone of the same sex.
Unintentional same-sex sex can happen under many conditions with someone alone, at a party, especially when you're
drunk. You can be curious, deliberate, or just caught by surprise. The situations are varied, but there are some common
important messages and lessons. Bottom line: Don't worry,
and don't be so quick to label yourself.

Also, there can be times in life when you go through
stages. You can be attracted to someone of the same sex,
and then have a stable relationship with someone of the
opposite sex, or change partners more frequently.

Ken: *"I had sex with my best guy friend once. He told some
of the other guys at school now and they're calling me gay.
I don't think I'm gay. I know I'm straight. What is the definition of gay or straight?"*

Basically I believe that the work of sex researcher
Kinsey still holds true, that sexuality is on a continuum—
that people can't be easily categorized as one thing or the

other. The so-called Kinsey scale rated people with only heterosexual behavior as 0, only homosexual behavior as 6, and people with both male and female partners as in between, in various degrees from 1 to 5. Category 3 represents equal heterosexual and homosexual experience or attraction. A meeting of world "sexperts" about five years ago upheld the usefulness of this scale, adding separate scales for love, attraction, fantasy, and self-identification, and allowing for changes over time.

Most studies suggest that from two to ten percent of people may be predominantly homosexual, with half the number of women as men. While the 1994 Sex in America study found that only about four percent of people identified themselves as either homosexual or bisexual, the Hunt study twenty years earlier found nearly one in four men and fourteen percent of women reported both homosexual and heterosexual experiences. The recent Kinsey Institute New Report on Sex found, similarly, that up to a quarter of men have a same sex experience at some point in their life.

Some cultures revere same-sex behavior, or require it as a rite of passage. One survey of 190 societies found that two thirds considered it socially acceptable for certain individuals at certain times (though it is more common in nonindustrialized societies, like those in Africa and the South Pacific). One tribe in New Guinea insists that prepubescent boys drink semen from postpubescent boys' penises to become strong hunters, but become exclusively heterosexual after marriage.

Social views of homosexuality have changed over the ages, from Greek times when it was revered for young men to go with older men, to Victorian days when it was highly taboo, to current times, when laws about marriage, adoption, and serving in the military are being reconsidered and liberalized, and front covers of magazines like *New York* and London's *Sunday Times* tout "Lesbian Chic." On TV, we saw an openly gay character on *L.A. Law,* and Mariel Hemingway kiss Roseanne. Celebrities have also helped reduce the stigma, including Elton John, Olympic Gold Medalist Greg Louganis, and tennis star Martina

Navratilova (although Martina believes she did not receive lucrative endorsement deals because of her homosexuality). Supermodel Rachel Williams proudly declared her lesbianism. And lesbian singers like k.d. lang and Grammy-award-winning Melissa Etheridge receive enthusiastic fan support. Etheridge spontaneously declared herself a "proud" lesbian at a gay inaugural bash for Bill Clinton to a roaring crowd, and enjoyed equal fan support for a hit album, *Yes, I Am,* that she said is an affirmation of her love for her female lover.

Others have fought rumors, like Nicole Kidman protesting hubby Tom Cruise is not gay, and Richard Gere and Cindy Crawford taking out the infamous full-page ad in a London paper proclaiming they're not gay, "We are heterosexual and monogamous and take our commitment to each other very seriously . . . we both look forward to having a family." (However, they announced their separation not long after.)

People get into many situations where they worry if it means they're gay when that's not necessarily the case.
Daniel: *"I was watching some videos on TV late one night and my roommate came in and he was pretty drunk. I'd had a few beers myself. He sat down next to me and started commenting on what the girl was doing to the guy in the video and laughing that he could do better than that. I was yukking it up, and before I knew it, he unzipped my jeans and stuck his head there and did me like the girl in the video was doing to the guy. Then he made me do him the same way. It felt pretty good at the time, but the next morning I was freaked. What if my girlfriend finds out? And what does this mean about me? Now, I haven't wanted to talk to him since then and I avoid him. I'm scared it'll happen again, but sometimes I have to admit I wish it would."*

I can understand how you are embarrassed and worried, but you don't have to panic about this. Nor should you keep avoiding your roommate. Admit to yourself that what happened wasn't a tragedy, nor does it have to change your entire life. You were both drunk; watch out for that.

Alcohol makes you do things you wouldn't otherwise do because your inhibitions are down.

Talk with your roommate about what happened. Even though I know in the back of your mind you might be thinking it would be interesting if it happened again, you might feel more comfortable telling him it's too complicated for you and set limits for him about what you do and do not want to do now. Be reassured that this experience doesn't mean that this is what you will choose for life.

Damon, from the British band Blur, as Honorary Love Doctor on *LovePhones,* advised, "Men kissing men is good (I noticed hickeys on his neck). Graham has given me lots of hickeys that gets me in trouble with my girlfriends. I hate to say I'm just a straight male, it's very boring. I don't recommend it."

In childhood, sex play with the same sex is more common than you think.

Janine: *"I remember when I was five humping my best friend on my bed. We didn't know what we were doing, but it felt good. Sometimes I think about this when I'm having sex with my boyfriend. Is that stopping me from enjoying it?"*

It shouldn't. You didn't do anything abnormal or wrong. Either put it out of your mind, or think about what you enjoyed and do it with your boyfriend.

One study in the '70s found that about 6 percent of adolescent females and 11 percent of adolescent males had experienced same-sex contact during their adolescent years, mostly with peers. In another survey of over four hundred children, half the males and a third of the females reported homosexual experiences prior to puberty, suggesting it's a normal part of growing up. The data from the Kinsey research also shows that regardless of what people call themselves—heterosexual or homosexual—or what their current behavior is, you can't assume that this determines how they will behave for the rest of their life.

When you're learning about your sexuality, it's normal to explore your body, and if you're surrounded by people of the same sex, as at a camp or school, it can happen that you will "play" with them.

Lance: *"My buddies and I jerked each other off all the time at boarding school. We would sit around and talk about what we'd do to girls when we get them, and do it to each other. Now that I'm out of school, I haven't dated. I'm not gay, I like girls and want to go out with them, but I'm scared to go out and I keep thinking I don't know what to do with girls."*

It's not uncommon for boys or girls in camps or school to play around with each other. Of course you might be scared when you finally get to dating. The dating game is often painful and stressful. Don't blame your shyness on your past. Grit your teeth and get into the game and build up your confidence.

Katie: *"I love my boyfriend, but one day my best friend came over and we were sitting on my bed talking about our boyfriends and what pain-in-the-necks they are. We were laughing and having a good time and then she asked me if I ever kissed a girl. I said no, I thought it would be stupid. She said she did once and it was better than a guy. Then she said we should touch each other just for fun, and we did. She was right. Now I think about her when I'm with my boyfriend. She pleased me the way he never did. It felt better than anything. It was like she knew exactly what to do to make me feel good, like she could read my mind. I'm really worried about whether I'm that way now."*

That's understandable. Unfortunately it's true that there are some differences between male and female sexuality, and in one sense, girls would know more what girls like and boys would "speak the same language" as boys. Your girlfriend may have been pleasing you the way she likes to be pleased, and so it seemed magically that she knew to say and do exactly what you like. Sometimes it works out that someone—it could be a guy or a girl—just seems to be on the same wavelength as you and instinctively does what you like. But someone who doesn't do that right away can also learn to do it, if you teach them. That doesn't mean they're wrong for you.

Give your boyfriend a chance to equal her skill. You don't have to tell him where you learned it, but tell him, "I love tenderness here, lingering there, more soft kisses, more flicks rather than hard presses," or messages like that.

Russian-born singer, Milla, who appeared in *Dazed and Confused* and starred in *Blue Lagoon Two,* shared when she was Honorary Love Doctor that she's been with different friends, one in particular in the bath, explaining, "it was a pretty natural thing, not anything we talked about, just hanging out. Any girl that appreciates her own body has got to appreciate other women's bodies because women are beautiful and that's all there is to it. It's perfectly natural to experiment, you don't know where you're going to end up but along the way you should try it." Now, she's very happy with her boyfriend.

Flo became obsessed with her young female friend after a fleeting, unexpected flirtation.

"I'm twenty-one and was best friends with this girl who is eighteen. I was like a big sister to her, helping her solve her problems with school and her parents and giving her advice. Then one night she was crying about something, in my arms, and we just started kissing. We touched through our clothes and it never went any further than that, but it was better than with guys I've been with. But since that happened, she won't talk to me. And I think about her all the time. I'm into guys and I like penises, and I know I want to get married and have kids. I didn't expect this to happen, but now I think about her all the time. I can't get her out of my mind. Now, whenever I masturbate, I think about her, about finishing what we started. What can I do?"

Sometimes it's more compelling when an erotic encounter has been left up in the air, it keeps you wondering and fantasizing. Also, having such an exciting, intimate experience, with someone you feel so in tune with, makes you want more. You have to realize that first of all, guys at your age are often not as open as women are with each other and they don't know as much about what women want, so the odds are that they won't immediately satisfy you 'til they learn more about women, and until you teach them about what you specifically like. Don't give up on them. Be more open with them about what you want.

Thinking about someone when you masturbate fixes that fantasy in your head. Either indulge it knowing you won't yearn for it in real life, or change it by purposefully thinking of someone else.

Sounds like she's really uncomfortable about what happened and afraid to face it and you. Tell her you think you should both talk about your feelings about it, and that you love her and promise it doesn't have to go any further than she wants.

As Honorary Love Doctor, Grammy-award-winning singer/songwriter Sheryl Crow was reassuring that she, too, (like Milla) has been attracted to women. "I have actually," Sheryl said. "There's nothing more beautiful than a beautiful woman. It's like a piece of art actually."

Eric, 18, was also confused.
"I've been a male 'ho the past two or three years. Women just come on to me, but I don't know why. I'm blond-haired and blue-eyed, but I don't think I'm that great. Sex has been wham-bam-thank-you-ma'am and I'm tired of it. What scares me is that lately I'm attracted to my roommate. I don't want to be gay, but I like him. He's not gay either, and tells me about his woman problems, how they string him along. The odd thing is that when guys have come on to me, I've hit them and broken bones. A guy I never saw came up to me when I was vacationing in South Carolina and asked me for the time and grabbed my crotch and I hit him and broke his front teeth. Am I gay for thinking about my friend?"

It was understandable for you to hit that stranger who grabbed your crotch; he assaulted you. But since it was a sexual advance, too, you sound a little homophobic. Sometimes people who are the most homophobic are terrified of their inner real attraction to the same sex, and are being what we call "counterphobic"—acting the opposite to feelings they find unacceptable. There are other factors in this situation: your roommate and you are commiserating over girl problems. You may be attractive, but you are not confident. You may also be so fed up with females, you're looking to guys. Understand and accept all these motives in yourself before you panic. You're learning about yourself and your sexuality.

People of all ages gossip—and kids especially pass all kinds of rumors, make fun of others, bully, or tell stories about others' sexual activities and particularly whether or not they're gay.

John: *"I play on the school football team and the other day I was in the locker room and I came out of the shower and I had an erection. The other kids saw it and now they tease me."*

Getting erections during sports, or other activities, or just when you're sitting in class, is normal. Of course you might get embarrassed, but know there's nothing wrong.

If the other kids tease you, resist letting them know it gets to you—without a response, bullies stop. Or make some innocent remark, like "I was just thinking about my girlfriend," or some smart-alecky retort, like "You only wish you were as virile (let them go look that word up)." Your attitude and self-esteem matter.

Movie megastar Tom Cruise has been beleaguered with rumors that he is gay. He told an interviewer in *Vanity Fair* that he's not a closeted gay. "First of all, I don't think it's an indictment . . . It's not true, but people are going to say what they want to say . . . I don't care. I don't care if people are Martians. Straight. Gay. Bisexual. Catholic. Jewish or Scientologists . . . I could go around saying that's not true and that's not true. But I've got so much stuff going on in my life that I'd rather spend the morning with my daughter and my wife and taking care of work." Cruise claims his wife, Nicole Kidman, is his soul mate.

If sex play happens between two people, no matter what sex they both are, sometimes one person may be more into it than the other person, or discover through the experience that this is what they prefer. Suppose the other person is gay, and you're not. Deal with it in the same way as you would if you were just not into the other person. That happened to Clark.

"My buddy and I jerked each other off," Clark said, *"and now he wants to keep doing it. He's bugging me. Finally he admitted to me that he's gay, but I'm not. I called him a faggot once already, but how do I get him off my back?"*

Please don't call him names or put him down. Just let him know kindly that you're not into a relationship with him, without making him wrong or bad. Tell him, "I have a girlfriend and I'm into her," or "I realize you like me but this is not going any further between us. What happened once is over. It would be better for us to be just friends and for you to find someone else you can be closer with sexually."

If someone imposes their sexuality on you, it's not right. But you have to give clear messages. Pete didn't.

"I was over my friend's house, and we were sleeping in different beds, and in the middle of the night he came into my bed. I was in cotton boxers and he was wearing pajamas but silk boxers underneath them. He started rubbing up against me first, and then he put his hand on my hips and started putting his hand down my underpants. I pretended I was sleeping the whole time, but I let it happen. He rubbed himself up and down and then took off his pants and put his hands between my legs and started rubbing my penis. It felt real good. Then he put his penis in between my legs by my crack and still rubbed my penis. Then I felt wet stuff between my legs. I never said anything. Now I don't know what to say to him. He looks at me funny sometimes."

Your friend shouldn't force himself on you, but you didn't object. Both of you can't admit openly to wanting the sex play, so you're pretending it didn't happen. I can understand your curiosity in letting it happen without openly confronting him about what happened. But if the vibes are awkward between you now, better that you say something directly to him about how you feel about it—yea or nay.

You don't have to be scared of same-sex advances; just know how to handle it.

Bob, 19: *"My floor leader at college is gay and I like to walk around with my shirt off. Won't he get turned on if he sees my bare chest? What if he likes to look at me?"*

He may look at your bare chest, just like a guy may look at a woman's cleavage. So handle it similarly; don't display yourself. But don't get self-conscious, either. Just act natural. If he makes any advances, you can always say directly and calmly, "I'm not into it."

A lot of people don't know how to handle it after one instance of same-sex play happens.

"A bunch of guys from work were all together in a stag party and we ended up in an orgy. Some of us are married, but now we can't look at each other in the eye. What should we do?"

Sex play like that happens even among married guys and fathers. All of you may have different feelings and degrees of interest in what happened. But there's no reason to make it ruin work. You have to go up to the guys yourself and say, "That happened, but let's put it behind us" (oops, pun). It's not a good idea anyway to get involved sexually with people at work. Make agreements about whether you're going to tell any wives or friends what happened.

Or they worry how to explain it to someone who finds out.

Michelle: *"I go with guys but I am attracted to a woman. We were in my bedroom and having sex when my sister came in and caught us. What can I do?"*

4 Non Blondes' Linda Perry: "I think you need to be aware of your feelings and come to terms with whatever it is that you're experiencing. I think seventy out of a hundred people look at someone of the same sex and say 'ah.' You shouldn't be ashamed or embarrassed. Go to your sister and say, 'I am not a lesbian.' Be honest with her. Figure out your feelings and talk to your sister about it."

You might wonder whether you should tell. Pat called LovePhones to say, "I'm married but I had an affair with a man. He's a truck driver so I hardly see him. Should I tell my wife?"

As Honorary Love Doctor that night, Van Halen's Sammy Hagar advised: "I have a hard time with that. I don't have any homosexual tendencies but I'm not down on that and I understand if someone else feels like that, but, I'd tell your wife. Forgive 'ya I won't do it again, and I would really try to get back into the sex with my wife because I'd think you'll feel better about everything. If you go the other way, it could lead to something you won't be happy with someday. I'd go with the old lady if I was you, man, especially if you were liquored up."

The same rules apply as to revealing an affair with anyone: decide what you want to accomplish in telling and assess the potential outcome.

Jonathan: *"My buddy and I were studying one night and we both got tired so started to sack out on the couch. He turned out the light, and then before I knew it, he pulled off my jeans and started licking me. I pushed his head off first, but it felt good, so I guess I let him do it. But I know I'm into girls and I have a girlfriend and I don't want her to find out. Do I have to tell her?"*

No. You can have private sexual experiences. You don't have to tell everything, and you can still feel honest. No reason to worry her if you aren't sure yet what this means to you anyway. There's plenty of time later, when you trust each other and you're clearer about what this meant to you. Remember, always be aware of why you want to share a sexual experience—as a turn on, to make the other person angry or jealous, or to absolve yourself of guilt.

Recording artist and actress Milla shared that she loved it when her boyfriend told her he got a "leg massage" from other boys at school. "It was really sexy," she said. "That really turned me on, after going out with someone a year and a half and finding out something you didn't know. It made me feel a little kinkier."

Other special situations can lead to temporary same-sex sex.

Mario was in jail for drug dealing. *"Some guys ganged up on me and butt-fucked me. It was hell, but I had to get into it to get through my sentence without being beat up. Now I'm getting out and I don't want my girlfriend to know. What can I do?"*

You had to do what you had to do to survive. Of course you may have unpleasant images in your mind, but forgive yourself and start your sexual life afresh just as you have to start all life afresh.

There are also behaviors you may do that might smack of being gay but aren't necessarily.

"I am a heterosexual girl who definitely likes guys, but the only way I get turned on when I masturbate is when I fantasize about girls having sex. Am I lesbian?"

Not necessarily. When you repeat a fantasy, especially when you have orgasm to it, you fix it in your mind. Change your mental channel to another fantasy, replacing the girl's face and body with a guy you know so you condition yourself more to other fantasies.

Use the fantasy to understand yourself. It's not bad to think of the same sex in a fantasy. Every character in our fantasy is a projection of ourselves. What is that girl like? How would you like to be like her? Act like she does in real life. What are you seeking from her? How do you think she treats you compared with a man? Act that way with a guy, too.

Shannon: *"I like to hump my boyfriend as if I were a man. Does that mean I'm really a dyke?"*

No. Women can like to experience the sense of thrusting and penetrating besides just receiving. It can also reveal a sense of integrating your "masculine" and "feminine" selves—using those stereotypes. Of course there is a possibility that you would prefer to be with a woman.

"I like to play with my anal canal when I get excited. Is there something wrong with this?"

No. This spot has nerve endings and muscles that tug on sensitive spots. Just make sure you're clean; there is lots of bacteria there. And practice safe sex, because the anal walls are thin and can be torn easily, making it easy to pass the AIDS virus (see chapter on Back Door Sex).

People have a lot of curiosity about what gay sex is like.
Grace: *"I have a friend who told me he is gay. I never thought he was. Now, whenever I look at him, I wonder what he does with a guy. What is the sex like?"*
Sex with a same-sex partner can be exactly like that with an opposite-sex partner, in your mind. After all, remember I've said sex is 90 percent between your ears and only 10 percent between your legs. The experience of penetrating and being contained can be similar in anal sex as in vaginal intercourse. Kissing, caressing, nipple stimulation, oral sex, anal stimulation can all be the same as it would be with a female partner. Some men don't like anal sex (especially given its association with high-risk AIDS transmission); studies show oral sex is the most common sexual activity between men, with mutual masturbation the next most common. Some are what's called "tops" or "bottoms" (you see that advertised in singles magazines), meaning, respectively, they like either being the one to penetrate, or be penetrated. Instead of playing one role, as old stereotypes about being "butch" or "femme," the "male" or "female," the "passive" or "active," the "top" or "bottom" partner suggest, people can be either or both.

Doreen: *"I want to make love to my girlfriend, but she's always been into men. Now she says she wants to do it with me, but I really want to please her and worry how can I do that if I don't have a penis. What should I do?"*
Do what comes naturally. Most women have the easiest time reaching orgasm with oral stimulation. But even though you don't have a penis, you can approximate one. Use your fingers, or a vibrator, or a strap-on, latex penis you harness on yourself. You can get on top of her, straddle her leg, or open your vaginal lips to expose your clitorises,

and rub them against one another, against the pubic bone, or against another part of the body (called tribadism).

Interestingly, studies show that lesbian women have orgasm more easily than heterosexual married women, yet the frequency of sex drops off twofold over time for lesbian couples compared with heterosexual couples.

Fantasizing about someone of the same sex is perfectly healthy. It also doesn't mean that you're gay.

Darcy: *"I have this fantasy often, that I'm making love to another woman. She's got beautiful flowing blond hair and we're walking in a field and she leans over and kisses me."*

Good for you! It can be very healthy to fantasize about someone of the same sex; it can mean that's a figment of you that you would like to be. Remember my theory of dreams and fantasies: that they are the movie of your mind. If she's sexy, you want to be more sexy in your real self. If she is beautiful, then feel more beautiful about yourself. If she is self-confident, then feel and act more self-confident in your real life.

In research on women's sexual fantasies for over a quarter of a century, author Nancy Friday found that one of the most "modern" popular fantasies for women is making love with another woman. It's the fantasy that "only another woman knows" how to please you. As Friday points out in her most recent book, *Women on Top: How Real Life Has Changed Women's Fantasies,* far more women than ever before want or need more than an occasional embrace from another woman. The trend began in the 1970s, when women were encouraged to turn to one another for acceptance and self-discovery, even to the exclusion of men. Friday insists the female-to-female contact goes beyond homosexuality or sexuality at all, but implies how women feel men have failed in giving them the tender, nurturing love they seek. But there are many more motivations than that.

At times in life we may just want to try everything and anything. Sometimes you go through a phase of trying out different sexual experiences, although it isn't what you continue to do for the rest of your life. I have a few helpful rules about it: don't label yourself so quickly; accept your feelings; allow yourself to explore, but certainly act responsibly and don't do anything that hurts yourself or others. By the same token, you don't have to try everything.

Allison called *LovePhones* when Salt-N-Pepa were Honorary Love Doctors. She said her boyfriend wanted to bring another girl into their lovemaking, so she did, and now she's worried that she's attracted to the girl. Salt-N-Pepa said it might be temporary and just her curiosity and not to worry. Usually it turns out the girl, as in this case, was more soft in her touch compared with the boyfriend who got hard and got it over with. He had to be taught to be a better lover!

People can love others of the opposite or same sex at different points in their life. Sometimes people who are with someone, or even married, either experiment with, or fall in love with, a same-sex partner. It can be a passing relationship, or lead to breaking up the first relationship. The partner who is left is usually devastated. If you discover your main squeeze with someone of the same sex, find out what it's about.

"My boyfriend and my best friend who is a guy were over my house one night and we were all going to the movies. The guys went upstairs to call the movieline, and when they didn't come down in a while, I went upstairs and looked inside my bedroom and saw them on my bed. My friend was lying on top of my boyfriend, who had his pants down. I was in shock and didn't say anything then, or throughout the movie, or since then in two weeks. But I'm real upset about it. What should I say to my boyfriend?"

Confront him. Say, "I've been upset since that night we were going to the movies. I saw you and Bill on my bed, making out. What was that about?" No matter what he says, ask, "I want to know whether this means any of these three choices: You were just experimenting, you're really bisexual and like men and women, or you're really gay and just dating me because you're afraid to come out."

Jenine: *"I love this guy I was dating for two years. The sex was never great between us, and in the past few months he never liked to have intercourse with me but just for me to suck him off. He wouldn't even touch my genitals. I got really hurt and he would never say anything about why he didn't want me anymore. Then I found a love letter in his closet from another guy. I confronted him about it and he admitted that he was in love with his guy and that he never really was attracted to me, and that he was fighting being gay. Now he's left me. I really love him and I want him back. He says he loves me, too, but he won't come back. Could I have been a better lover and he would have stayed with me?"*

Let him go. Don't blame yourself for not being a good enough lover. His choice to go with his male friend has nothing to do with you not being good enough. Some people try to live a heterosexual life, but then can't keep up the front. Imagine that it's better that he left you for a man than for another woman, which might make you feel even more insecure or inadequate. Bless him and let him get on with his life and you with yours. Forgive him for any deceit, as he was likely struggling with his own conflict. He may indeed love you, but he wants to share sexual love and a relationship with someone else.

Such a change happened for Julie Cypher, who was married for four years to actor Lou Diamond Phillips when she was working as an assistant director on lesbian singer Melissa Etheridge's "Bring Me Some Water" video. As reported in *People* magazine, Etheridge felt an immediate and "very physical" attraction, but Cypher said her own initial feelings were less clear: "I was drawn to her, but it never occurred to me that I could be a lesbian." But when her feelings grew too strong, Cypher, then twenty-five, started dating Etheridge, and separated from her husband, and divorced a year later. The two claim to be very different— Etheridge in jeans and shirts, with no makeup, an admitted slob, and California-chic Cypher, who is more "focused." But it works for them, just like it could in any male-female relationship.

BISEXUALITY: THE BEST OF BOTH WORLDS

Certainly the rock-music world facilitates a lot of acting out, sexually and otherwise. Lots of rock musicians have admitted playing around with their sexuality. Marianne Faithfull, a sixties singer who had an affair with Mick Jagger on and off for six years, claims that the real love of the full-lipped rocker was neither Bianca, nor Jerri Hall, but Keith Richards. She recently wrote in her autobiography, *Faithfull*, that many times when they were making love, Jagger would whisper in her ear, "Do you know what I'd really like to do? If Keith were here right now, I'd like to lick him all over."

Some people, like Mick Jagger, are just plain interested in both sexes. As Woody Allen joked, "Say what you will about bisexuality, you have a 50 percent better chance of finding a date on Saturday night."

There are many stories of people who find themselves liking both sexes.

Jade: *"I have a boyfriend and I really like being with him and having sex with him. I think I want to marry him, but recently I made out with my girlfriend. We went out and she had just been dumped by her boyfriend. I was driving her home after we went to a party and she was crying. I went to hug her, and then before I knew it, she was kissing me and reached in to feel my breast. She touched them more lightly than my boyfriend and I felt tingles inbetween my legs. She talked to me softly and told me she was getting wet and I should feel it. I did, and then I started rubbing her. She was groaning a lot and crying, and I was kissing her tears, and then she put her hand in my pants and I was sopping wet. She begged me to finish her, and I kept touching until she screamed and said that I was making her come. It was really fun and she called me a lot and I agreed to go to her house, and we've done it a few times since then. Now I think about her all the time, and I really am falling in love with her. Is there something wrong with this? Am I heterosexual, bisexual, or gay?"*

Clare: *"I was married to a guy who left me after I had my baby. Then I took up with a girl I met and was happy with her for a while, until we broke up. Now I'm dating a guy again, and I may marry him. I'm so confused. Do I like men or women?"*

Grant: *"I've been married nine years and my wife cheated on me. I was real hurt and a friend took me to a gay bar. I never thought about men before, but a guy started dancing with me and then I went home with him. He called me all the time and finally one night I let him have sex with me. Now I've started seeing him a lot. I really like him now, and I'm going to leave my wife and move in with him. What does that mean about me?"*

Being attracted to both sexes can seem confusing. But some people don't think about the other person's genitals; they are just attracted to or love a person for who they are and how they feel with them and about them. You can call this bisexuality. By this broad definition, it might apply to a lot of people these days, since over the past twenty years people have become less afraid to experiment, and society has less of a stigma against homosexuality. If you use a strict definition of bisexuality, counting only people who have sex with people of both sexes over a period of years, then it applies to about 10 to 15 percent of men and women.

Times and circumstances in your life can make you choose different partners. There are essentially different kinds of bisexuality: a real orientation, a transitory orientation, or a transitional orientation. It can also indicate homosexual denial, meaning you're afraid to really accept being with same-sex partners only, so you keep up opposite-sex activity. Or it can be an attempt to have the best of both worlds, so you can marry and lead a family life accepted by society, but also act out your inner desires. Don't force yourself to be one thing or the other. Resist labeling yourself until you observe your feelings and behavior over a long period of time.

After all, you can consider every body part equal. HOMEWORK: If you are having intercourse, play, "Who has the penis? Who has the vagina?" Imagine that you have his and he has yours; that all are exchangeable, and one.

Carole: *"I'm bisexual and for the past two years I was with a guy, but it's ending, so now when I go out with women, I tell them I've been with men and first they say, 'I'm fine with that,' 'I'm hip to that,' but then they get scared and can't deal with it."*

Everyone is scared of rejection, so you can understand, I'm sure, how someone starting up with a person who is bisexual would be under a double threat—because any man or woman is a potential competitor for your affection. It's natural. Be honest and then expect their fear, and reassure them when you genuinely care.

Julia: *"I've been into men all my life but this girl at work pursued me and I fell in love with her. She made love to me better than any guy and always told me I was beautiful, which made me feel great. She called me all the time, and insisted on coming over to my house. But she was married. She'd invite me to her house when her husband was there, and wink at me and grab me when he wasn't looking. When we had sex she would tell me she hated having sex with him and always gritted her teeth. I was really confused, so I still had sex with some guys. Once I got pregnant, but I had an abortion. Then she got pregnant, and told me that even though it was an accident, she was going to have the baby and pretend it was ours. As soon as she had the baby, she refused to see me or talk to me. Now I'm devastated. I can't believe she cut me off so cruelly and totally. And I'm so jealous she has a family now. How can she do this?"*

I'm so sorry you were hurt like that. Obviously she was acting out her own needs and totally insensitive to yours. She is clearly attracted to women, and has some antagonism to men, but her desire to fit in with society overrode the deep psychosexual nature that drew her to you and women. She is now cutting off her feelings, which were obviously very deep for you at that time. Feel somewhat comforted that her love for you was genuine once, but that she couldn't follow through. You need someone else to love you as she did, whose life is not so complicated. Create that for yourself.

Some gay men and women particularly like seducing heterosexual people:

Lyn: *"I'm only attracted to women when they're straight. I love being their first, and showing them how great a woman can be."*

Jon: *"There's a guy at work who's always telling me about his problems with girls and I'm trying to show him I like him. I always get attracted to men who aren't gay. What can I do?"*

You may be trying to use the heterosexual person to work through your own feelings about your sexuality. For example, you might be trying to relive the way you were seduced. Or you want to "convert" that heterosexual person to symbolically make the way you are okay. The person could symbolize acceptance you want from your father or mother. Or maybe you feel that the bigger the challenge, the better. If they're not interested, don't push yourself on them.

One of the most riveting calls to *LovePhones* was from a guy who said he was about to get married in a few weeks but that the other night he and his fiancée's cousin, a guy, were sitting around watching TV and started fooling around. Since then, they have had sex together a few times. Now he's worried about whether he should get married.

While he was talking to us on the phone, the door opened in the background and a woman started screaming, "Oh, my God, I can't believe you did that." Apparently, his fiancée had been driving in the car and heard him recount his story. He started apologizing as she was screaming, "How can you do this to me? It's over." She stormed out the door. He stayed on the line as I tried to calm him down. I told him that it was better that she found out about this now. It may mean the wedding is called off, but he'd have to understand that she couldn't walk down the aisle happily, knowing that her future husband had cheated and that he might not be into women.

Sometimes you might not want to actually be sexual with a person of the same sex, but you might want your partner to act like that.

*"What if I want my boyfriend to act like the girl and I want
to be the girl, too? I saw it in a video once and I'd love the
idea of putting a silk teddy on him and lace stockings and a
robe and then him acting like we're two girls together."*

If you have a guy who wouldn't be threatened, then go
for it. How exciting that can be! If your guy is really
uncomfortable, you may have to just do it in your head so
he doesn't label you as a lesbian.

Lance: *"I'm straight but I've thought about going with a
guy just to see what it's like. What would make a person gay
or straight?"*

The cause of people's sexual orientation has been a
subject of debate for many years. Years ago the popular
psychoanalytic theory held that gay men had dominant or
smothering mothers but distant or absent fathers. But
others discredited this view, showing that men who were
not gay had similar family relationships. Indeed, while
anyone's family history can be analyzed and used to
explain their behavior, homosexuals and heterosexuals
all seem to come from varied backgrounds. About twenty
years ago activist gay groups protested the professional
organizations' meetings (like the American Psychiatric
Association), insisting that homosexuality was a choice.
Then, some of these groups insisted that sexual orientation was inherited.

So, are you born gay? Some research suggests a "gay
gene" that could cause homosexuality. One recent study of
twins found that when one brother was homosexual, so
were about half the identical twins, compared with only
about twenty percent of the fraternal twins and ten percent
of the adoptive brothers. Yet there is also evidence that children raised by homosexuals do not necessarily grow up to
lead the same lifestyle.

I believe that sexual orientation is a combination of
inherited and learned behaviors, similar to many other
aspects of our personality and behavior. This makes sense
because most people experience "love" as something that
"just happens" and they can't force themselves to fall in

love with a particular person. But we are also affected by social conditions, family interactions, personal needs and fears, and experiences. The proportion of all these then varies from person to person.

In one typical example, twenty-five-year-old Dennis came to me for therapy because he had really low self-esteem. He was overweight and thought he was a nerd. He was attracted to guys who were really muscular and powerful. In therapy, he realized they were the projection of what he wanted to be. When he lost weight and got a good job and started to feel like those guys he wanted to have sex with, he no longer felt as attracted to them. He now was the object of his desire. So his attraction had been more narcissistic than lasting.

Regardless of which sex you relate to, getting comfortable with yourself is healthy. Eastern philosophy has it right: you should be comfortable with both your male and your female energy, your yin and yang, to be a full person.

BREAST FRIENDS

Dana and her best friend are using their sexual relationship to get back at guys. They've become "breast" friends; it's a *Thelma and Louise* thing.

"Guys bug me and my best friend at the beach because we have great bodies. One afternoon we were standing at the bar and touched each other's breasts and kissed and the guys went nuts. We looked so hot together—she's a Marilyn Monroe with brown hair and I'm a Kim Basinger with dark hair. We felt so cool teasing the guys. So now we're into being like an item. How do we pursue it?"

Sounds like you're doing a great job as it is. You and your friend have bonded big time against the bullies, and learned that the two of you can break those macho hearts! What power you're experiencing from taunting men, rebelling, and also gal-bonding! Now you know what guys have when they're buddies. Enjoy your fun.

Some guys, like Lance, want women to act more like men so he can be into them.

"I used to be into girls, but I had a hard time with them. They're so demanding and emotional that I got fed up with them nagging and whining about me not being there and not talking about my feelings. This guy on my block came on to me and then we started having sex. We'd just do it and there was no muss or fuss. We'd pal around and joke and go to ball games and fall asleep after jerking off together. Now if a girl would do that stuff with me, I'd like to meet her because I'd rather not be gay, so where are the women who can just act more like a guy and not that prissy stuff?"

Look for one. There are definitely women who are less emotional and needy, and who are more into their "male" energy. Keep looking.

Mike is also reconsidering.

"I was into women 'til I was eighteen, now I've been gay for years. I was living with a guy who I thought I would marry and we would adopt a kid. I really want a family. Then he turned out to be such a rat and tried to steal my money. We're in a court battle now over some property of mine that he wants. I hate him. I've been having sexual fantasies about women lately, and now I'm thinking of going back to dating women. Do you think I'm not gay anymore?"

I think you're angry—understandably—at this guy and generalizing your anger to include all men. You're hurt and need to be taken care of, so you're looking to bring mothering energy into your life. Obviously you yearn to be part of a family, so it's understandable you're thinking about women. That's fine. Let yourself go through whatever transitions you want. But this is a good time to reevaluate what turns you on to people and to evaluate your earlier family relationships with your mother and father.

Dean: *"I'm definitely into men, and I've been seeing my boyfriend now for five years. But lately, when I have sex with him, we'd be in the middle of me giving it to him in the rear, and I start thinking about being inside this girl I know. I never had sex with a girl and it freaks me out to be thinking about doing it to a girl when I've been with this guy. I don't want to break up with him. Does this mean I want to be with a woman?"*

Not necessarily. You can be gay and still think about sex with a woman. It's perfectly okay. Research studies show that six to eight out of ten gay men have had sex with a woman and even more lesbian women have had sex with a man. Only about four percent of men and up to three percent of women are exclusively homosexual throughout their entire lives. So it's normal to have a fantasy about the opposite sex, even if you prefer sex with a same sex partner. Think about how being with a woman would allow you to feel or act, and let yourself feel or do that with your partner. If the feeling really persists, you can imagine you're having sex with a woman. You can feel a man's chest and imagine they're breasts. You can be in a vagina and imagine it's an anus, or vice versa. Sex, remember, is 90 percent in your head, and only 10 percent between your legs.

Some people are really homophobic, which means they have fears or a range of feelings from dislike to hatred about same-sex activities or couples. Some actresses, for example, refuse roles where they have to be sexual with someone of the same sex. Others have no problem with it, like Tom Hanks, who played a gay lawyer with AIDS in the hit movie, *Philadelphia*.

Danny: *"I hate gays. This guy in my school walks funny and talks like a girl. I can't stand him."*

That's too bad. If you're so intolerant of others, there must be something you hate about yourself. Prejudice against homosexuals is the same as prejudice against any group. Studies have shown such people with negative attitudes to gays often don't know any, are authoritarian, and have rigid concepts about sex-role stereotypes. These people often feel persecuted themselves, and pick on someone else to restore their own flailing personal power. Turn your energy from hating others for their sexuality—or anything else for that matter—to doing something positive for yourself or others. Have some compassion. The statue outside Gurimayi's South Fallsburg retreat reminds us that if the creator created everything about us, then all of it is acceptable.

"Why do men get so upset seeing two men having sex together and don't when they see two women?"

Because men are more homophobic—scared about being gay, because it threatens their concept of being "masculine." Yet they like the idea of two women together, usually because they imagine that the women are both ultimately into wanting him, and playing with each other for his pleasure. Women are also more comfortable being close and cuddly with both women and men.

Even MTV has its limits about what it will show on TV regarding sex, between any two same-sexed people. *LovePhones* Honorary Love Doctors the "lipstick lesbian" group Fem2Fem made a hot video of their song "Switch" and two scenes were banned: one full-frontal nudity shot of band member Julie Ann Park, a self-described bisexual, and a scene with band member Lynn Pompey, an open lesbian, who pours a milky substance from her mouth into Julie's mouth. The milky substance was objectionable because it looked too much like ejaculate to censors. Julie just saw it as a loving act.

Homosexuality has also become heightened in people's minds because of AIDS. The deadly disease first spread rampantly through the gay community because of the amount of sex partners gay men tend to have, and their preference for anal sex, which more easily transmits the virus that causes AIDS. Fortunately, the gay community has done a great deal to heighten everyone's awareness of the disease and the need for safe sex.

"I've been very depressed about being gay and afraid to let people know about it. I feel different but I'm ashamed and worried how it'll be if I come out."

You need support from organizations to help you. I'm worried about you. But take courage from successful public figures who have come out, like Elton John and Melissa

Ethridge. Gay Olympic star Greg Louganis shared his powerful story about how he grew up an adopted child feeling neglected by his father, called names in school, and so depressed about being different, he considered suicide to end the sadness. The song, "Believe in Yourself," inspires him.

Jerry: *"I've always known that I'm gay, but I hate the life. I don't like going to bars and picking people up. Once I was in a public bathroom and I was sitting on the pot and I looked on the side wall and there was a hole. All of a sudden a penis appeared in it, and a male voice from the other stall said, 'Take it, man.' I got sick, and got up without hardly wiping myself, just to get out of there. My friend told me later that was called a glory hole. He told me about clubs where guys go in dark rooms and have sex with the first person they grab. I don't want to live like that. Why do gay men sleep around so much?"*

It's a shame that the gay community has fostered that kind of promiscuity. In one study of over five hundred gay men done over twenty years ago, 40 percent reported hundreds of sexual partners. In another survey, three out of four gay men reported more than thirty different sexual partners during their lives. More recent studies report that gay men are engaging in fewer sexual contacts, presumably responding to the threat of AIDS.

But you can have a loving, stable relationship. In one study, one half of the lesbians and one quarter of the gay men were in stable relationships. In fact, there is more acceptance of gay relationships these days in America than ever before. (In Denmark, gay people can legally marry.) And acceptance is growing for gay couples to adopt children. So there are many more options open to you.

True self-esteem and happiness comes from having respect for yourself and from others, and feeling in control of your life, and feeling confident, secure, and proud of your choices. Studies show that homosexual adults who have come to terms with their homosexuality, who do not regret their sexual orientation, and who can function effectively sexually and socially, are no more distressed psychologically than heterosexual men and women. Professional organizations, like the American Psychiatric Association and the American Psychological Association, have taken steps to remove the stigma of "mental illness" from being gay.

Xaviar: *"I've been with men but lately, but I think I want to get married and have children and lead a regular life. I don't like sneaking around. I liked women before. I had such trouble with them, it was easier to go with guys who didn't hassle you all the time to talk and be sensitive. But girls aren't so bad after all, I think. I didn't give them a chance. What chance do I have of changing?"*

Some men and women do turn to the same sex when they are unsuccessful or hurt in relationships with the opposite sex. There are some programs in hospitals that help people who want to be attracted to or have sex with opposite-sex partners. Behavior techniques can help "train" you to associate pleasure with women or men, by thinking sexual or pleasurable thoughts while you are with that person. Deeper psychological therapy may help you identify and resolve angers, fears, or resistance toward the opposite sex, or past relationships with rejecting partners or a smothering mother or unavailable father. Realizing that you are repeating avoidances from the past can help free you to approach, and risk, involvement with someone of the opposite sex. Some men have gone through a program called Aesthetic Realism they say helps then reconnect love and sexual feelings with women.

I want you to fully accept yourself. That's the only way you can fully love yourself and be open to love for someone else.

George: *"I've realized I'm gay. Should I tell my friends? I'm afraid they'll pick on me."*

Be careful. Pick wisely whom and when you tell. If you want to tell to gain acceptance, accept yourself first. Realize that you are not alone, so you don't have to suffer in isolation, guilt, or fear. But you can't always trust that everyone will be open and nonjudgmental. While there is more openness and acceptance of gay people, there is also still much discrimination. Investigate how your workplace treats gays and what policies they may have. Consult gay-rights organizations for information and support groups.

Some people want to taste everything, but can confuse the person they're experimenting with.

"I like my friend who's a girl and a lesbian but wanted to try a guy. I said I'd be the guinea pig. She let me kiss her, go up her shorts, and do her. But then she said it wasn't as good and she'd stick with her girlfriend. But I like her. What can I do?"

Oink. You agreed to be a guinea pig so you set yourself up for rejection and it happened. So accept the consequences. If it's a pattern that you take such far-fetched risks, you have to be prepared for the high percentage of losses. Consider whether you have low self-esteem, insecurity as a man, or set yourself up for failure because you really don't value yourself as a person or a man.

CAME OUT TO PARENTS

Gary: *"I'm bisexual and I just came out to my parents. They're very upset. What can I say to them to calm them down?"*

Give them some time to get used to the idea. Understand that it is traumatic for them and they need to readjust their image of how they would like your life to go. Set aside uninterrupted time for heart-to-heart conversations. Openly identify and discuss their fears and hurt, since most parents blame themselves, worry about their child catching and dying from AIDS, feel disappointment about possibly not having grandchildren or their child not having the family life they dream about. They may need the support from groups like PFLAG, Parents and Friends of Lesbians and Gays. Remind them that you are still their son and face many of the same problems as you would have before this announcement, and that you need their support because you may now have other potential worries and challenges in dealing with people and deciding your future. Hopefully, after they review all these feelings, they will get to the best resolution: that your finding happiness is of paramount importance, that your life cannot always be what they would like it to be, and that they love and support you for who you are. You have to love yourself, too.

I'm a lesbian and my girlfriend wants to strap on a dildo and stick it in me like a man. Sometimes I think she thinks she's the man. I don't like this. Should I tell her?"

Yes, always say what you like and don't like. But what does the strap-on penis mean to you? It is perfectly fine for women to make love with these sorts of toys. Are you threatened by penises or men? Did one hurt you in your past? Perhaps you were once sexually abused by a guy.

HETEROPHOBIC

Luis is an example of how when you dig deeper into a person's mind, the whole conversation can take a sharp turn, and the mystery is revealed. In Luis's call, he revealed himself to be "heterophobic."

Luis: *"I have wet dreams about Madonna, but I don't eat fish. I'm allergic to being with a woman, I don't feel nothing for them. I like guys only."*

So I asked him, "When did you ever do something you thought was very bad or dirty involving a woman, maybe your mother?"

It unraveled, as Luis recounted: *"I was very young and I saw my mother nude in the shower. I was watching her breasts but her legs were ugly, they had cellulite. I didn't like looking at them, but I kept looking. I don't like looking at women since."*

There it is! The early trauma relates to the current experience. We all are conditioned that way, in more or less subtle ways. It also makes sense that Luis would now be obsessed with Madonna, whose name, after all, stands for mother. So in this way, he gets to feel close to mother, without the negative guilt or fears associated with sexual feelings toward his real mother. "If you forgive yourself for looking at, desiring, or being disgusted by your mother," I told Luis, "you will be freer to love women."

It's important to understand three different concepts.

> Gender refers to how you're born (whether you have a penis or vagina).
> Gender identity refers to which sex you identify with (whether you think you are male or female).
> Gender role is a combination of what you do and say to show others you are male or female.

HERMAPHRODITISM:

"I went to have sex with this girl—I thought—and she had a hole that I couldn't get in all the way, and when I put my hand there, there was this thing that was like a penis. I was freaked and ran out."

It can be surprising, but there is such a thing as people who have characteristics of both male and female— called hermaphrodites, from the mythical Greek god Hermaphroditus, who was thought to possess attributes of both sexes. Some guys have claimed they've picked one up at a bar and discovered a surprise.

"Can a hermaphrodite fuck itself or get itself pregnant?"

No. The penis is usually small, and wouldn't go into the vagina, and sometimes the vagina is not fully formed and the rest of the female reproductive organs necessary for reproduction, like the uterus, are not fully formed either.

Karen: *"My twin was born dead and now I have some weird disorder with my genitals. At six months old, I had five operations at six months old to cut my clitoris. At eleven, they opened my vagina because I might get my period. At eighteen they cut my clitoris again. I had one relationship with a guy who abused me. I never had sex yet, and I'm terrified because of what my genitals are like. I take Prednisone and some other medication and am a recovering substance abuser from taking painkilling narcotics. Can I ever be normal?"*

It's hard enough growing up, much less having abnormalities with your genitals and wondering if your body is male or female. True hermaphrodites, who have both ovarian and testicular tissue and a mix of both penis and vagina externally, are very rare. More common are pseudo-hermaphrodites. Here are some types:

Yours sounds like you're a *fetally androgenized female,* who has female organs inside, but the outside genitals look more male (the clitoris looks like a penis). They grow up female, but feel and act very "male."

Androgen-insensitive males have a mutant gene on the X chromosome that prevents testerostone from entering the fetus's cells to do its job of masculinizing. So the body develops a short vagina and looks female outside, and the brain also thinks it's become "female." They grow up with big breasts and a rounded figure, so they're often raised as girls, but they don't have much interest in sex and they can't have babies because they have no uterus, so don't menstruate.

DHT-deficient males are called "penis at twelve" or "first woman, then man" because they have a Y chromosome, so they're genetically male, but their testes are undescended, and they have no prostate, and on the outside their genitals look more like a female, with a clitoral-like phallus and more or less fused vagina. Since they look more like females at first, they're raised that way until puberty, when more testosterone flows, so the penis starts to grow, and they get other male characteristics and start getting interested in girls. Some of these "girls" are raised as "boys" then, but some experts say they should get surgery at birth and be raised as girls.

GENDER BENDERS

Lots of guys have called up *LovePhones* saying they got drunk and picked up someone at a bar, only to be mighty surprised later when they go to have oral sex in the car or back at their place.

Like Chuck: *"I tried to stick my hand down in this girl's crotch, and I felt a penis. I was really scared and mad. She looked just like a girl. But she was so gorgeous, I ended up letting her go down on me. Boy, was it good! Now I'm worried, though, should I not have done that and what does that mean about me?"*

Chuck got tricked by a pretty transvestite or drag queen. Guys dressing and acting like a caricature of women can do the perfect act and look beautiful! A few are guys who want to be women. Called transsexuals, they are "transgendered" in that they have the sex organs of one sex, but feel that they were born in the wrong body and want to have surgery and other changes to become the opposite sex. A few are gay guys who dress up and act like women but want to stay men who like having sex with men while pretending they're female.

If you're drunk, it's easy to see how your "beer goggles" can get you into anything. Don't freak about it; remember, one in four guys has a same-sex experience for many reasons—curiosity, desire, or just circumstances. Some guys pretending to be women can be better at pleasing a guy because they act like a woman and really know what a guy likes to boot!

If you're a sexually adventurous kind of person, you might even get off on the idea of doing something wild, and also on the idea of somebody being male and female. Don't get weirded out. You don't have to repeat it, or be ashamed that you enjoyed it. If you have a girlfriend, maybe you can get into play-acting that you're different sexes. Mix it up. The more secure you are in who you are, the easier it is to do that without being afraid you'll go overboard.

CROSS-DRESSING

Dressing in clothes of the opposite sex has become a fashion statement. Women have traditionally gotten away with it more easily than men, from George Sand in the mid-nineteenth century and Marlene Dietrich in the 1930s, to Madonna. Donahue wore a skirt on his talk show about men who like to dress as women but who don't want to have sex with men. They're called transvestites (TVs), like Les.

"I love my girlfriend and I like being a guy, but I like to dress in my girlfriend's clothes. I'm scared to do it when she's around. I remember doing it for the first time, in the bathroom, after my father left my mother and she was out to work all the time, and one day her underpants and bra were hanging on the rod to dry. I put them on and liked them, and now I go sneaking into her drawers when she's out and put on all kinds of things. I like to look in the mirror and think I'm pretty like my mother used to tell my sister. I want to wear a dress and go out. What if she finds out and is there something wrong with me?"

It depends on how far you take it and whether there's a conflict in your psyche. Wearing women's clothes can be fun, and allow your "female" side out, but it is a problem if you can't get sexually turned on without doing that, and if you really aren't happy being your own sex.

Your story is common: losing mother's attention and being jealous of your sister. In the majority of cases, the behavior starts before age ten, when the boy over-identifies with a female figure, or is treated to or punished by being dressed as a girl. Or he grows up learning girls are favored or sweet compared with boys, and yearns to express this feminine side. He puts on women's clothes as a need for beauty or goodness, or as an escape from cultural expectations or sex-role stereotypes where a man has to be aggressive or excel in sports, sex, work, or marriage. In many cases, the item of women's clothing becomes associated with sexual pleasure when he masturbates.

Deeper Freudian analyses say the man dresses as a woman to avoid separation anxiety from the mother or female figure (if he wears her dress, he'll never lose her) or to avoid castration anxiety (if he still has a penis but dresses like a woman, then he can believe that women haven't lost their penis).

The Romans wore togas. In Japan, male Kabuki players take women's roles and girls play all men's roles in Tasarazuka. Men vamp as women in Broadway shows like *La Cage Aux Folles*, Las Vegas revues, French burlesques, commercials (Olympic star Carl Lewis donned red stiletto heels for Pirelli tires), and movies (Dustin Hoffman in *Tootsie*, Robin Williams as a divorced father trying to get close to his child in *Mrs. Doubtfire*, and Patrick Swayze and Wesley Snipes as drag queen beauty contest winners in *To Wong Foo, Thanks for Everything, Julie Newmar*).

Adam Ant told me he loved to wear make-up in the glamrock era because girls loved it! Duran Duran's Simon LeBon told me at our Z100 Madison Square Garden 10th Birthday Bash that he likes the idea of wearing stockings! Heartthrob Richard Marx feels the opposite: "I never had the desire to do that and I can visualize it wouldn't be a pretty sight if I did."

TVs can be in hiding. Drag queen pop singer, RuPaul, who shot to fame singing about being a runway model, gave up his big blond wig, penciled eyebrows, and high heels, to be himself, telling the *Advocate* (a gay newspaper), "Now that I approve of myself and I don't need that approval from someone else, I'm ready to take the mask off . . . I speak to everyone with pain in their heart. But now the challenge for me is to project that message when I'm not in drag."

Watch out for your girlfriend's reaction. A few might be really into it and flattered, but most will be shocked, like Karen: *"I came home from shopping one day and found my boyfriend parading around the living room wearing my red silk panties and stockings stretched over his knees, and one of my bras dangling over his chest. He's a little bigger than me, so he stretched it all out. I told him to go do the dishes, and called him names saying he was queer, and he got all upset and promised not to do it again. A few days ago in bed he begged me to let him do it, and admitted that he has been doing it awhile, and wants to do it in sex. What's wrong with him?"*

Your boyfriend may like cross-dressing but that doesn't

mean he's gay. Most men who cross-dress are heterosexual, and married with children. They work in all types of jobs and like being men, but feel there is a "second self" inside them, their female side, that wants to be expressed.

See if you can see his cross-dressing not as a threat, but a compliment, that feeling his feminine side, he's more likely than other men to appreciate women and less likely to have an affair. He might not want to give this up even if you insist.

A guy who started cross-dressing support groups rated female partners from "A" (enthusiastic and encouraging, using his fem name, sharing clothes) to "F" (considers him perverted and wants nothing to do with this "horrible thing").

Brenda is an "A" female partner. She digs it.

"I want my boyfriend to put on my panties while we're having sex. Is there something wrong with me?"

Critics would say women who like this are secretly man haters. But having the guy wear your panties, or other things, can be really erotic! Know what you want from it. If it's your way of getting him to appreciate you, and women in general, or if it's a way to get him more in touch with his female side or sensitivity, then ask him to act more sensitive and loving whether or not he wears the clothes. If you want to reverse roles and let yourself be more in control, allow yourself to act more like how you think the man would.

Jen takes it a little further: *"I want my boyfriend to dress up in my clothes and put makeup on him. I thought about doing it with a girl, but I wouldn't do it. He has a female voice, though, and he used to be a model for underground fashion and they put eyeliner on him. Is this okay?"*

Sounds like it's safer for you to dress him than to be with another woman. It also sounds like this is acting out a narcissistic fantasy, making him into a projection of what you'd like. By dressing him up like a doll, you get to control him. He may go for it, though, because he's already used to it, so you have the perfect set-up to act out your fantasy. Make the most of experiencing what it means to you.

Some cross-dressers are gay men who vamp it up, called

drag queens. My friend Miss Understood, explains how a lot of heterosexual men love to play with drag queens, and get oral sex. The exaggerated dress-up makes acting out all the complicated fantasies of having a female and a male less threatening. Miss Coco Peru called when Sandra Bernhard was Honorary Love Doctor on *LovePhones*. "When I'm out in drag and feeling wonderful, and all these straight men come up to me after they've had a few cocktails and all of a sudden they're all over me. They know I'm a man and yet I'm dressed like a woman. It's annoying because I get angry, as though they should be either out, or go back to their wife."

Sandra: "Well, it's a turn-on for them because they're gonna feel more comfortable with a man ultimately; all men would because they relate to the same sex. They know what to do and yet you're in drag, so they can fool themselves."

Vogueing, posing, and dressing up as a sexual turn on, made popular by Madonna's song, includes not only transvestism (wearing clothes of the opposite sex), but also "homeovestism," dressing in clothes of the same sex person, usually as a caricature, for masquerading purposes, like a Barbie Doll of exaggerated proportions, or an overly made-up Tammy Bakker. It can be a sign of high individualistic style—or hiding insecurity.

"What if I married him, what would happen to our children?"

I have interviewed several such families. Some keep it secret from the children. Others use the occasion of a costume party to say, "Daddy sometimes wears Mommy's clothes, but he is always a man." Some kids get used to it but hope their friends don't find out. While it's certainly possible that a boy whose father dresses as a woman will copy the behavior, no studies prove it has to happen.

"How can I give up dressing in women's clothes?"

Help consists of therapy to understand why you do this, and to undo rigid male-female stereotypes, as well as masturbation training to associate pleasure with other fantasies.

But most men don't want to change. They prefer to join

support groups, where transvestite men seek mutual encouragement, hold parties, and share referrals for wigs, size-
thirteen shoes, and coaches to teach them how to walk and
talk like women, like Veronica Vera's "School for Girls" in
New York, or the Tri-Ess organization, with chapters
around the country. A video called "How to Impersonate A
Woman" goes through the steps of transforming a man to
dress and look like a woman.

BOYS WHO WILL BE GIRLS AND
GIRLS WHO WILL BE BOYS

There is a difference between transvestites who enjoy
pretending or feeling like a woman but want to remain a
man, and transsexuals who want to be physically changed
into being a woman because they feel trapped in the wrong
body and get no sexual pleasure from their penis.

James: *"I want to be a woman, I hate being a man."*

Tracy: *"I feel like I don't want to be a girl. I'd rather be a
boy. I heard there's an operation for it. Can I get one?"*

When a guy wants to be a girl or a girl wishes she were a
man, the true test of whether they are a transsexual is
whether they feel "trapped in the wrong body." We say
these people have a "gender dysphoria"—they feel at odds
with their gender. Another test is whether they get no pleasure from their genitals. A man might feel, "I don't like my
penis, I don't feel it belongs on my body."

I used to be part of a psychiatric team that evaluated people who wanted a sex-change operation. They had to go
through what's called a "life test" before being admitted to
any surgery. This means living as if you are already the
opposite sex. Curiously, one factor we found in common in
the backgrounds of men who wanted to become women is
that they often had very close relationships with their grand-
mothers and suffered severe separation anxiety from them.
Males into females are called MTF and females into males
are called FTMs. They're also called he-shes and she-males.

People are infinitely curious about what happens surgically to the genitals when you have a sex-change operation.

In the male to female operation, the testicles and most inner structures of the penis are removed and the outer skin is turned into the body to form the vaginal canal. To give a female male genitals, you can reconstruct a penis with the woman's own genital skin (facilitating orgasm) or you can construct a penis by grafting other skin and inserting an implant (a silicone rod or inflatable type), making a longer, more visually approximate, phallus.

"Can a man or woman who has a sex change operation have orgasm?"

Some claim that they do. Body changes that indicate changes in the sexual-response cycle can be measured—like temperature and pressure pulse. But remember that a very important criterion for orgasm is your subjective *feeling* of satisfaction. People who have had sex-change operations can feel satisfied, although, depending on the operation, not all can achieve the physiological response. It depends on the extent, type, and success of surgery. If nerves are intact, sensation can be achieved. It is certainly easier in male-to-female surgery, where things are removed, than in female to male surgery, where a penis has to be constructed.

Denise, once Darnell, is going through it. *"I'm very happy that I'm living like a woman now. I haven't had the surgery to have my penis removed yet, but I've taken hormones, so I have big breasts and my body shape changed, so I have more curvy hips. I'm six feet tall, but I know how to wear makeup and I let my hair grow long and bleach it blond, so I look like a hot babe. I met a guy at a bar three months ago and he fell for me. He didn't know at first what I was because I didn't let him have sex with me. I taped my penis back between my legs so when he pressed against me, he didn't feel anything there. Then we tried anal sex once, in the dark, so he didn't see my thing, but it was very tight and I didn't like it. For a while he didn't know and he proposed to me. I love him and had to tell him. He was shocked but said he loved me anyway. So now, when we have sex, I still tape my penis back, so he feels I'm the woman I want to be. Our sex consists of me giving him blow jobs. I don't let him touch me. I certainly don't want to use my penis because it feels alien to me. I hope the blow jobs keep him satisfied until I can get enough money together to have the operation. What else can I do to satisfy him sexually?"*

You can use frottage—rubbing bodies against each other for sexual pleasure, or dry humping, with or without clothes, simulating intercourse. You're lucky to have found this guy. Some Freudian shrinks would say a man who is willing to have sex with a partner who still has a penis, even though looking and acting like a female, has a complicated psyche, and may be conflicted about his own sexuality. Just be careful, as we were when I worked on that team evaluating candidates for the operation. Some men—and their partners—had too high expectations that changing sex would bring them happiness and love, when in fact, lopping off their penises plunged them deeper into depression.

But go ahead, enjoy your life, if it's working for both of you.

Remember what Madonna announced on her Girlie tour:

It's not about being male or female,
it's about being a person.

Get in touch with, love, accept, and express, all the sides of yourself, for true happiness.

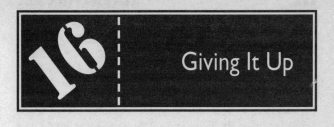

EXERCISE YOUR WILL POWER/ WON'T POWER . . .

That means you have the right to say yes or no to sex. For the first time, or for any activity. Exercise wisely your power to decide with whom, when, how, and why, you share yourself—what I call your Will Power/Won't Power.

Myths about giving it up destroy your will power/won't power.

Myth #1 (the biggest one of all): If I don't give it up, he'll leave me.

Girls are real prey to this myth. But falling prey to it is old. Give up the myth, not "it."

Tanya's story sounds so familiar: *"I haven't had sex with this guy, but I love him and he said if I don't, he's going to get another girl who will do the wild thing with him. But I don't want to lose him. What should I do?"*

Make him get lost. He's a loser. Obviously he only wants sex from you and doesn't care about you. Have more self-esteem, girl. Don't you believe you deserve to be treated better?

Tanya's situation applies to so many women—and guys—of all ages, in so many different situations, whenever they give in to a sex act because they're afraid the other person will find someone else to do it for them. Like Paulette: *"My boyfriend wants me to have sex with his friend, a girl we know and him. He doesn't stop going on about it and*

finally said if I don't do it, he'll find someone who will."
And Gina: *"My boyfriend wants to get into this fraternity
and for his hazing he wants to videotape us in sex and show
it to the brothers. They said if I won't do it he has to get
mother girl. I don't want him to have sex with another girl.
Should I do it?"*

You have to feel the right to say no, without being black-
mailed by your boyfriend to do what he wants or he'll leave.
It's a test of your self-esteem. You are not that desperate to
have anyone that you would sell your power to choose. Don't
let your fear give your will power/won't power away. Would
you tell him he has to do what you want or you'll leave?

I can understand you want to help your boyfriend but
don't be afraid to stand up for your point of view, no matter
what. You'll have to be strong to face the consequences. If
he drops you because of it, then the frat is more important to
him than honoring your feelings, and you know what type
of guy he is.

Guys worry about giving in or losing, too. Like Jason:
*"I'm fifteen and I'm a virgin and I'm dating a seventeen-
year-old and I'm afraid she'll think I won't like her if I
don't do it."*

Let this be a true test of whether she likes *you* or just
wants you to be what she wants. See this not about sex, but
about you learning how others respect you.

Guys need even more support than girls when they're
saying "no" to sex. They have just as confused inner feelings, just as many conflicts, fears, and needs. They want to
be loved and cared about as much as women do, for themselves, rather than as a sex object.

Myth #2: No guy in his right mind would turn down sex.

The truth is, of course they would.
Chris: *"I met this girl at a concert and offered to drive her
and her friend home and she invited me in and before I
knew it, me and her were in her bedroom. We were going at*

it and I had this thought like I don't even like her so why was I there. It just seemed like the thing to do. I couldn't finish, so I got up and left and she was mad."

Peter, 23: *"My friends make fun of me because I never did it yet, but I want to wait 'til I find the right girl, and I haven't yet. I like to date and make out, so I'm not a loser, but I don't think just 'cause I'm a guy I should do it. Is something wrong with me?"*

Everything's right with you. Congratulations that you are holding out for the right person and resisting pressure from your friends. You'll be very happy when the time comes. Trust yourself.

Preserve your will power/won't power. You always have a choice to go through with sex or not. Choose wisely. Think before, do I really want to do this? Why am I getting swept into this (need to feel desired, important, accepted, one of the crowd)? How will I feel after?

Guys especially have to know they don't have to have sex. It's a myth that you always have to be ready and willing.

Bob, 23: *"I broke up with this girl and now I haven't wanted sex. Girls don't understand I want to go out but just hang, no bang."*

Make it clear to them, say, "It's not a rejection of you, just where I'm at." If a girl can't understand, she's too insecure, or not right for you.

What a great phrase: **Just Hang, No Bang!**

Myth #3: Whatever you started, you have to finish.

The truth is, you don't have to follow through. You can always say "no."

Too often I hear stories about giving it up and regretting it. Like Mindy: *"I had sex with this guy I met at a party. He was gorgeous and every girl in the room had her eyes on him. He started telling me how pretty I am and asked me if I wanted to go into one of the bedrooms and talk private. I said 'sure,' and when we got there, he opened his pants and I did him. Then he walked out and started flirting with some other girls. I went home and cried for days."*

You don't owe anybody anything. Don't do it just because you're flattered. Sorry, but that shows you have low self-esteem. Remember, Respect (for yourself) Rules.

Myth #4: You should give it up just to get it over with.

The truth is, your first time is crucial. It sticks in your mind. You get attached to the person. Treat it carefully. When it should be a pleasant memory, why let it be a nightmare?

Like John, 19: *"I lost my virginity to a slut. I met her at a club and did it, but now I'm disappointed because I held out so long and I wasted it. After we did it she told me about so many other guys she did and how she wants to be a stripper. How can I get this out of my head?"*

And Brandi, 19: *"I'm feeling sick about myself. I lost my virginity last weekend in a one-night stand with three guys. I was drunk. It was my first time, and they all stuck things in me. One had his thing in between my breasts and I was puking from the alcohol. They didn't give a damn about me, and now I feel angry and hurt."*

I'm sorry you allowed your body to be used and you are disappointed about your first time. Put it behind you. Learn from the unpleasantness—never to get yourself in a situation like that again. Protect yourself. Ensure you have good experiences, don't just throw yourself to the wolves.

Horror stories when the first time didn't work out well should be reassuring to those who want to wait for the right person, time, and place, and serve as a warning to those who just want to give it up and are not being careful enough about making the first time a happy time.

It is a big present. So think, to whom would you give the most expensive, biggest present for Christmas? Treat your virginity and your body and soul that way.

Remember, Responsibility Rules: Before you open those pearly gates, investigate. Who is this person you are about to share intimacy with?

"It's better to stay friends first," Red Hot Chili Peppers' Anthony Kiedis told me backstage at the '93 MTV Awards, "you can't have sex 'til after that," recounting an as-yet-unconsummated relationship with a certain Mary whom he hoped to meet up with in L.A.

Myth #5: When you give it up, it'll matter as much to the other person as to you.

Truth is, they may not give a hoot. Christine was a virgin who found that out: *"The first time I had sex I was fourteen. I thought the guy was great. He was eighteen. My friends drooled over him. He drove a fancy car, but he took me for a ride. Right after we had sex, he never called me again. I was sick. I called him and he said he was busy and couldn't talk. Then I saw him with another girl in the mall, with his hand on her rear. He pretended he didn't even know me. I know now he just went with me for the sex. I hate him now. I'm sorry I did it."*

I'm sorry you had this experience. It's really sad to be so hurt, so rudely treated, and so disappointed in how other people can treat you, and in yourself for your judgment! It's a hard way to learn a critical lesson about treasuring your body and soul and exercising your will power/won't power wisely. Because you've been so burned, you'll be far more careful next time! Stop and Think before you do anything, think of your motives and needs, and think of the consequences, and then decide.

Myth #6: If you give it up to someone, for the first time, or do something special with them (that you didn't or wouldn't do before), that person has to matter to you forever.

Truth is, if it works out badly, you have to give him or her up!

Too many girls—and a few guys too—get so attached to

someone they did something special with sexually, that they lose their judgment about whether it's really a good relationship. I hear the story so often:

"This guy I'm dating is cheating on me and treats me bad."

"So why do you stay?" I ask.

"Because I love him," is the answer.

"But why do you love him?" I ask.

"Because I've been with him two years, and besides he was my first," is invariably the answer.

Sharing your body and soul is significant, but if the person turns out to treat you bad, s/he's not worth it! You've got to let it go. Don't get so emotionally invested that you're blind to their faults, or expect so much you end up settling for so little.

Having sex with someone does not automatically mean you love him/her.

Aiisha, 16: *"I've had sex with six different guys in the past year and I thought I loved them, but they don't say it back. I thought they did, but it never goes on. What's wrong?"*

What's wrong is that you are giving it up too quickly, thinking they're in love when they're just into having sex and not a lasting relationship. You want love so badly that you see it when it's not there. Love takes time to grow, so what you feel is the desire to be loved. I can appreciate that, but sex is not going to get love for you. In fact, you see that it brings you hurt and rejection. Wait before having sex the next time, until you know the guy cares about you for you.

Myth #7: Everybody's doing it.

Truth is, falling for peer pressure is old.

"I don't want to be the only one. My friends all say I should go for it or I'm a wuss."

A lot of teens have sex because of peer pressure—all their friends are and they don't want to be the only one who isn't. Peer pressure was rated the major reason for having sex by half of boys and three out of four girls in a Harris poll of twelve-to-seventeen-year-olds, funded by Planned Parenthood. Almost a third had sex. Over half of the seventeen-year-olds had sex.

"We hear so much about everybody's doing it. But how many young people are really having sex?"

Most surveys do show high numbers, at early ages, suggesting that "white weddings" are a thing of the past. More than half of students from ninth to twelfth grade report having sexual intercourse at least once, and one in five have had at least four partners. Other surveys show up to 70 percent of high-school students have had sex. One survey of 1600 college students found three out of four seniors were sexually active but only half of freshman were.

But is it right for you?

Bridget: *"I'm seeing this guy and he's pushing me to have sex with him. My friends are telling me I should do it already or I'm out of it. Should I?"*

Poison's Bret Michaels: "If you don't want sex, don't do it. If your body wants to, work it out with the guy. If not, say you aren't quite ready for it. Never be in a drunken stupor. I never had sex because of peer pressure. Girls are pushed into it more often than boys."

"This guy wants me to go down on him and said that all the other girls are doing it. My friends say they do, but I don't want to, but I don't want to be the only one."

Whether it comes to having sex for the first time, or doing a particular sex act, everybody's not doing it. And even if they were, that doesn't mean you have to.

Myth #8: "It just happened . . ."

URGGHHH. This boils my blood. The truth is: nothing just happens. You *choose* it.

Paige, 13: *"I was going out with this guy and we were fooling around and it just happened. Now I think I want it again."*

Nothing just happens! You chose it, you allowed it, you let it happen. See that you have a choice. That's a critical lesson for growing up. You're not ready to say yes to sex until you can say no.

Myth #9: When you're with someone, you owe them sex.

The truth is, you don't owe anyone sex.

Girls have to especially beware of their own feelings of intimidation and inclinations to please others. Girls get into doing what they don't want—from going out on dates with guys they don't like to having sex when they don't want to—to protect others' feelings, maybe to save a guy from embarrassment or being turned down. Why would you rather suffer inside than tell someone "no"?

"What should a girl do if she feels obliged to have sex with a boy because she owes him something to make him happy?"

You aren't obliged to have sex with anybody for any reason. You don't owe anybody sex for anything they do or say or buy for you. If it's implied that you should, then there's something wrong in the relationship.

Like Heather: *"I agreed to go on a date with this guy I don't like. When he came to the door I got sick, but I went. Then, when he dropped me off and went to kiss me I grit my teeth and scrunched my eyes but let him do it because I thought he'd be devastated if I didn't. I hate this. What can I do?"*

Tell yourself that you are not responsible for pleasing everyone and that you come first. It's great to be nice, but sacrificing yourself all the time is not a good quality; it's desperation and fear. Don't lose your sensitivity and kindness but also don't lose your self! Some people need to learn to be kind, you need to learn to be more selfish!

You are never obligated to have sex. Some guys think when you're their girl, or their wife, it's their due. Wrong.

Connie, 20: *"My fiancé said I'm obligated to have sex with him, but he won't go down on me. I put chocolate pudding on it and made it a pudding pot, but he still didn't. He wants anal sex with me, though, and said when we get married, 'I got papers on your ass.' I really love him, so what do I do?"*

Reassess what love means to you, since that sounds like being an indentured servant, not a respected partner. A marriage license is not an owner's license.

Beware the dudes who demand their due.

Vlad: *"Yo, I'm tryin' to get boonani from my girl. I'm like a brick. I respect her, but I'm not in love with her. I rub and lick her, frying her in the pan, but she won't go in the crib with me. She says, 'I'm not ready for this.' I tell her it's an ill line. I tell her she has to give up the boonani so I'll make her a woman. I smack her and hit, but she don't listen up. How do I get through to her?"*

Certainly not by smacking and hitting. How abusive. She's a fool for sticking around listening to your "ill" lines.

And watch out for the ones who only want sex.

Josh, 18: *"I'm dating this girl, but the bitch won't do the nasty. I send her flowers and she still won't give it up. I'm getting ready to ditch her because there's this other virgin I know is dying for it."*

Get a grip, you're acting like a butthead. Hopefully none of those girls will get with you, so you'll be left out in the cold, and be forced to learn more respect for women.

How come you have to treat girls like objects? You don't have to do that to prove something to your boys, or to protect yourself from being hurt. How about experimenting with caring about a girl for her more than for sex. Could you stick with this girl and think of enjoying each other's company and feeling something? Maybe not, but think about it.

Myth #10: Once you lost your virginity, you can never get it back again.

The truth is, you can be a virgin again: a Second Virgin. You may not get the tissue called the hymen back, but in your mind, you can consider that you still have not had that meaningful first time.

Both girls and guys may regret how they lost their virginity. I always say you can be a second virgin or a born-again virgin many times over. In fact it's always good to come to a sexual experience—or any experience—as if it's the first time.

My old friend, *Entertainment Tonight* host John Tesh, and his wife, actress Connie Selleca, became second virgins: waiting for sex until they got married, though they both had been married before. It was Connie's idea, to put a pure, virginal twist on their union.

WHEN IS THE RIGHT TIME?

"How old should you be when you first have sex?"
1. 14 years old
2. 16 years old
3. 18 years old
4. When you get married
5. Whenever you feel ready

When she was only fourteen, Melanie Griffith fell madly in love with then-twenty-two-year-old Don Johnson and wanted to do it, since all her girlfriends had, and all the other guys she knew were jerks. She invited him to lunch, but he was scared to death because the possibility of going to prison for sex with a minor was not an attractive idea, but she felt ready, not just physically but mentally and spiritually.

Candlebox lyricist and lead singer, Kevin Martin, lost his virginity at twelve: "She was in her late teens. It was a shocking time for me, but also beautiful." Danny Bonaduce gave it up as a kid on the set of *The Partridge Family,* where, as Danny told me, "there was sex everywhere. I was getting it all the time." And Lemonheads' Evan Dando, once one of *People* Magazine's "50 Most Beautiful People," was fifteen his first time with a sixteen-year-old girl, and wrote "It's About Time," musing whether a female friend would lose rock's most famous virginity.

For Madonna, "Losing my virginity was a career move." Maybe for the Queen of Sex, but not for millions of other young women and men.

I would like to say the right time to have sex for the first time is whenever you feel ready, but I'm afraid I've heard too many young people, no matter how mature they look or act, who are not "ready." The younger you are, the more confusion and complications you face about love and sex, so waiting is wise.

A real big problem is not knowing what real love is. Too many stories go like Tara's: *"I had sex with this guy, and then I found out he was cheating on me and then I dumped me. But I love him."*

What do you mean *you love him*? You only knew him a few weeks, a month! That's not enough to love someone on the deepest level. You can feel excited about them. You can be thrilled about the amount of attention you're getting or giving. You can be proud he's cute and you got him. Don't use the word "love" frivolously because what you say influences how you feel about something and what you do about it.

Unfortunately, this experience doesn't qualify for love because it's missing a critical factor. Sex without emotional intimacy is just sex; sex with emotional intimacy and trust is making love. But you haven't shared enough to truly love. Love means going through thick and thin together. Love is when you trust and respect each other for who and what you are and how you behave. This usually develops over time. Love leaves you feeling good, not bad. Why would you love someone who hurts you so badly? This just repeats a pattern of low self-esteem and abusive relationships.

MAKING THE DECISION

"I'm twenty-one and still a virgin, but I have an ex-boyfriend who I stay in touch with, even though he's going

with another girl. Sometimes when we talk I think I'd like to have sex with him, just to do it finally. Should I?"

You waited so long, why not wait until someone comes along who is totally there for just you. Your ex-boyfriend already has someone else. So you'd have sex with him, and he'd be off with her. And you'd be hurt. Relationships are hard enough, without starting out with someone who already has someone else.

Beverly Hills 90210's Brian Austin Green on virginity: "It's your right and it depends on what you're in the relationship for. If you're in it just to hit it, then move on and find someone who's down for that. If it's for love, respect the other person."

Actor John Stamos has a different view on sex: "Have as much sex as you can . . . you can never have too much."

VIRGIN SUPPORT

There's so much peer pressure to have sex, virgins need support.

Kristi, still a virgin at twenty-two, was told by her girlfriends that virgins are not real women. *"I'm a virgin and I still feel like I'm a woman and a woman of virtue. But am I cheating myself by not having sex?"*

About to be seventeen years old, Lisa has similar worries. *"I'm embarrassed to be a virgin still. All my friends are not virgins, but I am. I want to have sex bad just to say I did it, but I'm afraid it'll hurt. Some guys chase me at first but I've lost boyfriends because I won't do it. They say I'm no fun, but I am fun!"*

I'm glad you realize their criticism of you is not valid! You are fun even if you won't have sex. Don't let them intimidate you or break your confidence. What a way to be convinced to have sex anyway—a real lover would build your confidence, not destroy it! Just having sex to say you did it can hurt you more than anything in the long run. Physically you may close up (your vagina could get tight and it could be painful) because you're afraid and untrusting. And emotionally you could get hurt because you won't be selective about who you're doing it with.

Just because your friends did it doesn't mean you have to. There's nothing to be embarrassed about, thinking you're less attractive or desirable or mature. Never have sex because you think you have to for someone else. You need a guy who wants you for *you,* not for sex alone. Plenty of guys come on like sex matters because they think they have to live up to an image, when they're really as nervous or concerned as women are.

Gary Cherone from the rock group Extreme was *LovePhones* Honorary Love Doctor that night, and advised: "Let me just tell you something right off the bat. You're gonna be not a virgin a lot longer than you'll be a virgin, so don't worry about being a virgin when you're so young."

Lisa continued: *"I know a guy for a month I think I love. Should I do it before I run out of time?"*

Gary answered, "There would always be time. If you haven't had a serious relationship that you felt you could do that with, then don't bother doing it, because it's the best when you're with somebody you really care about. People could gain your respect if you hold out, because the second someone rushes you into it and then you have sex with them, suddenly the respect is gone. One of the main reasons why they may be chasing you is for your virginity. Personally I don't think you can be in love for a month. People say 'love at first sight' but I don't think you can know someone that well in a month. Let them wait; if they love you, they will."

Bassist Pat Badger added, "You're part of the limited few and we're running out of you guys. I think it affects women more mentally, losing their virginity, because of society. Men could take a facecloth and wash it off. A girl feels violated and wants to fall in love."

Take heart that despite all the talk about peer pressure to have sex, and the high numbers of young people doing it, there is some evidence that chasteness is in! Look how long the Donna Martin character played by Tori Spelling on

Beverly Hills 90210, held boyfriend David at bay. Across the country some teens are choosing abstinence. One USA Weekend poll found 72 percent of teens agreed with swearing off sex (that doesn't mean they'll do it, of course, as attitudes don't always predict behavior). Some organizations for chastity have sprung up, like True Love Waits and Best Friends. "Save Sex" is another campaign to "Keep Sex Pure," and touts "The New Revolution" with ads and posters of members, and the message: "First they questioned marriage. Said that love should be 'free.' But 'free love' turned out costly, very costly for some. Now they're pushing condoms. Saying sex should be 'safe.' But 'safe sex' can be risky (to your health and your heart). We think it's time for a new revolution. We think it's time for a love that is real . . . and lasting . . . and pure. A love that sees sex as a celebration of two lives shared together. Forever. That's why we believe in marriage. And why we're saving sex for it."

More than 750 students at three universities in Illinois, Wisconsin, and Oklahoma surprisingly said they preferred low sexual activity—meaning nothing more than kissing— not only in their potential mates but also in their friends. (Of course there is an explanation for this. Most people like to think they are the first or at least the truest of their beloved, so they don't like hearing of past exploits. And in the age of AIDS, getting involved with someone with many partners can be dangerous, making the person seem unattractive.)

Some people have more complicated reasons for staying a virgin. Like Gerald: *"I'm twenty-six and a virgin. I never even kissed a girl. I swore off sex because when I was six I saw my mother raped by a neighbor. I hit him with a toy, but he didn't stop. My mother never reported it. Now I'm thinking about having sex."*

I'm happy for you that you are allowing yourself to accept the natural feelings you have. And you're wise to connect your earlier trauma to your avoiding sex later. It must have been awful to see your mother being raped. How wonderful that you tried to protect her! But you must have been disappointed that you couldn't stop it, so you felt guilty and angry at men and probably decided that men treat women badly in sex, so you would avoid it when you became a man. Look for a female partner who doesn't play the victim role so you don't unconsciously repeat the pattern from your childhood. Reassure yourself that you would not be aggressive during sex like that abusive man.

Lucy: *"If a girl came up to you claiming she is a virgin and saving herself for you, how would you handle the situation?*

Poison's lead singer Bret Michaels: "Hopefully an attraction would have to be there. Then, if we were both single and it felt right—it's not something you want to do in the back of the tour bus or the bathroom, though I must admit the thought has crossed my mind. We'd have to be able to see each other again so it wouldn't be something that just happened, since if it's the first time for someone, it's a big deal for that person. The excitement for a guy is that she's not been with anyone else. It's a boost to your ego, you feel she's safe and pure. I have to admit my first time was all in three oops . . . she didn't even have time to get her cigarette out."

Poison's drummer Rikki Rockett: "First, I'd ask how old she is. Then I'd have to talk to her and be careful. I'd need a whole evening with her before anything could happen."

WHAT IS A VIRGIN?

Jasmine: *"If you have sex with a condom on, are you still a virgin—because you didn't have flesh-to-flesh contact?"*

Technically you're a virgin if your hymen—that membrane stretching around the vaginal opening—is intact. And you lose your virginity when you are penetrated by a penis. But this is a limited view of virginity. For instance, some girls' hymens are broken before having intercourse. Personally, I take a broader view. I think you're a virgin until you have engaged in any sexual activity with a partner that includes oral or anal sex, including penetration by fingers as well as a penis. If you had sex with a condom on, you're not a virgin anymore. It doesn't depend on the skin-to-skin contact, but person-to-person contact.

Guys from the British rock group Blur agree: "If two girls have sexual relations, does that mean that they have lost their virginity if it was the first time? You may try to get away with thinking if you're wearing a condom and getting off, then they are no longer a virgin. It's not so." Sex with a condom and two girls having sex would qualify for not being a virgin.

Come up with some new ways to define virginity!

One of my interns had a creative way of maintaining her "virginity" for marriage in modern times. She came up with a new definition of virginity. She insisted on having sex with a condom with her fiancé (despite being tested for AIDS and being monogamous), until they got married, when they would experience sex on their honeymoon for the first time, indeed—without a condom.

"I've been dating my boyfriend for two and a half years, but we want to wait to have sex. How can we survive another two and a half years 'til we get married?"

Decide that waiting until you're married is right for you. Do other pleasurable things together, nonsexual things that bring you close and make you feel "one" as sex would (e.g., write a book, or play a sport like tennis). Do really romantic things for each other. Do sexual things that stop short of what you decide is the line, like dry humping, and outercourse.

"I'm a virgin and don't want to have sex yet. What other ways can I satisfy my boyfriend without having intercourse?"

Outercourse includes kissing, hugging, rubbing (frottage), and all behaviors other than penetration. Dry humping—simulating sexual intercourse with your clothes on (i.e., no skin-to-skin contact) can be extremely exciting.

Personally, I believe that oral or anal sex is as legitimate sex as intercourse, so if you hold off intercourse just to be a virgin but do the other things, then you are what I call a Level II virgin ("vaginal virgin" or "penetration virgin"), but you're not a Level I virgin, because you had some kind of sex.

STARTING OVER

Susan: *"My boyfriend broke up with me today. Was it because the sex was bad? I liked him for two years and he finally asked me out. We went out three times. I was a virgin and gave it to him. But then he didn't call me, and when I called him he told me another girl asked him out and he was probably going to go. What is he doing?"*

He's telling you he doesn't want to be with you. I'm sad for you because you carried a torch for him for two years and then it seemed your dream could come true, but it didn't. Unfortunately, your mistake was making it more than it was. Set your sights on someone else who will return your attention. Feel like you're starting over.

Linda: *"I had sex for the first time when I was only thirteen. The guy was twenty-three, a musician in the band at the hotel my family was staying at while on vacation. It was a horrible experience because he never paid any attention to me except when we went to his room those few times. Now I'm eighteen and dating a boy who thinks I'm a virgin. I really love him and am afraid he will leave me if he knows it's not my first time. I'm tempted to lie since the other guy meant nothing. Is that okay?"*

No! One lie, regardless of the rationalization, endangers trust and respect, including self-respect! Though you regret sharing that significant first sexual experience with someone insignificant, it helped you to learn to value love in sex. Hopefully your boyfriend can appreciate this, too. If he leaves you over this, then does he truly love you? I suspect you are projecting your own negative feelings about your past. Find out how he really feels. He may be like other men today who fantasize both about a virgin they can initiate and also a sexually experienced woman who takes the initiative.

Don't feel compelled to confess your past; but if he asks, be honest.

Here's one new twist: Consider yourself a "mental virgin"—distinct from a "physical virgin," which refers to the unbroken hymen. I notice an increasing number of women with this story: single or married women, they have had sex but then become celibate—because there is no available or "right" partner; because other circumstances interfere with sex, like stress, overwork, illness, parenting responsibilities, or problems in the relationship; because of fears of AIDS; or because, like you, past experiences were painful, and they want to wipe their slate clean.

I first became familiar with "second virgins" in a Japanese women's magazine survey of three hundred women in their twenties and thirties. The survey found 36 percent of the single women had sex before, but not in the previous year; 61 percent felt nervous and 15 percent scared to resume sex. Your own insecurity may also be inflating your fears about your boyfriend. Relax; you can get back in the saddle fine! Some women may actually wish they coud reattach the hymen! But you don't have to go that far: virginity can be a state of mind.

Can you lose your virginity to yourself? Danielle wanted to know: *"I know this friend, right, who like told me this deep, dark secret that she lost her virginity while masturbating. It kinda grossed me out, but I was just saying I thought it was pretty nauseating, and I just wanted to know if it is normal? Is she not a virgin?"*

It's fine for guys, so certainly it's fine for women, too! Feel better. Don't worry. She's not a freak. Hymens break all the time before intercourse. She has nothing to be ashamed about and should still tell her "first" boyfriend she's a virgin because she hasn't been with another person.

Hot weather triggers hot times. Approximately 45 percent of young people lose their virginity in the summer months—and the most popular month for first-time sex is June. Researchers believe sex hormones may rage more freely during summer's long days and warm weather. Of course, summer vacation increases the opportunity for sexual encounters, with more free time, freer dress and lifestyles, and fewer responsibilities.

"When is the right time to do it?"

The same rules apply to having sex with someone as for deciding when to have sex for the first time:

THE TEN COMMANDMENTS OF SHARING YOUR SEXUAL SELF— Only when:

1) you know your own body and your emotional and sexual needs.
2) you trust him/her to care about your emotional and physical health.
3) you communicate openly about what you do and do not want in sex and relationships.
4) you fully understand where you both stand on dating, intimacy, sex, love, and commitment.
5) you have spent a lot of time together nonsexually, enjoying each other's company.
6) you've seen him/her treat others well.
7) you've experienced him/her coming through (for you, and in emergencies).
8) you express real caring for one another.
9) you're responsible enough to protect against pregnancy.
10) you've discussed and ensured protection against sexually transmitted diseases.

NOT READY

Brian: *"My girlfriend is a virgin and she wants me to pretend to rape her to lose her virginity. Should I do it?"*

Honorary Love Doctor Debbie Gibson's advice: "Don't do it. It means she's not ready. She can wait."

To me, the fact that she wants to be "taken" means absolutely that she is not ready to have sex; that she wants to absolve herself of choosing to do it, making up in her mind that you forced her. A condition for having sex is that you're ready to take responsibility for choosing it.

BLEEDING FROM BROKEN HYMEN

"I'm twenty and I've never have sex before, but I wonder when the first time happens, how much will I bleed? If I'm at somebody's house, will it go all over the bed and everybody will know?"

Bleeding the first time you have intercourse comes from breaking the hymen, a thin membrane around the vaginal opening. The amount of blood from its rupture depends on the thickness, flexibility, and diameter of the ring of tissue. Some are so impenetrable, they require an incision by a doctor; yet bleeding may still be minimal, hardly like the gushing Niagara Falls many girls anticipate. Others are so thin or partial, they tear easily (during strenuous sports or penetrations other than intercourse) with little noticeable blood or just spotting. In addition, intercourse does not always tear the hymen, but may simply stretch it, so pieces can be left. On a deeper level, your fears about bleeding might be a symbol of your fears of being hurt in love, injured in sex, or even punished for being sexual. You might not be so worried if you wait for the right man to share your special moment with. Give yourself permission to have love and pleasurable sex, without thinking that everyone will be judging you.

"I was a virgin, but when I had sex with my boyfriend for the first time, I didn't bleed. He won't believe me since I didn't bleed."

Tell your boyfriend that you are telling the truth and that the hymen may be broken by ways other than intercourse. Especially if it's thin or more delicate, it could tear from using tampons, or putting anything else in your vagina, or from activities (like riding horses or vigorous sports), or it may just disintegrate over time. As a last resort, call your gynecologist and have him talk to your boyfriend.

If he persists in thinking you lied, ask him to explain why he is so paranoid, so distrustful, so fearful that there was someone else. What is his real upset with you that this may be covering?

TELLTALE SIGNS

"Is there a way to tell if a guy has had sex before?"

Not physically. There is no equivalent in males to the hymen of females. You might be able to tell if he's inexperienced from his awkwardness, being shy about taking off clothes, not knowing how to undo your bra, being awkward inserting his penis, fumbling for your vaginal opening.

FEARS OVER FIRST TIME

Adam, 21: *"I'm a virgin but my girlfriend wants to get busy, but I'm afraid I won't get it up good, and that she'll see I'm scrawny when I'm naked."*

I'm glad you're in touch with your fears. A lot of guys have the same fears as you, about their bodies and their performance. Accept your fears and go for it anyway! Tell your girlfriend you're nervous about looking good and "doing it right" so she won't have grand expectations from you and the performance pressure will be off you. She may find your honesty and naïveté charming. Tell yourself that making love is about sharing and not having to "get it up." The best trick: no erection the first time. Tell yourself and your girlfriend that you may purposefully not have an erection the first time you have sex. You'll be surprised. Once you take those expectations off, you will probably have a fine erection.

Mike: *"When I pop the girl for the first time, am I going to get all those virgin juices on me?"*

Probably, but they'll be nice. Some might be blood, from the broken hymen, and the rest is the woman's natural lubrication, a sign that she's excited, just like your ejaculate is a sign you're excited.

HURT THE FIRST TIME

"I'm a virgin and we were trying to have sex, but it hurt so badly I couldn't. Even trying so many times, it still hurt. Is there something wrong?"

Dyspareunia, or pain in sex, can be physical or psychological. Infections or disorders can cause pain with penetration. If it persists, you need to have a checkup with a doctor. More likely it is in your mind. You might be very frightened and tightening up, so it's hard for your boyfriend to enter. Relax. Perhaps you have guilt about having sex. Give yourself permission. If you feel really guilty about having sex, perhaps you're not ready.

"I know a lot of girls who lose their virginity hurt the first time. But does the first time hurt for a guy, too?"

It can, for the same physical and psychological reasons for guys as for girls. If your blood isn't flowing freely, then it can create a feeling of discomfort or pressure in your penis or in your scrotum. You might also push too hard too fast, without her being lubricated enough, so the skin is being tugged and irritated. You might be very frightened and tightening up. If you feel guilty about having sex, either don't do it, or reassure yourself with permission. If you're worried you'll hurt her, make sure she's lubricated and don't force anything. If you're worried you'll get her pregnant or get an STD, take precautions. If you're insecure about what to do, reassure yourself that anything you do is okay and ask her what she likes.

BAD REACTION

The first time can be real confusing and disappointing. Apparently that happened for John Lennon. The late Beatle lost his virginity at fifteen to a big-busted beauty and is quoted as saying in *The Last Days of John Lennon* by a former personal assistant Frederic Seaman, "I got so frustrated and angry that I started to curse her, 'You dumb cow, what's wrong with you?' It wasn't her fault, of course, but what did I know? I was just a weird psychotic kid covering up my insecurity with a macho facade." Many guys do this, and the girls get the brunt of feeling hurt and rejected.

Hope, 19: *"I had my first experience and I thought it would be better. I was looking forward to something really passionate, but my boyfriend was so quick and I didn't feel much. He said, 'I hope I gave it to you good.' I couldn't tell him, but now I want to break it off."*

Don't measure the future by this first time. You both had too high expectations. He was obviously nervous (because he came so quickly). He's also obviously inexperienced, so he needs more time to get used to being comfortable being together and pleasing each other without thinking he has to do anything particular to perform, or prove himself. Next time, spend the time talking and touching, without shooting for some goal, like orgasm.

Clarisse, 19: *"I really like my boyfriend, but the first time we did it I screamed at him to get out of here. Why would I do that if I care for him?"*

You were scared and didn't know how to react. And you were probably a little ashamed of having sex, for fear that you had transgressed your morals, or would upset your mother if she knew. So you took it out on him. Apologize and explain to him so he doesn't get the wrong idea. Resolve that you made a decision to have sex because you love your boyfriend and give yourself permission.

DRY HUMPING

"I haven't had sex, but my boyfriend gets on top of me with our clothes on and makes all the motions. I get all tingly and I think I have an orgasm. Is this possible? I thought you had to have him in you for that."

Dry humping—simulating sex without skin-to-skin contact—can be extremely exciting, and can definitely lead to orgasm. In fact, it's the anticipation of sex without doing it, thinking it's forbidden or that you're withholding, that can build the excitement phase of the sexual-response cycle, and make you so mentally turned on that the orgasm can be exquisite.

ONE STEP AT A TIME

"I like this guy and want to go out with him, but I don't want to have sex. How do I let him know I'm interested in him without making him think I want sex?"

One step at a time. Let him know you like him. Smile and say something like, "It'd be great to go (bowling/to the movies/hang out) one night," and see if he picks up on it. Then when you're out you can get into a conversation about dating in general (how most people think they have to have sex, but it's so much better to hang out together first); then more specifically about *your* style (how you love being friends first); and then you can be direct about how you're not ready for sex and don't mean to imply you are, but would like to spend time together. Don't be afraid to be direct—if he's not on the same program, it's not going to work anyway. Better to know than get caught in an uncomfortable situation.

PHOBIC ABOUT TOUCHING

Damon, 18: *"My girlfriend doesn't want to do anything, because she wants to stay a virgin. But she wets my whistle. Whenever I touch her though, she freaks out, thinking one thing will lead to another."*

Talk with her openly about how far you will go so she trusts you. Then she won't freak every time you touch her, thinking that this time she'll give in, or you'll push her. Reassure her that she can set the limits and you'll respect them.

PARENTAL FEARS

Heather: *"I'm the youngest of five children and my parents treat me like the baby. If they find out I want to have sex, I'm afraid they won't see me like the angel anymore. I'm scared."*

Some girls like you want to give up their virginity just to be rebellious. They want to prove their independence from their parents, and escape from the prison of having to be their "good little girl." Don't be a rebel without a clue. It's best not to make choices out of rebellion, but because they're constructive to you. If you know you're independent in your own heart, you don't have to prove it. Since you've already made a choice, live up to the consequences of that. Talk to your parents about it like an adult and they will be more likely to treat you that way. Accept that they will be shocked and disappointed. Listen to their upsets. Explain your actions. See if you can make them feel you do consider their opinions, even though you made a different choice. Reassure them that you are being responsible. This way you are accomplishing what you set out to do in the first place, proving you are an independent and maturing woman, not only to them but to yourself as well.

PARENTS FEAR

"My parents are going to kill me when they find out I had sex."

Maybe not. Parents get upset over this news. Sometimes they threaten extreme things—even to throw you out of the house—but that could be just their initial shock, and they'll calm down and be more reasonable.

USES NONVIRGINITY TO CONTROL

Debbie, 18: *"My boyfriend brainwashes me. I lost my virginity to my first boyfriend and now my boyfriend says I'm worthless and used and that now only he will love me. Am I so worthless?"*

No! But this is his way to control you. He's so scared of being rejected, he's telling you that no one else will want you. But that's not true. You must feel worthless, though, that you accept this ridiculous brainwashing. Are you really so desperate for someone's love? What made you feel you are used? Are you that guilty about having had sex? I'd be afraid of what else is in his head about relationships. If he controls you in sex I'm sure he does in other ways. This is not a healthy relationship for you. It's a prison.

GETTING SMART

Kendra: *"I had sex with twenty-nine guys in the last few months. I be giving them what they ask for, but it's about time to say 'no mo' 'ho.'"*

Congratulations. You have the right to say no. HOMEWORK: Start out by saying no to three things that are not sexual that you ordinarily would say yes to. It'll get easier the more you practice. Then when you're with a guy, close your eyes and see "no" like a big stop sign and then just say it. Once you do, and you see it can be honored and things work out differently, you'll feel your power of saying no.

TAUNTED AS TEASE

"How do you handle being called a tease because you won't give it up?"

Ignore those taunts. Sticks and stones can break your bones, but names will never get you into bed. They can call you anything, don't take it to heart. You're allowed to be a flirt and enjoy making out and also to set your limits and say you won't go all the way. To prevent guys' misreading you, though, make it clear up front what your limits are. Then you won't feel guilty that you led them on, and there won't be any question that they misread your signals.

NO-SEX GUARANTEE

Jason, 18: *"My girl wants to wait 'til after we get married to have sex. But how can I tell if she'll be good? What if she never wants it enough after I already tied the knot?"*

You have no guarantees. But you can find out how someone would be in sex:

- by observing how affectionate he or she is;
- by asking about how he or she feels about sex (does she think married people should do everything they both want to?);
- by asking what his or her sexual fantasies are and if he or she will discuss them (to give you an idea how open she is);
- by observing how freely he or she uses their body (does she dance and walk with abandon and openness);
- by watching how he or she eats (does she seem comfortable using her mouth);
- by finding out what he or she learned about sex (if she was told it was bad or dirty, then she will have a harder time getting over inhibitions).

Girls will be happy to know that guys have the same dilemma about whether to say yes or no to sex.

"I have an ex-girlfriend who I still like. She left me and is going with another guy, but she calls me a lot and talks to me about the arguments they have. Sometimes she beeps me, just to talk. I think about her a lot and I'd like to do it with her again, and I think she would go for it. Should I?"

No. What for? She's using you as a backup to make her feel good when she has problems with her current boyfriend, so she feels reassured someone cares about her and she has somewhere to go if it doesn't work out with her boyfriend. You're the "mattress"—something to fall back on. If you still like her, you're only going to feel hurt when she goes back to him. You may have a momentary pleasure, but it's not worth it. Use that same energy to find someone else. You can go on being friends with her if you like, but I think it's usually better, when love, or lust, is unrequited, and the needs are lopsided (you're more into her than she is into you), to find someone else.

Austin: *"I hooked up with a girl and in three days I slept with her. Now I don't feel too well about it. She's moving to Texas. Should I have waited?"*

You're sweet to be thinking about this. Obviously, you cared for her and sex meant something to you—which is good—and now you regret doing it because she's moving and you'll miss her. Accept that you enjoyed the meaningful connection and tell her that it mattered and that you'll miss her. You'll feel better sharing your feelings about the separation after a meaningful sexual union, and hopefully being reassured that it mattered to her, too.

"Don't you think a woman should have sex with a guy regardless if she likes him or not?"

Absolutely not. Don't have sex with someone you don't really like—and who doesn't really like you in return. You'll feel empty afterward. Sex should be a meaningful sharing.

Love should be unconditional. But sex should be conditional. Make sure you're treated well.

Salt-N-Pepa put out these conditions for good sex when they were Honorary Love Doctors on *LovePhones*: "Wine and dine me, talk to me after and before, be positive you want this person inside you!"

HOW TO MAKE A GOOD DECISION

"How do you get rid of the stigma surrounding sex, parents pressuring you to abstain, fear of becoming a 'slut,' pressure from boyfriends—in order to decide for yourself what is best?"

Like the mature way of making any decision, think it through carefully first. Get all the facts, examine your feelings, consider all the possible outcomes. Take everybody's opinion into consideration. Feel confident that you can make a decision that is right for you even if it differs from your parents' or your friends'. Beware that some people want others to act in a manner consistent with their own rules for behavior to make themselves right. Don't do something just to justify someone else. Trust that you know what's right for you. You have to live with the consequences of your choices.

A STRAIGHT ANSWER

"How many no's really mean no?"

One no should be enough. The confusion comes in

because playing at resisting can be tantalizing. Years ago the message about no was even more confusing because women didn't want to take responsibility for being sexual. If she protested and he overwhelmed her, she didn't have to admit that she wanted it.

Now there are rules on some college campuses requiring verbal consent for sexual acts. Guys have to ask for a "yes" or "no" with every advance. "May I kiss you?" "May I touch your breast?" On the campus that pioneered these explicit verbal requests for physical and sexual contact, Antioch College, you could get expelled for not asking for and getting permission. It might dampen the romance, but it kills the confusion.

"My girlfriend and I get naked and fool around. First she says yes and then she says no. What should I do?"

Tell her you're going to honor the "no" and that she shouldn't say yes until she's real clear and sure that she means "yes" because otherwise she's confusing you. Talk with her about what her fears are about having sex. And ask her what she intends to do by giving you double messages. Sometimes doing this means you enjoy the conflict on some level, and get off on having the man take over and talk you into it. It's possible to play this game, but you have to know that's the game.

LEG-LOCK LISA

"My girlfriend is seventeen and I'm fifteen. She goes with younger guys a lot. She says she wants it, but when we try, she screams and gets tight and nervous and says I'm too big. When we get ready to do it and my penis gets close, she moves her leg to dodge it and I flop over. I call her 'leg-lock Lisa.' What's going on?"

She is conflicted. She thinks she's supposed to want it, but her body and mind are not ready. She goes for younger boys because they're easier to control (older guys might pressure her more), and because she feels young and naive herself. Don't push it, or blame yourself. Give her more time to be ready. Just date and have a good time.

STOP SIGN

Richie, 16: *"My girlfriend says stop right at the point when I'm about to come. Then she gets mad. How can I help it? Is that fair?"*

Not really. You have a point. Once a guy reaches that point of ejaculatory inevitability, it's almost impossible to stop the ejaculation altogether. This tells me she has to be more clear about whether she wants to have sex. Also, she may have some hidden hostility toward really letting men reach their peak, perhaps because at that moment she feels controlled. You also need to communicate more in sex. You should have some sign or word that alerts her to when you're getting close to ejaculating. And clarify your means of safe sex so you both feel confident about that.

STUDS VS. SLUTS

"Why are men studs for doing it and women are sluts?"

It's an old socialized principle that the guy who gets a lot of sex is revered and envied, but girls have to be pure and virginal. The difference has anthropological roots, where the goal, and proof of superiority, of male animals was to spread his seed and create as many progeny as possible, while the woman's goal was to ensure the survival of her children. Things are changing now, as women are allowed and even admired for their sexual freedom of expression.

> *I'll never marry again. Why buy the steer when you can sit on the horns for free?*
> — Roseanne at the 1994 MTV Awards

"I recently slept with a guy I really like, but I think I made a mistake by giving in too fast. Do you think he thinks I'm a slut?"

Don't think you're a slut yourself. Respect your decisions about when and with whom you have sex. If you think he'll spread bad stories about you, then he wasn't a good choice. Why get involved with someone you can't trust, who will hurt you—by hurting your reputation, or any other way? If you think you gave it up too fast, then you did. Wait longer, for your own sense of self-respect. You can never go wrong by saying no and trusting whether he cares about you to see you again, compared with giving in to passion soon and wondering after the fact whether he really cared about you or just the sexual conquest.

SEX ETIQUETTE

A guy should always call a girl after he sleeps with her, even if he doesn't like her, or doesn't want to see her again. It's the humane thing to do.

"I met this girl at a party and we had sex. I don't really like her, but my friend told me she's telling all her friends that she likes me. I just did it that night. When I see her at school, she looks at me funny, like a poor little lost dog. It makes me feel guilty. I try to look away, but it bugs me. How do I get rid of her?"

You're feeling guilty, and you save yourself from being a rat by showing that you have some real compassion for her. Obviously the sexual encounter meant more to her than to you. This should be a sign to you not to just do it with someone you don't want to be involved with because it complicates matters, hurts that other person, and hurts you because you feel guilty. Have a heart. Call her just to connect. If you don't like her, let her know kindly. Say something like "It was nice to be with you," just to make her feel okay, reassured, acknowledged, but add, "We can't take this too seriously." Notice I said "we"; making it sound like a joint decision (even if she wants you) helps her maintain some self-esteem and sense of power. Saying "I don't want to see you" would be hurtful and rejecting. If she doesn't get it, be more specific: "Let's put this behind us, because it's not right between us. I hope you're not too hurt."

"Is it harder to stop having sex after you've done it once?"

If it's been a good experience and if you liked the person, probably yes. Whatever feels good, we want to repeat. But of course, if you don't want to do it again, or regret it, you can control your behavior. Remember, you can even decide to be a "born-again virgin."

SAYING YES TO GET LOVE

"My fifteen-year-old cousin is very bitter about men and claims that all men are scum because they only want one thing and can't be trusted. Meanwhile, it seems like she'll date and apparently sleep with any guy who gives her a second glance. I know she's insecure, and when we discuss the topic of sex, she always agrees with me that sex is something you can't just give away. But as soon as I turn around, she'd in trouble again. I'm afraid she'll get in over her head and wind up pregnant, if not other things. What can I do?"

Help her release more of her anger toward men—have her tell you, or write out, the entire history of her patterns with men, how they treat her, and how she treats them. Tell her point-blank that you know she is talking out of both sides of her mouth—saying that men use women, and then letting herself be used. Ask her what she really wants from men. Likely she is looking for love, but gives in to the sex instead. Explain how she is giving off the wrong message to men and that she should hold off having sex until she knows the guy is more interested in her.

Tell her to call you when she feels the urge to have sex with a man she doesn't know. Sometimes just knowing you can call someone helps you feel not alone and you can follow through with resisting the behavior.

> When it comes to sex, yes or no, Stop and think, will you stay or go.
> Instead of instant gratification, stop and think of possible aggravation.
> Don't give in and don't bust, unless there's love and mutual trust.

GIVING IT UP TOO EASY

Jennifer, 18: *"I used to have pimples and be chubby and no one asked me out, but now I'm prettier and guys hit on me. I had sex with a guy who told his friends and they treated me funny, but then another guy hit on me and I had sex with him. Then I did it with another friend of theirs. Now they talk about me. How can I stop them?"*

It's you who has to stop feeling such low self-esteem. You don't have to make up for being unwanted when you had pimples. And you don't have to have sex to prove anything to them either. Tell yourself that you are pretty and lovable and worthy and that you don't have to have sex with anyone to prove it.

SORORITY SEX

Jenny: *"I was pledging a sorority and was told I had to have sex with a fraternity brother while three or four people watched. It was the 'in' thing to do. It was my first time having sex. I'm afraid now that people will think I'm a slut and that since I did it in front of the sisters, now I'll like having an audience. What can I do about this?"*

You liked the attention and the approval. Give it to yourself without others having to give it to you. HOMEWORK: Imagine the audience in your mind, so you don't have to have one in real life. What do you want them to be saying about you? How should they be cheering?

You also have to work on enjoying an experience for yourself, instead of just for others' admiration. So another homework for you is to do things that just you know about. Purposefully keep it a secret. Be your own best audience. Get inside your own skin and focus on your inner sensations.

Alcohol clouds your will power/won't power.

GETTING HER TO GIVE IT UP

Guys have all sorts of tricks to get a girl to have sex when she's resistant. They try alcohol to lower her inhibitions and impair her judgment.

A *LovePhones* caller, Jay, has a disarming trick: *"To get a girl into sex, I tell them I'm not going to do anything so they're lulled into security and safety and trusting me, and then I suggest the 'touching game,' where we touch a spot that feels good, and they get into it, and before they know it, they're touching what I want."*

"I told this girl if she doesn't give it up, I'm going to tell the whole school she's a 'ho."

Let him tell. Better to face that than him across the pillow, with that attitude.

SAYING NO WITH LOVE

"I love my boyfriend but sometimes don't feel like having sex when he does. How can I say no without upsetting him?"

Look at him lovingly and touch him warmly, for reassurance. Don't use the word "no," which immediately raises people's hackles; instead, say what you will do instead of what you don't want to do. Give an explanation. Suggest, for example, "I'd love to hold you while you pleasure yourself now, since I'm exhausted." Offer another time you will be wholehog into it: "Tomorrow night I'll be really into it." Don't give in when you're really not into it, and act like you can't wait for it to be over. That will only escalate into resentment. See if there's another way he can be satisfied (talk through a fantasy, watch a video).

**When you can really say "NO"
you can really say "YES"**

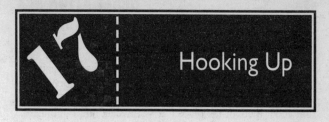

Hooking Up

EVER HAD A BOOTY BOMB? ARE YOU A LOVE Chicken? Help is on the way . . .

Dating isn't easy. You don't know how to make the first move. You're scared to be rejected. You're confused about whether he or she is the right one.

Everybody goes through it—and distress is rampant! In a survey of over three thousand listeners to *LovePhones,* questions about dating were the most common. You have to grin and bear it, throw yourself into it. Having fun and possibly falling in love is a whole lot more fulfilling than staying safely tucked away in your room. Just be emotionally prepared and choose potential partners wisely. Remember the Rules: Respect, Responsibility, and the Right to say yes or no. Keep up your self-confidence and go for it!

SEXUAL SHYNESS

Everybody is shy—even the loudest person can be inwardly insecure. It's good for girls to know how guys feel shy. Even good-looking guys may not feel confident. You may think he's being snobby when really he's scared.

Rob: *"A lot of girls come up to me at bars and talk to me. They say stuff like I'm a good-looking guy. But I don't know how to go up to them. My girlfriend broke up with me, and since then I can't talk to girls. I don't know what to say."*

Just be yourself. Stop thinking in your head that one girl rejected you, so you're not worthy. Put it behind you. Pay attention to the ones who come on to you, not the ones who reject you. So, you're afraid of rejection, like everyone else, welcome to the world. Being good looking didn't ensure you against it, but it's a magnet for moving on. Dating is a game of averages: expect twenty "no"s before a "yes"; eventually, you'll click with someone where it's mutual. Practice talking to the person nearest to you. For starters, make an observation about them or the place ("It's crowded, hot, fun in here," "Those are great shoes"), followed by an open-ended question ("What's your favorite place?" "Where'd you get the shoes?"), or a self-disclosure and appeal for help ("I'm shy, help me out"). Don't expect anything. If interest comes back, fine. If not, on to the next. One of my favorite lines comes from my favorite TV show *Silk Stalkings,* on cable TV's USA Network. The guy cop leading man is trying to pick up a beautiful woman at a disco, and says, "If I went out there dancing I'd make such a fool out of myself with everyone looking at me, but if you were out there with me, everyone would be looking at you and no one would notice me."

WINNING HER OVER

"What really gets a girl?"

(Same as for guys): Feeling wanted, adored, special. Say things like "I'm crazy about you" (reassurance), "You're one of a kind" (specialness), "You're beautiful" (flattery). Remember things that she tells you and ask about them ("How's your grandmother?" "How's your paper going?")— making someone feel acknowledged and appreciated is the best seduction! She'll be ecstatic you cared enough to remember.

In all my surveys on thousands of men and women, women still want a sensitive, caring guy. And a sense of humor is THE edge in the dating game today for both men and women! Be funny and warm, and you're in!

DATING DISASTERS

"I'm a reasonably good-looking, nice girl, but I seem to always date the wrong guys. When I have sex with them, it

never goes right. I try to be what they like, so I don't know why, but the magic isn't there."

Many women don't allow themselves to be who they really are in sex. If you were to write a sex personal, what would it say? "Shameless Sheila, looking for wild guy"? Or "Pristine Paula, in search of a pure Paul"? Be clear about who you are and what you want. Let the other person know right up front what you're like, what you like, and what you're looking for, so there are no misunderstandings.

PUZZLED OVER NO PASSES

Samantha, 16: *"I'm 5' 4" and my body is 36C-25-36. I wear tight bodysuits and big jeans. I look real cute, so why don't guys come up and talk to me? If I go talk to them, they'll think I'm easy. The rule in my 'hood is that shy girls are good girls who you don't hit on, and the girls who go for you are asking for it."*

You can be a third type of girl, one who talks to guys but is not asking for it. Guys are shy, too, especially if you're cute. And if you have big breasts, they may want you but don't want to look like that's all they're after. Don't be afraid to be friendly and sociable. Ask about homework, a new video, an episode of a TV show. Make it clear early in the conversation that you'd like to be friends, with the emphasis on "friends" as opposed to getting with them.

LOVE CHICKEN

Charlene: *"I'm hot for the guy sitting next to me in class, but he doesn't know. How do I let him know I'm interested?"*

Most people drive themselves crazy carrying a crush and thinking the other person doesn't like them when they might, but no one makes the first move. Test the waters. Lean over and ask to borrow a pen. Ask what the teacher said yesterday about a lesson. See how friendly he is back. Make three approaches before judging his interest, in case he's shy. Give him some space to let it sink in, and to approach you. It's what I call the "Seduction Dance." Make your move, then step back and give him or her a chance to let it sink in and to approach you. On the next approach, be more forward. Ask what he likes to do, where he hangs out. Once you know, suggest doing that activity together. Casually say, "We ought to . . . someday" and let him pick up on it. If he doesn't pick up on it, drop it. Play the game with someone else.

Dawn, 16: *"I like this guy but I'm afraid to embarrass myself by showing him I like him. What should I do?"*

Go ahead and be a fool. You won't be, of course; you'll be being you and after all, that's what you want him to like. What you think makes you seem foolish may actually be adorable to him.

My favorite story about being loved for yourself comes from the movie *My Bodyguard,* where a teen finally gets a chance to talk to the blond cheerleader he has a crush on, and tells her boogers fly out of your nose at a certain rate per hour. She cringes, and he's destroyed. Then he tells the same thing to a plainer girl who has a crush on him (but whom he had dismissed), and she laughs adoringly. Morale: it's not what you say but to whom. Sex appeal in the eyes (and ears) of the beholder.

Jillian: *"I'm crazy about a guy I've been seeing, and when we have sex, I feel so fulfilled and happy. I feel like I love him and want to tell him, but I'm so scared that he'll be frightened to hear it. He hasn't said that yet. Should I say it? How do I get up the courage?"*

Absolutely, tell him. Don't be afraid. How wonderful for you to feel love in sex—it's one of the greatest aphrodisiacs! Prepare yourself by saying to yourself that telling him is a beautiful gift. Second, open your heart. Don't be afraid of the consequences. Reassure yourself that if the love is really returned, he will welcome the message. Say "I love you" without an implied demand or expectation for him to say the same thing, so you're not disappointed. Taking the pressure off him makes it more likely that he will respond as you want anyway.

CONVERSATION CHICKEN

Vincent: *"As soon as I get face-to-face with a girl I want to talk to, I get tongue-tied. I don't know what to say. What are some great pick-up lines?"*

Make up your own; talking from your heart is best. A cute line is one Spencer Christian, the weatherman for *Good Morning America*, told when I was working with him on a TV talk show: "A guy goes up to a girl and says, 'Before I came up to talk to you, only God and I knew what I was going to say, but now that I'm standing here in front of you, only He knows!'" My co-host Chris Jagger's favorite line is, "My face is leaving here in fifteen minutes and I'd like you to be on it." A *LovePhones* listener faxed in this suggestion: "The word is 'legs' babe, let's go upstairs and spread the word." More romantic tries: "I hope you know CPR, my heart's fibrillating for you," or "If I could redo the alphabet, I'd put the U and I together."

A survey of two thousand bartenders found some standards still in operation, including: "If I don't find someone to marry by next Friday, I'll lose my large inheritance," and "You must be related to Cupid because you're breaking my heart." From women came: "I'm looking for a strong guy to flip my mattress," and the comeback line, "If you say my eyes are beautiful, then they're looking at you." Ex-Blondie Deborah Harry's suggestion: "All you have to do is tell her the only reason you get on the bus—or wherever you see her—is to see how fabulous she looks."

DATING DREAD

Men as well as women have fears about dating and not being attractive enough.

Tony: *"I'm 5' 8" and 300 pounds. I can't get a woman. What can I do?"*

One of my favorite techniques is to see how your problem helps you—even though you complain. How does being heavy help (protect) you? Some people use being overweight as a test: love me for me, overlook my fat. But that just makes love more difficult. Or they postpone love or sex ("I won't have sex until I lose weight"). Or they worry, "If I lose weight, will s/he only love me for my body?" Try it. Believe you're a wonderful person, no matter what. Famous talk-show host Oprah Winfrey was afraid to lose weight in case her audience wouldn't love her as much as a thin woman, but she faced this and other fears of getting thinner and did it, and her ratings stayed high!

ULTIMATE KISS

As my mother used to love to say, "A kiss is the juxtaposition of the *ubicularous oras* muscles in a state of contraction." Sounds simple, but doing it right can be a win-or-lose proposition. Kristin's date lost.

"I liked this guy until he went to kiss me. He dove into my lips and stuck his tongue into my mouth right away so deep I thought I was going to choke. I pulled away but he dove at it again. I kept turning my face so he'd stop. Now I'm turned off. How could he be so lame?"

Some people just don't know how to kiss, to be seductive. I must admit, it is a sign of intrinsic sensitivity and this guy sounds inexperienced and insensitive.

Some guys are smart to realize they need instruction. Like Danny. *"I don't know how to kiss a girl. How do you do this right?"*

Comic actor Pauly Shore's advice: "Start soft, then alternate soft and hard, then go at it, dude."

I'll add: build anticipation by thinking about the kiss before you touch lips. Look in her eyes and feel your eyes kissing. Feel the sensation build in your lips. Test how she likes to be kissed, so lean in and let your lips touch lightly and see how hard she presses back. Press again and withdraw and look in her eyes again. Next time, make contact on the sides of your mouths, or catch her bottom lip in-between yours. Dip your tongue in slightly to see how she responds. If she opens her mouth wider, put your tongue in a little more. Trace her teeth or the inside of her mouth. Try little pecks, then sink softly into her again. As you progress, get more daring. Let your tongues, lips, and mouths converse. They can "say" loving, soothing things, or get more aggressive to the point of dueling tongues, or dancing together either slow or widly like in a mosh pit.

MORE THAN FRIENDS

Isiah: *"I like this girl who's a friend and I want to hit the skins with her. How do I do it?"*

Chelsea: *"I've become attracted to my roommate. Once we kissed like friends but we haven't talked about it since. I really want to get with him, but I'm not sure if he likes me in the same way. I don't want to lose his friendship, so what should I do?"*

You have three choices: going backward, forward, or staying status quo. Why not go for it and if he isn't in the same place, then you will just have to accept it or move out. Carpe diem: seize the day.

The best way to advance a friendship into more of a romance is to escalate being friends—that means, spend more time and share more experiences together. Friendship is, after all, the best foundation for a good love relationship. Rather than come right out and declare that you want a deeper involvement, go slowly and see how it goes. Suggest an afternoon in the park, an evening at the movies. Invite him to a party or over to watch a particular show. Call to ask advice (on work, vacation plans) or share excitement over an experience, or ask about something he did (a test, ball game). Drop hints in a casual tone and spirit of fun, like, "I really have fun with you," linger on glances, lightly touch or hug. If he reciprocates, up the ante, and then confess your interest openly. Otherwise, set your sights on someone else who is more responsive.

TURNING FRIENDS INTO LOVERS: SEX BUDDIES

Paulie: *"I'm wildly attracted to this gorgeous girl who has been depressed because she just broke up with her boyfriend. We're friends and the last time we went out, we were lying in bed and she was telling me how upset she is and I said, 'I'll help you.' I started rubbing her butt and her breasts and gave her a massage and she got on top of me. The sex was great. The problem is I really like her and want to know if there's a chance to get her because she called us "sex buddies" and I'm afraid she isn't taking me seriously. What should I do?"*

Go for it. You have a wonderful opportunity to experience the fabulous high of having great sex when you're in love. You're headed toward a cosmorgasm, mixing sex and love. Her calling you "sex buddies" is either a way to go slow because she's getting over rejection, or she really doesn't consider you a likely candidate. I suspect it may be the latter, so enjoy your end of it without expecting more.

While I'm slightly encouraging Paulie, I'm much more wary for others, like Maria and Joe.

A SNAKE IS ALWAYS A SNAKE

Joe: *"I want to get with this girl Taylor and tell her I love her and she's beautiful, and ask if she's attracted to me. She has another boyfriend but says she doesn't want to hurt me but maybe someday she'll come around. Does that mean she wants me to keep on her?"*

She's keeping you on a string, using you as a fall-back in case something happens with her current man, and to boost her ego. Stop wasting your time unless you're into unrequited love.

Maria is also being dangled: *I've been dating a guy I really like but he's keeping his distance and I want to know if it's worth my while to keep at it. He keeps telling me 'Don't fall in love with me,' 'I'm not ready for a commitment.' Then other times he says to me, 'Let's see how it works out,' and calls me several times a day. What does he want?"*

He's giving you double messages: I won't commit, but keep trying, I may decide to. This is crazy. Of course, you'd be better off with someone who clearly knows what they want and better yet, is open to commitment without these problems. Suppose you hung on to a shred of hope he will change, expended all your efforts proving you can make him change, and then he said he never promised you anything. That would be a real drag. If someone says he's afraid of commitment, or doesn't want to commit, believe it.

HELPING FRIEND WANTS MORE

"My boyfriend and I have been going on and off for two years. Every time we break up my guy friend, Matt, helps me through the tough times. He's my best friend. This last time he admitted that he's falling in love with me. I haven't done anything about it. Should I tell my boyfriend or just let it slide?"

Why tell your boyfriend? Your business is with Matt. Tell him where you stand: that you like being friends but you're really connected to your boyfriend sexually and emotionally. Matt sounds like a typical confidant, who falls in love with the troubled committed person. You may have to let him go, so he doesn't keeping pining and trying for you. Or you may wake up one day, like Meg Ryan's character in *When Harry Met Sally,* and see that the nice guy/confidant/friend is the one you should be with, since he's more there for you.

SYMPATHY SEX

Mike, 18: *"I met a girl at a friend's house. She told me she was a virgin but didn't want to be anymore. She wasn't very pretty but I felt sorry for her, so I went up to his bedroom and popped her cherry for her. Now she keeps calling me, but I'm not interested in her. How can I get her off my back?"*

You had sympathy sex. Now you see how it gets you in trouble because sex can mean something more to someone than you think, especially if it's their first time. Stop and think next time. For now, let her down easy; she attached more meaning to the act than you, and likely because she's not that attractive and you are, she's flattered you went with her. Don't damage her self-esteem. Tell her she's a lovely person but you're not ready to get involved. Acknowledge that the experience was meaningful, especially since you know it was her first, and that you just want to be friends.

STUCK IN THE MIDDLE

"I like this girl, but she has an ex-boyfriend that I know. He's going out with someone else, but someone told me she still likes him. I don't want to get in the middle of it, so what should I do?"

It's a good idea to check out with an ex, especially if you're in the same crowd, to see whether they still have any leftover feelings. Better to go into it with your eyes open about what backlash or gossip could be generated, especially since you suspect she still carries a torch for him. If he still likes her, you can consider whether it's worth it to step into this potential land mine, or find yourself another playing field.

LOVE LOCATIONS

John: *"I'm not into the club scene. I'm a 'low hanger,' meaning I don't like to hang out much, so where can I go to meet someone?"*

My favorite suggestion: go where you can get involved in an activity you enjoy and be around people with similar interests. When you're totally immersed in doing something you enjoy, instead of self-consciously scanning a singles bar or shyly wondering what to say over dinner, you exude confidence and others find you attractive. That spells sex appeal. If you're the quiet type, hang out in bookstores that have coffee areas now. Take a workshop, to meet like-minded people, where you can work on a project together (that stimulates arousal). Go to health fairs. Join team sports clubs (bowling, volleyball, tennis). But if you're excitable, go where the energy is electric: a sporting event, concert, or amusement park. In my work with Universal Studios Florida, developing what I call "Theme Park Therapy," I found certain rides (E.T., Back to the Future, Jaws) are conducive to seduction and falling in love (ones that cause a medium amount of arousal, not extreme roller coasters that bring your lunch to your throat) because they stimulate a powerful cocktail of chemicals of attraction and throw you together physically and emotionally. Similarly, if you've ever been in the stands at a football game, or in a stadium at a rock concert, you know how excitable that turn-on can be, and how close you can feel to those around you.

HE LOVES ME BUT HE'S NOT IN LOVE WITH ME

"For two years I was having an affair with a man I was deeply in love with. Several times in the heat of the moment, he told me that he loved me, but many times he said afterward that he is not in love with me. Even though I knew this, I continued sleeping with him. Now he's dating another woman he says he loves. I can't bear thinking he didn't really love me at all. Is that possible?"

Sometimes the worst part of being left is feeling you were never loved. If he's kind at all, ask him to simply acknowledge that he did feel something for you. That'll help your ego. Surely he did care, so do not negate your experience entirely; but also do not embellish it. Some men or women will say, or feel, that they are in love at the height of a sexual experience in order to placate the partner or because they are swept away by the passion of the moment. But if, in more rational moments, they protest they are not in love, believe it. They are making a distinction between loving you during a transitory moment and longing to be with you more continuously.

LOVE OR SEX?

Negra, 18: *"I'm going with a guy and he just got locked up for drugs. I want to know from him does he want me for just a piece of ass or is it serious? He says once he gets out we'll spend a lot of time together, but you know guys say*

*that in prison just to keep the girl waiting. I don't want him
to mess with no other. What should I do?"*

Ask him outright and tell him that you want him solely.
But you already know that there's a chance he'll tell you anything you want to hear in order to keep you devoted, and once
he gets out it could be a whole different story. It sounds like
you don't trust him anyway, so keep your eyes open and don't
fall for lines. Being in the drug world, he's probably pretty
clever at manipulating you anyway. Use his time to get strong.

SEX GREAT, LOVE STINKS

Celeste, 24: *"My boyfriend won't break up with me because
the sex is great but our relationship is bad. We're always
arguing. Why is he hanging on?"*

Why are *you* hanging on? Sex is glue, so people have a
hard time leaving when the sex is good. Are you using each
other until you find something else? Or does the anger actually fuel your sex? If you decide to stay together, why not
examine once and for all what your problems are and
resolve them, or cut loose and find someone where the sex
and the relationship are both great.

ONE-NIGHT STAND-UP

*"After a one-night stand, does a guy put it out of his mind
or get attached like girls?"*
*"I had sex with this guy and it was really erotic and roman-
tic. We walked on the beach and laughed and sang together.
Then we watched the moon and kissed softly. We ended up
on a chaise lounge by the pool. There was a warm breeze
enveloping us, and moonlight in our eyes, plus the thrill that
we were outdoors but secluded so no one would see. It was
such an intense time, but I didn't hear from him after that. I
bumped into him a few weeks later, and he said hello, but
there wasn't that same magical connection. How can you
can have such intense sex with someone and then he can
just put it away as if it didn't happen?"*

It's depressing to share intense moments with someone

with no follow-through. If you cannot tolerate this, don't have sex with people when there is a risk that they won't call or see you again. You can tell by reputation, past behavior, flirting, or prior dating and sex habits, and his intentions for a relationship in general or with you. Likely he felt that intensity you described at the moment. But you obviously invested more into it, both at the moment, and afterward, thinking it would lead to more. You let your expectations run away with you. Rather than be angry with him, or dismiss your experience, value that you had a beautiful romantic exchange. You can feel sad that he doesn't want to repeat it, but learn from it what you want next time in a more lasting relationship.

DOORMAT

Some self-identified nice guys are really doormats.

Salvatore: *"Girls always use me. I give them clothes and roses and they stay a month and when I fall in love, they leave me. Why?"*

Because you act like a doormat. I know you feel you're giving—that's nice. But when you give out of a sense of desperation and needing to be appreciated, it turns people off; they get uncomfortable and resentful, sensing your insecurity and that gifts come with strings attached. Gifts are not the sign of being a nice guy. Develop an inner sense that you are worthy, without buying attention.

TRIPS ON TAUNTING

Alexandra: *"I treat this guy really mean. When I have sex with him I tell him he's terrible. I kiss other guys in front of him and cheat on him and he keeps coming back for more. I order him around, saying, 'Get this for me,' and he does. I think I love him but I feel bad being so mean."*

Who did that in your family? There's always someone you watched and learned from. At first Alexandra couldn't remember anyone, but then she remembered that her grandfather bossed her mother around the same way. Angry at her mother's helplessness, Alexandra identified with her grandfather, and became an aggressor, like him. At the same time, she still feels guilty about it, because a part of her identifies with her mother and her helplessness. So, she is vicariously abusing herself by abusing her boyfriend. Recognize such patterns from unresolved family feelings and say, "I don't have to repeat my past," "I am not my (father/mother)." Also confront any stereotypes you may have, like that women are helpless and men are brutes.

DOWN ON FIRST DATE

Too many women have sex on the first date because they're afraid to lose the guy if they don't. Or they're drunk. Or guys do it because they think they should. You don't have to give it up so fast. Teresa had to learn that lesson.

"I've had my eye on a man at work and he finally asked me to come over to his house next Sunday. I'm incredibly attracted to him and I know if he makes a move I'll go to bed with him. I'm worried that this may not be a good idea, though, since in my twenty-eight years I've had a number of experiences having sex on the first date and only once did I end up seeing the guy for a year. All the other times I never saw them again. Part of me figures if guys can get what they want, why can't I? But then I don't want to be a slut, so should I maybe not do it so fast?"

Women have earned the right to decide when, where, and with whom they'll have sex. So deciding you want to have sex with this man anytime can be a positive sign you are taking responsibility for your own sexuality and satisfaction. But there are some hitches. First, are you truly being responsible? The answer is no if you have sex on the first date because you're afraid he'll never ask you out again, or if you're plunging into sex when you really would prefer (but fear) waiting for love, or if you're trying to turn the tables on men by "using them for sex" just like you feel used by them, to insulate yourself from being hurt. It's generally best to wait and take time to find out who this man really is—his values, trustworthiness, lifestyle, even whether or not he's involved with someone else. If the chemistry is valid at the start, it can only grow in anticipation.

WORRIES AFTER

Denise, 18: *"I had sex on the first date with a twenty-six-year-old guy I've known two years and always liked. Afterward, I felt cheap. Alcohol was involved, but I would have done it anyway. What should I do now? He told me before we did it that he thinks I'm the nicest girl he's ever met, and he likes me a lot. The morning after, we hugged and kissed good-bye and it was a little awkward but sweet. Now my friends say not to call him or he'll be spooked. Should I wait to see if he calls me?"*

You can wait, but if you get antsy about it too much, call him. If he gets spooked that easy, after an important time together, then it's going to be a real rocky road for you, and you might not want to throw yourself into it head-first, or you'll have a lot of heartache along the way.

Tell him how you felt. It sounds like you need him to reassure you that he still thinks you're a nice girl. And you need to think that yourself.

WANTS LOVE IN SEX

Kerry: *"I've only had sex with men I love. But one night I got drunk and one thing led to another and I had sex with a stranger. Now I feel I made a mistake. I like him but I don't know if he wants a relationship. How do I get over this?"*

Forgive yourself. You feel you compromised your values, but you're allowed to do something you later decide you don't want to do again. Your rule is a good one: be sure that he cares about you before you have sex, otherwise you leave yourself more vulnerable to being hurt.

MAY–DECEMBER

Calvin: *"I like those younger women, man, they yank my chain. They're so sweet and listen. I don't go for those old chicks. One of them is after my body as she heard I was real good on the rack. Do you have a problem here?"*

It's as old as the hills: older men going for younger women. Enjoy yourself. But do consider, why do you do it? Perhaps to tap into the fountain of youth, stave off a mid-life crisis, fears of incest or dying, or maybe because you're stuck in emotional puberty. The Chinese leader Mao Tse-tung liked to have several young women in bed at the same time to restore his declining "yang" or male essence with their "yin" or female essence, copying China's first emperor who achieved immortality by making love to a thousand virgins. And Rod Stewart married three times to tall blond models, each time ten years younger.

Cable TV's *Up All Night* beauty, Honorary Love Doctor Rhonda Shear, may purposefully dress like a bimbo, but she doesn't believe in being one, or in young girls marrying rich old men: "They're like two parking meters," she says, "he's thinking how much money do I have to put in this thing and she thinking how long do I have to wait for this to expire." Shear was once an older rich guy's armpiece, until he took up with her best friend when she was sick!

But what about older women and younger guys? Cher was in her forties dating twenty-eight-year-old Rob Cameletti and a throng of younger men. Elizabeth Taylor was born in 1932 and her husband Larry Fortensky was born in 1952. R.E.M. guitarist Peter Buck, at thirty-seven, told me he likes older women because they have life experiences to share and ideas to discuss. Wholesome Richard Marx was really attracted to his now-wife who was seven years older, who originally thought he was a "nice sweet little boy but so young" and fixed him up with a friend, until he persisted in pursuit. And Candlebox's Kevin Martin, who at twenty-four was with a girlfriend four years older, said "older women are more inter-esting and more real." Kevin was used to the age span, since he lost his virginity at age twelve to a girl in her teens.

"I'm a divorcee in my forties and I've fallen in love with a twenty-two-year-old young man. We have great fun and

long talks in lovemaking sessions like I've never known before. I'm planning to have him move in to my apartment soon. The problem is although I look and feel in my thirties myself, sometimes I worry that even though I don't have children, by his age he could be my son. And while he works hard, he doesn't have much money, so I take care of everything. Am I silly to pursue this?"

There's nothing wrong with the older woman–younger man coupling. Statistics show 23.5 percent of U.S. brides now marry younger men. For women age thirty-five to forty-four, the number goes up to 41 percent. Such unions are becoming more popular as social taboos drop and women keep more fit physically, feel younger psychologically, and become more financially independent, so they can afford a younger guy not as far along in his career. One conclusion (in *Loving a Younger Man*) is that a ten year span can be the best match; such couples described their sex life as "the best ever."

For the relationship to work, overcome your fears ("Will he still love me when I'm old and gray?"), embarrassment ("I'm robbing the cradle to feel young again"), and other people's criticisms ("Why can't you find someone your own age?"). Beware, some older women enjoy "turning the tables," supporting a younger lover as they dreamed would happen to them. Initially you might enjoy the power and control, but later tire of it. Make sure showering him with presents is not buying his affection or submission, and that he is not with you to use you. If your love is real, accept age as a state of mind and prepare for your best love life ever.

In some cases the age difference is clearly not right—and a legal problem!

Samantha: *"I have a problem. Two weeks ago I was going to the store and I met this guy, this older guy. He's thirty-nine and I'm sixteen. He told me that he liked me and that he wanted to see me. So he called me up and we went on a date. I had sex with him. Now, he wants me to move in with him. It's been a week. Well, he says he is going to give me everything that I want. He took me shopping. He tells me he's going to get me everything I need. My parents are divorced and I live with my sister. So, I don't know if I should go and live with him. It feels like I've known him for like a long time. We get along with everything."*

No, you mustn't do it. You don't even know him. I am very suspicious about his motives. It sounds like you are being seduced by a "sugar daddy." I understand you miss being loved and having a home. But this doesn't smell good to me. It's illegal for him to seduce you. Not only that, you're desperate, and that's not a healthy way to make a decision. Stay with your sister for the time being. How about calling your mother and telling her you need her?

JUST SLEEPING

Christine: *"I met a man the other night at a party and we had a great time together, so I went back to his apartment after and we talked and made out. He asked me to stay over and promised we could stay in our clothes, but I went home. Now I haven't heard from him. Did his offer to just sleep together really mean sex and is that why he hasn't called?"*

If that's the reason, you're lucky he didn't call you. A man who purposefully tricks you into immediate sex is being unwise these days as well as disrespectful. You're sensible to suspect that sometimes an offer to just sleep together can be a ruse to seduce you into more serious action once your defenses are down. On the other hand, this man could have genuinely wanted your company, and now feels rejected, embarrassed, or afraid to contact you. The only way to judge which is true of him is with further information about his character, or call him and see if he's receptive.

BEST SEX

"What makes for the best sex?"

My theory is this: everyone has an ongoing, sometimes secret, sex script in their head of what they would like to have happen in the ideal romantic or erotic relationship. It's like a movie going on in your mind of what you would most like both of you to say and do. If the other person taps into that, or is on the same wavelength, magic pops in your head. That's what you call "chemistry" or "falling in lust." It's your movie. You are the producer, writer, director, and all the actors—even the props! If a potential partner plays their part perfectly in your love movie, you're mesmerized. If they don't, the "magic" isn't there.

BEYOND SLOPPY SECONDS

Peter, 15: *"I'm a virgin and have been going for sloppy seconds, sucking on her nipples for a long time. I'm ready to take the next step, and finger her. How do I find out if she wants this?"*

Ask. Tell her you enjoy being with her and love playing around and ask her how far she feels comfortable going.

GETTING TO BED

A lot of males and females call asking, "How do I get him to like me? or "How do I seduce her?"

Compliment her or him. Do fun things together. Share experiences. Be yourself. Let your inner self out. But fundamentally, see if your inner sex scripts match. Create a safe space for both of you to express that and see if they overlap and sparks catch.

It can be awkward, that first time, making it known you want to have sex, but not knowing what to say.

Jay: *"I like this girl and I don't know how to get her into bed. We were at my place and I was so close, but I felt weird about how to suggest we have sex. Do I just come out and say it?"*

It's best to go with the flow, so you trust it'll happen in its own time, given the energy between you, without forcing anything or asking directly. But if you feel your target is hesitant or shy, or your desire is so pressing, you have a few choices. You can just say in the heat of passion of the moment, "I want you!" That could send someone's heart racing or at least get a smile. Or try a cute line, like, "Your clothes would look nice on my floor," "I like your dress but

I like nothing better." Other callers suggested: "I got a thirst, baby, and you smell like Gatorade," "Want to see my hard drive? It isn't 3.5 inches and it ain't floppy," "I would die happy if I saw you naked once."

FIRES FIZZLED

Isaac, 18: *"Every time I have sex with a girl, the relationship dies. Just when I feel we're cooking together, she cuts out."*

If there's a pattern of dating in your life, there's a reason—likely it's something you're putting out without realizing it. You may be a player and they're anticipating they're going to be hurt so they protect themselves and withdraw. Realize the signals that you are transmitting to others. Remember my Mirror Law of Attraction: the people in our lives are mirrors of ourselves. If they all cut out just as you heat up, maybe you're the one with cold feet.

CONFIDENCE BLOWN

Valerie: *"I'm scared of guys. Two years ago I made out and the guy made fun of me. I didn't know what I was doing and he asked, 'What are you doing?' I nearly died. What can I do to go out again?"*

That was certainly a trauma! You were sweet enough to just go for it, doing what came naturally, and he was critical! I'm sorry you had that experience. The guy was obviously awkward, rude, and immature. Put that ghost behind you and don't let it kill your confidence. Try again. Pick a nice guy. You can always say that you feel inexperienced—he may like that—and ask him to teach you. Being honest also builds trust.

CONNECTING SEX AND LOVE

"I met a man I wasn't crazy about at first, but I went out with him. When I had sex with him it was good because he was very sweet, spending time touching me all over. At first it felt like it was just sex, but then I started to really like him. We

talked a lot and got close and I was falling in love with him. I've always wanted a guy to tell me that he loved me when he was inside me in sex, so one time I was going down on him and he was moaning so much and I asked him if he liked it. He said, "Yes, oh thank you, you make me feel so good. I'll do anything for you." So I got on top of him and as he was moaning more, I whispered in his ear, 'Tell me you love me.' At first he didn't, but then, he finally said, 'I love you, I love you' really low over and over until he came. I'm ecstatic, thinking he loved at the moment of highest sexual release. Now, my question is: Will he deny it? Did he really mean it?"

I'm happy for you that you took that big step—connecting sex with love. You made your big fantasy come true. Obviously at the moment, you didn't care if it was totally true. But, you're right, that was a good way to train a partner to fall in love with you: mix love talk with sexual release, and you condition him to love you.

STOLEN SEX

"Every time I have sex with a guy, I get into trouble because then I like him too much and I get wiped out if he doesn't call me. It's like he stole a piece of me. I get real upset that it didn't mean as much to him and I keep thinking that he's so happy going on with his life and I have nothing, even though I do have a good life with a good job and good friends. But when he doesn't call me after we have sex, I think I have nothing."

Hard as it would be for you, it's best not to have sex so casually—if there is a chance the guy won't follow up, since you know from your pattern that you always get hurt. Learn to love and value your own life. And don't always think the grass is greener. He may not be longing for you but that doesn't mean his life is so wonderful. Everyone has problems.

SEXUAL JEALOUSY

Laura suffers from the green-eyed monster: *"I can't go out with friends anymore, because wherever I go I keep imagining that everyone else around me is happy, having good sex and a great life, and I'm not. I'm always thinking my date is more attracted to the other girls, who are taller, prettier, and come from richer families. I lay awake at night wishing I were like them. How do I get rid of these awful feelings?"*

Don't get rid of your feelings, use them. Painful as jealousy is, it can be a helpful sign that you want to make changes in your own life. Instead of comparing yourself unfavorably to other women, notice what it is about them that you admire (their style, confidence, care in their appearance) and develop those traits in yourself as much as you can. What you imagine that your date wants is also what you want for yourself. Don't waste energy on things you cannot change; focus instead on what you can change.

Jealousy can also ruin your relationship.
Diane, 17: *"My boyfriend's best friend is a girl. I don't like it. Should I tell him to dump her?"*

No. Instead of being so jealous, remember he's with you! If he gets his ego fed with having a girl as a best friend, fine. Be happy he's not playing around.

LOSE THE LOSER

"I was seeing a guy for three years, but he rarely did anything for me, either sexually or even taking me out to dinner. Finally it got to me and I broke up with him. How much could he care ₍nat he hasn't called in three weeks and tried to get back together? But I'm lonely, so now I worry that I did the wrong thing."

Don't give up the progress you made in leaving a man who didn't treat you right. Instead, continually remind yourself that you made the right decision and that you deserve a man more generous and proud of you, both in and out of bed. Your instincts to question his love are correct, given his absence and lack of attempt to revive the relationship. The loneliness you feel is natural. Rather than trying to end that loneliness by returning to a dead-end relationship, turn it into motivation to get on with your life. Call friends who care about you and do things that make you feel good about yourself.

MORE LOSERS

Diana, 24: *"I'm seeing this guy for two years, but recently we moved from the city to the country. But he stills goes back to the 'hood and I think he sells drugs. He doesn't spend any time with me and he's so stoned we don't have sex anymore. A new guy friend of mine made calls me and I'm thinking about having sex with him. Should I?"*

Not yet. First dump your loser boyfriend.

FUELS HIS FANTASY

Melinda, 20: *"I met a guy I liked, but he didn't want anything to do with me. I heard that he thought I was too chubby. Then all of a sudden he started calling me, but it happened right after he found out from mutual friends I was into lesbianism. What should I do?"*

Tell the guy where to go. Do you want to be used as his plaything, to act out his fantasy of being with two women? Remember, Respect Rules. Don't give in just because you agree with him secretly that you're chubby and can't get a guy any other way.

STOPS SHORT OF SEX

Patty: *"I met a guy at a party and he came on to me real hard. He was tall, dark, and extremely handsome and a doctor. I was trying to play it cool, but he followed me into every room, and when people came to talk to me, he nudged over and would grab my hand or turn me toward him. Then when we were alone, he asked me if I wanted to get involved with him, and I said no, I really didn't want to get distracted by anybody now, which was true. I guess he liked the challenge, because he kissed me with real soft lips. He asked to take me home and kissed me again.*

Then he called me when he got home and asked me to go to the movies. During the whole movie, he would put his hand on my leg and then stroke my arm, and then lean over to lightly kiss my neck. I spent the whole movie aware of how he was touching me and didn't even follow the film. But when we got outside, he said, 'I'll get you a cab.' My heart sank, because I wanted to have sex with him. I said, 'Oh, can't we get something to eat?' He said, 'No I have a real stomachache.' Then I didn't hear from him, and when I saw him again at a party I avoided talking to him. I cried that whole night, what did I do wrong, why didn't he like me so fast after that big come-on?"

Nothing's wrong with you. He won your attention, and then he panicked. His stomachache was probably a fear of following through. Maybe he doesn't get erections. Many guys like this are what we call passive-aggressive, leading you on and charming you 'til you get hooked and want them, then cutting you off. Getting you to want him was enough to fill his damaged self-esteem. If he had gone further, he would have risked the rejection that he lives with in his head, so he cut out while he's ahead.

FLIPPED

"My boyfriend used to be obsessed with me. He wrote poetry all the time and told me he loved me. I didn't really like him that much to begin with nor did I believe that he loved me. Finally when I fell for him and everything was fine on my end, he changed his mood totally and broke up with me in a letter. Why did he do this? I didn't do anything wrong."

What you did wrong was turn his unrequited love into returned love. That apparently wasn't in his love map pattern. It sounds also like he likes the chase, but not the catch. Those people are usually so self-absorbed, or insecure, they're a nightmare as a boyfriend or girlfriend anyway. They remind me of Groucho Marx's famous phrase, "I wouldn't want to belong to any club that would want me as a member." It's frustrating for you because when you're the one who finally breaks down and gives in, the feelings are more real. You

also feel duped, since you were the one pursued. Chalk it up.
Tell him how you feel and ask him what was going on, just to
add to your computer bank of dating knowledge.

HIT AND RUN LOVER

*"I was dating a guy for four months who seemed head over
heels for me. We had a ball together and he was telling me
this was it. Then, out of the blue, he disappeared and a
friend told me she saw him with another girl. I'm wiped.
How can I ever trust another guy?"*

Your devastation and distrust are warranted! You were
hit by a hit and run lover; it's like being in a car accident.
But don't lose hope. It's still possible to find a true nice
guy. Appreciate how you opened up enough to enjoy this
relationship. Remember that proof of enduring loyalty often
takes longer than the four months you had together and
more tests through good as well as trying times, to prove it
lasts.

TESTING THE WATERS

Reesa: *"If you've only made love to one person, how can
you be sure he's the right one? Shouldn't you try others so
you don't wake up years from now after you're married and
wonder if it's different with anybody else?"*

It would be a beautiful thing if you fall in love with
one person and don't want to be with anyone else. Love
should be more important than variety in the ideal world.
But in reality it's easy to get curious if you've only had
one person, and most people would rather play the field a
bit and explore themselves as well before they make a
commitment.

HOLDING OUT

T.R.: *"I'm going with this girl and she won't give it up. I
like her, but I got to have it. There's another girl at school
who'll go with me. What should I do?"*

If you're the type of person who would only date someone if they have sex, then go for the girl who will do it. Don't hurt the girl who won't have sex with you by leading her on.

ROCK STAR ROCKER

Katrina: *"My friend got us backstage passes to a band I'm crazy about. I could hardly stand it. After the gig, I was standing around and the lead singer who I have a huge crush on came over and asked me what I was doing later. He told me to come to his hotel room. My heart was pounding. I went and he just wanted me to suck him off. Then he and his friends ordered steak and champagne and spilled it all over. He grabbed me and kissed me and fed me steak and dripped the champagne all over me, and licked it off my breasts, and told the other guys what beautiful breasts I had. Doesn't that mean he liked me? Then he said it was getting late and he had to go to sleep. I asked if I could see him the next night after the gig and he said sure. I was so excited all day, but when I called his room, there was a block on the phone. I went to the hotel and the guard wouldn't let me up and wouldn't put me through on the house phone. I felt so humiliated."*

He probably was too drunk—either from champagne or with his own ego—to know or care what he was saying. He got what he wanted—a plaything for the night, amusement, a blow job, showing off with his friends. On a deeper level, he escapes feeling humiliated by making you feel that. If he really had heart he would find a way to end the night with both of you feeling respected.

Donna: *"I was seeing this famous rock singer. He was flying me to his gigs or coming to my town on breaks. I met him because my hometown paper sent me to write about him. He told me he liked me better than any girl he ever met because he could talk to me and I was intelligent. We liked the same books and music. Then, he wanted me to leave my job and go follow him on the road and I said no. He got mad that I didn't want to give up everything for him, as he said millions of girls would. The last two times I saw him he wouldn't have sex with me. I talked to him on the phone last week and he wouldn't say why. Why won't he have sex with me?"*

It's his only weapon to get back at you for not giving yourself to him. You're in a no-win situation. If you became a groupie and followed him around, you would lose your independence—what drew him to you in the first place. And if you don't, then he can get angry that you don't care enough for him.

Sounds like this resisting was a true test of your self-esteem—reaffirming that you are a woman who cares about her own career and will not subjugate her life to a man.

SMOTHERING SYNDROME

Nicole, 18: *"My boyfriend thinks I hug him too much. When I go to hug him, he cringes or moves away. I get hurt. He always asks me, 'Why do you hug and kiss me so much? I'm not the hugging type.' I say because I love him, but he sneers. What's wrong?"*

You two are locked in an unpleasant syndrome I call the "smothering syndrome." Typically, the woman who is desperate for affection repeatedly showers it on her partner, but he, sensing her desperation and uncomfortable with affection, withdraws and puts her down. She feels further deprived and becomes increasingly demanding. This spirals into an unpleasant desperation on her part and further withdrawal on his part, criticizing her for being needy and nagging. The only way to get out of this mess is for both to realize the source of their behavior: She has to stop demanding so much of him. And he has to give in and be more available, not seeing her as the suffocating female ghosts from his past.

MAN'S BEST FRIEND

"It's been said about men that they're like dogs and that you can't teach an old dog new tricks. I've been seeing a

*man that I just started having sex with and now I want
him to spend more time with me rather than running off
and being with his friends to play golf on Sundays and
cards during the week. I have a dog and he likes being
with me more. How do get my boyfriend to be a good
puppy, too?"*

No disrespect intended, a clever book, *How to Make
Your Man Behave in 21 Days or Less, Using the Secrets
of Professional Dog Trainers,* points out that men are
similar to puppies; after all, they both have bad peeing
habits, pack behavior, and an obsession with their bone.
And both can be trained with simple learning theory techniques. Fill his bowl halfway so he's always yearning for
more; promise his favorite treat when he does what he's
told, as long as he begs first; never be extra-nice when he
misbehaves, in hopes of winning him over; if he runs
away, don't chase or he'll run faster—instead, act like
you're having loads of fun without him and he'll trot
eagerly back. Remember the 4 C's: always be consistent
about your demands, Clear in expressing yourself,
Confident in your authority, and Complimentary about
good behavior.

BEST FRIENDS?

*"My best friend is in love with a guy. She introduced me
to him last week and now the guy called me. He told me
he doesn't really like her and wants to date me. I feel
guilty about it. Should I see him? She hasn't gone out
with him."*

You decide whether friendship is more important than
romance. I generally follow the rule that if a friend puts
dibs on a guy then you should stay away. She'll inevitably
get hurt, be jealous, and it'll mess up your friendship.
Wouldn't you feel that way if the shoe were on the other
foot?

On the other hand, I can understand how it's not the
same as if she dated him. You can ask her how she would
feel and help her understand that it doesn't mean she's less

attractive. Telling her ahead of time is better than letting her find out after the fact and feeling betrayed.

CYBERSPACE DATING

Sandra Bernhard says she can't get on the information superhighway: "I still like face-to-face contact and an Aveda oil massage." But thousands of others are getting on-line.

"I'm looking for dates and tried those personal ads. Should I try all those computer services? Which are they, and since I don't write well, how would I get a girl to notice me?"

There are bulletin board systems (BBS) on computer networks that are divided into categories, such as 90210, soccer, and Keanu Reeves. To find a girl who is as into Green Day as you are, post a note on the boards or send her an E-mail. Some networks have "chat rooms" like on-line parties where you can join a live conversation.

Remember, though, that while it's great that you can be anything you want through the computer, hopefully that means you can be yourself. Beware of cybercreeps—sexual perverts who use computers to lure victims. If you suspect anything on the service, alert the network supervisor or "sysop," who'll tell him to stop or discontinue his service. Or contact your local police. Never give out your phone number.

COMPUTER FRIENDS FEAR MEETING

"I've been talking to a guy on-line for a few months. We don't know each other but we are planning to meet. Sometimes I don't want to meet him because I feel he wouldn't like me in person. What should I do?"

Being computer friends keeps you safe and protects you from insecurities (of how you look, rejection, being socially awkward). Don't expect this to be the perfect relationship, despite what it seems on-line. Go ahead and meet him; share your fears since it's likely he feels similarly. Be honest about who you both really are. Enjoy exercising your intimacy, but keep your hi-tech fantasies in check until you get a reality check.

ON-LINE OFF

Ken: *"I met a girl through AOL. We chatted on-line every night for a month and then I flew from New Jersey to Tennessee to spend a week with her. I'm six feet and weigh 210 and she turned out to be seventy-seven years old, 5'3", and weigh 240! I really didn't like that, plus she had a child from another relationship. But I had fallen in love with her on-line, so we had sex. But I lost my erection. I was disappointed she went to sleep and didn't finish me off with her hand or mouth. The next times I gave her oral orgasms and she reluctantly did me, but I kept losing my erection and asked for oral sex and she said she was depressed about it. Then she said she felt no love for me. I do feel there is love there, but the sex is not as good as it could be. I'm afraid she's going to end it anyway. Should I put sex on the backseat and work on putting our love together?"*

It sounds like you lost your erection partly because you were not excited about her physical appearance. You also sound so desperate to be loved that you are taking some abuse and feeling abandoned by someone who is not really loving you. Leave it be. It's disappointing to be so excited about something and have it not pan out. Find another who's more in tune with you.

CO-DEPENDENT

So many women think they're in love when they're really co-dependent.

Lisa, 24: *"I'm dating my boyfriend for two years and he has a violent temper. My father was also abusive. I'm like a mother figure to him, he needs me. I solve his problems and cover for him, like when he misses work. But every time I try to break up, he promises he'll be better and I go back with him. What can I do?"*

Marissa, 21: *"I'm engaged for three years but the relation-*

*ship is boring and I fake in sex. I know my fiancé calls the
900 lines and has phone sex because I see the bills. He also
has trading cards of girls. I can't seem to leave him,
though, and keep trying to make him interested in me. I take
Xanax because it makes me so anxious. How can I get him
to change?"*

We need to concentrate on what to do for you. You feel
like you are in love when really you are co-dependent,
meaning that you think you are being a loving, understanding girlfriend, helping your boyfriend through hard times,
when really you are "enabling" him to stay dependent on
you and continue his addictions to drinking and sex and
being irresponsible and abusive.

Signs of co-dependency are: being too concerned about
others' needs to the point of neglecting one's own; doing
anything to keep a relationship; irresistible attraction to others in need of rescuing; covering up for others; trying overly
hard to please. Often co-dependent women come from child-
hoods where the mother was co-dependent on the father or
with the children. There is often a history of alcoholism and
abuse, physical or sexual, and this cycle of abuse is repeated.

Women show milder forms of co-dependency when they
give up friends, interests, and their own career to live
through a man. Or they may continually give counsel or
money to others, or support and sex to lovers, when they
have little themselves or get little in return. Women are more
prone to co-dependency than men because of the expected
maternal role of caretaking, people pleasing, and putting others first. Women also learn to serve others and make them
dependent in order to achieve power and control.

Guys can be co-dependent, too, with the same symptoms.

DUPED INTO THREESOME

Michelle, 22: *"My friend encouraged me to have sex with
her boyfriend. She kept saying, 'He thinks you're pretty,'
and 'He's the best lover, why don't you try him?' She convinced him to sleep over at my house with her one night and
got us all in the bed. She moved him between us and got*

behind him and grabbed his penis from behind and he kissed me. I kissed him back and he put it in me while she was behind him rubbing his penis in me. He started to cry, blurting out that he thinks he's falling in love with me, and she dragged him out of the bed and pushed him up against the wall. Now she's saying I'm not her friend and blaming me for it. She said she was just testing me and didn't expect me to go through with it, and since I did, it proves that I'm not a real friend. I do like him, but what should I do?"

You should have seen this coming. You're not responsible for the fact that he doesn't care about her as much; she's upset and blaming you to make herself feel less rejected. Obviously she feels not only betrayed and rejected, but humiliated because her plan backfired.

Stay away from him now because the experience is too loaded for everyone. Let the emotions cool down. It's not the best way for you and him to have connected, but if it's meant to be, you'll still get together after the cool-down.

HARD BARGAIN

Jane, 24: *"Two months ago my boyfriend said he didn't love me, but that we should stay together and maybe the spark would come back. Meanwhile he wants me to tell him stories about me having sex with another guy and him watching, and then do it. I don't like that story, I want just the two of us. Can it come back?"*

It can, but it sounds like in your case it won't. He's holding out for you giving in to his fantasy in order to keep him. But the love isn't there. It'll just lower your self esteem to indulge his fantasy against your better judgment or desires, and have him leave you anyway.

NO FRIEND OF MINE

Joe, 18: *"My friend's girlfriends are all hot for me. They make passes at me, like one looked at me and licked her finger. I feel bad if I don't respond. But I already went out with one and I lost my friend. What should I do?"*

Put a lid on it. Recognize that pattern and stop it in action. Set limits on their behavior and, more importantly, your own. You don't have to prove you're better than your friends by snaking their girlfriends—and pretending you're the innocent bystander to the girls' flirtations.

TOO YOUNG?

Tabitha: *"I'm young but I'm really in love with my boyfriend. My parents think we're too young to be in love and don't know what it's like. I cry about that. Why can't I love him?"*

Oh, of course you can! You're never too young to feel love. And how exciting for you that you do. We feel love from the time we're infants. Love tends to evolve and change over time: at first, you might feel lust, idealization ("love is blind"), infatuation. This can settle into various degrees of comfort, security, and friendship, and later into genuine appreciation and acceptance of limitations and differences.

ULTIMATUM

"I'm dating a guy on and off for two years. All my friends are getting married. He hasn't said anything about it yet. Should I continue?"

It may feel bad to be the only one of your crowd not to be getting married, but look at the relationship you pick compared to theirs. You're in a yo-yo relationship not just because of him, but you. If you were ready to marry, you'd put your foot down and be with a guy who's ready for the big "C" commitment. Make an ultimatum: We're getting engaged by a certain date or it's over, and stick to it.

WHEELCHAIR LOVE

"A few years ago I met this guy who is in a wheelchair from a motorcycle accident. He's gorgeous and I'm falling in love with him. I'm afraid. Is it okay? Can we have normal sex?"

Good for you finding love, and looking beyond his body. Just be sure you're not being co-dependent, liking people to be dependent on you, avoiding rejection by picking someone you imagine has fewer options and so wouldn't leave you.

People with disabilities are now called "physically challenged," so look on the positive side of how your life can be normal, rather than just the limitations. Your boyfriend can have sex depending on where the damage to his spinal cord was done. Ask him about it; I'm sure he has asked his doctors. In most cases you can make adjustments for whatever kind of lovemaking he can manage physically.

PAGING SEX

Melissa: *"I met someone who pages me or I him to have sex. I only know his first name and I know nothing about him. He gave me his pager number and I page him when I feel I want him to come over. Is there anything wrong with this?"*

How could you possibly go with someone you don't even know these days? It's a favorite female fantasy to have sex with a stranger, but safer kept as a fantasy. Peter Hook, New Order bassist, as Honorary Love Doctor advised: "I wonder how many other pagers he has given out. Do you have other normal relationships while you see him? Seems a little devoid of love to me. In England, we don't have pagers. It seems clandestine."

WHO'S A BIGGER BOOB

Joe, 22: *"I'm dating this girl and want her to get a breast job. Marriage should be perfect and you should love everything about the person, and her bonkers aren't big enough. They're like mosquito bites. It's easy enough to fix. I'll even help pay for it. No other guys would go for those ant hills. How do I get her to do it?"*

She'd be lucky if she ran from you, fast. You're the big boob, not her. What arrogance to insist she enlarge her breasts to win your love. Yours is not love. Marriage isn't built on perfection, anyway. You have a long way to go to change your attitudes. Get smart. Women aren't their breast size.

BRAGGING

Russell: *"When I'm around other guys, they go off about how many women they had and what they did. I really find that uncomfortable and I don't know what to do about it. I feel like if I said that about women it would be degrading."*

Good for you. Extreme's lead singer, Gary Cherone, agrees: "That's part of the male ego to share stories, it's just barroom talk, locker-room talk. You don't have to do that."

DOESN'T LIKE SEXUALLY AGGRESSIVE WOMEN

"How do you handle a guy who appears to be turned off by a sexually aggressive woman?"

If you're sexually aggressive and he doesn't seem to like it, walk away—he clearly doesn't appreciate you. Don't take someone's rejection of your style as a sign that your style isn't right. You're just not the right match.

MAN-KILLER

Lema, 20: *"Every time I date a guy, after sex they don't want to leave or let me go. I don't want a relationship and they get possessive, saying they think they're in love and 'That's the best sex I ever had.' I do whips and chains and go on top, and one guy wanted to whip me. Why are men so easy and how do I get them off my back?"*

You love it. Don't kid yourself or anyone else. If you like whipping them, then of course it's part of the game to make them desperate and drooling for you. I'm sure not all guys would be begging for more of you, but you're very clever about your choices. Maybe deep down you want out of this trap of just being used or using them for sex and want to feel some real love. But first you have to get over your contempt for men. Obviously you must feel used by them, so you've turned it around to make them into objects. Connect with some deeper hurt you've had, and release it and you'll be attracted to and attract nice guys and feel some emotion toward them yourself.

GO-GO GONE

Dave: *"I was dating a girl and she had a great body, so I encouraged her to get a job dancing nude. I used to like going to the bars to watch her dance, knowing the guys were drooling but she was mine. But now she comes home tired and doesn't want sex as much and I've lost my libido, too. How do I get it back?"*

Your plan backfired. You wanted to prove to the other guys that you were a bigger stud, but instead, you sank. Of course she's tired. She's simulating sex all night for men, spreading her cheeks and legs. Being new at it, she can't separate what she does displaying and performing for men, to being more "normal" with you, so she's withdrawing. If she doesn't quit the job, you lost her.

See how some fantasies are best left in the mind.

DOES ABSENCE MAKE THE HEART GROW FONDER?

Mercedes: *"My boyfriend went off to college, and I'm afraid I'll lose him and he'll get attracted to other girls. I'd like to believe that 'absence makes the heart grow fonder,' and 'distance lends enchantment,' but is it more true that 'out of sight, out of mind'? It's coming up to our six-month anniversary and we're going to spend the weekend together. What can I do to make it special? What can I do to make him get his eye back on me only so he doesn't look elsewhere?"*

Separation can work either way—either bringing you closer because of anticipation and realizing how much you miss the person and how much you mean to each other, or it could leave you space and time and opportunity to explore other people. Obviously you don't feel very secure about your commitment, but don't force him to verbalize that you're the only one. That'll only reveal your insecurity and make him feel pressured and cornered. Plan the special weekend and make it very exciting so he does think of it and you when you're apart.

LONG-DISTANCE LOVE

John, 21: *"I'm in this long-distance romance with a girl and I miss her. We had great sex and I'm real horny now. What can I do?"*

Have phone sex. Write erotic letters and poems. Make a sexy video. One guy told me how he kept it up with his girlfriend when he was away at college: "I busted my nuts in film canisters and sent them to her." Have fax sex! My friend Danii Minogue, Australian pop singer and her handsome actor husband, Julian McMahon, exchanged faxes tracing their body parts to cross the oceans when he was on *Another World* in New York and she recording an album in London. Bon Jovi guitarist Richie Sambora said he loves the idea of fax sex.

DISGUSTED AFTER SEX

Debbie, 20: *"As soon as I have sex with a guy, he disgusts me. It could be the best sex imaginable, but he still disgusts me. I can't stand the way they eat, or how they walk. Why is this? A friend said it was related to my father, but I didn't know my father because he left when I was one year old."*

It makes sense. Because you didn't know your father—he abandoned you when you were so young—you hate men and punish them now. You grew up wondering why your father left and probably deciding that all men are pitiful and hurt women. So you turn the tables, and reject them before they get a chance to hurt you again. You don't have to keep repeating this pattern. You were hurt then, but don't have to be hurt now. There are some good men out there who will be loyal to you!

PRESSURE TO MARRY

Manny: *"I'm twenty-three years old and dating a woman I really love for six years, but now she's pressuring me to get engaged and married. I want to finish my education first and have a financial base."*

Candlebox vocalist Kevin Martin, as Honorary Love Doctor, advised: "Does she threaten you, saying you will lose her? If it is not right to be married now, don't be frightened by it. Sit down with a counselor."

And advice from Candlebox guitarist Peter Klett: "She needs to respect you for that. Look into her need to be married. Emotionally I wasn't mature enough for marriage when I was in your situation. I'd watch Kevin's relationships and see him argue with them because either he or they were insecure. Think about it, take some time away from one another."

MARRIAGE JITTERS

Joanie, 25: *"I'm getting married and I have cold feet. I went to a bar and met my old boyfriend and I'm attracted to him. Does this mean I shouldn't get married? I really love my fiancé."*

No. You're having normal marriage jitters—men are not the only ones that get them. So you're thinking of what it's going to be like to only be with your husband. Consider that you're presented now with this attraction to your ex to reaffirm that you love your husband. See it as an opportunity to resist temptation and to resolve the relationship with your ex by reviewing how you cared while keeping in your mind that it is in the past, and that you can set limits and not act on the attraction now.

Toad the Wet Sprocket drummer Randy Guss, as Honorary Love Doctor, said he could relate: "I've had a similar situation with my girlfriend for years. We've been going out for six years and there's been times I wasn't sure I wanted to be with her, no matter how much I love her. So you could love him and still be confused."

COLD FEET OR NOT

Dan, 32: *"I'm a nice guy and I'm seeing this woman who wants to marry. I think I want a commitment, too, but in sex the chemistry is just not there enough. I had a passionate relationship before, but the woman was ten years older and I thought it wouldn't be permanent, so I enjoyed it. Could it be that the pressure was just off in that past relationship, so I could really like the sex, while with this girl who's more right for me I can't enjoy the sex as much because I'm really one of those guys with cold feet?"*

Good for you, considering whether you have cold feet or if this just isn't the right one for you. The only way to know is to examine your whole dating history to see if you always seem more committed when there's an "out." Another trick is to pretend you have the most passion for your current girlfriend by acting toward her like you would to the one who wasn't right for you, to "jump start" the passion. If that doesn't work, then likely she really isn't the one. Keep on thinking and feeling you're ready and you will be!

FAULTED FOR FRIGIDITY

John: *"My girlfriend never had an orgasm but complains it's my fault that I last too long. She also tells me all the things that are wrong with me, like my butt is too hairy and my shoulders too small. Why can't she come?"*

She can't orgasm because she obviously doesn't love herself, so don't you blame yourself as she's blaming you. I bet she spends her inner life criticizing herself too, and grew up in a household where she, or others, were always being put down. Tell her you do not accept all this bad-mouthing and that compliments instead of criticism will lead her closer to orgasm.

BOOTY BOMBS

Usually it's girls who worry that once they give it up, they get dumped. But it happens to guys too, that after sex the girls may not be interested.

Isaac: *"What gives? Every time I have sex with a girl, the relationship dies. They call me to come over, I do, and then I call them and they say 'call me later' and then they don't answer."*

MTV comic Bill Bellamy was *LovePhones* Honorary Love Doctor that night: "Are you that bad, man? Think about how you answer that booty call! Did they say anything in sex about things you did or did not do? Maybe you're not affectionate, or you have too many going, so you don't come clean and they figure 'he doesn't really care about me.' "

USED FOR SEX

Sometimes guys feel used for sex, too.

Manny: *"I love this girl but I feel she just loves me for sex. We do it every time we're together. I'm afraid she won't be satisfied if I don't keep it up all the time. What can I do?"*

You may be making this up in your head—suffering from the myth many men have that they are always supposed to be ready for sex, and to perform for the woman. That's not true. Talk about it with her. Find out if she cares for you. Tell her you'd like to do it every other day instead of every day.

FIX IT OR FORGET IT

Michelle, 18: *"My boyfriend broke up with me, and now hangs out with a lot with his friends. But we still go out occasionally and have sex. Why did he break up with me then?"*

Clearly he didn't want such an intensive relationship. It sounds like it's painful for you to just cut back, so see if you have the strength to say no to him, and leave yourself open for someone else. Otherwise you'll still be marked as his girl. One person in the relationship shouldn't be calling all the shots anyway.

BOYFRIEND'S SECRET PAST

Sue, 18: *"My boyfriend wants to keep our relationship secret so his ex-girlfriend won't find out. He says if she knew he was sleeping with me she'd be upset. If he says it's over, why does he care?"*

I'm with you. Something's very fishy. He's probably still keeping the fires stoked with her, or he wouldn't care if she knew he was with you now. Refuse to be kept in the closet. There's nothing to love under these terms of his.

BEAT TO THE PUNCH

Norma: *"One of my friends has been gay and we've been really good friends and recently one of his other friends started getting attracted to a girl and fixed him up and now I think if I had said something a long time ago, it could have been me that he's with now, because I'm in love with him. Now he's with her."*

Sandra Bernhard, as Honorary Love Doctor advised: "Maybe it's not too late. Maybe the other girl wouldn't respond to him and maybe it'll open up him up to different possibilities. Let him explore with her and get comfortable with it and then maybe when he comes around to you, it'll be more well-rounded. Let him play it out and just be his friend because the closer you get as friends, the better it would be to segue into something else. Be patient and don't flip out, and just be there for him and help him through it and you never know."

SETS HER FREE

Lisa: *"My boyfriend broke up with me because his mother is dying of cancer and said he has to give her full attention. His parents are divorced, so he regrets leaving her to be with his dad. He said he doesn't want to hold me back. I thought I'd give him his space. Is this right?"*

He's probably scared to be a burden on you and would feel guilty about taking his own pleasure with you when he already feels guilty about abandoning his mom and responsible to care for her. Maybe he's also afraid to show he's vulnerable, or to risk suffering any further losses.

Respect his choice, but let him know you are there for him when he needs you. Maybe he'll realize in time that he doesn't have to sacrifice all his own happiness in the face of his mother's illness.

RUN-AROUND SUE

Morris: *"I'm seeing this girl and I heard she gets around. The other day I called her and she said, 'Who's this?'"*

I can see how you were hurt that she didn't recognize your voice. True, it's a sign of really being familiar when you recognize someone's voice just from a short "hi." Everybody likes to be known. But some people don't recognize sounds as well as others. She may have a lot of guys calling her, but that doesn't mean she's having sex with them. Sometimes popular people get a rep for sleeping around, when they're just friendly, and those who accuse them are jealous or insecure. Make up a special greeting she'd surely recognize.

SHE OBJECTS TO BACHELOR BLAST

Susan: *"My boyfriend is planning a bachelor party and I refuse to let them have nude dancers. I told him the wedding is off if he has them. Why should he need to look at those girls and maybe have wild sex with them when they all get drunk, when he has me. It wouldn't be the good beginning of the marriage. He's arguing and says I'm being unreasonable. If he sneaks it anyway, I'll be furious."*

You're being quite the boss at the beginning of the relationship. Will you always define what he can and cannot do, and stop him from doing things that threaten you? You could be so smothering that he ends up rebelling. Realize that you can tell a person not to do something but you really can't stop their wanting to.

SEX WITH AN EX

It's not uncommon for men and women to fall into having sex with an ex. You may harbor a fantasy that maybe this time it'll be better. With distance, problems and resentments can fade. You may try to repair old hurts. You may just be lonely. But it's usually not a great idea.

Tammy, 24: *"I'm divorced, but when my ex-husband comes over to see our son, I give in to having sex with him. But I don't want to. I don't want to get back with him. He treated me poorly and was always verbally abusing me, blaming me for getting pregnant. I've tried to stop, but he gets irate. When he calls to come over he says, 'I'll come and spend time but do you have something for me?' I know that means sex. If I don't, he won't be nice to our kid. What should I do?"*

He's a jerk and he's taking advantage of you and your fear that he will treat your child badly. Don't fall into bed with him. Instead, stop and remember how he treats you poorly; why let him abuse you by giving your body to him when you don't really want to? You're cheapening yourself and lowering your self-esteem. Remember you have the right to say 'no' to sex with him. If he abused your child because you won't have sex with him, tell him you will go to court to reduce his visitations or change the custody arrangements.

FEAST OR FAMINE

Jose: *"Why do girls want me when I'm dating someone, but when I'm not they're not attracted to me?"*

Yes, it seems like when you have it, you get more of it offered, and when you need it, it doesn't come! But don't fall into the trap of thinking that life deprives you of what you want. It's partly you and partly them. The part that's them is that so many people want what they can't have, unfortunately.

The part that's you is that maybe you, like a lot of other men and women, are more confident when you're with someone; you're relaxed and secure and more yourself, so you shine and other people pick that up. Confidence is sex appeal. But when you're not attached, you're looking too obviously, perhaps appearing desperate. Measure your "Desperation Factor" on a scale from 0 (none) to 100 (total). Do things that make you feel good and affirm "I am okay on my own," "I am lovable," until the score goes down.

OWES SEX

Carlos: *"I spent a lot of money on this girl on a date and she didn't put out. Should I take her out again?"*

Sure, but she'd be smart not to go out with you again. Since when do you think "you pay she plays"? If you begrudge spending the money on the date if you don't get sex, don't spend the money. Build the connection on liking each other, not on money or what she owes you.

One final word on dating:

Make it a two-bagger. Put a bag over her/his head,
AND over yours, and then test
how attracted you are to each other!

18 Cheating

Statistics show up to eight out of ten men and up to half of women cheat in America. The rest do it in Europe.

KRISTA: *"WE'VE ONLY BEEN MARRIED TWO YEARS, and I love my husband, but recently I ran into my old boyfriend and we just fell for each other again. We went to a hotel right then and there, and had the best sex, crying and laughing and talking. I was so happy but now I'm terrified because I want to see him more and more and what will this do to my marriage?"*

Tom: *"I'm on the road a lot, and since my wife had our baby she's gotten really fat which turns me off. I meet these women in the bars of hotels and even though I know the risks, I take them back to my room. My wife hasn't wanted sex, so why should I let myself go to waste?"*

Cheating. Over the past ten years, surveys have shown that up to eight out of ten men were having affairs. Recently, the most hopeful news for faithfulness came from the 1994 *Sex in America* study that reported the opposite trend—that more than 75 percent of men and 85 percent of women claimed to be monogamous. Yet, other current surveys insist that at least half of marriages are still rocked by infidelity, and a recent survey of over eight thousand people showed that even three out of ten people who considered themselves very conservative admitted to affairs.

So in this chapter, we confront some of the conflicts over cheating.

TRYING TO RESIST

Todd is twenty years old and in his second year at college. *"I don't know what they feed these Midwest girls out here but they're so good looking, I can't keep my hands off them. I love my girlfriend to death and I like being with her every time I go home on break, but I go to so many frat parties, and the girls get wild. One wanted to do me with a friend. How can I not tap it? But how am I going to face my girlfriend? I'm between a rock and a hard place."*

You always have a choice. Making choices is part of growing up and being responsible. You don't jump off a building or drink cyanide. What's best for you? If you want to sow your wild oats at college, clarify your agreement about fidelity with your girlfriend so you don't feel guilty. Breaking agreements feels bad. If you ask for a more open relationship, she may break up with you, but at least you're honest. It's normal to be attracted to people, but you don't have to act on it. You can control your sexual urges. If a hot chick comes on to you, smile and walk away, go change the CD, go talk to a guy friend.

One guy told me whenever he gets tempted by a woman other than his wife, he says "Dead Cats" over and over in his head. Associating a negative with an unacceptable behavior is a solid behavior training technique.

"The best sex is with someone you love . . . (so) be true to your heart and don't follow your wiener," warned Red Hot Chili Peppers bassist Flea when I met up with him at the MTV Awards. Rockers are always tempted, so how do they resist? Aerosmith's Steven Tyler says he stays faithful to his wife by keeping "learning new things about each other." Though he's single, Extreme's Gary Cherone advises, "Have will power 'cause if you're getting it regularly from your girlfriend, there's no reason to go elsewhere."

There's much debate whether the urge to have affairs is biological. Anthropologist Helen Fisher explains that in the animal world, monogamy usually lasts about four years or as long as necessary to protect the young. She hypothesizes that it's difficult to stay in love for more than a few years due to declining brain chemical levels. Animal husbandry researchers made a startling discovery that a bull exhausted from sex will go at it one more time if presented with a fresh cow. Sensing the smell of the "new woman," other mammals, from sheep to rats, also do it.

Other research suggests the female species may also have some biological drives that cause them to stray. A female barn swallow may stray with a male with a longer tail, suggesting better vitality. Certain female insects seduce many males for the ejaculate that protects her eggs. With such evidence against natural monogamy, you have to work at it, controlling your mind and your actions.

FALLING INTO IT

Having an affair with someone who is not really available—whether they're married, have cold feet, or are far away—is usually difficult, because you set yourself up for disappointment. But instead of always looking at the bad side, see how every relationship is a step in a progression that gets you closer to what's good for you.

Anne: *"I met this married man a few weeks ago in a restaurant. He just started talking to me. He said he loves his wife and his family, but they were away for a few weeks, and he wanted 'some nights of passionate sex.' He kept saying how turned on he is to me and I was lonely, so I did it with him. We met many nights at his apartment and the sex was just like I like it. He went down on me every time before intercourse, and told me he loved my snatch more than anything and could be between my legs forever, and that I was beautiful from every angle he looked. He warned me he would never leave his family but I couldn't resist, even though I like to be No. 1 in a man's life. Since his family came back, he hasn't called me. I know I have no right to be mad because he prepared me, but I miss feeling so good. Was I stupid to do it?"*

You went into this with your eyes open, but got blindsided by the pleasure. He was being selfish, but he was honest about the limitations of your relationship. Still, it's natural that you're upset, angry and even jealous that he has his family as well as you, and you have to take a back seat. Better return to believing you deserve to be No. 1. Remind yourself that you chose to allow yourself to have this beautiful sexual and emotional experience. It is a step in your life on the ladder to true love and sex with someone who is more appropriate and available to you.

Debbie, 24: *"I'm in love with this married man and I cry about it a lot because he won't leave his wife. How long can I let this go on?"*

As long as the payoffs for you outweigh the debits. What are you getting out of it: a few nights of great sex, intimacy, presents, security of knowing someone's there? How much is that worth, compared with the loneliness, frustration, emptiness? Make a balance sheet. Are you getting a good deal? If not, end it.

Everyone operates in relationships on a balance of their needs for closeness and separateness. Probably his being committed is safe for you. When the balance tips and you need more closeness, you'll likely let go. If you feel empty, or bad about compromising yourself or your morals, trust that you can find something else that makes you feel better.

Having an affair is always about setting up a triangle, the roots of which are always in your family relationships. How does this repeat your family dynamics? For example, one woman, Pam, was having an affair with a married man whom she was "serving" like a slave. Turns out she also served her father that way when he was sick and her mother was out working, thereby repeating her childhood, winning daddy over mommy. Are you trying to replace a parent, punish a parent, compete with a sibling? When you identify the pattern, you have more control over doing it or not.

Married sex is always the butt of jokes—but it doesn't have to be so bad!

A guy comes home from work early and finds his wife in bed with another man. "What are you doing?" he screams and the wife says to the other guy, "See, I told you he was stupid."

The prostitute says, "Faster, faster,"
the girlfriend says, "Slower, slower,"
and the wife says, "Pink, I think I'll paint the ceiling pink."

Q: What do you do after good sex?
A: I call my wife.

BORING BEAU

Cindy: *"I married really young to get out of the house and now I lost my attraction for my husband. I started an affair with someone in my office who is really lustful. But I wish I had those feelings toward my husband so it wouldn't be so complicated. He's a boring guy. What can I do?"*

Treat him as you do this lustful guy; you might unearth some hidden lust in him. Do a project with him (like remodeling your house, painting a room, doing a puzzle) since working on something together generates eroticism. Watch some sexy movies or read sexy books together. If you want to stay in the marriage, reconcile yourself to the fact that you chose security over lust. People do have different styles, and though you can spark up your husband, you can't change his personality altogether. Rechannel your sexual desires into other activities on your own.

FEARS FACING UP

Many people have affairs because they're afraid to face what they want.

Theresa: *"I have this fantasy of being a dominatrix—making guys do what I order. I haven't had the nerve to do it with my boyfriend because I'd be afraid to face him after that, and because he thinks I'm a nice girl and nice girls wouldn't act like that. So I did it with this other guy, and now I don't enjoy sex as much with my boyfriend. What should I do?"*

It's classic that people, like you, seek an affair for a certain kind of sex they're afraid to do with their partner. A common secret fantasy is to act bossy or order someone around. You worry that you'll lose respect for your partner if you act the dominatrix and put him/her down, or that you'll get stuck acting that way all the time and it'll ruin what you have. Risk it. You could enrich your relationship.

ON-LOCATION LOVE

Some famous couples have managed to keep their love alive for years, like Paul and Linda McCartney, Candice Bergen and Louis Malle, Susan Lucci and her businessman hubby Helmut Huber. Kevin Costner was touted as faithful, until gossip columns went afire with news of his wife leaving him after hearing of a hula dancer in his room while on a movie set in Hawaii.

Some situations throw you together in temptation. Hollywood is replete with stories of romance on the set. Celebrated leading men who fell in love with their leading ladies include Dennis Quaid and Meg Ryan, Alec Baldwin and Kim Basinger, Tom Cruise and Nicole Kidman. But then some of these couples worry about the starring roles.

Trish: *I feel terrible that I succumbed to my leading man when I played Maria in* West Side Story, *when I love my boyfriend."*

Forgive yourself and move on. Being cast as lovers— or partners in any venture—where the world recognizes you as a good pair—is seductive. Accept the reality of the situation, and force yourself to control your actions next time.

"Trust me with your life, not your money or your wife."

IS IT CHEATING?

Dave: *"I'm worried whether my girlfriend will know I cheated. Do you think she can tell?"*

Van Halen's Sammy Hagar, as Honorary Love Doctor, warned: "A woman always knows when a man has been with another woman . . . you walk in the door with the smile on your face they can smell a mile away, man. A woman knows like that but men don't. They sit at home and think of all the weird crap and get themselves wound up and you could be way off."

Yet many women don't want to believe there's an affair going on, no matter what evidence they're faced with.

Jessica's boyfriend goes to pool parties without her and when she asks him where the condoms are that she knows he had, he claims he lost them. She wonders, *"Should I trust him?"*

Joanne found fake nails on the floor of her boyfriend's car and a long blond hair on his sweater, when her hair is brown. But she worries, *"What if it's an innocent thing, won't I look like an ass to accuse him of having an affair, and make him angry at me?"*

Sherry is supposed to get married in a few weeks but her fiancé came home with a hickey on his neck. When she asked about it, he said, "I don't know what you're talking about.' She wants to know, *"What should I do?"*

Don't buy the denials. Find out what's up, for the sake of your self-esteem and the future of your relationship (if there is one). Take a deep breath and say to yourself, "I'm entitled to ask what I want to know." You may decide to stick with the relationship in any case, but at least you'll know what you're up against.

Some telltale signs of an affair are: being happier than usual, changing underwear style, making more excuses, taking time off, mysterious phone calls or messages, new sexual behaviors, new interests in subjects or events, working out or losing weight to look better, evasive responses about the future, and either protesting everything is fine between you or bringing up new complaints.

Like Jessica, Joanne, Sherry, and so many girls, Brenda

is so desperate to keep her boyfriend, she'll accept anything. *"Sometimes he says he's going out and will be right back but then he doesn't return for hours. I think he may be messin' with other girls and playing me dirty. But I have sex with him even if I don't want to because I'm afraid of losing him."*

If you keep giving him sex just to keep him, and let him play you for a fool, you may win in the short run, but you'll lose in the long run—his, and your own, respect. Such fooling is a painful relationship. Do affirmations: I deserve to be happy.

Vanessa, 22, did put her foot down and hopes it's right: *"My boyfriend said he went camping with his friend but while he was away I looked in his closet and found a shoe box with some letters in it from a girl who said making love to him is so great. He came home and after he said hello, I dropped the letters in his lap. He said it was the girl's fantasy and never happened. I told him to pack his bags and he did. Now I'm upset, should I have thrown him out?"*

If he wasn't feeling guilty, he wouldn't have left. It's a lame excuse that the girl wrote a fantasy. He's the one who has to come back with apologies and a new agreement with you. Stand your ground. Remember, Respect Rules.

SNOOPER

Danielle: *"I slept at my boyfriend's house and I found a letter in his computer to his friend about a girl who's tall with her legs up in the air. I'm short so he couldn't have been talking about me. I woke him up and he left on his bike. I was shaking so much, I told his parents. I've been seeing him for two years and don't want to have wasted all that time. Besides, all my friends have boyfriends. What will they think of me? What can I do?"*

From the way you describe this, you're less concerned about the relationship than you are with being lonely or the only one in the crowd without a boyfriend. Coupled with your snooping, and telling his parents, it sounds like you're so needy, it turns him off. Comfort yourself and try to understand that you are okay on your own. Give your boyfriend some space and then talk to him about what's going on between you. Sometimes, as with investing in the stock market, you just have to cut your losses and move on.

GETTING HIM BACK

Darcy: *"My boyfriend and I have been together a few years. Our sex life has gone down the tubes to practically nothing and I think he must be having an affair. How do I get him back in my bed?"*

There may be nothing you can do; it may be all his problem, so don't blame yourself. But if there was trouble between you, figure out what made you drift apart sexually or emotionally and fix that. If you argue, make peace and decide to bite your tongue for two weeks to see how that goes. If you take each other for granted, pretend he's a new lover that you have to impress. If you stopped being seductive, plan a new surprise for him each night. If you both have deeper interpersonal problems, see a therapist to work them out.

FORGET THE AFFAIR

"My husband had a one-night stand four years ago. I forgave him and he promised never to do it again. I'm sure he hasn't, but occasionally when we're making love, I can't stop thinking about what she did to get him. How can I get rid of this thought?"

Think of your brain like a computer. Every time the thought of your husband with that other woman crosses your mind, hit the delete button. Since obsessive thoughts arise from unacceptable feelings, identify that underlying feeling and cope with it in a more constructive way. For example, if you start thinking of your husband cheating on you when you feel insecure about your own desirability, instead of obsessing about how good a seductress she must have been, concentrate on what you can do at that moment to feel better about yourself.

Bobby: *"I found my girl two-timing me. I threw her right out. She can't do me in. Women are getting too fast. What kind of women cheat so I can avoid those bitches."*

Oops, watch your language. If you talk like that and treat her like that, she should have left herself before you threw her out. If you weren't so ego-involved, you'd be calmer and fix what's wrong between you. And if you really cared about her more than just yourself, you'd give her another chance. Men are often so much more unforgiving of a straying love because their ego is busted. The profile of a woman who is likely to have affairs: mid-20s to mid-30s, who works, makes family decisions, and has had considerable premarital sex. But you really have to figure out the woman's character, her needs, and whether the two of you are getting along. You sound so angry and hostile to women, though, that you'll have to get over that before any smart woman really gives her heart to you.

IS AN AFFAIR EVER GOOD?

Mary: *I found out my boyfriend cheated on me and he begged for me to forgive him. He's been so good ever since. Is that possible?"*

Pop singer Alison Moyet as Honorary Love Doctor: "I have been in the situation where one person shags somebody else and it's ended up perfectly well. Sometimes it can be a real building thing. It can make you decide you want somebody more than you thought you did. You have to want a clean sheet and just drop it."

DOGGED BY SUSPICION

Since history often repeats itself, it's inevitable that if you were the other woman, if he becomes yours, you'll wonder if there's another "other woman."

Willa, 20: *"Every time my boyfriend goes out with his friends alone, I'm scared that he's cheating on me. I know he cheated on his ex-girlfriend but after a year he's never done anything to make me suspicious. Sometimes I beep him ten times a day and ask him where he be. Am I wrong to be checking up?"*

Of course you'd be suspicious. If he cheated on someone else, he could cheat on you. Be wary (don't overlook any signs) but also wise (rather than harp about his past, spend that time making your relationship good). Do find out what drove him to cheat before (insecurity, unfulfilled fantasies), so you can fix any problems that may come up between you. But realize, the more you obsess and remind him about a past affair, the more you could sabotage what you have, suffocating him. Bite your tongue before you check up on him so much. Turn your mind to something else. Give him a chance to prove that he's worthy of your trust again.

Men get overly jealous and suspicious too. Carrie's fiancé is in the Army, so he's away a lot. *"The last time he came home and we had sex, he said I wasn't as tight, so I must have had an affair. It's not true. How can I convince him?"*

Just tell the truth. Tell him he's just being insecure because he's away, and turn it into something positive, like that he must mean he misses you.

"Is once a cheater always a cheater?"
Not necessarily. But:

> **Q.** How many psychiatrists does it take to change a light bulb?
> **A.** One, but the bulb has to want to change.

A cheater has to want to stop, and has to make an effort. It can work both ways. Cheaters can do it once and get it out of their system or be frightened to lose what they have with you and stop. Or it can be like anything else: once you do it once you're not so scared to do it again. It depends on why he or she is cheating. If a problem remains unresolved, the desire to cheat will persist. If the cheater's needs (to be wanted or wild) persist, and no partner sets any limits, then the cheating will likely persist unless the needs are satisfied in another way.

Mike: *"I got my girl and I got a slice on the side. Now they're both pregnant and they both mean to keep it. I'll do my duty to both of them but my man tells me I should move them all in so it doesn't cost me so much."*

A lot of women will look the other way about everything after they have a baby with a guy, to keep him in the picture, but they'd have to be real desperate to go for your group home idea. How cocky.

SETTLING FOR CRUMBS

Tracy: *"I'm dating a guy for three years and he's cheated on me four times in the last six months. But I love him. I don't think I can get anyone else because I'm a little heavy."*

URGGHHH! It makes me cringe when I hear that: he did this or that terrible to me . . . "but I love him." That's not love; that's dependence and a fear of being abandoned and alone. Taking crumbs makes him lose respect for you, and you for yourself. Love yourself and your love antennae will draw people to you who love you.

NEWLYWED STRAYING

Newlyweds between the ages of eighteen and forty-nine are the most likely to cheat, according to a poll by the Opinion Research Center in Chicago. On a recent *Sally Jesse Raphael* show I was on, I talked with spouses who had affairs right after walking down the aisle. One, a fourteen year old girl, cried, telling how she was in love with her old boyfriend, who is eighteen, and had sex with him on her wedding night.

"I love my husband," she said, "but I can't give up my boyfriend. I don't go to work or school and just spend my time thinking about him. I love being with him and having sex with him."

She and her husband had not had sex at all. The audience went ballistic. A representative from a religious group said she was doing evil. A guy in the audience called her a "'ho." I was upset. "She's just a kid who wants a family, not a husband," I explained, as she never knew her father, and her stepfather beat her, called her a bitch and a whore, and paid someone to rape her when she was twelve. After all, her mother got married and gave birth to her at the same age she was now. I thought the marriage should be annulled, and she should be in a foster home so she could have the family she needs, and grow up like the adolescent she is.

On the same panel was "Katrina." Married a year and a half, she began cheating on her husband only two days after the honeymoon. "I have no intention of getting divorced," she said, "and I will keep my lover because he satisfies in me what my husband can't."

She explained that she never paid much attention to her husband when she met him in high school, but he pursued her until she said "yes." But she couldn't get an ex-boyfriend out of her mind so she called him and he admitted he still loved her—he'd driven by the church the day she got married—so they got together and had sex. Once she felt guilty and told her husband, who made her promise she'd never do it again, but she says, "I won't give it up. The sex is great and we talk, and a little part of me loves sneaking around."

Normally, the appropriate therapeutic advice would be to stop that affair and to figure out what her needs are and give the spouse a chance to fulfill them. But as psychologist Sonja Friedman's study of 109 women in affairs showed (reported in her book *Secret Loves: Women with Two Lives*), some women opt to "have it all" by keeping a husband for security, financial support, and family cohesiveness, and the affair on the side for excitement, friendship, or other needs. They feel no one is getting hurt, they have no desire to change, and it works for them.

Some people will defend to death the notion that having an affair helps their marriage, giving them an outlet, allowing them to stay with their spouse while satisfying other needs outside the marriage. Though not admitting to outright affairs, in her book *Dolly,* Dolly Parton says of her long-time husband Carl Dean, "He seems to know that I'll be back, and that love affairs and relationships are just a part of my dealings with people."

Newlywed men stray, too. Irene is only eighteen and

married only three weeks. *"My husband told me he had sex three days before our wedding with a girl he met on a train. He cried and said he was thinking of me. I tried to strangle myself with the cord of a lamp. How can I get over this?"*

You're hurt and angry and taking your anger out on yourself. There is never no hope. Discuss why he did it and your fears about ever trusting him again. Your dreams and illusions about perfect love are shattered, but he obviously wanted to confess to end it, so move on and see how you can re-constitute your marriage.

BALLISTIC OVER BETRAYAL

A wailing Vince, 18, called one night: *"I caught my girl-friend doing coke with my brother, and he had his pants down. I knocked his head against the bathroom wall, and it bled. I went to a friend's house and now I want to get a gun and kill them both. I'm not afraid to go to jail."*

You're out of control, crying one minute and furious the next. You need to see a psychiatrist and get treatment as soon as possible. Then you have to let out all your hurt, so you don't turn it into murderous acts. And you have to control your anger. Learn to express it in a safe place. Then verbalize your hurt and anger to the real people who triggered it, like your brother and your girlfriend and others in your past, with-out having to hurt them. Tell them you expect Respect.

ENDS IT BUT FEARS EXPOSURE

Amy: *"I slept with the husband of this girl I've known two years. We got together four times in two months, but now I want to end it with him. But I'm afraid he'll tell her. I saw her and her baby and I just can't go on."*

It's good that you want to break your pattern and restore your self-esteem. Tell him outright it's over. You'll have to face the consequences if he tells, but he has more to lose than you do, so he probably won't.

Always have an affair—with your love partner, that is!

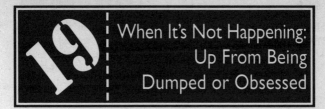

AS THE R.E.M. SONG GOES, "EVERYBODY LOVES sometime/Everybody hurts sometime." It never feels good when you lose someone you want. But don't *lose it* in the process.

Even if someone you want doesn't want you, you better want you. Stepping over the landmines of being dumped, or getting over an obsession with someone is tough, but here's how you do it:

GETTING THE NEWS

Jason: *"What does it mean that this girl I was seeing just wants to be friends? What's the woman's scheme in proposing that? Is that like putting me on the "layaway" plan?"*

I'm afraid so. Read her lips. "Let's be friends" means "Let's not have sex," "I found someone else," "I like you but I don't love you." Get it. It's difficult to be friends anyway, you'll just end up feeling used and hang on to false hopes. So don't buy into her and you won't be laid away.

Sara, 22: *"Since my boyfriend broke up with me, I can't get sexual with anyone else. He said it's over forever but I can't believe it. I'm freaking out. What can I do?"*

Believe it. You have to move on. You're hurt. Give yourself time, but don't put yourself on hold for him forever in an illusion that he'll return. Meanwhile, you learned a great lesson about yourself: that sex means a lot to you and you don't want to give your body and soul to just anyone else now. Value that as you recover; it's your silver lining in the dark cloud.

Disbelief and desperation are two common reactions to being dumped. If you shared your body and soul with someone, and it's over, you can go into what's called love shock.

LOVE SHOCK

"I'd been dating a guy I'm really crazy about for almost a year when all of a sudden he called me on the phone and said it was over. I see him around school and he pretends he doesn't know me. I'm devastated. I can't stop crying, and some days I can't get out of bed. My friends tell me to get over it, but I can't stop wishing I were back with him and I can't imagine ever being in love or having sex with anyone else. Can I ever get over this?"

Being rejected is upsetting enough, but you're suffering from Love Shock: being rejected by a loved one precipitously, without warning or reason. It's even worse that now the guy pretends you don't exist, which makes you really feel negated and wiped out. It's like you've been through a war, as New York behavioral scientist Stephen Gullo described it.

Love Shock victims like you fall into pitfalls. They "futurize," thinking they will never recover or find another love. They magnify the rejecting partner's assets and their own deficiencies. And they blame themselves, wondering, "Wasn't I enough?" or "What do other women have that I don't have that he wants?" The answer is that there is nothing wrong with you. No new hairdo, weight loss, or wild sex will bring him back. He may have left you, but you should not leave yourself; convince yourself that it's his loss.

Expect the stages of dealing with any loss. First there's denial: he can't possibly not love me. Then bargaining: "I'll do or be anything you want if you'll come back." Then anger, or depression, in either order. Focus on your positive qualities that someone else will appreciate. Choose to be with friends and family who adore you now to rebuild your confidence and form new associations to the things you once did with him.

Time heals all wounds, but research suggests it can take half the time the relationship lasted to get over the loss and even then about ten percent of the pain remains. Feel sad but don't wallow; immediately do something else that makes you feel good. Let out your anger: picture him in your room and let him have it, full force. Treating yourself well is the best revenge: get a massage, call a good friend. His exit leaves space for someone more wonderful to enter or something exciting for you to create. BRAIN RETRAIN: Say, "I'm worth it, his loss, the next person's gain." As my mom says, wisely, "A door closes, the window opens."

A chorus from the guys in Urge Overkill: "Get on with your life." Gin Blossoms' lead singer Robin Wilson says he got over a lost love—even after asking the girl to marry him—by writing songs and distracting himself with someone else. He hasn't seen her since and doesn't mind.

SEX HOLD ON HER

Sally, 29: *"I'm so devastated that this guy broke up with me. He went down on me even when I had my period, and licked me front and back. I can't get sexual with anyone else. I still feel my knees get weak when I see him. What can I do?"*

If you like steak, wouldn't the sight of that make your mouth water too? Obviously his licking you all over made you feel really loved and adored. It's normal conditioning that the sight of him would trigger the memory traces of that in your mind and body and make you drool for it. Sexual pleasure is powerful glue. It'll continue for a while, and probably until you find someone else equally exciting. BRAIN RETRAIN: Whenever the thought of him comes in your mind, snap your fingers (to interrupt it) and think of someone else exciting (whom you know or a stranger), or of doing something else you like.

DO THE DRAMA

Mark, 20: *"My girlfriend called from camp and said it's over. She's attracted to someone else. She didn't want to hurt me but it did. She calls me to talk and I ask her if we can get back and she doesn't answer. I'm lonely and I cry. I have to have her back. Is there any hope?"*

I love this technique: purposefully overdramatize your feelings so you can get to the bottom and come up again. Pretend you're in an improvisational acting class, and exaggerate. Escalate your crying to wail, "Oh, I'm going to die, this is terrible, I'll never get over it. She was the only one . . ." Doing this can purge your emotion, or help you see the absurdity of the situation and therefore, neutralize its power over you!

The girl calls you because she doesn't want to hurt you, and she probably likes you because you're a nice guy anyway. But she doesn't want you back or she'd say so. She's playing ping-pong with your heart. Stop being a masochist. Self-respect Rules. Let her go. Maybe she'll miss you; if not, her loss. Make room for a more fulfilling, constant love.

Guys take rejection harder than girls sometimes. Research with monkeys suggests how poorly males deal with sexual rejection. When male monkeys were presented with a female with whom they were unable to mate (she was plugged up with a tampon), they withdrew into a corner, picked at their skin, threw themselves against the wall, or hit the females. Even a year later, when the females were unplugged, willing and able, the males still behaved bizarrely. Don't be one of those monkeys; be open to the unplugged females.

Aside from the hurt at being dumped, you can get real angry—even go ballistic.

UPSET SPILLS OVER

Anne: *"I had great sex with a guy and now he's seeing me less and less. I'm so upset, I yelled at my super for not fixing the stove. I screamed at my hairdresser for cutting my bangs too short. I'm on edge with everyone. Why am I losing my temper?"*

You're hurt and angry. You had what you liked and

needed, and it was taken away from you, so you're like a pressure cooker, spitting out upset. Think what a temper tantrum a two-year-old goes through when a favorite toy is taken away. You may have been spoiled as a child. You'll have to develop frustration tolerance of not having what you want—part of growing up. Clarify with the guy about what's going on, so you're not in limbo.

CAN'T TAKE BEING REJECTED

Jennifer: *"I had sex with this guy but I didn't ask him to go down on me. Now he's not seeing me as much. When I think about his not calling me, I feel like punching him. I want to flatten his tires, and take him out. He led me on. Now I want him to suffer."*

Sounds like your anger has something to do with you not asking for and getting what you wanted along the way. His not going down on you means he didn't give you enough, nor did you have the confidence or balls to ask. HOMEWORK: (1) Purge your anger by pounding pillows and yelling at all the ghosts from your past who never gave you what you wanted. (2) Mentally rehearse asking the next guy to go down on you or whatever you want. Each relationship can be a stepping stone.

REVENGE

Nicole, 18: *"My boyfriend was seeing a lot of girls while he was having sex with me so I dumped him. Now he's hurting a lot of other girls. I want to hurt him. I don't want him with anyone. I hope he never has any sex with anyone as good as me. I'd like to beat the crap out of him. How can you stop me from hurting him?"*

You are obviously furious at his two-timing. But your fury is not just at him, but at other guys who have already, or whom you imagine will, hurt you. Picture all those guys lined up in your room, give 'em hell. Tell them what rats they are, and then torture them mentally all you want. Get it out of your system. Don't do it in real life. Resolve to yourself that what goes around comes around: his behavior will catch up with him someday. If only women wouldn't take crap from guys, they couldn't dish it out on you, or the next girl.

Stop wasting your time thinking about what he has or doesn't have, and concentrate instead on yourself getting what makes you happy. Wanting him to be deprived is a waste of time you could be spending on your own life. Living well is the best revenge.

LOSES CONTROL

Mike: *"I was seeing this girl before, and once I was at a bar and I saw her giving out her number to another guy. I saw red thinking if she had sex with him, I'd kill them in bed. I grabbed her arm and said, 'Don't you ever do that again in front of me.' She hit me in the head and ran out. My own blow-up bothers me. I never did that before. Could it happen again?"*

Yes. Get a hold of yourself, man. You have a serious temper-control problem. No matter what someone does, you're not entitled to be abusive to them. Losing it over your ex-girlfriend's flirting with another guy shows how fragile your ego is. Next time, see if you can stop and take a breath and count to ten and say to yourself, "This hurts me and I am furious." Take her aside calmly and ask her if she can respect your feelings.

Adam Ant: "Men are carnal. They're not in touch with really loving the girl, but if they see her with someone else, they lose control. But that's possession, not really caring about the person. Men have to learn to feel something before."

Urge Overkill's lead singer Nash Kato's advice: "It's always tough rebounding when it's over. You gotta believe in yourself."

UO's bassist Eddie King Roeser adds, "Get on with your life, man, it's not the new guy's fault. He doesn't mean to bum you out. You better not beat him up."

If you can't accept it's over, you may have developed an addiction.

AFTER-SEX ADDICTION

Kaity: *"I'm crazy about a guy who dumped me. I had sex with him for my first time. Now I want to kill the other girl he's seeing."*

Margaret: *"I went out with this guy Mike a few times. He told me I was interesting. I slept with him once and I thought it was amazing. He told me "wow" in the middle. Then he didn't call me. So I called him to talk and he said he was studying. I hung up and then five minutes later I called him back and asked him what he was studying. He said he'd call me back Wednesday. Then I remembered that I might be out on Wednesday, so I called him back to say maybe I'd be out and he was very rude and hung up. I cried and felt like I was going to die. I keep calling and getting his machine. Why is he so mean?"*

Because you're pestering him. I'm sad to tell you he doesn't want you like you want him, and he's liking you less the more desperate you become. You've gotten real attached, most likely because you had sex with him (especially if it was your first time), and you're blowing it into more than it was for him. You're typical of millions of women in America who have what I call the "After-Sex Addiction." Test if you have it:

AFTER-SEX ADDICTION TEST

Do you:

❑ have to know it was as good for him as for you?

❑ have sex once, and immediately decide he is "the one"?

❑ feel extreme "highs" having sex with him, and "lows" when you don't?

❑ lose interest in everything else after having sex?

❑ stop accomplishing what you have to, thinking of him?

❑ panic or feel the world has come to an end if he doesn't have sex with you?

❑ fantasize that no other partner can be as good as you?

❑ see red if s/he is with someone else?

❑ feel worthless and unattractive without his/her sexual attentions?

❑ imagine constantly how you could please him/her?

❑ plan how one day you will be together?

Scoring: More than four "yes" answers and I'm worried.

Stop focusing on him, and notice the big black hole inside you—that feeling of being unloved. You have to fill it with things other than some guy or girl. Realize that your pain comes from the ghosts of the past. Do other things that make you feel whole. What can fulfill you? A new hobby. A good movie. Retrain your brain, from "I need sex with this person to be happy," to "I would like to have sex with this person, but my life is full anyway." As soon as the thought of him crosses your mind, immediately dump out of that mental computer file and open another. Review your relationship history to clearly see the pattern that leads you to that roller coaster—how it starts, how it ends, and your reactions. See how you always got attracted to exciting but noncommittal people who jump into bed with you because you're fun and attentive to them, but then dump you. Also see how you misread people, blowing things out of proportion (like thinking his telling you "wow" in the middle of sex means more than it does to him). It hurts when you feel more than the other person, but don't think he took something away feom you—you got something out of it, too.

Society is partly to blame for women being addicted to a partner after sex. Women are brought up being taught to use sex to get love. Advertisements, soap operas, and romance novels extol the drama of falling in passionate love. There's a biological basis, too: when you have good sex with someone you care about, you get a "rush" from your quickened heartbeat, sweaty palms, and pumping adrenaline and other chemicals. It's like a drug. Recognize this and refuse to be the victim of it. Don't have sex until you know the person cares a lot. When you have higher self-esteem, you won't be so vulnerable.

TAKES CRUMBS

Erin, 16: *"My boyfriend stopped calling me for a week, and I got so mad, I broke up with him. I wanted to hear him say he missed me and to come back, but he didn't. He said if that's best for me, he wants what's best for me. Then I*

*found out he was two-timing me. He's already gone out
with two other girls, but I'd have sex with him even if he's
seeing other girls."*

Don't be a fool, man-sharing this player. You shouldn't
be willing to settle for crumbs, just not to lose him entirely.
You let him off the hook by breaking up, and he's using it so
he doesn't feel guilty. Self-Respect Rules: don't let him get
away with treating you like dirt, or that's just what you'll
get. Don't take from a lover what you wouldn't take from a
friend. Better to have none of him and all your self-esteem.

Like in the Kenny Rogers tune, "The Gambler," know
when to fold your love cards. Or in playing the stock market, know when to cut your losses.

SOUVENIRS

Kenneth: *"My ex-girlfriend called me up one night out of
the blue and said it's over. I was very upset. She asked me
to pack up her stuff, but I kept a pair of her panties. I have a
few others in a collection from other girls that left me. Was
I wrong to keep them?"*

A keepsake is what we call a "transitional object"—a
reminder of a person when we don't have the person. Teddy
bears are the first important transitional object; soft and
cuddly, they remind us of mother's comfort. Collecting
panties is your way to prevent feeling loss, rejection, and
severe unworthiness. Do affirmations: "I am lovable," "I
can have a lasting love." Decide if people leave you, it's
their loss.

HANGS ON TO PAST

Joe: *"A year ago my old girlfriend was raped. She was sent
to her relatives and she killed herself. I thought love was
perfect once, but now when women come on to me, there's
nothing there. I compare them to her and no one lives up.
Will this ever change?"*

Yes. It's hard to believe your love is gone, but she lives

on in your heart, and you need time to mourn. Forgive yourself for not saving her from rape and suicide. Express your anger and sadness. Have imaginary conversations with her, to complete what we call "unfinished business" (asking why she did it, saying you care), and eventually imagine her giving you permission to get on with your life and new loves without feeling unfaithful.

Actor Ricky Paull Goldin agrees: "You can't be alone for the rest of your life, mourning. She probably understands that. Turn it around, you would probably let her go. You have to move on."

Putting the pieces back together takes emotional effort.

AN OUNCE OF PREVENTION
WORTH A POUND OF CURE

Andy, twenty-one, is a walking example of how you better know someone before you take the plunge. *"I met this girl three years older than me in church and we got married three months later. She was a lesbian before, and likes to touch my butt for three and a half hours at a time in sex, but nothing else. She tried to rule my life. It was horrible. I separated from her, but how can I ever get my life back?"*

Recognize that no one ever takes control away from you; you give them control. You're an example of how not to rush into anything. Know someone well before you fall in love, much less marry. Wait six dates to decide if someone's really worth your while, and six months before you think you know who they are.

What's the last thought you couldn't get out of your mind? When you can't control your thoughts you have an obsession. Sexual thoughts can become a mild or severe obsession.

BEACH BONGO

C.J., 19: *"I'm a lifeguard, and every time I see a girl walk by, I picture her naked. I can't keep my mind from looking around. I blame the job for making me this way."*

Force yourself to keep your mind on something else. When you watch the girls go by, before you get to the picture in your mind's eye of them naked, delete the program, switch your attention to people in the ocean and thinking of going in to save one. That's what you're there for. Undress the girls mentally on your time off, if you want. You're indulging your fantasy too much. Exercise a little self-control.

OBSESSION

If you've ever wanted someone so bad you couldn't eat, sleep, or drink without thinking of him/her, you know what it feels like to be obsessed. Have you ever pursued someone who didn't want you and called and hung up when they answered? Driven by their house? Beeped them twenty times a day? That's not love, but obsession. Like for Margaret, who wrote to me at my newspaper column in *Newsday: "I'm eighteen and last October I met this guy who's nineteen and plays drums in a band. I fell for him instantly. I found out his name and what college he went to and started following him. I would sit outside the college for hours, and when he was playing outside the college, I would go and watch him. I started dreaming about him day and night. In December he noticed me and introduced himself, but I played stupid and pretended I never saw him before. We became good friends and he gave me a list telling me when the band would be playing at the clubs. Every night that the band played, I made sure I was there, just to see him. One night he brought his girlfriend and I was so depressed. I never cried so much as I did that night. About three weeks later I finally found the courage to tell him how I felt and he told me, 'I like you, too,' but we can only be friends because his girlfriend would be mad and he couldn't hurt her that way. I said 'okay' (better than nothing, right?). Please don't think I'm crazy! I've been out with boys before and this has never happened. He sings a lot, so when I listen to a song he sings I can't help but cry, because*

I want him and I know I can't have him. I don't want to let him go. Just tell me what to do? I'm so confused and I feel like my heart is breaking. Why am I doing this? Why am I waiting for him when I could be going out with other guys and having a good time? I wish I could forget about him for just one day. Please help me."

I feel so sad for you, because you know that you should move on and get on with your life and yet you are hanging on to a fantasy that is giving you nothing in return. But you can get free before it gets more dangerous—with you totally sacrificing your own life, stalking him, and getting into trouble with your own school, friends, family, and even the law.

What is the need he satisfies in you? You've made him into some icon—a rock star who can give you the life you want—fun, excitement, fame, money. You have to get these things for yourself or you will never be happy. Remember this: become the guy you desperately want to have. HOMEWORK: Make a list of five things that make you feel good and be sure to do them every day.

Examine your family history. Who do you know that lived through another person? Did your mother put all her hopes and dreams into you, or live through your father? You are likely copying someone who devoted herself to another person. Recognize your desperation about him as a need to make you feel important. Make *yourself* important.

The severity of your obsession is measured by the time you spend in it, degree of distress it causes, lack of control, and interference in your life and responsibilities. In severe cases, medications can help. As many as one in forty people, or five million Americans have some sort of obsessive-compulsive disorder.

<u>EROTOMANIA</u>: Some people get so sexually obsessed with a person who rejects them that they're driven to stalk, or kill, the object of their desire. It's called erotomania. *Baywatch* bombshell Pamela Anderson has had strange men follow her home from the set. O.J. Simpson was accused of snoooping in his ex-wife Nicole's windows. And a drifter,

claiming to be Madonna's husband, was sentenced to a year in jail for stalking her and scaling the fences of her estate.

Erotomaniacs are out of control and sometimes driven to violence.

Louis described how: *"I was in love with a girl who told me we'd be together forever. Then she broke up with me. I told her if I can't have her, no one can. I got a gun and she told my parents. They put me in a hospital. Now I have a new girl and she says she loves me. But the last time the word 'love' was used to hurt me. Should I trust her?"*

I'm happy you got help. I hope you learned your last lesson: you cannot let your fears and desperation to be loved get out of control. It's dangerous. Control your fears. Understand that everyone gets hurt sometime. Let your frustration and anger out in a safe way. Yell in your room, punch pillows, talk about how you feel to people who care. Do something active and physical like working out, boxing. Let yourself risk loving again. You deserve it. But understand that people cannot always make promises about forever. It sounds romantic, but reality is often harsher.

Tori Ann: *"My boyfriend is so jealous and possessive, he says if I break up with him he'll murder me. I can't talk to guys, or if I dress a certain way he goes ballistic. I broke up with him a few weeks ago and he was with another girl, but he tried to run me over. He came over to me and pushed me and punched me on the arms and legs. What can I do?"*

Go to the police. This is dangerous. Get an order of protection. Even then, I'm scared for you because you know there are news stories of guys who do this and then really kill the girl. After you've gotten some kind of protection, you have to examine how you got involved with someone like this. Without blaming yourself, examine why you draw someone like this to you. Following my Mirror Law of Attraction, what does wanting him say about you? Like him, how are you possessive and jealous, too? Or you are so insecure about being rejected, you pick a guy to pursue you so you never have to feel you'll be abandoned—even if the attachment is not a healthy one.

Obsessed lovers are often addicted to abusive people.

Tanya, 21: *"I had sex with my friend's brother, and I'm now obsessed with him, but he's a rat. He had a baby with another woman, but now he doesn't want to be bothered with her and says she tricked him into having the baby. I want to be with him, but my other friends say I'm a fool. How can I stop wanting to get with him?"*

Associate him with unpleasant instead of pleasant thoughts. Remember how badly he talks of this other girl and think he's talking about you that way, too—he could be. Following my Mirror Law of Attraction that the people we want are mirrors of ourselves; you need to stop being a rat to yourself. Get a job or help some runaway girls to raise your self-esteem.

FIFTY WAYS TO LEAVE YOUR LOVER

How do you get rid of someone's unwanted attentions? Be kind when you end it, as you would like others to be kind unto you.

Wendy, 20: *I was going with this guy for a year and the sex was just okay. He was nice enough, but I realized I didn't like his being so disorganized and possessive. He keeps calling me. How do I let him down easy?"*

I'm proud you want to end it without hurting him. Always be as kind when you end it as you would want the other person to be to you. Explain that it's not working out. Never blame or point out his/her inadequacies; that'll only destroy his/her ego or incite defensiveness or pleading. Say how both of you will be better off. Allow some discussion (best in a public place), so the rejected one can express hurt and get some closure.

Advice to end it:

Tell 'em, "We ain't the two and you're not the one."
—Corey Glover, lead singer, Living Colour
(one of the few Black hard rock bands;
toured with the Stones.)

EX STALKS

Actress Sean Young knows about obsession. On screen, her movies *Love Crimes* and *Fatal Instinct* (a spoof of *Fatal Attraction* and *Basic Instinct*) were about obsessed characters. And off screen, she became the target of the tabloids, accused of stalking a co-star in one film, and a movie director for the part she wanted in another. But when I did Joan Rivers' TV show with Sean, she was appalled at the portrayal, and felt misunderstood for her intensity. Knowing the issue of obsession so well, she had level-headed advice when she was Honorary Love Doctor on *LovePhones* on that topic when Jason called to say, *"I broke up with my girl about two months ago and she keeps coming back around and she won't leave me alone and I . . . Someone was talking about obsessions before and I can't get rid of her. I told her I am just trying to get on with my life and she won't leave me alone."*

Sean: "There's something you need to do to help her feel a little more complete about this separation. Instead of like making her feel rejected. That's what you need to find out, how you can make this person feel complete about her loss of you.

"For me, seeking balance is a big part, because I live in such a topsy turvy world, going from living in Arizona and being very content at home to going off and being on location and then coming home to my husband and being like, 'Hi, honey. So and so was an okay kisser . . . ' Balance is what I seek. I don't always feel it but that is what I strive for."

Andrew, 19: *"My girlfriend's ex-boyfriend won't leave her alone. He always follows us and he leaves her notes and threatens that he's going to kill himself if she doesn't see him. What can I do?"*

It's touching that you care and that you want to protect her, but it's best for you not to intervene. Encourage your girlfriend to be firm in telling him that it is over, reassure him that she cared for him also (to salve his ego), and that they both have to move on for the best. She should suggest he get help, and say that because he threatens suicide, she is going to tell either his parents or the school counselor, for his best interests. Then, she has to let him be.

Erotomaniacal obsessions with celebrities are dangerous, but some fan adoration can actually be useful.

Stevie: *"I'm obsessed with Madonna. I imagine having sex with her where she tells me I'm the best she ever had and invites me to go on tour with her. Is this bad for me to do?"*

When you have an obsession about having sex with a celebrity, use your obsession constructively to figure out how being with that person would allow you to feel about yourself and feel that way in your real life. Imagining being desired by a person celebrated for sex likely means you want to build your sexual confidence and overall self-esteem. What inhibitions and fears about your own attraction and possibly gender identity do you want to overcome?

Feel yourself worthy and desirable from inside. Tell yourself what you imagine the famous person telling you—that you're the best. Instead of longing to hitch onto their life and bemoaning your own as boring, create exciting adventures that are possible for you. Be as much of a celebrity in your own mind as you wish you could become by reflecting in their glory.

Heather: *"I'm in love with a guy in the Red Hot Chili Peppers. I've been close to the stage and thrown him flowers, and sent him my bra several times in the mail. I can't understand why he doesn't write back. My body is beautiful and I deserve to have him. He should know me. When I see him perform, I get wet and shaky all over. It's better than an orgasm."*

Having been at their concerts, I can understand how being in a thrashing crowd watching this punkedelic group generates a lot of sexual energy and a high. The chemicals that flow in your body during such an event, with the energy from the band and the crowd, definitely create a physiological sexual charge.

I'm certainly one to say go for your dreams. Anything is possible, even meeting a star and really getting together. A work assignment can bring you together, as it did for Linda

Eastman, who did her first photo shoot of Beatle Paul McCartney, and ended up marrying him. You can just meet by chance, too; you don't have to be a celebrity yourself. Guys in grunge bands these days have told me they met their girlfriends getting a haircut, playing pool in a restaurant, waiting in an airport. One girl supposedly did what you did— mailed her bra—to a *90210* hunk and ended up snagging him. Always go for your dreams—so do whatever you want to, to make contact, but also get on with your life with out it.

Georgina: *"I was backstage at a concert for Extreme and I'm madly in love with Gary Cherone. I'd love to have sex with him, he seems so sweet."*

He is. Gary has been an Honorary Love Doctor on *LovePhones* and I saw him in concerts here and at the Monsters of Rock in England. Friends agree that he is not into the typical rock-star wild sex life. One even tells the story of beautiful models being in his room on his bed, waiting for his move, and Gary enjoyed just talking to them and reading from the Bible. A good man loves his mother, and Gary apparently does that (he even wears saddle shoes on stage that remind him of her, as good luck charms). So, know that you have good taste—and find a man who is equally exciting and not a run-around.

Debbie: *"I'm obsessed with Bon Jovi. I play his music and think of him while I'm having sex with my husband. Sometimes I ask my husband to pretend he's Jon. He's getting sick of it. What should I do?"*

What does making love with Jon Bon Jovi allow you to act like? What does Jon mean to you? If you think in your head, "Oh, he's so cool, he's gorgeous," you can think those things about your husband. Switch the picture of Jon in your head with the image of your husband, so they merge.

My final word on this subject of loss and obsession is, like my friend Reverend Ruth Green, says:

There is no such thing as rejection, just someone going in another direction.

*"I WENT TO VISIT MY FRIEND AND HIS MOTHER
was there and she looked good and one thing led to
another and . . . it just happened."* URGGHH.
*"We were hanging out and my boyfriend's best friend
put his hand in my lap and . . . it just happened."*
URRGGGHHHHH.
*"I was just watching a video and he came over and put his
hand on my thigh, and . . . IT JUST HAPPENED."*
URRRGGGHHHHHHH.

HELLO. NOTHING JUST HAPPENS.

When something happens you know maybe wasn't right,
have you ever said, "It just happened"? I can't tell you how
often I hear that story. Baloney. Nothing just happens.
People make it happen. You choose it. Everybody's
Responsible. You have to take responsibility.

There are two kinds of Sexual No-No's: the sexual things
you do that you excuse by saying, "It just happened," when
you really have to take responsibility for it, and the sexual
abuses that happen that are really not your fault. In this
chapter, we'll go through how to deal with both of those.

You know I'm pretty reasonable when it comes to what
you want to do. I help you be strong enough to get what you
want, and reassure you when you're worried about whether
what you do is normal. I want you to feel good about your
desires and yourself.

But there are limits. There are some things I am just not
down with. And neither should you be.

Remember, the Three R's Rule: **Respect yourself and others; Be Responsible** (think about what you do and consider the consequences); and the **Right to Say Yes or No to Sex.**

Here are some things you should say a resounding "no" to.

SEXUAL BETRAYAL

Whatever happened to good old-fashioned loyalty? It seems to have disappeared these days, when people would rather gratify their immediate urges than think about how others would feel. If there's an attractive offer, they go for it, throwing caution, better judgment, and loyalty out the window.

But trust is a nurturing, comforting feeling—knowing someone would not hurt you. And being trustworthy—knowing you wouldn't hurt others and can be counted on—is an important element of self esteem. It means you would defend, support, care for, and protect someone, or that someone would do this for you.

Betrayal of trust is devastating, and when it involves sex, it ups the ante. I hear so many tales of sexual betrayal on *LovePhones*. The "it just happened" story of sex betrayal ("I couldn't help myself") comes in all combinations.

Danny: *"I was over my girlfriend's house, sitting on the couch, waiting for her to come home and her mother came in and asked me if I wanted something to drink. I kidded around and said I'd like a beer, and to my surprise she brought me one and one for herself, and sat down on the couch next to me. We had the beer and she asked me what was going on with my girlfriend, and if we were having sex. I got into telling her what it was like, and she said I must be a good kisser, so I showed her how I kiss. Then she put my hand inside her blouse, and before you know it, I was doing her right there in the living room. It just happened. Now I go over her house and we haven't said anything about it. I try not to look at her mother, but sometimes she brushes against me, and I can't help thinking that she gave me better head than my girlfriend. I'd like to get with her again, but what if my girlfriend found out?"*

You should have been thinking about that before you showed her mother how you kiss. Nothing just happens! *You* choose what happens. Now you've gone and ruined your girlfriend's life. If she finds out, there is no way she can ever ever forget the pain of such a double betrayal—by her boyfriend and by her parent. Life will never be the same for her. She will never fully and innocently trust anyone again. And understandably so. The two people she should have felt most cared for her, and had her best interests in mind, betrayed her.

You and her mother have some real deep problems. There are always deeper motives for any action. Examine what they are. Her mother may have wanted to prove she is attractive, or maybe she's really competitive with her daughter. It's likely she's frustrated and angry at her husband and getting even with him; she betrayed him, too. Possibly she had incest in her own family and is reenacting the pattern, as many people do. Maybe you're both buying into the Oedipus complex, sex between the mother and (symbolic) son.

As for you, similar dynamics may be at work. You may think it was just fun, or that she seduced you, or that the thrill of sex with an older woman overcame you, but look deeper. Having sex with your girlfriend's mother may be an unconscious incest, to win your own mother from your father. Or a sibling rivalry to win maternal favor from your brothers and sisters.

Beware when the trap is set for you to betray others:

- If you are having family problems (your parents are breaking up);
- If you need to compete with others to prove you're desirable;
- If you give in too easily to your sexual impulses or others' seductions;
- If you define yourself by particularly difficult sexual conquests;
- If you get turned on by risky situations;
- If you're jealous of others' sexual liaisons.

In any case, when you betray someone's trust, you erode your own self-esteem. Remember my "Mirror Law" of

Attraction, that every relationship is a reflection of what you're creating in your own life—in this case, distrust. What you do to others is what you do to yourself. Take a look at what you are creating, and hesitate before you act. Walk a mile in the other person's shoes. How would you feel if your girlfriend did that to you? Not good, I'm sure! Always consider the consequences of your actions. Even if your girlfriend doesn't find out, you have to live with the guilt of doing this—so I doubt this is a good relationship to continue.

Evan, 21: *"My stepmother is twenty-four, only three years older than me. My father is fifty-two. She's always been attractive to me. She's real hot, someone does her hair and she rides in a limo. When my father went to a conference out of town, I went shopping with my stepmother in the limo. Then she took me for a fancy dinner, and on the way home we got stuck in traffic. She asked me what I thought about her and as I was saying how I like her, she said come close to her and kissed me. We continued when we got home, in their bedroom all night. I'm sure she liked that I'm a young thing like her. When my father came home we pretended like nothing happened. But I feel bad because he's my dad but we never got along because he always had affairs, but I have a trust fund I don't want to lose. Maybe she should feel guilty, but it was building up and like a cork had to pop."*

There are no excuses, but I can see explanations. You're angry at your father for leaving your mother and for cheating on her so you got back at him. You better resolve your anger with him more maturely, like have it out with him. Meanwhile, you better never go near your stepmother again.

It depresses me to no end that people are so selfish today. If you think the '70s were the age of the "Me Generation," I think we're in a New Age of Narcissism now. People are so fearful that they don't have enough, so worried about money, so disillusioned about relationships and government, that they don't care about others. I so often see people do what they want without considering the impact of their actions on others.

With friends like this, you don't need enemies.

John: *"I went to visit my girlfriend and I went upstairs to her bedroom, but she wasn't there. Her younger sister was in her room, looking through her drawers. She was going to borrow a shirt and when she pulled it out, she asked me if I would tell her if it looked good. So she took off her T-shirt right in front of me and put this other tight thing on. Then she asked me if it was too revealing, and too sexy. It was too much. I pushed her on the bed and we did it. It just happened. She was always so hot looking and she was a better lay than my girlfriend, so much freer. I never realized how uptight my girlfriend is. Now I'd rather be seeing her sister."*

You already ruined your girlfriend's life by doing it with her sister. Now if you dump her and date her sister, she'll be devastated constantly. How can you be so cruel? If you want to break up with your girlfriend, fine, but find someone else not related to her.

Hah, you were used too! Her sister, just as selfish as you, must have some sibling rivalry competition going, to steal her sister's boyfriend. Don't let yourself be a pawn in the sisters drama.

And don't give me the "raging hormone" defense that you just got turned on and carried away. Always take responsibility for your actions. Use the "Stop and Think" technique. Hesitate before you act and consider (1) Do I really want to do this? (2) What effect will this action have on others? (3) How would I feel if the shoe was on the other foot (if your girlfriend slept with your brother)?

Restate saying "It just happened" to take responsibility. In your case, say, "I went to visit my girlfriend and her sister looked good and I DECIDED to have sex with her." It's a whole new ball game when you see that you choose every thing you do.

Advice from Bob Guccione, Jr., *Spin* magazine editor: "In the name of decency, if you're not happy with your girlfriend, break up. At least if she ever finds out, you're not two-timing her."

Have you heard about Rodeo Sex? That's where you make love to your girlfriend from behind and you say "from behind you look a lot like your sister" and you try to stay on her for at least eight seconds without getting thrown off.

If you become aware of something hurtful, call it. Painful as that may be, better to get it out in the open.

Carrie, 16: *"I came home and saw my mom French kissing my boyfriend on the stoop. She's divorced. Should I say anything to her?"*

Absolutely! Tell her how she hurt you badly and ask her to explain how she could ever do that. Tell her it was so selfish. You must talk about it. You can't keep it inside you. I'm so sorry this happened. Your mother should know better.

No matter how devastating betrayal is, you must not think you cannot face it, or that you are so wiped out that you are driven to kill the other person, or yourself. Like Steven: *"My girlfriend had sex with my best friend on my couch and I caught them and now I feel like shooting her in the head or banging my head against the wall."*

It's helpful to let yourself purge the feelings by imagining the worst punishment you would dole out, but don't fixate on this negativity. Words have a possibility of becoming reality. Say more positive things to yourself. "I'm wiped or angry but I can handle this." Nothing ever warrants that loss of control. If people act so low, that doesn't mean you have to ruin your life over it. Living well is the best revenge and the only salvation.

Friends often let themselves get busy with their friend's boyfriend or girlfriend.

Kelly: *"My friend Kyla's boyfriend did it with her older sister. But he also did it with me. Me and Kyla were best friends, but I knew him before she did. One time I just asked him what's going on with them and he was telling me the intimate things he did with her, and then he kissed me. How can Kyla think he loves her if he did that to me? How does she know he won't do that to a hundred other girls? He said Kyla wouldn't have sex with him. What should I do?"*

Get out of it. He's obviously not having sex with his girlfriend, so he's getting the action elsewhere and he's getting three women—all of whom are close to each other—involved in a fighting match over him. What's so great about him? He's a troublemaker. So what if you knew him first? All of you should dump him and make up.

Fortunately, people sometimes call me before betrayal happens.

"My girlfriend's sister is making passes at me. I'm close to taking her up on it, especially since my girlfriend is withholding sex from me since we had an argument."

Don't do it. Do you want to be used by your girlfriend's sister—for her own purposes, to get back at her sister, to prove she's more attractive, whatever? Don't get into a pattern of revenge against your girlfriend even if she's withholding sex. Tell her I said you shouldn't use sex as a weapon when you're angry. Talk about why you're angry and fix that.

You have to be willing to see the impact of your actions and get control of your impulses. Think and talk it through. Where does it lead? What do you stand to gain or lose? Who gains and who loses?

Chris: *"I have a little problem. I am a senior in high school and I have been going out with this girl who's a senior in college for about a year now. I knew she had a sister who's a freshman in college. I had never seen her before, I had only seen pictures of her. She came home for the weekend and I saw her. I saw her and I automatically fell in love. I feel bad. I have been calling her and my girlfriend would answer the phone and I would ask for her sister. I feel bad about it. We went out once or twice. It's like completely cheating on my girlfriend. I feel really bad."*

But, Chris, let's think this through. If you feel badly about something you are doing, why would you persist in doing it? Who are you hurting?

Chris: *"I'm hurting my girlfriend. I am hurting her sister probably right now."*

And who else?

Chris: *"I am hurting probably myself because I will get screwed in the long run. If I go out with her and I keep going out with her sister, it would work for a while, but once they find out I am cheating on her, it'll be bad, and I'll have a really hard time getting some other dates. I understand that now. I am probably going to apologize to both of them and probably buy her a dozen roses and treat her right from now on. I am going to dump her younger sister."*

Good for you. You figured it out.

It's better to be safe than sorry—like when it comes to dating a friend's ex, as Patty wanted to know:

"Should I feel guilty sleeping with my best friend's ex-boyfriend after they broke up?"

There are lots of fish in the sea. Pick one who doesn't trigger complications. Even when people break up, they have residual feelings, which take a long time (up to half the time of the relationship) to get over and even then some of the pain remains. Seeing you with her ex, even if she broke it off, is a constant reminder. Why have that residue potentially interfere with your relationship with a boyfriend? If you do, it only means you're unconsciously inviting a rivalry or competition with her. Best to find your own boyfriend from scratch.

If you have to do it, talk to both of them about how they feel about it. Tell your girlfriend you don't want to start anything with him if it will hurt her. Wait up to six months 'til after they have stopped seeing each other. Be prepared for the complications that will come from all of you being together.

DECEPTION: SEXUAL LIES

People usually lie in order to avoid arguing and to control a situation. By telling the truth, you could risk losing the person, or a situation you want. But remember the old saying,

"Oh, what a tangled web we weave when first we practice to deceive." People go to confession for a reason—to unburden the guilt of lying. Most people want to confess, they want to be found out, they want to live more authentically.

I once did a *Richard Bey* show on sexual secrets people wanted to unload. One girl wanted to tell her ex-boyfriend that she purposefully didn't take her birth-control pills because she wanted to get pregnant (which she did; they have a five-year-old now), so she could keep the guy forever. Nyeaijah was posing as a guy's cousin to live in the house with him and his girlfriend, Tataneisha, and have sex with him behind her back.

I'm always in favor of honesty, but not at the expense of damaging another person's life. Avoid lying, but there are rare situations when the whole truth is very hurtful and silence is kinder. I think if you're not too deep into a relationship where betrayal has taken place, you should end the relationship. Otherwise you're constantly carrying around that negative energy of keeping a hurtful secret or taking advantage of someone's innocence.

The second type of No-No's involve situations where you're being treated poorly. In some cases you take the crumbs, because you think you love the person. In others, you know what's going on is wrong, but you feel too scared to deal with it.

SEXUAL HARASSMENT

"Hostile Hallways" are plaguing students. One Harris poll showed sexual harassment in junior high had reached epidemic proportions—with eight out of ten girls and nearly as many boys reporting it. A similar poll of over 1,600 8th-through-11th graders in seventy-nine schools showed three out of four girls and over half of boys complained of being the butt of sexual comments, jokes, or looks. The next complaint was being touched, grabbed, or pinched. Thirteen percent of girls and 9 percent of boys

had been "forced to do something sexual other than kissing." Of all students, 18 percent said they had been
harassed by a school employee. The seventh grade seemed
to be the most vulnerable. And the hallways were the most
dangerous.

Michelle, 15: *"This guy at school keeps telling me I'm flat
and rubs the wall moaning, 'Oh Michelle.' Why is he doing
this to me and how do I get him to stop?"*

This guy is harassing you. He's being a bully, trying to
show off in front of his friends, or showing his power
because deep down he feels powerless. Probably he's been
picked on at home, or is mimicking someone else's bully
behavior. In some cases, if the comments are awkward but
not offensive, a young guy may be really embarrassed or
uncomfortable about showing he likes someone, and have
poor social skills, so he acts stupid, like this guy, or ends up
showing his attention in exactly the opposite way than he
intends, offending rather than pleasing you. Next time, test
if that's the case, by saying something to turn him around,
like, "If you like me and don't know how to show it, say
something nice instead of doing these stupid things." If he
doesn't respond, and keeps harassing you, tell him to stop it
and then ignore him. If it persists, tell him you're going to
report him. You don't have to stand for this.

TITTY GRABBER

Steve, 14: *"I see girls in the hall and I have to grab their
titties. They like it. Three out of ten say they like it. One girl
yelled. Why would she do that?"*

Stop this right away. They do not like it. Your thoughts
and perceptions of women are all wrong. You are headed
for big trouble. Your behavior is harassment, not cute.
Some girl could complain to the school and file a suit
against you with the police. You could get arrested.

You have a need for attention, but this is negative attention.
Also, you don't think girls will like you for you, so you're acting like this. Develop some other attention-grabbing
behavior—like being the smartest or funniest kid in school.

Participate in the school play since you have a flair for the dramatic. Or write some article for the school newspaper, or start a new club for whatever you're interested in.

In some surveys, half of women report having been harassed. Men get harassed, too. Recently the laws changed to define harassment not just as actions but anything that creates a "hostile work environment." Mario was harassed by a rich guy he went to for a job interview. The guy said to him, "Sure, there's a position in my company for you. It's called, 'bend over.'" That's your cue to walk out. Say with dignity, "That kind of unacceptable behavior means this is not the place for me, nor should it be for any other self-respecting person." Consider reporting the guy.

It's crackdown time. People are not getting away with grabbing and forcing anymore. Mike Tyson went to prison for it. Even Hollywood kick-boxing tough guy Jean Claude Van Damme was hit with a multimillion-dollar lawsuit accusing him of sexually assaulting a Louisiana woman in a New Orleans hotel room, barging nude into her room with his exotic-dancer date and getting into her bed, groping, fondling, and forcing her to perform oral sex on him until she feigned passing out.

"I was swimming at my girlfriend's house, and when I went upstairs to get changed, I was standing there with nothing on and her father barged in and stared at me nude. I told him to get out, but he just stood there. When my friend started to come up the stairs, he sneaked out. I was very upset but made up an excuse, telling her I was sick and had to go home. Should I never go back there again?"

Of course you were upset. Your girlfriend's father's intrusion in your room and staring at your naked body was inappropriate and should not go ignored. Like in any abusive experience, you must trust it is not your fault, you are not to blame for his lewd behavior. You might be petrified to tell anyone, intimidated by authority figures, or fearful that they would assume you asked for it (leaving the door open, wearing a skimpy suit, not complaining at the time), or think they would doubt it really happened (as he would likely deny it, pitting your word against his). Take back control by doing something about it. Tell your friend (she may deny it or be accustomed to such behavior and accept it, not realizing it's wrong). Tell your parents and discuss the difference between an innocent intrusion (with immediate apology and retreat), casual looking, and lewd invasiveness that deserves a stern response. For more information about what constitutes sexual harassment, how to confront the harasser, and what to do if it continues, call the 9 to 5 National Association of Working Women hotline.

Carin: *"My boyfriend's stepfather was driving me home because my boyfriend's car broke down. He stopped the car a few blocks from my house and said he wanted to talk to me. He was worried abut my boyfriend not doing well at school and thought maybe he was spending too much time with me, and maybe he should dock him. I was upset and started to cry and he started kissing my tears up. I told him we shouldn't do it, but I let him kiss me. We didn't go all the way, but he put his hand down my pants and I did him. Now I feel disgusted about it and I can't face my boyfriend. What should I do?"*

It's what you should have done then—told your boyfriend's stepfather where to go and gotten out of the car yourself. But that's hindsight. This is surely a stark lesson. Unfortunately, you never said no, but it is still sexual harassment, since he is an adult and an authority figure, and manipulated you. You should tell him off, to get back your power. Then you can tell your parents and decide whether to press charges. Don't ever be around when he's around.

Tina, 15: *"I baby-sit for this guy and sometimes when he and his wife come home and she goes up to bed and he's supposed to drive me home, he says to me, 'Oh, stay, come downstairs in the basement with me and watch a video.' I say I have to get home, but he's really attractive and I'd like to do it. I like his kids and don't want to stop baby-sitting for them, and I'm really friendly with his wife and I like her. Can I watch the video with him?"*

You're asking me if you can get sexual with him and get away with it. No! You'll ruin your friendship with his wife, you'll ruin their marriage, and you'll end up suffering—being thrown out of their family, feeling guilty, and getting angry at yourself for giving in and at him for using you.

You dig it that he comes on to you. What family scenario might you be acting out—having the daddy come on to you while the mommy isn't around? Is that what happened in your own family? Recognize the ghost of the past and don't fall prey to repeating it. If you can't stop your attraction to him, then stop baby-sitting there. Granted you'll miss the family, but you will have saved yourself a lot of trouble!

HARASSMENT ON THE JOB

Long Dong Silver raised our nation's awareness of sexual harassment in the past few years. That was the name now Judge Clarence Thomas supposedly gave his penis, according to his former employee who accused him of unwanted sexual advances, including leaving pubic hairs on a Coke can.

Judge Thomas got confirmed, but the laws against sexual harassment have changed. Now, rather than just unwanted, unwelcome, or repeated advances that are objectionable (like fondling or suggestive remarks), sexual harassment includes creating a "hostile work environment," like gestures or posting pornographic pinups, and threats about firing if an employee doesn't comply with a boss's sexual invitations.

Studies show that over half of working women have experienced sexual harassment at some point in their careers. Only a small percent were assaulted, one in ten were pressured for sex, and a quarter were touched; the largest number, one third, were subjected to unwanted sexual remarks. You don't have to put up with any of it.

Gloria: *"I love my job, but my married male supervisor is making passes at me. Once at a business dinner I ordered juice, and he leaned over and whispered in my ear, 'If you want juice, come back to the office and I'll give you all the*

*juice you'll ever want.' I didn't know what to do and just
laughed it off, pretending he didn't mean it. But it bothers
me. He does it a lot, patting me on the tush when I pass him
in the hall and asking me what I'm wearing on my dates.
Last week he told me if I was nice to him, he'd be sure I get
to own my own business someday, which is exactly what I
want! He's a nice guy other than that, and I don't want to
lose my job, because I'm doing well now and learning a lot,
and because I do want to open my own company like this
for my future. What should I do?"*

Stop laughing it off, pretending you didn't hear, and
making excuses for him, which can give him a mixed message or make him push more. You're being harrassed. You
have to have courage; overcome your fears about "not being
nice" or speaking up, and don't give in to his threats. Tell
him to stop. Better than saying, "You're lewd," or "That's
gross," which may only make him defensive, say things
like, "I don't appreciate your making comments about my
body," or "I prefer that you don't talk to me that way," or
"We have a valuable professional relationship and if I've
done anything to give you the impression I'm interested in a
sexual relationship, I didn't mean to." Studies show that
some men aren't aware they're offending you.

Find out about your company's sexual-harassment policies and resources (since the Thomas–Hill hearings, many
companies have beefed these up). If he doesn't stop, go to
the human resources person. Call the women's organizations who deal with this, for support and steps to take.
Meanwhile, keep notes on what he does and your stress
about it, get any witnesses, and then stay away from him.
Find out if other women on the job have similar experiences. You may have to leave the job. Have confidence
you'll be better off elsewhere. No job is worth your self-
respect.

IT HAPPENS TO HIM

As more women rise in the corporate world to positions
of power, men are becoming subject to sexual harassment,

too. *Disclosure*, the Michael Douglas–Demi Moore movie about this, brought the problem out in the open.

Frank had the experience: *"I work in a doughnut shop and the owner of the shop is coming on to me. She licks her fingers in front of me and told me if I'm nice to her she'll make me manager on the weekends. I need the money to finish school, but I really don't want to have sex with her. She's married and she's pretty ugly. How do I make her stop without losing my job?"*

In one study of a thousand men and women, 67 percent of the men (compared with 17 percent of women) said they'd be flattered if propositioned at work. But don't think you're not a man if you don't like it. A woman using her power over you, when unwanted, is not fun, it's harassment. Guys who are harassed can be more distressed than women because they're not taken as seriously, since men are expected to like come-ons.

The rest of my advice is the same as it would be for a woman in this situation: avoid being alone with her, but make it clear the next time she makes an advance, in a polite but firm voice, that you love working there, but it's not a good idea to have a personal relationship because it's too complicated and not right for her or for you. If she doesn't back off and respect that, look for another job. You'll be better off anyway. Consider reporting her.

Studies show up to 15 percent of male workers feel victimized. In August 1994, actor Jon Voight, the star of *Coming Home, Midnight Cowboy,* and *Deliverance* sued his former business partner, saying she was more interested in making sexual moves on him than making movies, that she constantly asked for "more hello-hugs and longer good-bye kisses on the cheek," and when he didn't respond, she sabotaged their production company.

A'S FOR LAYS

I know you'd heard about the infamous Hollywood casting couch, but schools are another breeding ground for trading sex for grades or other favors.

Genie: *"My hockey coach came on to me after practice the other day and I want to make the junior team so I'm thinking of going along with it. Is this a bad idea?"*

It's not a good idea to start a pattern of trading sex for favors. Get ahead on your ability, not sex.

I can understand your falling for an attentive and attractive teacher or coach. It's seductive to have someone in authority support, encourage, and appreciate you. Special attention is seductive! Set limits. Get his attention for your being a sports star or student, but don't take it any further. Instead, notice the qualities that you like in him and how he makes you feel, and look for it in an appropriate boyfriend who has these same qualities.

Also, the coach, teacher, or authority figure can get into a lot of trouble, like being fired. Take a horrifying lesson from Alex's situation: *"I teach high school and I had sex with one of my students. I met him at a bar one night and I drove him home and we did it in the car. I saw him a couple of times after, but he kept hanging around wanting to see me. One night he went over to my house and I came home and found him in the kitchen with my wife. I threw him out and the next night I came home and my wife said he called and told her I had sex with him. She called the police and now the school's going to find out. We have a three-year-old daughter. What can I do? Why did he go and tell?"*

Guess you'll have to face the music now. It's tragic how acting on impulses and needs with inappropriate partners can lead to such disaster. Truth is, your life as you know it now is ruined and about to drastically change. You need a lawyer and counseling for you and your wife, as likely she is devastated and angry.

Many schools are discouraging even consensual faculty-student sex. Harvard's code not only says the teacher and student can get in trouble, but if you know about it and don't report it, you get in trouble too. The University of Virginia tried to ban all sex between students and teachers, but when the ACLU (American Civil Liberties Union) challenged it as unconstitutional (violating privacy rights), the faculty limited the ban to sex with students they teach or supervise.

DOCTOR-PATIENT

Maira: *"I have a weird question. I have a girlfriend who goes to the gynecologist and she tells me he sniffs the tools and sniffs the gloves to find out if there is an infection. Is this normal? I am not kidding. She had another gynecologist, so she tells me, that after he gave her an internal he said, 'You must be good in bed.'"*

These are terribly unethical doctors. Certainly, some of the symptoms of some female disorders do have a distinct odor as a sign. But it would not be appropriate for him to do a sniff test. You should never go back, and the one who made a sexual advance should be reported to a professional licensing board. Jagger's suggestion: "Send a ninety-year-old woman in and see if he does the same examination!"

Actress Sean Young, as Honorary Love Doctor, thinks if you feel "odd," something's wrong: "I am afraid to sniff my own vagina, let alone somebody else's. Cheesy-peesy. I would be really suspicious of my doctor if they started sniffing around. "

It is egregious—and unethical—for any person in authority (therapist, doctor, teacher) to force you to have sex. But it's understandable how it can happen.

Sandra fell prey to her therapist: *"I've been going to a counselor for a year and we have special sessions. He knows how I feel my father didn't love me, so he promised to teach me that not all men are bad. I'm not supposed to have sex with my boyfriend until he shows me how to trust men. One time when I was crying about my father he kissed me on the mouth and the next few times, I had to lie on the couch for relaxation therapy, where he would lay down on top of me, so I could feel that he cared for me like my father didn't. He massages me while I talk about my problems, and last time, he said I was ready for the next step where I took off my clothes. I was shaking, but he insisted I was learning to trust, and I do want to go back to my boyfriend. Am I doing the right thing?"*

It's your therapist who is doing wrong. He is abusing you and violating the code of ethics. You should report him and never go back. Like other abusers, he twists the facts to get you to do what he wants. Ethical therapy helps you talk through your problems and build loving relationships with real people in your life. You need a support group and a new ethical, qualified therapist to rebuild your trust.

FORCES BROTHER TO WATCH

Bill, 17: *"My older brother brings slutty girls into the house and makes me sit on a chair and watch him have sex with them. He says it's for me 'to be a man.' He puts the girls' ankles behind their head. One girl played with me. I don't want to do it, but he'll beat me up if I don't."*

Your brother is being abusive, cruel, and crude. It sounds like he is a real obnoxious exhibitionist who can't have healthy relationships with women, and picks slutty ones so he doesn't have to respect them. Since he said he wants to teach you to be a man, he may also be concerned that you may be gay. Or he could be concerned about his own gay tendencies, so he has to choose women he can use or put down, and have sex with another guy in the room. Whatever his reasons or problems, refuse to participate. If he doesn't leave you alone, tell him you're going to tell your parents.

SEXUAL BLACKMAIL

Like sexual harassment, there's an insidious behavior, now pervasive, I call "sexual blackmail." I hear so many stories about sexual blackmail—people forcing others to do things they want by holding something over their head. It's despicable. And it seems more prevalent than ever because of the current new wave narcissism and disrespect for others. It often happens between peers, as well as, like harassment, from an authority figure to a subordinate.

Leslie: *"My boyfriend has pictures of me nude and said if I don't have anal sex with him, he'll show the pictures to all his frat brothers. Should I do it?"*

Veronica, 17: *"I slept with this older guy, and now he's*

*calling my house and told me if I don't see him that he'll tell
my boyfriend we had sex."*

Dreyfuss: *"I had sex with my friend's girlfriend. She offered
me money and more sex if I don't tell the guy. Should I take
it?"*

Ryan 21: *"I have a foot fetish and I was flirting with my
good friend's girlfriend, touching her feet and telling her
I wanted to suck them. She said if I didn't have sex with
her, she would spread it all over school that I'm into
feet."*

Rob: *"This teacher let me put my hand up her dress in the
teachers' lounge. I know she just got married. Now I have
her where I want her, because I can tell on her unless she
gives me a good grade."*

Steve: *"My boyfriend pours hot wax on me. I don't like it,
but he said if I don't do it he'll tell the other kids that I'm
gay, and he'll find someone else who will do it."*

Vanessa: *"I met a guy I really like but he's a little strange
because he makes his dog more important than me.
Sometimes when I come over, he tells me I have to wait
until he finishes shampooing the dog. A lot of times he
strokes him and makes me look when the dog's pink thing
comes out. The other night, he told me he wanted me to
do it to the dog and if I didn't he would tell my parents
that I had sex and that a friend of mine did, too. I started
to cry. Our parents would kill us if they found out. What
should I do?"*

This guy is a dog. This is sexual blackmail! I know you
feel trapped, but definitely don't let him coerce you into
having sex with his dog. Never see him again. He doesn't
care for you, except to use you. Would you let a friend treat
you like that? If he tells, you'll have to face the music with
your parents. Turn the obstacle into an opportunity to talk
with your parents anyway.

A more subtle form of blackmail is the taunt, "If you
loved me, you'd . . ." Like Josephine's boyfriend saying, "If
you loved me, you'd do it with my cousin and let me
watch." Or Laura's boyfriend pressuring her to prove her

love by having sex with another woman and him. Or Carly's guy insisting she doesn't love him unless she has sex with him every night he wants it.

You have the right to set your limits. Consider if this person is making such demands. Is that love? If you give in to this blackmail, what else will they demand of you?

BUTT OF RUMORS

Another form of sexual blackmail, and a big issue with friends today, is that a friend will spread a story about you. Christy: *"I have a friend who told me she goes both ways. I told her I didn't and she had to respect that. But after a few times of staying over at my house, she went around telling everyone we slept together. I didn't. I don't know how to confront her about why did she tell other people we slept together. She has a man and they like to have sex with another woman and she's trying to get me and my other friends to sleep with her and her man."*

She wanted to get you in on what she's doing, to make what's she doing right. Don't give in to her sexual blackmail. Go up to her and tell her you don't appreciate that she's spreading stories, and to stop, and that you won't let her manipulate you. You can't stop her from making up and telling stories, so just know in your heart you didn't do it and tell your friends she made it up and hope they believe you.

OTHER OFF-LIMITS BEHAVIOR:

TOO ROUGH SEX

Dvonne: "When my boyfriend and I try to have sex, he handcuffs me to the bed. I like it at first, but then it drags on, and after that it gets violent. He slaps me around and I tell him to stop and he says he's sorry and calms down. He bought Madonna's book, Sex, *and he says he wants to try the different things in there."*

I'm glad he stops when you say so, but it sounds like it's getting out of hand. Salt-N-Pepa, *LovePhones* Honorary

Love Doctors for the night, agreed: "If he keeps doing that, don't let him tie you up. Let him know that you are serious. You should really tell him that it hurts and that you don't like it. It sounds like you're under pressure to please your man, and while you're pleasing him you're going through things that you don't want to go through and that's never good! He also has to respect your feelings and your wishes."

This is definitely a No-No: doing something just to keep someone! URGGHHH!!! Self-respect rules!

Amanda, 25: *"My boyfriend is rough in sex. When he goes down on me in sex, he presses real hard right on the tip of my button. I beg him to go around it, but he presses harder."*

Your boyfriend is an oaf. A hardheaded thick-skulled, self-ish macho, who can't take directions and clearly is more concerned about what he wants to do with your body than what you like. You can try to give him some suggestions about what you prefer in a positive way so he's not threatened, but I doubt he cares what you want. Dump him.

BREATHLESS ORGASM

Francine: *I was having sex with my boyfriend and then he suggested that we do something he heard about. He wanted to get some rope and tie it around each other's necks and then make it tight so when we reached the peak of our orgasm that it would be a real high. He said it would be like having a hard time catching your breath, like your mind would pop like it does when you do some drugs like pop-pers. I don't know because I never tried any of that. It sounded scary but I like to do whatever he wants to please him, but I want to know if this could be dangerous.*

Damn straight it's dangerous, and downright deadly. Forget about pleasing your boyfriend, you could both end up dead, or you dead and he in jail for murder. You know that love-struck phrase, "You take my breath away"—well some people desperately seeking the "breathless orgasm" strangle themselves or a partner to bring on a sexual high.

It's called "sexual asphyxia," or "asphyxiophilia," or simply "rough sex." It was a murder scene in the movie *Rising Sun,* but a real life disaster in the infamous case of the "Yuppie Murderer," Robert Chambers, who went too far with "rough sex" with a girl in Central Park. She ended up dead, and he's in jail. It can be called murder, or if you're lucky, manslaughter with the death ruled as "inadvertent strangulation during consensual sex." One twenty-two-year-old guy faced three to seven years for tightening a rope around his girlfriend's neck while she squeezed his throat; as he passed out and slumped, the rope pulled deadly tight. When I was at a speaking engagement down south, a mother alerted me that kids in the local high school were all doing it, as a craze, like the once-popular inhaling glue or the gaseous capsules for industrial whipped cream dispensers called Whip-Its. Parents were suspicious that in some cases where kids were found strangled with their own belt, suffocated in plastic bags, or suspended by a tie from a lighting fixture, police were calling it suicide when really it was strangulating sex in attempts to stimulate. Very stupid.

Don't think that you can pull a rope tight and if it's too much that you will faint or pass out and it'll be released. When you pass out, the rope can get tighter; any 'accident' can happen to make it choke, not release, you. The best sex is when you breathe deeply, not HOLD your breath!

See the chapter Am I A Freak, on where to draw the line with other types of rough sex and S&M games.

CALLS ANOTHER NAME IN SEX

"Three times my boyfriend has called out his ex-girlfriend's name while we were having sex. It's upset me so much, but I was afraid to say anything. What should I say to him?"

Tell him when he does it. Of course it's upsetting to you—it shows he's still thinking of her. If you're sure of your relationship, tell him he better make an effort not to do it. He can practice by deliberately saying your name aloud during lovemaking many times, so it becomes a habit and sticks in his mind.

"T": The only other guys' names I don't mind
my girlfriend calling out when we have sex are,
"Oh Jesus, Oh Christ, and Oh God.

OBSCENE PHONE CALLER

Kaity: *"Me and my best friend were getting perverted phone calls. This guy would call and say, 'Take off your panties. Look at my big hard cock. Put your wet mouth on it. I'm stuffing my cock in your pussy.' We put a phone trace on our phone and it turned out to be my best friend's new husband. They charged him with disorderly conduct and he got fined, but how do we face her now?"*

It's a shame he did that! Guys can seem normal and still do things like that. There was a big story about a professor at American University who was leading a "normal" life to the outside world, "happily" married, yet making obscene phone calls to strange women. He got caught when he called a policeman's wife and she traced the calls. Then he wrote a book about it, tracing his actions to his childhood, when he was sexually abused by his mother, and explaining how this was his way to both get back at her by shocking women about sex, and repair his hurts. Tell your friend you understand and you don't blame her. She's likely ashamed; so tell her you understand that her husband's behavior is not really meant to hurt you, but because of his deep-seated problems which you hope he gets help for.

PICKUP HORROR

Anthony, 22: *"I picked up a guy at a gay bar and took him home with me. He robbed me and tried to smother me with a pillow when we were having sex. What can I do?"*

Go to the police. And stop picking up strangers. You could have been dead. Don't treat yourself like a piece of meat, a nameless sex bang. Do affirmations: "I am a lovable person who needs to be loved, not abused and robbed."

DEFILES FOOD

Coty: *"I work in a bagel shop and after the bagels are done we do them. We ejaculate into the bagels and serve them to steady customers we hate who are bastards who come in and catch an attitude like, 'Hurry up, give me my food.' We have a special basket we put them in and get a thrill giving them one of the hot bagels. They deserve it."*

What a disgusting thing to do. A stewardess once told me she put powdered laxative in the food of passengers she felt were obnoxious. And people who work in restaurants have all kinds of stories about how the help sneeze into food, drop it on the floor, or worse yet ejaculate into all kinds of foodstuffs and serve it to people. As far as I'm concerned, you're hostile—and abusing your job and people. If you don't like someone, have the balls to say something, like, "I'd like to be spoken to nicely."

SEXUAL ABUSE AND INCEST

So many times when I hear tales of woe like, "He cheats on me," or "I'm never satisfied," with the aggravating, "But I love him." I'm upset you let yourself be abused. URGGHHH. But I'm also suspicious there's been sex abuse in the past. So, I always ask, "Who ever treated you as badly, or sexually abused you, before?"

Kathy was married two years. She initally complained to me, *"I flirt with guys a lot and feel guilty."* But that wasn't the real problem. What else is wrong? *"My husband is cold and nasty to me,"* she admitted. Who else treated her so badly, I asked. *"My sister's boyfriend,"* she said. *"He came into my room when I was seven and he touched my breasts and put it in me. I never told my sister and now she's married to him, and when I see him I still get sick. He acts to me like nothing happened. But I hate him. My husband is just like him."*

Monica likes to hurt guys and wonders why. "How have they hurt you?" I asked. *"Someone was bad on me,"* she said, remembering when she was little how her cousin made her rub his penis. Her mother didn't believe her. No wonder Monica's angry; no one protected her.

Shocking statistics show that up to one in four girls and one in seven boys are sexually abused. In a study that was done by my interns, over a third of the callers to my *LovePhones* radio show admitted to having been sexually abused.

Many stars have recently been open about their sexual abuse, including television comedienne Roseanne and her ex-husband Tom Arnold. LaToya Jackson, who wrote a book condemning her parents, said, "I'm just not interested in sex. The abuse I went through as a child had an effect on my adult life." Tori Amos was raped and, around the time of her touring with a major superstar and having to deal with the big time music machine, Sheryl Crow felt sexually harassed. Both women wrote a song about it to help purge the pain.

First Brother Roger Clinton does motivational speaking about the physical abuse in his childhood, mostly at the hands of his father (who died when he was young), who also abused his mother. "It was tough growing up where every memory of my father was one of violence," Roger told me, "but good things can come from pain."

Hearing our heroes' stories can ease our personal pain. TV talk show queen Oprah has also talked about being sexually violated in her youth—a teenage cousin fondled and raped her. "I didn't tell anybody about it," Oprah once said, "because I thought it was my fault, that something must be wrong with me, and that I would be blamed for it." The feelings create a confusing mixture of pleasure and guilt that led to rebelliousness and promiscuity. Oprah ran away from home and got pregnant. Finally she told her family what was going on, even though, as is typical, they didn't want to believe it.

PSYCHOLOGICAL SEXUAL ABUSE

There's a kind of sexual abuse people don't easily recognize—it's not physical, but psychological.

Being undermined and verbally abused is just as destructive as being hit. You're being hit in your heart instead of on your body.

Jasmine's boyfriend makes her miserable. *"He played on me, flirted and grinned all the time and smiled at these girls with great bodies, but if I did anything he called me a porker."*

Lynn's boyfriend also psychologically abuses her. *"After I have sex with my boyfriend he tells me I'm fat and calls me a dope. Am I?"*

Of course not. The only dopey thing you do is put up with it. Prove you're not a dope by dumping him. He's obviously acting out his own abusive scenario probably that he learned from his family, and drawing you into it. Refuse to play into it. He probably feels guilty and, by punishing you after sex, is projecting his own feelings of being "bad" onto you. Remember:

> **There is no enemy without**
> **if there is no enemy within.**

People we choose to put in our life are mirrors of ourselves. He tells you you are fat and stupid because you are telling yourself that. Change your message to yourself. Do positive affirmations: as you tell yourself, "I am beautiful, I love my body," you will come to believe it and put people in your life to reflect that.

CHILDHOOD SEXUAL ABUSE

Caitlin, 16: *"I baby-sit for this little girl who's six and she told me her mother's boyfriend 'made me make sex with him.' I told the mother and she got mad at me and told me never to come baby-sit again. I was really upset, so I told my mother and she called the authorities at the Child Protection Services. Apparently the older brother is in jail because he sexually abused a woman and someone told me the mother abuses the little girl physically. Did I do the right thing? What if it's not happening?"*

Of course you did the right thing. If it's true, you saved the girl's life and proved people will protect and believe her. Likely the mother denied it because she was shocked and ashamed. Let the authorities investigate. Even if it's not true, it's always better to err on the side of protecting the child.

It helps to recognize the common feelings after a trauma so you don't feel alone or abnormal.

Going numb is one of those. Jen experienced it: *"I can't feel anything in sex. I flirt with a lot of guys but then I'm scared to go through with it. I had sex once and felt in control at first but then I got angry because I lost control and felt like a dead fish inside and acted like a robot. What's wrong with me? I was raped when I was four. Does this have something to do with it?"*

Definitely. When you are sexually molested, the most common reaction is to detach from your feelings and the experience—you go out of your body so to speak, in order not to feel the pain, or the guilt. It's common to experience yourself on the ceiling, looking down at this thing happening, or to "go away" to you don't know where. This "dissociation" continues in sexual interactions even with appropriate partners. Because of the earlier sexual abuse where you felt powerless, you are only comfortable in sexual experiences where you do feel in control; but this sense of control is shaky, so you lose it easily. Shed those ghosts from the past.

You can revive your sensitivity with "sensate focus" exercises. Touch yourself (or have your partner touch you) in nonsexual places while you focus on the tiniest sensations. Notice how smooth the skin is, or how soothing the touch feels. Build slowly, constantly giving yourself permission to feel pleasure. Choose only loving partners you can trust. Be in the present instead of the past.

Sometimes the abuse is so traumatic, the dissociation becomes so extreme that you develop "multiple personalities."

Like Trisha: *"I had a boyfriend I loved a lot but when he was making love to me he said he had a surprise and I thought it was a bracelet but it was handcuffs and he grabbed me and I cried. I can't tell anyone."*

I sensed there was another side to Trisha. "Who does know anyway and might get back at him?" I asked her.

"*Kat*," she said, "*she's the bitch who will get him.*" Kat turned out to be her other personality, the tough, "bad" girl side of her. Trisha is typical of girls (some boys too) who have been so abused, they cut off a part of them and put it off to another personality. The "bad" girl doesn't take abuse and may even repeat what the victimizers did, wielding knives, being a bully, while the "good" personality is innocent, helpless, and loving. In a famous book, the story is told how Sybil developed many personalities like this after extreme abuse from her mother, including putting knives in her vagina. In her book, *My Sister Roseanne*, TV's Roseanne Barr's sister, Geraldine, said Roseanne developed twenty-one personalities from being abused.

Some people develop sexual fantasies later in life that protect them from the memories. Like Vance: "*I was raped at fourteen by my father's friend who gave me a massage on the kitchen floor and then did it to me, and now I want to have sex with transvestites.*"

Wanting sex with a transvestite (a man dressed as a woman) is a way for Vance to neutralize the aggression of a man by making him into a woman, and to re-live the experience of sex with a man without fearing he's gay.

THE ABUSERS
"*What kind of man would sexually abuse a child?*"

Many pedophiles are married men with children, so not having a sexual outlet is generally not the reason for abuse. Psychologist Nicholas Groth, director of the sex offender program of the Connecticut Correctional Institution, says 80 percent of the men he treats for sexually abusing children were sexually victimized when they were children, and need to feel dominant and control a sexual partner. These men can appear to be upstanding members of the community. Since they like children, they often choose jobs where they can be around children.

I believe there are two general types: men who feel powerless and need to control helpless youngsters to exert power, and men who are so developmentally stunted, they feel like youngsters themselves, no older than those they abuse.

There's an organization, NAMBLA (the National Association of Man-Boy Love), that supports sex between male adults and young boys—what a sick notion.

Twenty-three-year-old Tony is in trouble as a budding abuser: *"I have a fixation for young girls, eleven or twelve years old. I fantasize about them and think of them when I have sex with a girl I go out with. They seem young and have no worries. I fantasize that they come on to me and I promise to teach them and then they give me oral sex. I think about a neighbor girl most of the time. I'm afraid it's not right and that I'll do it, but I don't want to. It's harder with someone of my own age."*

I'm glad you realize the danger of your fantasy. Stop thinking about these young girls. As soon as the image of a young girl pops into your head, replace it with a girl your own age. You have to retrain your mind; you have do it.

You're clearly insecure and afraid of a real relationship with an equal. You need serious psychiatric help and you need to learn social skills—how to get over being shy and fearing rejection, and practice talking to girls your age and asking for what you want in sex. Get over your own worries, so you feel the childlike innocence you desire. To stop the fantasy, retrain your brain: every time this dangerous fantasy comes into your head, snap your fingers (to interrupt the thought) and subsititute it instead with a healthier one: you with a girl your age smiling at you. You can control your mind!

Females can commit sexual abuse, too—though they don't as often as men, because sex abuse is a power trip and women don't play that game as often as men.

Andrea: *"My friend Jen is twenty-three and likes young boys who are twelve or thirteen and thinks they're so cute. She likes to blow them. Is this wrong?"*

Yes. They're underage and she is committing child sex abuse. She has a problem relating to people her own age, and probably doesn't think of herself as doing anything mean to these boys, but rather pleasing them. Your friend needs to stop this right away and start paying attention to what she finds so frightening about growing up and being a mature woman. She may have been sexually molested as well, and is just repeating this pattern. Tell her, as a good friend, that she needs some psychological help.

INCEST

As if childhood sexual abuse isn't bad enough, it can be even more devastating at the hands of a close family member. But the horrible truth is that this happens all too often.

Ashley called *LovePhones* recounting one of the most compelling, upsetting stories. She was sobbing as she told us that her father was coming home and that she was afraid of what would happen when he got there. He (a prominent businessman in an upper-class neighborhood) and a police officer friend of his, would play sex games with her. Once, she said, they put an unloaded gun in her vagina and shot it off, laughing as they did it. Ashley said the abuse only stopped for a brief period when she was raped by a stranger and the police were investigating. Now, she also feared for her little sister.

I insisted she get out of the house, get help, and report her father. We asked her to call again, and notified the authorities to investigate. Many listeners were riveted by her story. People called who thought they knew her, but to date, we haven't found her, and can only pray she got the help she needed.

With the horror of childhood sex abuse, many people wonder, like Candy, *"My girlfriend told me her stepfather abused her sexually from the time she was five years old until she was eighteen. How can it go on that long and how does it ever stop?"*

Often the story of childhood sex abuse goes like this: The child is young (maybe five or six) and alone with daddy (or grandpa, uncle, older brother, or any authority figure) who starts a fondling "game." Then daddy comes in at night to tuck her into bed and coos that he will help her go to sleep. He slips his hand under her nightshirt and starts rubbing her thighs, saying how proud he is of his little princess. His fingers find a spot between her legs that feels all mushy. It feels good. She hopes that daddy will come say good-night to her again.

Daddy does come again, many times, to put her to sleep in the special way. He tells her, "It's our secret," and warns her that if anyone found out it would ruin their special time and she might be taken away and never see the family again.

The trap is set. Even if she worries it's wrong, she's a prisoner and doesn't know how to stop. She worries if she brought it on herself, if she's to blame. She is consumed with fear, that daddy will be angry, that she'll be taken away from the family. So it continues.

All her friends are dating at school, but she can't go out because she has this nasty secret. If the girls knew, she'd be ashamed, and the boys would make fun of her. She lives in terror. Finally a boy asks her out and he kisses her, but she freezes, worrying if he'll know or if he'll want to go further. How can she trust any man, any person, ever again?

Some women suffer for years with guilt, sadness, anger, and distrust—whether it happened once or over many years—and don't face it until their thirties, forties, or even fities. The memories get buried, often until they face some other problem—like a bad rejection, eating disorder, panic attacks, or addiction to alcohol, drugs, or sex. Then a connection can be made to the early abuse, and it can be uncovered and healed.

A helpful technique: in your imagination create a new father figure who treats you lovingly.

Lara, 18: *"I have a problem with multiple addictions. I can't stop eating and every time I go out with a guy, I want to have sex with him. But when he gets close, I get revolted, and want to kick and scratch him. I thought I was going out of my mind, but then I went to a therapist who said I was probably abused. I thought she was wrong but now I am getting flashbacks of what my grandfather did to me for years when I was young. What can I do about it?"*

Flashbacks can be scary, but seeing clearly what happened back then is the first important step to healing. Then you need to reexperience the feelings—the conflict between some pleasurable feelings and the guilt, anger, confusion, and helplessness of being controlled. Forgive yourself; it's not your fault.

Remember:

Shed shame and self-blame, say no and tell to get well.

Separate selfish, controlling, abusive men in your past from loving, caring, healthy men you can have now.

"Why me?" you might ask. Every hurtful experience is a building block, to understanding, to compassion, to sensitivity, to a rebirth, and perhaps to a mission to help others. You can "Get Strong at the Broken Places" (the title of a wonderful book about getting over abuse).

Sex abuse and incest happens to boys, too.

Like nineteen-year-old Patrick: *"I was molested by my stepfather. When I was eight years old he came into the bathroom when I was taking a shower and pulled the shower curtain aside boasting that he had to see if I was becoming a man. Then he took his shorts off to show me what a penis would look like when I got mature. He made me touch it until it got hard. A few weeks later I was in the garage making a biology project for school and he came in and told me I should see a real human body and took his penis out and put it in my mouth and told me to suck on it. Times after that, he would come into my room and throw me against the wall and put his penis inside me from the back. To find me alone, he'd come home early from work and make me watch porno tapes and copy the positions. He told me it was important training to be a man, and that not all fathers and sons could be as close as we were. I believed him because he was my father. My mother came to my door one time and I thought she saw, but she turned around and never said anything. Since then, I got depressed, crying a lot, feeling ugly. Now in college I'm terrified I'll do something weird to one of my roommates. I made out with a girl once but I couldn't let her touch my penis. The worst thing I'm worried about is whether I'm going to grow up to be just like my father and do this to my kids if I have them. Will I?"*

I feel so sad and angry with you. Your stepfather has a severe problem and needs serious psychiatric help. You must feel betrayed by him, and by your mother, for not protecting you. Some mothers sense abuse is going on, but are unable to face the truth. She needs psychiatric help, too.

Your fears—of being gay and of copying your father (being sexually aggressive or worse yet, abusing your own child when you become a father)—are common ones for guys who have been abused. They are just fears and don't have to be reality.

Also, not being able to have sex right now is understandable; you're remembering the trauma. Shed shame and self-blame. You must purge and talk through your feelings with a therapist you trust. You also have to decide what legal steps to take.

With time and therapy, you will learn to separate the ghost of the molester in your past from a real potential love partner in your present, so you can have the healthy, mature, loving, sexual relationship you want and deserve.

Although father-daughter incest is more common, mothers also sexually abuse their kids. It happened to seventeen-year-old Mike: *"My mother used to come into my room at night and get under my covers and stroke my penis. Now I can't let a girl do it. Help."*

Your mother abused you. Don't let her continue to own your mind. You were helpless and needed her love then, so you had to go along with what she did, but now you can free yourself. Say symbolically to her, "Good-bye mother, I hate what you did to me but I am free now to get on with my life."

Incest is most common between children and parent-figures but also can happen among other family members.

Jim called *LovePhones* when the British band Blur were Honorary Love Doctors. He said: *"My sister and I have had sex. She's twenty-six and I'm nineteen, and I'm engaged to someone else, but it's my sister so it doesn't count. What should I do?"*

Blur's guitarist, Graham Coxon said: "That's rubbish. You can be in love with someone but not help what your dick is doing because you can't control your penis unless you cut it off. It gets to the point where your cock is in gear and your mind is in neutral and you just go, you can't help it. So you have to break it off. Something inside you has to say no. If you do it to your sister, you're likely to do it if you have a daughter or something like that."

Graham's right that you have to control your mind and your actions.

Sometimes justice is done, but fears persist.

Angela, 17: *"My dad is in jail for sexually abusing me. He got off easy with three years, but he gets out in January and I'm scared he'll find out where I am. My brother committed suicide right before his trial, by setting himself on fire with gasoline in the house. My father sends letters trying to say he loves me, and I get confused. How can I escape him?"*

I'm riveted with pain with you. You have endured much, with courage. I'm sure you still suffer with anger and guilt about the abuse and your brother's horrible suicide, and also from prosecuting your dad. But your brother couldn't cope, and you did the right thing. Despite what he did, your dad can still love you, and part of you may still love him, too. But trust that you are not under his power anymore: you don't have to see him if you don't want. Don't fall prey to him anymore. Ask other family members to protect you.

Linda, 25: *"Between age seven and eleven, I had sex with my brother who is two years older. He made me perform oral sex on him. Now I cry about it. In my dreams I think about him dying. Is this bad?"*

You're hurt, that's what is bad. He forced and humiliated you. It's good for you to finally get in touch with these feelings. Your dream is allowing you to feel your anger and wish to punish him.

After you've gone through the stages of healing—hurt, confusion, guilt, anger, disappointment, and finally, restored self esteem—you may want to share some of these feelings with your brother if you feel it would help you, or if you want to heal the relationship. A sex-abuse support group may help, so you don't feel alone.

PSYCHOLOGICAL INCEST

There's a kind of incest that people also don't readily recognize; it's not physical but psychological. Sandra Bernhard described it very powerfully when she was an Honorary Love Doctor on *LovePhones,* and a young girl, Jasmine, called to say she was confused about whether she was incested. *"My father never put it in me but it felt like he owned me."*

Sharing her own story, Sandra (brilliantly) called it "emotional incest."

"My father didn't really have sex with me," she said, "but the effect of incest was the same because he treated me as if I were his substitute wife. He turned me into my mother (with whom he had a horrible relationship and whom he left years ago), and of course I was angry at him, and at her for letting him do it. He made me feel he owned me sexually. It was so meshuga and so twisted."

The dynamic affected her later sexual relationships. "I tried to re-create it a long time . . . I played my mother and my father in relationships," she explained. "It made me frightened of men (and) I didn't want a relationship like I had with my father with any man or woman."

But there is healing. "As an adolescent you don't understand it, so you accept it. But I've extricated myself from those kinds of controlling relationships and dealt with it in therapy. It's led me to saner relationships, not victimizing people."

ABUSE TRUE OR FALSE?

Vinnie: *"I was walking a girl home and she was drunk and we had sex and then she said I raped her. The police arrested me and she dropped the charges but it was awful. She has a record herself."*

Yikes. What a bad experience. I'm sorry you had to go through this. Some people use crying rape to punish others wrongfully. Your experience also shows how you have to be careful who you get with!

There have been a number of celebrated news cases of abuse, also, that have been recanted or proven false. In a famous "baby-swapping" case, the girl's charges of sexual abuse against the man who raised her were proven false.

The truth of incest memories is also a big controversy these days.

Pris: *"I just went into therapy because I can't enjoy sex with my husband and I started an affair with a guy I'm obsessed about who treats me meanly. My therapist thinks I was sexually abused by my stepfather when I was young because of things I said about him. I came from a good family, so how can this be so? Did this really happen or is my therapist making this up?"*

Your therapist is doing her job by considering whether sexual abuse contributes to your current problems, because incest is so prevalent, because it can happen in even fine homes like yours (remember a former Miss America told *People* magazine she was sexually abused by her very prominent father), and because it can cause some lasting scars unless dealt with. Certain aspects of your situation may "fit" the profile of sexual abuse, including your distrust, fears, anger and sadness involving men and sex, conflicts over being loved, and repetitions of abusiveness. Since many people repress such traumatic memories, therapists sometimes have to help dig them up. But you're right, they can be suggested when not true—leading to false accusations of innocent people. To solve this problem, organizations like the American Psychological Association and the False Memory Syndrome Foundation in Philadelphia offer information.

Make sure you're seeing a qualified therapist whom you trust. If the abuse did happen, dealing with the past is crucial to healing you, so you're not a victim but a survivor.

CUTTING IT OFF AT THE PASS

"My brother jumped on my bed and I got aroused. Am I sick?"

"My friend got turned on when he saw his sister undressed. Is he a freak?"

Steve, 14: *"I think I like my mother. She's so sweet and has a nice body. Is this real bad?"*

You can be attracted to someone with whom you shouldn't have sex. When you're young and just having your first sexual feelings, it's understandable how those feelings could get attached to people close to you. Instead of continuing to think about that person, figure out what qualities you like and how they make you feel, and find those qualities with someone appropriate. Switch the fantasy in your mind to someone your age, or a made-up person.

Beth: *"I'm attracted to my stepbrother. We knew each other before our parents married, but now my body says yes but my mind says no. I think it's morally wrong and will ruin my mother's marriage and may cause arguments between her and my stepfather."*

You're not related by blood, but it is too complicated, considering the family ties. If you live together like a family, regardless of not being blood-related, you are a family. Cut it off at the pass before things get too involved in a messy family drama.

SEXUAL BATTERY

Statistics show that every fifteen seconds a woman is beaten by a man and that of the nearly 4,500 women murdered in the U.S., almost 30 percent were slain by angry husbands or boyfriends.

It doesn't help when celebrities engage in unacceptable

behavior. Red Hot Chili Peppers' Anthony Kiedis was convicted of sexual battery and indecent exposure in 1989 (that got him booted from a safe sex campaign). Guns N' Roses' Axl Rose was slapped with a seven-figure lawsuit for sexual abuse and beatings (kicking, spitting on her, dragging her by the hair) by his ex-wife (Axl, diagnosed with a mood disorder, and with a history of arrests, claims his violent temper is the result of childhood sexual abuse).

Devon called *LovePhones* when Salt-N-Pepa were Honorary Love Doctors. She said: *"I cheated on my boyfriend once and now he freaks. When we have sex, he raises my legs too high and pushes into me when it hurts. If I say stop, he just says 'you know you want it baby'. He slaps me around and I say stop and he says he's sorry but keeps at it next time. I left but he wants me back. Should I go?"*

Salt-N-Pepa advised: "Tell your man, 'We're not going to play this game anymore.' You're not under pressure to please your man. He has to respect you. You're #1. Put your foot down."

I'd add, make sure you're not giving him double messages, that part of you isn't buying into the rough sex. Do affirmations: "I deserve to be treated well."

Rico: *"I caught my girlfriend tongue-kissing a guy in Burger King. Then she got pregnant by some other guy. Since then I pick up girls and treat 'em bad, using whips and chains. When I have sex they masturbate me and I don't come. How can I come?"*

Not coming is the least of your problems. You have to be cured of your abusiveness first. Get out your anger by punching pillows instead of people. Force yourself to control your anger and express your hurt, humiliation, and desperation to be loved instead. Change your view of women—no man gets to own them. Get some serious therapy.

Not being able to come means you feel alienated and afraid to be open and vulnerable or to give women anything of yourself. You have to learn to trust again, and fill your soul with love rather than hate.

Women can be sexual batterers, too. Seventeen-year-old Dave has a girlfriend who is. She has low frustration tolerance, low self esteem, and a trigger temper.

"My girlfriend thinks I'm cheating and throws stuff at me. She calls my house threatening me. Last week she sliced me on the arm with a razor. I think the cops are following me now. They're parked wherever I am. I stay with her because I care about her. How can I get her to calm down?"

She needs therapy and maybe medication. She's insecure and obsessively jealous. Possibly she's been abused and now she's abusive. And you sound co-dependent—her abuse satisfies your needs to be treated poorly. You both have to learn self-control to deliberately choose to act calm instead of creating a high drama.

If that's the dark side of love, then what's the light side? Respect, support, and high esteem for yourself and others. Facilitating each other's growth and self-actualization. Accepting loss of love and moving on. Going for your dreams but accepting disappointments along the way, as the roller coaster reality of life. Celebrating the inner being in yourself and others, without attachment to them or what is supposed to be; focusing instead on what is, allowing all to change and evolve.

SELF-ABUSE (MASOCHISM)

Cecile: *"My boyfriend promised to have sex for the first time with me, but then told me another girl beat me to it. I asked him what happened to us and he said it's over. I hung up and cut myself with a steak knife. I've sliced my legs and arms before, and poked my stomach with pins. I'm scared I may really hurt myself one day. How can I stop?"*

You hurt yourself when you feel really hurt or abandoned by others. Some women with low self esteem indulge in mild self-torture when men leave them—like chopping their hair or biting off their nails. In more extreme cases like yours (about one in a hundred), typically attractive and intelligent girls, with a history of abuse, rejections, or addictions, become either promiscuous or fearful of sex in the face of rejection, and prick, scratch, or burn themselves. Sometimes a parent has committed suicide, teaching the child to turn anger inward.

Before you do something destructive, follow the Four Steps: (1) Stop and think. (2) Identify your needs and feelings. (3) Assess the possible outcomes, and do something else that's healthy. If you feel self-hatred and guilt, forgive yourself for any imagined bad deeds. If you feel empty and numb, seek love instead of pain. If you're angry, pound pillows or express it verbally. Confront the person involved; in your case, tell your boyfriend how despicable his betrayal is.

When your emotions are so intense you feel violent, realize they are likely fueled by previous losses, hurts, and betrayals. Rather than take it out on yourself or your boyfriend, recall hurtful people in your past. In your room or another safe place, vent your most extreme secret fantasies of revenge and punishment without acting it out. Therapy with a trained professional and occasionally medication can also help inhibit these self-destructive impulses and relieve depression.

SEXUAL ASSAULT: RAPE

Studies around the country show that up to twenty-five percent of college students have been victims of attempted or completed sexual assault. There is a game called Rodeo, where a group of guys busts into a dorm bedroom while a couple is having sex. As the woman struggles to get away, her date pins her to the bed, the winner being the guy who can pin his date the longest. Or the guy invites his buds to peek through the window or closet while he makes it. Or he secretly videotapes the sex session.

Singer-songwriter Tori Amos wrote about her own rape experience in the song, "Me and a Gun." She's adamant that one way to heal is to help others—so she cofounded an organization (RAINN—the Rape, Abuse and Incest National Network) to provide a national hotline for free counseling and referrals. As an Honorary Love Doctor one evening, she took Joe's call about his wife's sexual coldness:

Joe: *"My wife says she doesn't need masturbation or sex. But I want more of it, like oral sex. You know when a person has been sexually abused? That is how she acts. When I was younger I was molested, and she shows signs I showed years ago, like fear, never talking about sex, being afraid of sex, everything. What can I do?"*

Tori offered her support: "I feel for you both. When I was raped it changed my life. I was in a car and held hostage. When it's happening you feel so much hatred coming at you and you're there, thinking you're going to be mutilated and just trying not to be murdered. It showed such hatred men can have for women. I felt so vulnerable that I took it in and numbed parts of myself for years.

"I made a mistake and didn't get help. I retreated into myself. I did not want to put myself through a heavy interrogation that is the second rape—the system. It affected my personal relationships so that when I was with a man I had to pretend I was a whore to have sex. I had to be in control and I had to become another person. I took on different identities for a long time. Writing the song 'Me and a Gun' was the first step in acknowledging what happened. I take a lot of time every day not sweeping things under the rug when I see that man's face again or when I want to pull away.

"Guys can do a lot. I'm in a relationship with a man for a while who knows the signs and respects my space but does not allow me to retreat into myself. He turns on the lights and says, 'What is my name?' and we go through his identity and remember things we have done together. He reminds me, 'I am not the man who hurt you,' and he'll go 'What am I doing? I am making love to you and I love you.' And then I repeat it. He is an amazing man. He is a wolf. It's really healing. 'Baker Baker' was written about not being able to be open. I am passionate on the piano but in the rest of my life I was a Dorito, dry and a bit stale. We can all put on a front, but in our personal lives we just push the passion away. But the message is that we can have love and passion in our lives again."

You go girl, Tori. Excellent advice! Right on target, especially about how the partner can help.

IS IT RAPE?

Sometimes you wonder whether what you experienced in a certain situation amounts to sexual assault. Of course the laws of each state vary. But psychologically, it could be a different story.

Minday and Erica, nineteen, needed my reaction to validate their feelings. *"We were driving on the highway and this guy in a beaten down Escort was next to us and then we saw that he was jerking off. He had his whole body in the air, going 60 mph. He came all over himself. We were screaming and laughing, but after I had to pull over to the side of the road and I gagged. It ruined my night and now we're upset. We feel victimized, but are we right to feel that way?"*

Absolutely! He took advantage of you. Sure you thought it was funny then, but you were caught off guard. You were excitable (laughing) but also nervous. He was an exhibitionist and you felt invaded and taken advantage of.

ACQUAINTANCE/DATE RAPE

Some people think Stone Temple Pilot's Weiland looks like he's having a date-rape fantasy in the video "Sex Type Thing," thrashing around topless in a dungeon-like setting, singing, "I know you want what's on my mind . . . Here I come," as an aging prom queen chews her gloves and another guy flies around her head. But really the song is supposedly about the misogny of the music world.

Debbie Gibson wrote a song, "When I Say No," about date rape. As she told me, "Date rape was in the papers that week so I decided to write about it because I think a lot of how young girls look to guys for self-worth and self-esteem and get in over their head."

A patient of mine experienced it, and told me, *"I shared a summer house with a bunch of people and one night there was a big party and everybody got drunk and was sleeping over in different people's rooms. I had a big double bed to myself, so this guy who's the most popular guy in the group asked me if he could sleep in it with me. I told him he could just sleep, and would have to keep his clothes on, and he said okay. I dozed off, and then woke up with him on top of me, humping away. I screamed and made him get out. But I was shaking and couldn't fall asleep all night. Now I'm afraid to face him and feel ashamed to go back there!"*

That was acquaintance rape. The guy performed sex acts on you without your consent and ignoring your specific requests to the contrary. Oh, what happens when people get drunk!

Why should you be ashamed? You didn't do anything wrong. You should be angry. You could have reported him if you wanted. Certainly you should tell him off, to restore your feelings of self-respect.

Mia, 19: *"A guy I went out with made me do oral sex on him, and then did it to me, but I really didn't want to. It was the first time I had sex and it was horrible. But I didn't make it stop so it must be my fault. I saw a penis for the first time and it was ugly. Does this must have something to do with being raped when I was young? Does this mean I'm not a virgin?""*

You can consider yourself still a virgin, because that wasn't sex, it was a date rape—him controlling and assaulting you—and it was not your fault. One day you will have an experience of love, and you can consider that your first.

You now have penophobia—an inability to look at or touch the penis—because a penis once hurt you. As you work through your fear and anger, and learn to trust your boyfriend, you will come to see a penis, and the man attached to it, as making you feel good.

Have the guts to say no and reject abusers. Michelle needs to do this. *"I went on a blind date and we were sitting in the car and the guy asked me if I liked oral sex and opened his zipper. I said no, but I'm still upset that the whole thing happened."*

Feel proud you said no. Like most women who feel intimidated, you feel you didn't have the right to say "no," or fear that you'd insult the guy if you told him to stop or get away. But don't be afraid to speak up.

To heal this, and complete the experience as you wish it would have gone, imagine facing him now and tell him what you think of him in the strongest terms. Feel the inner strength that comes from saying exactly what you do and do not want. That way you turn a scar into a star. As I mentioned before, this is called "getting strong at the broken places."

Tianna needs to do that, too: *"This guy I went out with is big, real big, and when we had sex, he threw my legs over my head and shoved his nine inch thing in me. I told him to stop, but he said, 'You know you want it baby.' He gets mad if I don't ride him and shoots and gets up to take a shower. What should I do?"*

Dump him immediately. Don't be okay with any of that. Make your word stick. **"No" means "no."** Expect to be respected and treated well.

Don't get sucked into anything, like Shannon: *"I'm used to guys who tell me what to do. I was raped by a guy at school but I see him now and I want to go out with him. He said he's sorry. I find him irresistible. Should I go out with him?"*

Absolutely not. You have to get over playing the victim role. You have the Stockholm Syndrome—whereby a captive falls in love with the victimizer. Stay away from him!

It's fine to be passive at times, but you have to expect to be treated with respect. Instead of being intrigued by his power, feel your own. You should report him. Tell your parents about the rape and visit a rape crisis center for counseling.

Lisa: *"I was raped by a guy when I was twelve and he was fifteen. He came inside me. Now when I get horny, white discharge comes out of me, like milk. Is something wrong?"*

I'm so sorry you were raped. You may worry your

insides are corroded or polluted, but this discharge is not his ejaculate, left inside you after years, but your normal vaginal lubrication from being turned on.

Watch out how far you let fun go, so you're not like James. *"I was thinking I'd have sex with this girl and film it and show my buddies. Is that a good idea?"*

Sure, if you want to get in big trouble. Take a lesson from famous rock 'n' roll legend Chuck Berry, whom a bunch of women sued claiming they were secretly videotaped while using the bathroom at his recreation complex restaurant.

Myth: Men can't be raped.
John, 19: *I feel I was raped by a girl. She was a hot babe and we got drunk and she went down on me and got me hard and made me stick it in her when I didn't want to because I didn't have anything to put on. I pushed her head off but she came back at me. My friends don't believe it."*

Shame on them. If you feel taken advantage of, you were. It's harder if she's even attractive to the point where your buddies would die for her. You're entitled to the same anger and sadness and feelings of powerlessness as any other rape victim.

Men can get raped too, but we don't acknowledge it because we think men always want and enjoy sex. We also don't think a woman can rape a man without a penis to penetrate him. And we assume he must have had an erection for the act to occur, and if he had an erection he must have wanted sex. But a guy doesn't have to have an erection (she can "stuff" him in), or an erection can result from fear that triggers the flow of adrenaline and blood to the penis.

TELLING

"How do I tell my parents that my father's best friend raped me on my seventh birthday?"

Tell them you have something very important to share with them and plan an uninterrupted discussion time. Say something happened a long time ago and you just now feel able to talk about it. Say it directly, "So-and-so raped me on my seventh birthday." I'm proud of you that you want to tell them. You will heal better by getting it out, and hopefully they will support you.

"Should I tell my husband I was raped?"

Telling a partner can help him understand your reactions and feelings about sex. One woman I was counseling found herself crying uncontrollably during sex one night with her husband, and started to tell him about the abuse. Though normally understanding, he was going through a great deal of stress that week over possibly losing his job, and her confession only escalated his fear and guilt that he was not a good protector and provider. He didn't want to hear about it, leaving her feeling devastated and abandoned. Fortunately, some months later, when he felt emotionally stronger himself, he could be supportive to her. Expect that partners will feel the same emotions of anger, depression, and helplessness as you do. Talking about it together and planning what steps to take—like legal action—is healing for both.

My final word on "No-No's" is not to be down with any of it:

> Shed shame, shed self-blame.
> Say no, and tell, to get well.

CHARLES CALLED *LOVEPHONES* TO SAY HE WAS sticking pencils up his rear. He couldn't stop the urge when he was sitting in class. It was consuming him! My producer, Sam, said, "I guess that's what's called really having lead in your pants." Which end did he put in first? The eraser. Was it #1 or #2 lead? Any lead would do.

Sounds like a freak, right? Not so fast. I asked Charles, "What's making you so depressed?"

"I tried to kill myself a few weeks ago," he replied. "No one knew. I jumped off the top of our building, but I told them I was trying to adjust my telescope and slipped."

What triggered such desolation? The same thing that causes most teen depression: family, school, drug, and love problems. Usually being rejected is the crowning blow. Charles's girlfriend of thirteen-and-a-half months—whom he hoped to marry—said it was over. He couldn't face it.

Fortunately, I convinced Charles to tell his parents the truth, so he could get the psychiatric help he desperately needed.

Sex can't cover, or cure, your ills, as Kurt Cobain's widow, Courtney Love, also found out. At a summer '94 concert in Cleveland, Love grabbed the mike and shouted, "I made coffee and gave Kurt head every morning and he still left me."

The crowd went wild. There are no guarantees that even "polishing the helmet" at the start of the day will make your mood shine.

Anytime you feel you've reached the end of your rope, when sadness or fears get you down for more than a few weeks, when you start to think it's hopeless, when your career and love life are falling apart, you need to seek professional help.

Fears about sex are irrational feelings of being out of control, a dread of impending disaster. They can range from mild upsets to extreme panic. But you *can* always get back in control. Here's how.

SWEATING LIKE A PIG

Keith: *"When I go out and get close to having sex, I start sweating like a pig. What's wrong with me?"*

Nothing. You're anxious and having symptoms just like you would before an exam, presentation, or any other experience that makes you nervous. The autonomic nervous system's response to a real or imagined fear is the flight-or-fight response that leads to symptoms like a panic attack: sweats, changes in breathing, weak knees, palpitations. Once you know what it is, you feel better. Acknowledge the feelings: "I am just frightened." Reassure yourself that you're okay; say to yourself, "I am safe." Since your sweats mean you feel out of control, take as much control as you can over the situation. Reassure yourself, "I don't have to do anything I don't want to do." Stop the escalating closeness at any point you want. Certain Dri is excellent for heavy perspiration—it works by "sealing off" the sweat glands. HOMEWORK: When you are home and relaxed, imagine the dating situation. Alternate deep breathing and feeling relaxed with picturing yourself in scenes getting closer and closer to sex. Start with simple, easy scenarios and build up to the scarier ones. This is a way to systematically desensitize you to the fear, and build up your confidence that you are safe and can handle any situation.

CAN'T TOUCH

Jackie: *"I get real uncomfortable whenever a guy puts his arm around me. I like him to, but if we're out dancing and he grabs my waist I pull away. I once slept in a bed next to a guy but it was okay because he didn't touch me. Why can't I let a guy touch me?"*

Likely you grew up in a strict home where you were told to be a good girl and you're afraid to do anything bad. Give yourself permission to be touched without having sex. Likely also, you're afraid that if you let them touch you, it'll mean you're giving permission or will be obliged to go further. Only go out with guys you trust. Tell them flat out that you don't intend to go far, but you like having fun. I bet you're also afraid you would like to go further yourself and that thought is unacceptable to you. It's okay for you to secretly want to be wild and to really let go, but remember that you can still decide to stop at whatever point you feel is right for you for now. HOMEWORK: Like Keith, you can benefit from systematic desensitization. In a relaxed state, imagine a guy near you, then touching you lightly, then holding you firmly, building up to more and more contact.

CAN'T LOOK

Angie, 22: *"My husband can't look at naked women. If he sees a magazine with women in bikinis, he rips out the picture and rips it in pieces and puts it in the garbage. If we're in the movies and a girl's body is exposed, he puts his head down to the floor. One time a woman was breast-feeding a child at a wedding and he had to leave. Once in a conversation, someone brought up the fact that a girl posed in a magazine and he called them a 'fucking slob' and almost slugged the guy. What's wrong?"*

Your husband has a severe phobia against nudity and a great deal of anger toward women. I bet he was severely punished when he was a boy for something related to nudity and women—maybe for looking at pictures in magazines, maybe for looking at his mother, or touching a woman. It could have been an innocent act, but he was punished out of proportion to the situation. This is the powerful way early experiences condition our behavior through life.

He has to connect his behavior now with those early

traumas, to see the seeds of his fear and anger at women. Then he needs to "tell off" (in the privacy of his room, or in therapy) whoever punished him—to resolve that healthy nudity with sex and love is appropriate and permissible for him now even if it was punished then.

SEX PANIC

Christian: *"I can't touch my girl's vagina with my hands."*

Likely you were punished for touching when you were a kid. We have to do some systematic desensitization with you, to reduce your anxiety. Think about touching your girl's lips and take a deep breath and say, "I am safe, this feels good." Now think about touching her stomach, take a deep breath, and say, "I am safe, this feels good." Now think about being an inch from her vagina and repeat deep breathing and affirmations: "I am safe, this feels good." Continue like this, as you get closer to her vagina, and then in it.

PANIC ATTACKS

Panic attacks are a common problem people face these days. They're often intertwined with depression, and can ruin not only your sex life but your entire life.

British singer/songwriter Seal (whose real name is Sealhenry Samuel) knows the pain of panic. As he shared on *LovePhones,* "I had a meteoric success. Success triggers anxiety which stems from some kind of insecurity in your childhood. It feels as if you are outside your body. There is an increase in the heart rate, then hyperventilation. The adrenaline balance gets upset and one hallucinates. One must see the danger signs and get therapy. You have to dig down in the dirt. Anything can trigger anxiety when you least expect it. In my case, it had more to do with the fear of being reprimanded by one of my teachers or a lack of attention from parents. You worry if you deserve the adulation of your fans. It's nice to own a black Porsche and a house in west London when you've been on the dole and living in a squat, but when you make it, you wonder, 'What does this person want from me?' Now, I don't suffer as I used to. It forced me into a position when I had to deal with it and overcome it."

The hardest period of self-doubt for the Nigerian/Brazilian Grammy nominee occurred after the success of "Crazy," when he wrote "Whirlpool" because, as Seal says, "everything was like a whirlpool, worrying about how the album would be received and whether the songs were any good and coming to grips with the fact you are worthy."

A fan called to say she'd be waiting for him outside the stage door when he got off the Letterman show. "That makes me happy," Seal said. "I will think of my fan standing outside and maybe it'll help me to perform on the show."

DESPERATION

Erica has a common problem: *"I was seeing this guy and having great sex with him and we had a wonderful intimacy too. Then he got real involved with his work and didn't see me for weeks on end. I went into a withdrawal and was so depressed. I had been fine and liked my life before, but when he didn't see me anymore, I didn't enjoy the things I did anymore. What's wrong with me?"*

You are suffering from a common problem successful women of the '90s have: they have a great life and feel fine on their own, pursuing a career and enjoying friends and activities, until they get with a guy they like and their independence falls apart. Worse yet, when the guy withdraws, they feel devastated and all the wonderful things they previously enjoyed about life seems empty. The problem is that they started to live too much through the guy, needing his appreciation and approval. Of course, the appreciation of others is nice, but shouldn't be essential.

Your self-esteem and independence was on shaky ground to begin with, so you need to do things and see people who reinforce your good thoughts of yourself as a strong, competent person. Live in the present. Think about the possibilities for the future. You didn't give away your soul when you had sex with that guy.

The blues are a close cousin to dread, and just as destructive to sex and your self-esteem. But you can get up from being down. Here's how.

DUMPED AND DOWN

As Beck sang, "I'm a loser baby, so why don't you kill me."

Allison: *"Since my boyfriend broke up with me, I can't get out of bed. I keep thinking about the times we were in bed having sex and it felt so good in comparison to everything else which feels so bad. I can't concentrate on my homework and I'm getting bad grades. I'm a real loser, like the song says. I cry all the time and feel stupid about it. My parents are yelling at me because I was a good student, but they yell anyway because they're fighting a lot and talk about splitting. Will this black cloud ever lift?"*

Everybody gets blue and down in the dumps at times over a sex or love problem, or something that happened in school, at home, or at work. But when the struggle stops you from functioning, you have a serious problem that needs professional therapy. First, you have to tell your parents that their arguing is affecting you. Since you feel insecure about your family, your own break-up makes you even more insecure. You're going to make it, though. Talking through your problems will help you turn them around, but you might have a chemical imbalance; in that case, medication can be helpful. Some deep crying is not stupid, it can help you connect with your deep pain. John Lennon experienced a real deep purging from intense crying, when he went through primal therapy, and chronicled it in his album "Imagine." The deep breathing and build-up and release of tension in crying—like in orgasm—can release chemicals in the brain that make you feel better.

HOMEWORK: Be careful how you verbalize what you feel. Don't exaggerate the negative. Say, "I'm frustrated," not "I'm a loser." Next step, escalate the positive; instead of "I feel good," say, "I feel fantastic." Even if the positive feelings don't feel real, the negative ones aren't any more real. Exaggerating the positive feeling gives you a chance to experience it that way.

In the era of grunge, brooding has become cool. But I ask you, where's the heroism in shooting dope and then yourself in the head? Kurt, you done us wrong. It was punk Sid and Nancy who were expected to self-destruct. As Sandra Bernhard said, "I'm sick of the (alternative) brooding . . . just do the three S's—shit, shower, and shave—before I kill you. Relax." (After all, Sandra was alternative before there was a name for it.)

Sheryl Crow, after hitting it big and being picked to be duet partner for Michael Jackson on his Bad tour, and then going out on her own, admits to being depressed at one point in her life and not getting out of bed for six months (it was related to being sexually harassed). Tori Amos also got depressed, and once, while on the road, called Nine Inch Nails friend Trent Reznor, who commiserated but reassured her that he had been in the same hotel room and knew the windows didn't open, so he was reassured she couldn't throw herself out.

Jim Kerr of the band Simple Minds also sunk into depression, as did Lemonheads' sex symbol, Evan Dando, once voted one of the "50 Most Beautiful People" by *People*. As is typical, Dando's downs started when his model parents (they actually had worked as models) split, and by thirteen years old, he was into mushrooms and acid, looking for an escape. Off drugs, he said he doesn't get moody anymore.

Being Down is on the Rise. Every sixty seconds an adolescent attempts suicide. Estimates show that up to 640,000 teens attempt to take their lives each year. One in two hundred succeeds. The rate more than doubled in the past twenty years.

More frightening is the risk for kids ages ten to fourteen. In 1990, 264 young people of that age took their lives—a 75 percent increase in the past ten years. Broken families, drugs, the availability of guns, and all the stresses young people face today, all contribute to the crisis.

Many serious life situations involving sex lead kids to feel hopeless, with no way out:

Bernice: *"I was seeing this guy and I just had a baby and he left me. I can't stand it. Why did he leave? I'm all alone and want to kill myself."*

Bret: *"I had sex with my stepsister for seven months and now she's pregnant. She's eighteen. I tried to kill myself by overdosing with sleeping pills. I lost my job. Now what?"*

There's always a solution, even if it doesn't seem like it now. Kids often have kids because they need to be taken care of themselves. But there is hope, forgiveness, and people willing to help. Ask, and let them be there for you (counselors, support groups, community centers, friends, religious leaders).

The problem can erupt into violence—against others or yourself.

Mark: *"My girl Nancy was sixteen and her father was a police officer who didn't approve of me. He caught us having sex on the couch and slapped me, and she grabbed his gun and shot herself in the head. Dead. That happened two and a half years ago, and I can't get over it. Every time I'm in a relationship, I get dumped, and every rejection brings that up. The last girl said I was a loser. I was in the hospital because I tried to kill myself, slicing my wrists with a razor. Then, I OD'd on sleeping pills a year ago. I've been thinking about it again, a lot, in the last two weeks."*

You have got to pull yourself together. You were not responsible for your girlfriend's death because you were making love. Forgive yourself. You indeed have a terrible trauma to mourn, but you can get over it. It was a tragic accident. I'm sure you're also angry at your girlfriend's father for causing such fear and despair that led her to kill herself. And you feel guilty that you could not save her. Accept these feelings and allow yourself to live.

SUICIDAL WARNING SIGNS

- Suicide threats. Take talk about dying or "I might as well be dead" seriously. Don't be afraid to ask, "Have you thought about killing yourself, did you plan anything?" It won't plant ideas in their heads, and the potential gain of the person opening up about problems is worth any potential risk.
- Depression symptoms: sleeplessness, sadness, crying, low energy.
- Behavior changes: sleeping and eating more or less, sudden withdrawal from social activities.
- Prior attempts. Of those who successfully kill themselves, 80 percent have tried before.
- Final arrangements. Giving away prized possessions, suddenly acting as if everything's fine.
- Preoccupation with death and philosophical discussions about the meaninglessness of life.

Pearl Jam's song, "Jeremy," about teen suicide won the 1993 MTV Awards for best group video, best metal/hard rock, and best direction. "If it weren't for the music I think I would have shot myself," lead singer Eddie Vedder said in accepting the award. Unfortunately, not long after, fellow grunger Kurt Cobain did just that.

Cobain didn't help matters when he checked out. Four deaths of kids in Washington were blamed on his suicide, the forlorn youths copying the rock star's exit from agony.

It was a typical story. Cobain seemed to have everything. He was at the top of his career, rich, famous, and with a family to boot. He said his daughter mattered to him so much—but apparently not enough to overcome the inner demons.

Cobain had a troubled youth: taking Ritalin for hyperactivity, suffering from chronic stomach pain (on which he blamed his drug abuse), feeling "his lights went out" when his parents got divorced when he was eight years old, being shuffled from relative to relative, not liking his alcoholic stepfather, never fitting in at school, flunking classes, smoking pot, stealing food . . . or getting food stamps. He wrote songs like, "I Hate Myself and Want to Die." He "felt like a turtle," stuck in a tank, miserable. It's not unsymbolic that he called his first band Fecal Matter. Nirvana promised more, yet did not deliver, as he ultimately announced to his fans, "I hate you and won't perform for you." Sadly, he announced in his suicide note, "I don't have the passion anymore." Apparently he could find no more joy in his music, and no more escape in it from his pain.

Steve was affected by Cobain's death: *"When Kurt Cobain checked out, I got drunk. Nothing was right anymore. I was in love with this girl and I thought she loved me. But she left me for another guy. I got so depressed I wanted to kill myself. I tried to kill myself by cutting myself, but I couldn't go through with it. Nobody knew, they just thought I had an accident. I can't seem to shake it. I feel I'm useless, I'm nothing. She doesn't love me."*

I feel so sad with you. Losing someone you care about feels awful. But you have to understand that you don't want to die, you just want the pain to go away. Young people who kill themselves think they're ending the pain, and don't realize that suicide is final.

It feels bad when you can't have what you want and you don't know where to turn. Everything seems meaningless. Your dreams crushed. But, I promise you the pain will end, so don't end your life. Take one minute at a time. Later you'll look back and see that it was worth living. Something wonderful will happen that you would've missed. Nothing you lose—or no mistake you make—is worth dying for.

Scale back and simplify your life. In the computer of your brain, dump out of the "Hurts" file and go into another program, "Simple Pleasures," or "Things To Do," or anything that keeps you busy and otherwise occupied. Take pleasure in simple acts, like folding your socks or alphabetizing your CDs, blocking out negative thoughts. Every minute you are occupied with something else, you are farther away from the pain.

You deserve to live. There is always a brighter day. You'll see, one day you'll look back and be glad you didn't end it all. Love who you are and treasure every minute of life.

DR. JUDY'S SEX RULE: TURN AN "A" INTO AN "A": Anytime you have Anxiety about anything, take Action— get an Answer. Check it out. See a doctor. Besides general physicians, you can go to specialists, like a dermotologist (for skin problems), a gynecologist (for female problems), a urologist (for male problems), a psychiatrist or psychologist (for emotional problems).

David, 16: *"I got a blotch on my penis. I should go to the doctor, but then I'd have to tell him I stuck my penis in a Crisco can to spank the monkey."*

Even if you're embarrassed or ashamed over what you did, take a deep breath and tell the doctor anyway. I'm sure s/he's heard worse. You can't ignore a problem at the expense of your health. Why should you suffer with discomfort and worry? Always conquer anxiety by taking action to do something constructive about it.

FEARS ABOUT BEING FOUND OUT

Crystal, 17: *"I have a sore on my genitals but I don't want to go to the doctor because then he'll tell my mother I had sex. What should I do?"*

One of the biggest reasons young people don't go to the doctor is because they don't want their parents to find out they're having sex. But you know what, you can't let that stand in the way of your heath. If you're too young to go to the doctor yourself, you gotta ask your parents to help you, and face the music. You can ask them if you can talk to the doctor privately in the examination room (everybody is entitled to privacy), and have them join you in the office afterward. Think about turning an obstacle into an opportunity, and treating this as a turning point to begin being open with your parents about things you haven't discussed before. If something really bad came from this problem, they're going to find out in an even harder way.

BROKEN PENIS

Paul, 25: *"When I was doing my daily duty of sex one day, my penis cracked at the base. It got swollen, but I kept going because I figured 'no pain, no gain.' Now it's hard to ejaculate and stuff doesn't come out as much from my penis."*

The penis usually tolerates a lot of action without injury, but occasionally, with extremely athletic intercourse, you can bruise it. I've heard guys joke about their "broken bone," and though there is no bone, a fractured penis can happen, and it is no joke! Most typically, the veins that bring back blood from the tip along the top of the penis can be ruptured and get clotted or hard. Left untreated, the resulting scar tissue can lead to damage of the chambers in the penis, and impotence that requires surgery and a penile prosthesis to fix! No delay, see a urologist right away.

NAILED

Jill: *"My boyfriend stuck his big toe in my vagina and the next day it really hurt and was bleeding a little. What's wrong?"*

I guess you really got nailed! It sounds like his toenail bruised your delicate vaginal walls. Likely it's not drastic and will heal, but to be safe, check it out (see a gynecologist). Make your boyfriend take better care of his toenails, and give him a pedicure as a present.

CUMS BLOOD

"I'm scared to death. When I come, blood comes out. What's wrong with me?"

This happens to women and men and in the vast majority of cases, urologists and gynecologists insist, it's nothing to worry about at all. A little blood in the ejaculate or lubrication can just be a by-product of normal functioning if you are having bouts of prolonged sex. In men it's called hematospermia, and the color of the blood can range from light red to dark brown. My buddy, California urologist Dudley Danoff reassures me that in the thousands of penis problems he's seen, a little blood coming out is as minor as seeing a little blood when you blow your nose (from tiny tears in the delicate nose tissues). The solution, he suggests: "Turn out the lights!"

There's always a warning, however, that if it persists, it could be a sign of some infection or cancer of the prostate, ejaculatory duct, or seminal vesicles. So, check it out.

PAIN

Tim: *"It hurts when I get turned on. What's wrong?"*

Your pain, called dyspareunia, could be physical or psychological, in both males and females. Physical reasons range from minor causes (like pressure which can go away once you orgasm or if you change position) to major problems like tumors. Obviously if pain persists, you have to check it out medically. If it's psychological, you know my favorite technique to find out what it's about: pretend you are the pain. Ask it, "What do you want?" It might say, "I'm angry at (your partner)," or "I feel guilty about having sex." So get over your anger, or give yourself permission to be sexual. Another technique to reduce the pain is to focus on it, describe its color and exact dimensions, maybe even, if it were an animal, what animal would it be. You'd be shocked how just focusing on it like that can make it dissolve.

SOFT IN HEAD

Joey: *"When I get an erection, the head is still soft. If I push on the vein, it gets fatter. What's wrong?"*

You might have a venous leak, so when you stop up the

blood, it goes into the extremity (head) of your penis. Check it out.

SEMEN: FACIAL OR FATTENING?

"My girlfriend told me that a guy's ejaculate is very healthy and can even be the best facial or hair conditioner. Is that true?"

Semen is not harmful if swallowed. It's made up mainly of a milky alkaline fluid secreted from the seminal vesicles, prostate gland, and Cowper's gland, consisting mainly of water, mucus, and a large number of chemical substances like fructose sugar, bases, and prostaglandins. The ingredients include citric acids, enzymes, sodium, and chloride, with small amounts of ammonia, ascorbic acid, acid phosphatase, calcium, carbon dioxide, and cholesterol, with sperm accounting for only 1 percent of the product.

Proteins are what make the semen frothy, like stirring up egg whites, and may be thought of as healthy, but there is not enough to make a significant difference in your diet or general health. Conversely, it is normally not dangerous to your health unless of course the man has an infection or sexually transmitted disease, or you have an allergic reaction. Beauty experts, like celebrity esthetician B. Genesco of Mario Bedescu, say some ingredients they use in facial masques (like fruit acids, glycolic acid, proteins, cholesterol) or hair conditioners (like enzymes and sodium) may be similar to those in semen, but the combination and preparation makes them significantly different. No doubt, the perceived similarity also lies in their consistency. Like masques, seminal fluid ranges in color from whitish to tones of yellow or gray and has a creamy, smooth, yet also sticky texture. Right after ejaculation, semen is rather thick, but then liquefies quickly. If exposed to air on the skin, it dries, seeming to create a temporary "tightening" effect as in a masque, but then evaporates. There is no evidence that this process is effective for skin lubrication or rejuvenation, though certainly there may be psychological benefits if you *think* it's good for you!

"Can you get fat from swallowing semen?"

No need to worry about semen being fattening: a normal amount, usually one teaspoonful, contains only about five or ten calories. The calories come from the fructose (a sugar-like substance) that is secreted in the seminal vesicles and becomes part of the semen.

SEX AND STRESS

"Does sex relieve stress?"

It can. Sex is the buildup and release of tension, so if you go through the sexual-response cycle, you can feel relaxed afterward. Chemicals are released in the body that act as natural sedatives. But sex can also cause stress if you do not complete your sexual-response cycle and feel the pressure of nonrelease, or emotional stress if you feel pressured by your performance, or by the relationship, or feel dissatisfied or unfulfilled by the experience.

BAD BREATH

"I'm dating a guy who has bad breath. How do I tell him?"

Test if his bad breath comes from poor dental hygiene. Some people are sloppy about not brushing their teeth before sex. Suggest that you both go in and brush your teeth before you kiss and make out. Brush your tongue, too; many bacteria lodge there. Teach by example: Keep a breath mint or spray in your purse and use it before you kiss him and pass it to him casually to use. His bad breath can also come from stomach problems, in which case he needs to see a doctor. If simple remedies don't work, gently say, "I love to kiss you when your breath is fresh. Sometimes I worry that you may have a stomach problem because I sense it on your breath."

SEX SNEEZE

Mike: *"When I have sex or even think about it, I sneeze . . . for example—three hours ago I thought of Christina*

Applegate from Married with Children *and Heather Locklear from* Melrose Place *getting it on together and a second after that I sneezed."*

Sneezing is a reflex action controlled by the medulla in the brain. When an irritant enters the respiratory tract, it stimulates the sensory neurons to send a message to the brain, which stimulates other neurons, which causes you to take a deep inhalation and blow the irritant out the nose.

You might sneeze when you are turned on because more blood is at the surface of the skin, making your mucous membranes more sensitive, so any irritant will more easily set you off. Histamines, responsible for the well-known allergy symptoms like hives and runny noses, may also trigger your sneezing.

Enjoy your sneeze—see it as a mini-orgasm, making your body shake. Maybe it's a mating call, cut short.

Sneezing can also be a stress response, with psychological causes. If you were the sneeze, what would you be saying? Perhaps, "I am scared," "Get away, danger is here," or "I want this but I can't have it"? If the message is that you're frightened, retrain your brain to think reassuring thoughts, like "I am safe, I can have this." Of course, there is always the superstition that three sneezes means you're telling the truth.

The same things could be going on if you cough in sex. What is your throat saying? HOMEWORK: Figure out what you want to say that your cough is covering up. Say it!

TROUBLE URINATING

"I like sex when my fiancé puts my legs all the way over my head so they touch the bed. But after, it's hard to pee. Is something wrong?"

Sometimes certain positions make you feel like urinating, because of pressure on the bladder (especially if you have a tipped uterus). In that case, urinate before sex and don't put your legs up or aim for such deep penetration.

The opposite can also happen, where you have a hard time urinating after sex. If this happens all the time, you could have an obstruction in your urinary system, or a problem with the urinary muscles not opening again when sex is over. Or if you can't pee, you may still be turned on so your body is registering that it's still in the sexual response cycle, which shuts off the urinary system.

A guy urinates through the same tube as he ejaculates, so sometimes urinary problems are linked to sex. Even if the problem is physical, there could be a mental connection, as in Peter's case: *"My pee gets stopped up and the doctor said I had something wrong with my urinary valve. I remember when I was about ten, I was lying in bed and I didn't want to go to the bathroom, so I pressed my penis against the bed and had a really pleasant sensation that now I think was probably an orgasm, though nothing came out. Now I don't get really full erections. Is there a connection?"*

Yes! Obviously you connected urinating with sexuality. It's understandable that young boys would confuse these until they get comfortable with being sexual and separating the two sensations. I bet you have conflicts over really allowing yourself to be sexual. I bet you want to have really big stiff erections, but somewhere along the line you learned you shouldn't. Think about your urinary tract, prostate (where the sperm gets manufactured), and that whole area. Tell it, "You can function. I let you spurt out your sperm and pee and show your power."

PEEING DURING SEX

"Can a guy urinate while having sex?"

If a man is healthy, he shouldn't. Think about it physiologically—the guy has two tubes inside his penis like two twin train tracks—one feeds the urine from the bladder, the other feeds the semen from the *vas deferens*. They meet at a checkpoint, the prostatic urethra, where there's a sphincter muscle, and then feed into one single tube that runs through the middle of his penis and out only one hole, through which either the semen or the urine travels. The sphincter muscle shuts off the urine when the sexual-excitement cycle kicks into gear. So the semen passes through the tube instead of the urine from the bladder. If a guy has a medical problem, like with the sphincter muscle, of course, then, some urine might sneak into the tube in the penis by accident.

"What about a woman peeing during sex?"
"I was having sex with my boyfriend and I am so ashamed; I'm sure I peed. It smelled like pee. Now I'm scared to have sex again. Is something wrong with me?"

If it happens a lot, you may have a physical problem, and need to see a doctor. It is easier for a woman to pee in sex than for a man because she not only has two different tubes; but each feeds a different opening. Open the inner vaginal lips and see how the urethral opening is a smaller hole, between the clitoris and the vaginal opening. So lubrication and urine can more conceivably come out at the same time. But like men, women also have a sphincter muscle that shuts off the feed from the bladder when the woman is excited, except if she has some physical problem. Some women who have weak muscles—from childbirth or other stresses or operations—have a tendency to leak urine. The penis may have been pressing against your bladder, causing you to feel the sensation of wanting to urinate. Or inexperienced women may "let go" in sex, and relax the bladder and urinary system, so they urinate when they're sexually excited, or have orgasm.

You can learn to control this easily by focusing on the muscles in the different areas: squeeze as if to stop the urine flow, or push down as if to squeeze the last drop of urine out. Those control your urinary system. Focus on them to stay closed in sex. Now squeeze and focus on the "love" muscles around your vaginal opening, a little further back. Twitch those. (You can also go a little farther back and distinguish the muscles around the anal opening).

NOT TONIGHT DEAR, I HAVE A (REAL) HEADACHE

Eugene: *"After I ejaculate I get a headache. It happens when I masturbate or if I'm with someone, no matter how much sex I have. First I thought it's because of not having enough, then I thought it was from having too much. It's been happening for a year. It happened one week straight and then not for a while. The vein in my head throbs. What's the problem?"*

Frederika: *"I know people joke that women say they have a headache as an excuse for not having sex, but for me it's no joke: my husband is the one who says he gets headaches in sex. We have a very happy marriage and always enjoyed sex, but now we hardly do it at all. Is something suddenly wrong with me or does he really have them?"*

Don't think you're not attractive enough! Sexual headaches may be real, not just an excuse for calling off sex. About half a million Americans suffer from what's called "benign sexual headache," called BSH (different, as my *LovePhones* co-host Jagger says, from B.S. headaches that really are an excuse from sex). Men get them more than women, since men are more susceptible to sudden or extreme blood pressure changes during sex. Yet people with sex headaches suffer in silence because they're ashamed to admit it! Be happy your husband admitted it.

Tension-type sexual headaches (also called coital headache or orgasmic cephalgia) can happen after sex, or during the excitement phase of the sexual-response cycle, with rapid increases in body tension and blood flow, altered breathing patterns, and muscle contractions literally from head to toe. They often pass, but persist if you have high blood pressure, stress, obesity, migraines, or heart disease. An aspirin prior to sex can help. So can recognizing fears and worries (of rejection, pregnancy, distrust) since anxiety or "holding back" in sex triggers physical reactions, which in turn escalate anxiety in a vicious cycle. HOMEWORK: Relax, give yourself permission to be sexual, practice breathing regularly, rather than holding your breath.

Another kind, an "exertional" headache, comes from increased blood pressure from being too active, as in any exercise, and can last from seconds to hours. Seek medical advice. Danger signs include nausea, vomiting, altered consciousness, or lasting pain, which can signal stroke or blood or spinal fluid leaks. Be wary of highly charged sex activity, such as attempting several orgasms! But keep in mind, studies show making love can also cure headaches: by stimulating blood flow, reducing body tension, and releasing pain-killing chemicals!

NAUSEOUS IN SEX

Christina: *"When I have sex with my boyfriend, he throws up. It doesn't matter if we've done it right after we eat or in a few hours. He gets dry heaves. Then he can't perform. What's wrong?"*

Amy: *"I broke up with a guy and now when I think of sex with him, I feel like puking."*

Angel: *"In the middle of sex, I feel like I want to throw up, and then at the end I feel grossed out. But I want to be with the girl forever. I had a traumatic youth. My mother beat me all the time and my aunt raped me when I was eleven. Does this have anything to do with it?"*

Certainly. A history of abuse can trigger many physical and psychological symptoms during sex, including headaches, dizziness, dissociation (feeling like you're not there), and nausea. Sex can bring back the painful experience of feeling angry, powerless, trapped, depressed, anxious, and a whole complex of emotions that made you feel "sick" about it happening. So it's no wonder that having sex now would reawaken some of those earlier traumatic experiences and the physiological responses that were associated with them. You are remembering the experience of somebody forcing rough sex on you, and being repulsed by it. Add to this difficult situation an overwhelming need to be loved and terror that you will not be loved. That emotional fear can then trigger activation of your autonomic nervous system, which in turn activates your stomach, causing you to feel nervous and nauseous, as would happen in any panic attack.

What is your throat saying (love me, hold me)? Ask for that. If it's saying, "I'm angry," express that. Tell off whoever you're angry at. Vomiting is a way of expelling strong feelings—getting them out of you. If you can't scream, you may vomit. It's getting out what's down in your guts—deep buried feelings you're afraid to express. You may want to, but fear saying "no" to some act your partner requests, but give in instead, and feel nauseous. Your body is saying "no" for you.

Vomiting (like coughing and sneezing) may also be a mini-orgasm! After all, your throat is contracting; it is even emitting stuff! Also throwing up releases chemicals in the brain that induce pleasure and reduce depression (which is, by the way, one reason bulimics do it!). If you can't allow yourself to get excited, then you transfer the feelings into another strong physical outlet that is more acceptable to you (as in hysterical crying or laughing).

Get therapy for your earlier trauma, to accept and unleash all your pent-up feelings. Few men get help to heal because they invalidate the experience, and consider complaining about sex as unmanly. Choose a trusted love partner when you have sex and explain how you feel. Reassure your partner that your reaction does not mean you don't care for him or her, but is due to early unresolved traumas. Ask to be held and nurtured rather than pulling away. Feel the security of another's loving presence, and connect with the depths of your soul.

SCREAMS OBSCENITIES

"I have Tourette's syndrome, where I yell out expletives that can shock people. It's hard for me to find a girl. I could be in the middle of something, like the movies or driving, and all of a sudden without my being able to stop it, I yell sick, sometimes lewd things like 'Stick out your breasts' or 'You slut, fuck me now.' They think I'm weird and run. What can I do?"

You'll have to only go out with girls who are sweet and understanding and whom you can trust to tell them about your condition. Emphasize that it is not something you can control, and not aimed at them.

Tourette's syndrome affects males usually between the ages of two and fourteen, and seems to run in families. The problem was given respect when portrayed so accurately and sympathetically on an episode of the television series *LA Law*.

EATING DISORDERS:

Food symbolizes love and both men and women use eating to stuff down a range of sexual fears and feelings. Eating disorders come from stress. Remember all the newspaper articles about Princess Diana's bulimia, and Paula Abdul's weight fluctuations when she was having trouble with her husband Emilio Estevez?

BULIMIA

Melissa, 17: *"I have trouble deep-throating because I used to be bulimic and stick my finger down my throat and vomit up food I binged on. But my boyfriend does it to me. I still look in the mirror and feel like I'm too fat even though I'm 5'6" and weigh 120, which is normal. What can I do?"*

You have to tell your boyfriend why deep-throating bothers you. You have conditioned your throat to start reverse peristalsis (retching up) by sticking your finger down it to throw up food. Be on top, so you don't feel out of control (which is what your bulimia is about anyway). Go down only as far as you feel comfortable; you can hold his penis in your hands to make him feel fully "taken in."

Much discussed in the 1980s, bulimia persists today. It is common among actresses, dancers, and college women who feel pressured to be thin. They try to control food—by stuffing it down and then throwing it up—when it seems the only thing they can control. About 95 percent of bulimics are women, especially those who feel more pressure about how they look, overwhelmed by feelings, and unable to get their needs met in some way. The vomiting as I mentioned above can trigger a chemical high, but beware, making yourself throw up a lot can lead to problems with your throat, stomach, and breathing, and even to death. Breakthrough research at places like the New York State

Psychiatric Institute are finding that some medications (like anti-depressants) help.

HOMEWORK: Follow my four steps: Stop and think. Recognize your uncomfortable feelings. Assess the consequences of your actions and do something else more constructive. If you stuff down food, ask yourself what feelings you are trying to stuff down. If you're angry, express that. If you need more love to feel filled up, ask for it. Identify thoughts that go through your mind when you're stuffing. If you're eating because you're nervous, recognize what you're nervous about and reassure yourself that you're safe. Hesitate before you eat and ask, "Do I really want this?" Retrain your brain: instead of thinking, "I can eat this and get rid of it," think, "What do I really want to do to make myself feel better now that is healthy?" Resolve, I will not do something and then immediately reverse it; I will do only what makes me feel right from the start.

ANOREXIA

Laura, 21: *"I want to hear my husband say he loves me in sex, but he says I should know. He upsets me but I can't leave him because I have a sickness where I don't eat. I almost lost a child a few years ago and didn't tell him, so he was angry at me. When I was fourteen I was date-raped by a guy, and since then I really don't like being touched by anyone. I am five-three and got down to seventy-nine pounds. Sometimes I take so many laxatives, like eating candy. I hated my breasts and lost my period for a while, which made me happy. When I look in the mirror, I see that I'm fat."*

You have all the classic signs of being anorexic—starving yourself to death because you feel out of control of your life and feelings, and the only thing you think you can control is your eating. Depriving yourself is a way to punish everyone who's been mean and depriving to you. You also disparage being a woman because that means being powerless.

You know you are killing yourself. You have to stop and you need serious psychological help. You can control your life, and express your feelings. A woman can be powerful.

You don't have to punish yourself to punish men like they once hurt you.

Tina: *I am eighteen and never had an intimate relationship because of how I see myself. I'm a compulsive overeater and I know now that I'm trying not to feel anything. What should I do?"*

Singer/songwriter Tori Amos, as Honorary Love Doctor, gives some good advice about relaxing and also about integrating different parts of yourself, to make friends with parts that you hate, and ways you treat yourself badly: "It might be a good thing to get a baseball mitt and play with your ball. This is the thing I have been doing for a while. I spend fifteen minutes a day in the bathtub because it is the most safe vulnerable place I could be. And if you go in there and you say, 'How do I really feel about what I did today?' if you are lucky you will do about thirty-seven things that are stupid. And now that I accept that I do thirty-seven things that are not so stupid, I am not so hard on myself. You start loving that coward, that part of me. And I've started taking all the parts of me shopping; I take the coward and the ugly one. I go, 'come on, ugly one.' And if I don't love me, nobody else can. I have created my own mom and my own prostitute and my own virgin. And the virgin and the prostitute, they love sitting next to each other. They trade stories. And it's becoming where it's okay when we are not okay. It's okay when I feel like I don't have answers or am not feeling superior."

NO SEX AFTER EATING

Ro: *"How come when I eat I have no desire for sex for about eight hours?"*

Psychologically it sounds like you connect being fed with sex, so when you feel full, you don't need to be filled up in sex. Also, physiologically your body might be metabolizing and so your body chemistry is activated, chemicals are flowing, and you are in a state of equilibrium; when this state changes, or chemicals drop, you feel the urge to activate again, which can be channeled into eating or sex.

M.D. HOAX?

Nancy, 20: *"I thought I was pregnant and went to a gyne-cologist I found in the Yellow Pages. He gave me some pills and told me how to take them and didn't say what they were for. He told me to take off my shirt and panties and to uri-nate in a cup. I told him I was spotting all week and he didn't ask why. Could he be a fake?"*

Some women aren't used to the procedures of a gynecologist. They do take urine samples in a cup. For the examination, you do get undressed and put on a gown and lie on a table with your legs up in the air while the doctor looks into your vaginal canal with a speculum and feels your abdomen and does a breast examination. There usually is a nurse in the room, too. Some doctors don't give any explanations for what they're doing. That's too bad, but then it's up to you to ask questions. Always check a doctor's board and state certification. It is best to choose a doctor by a personal recommendation from a friend.

If you are uncomfortable, don't go back. Find another doctor. Personal comfort is just as important as professional ability.

SHAVED PAINS

"I used a lotion to take the pubic hairs off and now I have a rash and it's growing in with all bumps and prickles. What can I do?"

Check the label on what you used for any specific treatments. Get an anti-inflammatory at the pharmacy, like hydrocortisone cream. See a dermatologist. You may also need an anti-infective if any skin came off. This would be treated like a chemical burn, requiring a prescription medication like Silvadene.

Why did you want to shave (curiosity, to feel like a kid again)? Don't think you got punished for what you did. It's okay.

Don't want to get stoned.
But, I don't wanna not get stoned.
—from "Style," sung by Lemonheads' Evan Dando.

> *I'm too much with myself.*
> *I want to be someone else.*
> —Dando, singing about speed, in "My Drug Buddy."

MARIJUANA

Ryan, 23: *"My girlfriend and I smoke pot every day. I like the way it makes me feel in sex, but will there be any long-term damage I don't know about yet? And when it comes time to having a baby, will we have a problem? I know it can hurt the baby, so what if we stop smoking when we know she got pregnant?"*

You may think sex is better on pot, because time slows down, making lovemaking seem to last longer, you feel relaxed, and your senses are heightened. But there could be trouble for both of you sexually with your chronic pot smoking. There is some evidence that too much THC (tetrahydrocannabinol, the ingredient in pot) can reduce the number of a man's healthy sperm and decrease testosterone level and therefore sexual desire. In women, it can interfere with ovulation. This would create fertility problems in both of you, making it difficult for her to get pregnant. Also the insecticide used on some weed can cause health problems and infertility.

As far as stopping when your girlfriend finds out she's pregnant, that won't work because you don't know you're pregnant 'til after the fact; she'd notice her missed period two weeks after the sperm already met the egg, so the embryo is already being affected by the smoke.

DANGEROUS MIX

Seventeen-year-old Angel faced the devil when drugs got involved with an already dangerous sexual attraction: *"I had sex with my best friend's mother and told the guidance counselor we did it and used drugs, cocaine and Valium one time, and she told my parents and now they're putting me in a drug program and threatening to sue the mother for endangering a minor."*

It's sad that everything has blown up, but you were playing with fire, and you really wanted it to stop because you told someone. Even though you're angry the counselor told on you, I bet you're also relieved.

HARD DRUGS

"My homeboy told me all's I had to do was some of that crack and I'd be keeping the ladies happy for long clock time. Is he steering me right? Some other dude told me I'd have a hard time getting it up."

Big trouble is ahead. Cocaine, or crack, does keep you hard for a long time, but not only do you end up having trouble ejaculating, but you can get addicted, and then you're in real hot water. It makes you feel euphoric by preventing dopamine (that causes excitement) from being absorbed, but if you use it a lot, it destroys dopamine and your sexual drive. Don't you be letting anyone talk you into it.

Horse is bad news, too. You may feel more relaxed, but heroin slows you down and causes delayed ejaculation and impotence, by blocking the alpha-adrenergic system responsible for opening the blood vessels.

Aerosmith's Steven Tyler had been there, and knows you get performance problems on it: "Yes, when I was doing a lot of cocaine . . . for a while it works, rubbing the coke on the head of your penis, but it causes derailment. And the same with heroin. It keeps you hard forever, but you don't come. But boy, when you take that stuff away, it's like Good Morning!"

LSD

Jason: *"I had a bad acid trip. I was hallucinating and blood came out of my penis instead of cum and my girlfriend's face looked like a skull. Now I can't have sex anymore without thinking of that. What can I do?"*

Treat it like a bad memory. You couldn't control your thoughts because you were under the influence of the drug, but you can control your thoughts now. Why choose to reinvent the bad trip over and over? When you think of those horrible images, imagine your brain like a computer and press the delete button and program a pleasant image instead. What could that pleasant image be? Picture flowers coming out of your penis and her face looking angelic.

Dare I need remind you of the dangers of playing with your mind with this drug?

VITAMIN X

"I'm planning to take ecstasy with my girlfriend. Will it turn us on?"

Ecstasy, the "love drug," can create an increased sense of intimacy and heightened sensitivity to touch, that makes you feel like lovemaking is extended and touchy-feely. It's used in a lot of clubs and at "raves" these days. But be aware it's illegal and there are questions about its long-term effects, as with any mind-altering substance.

ALCOHOL

Madonna wrote in her book *Sex* that you should have a couple of beers before you give a blow job—to loosen up. A guy on the panel when I was on the *Ricki Lake Show* about jerks and nice guys (he was in the former category) said he gets action by getting girls drunk, calling wine "liquid panty remover."

So many young men and women call me about escapades they fall into that they regret, or get into trouble over (being rejected, getting pregnant, having sex with a friend's lover or mother), and it turns out they were drunk. Skip the juice to be loose, or you'll lose.

Remember, Responsibility Rules.

Leslie, 22: *"My boyfriend calls me when he's drunk and says, 'I love you,' and 'I want your children,' but in person he doesn't remember. When we have sex he won't say it. What can I do?"*

Poor boy, he's using alcohol to reduce his inhibitions.

One drink can loosen you up, but research shows that three become dangerous. He may genuinely have those loving feelings he expresses, but he's in trouble because he's obviously fearful of intimacy because he has to be so drunk to say them. Better tell him to get help for his alcoholism because he's headed for disaster. Meanwhile, if you're not too involved, let go until he starts recovering.

Alan, 23: *"I've been drinking a lot since the last three years. Before I had a high sex drive. Now I'm not interested. Could this have something to do with my drinking and if I stopped, would it come back?"*

Drinking a lot dulls desire and causes erection problems in men and orgasm problems in women (partly because it constricts blood flow). You get caught in a vicious cycle: drinking to forget you can't perform, not being able to perform because you're drinking, getting more depressed you can't perform, so you drink more. If you stop in time, you can get back your functioning, but if you drink regularly over a long period of time, you can kiss your sexuality, along with your liver, good-bye. Too much too long (it varies for different people) lowers your testosterone and sperm count, leading to the possible shrinking of your testicles and sterility.

"What drugs are good and bad for sex?"

Bad news drugs: certain antipsychotic medications (like Thorazine and Mellaril for schizophrenia), anti-anxiety agents (that depress the central nervous system and therefore decrease libido and inhibit orgasm), some cholesterol-lowering drugs, diuretics, and some medications for hairiness and stomach ulcers (that increase prolactin and decrease libido).

Some good news drugs: L-Dopa, originally for Parkinson's disease, that produces dopamine and increases ardor; hormone replacements in case of deficiencies; the anti-diuretic hormone Vasopressin, called the "brain hormone," was touted to prolong orgasm.

In-between news: Some antidepressants can work wonders to help sex (because you're in a better mood) and others wreak havoc with your desire or performance.

"When I had a cough and took cough medicine, I couldn't come. Can that be?"

This is pretty rare, but codeine in cough syrup, or the synthetic codeine called hydrocodone, can interfere with urinating and orgasm. You can be fine when you stop taking it.

> **Q:** Do you smoke after sex?
> **A:** I don't know, I never looked.

SMOKING

"I like to have a smoke after sex, and everyone says smoking'll kill you, but will it ruin my sex life before I die?"

Smoking has paradoxical effects—it first relaxes, then stimulates. Ultimately, it constricts your blood vessels, so blood can't flow, which is what erection and vaginal swelling is all about, so you wouldn't get as excited or have orgasm.

If you want to be less anxious in sex, use deep breathing instead. Also, sticking a cigarette in your mouth is like a pacifier—you're stuck at the oral phase of development. Chew on something else (a pencil, or better yet, your thoughts). If you need to be suckled, nurtured like a baby, get the real love you need.

Carole: *"My boyfriend chews a lot of tobacco and it bothers me when he kisses me."*

Richard Marx hates smoking and does a lot of charity work against it. So it made sense he'd get incensed: "That's disgusting. I think you should put something in your mouth that is the rankest, most disgusting thing and then put your tongue in his mouth and say now you know how it tastes. Follow through with your ultimatum not to kiss him unless he stops chewing tobacco."

Lee: *"My girlfriend likes to "huff" inhaling VCR cleaner or whip-its and won't have sex unless she has it. Then she hits me and passes out. I'm scared."*

You should be. She has a serious drug habit. Refuse to have sex with her when she's using and insist she go for rehab. You need to go to Alanon, the 12 step program for people addicted to addicts.

FEARS SEX IN PREGNANCY

Jennifer, 20: *"I'm nine months pregnant and my boyfriend won't have sex with me. My doctor said it's okay. What's wrong?"*

Better check again with your doctor. Many say you can continue intercourse until the last two weeks, at which time having orgasm may trigger contractions that could put you in premature labor. There are other ways of lovemaking without intercourse! Also ask your boyfriend what his fears are—that he will injure the baby, that his sperm will spit in the baby's eye? Prepare yourselves for the transition to being parents, and continuing to be lovers even though you're now about to become daddy and mommy. Let him know that you need sex to feel attractive.

HEART AND SEX: THE BEAT GOES ON

"I'm only twenty-one but my husband is fifty and had a heart attack, and now he's afraid to have sex. I want to, but I'm scared, too. Could he die in bed?"

It's natural that you and your husband are scared—his very existence has been threatened. But there is good news: the cases of a heart attack during sex are extremely rare (though the risks go up with extra-marital affairs, with presumably more strenuous sex!). Check with your husband's doctor and send for information from the American Heart Association, but the generally accepted advice is that you can resume sex once you can climb two flights of stairs or take a brisk walk effortlessly. A lot of people don't start sex again because they're afraid or have marital problems. You sound fine. Reassure your husband and start sex in a relaxed place and position. It'll boost your spirits. He can even wear a portable monitor, for extra reassurance. As one caller to *LovePhones* said of her dating a man with heart trouble, "I didn't give him angina, I gave him vagina."

URINARY-TRACT INFECTIONS

"My boyfriend lives far away, so I go for months without sex, then when we see each other, we go at it for hours. I love it, but the worst is after one of these marathons, I had some blood come out and it was painful when I urinated. What was this and can he get it?"

See your gynecologist right away. Likely you have a recurrent urinary-tract infection (UTI) that comes from sexual activity when bacteria from the vagina, rectum, or a partner's hands or sex organs are introduced into the urethral opening either by hand or the motions of intercourse. It often happens (within twenty-four hours) after a lot of sexual activity with a new partner (called "honeymoon cystitis"); after intervals of abstinence; when you wipe from your rear forward; from holding it in when you have to pee, creating a pool of urine that breeds bacteria; from a diaphragm, nylon panty hose, or tight jeans pressuring or bruising the urethra; from vaginal douches, deodorants, and bath preparations; and from contraceptive use (e.g., an improperly fitted diaphragm can block urine flow and spermicide use can kill "good" bacteria in the vagina, leaving an imbalance of "bad" bacteria). Guys can get UTIs, too, but it's more common in women, since their openings are closer together and their urethras are shorter. Get a urine test. Antibiotic medication kicks in within half an hour.

True old wives' tale: bicarbonate or cranberry juice can help (depending on which medication you take). To prevent it, drink plenty of liquids (to flush bacteria from the urethra); urinate before and after sex; wipe from front to back; be clean before and during sex play; avoid the rear entry position, coffee, tea, or alcohol, which irritate bladder tissue; and reconsider your contraceptive (refit diaphragm); and wear cotton panties!

SCHIZOPHRENIC BREAK

Barry: *"I masturbate so much I get burns on my hand and penis. I go in my sister's room and take her dolls and pretend they're talking to me. I put the dolls' clothes on my penis and invite their buddies, my testicles, to get in the action. I like the big breasts on the Barbie, and when I'm in school, I grab the girls' breasts. They deserve it because they're sluts."*

Vance: *"I'm afraid I'm going crazy. After I masturbate I hear voices. It started five weeks ago after I had an experience masturbating with a guy friend, who went off to school. I have been masturbating thinking of him, and the groans come. I don't feel bad about thinking about him, but the voices say that I'm a whore, so what are they?"*

I'm scared for you both. You could be having the beginnings of a psychotic break. You may be guilty about what you've done. What are the moans saying to you? Do they tell you that you've been bad? They're wrong. Have a psychiatric evaluation. You could have schizophrenia, a thought disorder where you lose the ability to tell fantasy from reality, and end up doing weird things. People who have it can become either withdrawn into their own world, or paranoid, thinking the world is out to get them, accusing others, and even hearing voices that aren't there, usually threatening, or accusing them of vile acts. It's like a bad acid trip. There is considerable evidence that this is a biologically determined disorder, not something you can control. An event like the sex with your friend can trigger the episode, but cannot cause the problem. Medications, like phenothiazines, can help stop the voices in your head and any troublesome acts you do.

MANIC-DEPRESSIVE

Jane: *"I want to teach my boyfriend to be a wilder lover. My fantasies come so fast. I'm a sexy, wexy, lexy lover, who can swing him around my head, 'til he's dead, and feels like lead, and his name isn't even Ched. Sometimes I fly like a bird, and I go out and spend a lot on new clothes to amuse him. There isn't even time to do all the things I want to do. I should write a morality play about good and evil with Michelle Pfeiffer and Keanu Reeves as the leads. I think I can direct them to have some real love scenes that will scorch up the screen. Should I do it? The problem is some-times I get close and then I crash and I can't get out of bed for days, so it would hold up the shooting."*

How distressing to have so much energy and excitement that you feel you can do anything one minute, and then to be so paralyzed you can't get out of bed.

I suspect you have some disorder like manic depression, where you go through swings of mania, feeling like you're on top of the world and can do anything, and then bouts of severe depression, where black clouds descend down on you. Your rhyming gives it away. You need a psychiatric evaluation. The predisposition for this disorder is also inherited—if your parents had mood disorders, your chances of getting one are greatly increased. Medication helps ease the big mood swings—though you might resist because the highs feel so good. But if you're in enough dis-tress, you'll do something about it.

There was some suggestion that Kurt Cobain had manic depression, along with other physical ailments like back trouble and hyperactivity as a child. Guns N' Roses wild-man lead singer Axl Rose also reportedly had extreme mood swings.

FEARS FOR LIFE

Jose, 19: *"I think my wife is trying to kill me. One night after sex, I woke up and she was holding a pillow over my head. She said, 'I'm trying to make you more comfortable.' She has a history of manic-depressive illness but I don't think she's taking her medication. We've been married six months. One time she punched me after I called her a name because she was eyeing another man in a grocery store. What can I do?"*

People who suffer from manic-depression can do irra-tional things, in sex and at any time. Unless she takes her medication, her psychosis can wreak havoc. Go to see her psychiatrist together and report what happened; don't hide your fears or you could wind up dead.

Gary: *"My girlfriend has bad PMS. I try to kiss her and she says, 'Get away, I'm in a bad mood.' It's gotten worse since we had our daughter two years ago. Now, we both refer to her as 'the bitch is back.' What's wrong?"*

She needs a full evaluation for PMS and possible hormone therapy if she has an imbalance. Many women experience swings of mood according to the time of the month, with the most extreme being just before their period. It's due to the balance of the estrogen and progesterone, the female sex hormones. PMS can be managed with relaxation, knowing and controlling your moods, rest, and healthy diet and exercise. Have her keep a diary rating her moods to track her patterns; knowing what to expect helps you both from getting angry at each other for no reason or taking it personally. If it gets extreme, she needs medical attention.

Sean Young, Honorary Love Doctor, identified: "My husband would agree with your situation. I never really noticed that much about myself until I started studying my period in order to get pregnant. Now I know every twenty-eight days when it happens. I know when I am supposed to ovulate, and I started to notice that three days before my period or sometimes during it I wanted to kill my husband, I would get really irritable, like, 'You never do enough around the house!' There is for me a definite connection."

STEROID MADNESS

"My boyfriend is into bodybuilding and is going to a competition, so he's shooting steroids. We fight about it because I worry about him and also I want to have a baby. He yells that I never supported him in his dream to do these competitions and our relationship isn't working. I get hurt and cry. Then he came to me finally and said, 'I'll throw away my dream for you.' Do you think he means it?"

I hope so, but I wouldn't count on it. A dream is a powerful driving force. He may say he'll stop the steroids just to get you to support him so he can go through this competition without stress. But taking steroids is also a powerful addiction. Usually a guy would need a lot of therapy to stop it, unless of course he starts feeling the negative side effects. You have a right to worry because excessive steroid use shrinks the testicles and can lead to infertility.

ASTHMA

Sharon: *"My boyfriend has asthma and it's hard to make love. He had an asthma attack and we both freaked. I called an ambulance, I was so scared he was going to die. Now I'm wondering if I can go through this."*

Of course you're scared—it's frightening when someone is gasping for breath! And it can make you feel guilty that you, and sex, are endangering his life. What a horrifying thought that he might suffocate in the middle of the act. Some studies show that men with asthma have erection problems because of emotional rather than physical reasons: imagine that not being able to catch your breath means you need to be taken care of and are frightened of separation. As with various allergies, they can get started, or worsen, when the nasal membranes get congested, as can happen in sexual activity. This can be helped by taking medication timed for the sexual activity, and by keeping inhalers and other medication by the bed.

Since positions and sexual activity that require more oxygen—like being on top or very acrobatic—cause more strain and therefore breathing problems, stick to his being on bottom, or a side-to-side position with less thrusting and relaxed, pressure-free sex.

OBSESSIVE-COMPULSIVE

Michael, 18: *"I've been diagnosed as obsessive-compulsive because I do silly things, like wash my hands 'til they bleed, and check that I have my homework in my bag fifty times. I repeat myself over and over 'til it drives people crazy. I masturbate seven times a day, and sometimes to stop myself, when I get real anxious, I call up those sex lines. The worst part is I pull out my pubic hair all night. I can't stop myself. Will anything help me?"*

All these behaviors are classic signs of obsessive-compulsive disorder, which means you are out of control of your actions. In some severe cases (like yours) medication (like anafranil) helps reduce the pressure to repeat annoying behaviors. Otherwise, use my Four Steps: stop and think before you act. Recognize your needs (usually it's to prevent thinking or doing something else unacceptable, like getting angry or feeling sexual), assess the consequences of your actions, and choose to do something else (check out the chapter on When It's Not Happening).

SPERM IN YOUR EYE

"My boyfriend ejaculated into my eye the other night. My eye was sore. Could there be a big problem? Can I go blind?"

My cousin, Joel Spielberg, a noted ophthalmologist in New Jersey, says semen itself is not toxic to the eye. But since the eye is an open area through which fluids can get into the blood, if the person has some bacteria or sexually transmitted disease, it can theoretically be transmitted by getting semen in your eye. Fortunately, there are no cases of getting AIDS this way to date. Wash your eye out. If you wore soft contact lenses, replace them. If the irritation persists for more than an hour, definitely see an ophthalmologist, or go to an emergency room.

To prevent this problem, if you're doing oral sex, put the tip of your tongue on the tip of his penis when he ejaculates so it doesn't spurt out. Aerosmith's Steven Tyler suggested goggles.

HE'S PREGNANT

"A guy I work with was always in good shape, but since his wife got pregnant his growing paunch makes it look like he's the one having the baby. He's also moodier than he was. Could he be having a sympathetic pregnancy like some people have sympathy pains?"

Yes, there is such a thing as sympathetic pregnancy in men (called the couvade syndrome, for the French word "to hatch"), where the man identifies with his wife's state to the point of experiencing similar emotional and physical symptoms, like anxiety, depression, nausea, and stomach pain. More men have it now because they're more into fathering, going to Lamaze classes, and doing natural childbirth. He may also unconsciously mimic pregnancy because he's jealous of the baby, or wants to merge with mother! The guy needs more attention.

COLD GERMS

Rose: *"If the guy has a cold and does oral sex on you, can you get sick?"*

Technically, yes, the germs from his mouth can get inside your body through your sensitive genital tissues.

EMBARRASSED OVER GYN EXAM

Katrina, 17: *"My mother took me to the gynecologist for an exam to get birth-control pills and I was so embarrassed when he stuck his finger up my rear. I could feel that he could feel doody in there. Ugh. I never want to go back again."*

It's normal for you to feel embarrassed at your gyn exam, but know that gynecologists (urologists, proctologists) are used to doing all those procedures, so you don't have to be embarrassed. They have seen lots of genital and anal openings, and things inside, including feces. To feel confident, wash well before you go. You can take an enema to clear out the feces (do it a half hour before, so any excess liquid drains out, too).

NARCOLEPSY

Benjamin, 24: *"I could be in the middle of caressing my girlfriend's breasts and she gets knocked out unconscious. Could I be that good? Really, what's wrong with her?"*

She could have narcolepsy—a disorder in which people seem to fall asleep in the middle of something. Have her see a doctor. It's not your fault. You're not doing anything bad, or good, to make it happen.

STIFF HANDS

Stephanie: *"My hands get paralyzed in sex and I can't open them. It happens before I have orgasm, so I stop what we're doing. I'm scared I'll get paralyzed and have some kind of carpal tunnel syndrome."*

Don't worry. Your stiffened hands are most likely a sign you are excited! Muscle stiffness or myotonia (spasms) can happen as part of the normal stages of the sexual-response cycle. A lot of people feel that stiffness in their toes, which cramp up.

Relax. Do some deep breathing. If your fingers could talk what would they say ("I'm scared")? Tell yourself, "I'm enjoying this, I'm relaxed." Ease your mind by going to the doctor. Don't be afraid to say that you got this in sex. Carpal tunnel syndrome develops when certain tendons in the wrist are overused (most often by typing at a computer or even doing surgery). You could have arthritis, but then the stiffness would be there at other times, too.

So, check it out, my last word on keeping your body fresh is that if you take care of that temple you could get a Rolling Eye High:

ROLLING EYES

"My boyfriend's eyes rolled up during sex and I got scared. Is that okay?"

The sexual-response cycle can make you so relaxed that you go into a trance-like state. Also, in sexual arousal the brain waves change from delta (the busy state) to alpha (a semihypnotic state), so he would seem sleepy and other-worldly. Good time to talk to him and croon in his ear how you love him so he gets it on his semiconscious level.

"Are you having killer sex?"
"Are you sleeping with someone to die for?"

ARE YOU? THESE ARE GREAT QUESTIONS I HEARD
at the Planned Parenthood meeting where *LovePhones* got a
Maggie award for helpfulness to young people.

Simply put, are you having unsafe sex? If so, don't be a
sex dope. You could get a nasty STD.

What is an STD? It stands for sexually transmitted disease, any disease you get primarily by sexual contact
(though colds and the flu can also be transmitted by sexual
contact). STDs are caused by germs entering the body
through mucous membranes, including the vagina, urethra,
anus, and mouth.

Myth: STDs develop on their own, come from poor
hygiene, or may be transmitted without sexual contact
(from doorknobs, toilet seats). Truth: Except in rare cases,
STD germs are transmitted between people, and usually die
within minutes when outside the body or exposed to heat or
cold.

Respect Yourself, Protect Yourself

Remember, **Respect, Responsibility,** and the **Right to
Say Yes or No Rule.**

You should be scared about STDs—you may have sex
thinking you're in love, but end up with a disease or dead,
since STDs have reached epidemic proportions. This is the

Era of Sexually Transmitted Diseases because more young people are having more sex, because people have fewer sexual inhibitions, because using drugs clouds judgment, and because people think they can be treated more easily so they're more cavalier about what they do.

Do you think, "It can't happen to me?" Wrong. Listen to what happened to Lacey:

"A tisket, a tasket, a condom or a casket," she recited. *"I was a runaway when I was fifteen and had sex one time with a guy who took me in one night when I was on the street. I didn't know it then, but he was an IV drug user and he was HIV positive, and I had sex with him just that one time and now I have the virus and my life is ruined."*

Ethan's is another heart-breaking story. He recounted, *"I went to a party and got drunk. I met a guy who offered to take me home in his car, and he went somewhere and parked and said I have to go down on him and that if I didn't he would put saline in my friend's hypodermic needle who is a diabetic. So I went down on him and I got sick and went to the doctor and I found out I was HIV positive. He was the only guy I ever didn't have safe sex with. No one knows yet that I'm going to die. I can't bear it. I'm scared. Why did this happen to me?"*

You poor dear. You got really tricked, and that guy committed a terrible crime against you. You need a lawyer— there are cases like this now, where people who knowingly infect others could be accused of a crime, like assault with a deadly weapon. But you also need lots of love and support. Tell your friends and family. Don't be ashamed. Join support groups. You must have hope. You can live a full life being HIV positive. You have to be courageous, like other people "living with HIV"—rather than sink into depression. You have to feel, "I'm meant to do something with this." One good purpose is to be of service now to others. Your spirit can inspire other people that you touch.

If Lacey and Ethan's sad stories don't convince you that it only takes *one* time of a risky behavior to get infected, I don't know what will. Statistics don't count, it can happen to you.

Remember, *just once unprotected and you can become infected!*

Remember, too, you cannot tell from looking at anyone (except if they have obvious skin sores from Kaposi's sarcoma—a kind of cancer) whether they are infected. **And when you have sex with someone, you are having sex with everyone else they ever had sex with.** Any male or female who has had unprotected sex as long ago as even ten years (or sometimes more), especially with multiple partners, is at risk for infection with the HIV.

Shocking statistics:
  • Currently there are twelve million *new* cases of sexually transmitted diseases every year, with the largest number (two thirds) occurring in people under age twenty-five, including three million teenagers.
  • Over fifty million Americans currently suffer from STDs.
  • About one in every four Americans will contract an STD in their lifetime.
  • The number of STDs is increasing (there are now more than twenty), and "old" infections, like gonorrhea, syphilis, and warts are on the rise.

The safest sex, of course, is no sex.
An advertisement from a religious group asks:

Want to know a Dirty Little Secret? Condoms don't save lives. But restraint does. Only fools think condoms are foolproof. Remember, better safe than sorry. Short of abstinence, there is no totally safe sex, just safer sex and reducing risks.

Keith: *"I hear a lot about AIDS and what we shouldn't do but is anybody really doing anything different? I don't think my friends pay attention. Are condoms enough to keep you from getting those awful things?"*

No! It's true that rigorous tests have shown the HIV virus and other small viruses do not pass through *latex* condoms when they're properly used. But people get sloppy. They don't put them on right or they use non-latex ones with lubricants or spermicides that can break them (like oily substances—you have to use water-based substances). Being in the heat of passion can ruin your judgment. Also a condom isn't foolproof, since it doesn't cover everything (for example, you could have herpes sores in the anal opening).

Shocking: Even Madonna has admitted that she doesn't always practice safe sex. Answering Norman Mailer's questions printed in *Esquire*, the Queen of Sex said, "I'm not going to sit here and say that from the time I found out about AIDS, I've always had intercourse with a man with a condom on. That would be a lie."

One study showed that up to eight out of ten men and women believed that condoms were effective against AIDS, and up to four out of ten have at least one risk factor for contracting the disease (like having more than two sex partners in the past five years), but less than two in ten use condoms. The reasons: feeling less sensitive wearing them, or clumsy or embarrassed to buy or use them.

Simon: *"I hear so much about AIDS and HIV, and even this thing called ARC, and AZT that I think is a drug, but I'm embarrassed to say I still don't know what all this alphabet soup is really about. Are AIDS and HIV the same thing? What is it?"*

The deadliest STD, AIDS is the term for Acquired Immunodeficiency Disorder Syndrome, that refers to a variety of illnesses that happen when the immune system is broken down from infection with HIV (human immunodeficiency virus). In short, HIV is transmitted through the exchange of bodily fluids (blood, sperm, organs, or tissues from an infected person). An estimated one million Americans are infected, with the largest risk groups still including gay men and intravenous drug users, and increasing risks in heterosexual women and teens. If you're infected with other venereal diseases, you're more vulnerable to infection by HIV. Symptoms can go unnoticed (dormant) for up to ten years, and then show up in flulike illnesses, swollen glands, fatigue, diarrhea, weight loss, and other infections.

ARC is an outdated term that refers to AIDS-related-complex diseases. The antiviral agent AZT seems to slow progress of the disease (Olympic diving champ Greg Louganis has taken it and lived with being HIV positive since before his Gold Medal wins), but no known cure is available.

"Can you get an STD or AIDS from kissing or oral sex?"

No one likes to admit this—to prevent public panic—but it is not totally safe to have oral sex without protection against STDs or the HIV virus. Viruses and bacteria don't live easily on nonorganic material (like toilet seats, towels, toothbrushes), and usually die after exposure to air (though this doesn't apply to cold viruses), but other body contacts are not invulnerable to infection. Since the virus is transmitted by exchange of body fluids, if you have a cut in your mouth (haven't you ever bled when brushing your teeth?), and your partner has a cut on the mouth or genitals, a point of entry is possible—for HIV or any other STD.

It was shocking to find in the study on *LovePhones* callers, that lots of teens interviewed said they did not practice safe oral sex (even if they did practice safe sex with penetration). You *must* be careful. For example, you can get herpes on your mouth and then transmit it to your own or someone else's genitals.

AFRAIDS

Anxiety about AIDS is so high, it generates stories and myths that can get out of hand. In June of 1994, a high-school kid called *LovePhones* and said that a bunch of kids at his high school were sent a letter saying that they had tested HIV positive.

After much to-do the next day, it was discovered by calling the school and the Red Cross that the kids had misunderstood. Over a dozen kids were turned away from giving blood, not because of being HIV positive, but because of having colds, temperature, taking antibiotics, or other innocuous reasons. HIV testing wasn't even done.

Such rumors are testimonial to what my good friend, Frank Hagan, formerly on a Presidential Commission on AIDS, calls *AFRAIDS*—the fear AIDS generates! The Red Cross told me that such rumors erupt about once a year.

Turns out the kid who participated in the rumors had sex for the first time, unprotected, so he had a reason to be frightened that he would get AIDS! He needed to be careful.

"How do you convince college kids of the true threat of AIDS and other illnesses? I don't believe AIDS is really a problem for young people. I don't see any of my friends dying from it."

I'm happy for you that none of your friends are dying from AIDS; it's a very painful experience. But here's why: unlike catching a cold where you get the symptoms two weeks after being exposed to the virus, the HIV can take years to unfold. So you can be exposed to it now and it will not show up until you are much older!

Teens get infected because they take more risks and fall prey to pressure to do unsafe things by friends or strangers, like the girl who had sex for the first time with a cool guy who turned out to be an IV drug user but she thought he was "so nice" because he drove a BMW and wore an Armani suit. More teens are having sex, and don't know enough about it to make safe decisions. And they use needles to pierce their ears, or inject steroids, or play vampire games. And they get drunk so they don't know what they're doing.

Will shocking statistics convince you of the severity of the problem to teens?

- One survey from college campuses found (shockingly) nearly one in three hundred college students infected with the AIDS virus.
- Since one in five of all reported AIDS cases is diagnosed in the twenty to twenty-nine-year-old age group and the median incubation period between HIV infection and AIDS diagnosis is nearly ten years, most of those people in their twenties who are

diagnosed with AIDS were adolescents when they became infected.

- AIDS is the fastest growing health risk to teens. It was the sixth leading cause of death among young people aged fifteen to twenty-four in 1990.

Since some surveys show more than half of students in grades nine to twelve report having sexual intercourse at least once in their lifetime and 19 percent say they engaged in sex with at least four partners, the risks are there!

The numbers become real when you know real people who get it. Look at heroes and celebrities who have gotten it. Some, like basketball star Magic Johnson and Olympic diving Gold Medalist Greg Louganis (who created a stir when he revealed how he had hit his head on the diving board and bled in the pool at the Olympic games), survive. Others, like tennis star Arthur Ashe and movie star Rock Hudson, have died.

Elton John, open about being gay, has made fighting AIDS a life-long passion, as has Elizabeth Taylor (who has a daughter by marriage who is infected). Red Hot Chili Peppers' Anthony Kiedes would have made a good peer model for a government AIDS-prevention program (for which he did a radio ad, a verbal striptease, "Now I'm naked, with a condom") except he was dropped when they found out he had a conviction for sexual battery and indecent exposure.

Madonna presented her racy *Sex* book as a testimonial to safe sex. (But not everyone agreed; for example, Debbie Gibson criticized, "I've liked everything she's done up to the *Sex* book. I feel that the core of pop-music fans are kids. They are the ones most influenced by their role models. I think Madonna's book, which she referred to as a 'fantasy book,' is difficult for kids of twelve years old, who can't distinguish fantasy from reality. They don't know from Madonna's fantasy, they just know what they see. On every page she's with a different partner, that makes sex look too casual. The text was about casual sex. It was selfish. She's a great role model in lots of ways, but as a role model for kids, she crossed the line.")

GETTING IT FROM HER

"I love doing oral sex on women, and I heard that a guy can't get AIDS from going down on a woman—that it's really rare. So can I just do it without being worried?"

"How does a guy get the HIV virus into his body from the girl in intercourse if she doesn't cum in him?

"I just turned lesbian, so I've heard that the chances of getting AIDS from a woman are slim. Do I have to do anything to protect myself?"

It's ten times more likely a woman will get an STD or the HIV from a guy than he from her. That's because a woman's urethra is shorter (the man's extends the length of his penis, an added distance from his bladder) and therefore the bacteria travel a shorter distance into her body and have less chance of getting killed by the acidity of the urine; because her genitalia are more exposed than the encased penis; and because her lubrication makes her genitalia more moist, creating a welcome place for certain invasions.

True, the statistics of woman-to-woman transmission show the lowest risk, and female-to-male transmission is also rare—but it is still possible. The HIV virus is very small—1/10,000th of a millimeter in length—and microscopic skin openings inside the vagina are quite common in healthy women, so if you both have cuts on the genitals or mouth, the body products can travel from one to the other.

For safe oral sex on a woman, use a dental dam, a rectangle of latex that looks like a condom cut open, that you stretch over the genital area (so it's difficult to insert your tongue deeply). The sensation is like having oral sex on a man wearing a condom. You can get them from sex specialty shops, condom shops (like Condomania), or mail order companies like Eve's Garden in New York. The female condom also provides safer sex—it's like an inverted male condom that fits along the inside vaginal walls, and flops over to cover a little bit of the external genitalia at the entrance.

Will the statistics help convince you that AIDS is an increasing problem for women?

• Women are the fastest-growing group infected with

HIV. From 1990 to 1991, the number of AIDS cases among women reported by the Centers for Disease Control grew 37 percent, as opposed to a 4 percent increase among men. The risk is even greater for African-American and Latino women (three-fourths of all women with AIDS).

- By the year 2000, women will make up the majority of the newly infected.
- More than 70 percent of new HIV infections worldwide are contracted through heterosexual intercourse.
- By 1990, AIDS was the seventh leading cause of death in women aged fifteen to twenty-four and the sixth leading cause of death in women aged twenty-five to forty-four.
- The CDC estimates about 110,000 women in this country are infected with HIV. An estimated six thousand are expected to give birth, resulting in up to two thousand infected newborns.

"What are the safest sex behaviors?"

The only way to be sure not to get the HIV virus is to avoid any activities that expose your bloodstream to the fluids or tissues of anyone who is infected with the HIV virus or who is at risk. That means not having sex, or having sex only with a partner who is not infected (who has been tested twice), who only has sex with you, and neither of you shoot drugs or share needles or syringes.

Practice mutual masturbation, give body massages, hold each other warmly, have phone sex, share sexual fantasies, strip, or perform for one another.

"How can I have anal sex and not get AIDS?"

Anal sex is one of the highest-risk sexual behaviors. You must use a latex condom, and add spermicide. Don't insert anything or have penile penetration in such a way as to tear the delicate linings of the anal canal, causing a passageway for the virus to get into the bloodstream.

Get high . . . get stupid . . . get AIDS.

"Do drugs and alcohol make it more likely you'll get an STD or AIDS?"

Yes. You won't get it directly, but your judgment will be impaired, so you'll be more likely to do things that put you at risk, like have sex with someone you don't know.

Before you enter those pearly gates . . . investigate.

That means examine each other's genitals—to see obvious sores or signs of disease.

"What are the questions to ask if you want to find out if someone can give me AIDS?"

Get a full sex history and give yours. Like a good reporter, find out the five W's—when, with whom, where, and in what ways have they had sex, and what they know about the people they have had sex with. Have they injected drugs, had sex with prostitutes, had sex with a man, had a blood transfusion (especially before 1985 when blood wasn't tested), or had sex without a condom?

"If someone says they're safe, aren't they? How can I be sure he's telling the truth?"

You can't necessarily trust someone saying they're not infected. You can't tell by looking at someone if they don't have an STD. They may not know themselves, because some STDs don't have noticeable symptoms. Or they may be too embarrassed to tell. Or worse—they may be angry they have it and want to spread it to others. You can't trust an answer unless you really know the person.

"Is there nothing you can do to prevent getting a disease?"

Be responsible. You can say no to sex and drugs, don't share needles, don't give in to pressure from friends to do things you know are wrong for you. Make your own smart decisions. Think ahead of possible consequences. The only people who don't have control over getting infected are those who got blood transfusions and babies who get it from their mother.

"What's the AIDS test? I'd like to get tested but I don't know where to go. What do I do?"

The test for HIV is actually a test to see if any antibodies to the virus are present in your bloodstream, meaning your body is trying to fight it off. To be sure that you're not infected, you take the test one time and then again several months later, without having sex in-between (since the body takes several months to produce antibodies). You can get free testing from special state-funded clinics; unfortunately, they often have long waiting lists. Or you can go to your doctor. It's a myth that doctors automatically test your blood for HIV; some are concerned about legal issues like confidentiality in testing labs, and require that patients give specific requests and permission before they order the test.

Since the antibodies do not show up until a few weeks after the infection has invaded the body, you need to take one blood test, and then another after several months.

Be "positive" about being "negative."

Buddy: *"Should everybody take an AIDS test?"*

Debbie Gibson, as Honorary Love Doctor: "I think so. I am far from a promiscuous person and I got one because there are stories in *People* magazine about people getting it from their dentist. I believe in ruling everything out. I'd take a pneumonia test if people got pneumonia. I'm into raising awareness to AIDS."

Testing is recommended for anyone with a history of STDs, or who has sex with multiple sex partners, or who belongs to a high-risk group. You have to be tested once and then not have sex and get tested again. Go together. The good news about testing is that people who test negative are more likely to ask their lovers whether they're infected. A study showed college students were twice as likely to talk about AIDS with prospective lovers when their AIDS education included an AIDS test. But caution: testing negative doesn't mean you won't get exposed to the HIV the next day—so don't get sloppy about safe sex.

Angela: *"I love my fiancé and we plan to marry. Now I'm pregnant with his child. The other day I was going through some of his papers and came across his medical records and found a blood test that said he was positive for HIV. I'm in shock. We have been using a condom all the time, but he never told me. What should I do? Should I marry him?"*

I can understand your shock. You *must* talk to him and find out the whole story. Being HIV positive is one secret it is inexcusable not to share with a loved one. You must get tested yourself. Hopefully you do not have the virus. The good news is that recent reports show that babies born to HIV-positive mothers do not necessarily have HIV-positive blood themselves.

Rosie: *"My best friend's boyfriend made her HIV positive. How can I ask my boyfriend if he is, without insulting him?"*

Follow what I call The New AIDS Etiquette, that's **SAFER: Speak up, Ask questions, confront Feelings, talk Early in your relationship,** and **Require testing.** Obviously, you fear the crowd he hangs with is at risk, so you should be extra careful. If he gets insulted, be suspicious about his character since he should be concerned for both your safety and health, or he's not worth it.

Rafael: *"My friend just died from AIDS. He was just nineteen and his mother didn't know he was gay and she's in shock. What can help her?"*

Tell her there is nothing to be ashamed of. Recently I met Ryan White's mother at a rally we both spoke at for the AIDS and Adolescents Network of New York. She said something very powerful: "We must not think of people who get AIDS as 'bad.'" Other parents spoke about their pain at losing a child to this terrifying disease. Mother's Voices is a nationwide information, advocacy, and support organization for parents.

"I have AIDS. My girlfriend also has it from dating a drug addict. About five years ago my wife passed away from pneumonia because she got AIDS from a bisexual guy she

dated before meeting me. I was so angry I started using women. I must have infected twelve to fifteen women. The anniversary of my wife's death is coming up and I'm very depressed. What can I do?"

Report yourself to the Centers for Disease Control for infecting all those women. And to the police for attempted murder. You have no right to go around killing women because you're angry with your wife for dying. I'm sorry you have AIDS, but you're assaulting people with a deadly weapon.

Some people are so sadly dysfunctional, they actually want to get infected.

Roberto, 24: *"Both my parents are HIV positive. My father was a drug user. My mother, too. My brother who's six years older than me is also a drug user and his daughter was born HIV positive though she seems to be in remission. Somehow I always get attacked. Five kids assaulted me and cut me with a razor. I'm depressed, sleep all the time, and am afraid to go out. I used to do alcohol and cocaine, but now I just started doing IV drugs. I guess I want to get AIDS, too, like them. Why should I be the only one?"*

Please stop thinking of yourself as a victim. You're being attacked from so many angles, but that doesn't mean you have to do it to yourself. My heart breaks for you. You need support groups because you need a family—I bet a big reason why you want AIDS is not to feel left out of your family. Because your family is all sick, you have what we call "survivor guilt," like people who have lived through wars when their loved ones or buddies died, who wonder, "Why me? I don't deserve to live when they died." But you *do* deserve to live. You have to get professional help to get over your depression, and you CAN find happiness.

Sixteen-year-old Jessica also has a family who all are HIV positive—her mother, her stepfather, and her little brother. She called *LovePhones* with such a heart-breaking story, and lots of people faxed and phoned to offer to be her friend. She said, *"My mother has just gone into the hospi-*

tal. I expect she'll die soon, but I haven't been able to talk to her. I don't know how to do it. My aunt gets legal custody of my little brother if my parents die, and until I'm twenty-five I'm supposed to live with my uncle, whose wife just had a little baby. My father was an alcoholic who beat my mom and left when I was just a year old. I saw him a few years ago, but he never sends me any birthday cards. My brother is getting medication and is part of a special study, since he was born with the virus. How can I talk to my mother before she gets really sick and dies?"

I'm so glad you want to do this. It is important to bare all your feelings to people you love when you sense you might lose them—otherwise you are left with what's called "unfinished business," which haunts you. You need to tell your mother that despite everything, you love her, and you need her. Be yourself (crying if you have to), rather than trying to act grown up, which you probably do too often, in order to hold the family together. Join special youth programs for support for yourself.

Bill, 23: *"I recently met a guy I liked, and on our second date he told me he was HIV positive. I decided to continue seeing him and now we've progressed to having sex. We fool around and masturbate each other and wash. We've kissed, but no penis action. Should I continue the relationship?"*

Kudos to the guy for telling you his HIV status. That's a good sign he can be trusted. Be careful about your sexual activities, unless you have some unconscious desire to get sick. Do not engage in any activities that can transfer body fluids, because after all, that is how the AIDS virus is transmitted. Otherwise, you can be close and loving with this guy. Be prepared for some of the health crises he may face. You could benefit from joining an AIDS support group to share your fears and get practical advice and information.

DISCLOSURE

Scot: *"My friend is going out with a girl we know is HIV positive and she doesn't know I know. I know through some-*

one who works with a doctor who said so. Should I tell my friend?"

I'm shocked that the person who works with the doctor would tell—lawyers tell me there is a possibility that person could be legally liable for invasion of privacy, spreading damaging information about another person, obtained through a breach of confidentiality. A number of lawyers say this type of situation is more a moral question than a clear legal question. Cases related to such issues are just being brought before courts and there are not many precedents. States are passing laws making it a crime to knowingly infect another person, so it would be a crime that the girl doesn't tell your friend herself if she intends to have sex with him (since it can cause his death). But the law does not generally impose that you have to "rescue" another person from being harmed without your having a legal duty (for example, you being her doctor treating her). It's like, if you saw someone having a heart attack, you are not legally bound to help.

Many people would probably say you should tell the friend, but if I were you I'd tell the girl who is suspected. If it's true, she will certainly have to tell the guy, and she'll never act irresponsibly since it's out in the open. If it's not true, it would be horrible to be passing around further rumors. Also, whether or not it's true, she needs to find out who leaked such information, for her own protection.

Poison's drummer Rikki Rockett: "Why do people suppress the fact that they have a sexual disease. They tell about a cold. The guy who is having sex with your friend is going to need a lot of love and affection. I wouldn't want to be in that guy's shoes. The guy's life is at stake. We don't know what we're dealing with. You are doing right by telling him."

As I mentioned to you, not long ago, I was asked to participate in a rally for the AIDS and Adolescent Network of New York. The rally was really moving. People of all ages paraded through the streets of New York carrying placards with the initials of young people who had died from AIDS, their age, and the date of their death. Friends and family members, including Ryan White's mother, made speeches, and a youth group did an improvisation about how to talk about safe sex. In thinking about what to say, I devised the following bill of rights about AIDS for teens.

You learn in high-school history class about the bill of rights, and that for every right there is a corresponding responsibility. Teens are always lectured *you have to be responsible*. But today when it comes to the very real and increasing threat of AIDS, I believe you need to know "for every responsibility, you have a corresponding right." Hence, the following bill of rights for teens regarding the threat of AIDS.

TEENS BILL OF RIGHTS ABOUT AIDS

- You have a responsibility to know about AIDS . . . but you also have a *right* to accessible and better education about all the risks and options.
- You have a responsibility to practice safe sex . . . but you also have a *right* to have the means to do it readily available to you.
- You have a responsibility to protect yourself and others from the risk of AIDS . . . but you also have a *right* to expect that others will protect you equally.
- You have a responsibility to be honest with your sexual partners or selected others about your sexual health and HIV status . . . but you also have a *right* for them to respect you for it.
- You have a responsibility to be honest with others about your sexual health . . . but you also have a *right* to trust others will be honest with you.
- You have a responsibility to talk to your parents about sex and AIDS . . . but you also have a *right* for them to listen and love you no matter what you say or do.
- You have a responsibility to be supportive of your friends who have questions about AIDS or who are living with AIDS . . . but you also have a *right* to trust that they will not put you at risk.

> ### TEENS BILL OF RIGHTS ABOUT AIDS
> #### (CONTINUED)
>
> - You have a responsibility to get services and help for any questions or problems you have . . . but you also have a *right* that this help can be available to you.
> - You have a responsibility to take advantage of whatever services (agencies, counselors, caseworkers, etc.) are available to you . . . but you also have a *right* to know they are qualified, well trained, and sensitive to your needs.
> - You have a responsibility to take control of your life and ask for what you want and need . . . but you also have a *right* to choose how to do this, to take action yourself or have advocates, and to be supported and empowered in all your choices.

OTHER THINGS YOU CAN CATCH

The black cloud of AIDS overshadows other serious, though less life-threatening, sexually transmitted diseases. But fifty-six million people are infected with an STD, some of which are becoming epidemics.

Myth: the "old" diseases are gone. Truth: they're back: there are over a million cases of gonorrhea and half a million new cases of herpes. And there are other STDs people are not so familiar with, like condyloma and chlamydia.

Myth: that certain STDs, like yeast, are just "female" problems when truth is, they can show up in males, too.

Myth: that you can tell when you have an STD, when truth is, many are what's called "asymptomatic" (especially in men), meaning the symptoms are not obvious, so he could have it and not know it. A dangerous cycle can result, called "ping-ponging," where the couple ends up passing it back and forth, reinfecting each other.

HERPES

Herpes is one of the most complicated infections, because there is no treatment to get rid of it, because people who get it feel great guilt and shame, and because it varies so much from person to person that doctors can't even tell you exactly what to expect. But it is not the end of your sex life!

Raymond: *"I am twenty-six years old and was diagnosed with genital herpes a year ago. I use a condom but occasionally have oral sex with the girl I live with. I worry that she could get it, whether we can still have healthy children, and what'll happen if we break up and I'm in the dating game again."*

You are among forty million American men and women with genital herpes; there are half a million new cases a year, suffering similar emotional and sexual problems. In a survey released last year by the American Social Health Association, over two thirds of sufferers reported a decrease in sexual pleasure and over three quarters were depressed. But be reassured, herpes is unpleasant but doesn't have to stop you from a happy sex life and having a family. Just be careful. The virus is transmitted by contact with open lesions (chancre sores) and you can spread it from the genitals to other body parts or partners by touching a genital sore with a finger or mouth. Warning signs you have it include itching, tingling or burning, swollen glands, a blah feeling, and cold-sore, blisterlike lesions, *but* there is always a risk, since the virus can be present where you might not notice, like inside the genitalia, as well as on the thighs, buttocks, anal area, and other mucous membranes like the eyelids and throat. The lesions can shed without symptoms in the first six months you have it and then about three to four days a year *but* you cannot predict which days. Condoms reduce the risk, *but* do not cover all areas where the virus may be present. The lesions heal in about three weeks, and flare-ups are less severe over time and can be tamed by stress control and medication (like acyclovir), *but* outbreaks are unpredictable (since the virus lodges in the nerve cells near the lower spinal cord).

When you have an outbreak, don't have sex. Keep the area dry and frictionless (wear cotton underwear and avoid tight-fitting clothes or sitting in tubs that soften tissue and spread clusters). Be honest with a potential partner, but don't hide behind the herpes as an excuse for avoiding dating. You can have a healthy baby, but an infected mother can transmit the genital virus to a baby's eyes during delivery.

CHLAMYDIA

Eve: *"I had this whitish mucus coming out of my vagina and a lot of pain in my stomach, so I went to the doctor and she said I had this thing called chlamydia and gave me some medication. My boyfriend and I have had sex a few times since then and now he's complaining of pain when he urinates and says I gave it to him. I thought I had a female's disease, so can it be my fault?"*

It can be your fault, or his. Since this bacterial infection is thought to be more easily transmitted from male to female than from female to male (the woman's anatomy makes her more vulnerable), it is conceivable your boyfriend got it first and then infected you. Chlamydia is considered the fastest growing STD, with an estimated four million new cases a year among both women and men. As with many other STDs, it can "ping-pong" between partners who pass it back and forth, and you can be "asymptomatic" (where symptoms go unnoticed), as happens in one in four men infected with it and three out of four infected women. Similar to gonorrhea, the most common symptoms are the persistent urge to urinate, pain on peeing, or whitish discharge of mucus or pus. Women may have pain in the lower abdomen or during intercourse. Men can have inflammations around the prostate, testicle, and anal area. Called a "great masquerader," this infection can live in the body for years without being noticed, causing damage to your reproductive organs, tubal pregnancy, newborn illnesses, possible infertility, and even death.

Instead of blaming each other, you and your boyfriend should cooperate: be treated simultaneously (broad spectrum antibiotics are used), get annual tests (that analyze genital secretions), and reevaluate your contraceptive choices.

A distant cousin is psittacosis, a common disease among birds and people who feed birds (particularly parakeets).

THE YEAST OF THEIR TROUBLES

Yolanda: *"I'm a twenty-five-year-old woman with a bad yeast infection. Is it true that if I have a flour-and-egg douche, I could give birth to the Pillsbury Dough Boy?"*

Kevin: *"I put my finger in my girl and when I came out it had white stuff under my fingernails. What is it and can I get it?"*

It could be her normal lubrication, which has more mucous at the time of the month when she is most fertile. But it could also be some infection; so, she should check it out with a gynecologist. The thick, white or curdy discharge is often the sign of a yeast infection (also called "monilia" or "candida vaginitis") that comes from a microorganism fungi. Other symptoms: itchiness, redness, swelling, foul odor, and a red rash around the anal area that can extend down the thighs. It's not real serious and can be easily gotten rid of in three days to two weeks with antifungal medication you put in the vaginal canal and that you can get over the counter (I'm sure you've seen TV commercials for GyneLotrimin or Monistat 7). But since the symptoms can indicate other, more serious conditions, you should see a doctor. Since the same fungus also grows in the digestive tract, it can appear in the mouth (known as oral thrush) or be transferred there by scratching and getting it under your nails—so wash thoroughly to prevent spreading it. Cut down on sugar intake, but if infections recur, get tested for diabetes. Cut out intercourse 'til it's cured, or use condoms, because men can harbor yeast (like in their foreskin), even though they have no symptoms.

Susan: *"I've been divorced and haven't had sex in a while, but I keep getting those nasty yeast infections. Why is this happening, should I be worried, and what can I do to get rid of it?"*

A vaginal yeast infection is not always related to sex. It's caused by an imbalance in the vaginal chemistry, allowing overgrowth of a fungus that lives naturally in the vagina.

The fungus (*Candida albicans*) thrives when the bacteria that control it are destroyed or when the acid level of the vagina drops. Thus, you're at risk if you use douches or deodorants, antibiotics, an IUD or sponge, or during hormonal changes like menstruation, pregnancy, or contraceptive-pill use. Replace your diaphragm or cervical cap.

Two "old wives' tales" have some merit: (l) Eating yogurt helps, by getting live Lactobacillus *acidophilus culture* in your system; and (2) Since the fungus likes a warm, moist place to grow, microwave your underwear (for thirty seconds), wash it in chlorine bleach, and wear cotton or silk rather than nylon panties, panty hose, or workout gear, to let your vaginal area "breathe."

Anyone is vulnerable to an STD, regardless of age, sex, socioeconomic status. But the high risk groups include women more than men (because they show fewer symptoms, go untreated longer, suffer complications in childbirth, and because government funded programs are more often in clinics servicing men); inner city people who have more sex at younger ages with at-risk sex partners and inadequate health knowledge, care, and services; drug users; travelers and others prone to having casual and unprotected sex with multiple partners, or sex with known infected partners; gay men (Note: many now practice safer sex, reducing the risk); pregnant women who can pass infections to the fetus in the womb or on childbirth, causing blindness, brain damage, or death.

You can have two STDs at the same time (chlamydia and gonorrhea), and once you have one, you're more at risk for another.

It's really important to examine your own and a partner's body, including their genitals, to see any obvious signs of an STD. After all, you don't want to become infertile or blind, or get cancer, from a roll in the hay, do you?

THE CLAP

Hernando: *"I went to the doctor with this gook coming out of my penis and it really hurt when I peed. He said it was the clap. I thought the clap was that thing that starts the lights and the TV when you clap your hands."*

The clap is an STD called gonorrhea. It dropped off from many years ago, presumably due to safer sex, yet over one million people still get it each year, and drug-resistant strains have increased threefold over the past five years. The bacteria live in moist, warm cavities—your mouth, throat, rectum, urinary tract (and cervix in women). Symptoms pop up two to ten days after infection and include frequent urge to urinate and painful urination, and genital burning, itching, or unusual yellowish discharge from the penis or cervix.

The clap can be confused with other infections like cystitis, so it's important to see a doctor, who will send a smear of your discharge to a lab. It can be cured with penicillin, but if you ignore the symptoms, the infection can spread to other reproductive organs (causing infertility) or to joints, the heart lining, and the liver.

PID

Deandra: *"I have a lot of pain when we have sex. We tried different positions and I've taken pain pills but nothing helps."*

Severe pelvic pain is a big sign of Pelvic Inflammatory Disease (PID) that occurs when you neglect a bacterial infection and it spreads from your genitals to your reproductive organs (tubes, womb, ovaries, abdominal lining), causing scars that prevent passage of fertilized eggs, and complications leading to infertility or tubal pregnancy. PID can come from an STD (gonorrhea or chlamydia), IUD, or douching. Though decreasing, it still affects about one in nine women aged fifteen to forty-four during their reproductive years. Symptoms include a yellowish discharge, painful urination, spotting, fever, nausea, vomiting, and pelvic pain from swelling or tenderness in the cervix, uterus, or surrounding tissue, which are easily spotted during a pelvic exam, confirmed by cervical smear (to distinguish it from appendicitis, cysts, and tumors), and treated with antibiotics, though surgery is necessary in severe cases. Caution: PID can get worse from douching or intrauterine devices that force the infection further into the reproductive canals.

GENITAL WARTS

"I am horrified that I have these revolting bumps on my penis that are hard and look like little flat mountains. What the hell are they?"

When you have some abnormality on your genitals—or anywhere on your body—you have to check it out with a doctor to find out exactly what it is. What you describe sounds like genital warts, or HPV, human papilloma virus. About one million Americans and two thirds of their partners get them every year. They're something of a medical mystery: it is unknown how many people (possibly up to forty million) carry the infectious strains of HPV (of which there are more than sixty types). HPV is spread by anal, oral, or vaginal sex, leading to hard fleshy bumps that appear within three months. Be careful: Like herpes sores, warts are generally obvious on the external genitalia, but can be hidden well inside the vagina or the cervix in women. Usually they're harmless and just a discomfort, but there is the danger of a possible link to cancers of the penis, vulva, cervix, and anus. If you have them, men should have annual urological exams and women annual Pap smears. Warts may disappear on their own but also can be removed by a doctor by freezing, burning or chemical solutions, laser therapy, or when necessary, surgery.

SYPHILIS

A serious STD, syphilis is caused by the spirochete (a corkscrew) bacterium that can attack any body part and, if untreated, progresses to disability, dementia, and then death. I'm sure you heard about it being an epidemic during WWII days, when soldiers were getting it from prostitutes, until the 1950s, when the antibiotic penicillin was discovered. You get syphilis usually through vaginal or oral sex. Surprisingly, reported cases doubled over the past decade to 130,000 a year. The disease starts with chancre sores (pimplelike reddish-brown painless lesions) that appear within six weeks of infection and heal by themselves while the disease progresses (if untreated) to fevers, aches, rashes, hair loss; then spreads to the mouth, and ultimately attacks the eyes, heart, nervous system, bones, joints, brain, and other organs. Caution: the contagious period lasts up to two years. Since the symptoms "mimic" other diseases (heat rash, measles), you have to go to the doctor for microscopic tissue inspection or blood tests (Wassermann test, VDRL) that reveal antibodies. Penicillin cures it.

Here are a bunch of other things you can get from sexual contact. Check out some of these names!

TRICHOMONIASIS, a whiplike bacterium found in one third of all women that causes no trouble until overgrowth makes greenish or yellowish smelly discharge, itching, and swelling. Men who get it may experience pain on urination or intercourse.

GARDNERELLA also normally lives in the vagina and can overgrow, making a thick, grayish pasty discharge with a strong fishy odor.

MONILIASIS (thrush) is caused by yeastlike fungal organisms on moist linings, producing a whitish thickish discharge in women and raw red skin on men. Caution: uncircumcised men are more vulnerable.

MYCOPLASMAS of many subspecies can cause various infections in the urethra and prostate gland.

SALMONELLA, GIARDIA, and AMOEBIC INFECTIONS, transmitted through anal intercourse, cause intestinal symptoms (diarrhea, cramps, bloody stool).

MOLLUSCUM CONTAGIOSUM, a viral wartlike skin disease of pearl-shaped, painless, bumps that may go away on their own within up to a year, or can be dried up with a drop of Spanish fly, or dug out with surgery.

BACTERIAL VAGINOSIS (BV) causes a thin discharge with

fishy odor, burning, and mild pelvic pain, not usually an STD, but reinfected with contact.

NON-GONOCOCCAL URETHRITIS (NGU), a broad category for several infections with symptoms similar to gonorrhea, though milder, with difficult diagnosis.

HONEYMOON CYSTITIS is a bladder infection usually gotten from frequent sexual activity.

GROUP B STREPTOCOCCUS, present in the gastrointestinal tract bowel flora, can cause sore throat and other symptoms, transmitted by kissing.

CYTOMEGALOVIRUS (CMV), found in up to ten percent of healthy adults (in semen, saliva, or on the cervix) and transmitted through kissing or intercourse, it can lie dormant and flare up in fever or fatigue.

INFECTIOUS MONONUCLEOSIS (the "kissing disease"), caused by the Epstein-Barr virus, leads to mild to extreme fatigue and fever.

PUBIC LICE OR CRABS is one of the few STDs you *can* get from clothing, bedding, towels, and possibly toilet seats, besides direct sexual contact. It is cured by Rid or Kwell.

Other conditions that may not be an STD:
- Jock Itch: *"I get jock itch. It drives me crazy when girls see me scratching my crotch and they don't want to have sex with me. What can I do about it?"*

     Itching of your genitals can be due to a yeast infection that you can catch from a woman, or it could be a fungus (*tinea cruris*) you get from too-tight clothes, an allergy to chemicals in detergents or soaps, or exposure to moistness as sweating in hot weather. See a urologist or dermatologist. Treatments include cool wet dressings, corticosteroid creams, and keeping the area dry.
- "Jean" Folliculitis (from too-tight jeans).
- Lichen Planus—common itchy ringworm-like scaly lesions on the penile tip or shaft that are not venereal, that go away in up to ten weeks or can be relieved with steroid cream.

- Whitish, non-irritating vaginal discharges (due to ovulation, objects left in the vagina, douching).
- Fungal itchy skin irritations, like ringworm (*tinea cruris*), treated by Lotrimin.
- Pityriasis Rosea—itchy, scaly condition that goes away and is not an infection nor venereal.
- Allergies (to creams, deodorants).

HOW TO RISK-PROOF YOUR SEX LIFE

- Know about sexual behavior and STDs.
- Responsibility Rules—about partner choices (including monogamy and abstinence) and sexual behavior (caressing versus high-risk behaviors).
- Early detection by self-examination and regular medical examinations.
- Good general health practices, including cleanliness, diet, rest, exercise.
- Use of barrier contraceptives (Note: the pill and IUD do not provide protection).
- Get involved in developing school and community education programs.

IF YOU HAVE AN STD

- Overcome psychological distress (guilt, shame, fear, feeling victimized, anger), which can affect self-esteem, relationships, work. Get psychological help or join self-help groups.
- Inform sexual partners (required by law for some STDs like gonorrhea and syphilis).
- Get early medical attention. This is especially important to youngsters who fear being found out.

Renee: "I have an itch and I'm really worried that I have one of those contagious things, but I don't want to go to the doctor, because then my mother might find out I've been having sex. What should I do?"

I absolutely insist you check it out with a doctor. It is very dangerous to allow symptoms to go untreated, as you can become infertile, or die. You can get a confidential exam at a Planned Parenthood center. A doctor will normally feel it's ethical to talk with your parent(s) if you're a minor; but if you're not, no one need know. Even if your mother goes with you to the exam, you can request privacy in the examination room. But I much prefer that you consider talking honestly with your parents about whether you've been sexually active.

My final word on this topic:

Respect Yourself, Protect Yourself

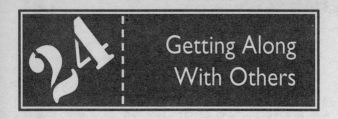

HEARING FROM MOTHER . . . AND OTHER SIGNIFICANT
Others in Your Life . . .

> *Gal, you keep your dress down, y'hear.*
> *Don't you make me shame of you.*
> *Don't you do nothing nasty with boys.*
> *Don't you come up pregnant.*
> —Dr. Rosie Milligan,
> *Satisfying the Black Woman Sexually*

Whatever you think, feel, and do, in sex is affected by
your family relationships, and affects how you raise kids
and relate to the important people in your life, including
your friends. So here's how to cope with dilemmas you face
with them. Rule: Always talk it out.

PROBLEMS WITH PARENTS:

It's one of my hopes that parents and kids talk
together—about sex and everything. In *all* the following
dilemmas, take it as a given to be respectful and considerate
of parents' opinions and rules.

UPSET MOTHER

Tracy: *"My mother found out I'm not a virgin and she's
upset. I guess she found some spermicide in my drawer and
came into my room and asked, 'I'm going to ask you a*

question and want you to be honest, are you having sex?' I said yes and she said, 'Why are you doing this to me? Why didn't you wait 'til you were married? People will laugh in my face.' What can I say to her. I feel terrible."

Talk to her. Tell her you're sorry she's so upset. You hope you can repair being close. You didn't try to hurt her, and you're proud you were honest. Hopefully you can say you love your boyfriend. Let her express everything she wants to say without you being defensive. Tell her you understand she feels ashamed in front of her friends or disappointed you didn't tell her, but that she doesn't have to feel that way. Ask if she can see any differences between what she learned and what's right for you. Reassure her you're not being loose or careless. For the next few weeks talk to her at different times about sex, what it means, what love is. See if there's anything about what she wants for you that you can agree and go along with—it will make her feel better and will probably be good for you! Hopefully this can deepen your communication together.

Frances is not having sex but her mother doesn't believe her.

Frances: *"My mother and I have been close. The other day she said she thought I was having sex, but I'm really a virgin. She didn't believe me. I told her I was going to wait 'til I'm in love with the guy. Why won't my mother believe me?"*

She's obviously feeling less secure about her closeness with you than you are with her. Reassure her that you love her. You can only state the truth, and if she doesn't believe it, then assume she has her own conflicts over honesty right now—maybe she's being dishonest with someone who thinks she's telling the truth, or she's suspicious someone else in her life is dishonest with her. Ask her to explore who else she mistrusts.

CAUGHT IN THE ACT

Getting caught in the act is a terror.

"I was having sex with my boyfriend in my room with the door open because I thought my parents were out at a

movie, but they came home earlier than I thought. We didn't hear them, but they flicked on my light and my boyfriend was doing it to me doggie-style. My father told my boyfriend to get out, and now they won't let him come around."

"I had sex with my boyfriend and my parents found out because my boyfriend tried to flush the condom in the toilet and it got stuck and my father found out. Now he won't let my boyfriend in the house. He thinks I'm too young to have sex. I'm his little girl. I stopped having sex with my boyfriend because I don't want my parents to hate me. How do I get my father to see I'm growing up?"

I'm sure you think your parents are being unreasonable and not keeping up with the times. If you disagree with parents about sex and dating, strive for open-ended discussion. Exactly what do they object to? Just revealing their objections takes some of the cold chill out of them. Also, once their objections are identified, you can address them.

HOMEWORK: Talk to them about where they got their ideas from—always get them to discuss what they learned from their parents when they were growing up. Parents' ideas are always influenced by either repeating what their parents did, or trying to do the opposite. Getting them to trace the source of their ideas helps them to put their opinions into perspective.

Ask questions rather than attack. Instead of making your arguments, reformat them as questions. Ask, "Do you think there is a difference in the generations?" and "How have the times changed to make things different?" rather than criticizing them as being "out of it." Walk a mile in each other's shoes, seeing how you each feel. Ask, "if you were me, what would you do?" Examine their deeper fears and needs from their point of view. If they don't want to let you grow up, then ask, "What are you really afraid of?" Discuss safe sex. Talk about what love means and how to make good decisions. Reassure your mom that she raised you with good judgment and you appreciate her trust. She wants to be a good parent and thinks she's behaving in your best interests. Acknowledge that.

WANTS TO TELL MOTHER
SHE'S HAVING SEX

Christine, 14: *"I used to be close to my mother, but I know it would disappoint her to know I'm having a lot of sex. But I still want to tell her because it's on my mind. I had sex about forty times with thirteen different guys and I think I'm pregnant now because my boyfriend's condom broke. My mother was always overprotective of me, wanting me to stay in the house, but I had sex with them in the house. She's got no right to complain about me because she got pregnant with me when she was fifteen. What can I say to her?"*

It is essential for you to tell her, not only to maintain your openness, but because you think you might be pregnant. Obviously you need your mother's support. Start the conversation honestly by saying, "We haven't talked about sex lately and there are a few things I need your help about." Then explain why you went against her rules, and listen to all her protests. Discuss her growing up in the times she did, and the climate you are growing up in. Talk about how you unconsciously may be following in her footsteps. Let her express her disappointments, hopes, and worries about your life. Then discuss making decisions about sex and love now that you already are sexual. She may become more restrictive in the household rules—after all, you are fourteen and should follow those rules.

Practicing what you want to say to others makes it easier to really say it.

SEXTEEN

"I'm sixteen years old and have been going with my boyfriend for three years. I wanted to wait for sex, like my mother told me to, but recently my boyfriend said he loved me and wanted to get married, so I did it. I'm very close to my mother and tell her everything, but I'm scared to tell her this because she said she would kill me if I did it. Should I tell her?"

Yes. I'm proud of you that you want to tell your mom and happy for her that you trust her with your confidences.

You're a good example to offset the sad statistic that fewer than two in ten parents and kids talk openly about sex. I'm sorry your mom made that extreme threat; probably she was so worried you'd join the alarming number of teens having sex at younger and younger ages. Have faith in your love for each other that she will forgive and understand. Ask her why she feels as she does. What did her mother tell her about sex? Did she have a bad experience when she was young? What is she afraid of for you? Likely your mom believes—as I do—that teens too often rationalize having sex by professing "love" when they are really experiencing infatuation, and so they are not as ready for sex as they think they are. Talk together now about safe sex, pregnancy precautions, and what it means to be in love and responsible about sex so you and your mom enter a new level of mother-daughter sharing.

BUSY MOM

"I've tried to talk to my mom about sex, but she's always busy. I have three brothers and sisters. I've been upset about my boyfriend, but she's always on the phone."

My heart goes out to you. Sometimes parents seem too busy for you, but they just have to be pinned down. You have to get their attention by insisting you have time together. Make your mother write it down in her book, if she's that busy. There's also a technique called family meetings, where once a week families sit together, just like at a board meeting in a business, and talk about who's doing what, who needs what, dividing chores, sharing gripes and good news.

Say real clearly to your mom, "I know you're busy, but I have some things I want to talk to you about. It's important for me now. I feel lonely and neglected and ashamed to tell you that." I'd be really upset if she doesn't respond. If she doesn't, it doesn't mean that something is wrong with you, or that she doesn't love you, but that she has her own problems and distractions now. Maybe she never learned to be loving. Can you get that mothering you need from a big sister, aunt, or teacher?

PARENTS STRICT

"My parents are so strict, they'd kill me if I ever had sex before I got married. They won't even let me go out on a date without going with a group. They're from Guyana, and that's the way it is there. I can't sleep over like all the other girls, and I have to be back so early, it's ridiculous. I do nothing but do my studies. But I like this guy at school and I want to go out with him. What can I do?"

You're not the only one with such strict parents. There are many cultures that are still extremely protective, particularly of girls. I had the wonderful occasion to address a group of selected high-school students from the Youth Multicultural Task Force at the Queens (New York) borough president's office. The students were from all cultures, and we talked about how restrictive so many of their parents were. Young women and men whose parents came from the West Indies, West Africa, India, Italy, and Muslim countries shared how their parents won't let the girls go out at night, date, or sometimes even touch a guy, until they get married. Orthodox Jewish rules say women can't even be in the same room at times with the males. Boys, on the other hand, are allowed much more freedom than the girls. Neither are allowed to date anyone who isn't from the same background. When parents are so rigid, it is often impossible to buck their system. When there is a little leeway, however, you can reason together and find compromises. One of the girls in the group shared her solution, how she eased her parents up a bit: "I proved to them I could be trusted. I always brought the boy home and introduced him to my parents. I told them where I was going and gave them the phone number. I agreed to a time to be home and never missed it. I assured them I wouldn't have sex."

Remember that parents have good intentions for their kids, however unreasonable their rules may seem.

TELLING PARENTS ABOUT PREGNANCY

Jimmy, 16: *I'm Greek and my parents want me to marry a Greek girl, but I went to my junior prom and had sex with a girl and now she's pregnant. I know it's the right thing to do to tell my parents, but how do I do that?"*

Bite the bullet. You know you made a big mistake not practicing safe sex. Expect their wrath and disappointment, but trust that after their blowup they will realize they love you and have to support you through a solution to this crisis. Ask for a family discussion at a time when everyone is relaxed and not distracted. The girl has to tell her parents, too.

HYPOCRITE

Ruby, 16: *"My mother told me if she caught me kissing a boy she'd cut out my tongue. She don't want no guy messin' with me 'til we got married. But she had me when she was fifteen. Then I got up one night and saw her on the couch fingering herself. What's with that if that's supposed to be bad until you're with the man from what she says?"*

Your mother was a little harsh, I'd say, about kissing being evil and due such punishment. Talk with her about why she says that. You already know she got pregnant when she was fifteen, so she probably wants to protect you from that, and strict rules are the best way she knows how. Ask her more about her experience, and what she thinks about men. I bet she thinks men only want sex from a woman.

PARENTS' DISAPPROVAL

A lot of people suffer from their parents' disapproval of who they like or date—because of religion, race, background, age, whatever. Parents have an idea of how they want your life to go. If you differ and want it your way, be prepared for the strife and taking the consequences. Many young people ultimately decide not to give up their family to date someone they disapprove of. Since this is easier before you get too involved with someone, think of it all early in the game.

"My boyfriend is twenty-three and I'm fifteen and my parents don't like me going out with an older guy. Could there be any trouble?"

Besides your parents' disapproval, your boyfriend could possibly go to jail for having sex with someone underage—it could be called rape or child abuse depending on how each state's laws define a minor. I once did a *Sally Jesse Raphael* show with a nineteen-year-old guy and his four-teen-year-old girlfriend he'd gotten pregnant, who subsequently pressed charges. They had the baby and married, but despite her efforts to withdraw the case, he was convicted and sent to jail. Despite their love, the law was sticking. Sad story; big lesson.

DIFFERENT RELIGIONS

David: *"I've been seeing this girl for about five months and I'm really crazy about her. I never thought I'd find someone who's my equal. But she's Jewish and I'm not, and her father's adamant about her dating someone of her own religion."*

When Sheryl Crow was the Honorary Love Doctor, she advised: "She should have a little faith that her parents are going to like you. It's the nineties and people gotta start accepting you. I'm sure he loves his daughter enough to want her to be happy."

Charles, 16: *"My girlfriend's mother doesn't like me because I was banging her daughter and got her pregnant. She had an abortion. I sent roses to her and her mother sent them back. She hangs up on me when I call."*

The mother obviously blames you for getting her daughter in that predicament. It's understandable she wants you out of her life. You feel hurt, too, and left out, but you'll have to be mature and accept her decision. This is a hard lesson to you. Also, you may have further alienated her by your attitude. Saying you banged her daughter may be slang, but it's disrespectful. It alienates people, so you better learn a more respectful and gracious and gentlemanly way to be if you want people to respond to you better.

LEARNING ABOUT SEX

Surveys show most kids learn about sex from their friends. Eight out of ten kids feel they can't talk to their parents about sex.

"I don't think any of my friends really know the real way that you should have sex, so I should talk to my mother. But what should I say to her?"

Just say simply, "Mom, I'd like to talk to you about some personal things." You can start with talking about something you read in the papers, heard on the radio, or saw on TV. Malcolm-Jamal Warner, a spokesperson for Planned Parenthood, asked, "If you're too embarrassed to talk about sex to your parents, how would you like to tell them they're going to be grandparents?" When I got the Maggie Award from Planned Parenthood for our work on *LovePhones,* I spoke with the celebrities there about where, when, and from whom they learned about sex. *Cosby Show* daughter Sabrina LeBoeuff got the whole scientific truth from her parents at a young age. *Fatal Attraction* actress Anne Archer learned from "growing up in the sixties when everyone was talking about sex." And character actor Richard Masur, once on *L.A. Law*, was eight when his eleven-year-old sister got her period and he thought she had spilled something.

Myths also abounded for veteran actress Polly Bergen, who thought she hurt herself when she got her period and was led to believe that just a man's touch could get you pregnant, until age seventeen when friends taught her otherwise, but said it was "disgusting." Vowing to teach her own kids better, she was wowed when, in response to learning the facts of life, her nine-year-old daughter said, "I don't have to do that, do I?"

TROUBLE TALKING

"Why do I have trouble talking to my kids about sex?"

There are two reasons:

1) You don't know the answers. That's okay; tell them you don't and will get the answers. Get a book or a video to watch together. (See referral list).

2) You're uncomfortable talking about it—either because of your own attitudes about sex in your childhood, or your own sex problems now.

British pop singer Alison Moyet, as Honorary Love Doctor, tells how she talks to her two kids: "I'm just kind of open with them. They ask me questions and I answer them straight up. My eight-year-old son asked me about procreation and I said that it comes to a point that you want to have a relationship with somebody and we talk about where the babies come from and you start off and you know you have to use fourex because of this disease that happens bla bla . . . I am sure that there is stuff that he doesn't quite understand but if you keep telling them things when they ask you questions it all kind of fits into place when they are ready for it, you know. You have to be careful about drawing the line between kind of like explaining the process without it becoming kind of like a sexual conversation. You explain the woman has an egg and the man has semen, you don't actually explain how it is passed. I don't want to start going into erections and penetration at this age, but it's when a couple loves each other and they want to have a baby. My five-year-old daughter said, " My mommy eats willies."

Aerosmith's Steven Tyler says he tells his daughter that her heart's gonna thump and she'll feel feelings she never felt before that are a real high, higher than drugs. In fact, he teaches, sex is a real strong drug, "You can get hooked on it, like the heroin that took her daddy. You have to be real careful about things that make you feel real good."

REPEATING HISTORY

"I heard in health class that you end up repeating the same relationship your parents had, even if you don't want to. I never saw my parents be affectionate and I'm afraid that I'll be the same with whomever I marry. How can I do different?"

Say to yourself that you don't have to repeat your parents' behavior and attitudes. You can be your own person.

HOMEWORK: When you notice yourself thinking or doing something that is not affectionate like them, think, "That is my mother/father, not me."

OVERHEARS PARENTS' SEX

"I hear my mom moaning when she and my stepfather have sex and I don't like it. How can I tell her to stop?"

While it is wonderful for children to know their parents love each other, and reassuring to know they continue affection, no kids like to be faced with the evidence of their parents having sex. Nor is it appropriate for them to be. Definitely tell your mother that you have heard her in private moments and that it is distressing to you. She should respect your request, and find personal time or adjust her style (making no noise) so as not to disturb you or make you so keenly aware of what they are doing.

Is there a chance you don't like your stepfather? Every child of divorce (of whatever age) resents their family breaking up and blames a stepparent (even if they like him or her), and hearing them in the most intimate moment may remind you of the sadness you feel over your dad being gone.

SEES PARENTS' SEX

"I walked in on my parents having sex. It's nasty. Now when I do it with my girlfriend I picture my parents. How can I get this picture out of my mind."

BRAIN RETRAIN: As soon as the picture of your parents in sex comes in your head, see a stop sign, or snap your fingers or tap the side of your head (called a "trigger" to break the connection in your mind), and immediately switch your mind to something else. Figure out what the scene means to you, that you keep thinking about it. Does it make you feel loved and wanted, or that you are in a secure family? Or does it give you permission to be sexual yourself and reassure you that sex and love in marriage can last? Once you know what it means, you are halfway home to being free of having to repeat the behavior. Then, you satisfy the need by reassuring yourself that the need is satisfied (that you are loved, that you can be sexual, etc.).

MOM EMBARRASSED BY DAUGHTER'S SEXY DRESSING

Diane, 15: *"My mother always nags me about the way I dress. But I'm my own person and will dress the way I want no matter what she says. I told my mother I wouldn't go to school unless I could wear what I want. My mother says she wants to crawl in a hole when she sees me in Daisy Dukes. She thinks all people are looking at her when we're out together and wondering what kind of mother she is. When we go shopping we fight in the store, and sometimes I storm out, so she really gets embarrassed. She tried to get my older brother's girlfriend to get me to change the way I dress, to be more Saks Fifth Avenue like her, but no way. Now my mother is worried because she thinks my little sister will copy me, because she thinks I look really great. We went to some family affair and she freaked that I wouldn't wear a prissy dress. Don't you think I should have the right to decide what to wear and my mother's stopping me from growing up?"*

Actually, growing up means you might wear the dress just to please your mother—that it wouldn't be so important to you to make a statement in your clothes that you can decide for yourself. When you truly know you are independent and in control of your life, you don't make such a fuss about proving it in everything you do, say, or wear. You can know inside yourself who you are and can do things to accommodate others if it's that important to them.

Aside from that, I do agree that you should follow your own sense of style and dress. But not if it is purposely to shock, or if it gets you into trouble at school or home. If it does, then your intention is to get into trouble, to stand out, to purposely get negative attention.

MOM UPSET WITH DAUGHTER'S FLIRTATIOUS BEHAVIOR

Patio, 15: *"My mother gets all bent out of shape over how I act with guys. She calls me a little tramp, and when we go out to a mall or something, and if any guy starts talking to me, she'll tell them it's so sad that I have an incurable disease. I have a great body and I want to flaunt it while I am young. She's fat and my father left her, so she's unhappy, so don't you think she's jealous of me and should bug off?"*

I have to admit that your mom may indeed be jealous of you, if she's unhappy being left by your dad, and worried about how attractive she is to other men. Though it certainly is not great for a mother to be jealous of a daughter's youth or beauty or opportunity, the truth is, it does happen. But you should be willing to see that maybe she also has a point—that you are flaunting yourself, when it would be more mature for you to act more sedate and subtly. Why do you need to be so obvious in your flirtations and solicitations of attention? Too much flash can send out a message that you are a loose girl, and send you in a spiral of using sex to get love, which would not be a happy pattern. Your mom is trying to get you to see that.

CONFIDING IN DAUGHTER

"My parents are divorced many years and I live with my mother. She just started dating again and allowing herself to be intimate with men. She's telling me what she's doing and who she's sleeping with. I like that she's more open with me than my friends are with their mothers, but I'm sixteen and is it right for her to be telling me these things?"

You're asking me the question because you're not comfortable with her telling you these things. It's one thing to have great open communication with your mom; it brings you closer. But it's another matter for you to hear too intimate details about her life when you don't want to. Besides, you're probably not sure what response she wants from you— approval, permission, advice. You probably still need your mother to be a mother more than a friend. You're struggling with your own dating and sexual choices, and need to feel that you can come to her as the adult, who has her life more or less together. And though you might not admit it, you probably need her to discipline and set some limits for you.

This takes a lot of courage, but tell your mom you're not sure why she tells you about her sexploits. If she wants to prove you're close, then tell her you can feel that way without talking about her sex life. Ask her if she feels guilty and wants your approval for developing intimacy with men other than your father. Maybe she wants to feel young like a teenager again herself. Tell her you're uncomfortable being buddies when you want her to be the mother.

CAUGHT PARENTS' INFIDELITY

"I came home and found my dad in bed with another woman. I haven't been getting along with my father. Should I tell my mother?"

Instead of ratting, tell your father you want to talk to him. Tell him you're angry at how he treats you and how he treats the family. It's too big a secret for you to keep. I think you need therapeutic support, so tell your family you want everybody to go into family therapy. If he refuses, then say calmly, not as a threat, that you think you have to have this all out in the open.

CAME OUT TO PARENTS

"I'm gay and my parents are very intolerant. What can I do? This hurts me a lot."

Parents are usually shocked on hearing such news. They often react with anger or guilt about what they did "wrong." Or they are embarrassed to tell their friends, disappointed they won't be grandparents, and worried about your health. They can get support from the self-help group, Parents and Friends of Lesbians and Gays. Over time, they will get that you cannot "change" to make them happy. Hopefully, their love will override their prejudices or fears. It'll be rough for a while, though, for you.

MOTHER FRIENDLY WITH EX

Debbie, 21: *"I broke up with this guy I was dating for three months and I'm dating someone else, but my mother has my ex over to dinner. She always liked him and says she feels sorry for him. Isn't this wrong?"*

I agree. It's nice that your mom is sympathetic, but he was your boyfriend, not hers. She doesn't have to make up for your breaking up with him or breaking his heart, by playing savior, or filling in for you. She is being inappropriately sympathetic. If having him around makes you uncomfortable, she'll have to tell him that, apologize, and express her sadness that it's over so she can complete her relationship with him as you did. After all, you were only dating him three months, and that's hardly integrating him into the family. To help her separate from him, ask your mother to explain how she empathizes with this boy about being rejected, and what experiences or past guilt she has over rejecting men or being rejected herself by them.

Many times it's hard to tell parents what's bothering you. I give you permission to say it, and invite you to practice saying it, so it's less scary.

MOM'S GAY

Chris: *"My mom is a lesbian and she brings my other mom to school and they hold hands and people stare. My friends call her a dyke, and I pushed one kid for it and punched him. If I tell her to stop, she cries that I don't love her."*

Instead of getting angry and losing your temper at the other kids who make fun, Stop and Think. They're uncomfortable. You get angry at their response because you're uncomfortable, too. If you felt more at ease with your mom having a girlfriend, you wouldn't be so defensive about it. Remember, there is no enemy without if there is no enemy within. Decide that your mother is fine, and when kids jeer, you can ignore them or blankly smile, or say some smart remark, like, "We're New Wave," or, "If everyone loved in this world, there wouldn't be war," or anything that comes to your mind.

Share with your mom that her behavior in public is causing you problems. Ask her why she feels she has to do that. If she's trying to prove something to the world, ask her not to do it at school! Say, "I love and accept you but it's hard for me. . . . I need you to do something to help me. . . ." She should be understanding and stop making a scene.

DAD GRABS MOM

"My father is always grabbing my mother's rear and breasts in front of us and she gets mad at him. I don't like seeing this. How can I tell him to stop?"

Just tell him. Don't be afraid. Say, "I get upset when I see you do that to Mom and get her upset." Your parents should care about how you feel. And they should know how their behavior affects you.

DEALING WITH KIDS:

CHILD WALKS IN ON SEX

A child walks by her parents' bedroom and sees them having intercourse and asks her mother the next day, "What were you and daddy doing last night?" The mother says, "That's where babies come from."

The next night the child sees them again, this time the mother is going down on the father. The next morning she asks, "Were you and daddy doing that thing where babies come from again?"

"No," says the mommy, "what you saw the other night was where babies come from, what you saw last night was where jewelry comes from."

Renee: *"With three kids, my husband and I hardly get any time to be alone, much less to be spontaneous about sex, but one afternoon we decided to risk it and make love. Sure enough, to our horror, our four-year-old came in. My husband was frazzled and screamed at her to go outside and shut the door. I don't think she saw anything, but I'm wondering if I should say something about it."*

Your husband's upset on being interrupted in the middle of your intimate act was understandable but unfortunate. He was caught off guard, but need not feel guilty or worried. Kids walk in on parents having sex (called the "primal scene" in psychoanalytic terms) either innocently needing you, or worried the noises they hear mean you're arguing.

Seeing you in the act will not harm them as long as they know you weren't fighting. If you stay calm, they'll have a better view of sex as normal; if you panic, they'll think something about sex is wrong. Explain that you're expressing affection, that "Mommy and Daddy love each other that way." They'll be happy about that.

TODDLER TOUCHING

"The little girl I baby-sit for is three years old and I saw her rubbing herself against the corner of her bed. I guess she was masturbating. Should I stop her from doing that or just ignore it?

"When I went to pick up my little boy from preschool the other day, they told me he puts his hand between his legs all the time. I've seen him do this at home and he even gets a bulge. My husband laughs it off, saying all baseball players grab their crotch so our son will be a great pitcher. Is something wrong with my boy and will he grow into a sex maniac?"

Don't panic. It's widely accepted child psychology that toddlers' touching behavior is normal. In several studies, up to one third of the females and two thirds of the males reported masturbating prior to adolescence. A famous sex researcher has even taken ultrasound pictures of male fetuses with erections in the womb, proving that genital responses begin even before birth. They continue in infancy when the child is nursed, cuddled, or bathed.

Haven't you seen infants explore all their body parts? They do it so naturally, and discover that genitals feel better than noses or toes. By two years old, kids are curious about everything. By four or five, they become intrigued with parents' bathroom activities, how babies are made, and sex play with other kids (which peaks from age six to ten). Connecting arousal to sexuality usually begins by age eight or nine, when hormones trigger physical body changes and when thinking changes from concrete to abstract (allowing more understanding of complex sexual ideas and intentions).

If parents panic or punish kids for such behavior—mistakenly ascribing adult interpretations to their "innocent" child explorations—they can grow up with problems in their body image, self-esteem, and relationships. Criticism would convey a destructive message that sex is "bad."

Discuss a plan with the child-care center. Since such public displays are inappropriate, distract the child by putting something else in his hand, sweetly say, "That's something you do in private," and give praise and a reward when he doesn't do it in public.

Having said all this about normality, I must add that excessive touching like any overboard behavior can indicate a problem that requires professional help. Since childhood self-stimulation is like thumb sucking, consider what is upsetting your child that he needs to calm, console, or comfort himself. Often he's angry, sad, insecure. Spend time together, encourage emotional expression, and offer extra hugging and cuddling, so he reaches out to others rather than turning inward to touch himself.

SEX WORDS

"What do you tell a seven-year-old when he asks you what sexually explicit words mean?"

Be an askable parent. Show that sex is not something to be ashamed or embarrassed about. Ask where he heard the words. Ask what he thinks they mean and say what they really mean. Explain that sex is beautiful when you're in love and sometimes people use nasty words when they're anxious or uncomfortable about sex, or angry about something else in life. Explain that they're not nice to say, though he'll probably hear these words throughout his life.

DIVORCED MOM'S SLEEPOVER

Denise: *"I am divorced and have been seeing a man I like. He wants to sleep over but I'm worried about my five-year-old's reaction. Can I do this and how can I get my son used to it?"*

Whatever their age, children are not happy when their parents are divorced and a new man or woman appears on the scene. They always harbor a fantasy that their family will be back the way it was. So, expect your son to be moody or angry. Let him get to know your new guy before he stays over. Do it on a fun afternoon outdoors so they "bond" in an activity. Then have him over for dinner. Save sleepovers for someone you are really serious with. Warn your son first in case he gets up in the middle of the night and discovers you. Reassure him that you won't be further alienated from his father.

TO CIRCUMCISE OR NOT?

"I'm nine months pregnant and want my son circumcised because my husband isn't and I don't like it."

It's definitely a choice you can make, as a parent, though there are organizations now that are very actively against infant circumcision, insisting the decision be reserved for the man as an adult. Groups of circumcised men are even hanging weights from their foreskin, to stretch it back. Circumcision— removing the foreskin, the fold of skin surrounding the head or glans of the penis—is done routinely in some religious and cultural groups (like Jewish and Muslim faiths) early in a child's life. However, the procedure may also be done later in life for medical or hygienic reasons (collections of cheesy smegma can cause irritation, infections, or foul odor).

The American Association of Pediatrics doesn't say yea or

nay to it, but recommends knowing the benefits and risks. Some investigators suggest that uncircumcised males may be more at risk for contracting urinary tract infections, penile cancer, and AIDS, and their female partners more at risk for developing cervical cancer—assertions unconfirmed by other studies. Personal reports also very. Some guys say the foreskin helps protect the delicate penile head, making it more sensitive for sex, but others claim cutting the skin and exposing the head allows for plenty of pleasure, and prefer how it looks.

SURROGATE OFFER

Dawn, 22: *"I want to be a surrogate mother, to give my godfather a son. He is thirty-six and in a wheelchair from an accident. He can only move his arms. His wife left him after the accident. I'm divorced and have a four-year-old daughter already. I could just have sex with him once and then carry the baby and give it to him for custody. I love him very much and want him to be happy."*

These days, surrogate parenting is certainly possible and much more socially acceptable than it used to be. There are guys who want to give their sperm to sperm banks, to make money, and to feel they have a lot of progeny (offspring), possibly as a sign of their virility. It's always important to know your motives when it comes to having a child. In Dawn's case, it's touching that she loves this man and wants to bring him happiness. However, it might be very difficult for him to raise a child alone in his condition, so perhaps she ought to consider if there is anyone who can help him. Maybe they could form a family unit. What would be in a child's best interests?

TELLING THE TRUTH

"I grew up as a good girl in a Hispanic family. I thought I'd be married forever. I married the first guy I dated, but he had an affair with my friend and they had a baby boy. I agreed to raise the baby, but now he left me and I'm bringing up his illegitimate child. What do I tell the child?"

It would be best to wait until he's old enough to understand these complications. Kids' ability to understand more complex issues starts when they're about eight. But, as in the case of adopted kids, if he asks when he is young, tell the truth, emphasizing that you love him very much and that you're a family. Saying too much to a young child risks that he feels guilty, unloved, and abandoned.

BROTHER LOVE

Kristin, 17: *"My ten-year-old brother said he's in love with me. I've been raising him, since my father took off when I was born, and my mother is always drunk. What should I say to him?"*

Tell him of course he loves you, and you love him. It's not a sexual love, he desperately needs you. You've been like a mother. Share with him how scared you both feel that you've been abandoned by your father, and that your mother has a serious drinking problem. You've both grown up too fast and need each other for support. Is there a relative who could help you in the parenting? You need to be in a support group; contact Alanon, for families of alcoholics.

KID DRESSES LIKE MOM

Robin: *"My five-year-old loves to wear my high-heel shoes, and I can tell he really likes women in skirts and heels because he tugs at them all the time. Is this a problem?"*

Are you encouraging him? Does it secretly make you feel good to know he admires you? Some women subtly and unwittingly encourage this when they feel unappreciated by men in their lives, because now they have a little boy who adores them. He obviously needs to be close to you, so when he puts on your heels, take them off and distract him with playing a game together or talking, so he associates a relationship rather than the object, as a sign of being close to you.

CHILD SEX PLAY

Christine, 16: *"I was baby-sitting and found the five-year-old little girl naked under the blanket in her room with a lit-*

*tle neighbor, saying, 'Oh I can't have your baby.' I got real
upset and made the other girl go home, but I remember
when I was six and there was an eight-year-old boy who, if
I wanted something from him, would make me pull my pants
down and touch him. Is this child sex abuse?"*

It can be innocent child sex play, and lots of kids do it.
When children examine each other, play doctor or family,
or simulate what animals or parents do, it doesn't have the
same implications as real sex for adults. Legally, up to a
certain age, it's not considered child sex abuse. But if one
child is considerably older and there is an element of force,
then the emotional result is the same as any abuse: you
grow up feeling guilty, mistrusting, storing anger, feeling
confused about whether you, and sex, is bad or good.
Sounds like you had a painful memory from childhood
where this older boy manipulated and controlled you. You
need to work through that stored-up anger, to recapture the
innocence *you* cherish.

NUDISTS

*"My neighbor is a naturalist. Their kids are thirteen and four-
teen. When my son goes over to their house, they're naked.
Sometimes now their kids come through the hedges to my
house naked. I don't think it's appropriate. My wife is afraid to
upset them and says they're not hurting anyone. Who's right?"*

You two have to agree, but my vote would be that they
can do whatever they want in their house but you have control over your house rules and can tell them that in your
house you wear clothes. Besides, are you concerned about
potential child-sex-abuse charges if someone saw them in
your house nude? Your wife has to get over her fear of
offending anyone and stick to her guns.

HISTORY REPEATS ITSELF

Dennis freaked when he caught his sixteen-year-old son
making out with a thirty-year old woman and was thinking
about pressing charges against her for corrupting the morals

of a minor. His son ran out the door, furious at him! *"What should I do?"* Dennis asked. He only calmed down when I asked him how this related to his own life. Turns out he got his now-wife pregnant when he was only sixteen—and had to give up his dream of becoming a lawyer so he could get a job right away and support the child. She was ten years older. Aha, doesn't that sound familiar! He freaked because he's afraid the same thing will happen to his son. Realizing this, he decided to calmly tell his son why he reacted so strongly, and what his fears are.

Parents and kids have to talk about sex!

GETTING ALONG WITH SIBLINGS:

BROTHER SNOOP

"I have a brother who videotapes everything. He came into my bedroom when I was in my underwear and photographed me. Then one day I went to open the bathroom door and he was in there masturbating while the camera was propped up on the sink. Then he has his friends come over and watch. Is something wrong with him?"

The video camera has become quite a toy, with people videoing sex in many situations. But imposing on others and being obnoxious, like your brother is doing—is something else. He's obviously into being a "bad" boy, enjoying his reputation with his friends as a wild man. Tell him point blank he's intruded on you. Demand he erase the tape of you. Watch him do it. If he doesn't, tell your parents. Warn him that his pranking could go too far and land him in trouble with the law. Advise him to try to get a rep with his friends as "cool" in another way.

SISTER'S MISTAKE

Amanda, 16: *"My sister is in love with a deadbeat. She's twenty-two and got pregnant on purpose to keep him. She pays the rent and he cheats on her. The family is upset. Her last boyfriend treated her like a queen and she cheated on him. How can I help her?"*

Continue to tell her how she is being masochistic. Point out the truth of how he behaves. Then she has to want to see it herself. Your sister is likely attracted to deadbeats because she has low self-esteem and doesn't feel she deserves a guy who treats her right. Don't you be like that. She has to live her life; you can help but you can't save her, and you certainly don't have to be afraid you'll be just like her. Also, don't think that her picking losers reflects on you.

BROTHER SCORES

Danny: *"I have a problem with my brother. If we go out to a bar, I'll be there picking up women and he'll just stand there and attract tons of them. This makes me crazy because I know he's gay and doesn't have any interest in them."*

My *LovePhones* co-host, Chris Jagger suggested, "He should be hooking you up man if he's a good brother."

The reason these women are so attracted to your brother is because he's not worried about being attractive; he's just himself. So, don't be predatory or desperate, be as natural as he is. Ironically, when you don't care is when you are most attractive.

GETTING ALONG WITH FRIENDS

(See the chapters on Hooking Up, No-No's, and Guys Who Like Guys Who Like Girls . . . for more issues about friends and roommates besides the following.)

SELF-CENTERED CONFIDANT

"Every time I try to tell my best friend about the sexual problems I'm having with my boyfriend, she always says, 'The same thing happened to me,' and goes on to tell me about her experiences. I never get to finish talking and end up feeling frustrated and disinterested in what she's saying. Am I being a bad friend?"

It is natural, reassuring, and helpful when confidants relate similar experiences or advice from their own life. Unfortunately, too many people like your friend selfishly turn all the attention back onto themselves, leaving you feeling frustrated, unheard, and even guilty that you don't become fully absorbed in them. The best listeners practice "active empathic listening," affirming genuine interest in what you say ("I see what you mean"), filtering through your experience rather than their own ("This sounds like what you told me about your last boyfriend. . . ."), asking facilitating questions ("How do you feel about . . . ?"). Let your friend know how you like to be listened to. Gently suggest, "I really need you to listen to my whole story as if you were me, and to ask me more about it so I can understand my feelings. Then I can listen to your story." Selfish listeners can change by realizing they can receive attention by giving it, and by rephrasing their own experience into a question: "What would you do if . . . ?"

If your friend persists in sole self-interest, gain what you can from her stories and seek others more capable of reciprocal sharing. Granted there is some value to sharing with a trusted friend before confronting a love partner, but complaining to a third party can reveal your resistance to communicating with your love partner. Since good communication is at the foundation of a good sexual relationship, you can only solve your sexual problems with your boyfriend by talking with him directly.

STEALS BOYFRIENDS

Dana: *I steal my friends' boyfriends. I've done it three times. The guys are obviously no good if they go for it. It's a joke. I get satisfied that I can get any guy. It doesn't take much, it's so simple. When I see them, I picture how he is in bed. I look for that challenge and like controlling them. But once it's over the girls can have them back. I'm off to another prize. But I want to try and stop it.*"

I'm glad your boyfriend-stealing is getting old. Obviously you're trying to prove you're attractive enough to snare them away. But you'll end up losing rather than boosting your self-esteem, by realizing you're being a rat. Build your confidence on something other than getting guys to want you. Believe you're worth it. How many guys will it take to prove it? Enough, already.

You also sound like you have contempt for men. Clearly they've hurt you and you're getting back at them. Where did you learn they are sheep that can be led to pasture so easily? I suggest you stop manipulating them. Turn your attention to getting what you want in a career, and to proving you can trust and love somebody—if you do this with as much vigor and success as you do proving they're stupid, you'll be a huge success!

Sometimes you can push your friend into having sex with your lover, without realizing it.

David: *"I kept telling my girl about my buddy Bob's sexploits to try to get her to do the same things, but little did I know that he was scamming me behind my back. I mean they were talking on the phone a lot and once I saw them kiss a little too cozy. What can I do about it?"*

Talk to your girlfriend. Instead of accusing her of going for him, be specific about the behavior that makes you unhappy. Tell her, "I get uncomfortable when you and Bob kiss so close." Tell your friend the same thing, without accusing him of stealing your girl. Stop telling her about how great he is in bed; why wouldn't she get turned on to that? Examine your own unconscious desires to set up a three-way or a triangle where you are battling over the woman as competition, a show of power, or a repetition of some family dynamics.

TATTLING

"My girlfriend's boyfriend came on to me a few weeks ago. I didn't do anything to encourage him, and I haven't said anything to her about it. But now I'm thinking I should let her know, because if he did it to me, he probably does it with other girls, and she should know how he is. Should I tell her? What if she doesn't talk to me after that?"

It's certainly risky to tell a friend that her man is flirting with or, worse yet, propositioning others, since it's certainly unwelcome news. First examine what his flirtation means to you, and your own motives for needing to tell. Even if you think you just want to be a good friend, is it possible you, too, have been hurt by men, and protecting her vicariously heals yourself? Or were you unable to get angry at him, and want her to get back at him for you? Telling her why you want her to know might help her accept the news. Then be prepared for her possible reactions. She may get angry at you for telling her what she doesn't want to hear. Or she may not believe you; denial is a common reaction to any shock. In both cases, you can apologize for causing her any pain, acknowledge that you know she loves him, and gently suggest that love can be blind and that she should be alert to any further clues. Hard evidence—like something he wrote or said, documented on paper or tape—can help, but don't go out of your way to entrap him or you'll look suspicious. Be absolutely clear that you were not subtly or unconsciously inviting his advances, so if she accuses you of being jealous, trying to ruin her happiness, keep her for yourself, or steal her man, you can reassure her none of these are true. If she severs your friendship, reassure yourself and her that you acted in good faith, pledge your loyalty, and let her go until she comes around.

SEXUAL BETRAYAL

Michelle, 18, is not so innocent.

"I told my friend I'm sleeping with her boyfriend, but she doesn't believe me. They've been going out for a year, but he's been seeing me for two months. I want her to know that he told me I'm better in bed than she is. She's straightforward and I'm wild and will do anything he wants. He tells her he's faithful then he drops her off and comes to see me. I'm upset, though, that he said he loves her and he asked me to act like her and whether he can call me by her name. He convinced me that it as okay to do what we're doing, but along the way I really fell in love with him. Then I realized

both of us were wrong. My friend said her whole world revolves around him and he wouldn't do that to her. How can I convince her he did?"

Boy, are you angry at him. He is really hurting you. Even though he flatters you that sex with you is great, you are finally realizing that he is using you. He loves her but gets you to do sex acts she won't, while he imagines he's with her. So he gets it all and you get just empty, kinky sex—and the humiliation of letting him do anything to you while he pretends you're someone else he loves.

Examine why you wanted to tell her. You're jealous; did you want to ruin what she has with him, because you can't have it? Telling her was a way to really get back at him! Telling her gives you a moment of feeling the power of revenge. Unfortunately, your friend is in a state of denial. Hopefully, she will see the truth, so she won't continue to surround herself with betrayals.

Eileen, 18: *"My roommate's boyfriend came over and she wasn't in, so he sat down and said he wanted to talk to me and told me he's bisexual. I told him I didn't want to know that because she doesn't know. He asked me to keep it a secret and I said yes, I would. Should I tell her?"*

Think about his motives for telling you (to get it off his chest, to ease his guilt). By telling you he gets you to share the load and implicitly sanction his deceit and ease his conflict. Maybe he also secretly wanted you to tell her. Tell him you made a mistake and cannot keep the secret. You'd like him to tell her, and if he doesn't, you feel you have to.

COMPETITION

Carrie and Ariel, 17: *"We're both after the same guy and we both slept with him, but who should have him?"*

Sounds like you two care more about competing with each other than you care about your relationships with this guy. Are you reenacting some sibling rivalry (competition with a brother and/or sister during childhood), or using him to prove either one of you is more attractive? Friends should honor each other in dating. Stake your territory and don't go for each other's flames.

COPYCAT

Tara, 16: *"My friend is a copycat. She buys all the clothes I wear and wants to have sex with all the guys I go out with. It annoys me. What do I say to her?"*

Realize her copycat behavior is a compliment that she admires you. Be confident that she can't take over your life. Tell your friend you appreciate her admiring you but you think it would be best for her to make some of her own choices.

MAN STEALER

"What do you do if your best friend steals your boyfriend?"

Write them both off. Tell them calmly how upset you are with their betrayal. Feel your hurt—what a double whammy. But don't swear off boyfriends and best friends for all time. It'll take time to trust men or women again, but you have to. See if there were any signs that they were not worthy of trust to begin with—you may have to sharpen your skills in picking people to get close to. Were they too selfish? Did you know they lie or were sneaky in other situations? Every unhappy experience is a lesson. See it as a step along the way for you to keep improving and getting closer to your goals of happiness and loving relationships.

FRIEND HAS AIDS

Diane, 26: *"A girlfriend of mine has AIDS. Other friends of ours say she's bad news, and warn me 'lose her or lose us.' What should I do?"*

Decide whether or not you want to be her friend. If she's untrustworthy, disloyal, or engages in illegal or immoral behaviors, then don't be friends. But if she's a good friend to you, be there for her through this terribly difficult time in her life. People with AIDS—or anyone with a terminal illness—need good supportive friends.

BUDDY SEX

Dawn: *"I was flirting with this guy friend of mine who I always liked. We were in a dark booth in a restaurant and talking about sex, and I just hiked up my skirt and he went down on me. It just happened. It lasted about fifteen minutes and it was really nice. Now he won't talk to me. What can I do, I really like being his friend?"*

URGGHHH. Nothing just happens.

Your friend is likely embarrassed, or feeling guilty because he let himself do it, or he's confused about where to go from here. Maybe he's also a little miffed that you didn't do anything back to him. Talk to him about what happened. Say you really enjoyed it, reflect what you think he feels or fears, and say you need to agree on your future: whether you stay friends and put this behind you, or get closer.

FLASHER

Angela: *"My friend Jill is always flaunting her breasts. She lifts her shirt to show us her breasts, and sometimes she does it to her little sister, who is flat. Isn't this wrong?"*

She needs attention. Ask her what she is feeling right before she lifts her shirt: does she want "oohs" and "aahs" to show how developed or pretty she is, or how she is better or more mature than her sister? Once she knows this need, she can hesitate before she does it, and take a deep breath and say, "I need attention," and get it in another more socially appropriate way (even if she has to just say, "I'm so proud of how my body has developed!").

NOISY ROOMIE

Christina, 18: *"My roommate in college is in the bunk bed above me and she masturbates in the middle of the night. It makes noises and wakes me up. I'm a virgin and don't do it, so it irritates me. It lasts about five minutes. What should I tell her?"*

Do I detect a note of jealousy that she is more experienced, or comfortable with her body and sexuality? Unless she's purposefully trying to flaunt her sexuality in front of you—which I doubt because she waits 'til she thinks you're sleeping—give her privacy. It's hard being roommates and sleeping in the same room since masturbation is often best at night when you're sleepy, feeling sexy, or need help falling sleep. Find a time when you are both feeling close and have a conversation about sex. Suggest she find a time when you're not in the room to pleasure herself. But, if you're curious about what she's doing, don't be afraid to ask her so you can learn.

Gotta love all those people who love you . . . they may make some mistakes sometimes, but when you got a few good people in your life, it makes it all worth living.

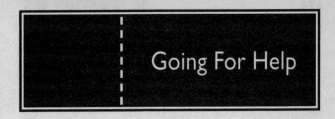

INFORMATION LINES:

ABUSE
Child Abuse: Child Help USA (800) 4A-CHILD.

ADDICTIONS (various)
Hazelden Foundation (800) 328-9000, in Minnesota (800) 257-0070. Outside U.S. (612) 257-4010. For books, pamphlets, videos, and treatment.

AIDS
AIDS hotline (800) 342-AIDS, including a Spanish service (800) 344-7432 and service for the Deaf (800) 243-7889, operated by the American Social Health Association under contract with the Centers for Disease Control.

ALCOHOL
Alcoholics Anonymous/Alanon/Alateen (800) ALC-OHOL.

DEPRESSION
National Foundation for Depressive Illness (800) 248-4344.

DRUGS
Cocaine Hotline (800) COC-AINE.
National Institute on Drug Abuse (800) 662-HELP.
   Spanish: (800) 66-AYUDA.

EATING DISORDERS
National Association of Anorexia Nervosa and Related Disorders, Box 7, Highland Park, Illinois 60035, (708) 831-3438.

HOMOSEXUALITY
Parents and Friends of Lesbians and Gays (PFLAG) (202) 638-4200. Offers local referral numbers.

MEDICAL DOCTORS

Ask friends, family, or coworkers for a referral to a medical specialist or call your nearest hospital or medical school, and ask for the number of the specialty clinic (gynecology, urology, dermatology, plastic surgery, etc.).

American Medical Association, 515 North State Street, Chicago, Illinois 60610, (312) 464-5000.

MENTAL ILLNESS

National Alliance for Mentally Ill (800) 950-6264 for information.

PREGNANCY

Planned Parenthood (800) 230-PLAN.
Catholics for a Free Choice (202) 986-6093.

RAPE

Campus Violence Prevention Center, national information clearinghouse on campus rape and violence, Student Services, AD 108, Towson State University, Towson, Maryland 21204, (410) 830-2178.

National Victim Center, 309 West Seventh Street, Suite 705, Fort Worth, Texas 76102, (817) 877-3355. Operates 8:00 A.M.–5:30 P.M. Monday–Friday. For referrals to organizations for counseling, support groups, legal advice.

SEX ABUSE

Sex Abuse Hotline (800) 656-HOPE. Twenty-four-hour hotline refers callers to rape crisis centers around the country. Run by RAINN (the Rape, Abuse and Incest National Network), the Washington, DC–based organization cofounded by Tori Amos.

SEX ADDICTION

Sex and Love Addicts Anonymous, call local information for chapters.

The Masters and Johnson Sexual Compulsion Programs (800) 733-3242.

SEX INFORMATION

SIECUS (the Sex Information and Education Council of the United States), 130 West Forty-second Street, New York, New York 10036, (212) 819-9770.

The Alan Guttmacher Institute, 111 Fifth Avenue, New York, New York 10003, (212) 254-9891.

SEX THERAPY
American Association of Sex Educators, Counselors, and Therapists (AASECT), 435 North Michigan Avenue, Chicago, Illinois 60611, (312) 644-0828. For referrals to sex therapists around the country.

SEXUAL HARASSMENT
9 to 5 National Association of Working Women Hotline (800) 522-0925.

SEXUAL IDENTITY
International Foundation for Gender Education (617) 899-2212.

SEXUALLY TRANSMITTED DISEASES
STD Hotline (800) 227-8922, operated by the American Social Health Association.

Herpes Hotline (919) 361-8488, Canada (800) 478-3227, and the Herpes Resources Center (800) 230-6039, developed by the American Social Health Association. PR41, P.O. Box 13827, Research Triangle Park, North Carolina 27209.

UROLOGY
Association for Male Sexual Dysfunction, 55 East 9th Street, New York, New York. 10003, (212) 794-1616.

BOOKS AND VIDEOS:

AIDS
You Can Heal Your Life by Louise Hay (Hay House, Santa Monica, California).

CO-DEPENDENCY
Codependent No More: How To Stop Controlling Others and Start Caring For Yourself by Melody Beattie (Harper/Hazelden, 1987).

EASTERN SEXUALITY
Sexual Energy Ecstasy by David and Ellen Ramsdale (Bantam, 1993).
The Art of Sexual Ecstasy by Margo Anaud (Tarcher, 1989).

FANTASIES
Women On Top by Nancy Friday (Pocket Books, 1991)
Videos from Femme Distributors, 588 Broadway, New York, New York 10012.

Selected videos from Penthouse Video, A-Vision Entertainment, New York, New York.

FETISHES
Lovemaps, Clinical Concepts of Sexual/Erotic Health and Pathology, Paraphilia, and Gender Transposition in Childhood, Adolescence and Maturity by John Money, NY (Irvington Press, 1986).

GYNECOLOGY
A Woman's Body, The New Guide to Gynecology by Niels Lauersen, M.D. and Steven Whitney (Perigee, 1987).

INCEST
Incest and Sexuality: A Guide to Understanding and Healing by Wendy Maltz and Beverly Holman (Lexington Books, 1987).

MALE SEXUALITY
The New Male Sexuality: The Truth About Men, Sex and Pleasure by Bernie Zilbergeld, Ph.D. (Bantam, 1992).

The Myth of Male Power by Warren Farrell, Ph.D. (Simon & Schuster, 1993).

Superpotency by Dudley Danoff, M.D. (Warner, 1993).

MASTURBATION
Sex For One: The Joy of Self-Loving by Betty Dodson (Harmony, 1987).

"Self-Loving" video by Betsy Dodson. Box 1933 Murray Hill, New York, New York 10156.

MASSAGE
The New Sensual Massage by Gordon Inkeles (Bantam, 1992).

"Sensual Massage" video, Playboy Enterprises. Sharper Image stores.

OBSESSIVE LOVE
Obsessive Love by Dr. Susan Forward (Bantam Books, 1991).

How To Break Your Addiction to a Person by Howard M. Halpern, Ph.D. (McGraw-Hill, 1982).

ORGASM (FEMALE)
For Yourself by Lonnie Barbach (Anchor Press, 1975).

"Becoming Orgasmic" video. Sinclair Institute P.O. Box 8865, Chapel Hill, North Carolina 27515. (919) 929-3797.

PARAPHILIAS
The Encyclopedia of Unusual Sexual Practices by Brenda Love (Barricade Books, Ft. Lee, New Jersey, 1992).

SEX ABUSE

The Sexual Healing Journey: A Guide for Survivors by Wendy Maltz (Harper, 1994).

SEXUAL HARASSMENT

In Case of Sexual Harassment: A Guide for Women Students from Center for Women Policy Studies, 2000 P Street NW, Suite 508, Washington, DC 20036, (202) 872-1770.

OVERALL:

Heterosexuality by William H. Masters, Virginia E. Johnson, and Robert C. Kolodny (HarperCollins, 1994).

How to Make the World a Better Place for Women by Donna Jackson (Hyperion, 1992).

Our Sexuality textbook by Robert Crooks and Karla Baur (Benjamin/Cummings Publishing Company Inc., Redwood City, California, 1993).

Satisfying the Black Woman Sexually by Dr. Rosie Milligan (Professional Business Consultants, Inglewood, California, 1991).

"101 Ways to Excite Your Lover," and other videos from Playboy Video Enterprises and the Sharper Image.

"101 Ways to Make Love Without Doing It," call for pamphlet, (800) 321-4407.